Contemporary Readings in
Social Problems

THE CONTEMPORARY READINGS SERIES

The new Contemporary Readings Series is unique in undergraduate education. The editors of titles in this series have selected both contemporary journal articles and material from the popular press to create books that are both research focused as well as accessible to introductory students. The journal articles within this series have been carefully edited to ensure that students can easily grasp the concepts discussed while learning from original sources. This, combined with carefully selected magazine and newspaper articles, makes for a practical and informative series of readings.

This new series is inexpensive, interesting, convenient, and stimulating. Each reader offers the latest research tied to the curriculum in an easy-to-use format.

Books in the Contemporary Readings Series to date include:

- *Contemporary Readings in Sociology,* Kathleen Odell Korgen, editor
- *Contemporary Readings in Globalization,* Scott R. Sernau, editor
- *Contemporary Readings in Criminology,* Gennifer Furst, editor
- *Contemporary Readings in Social Problems,* Anna Leon-Guerrero and Kristine Zentgraf, editors

Contemporary Readings in
Social Problems

Anna Leon-Guerrero
Pacific Lutheran University

Kristine Zentgraf
California State University, Long Beach

Editors

Contemporary

CRS

Readings Series

PINE FORGE PRESS
An Imprint of SAGE Publications, Inc.
Los Angeles • London • New Delhi • Singapore • Washington DC

For information:

 Pine Forge Press
An Imprint of SAGE Publications, Inc.
2455 Teller Road
Thousand Oaks, California 91320
E-mail: order@sagepub.com

SAGE Publications Ltd.
1 Oliver's Yard
55 City Road
London EC1Y 1SP
United Kingdom

SAGE Publications India Pvt. Ltd.
B 1/I 1 Mohan Cooperative Industrial Area
Mathura Road, New Delhi 110 044
India

SAGE Publications Asia-Pacific Pte. Ltd.
33 Pekin Street #02-01
Far East Square
Singapore 048763

Printed in the United States of America

Library of Congress Cataloging-in-Publication Data

Contemporary readings in social problems/edited by Anna Leon-Guerrero, Kristine Zentgraf.
        p. cm.
Includes bibliographical references and index.
ISBN 978-1-4129-6530-9 (pbk.)
    1. Social problems—United States. 2. Social problems. 3. Sociology. I. Leon-Guerrero, Anna.
II. Zentgraf, Kristine M.

HN59.2.C65 2009
361.1—dc22   2008028581

This book is printed on acid-free paper.

08   09   10   11   12   10 9 8 7 6 5 4 3 2 1

Acquisitions Editor:	Jerry Westby
Editorial Assistant:	Eve Oettinger
Production Editor:	Astrid Virding
Copy Editor:	Renee Willers
Typesetter:	C&M Digitals (P) Ltd.
Proofreader:	Gail Naron Chalew
Indexer:	Gloria Tierney
Cover Designer:	Candice Harman
Marketing Manager:	Jennifer Reed Banando

CONTENTS

Topic Guide   viii

Advisory Board   xiii

About the Editors   xiv

Preface   xv

PART I. THE SOCIOLOGY OF SOCIAL PROBLEMS

1. The Promise   2
   C. Wright Mills

2. The Art of Savage Discovery: How to Blame the Victim   6
   William Ryan

3. Where Do We Go From Here?   16
   Martin Luther King, Jr.

PART II. THE FRAGMENTATION OF SOCIAL LIFE

4. The Fragmentation of Social Life: Some Critical Societal
   Concerns for the New Millennium   26
   D. Stanley Eitzen

5. Capitalism, Class, and the Matrix of Domination   32
   Allan G. Johnson

6. Consumer Culture: An Interview With Juliet Schor   38
   Douglas B. Holt

PART III. THE GLOBAL FRAGMENTATION OF SOCIAL LIFE

7. Neoliberalism as Creative Destruction   48
   David Harvey

8. Poverty and Inequality in the Global Economy   62
   Michael D. Yates

9. The Making of International Migrants   69
   Saskia Sassen

PART IV. MEDIA

10. The New Media Giants: Changing Industry Structure   78
    David Croteau and William Hoynes

11. Reviving Lolita? A Media Literacy Examination of Sexual Portrayals of
    Girls in Fashion Advertising   97
    Debra Merskin

12. Tripping Up Big Media   104
    Gal Beckerman

PART V.   WORK

13.   America Transformed   112
      Gary Hytrek and Kristine Zentgraf

14.   21st Century Slaves   126
      Andrew Cockburn

15.   "Aqui estamos y no nos vamos!" Global Capital and Immigrant Rights   132
      William Robinson

PART VI.   EDUCATION

16.   Constructively Challenging Diverse Inner-City Youth's Beliefs About
      Educational and Career Barriers and Supports   142
      Margo A. Jackson, Jaclyn Mendelsohn Kacanski, Jonathan P. Rust, and Sarah E. Beck

17.   The Paradox of Poverty Narratives: Educators Struggling With Children Left Behind   151
      Cynthia I. Gerstl-Pepin

18.   Ideological Success, Educational Failure? On the Politics of No Child Left Behind   162
      Michael W. Apple

PART VII.   HEALTH CARE

19.   Pills, Power, People: Sociological Understanding of the Pharmaceutical Industry   172
      Joan Busfield

20.   Tango Immigrants in New York City: The Value of Social Reciprocities   183
      Anahí Viladrich

PART VIII.   POVERTY AND SOCIAL WELFARE POLICY

21.   Welfare Reform in the United States: Gender, Race and Class Matter   198
      Mimi Abramovitz

22.   An Understanding of Poverty From Those Who Are Poor   212
      Stephanie Baker Collins

23.   Child Labor in Bangladesh: Are Children the Last Economic
      Resource of the Household?   226
      Claire Salmon

PART IX.   CRIMINAL JUSTICE

24.   Crime   244
      Michael Tonry

25.   Prison Health and the Health of the Public: Ties That Bind   254
      Natasha H. Williams

26.   The Global Impact of Gangs   264
      John M. Hagedorn

PART X.   ENVIRONMENT

27.   Nature's Trust: A Legal, Political and Moral Frame for Global Warming   274
      Mary Christina Wood

28. Katrina and Power in America   288
    Peter Dreier

29. Integrating Environmental Justice and the Precautionary Principle in
    Research and Policy Making: The Case of Ambient Air Toxics Exposures and
    Health Risks Among Schoolchildren in Los Angeles   300
    Rachel Morello-Frosch, Manuel Pastor Jr., and James Sadd

PART XI.   WAR AND VIOLENCE

30. Poverty, Inequality, and Youth Violence   314
    Ronald C. Kramer

31. Learning War/Learning Race: Fourth-Grade Students in the Aftermath of
    September 11th in New York City   324
    Maria Kromidas

32. Combat Casualties and Race: What Can We Learn From the 2003–2004 Iraq Conflict? 336
    Brian Gifford

    Internet Resources   **349**
    Index   **353**

TOPIC GUIDE

This topic guide is designed to help instructors easily integrate these excellent and contemporary readings into their course. This brief guide also helps instructors and students find interrelated articles, which can help support both learning and research.

CAPITALISM

5. Capitalism, Class, and the Matrix of Domination
7. Neoliberalism as Creative Destruction
8. Poverty and Inequality in the Global Economy
19. Pills, Power, People: Sociological Understanding of the Pharmaceutical Industry

CONSUMERISM

6. Consumer Culture: An Interview With Juliet Schor
11. Reviving Lolita? A Media Literacy Examination of Sexual Portrayals of Girls in Fashion Advertising
19. Pills, Power, People: Sociological Understanding of the Pharmaceutical Industry

CRIME

24. Crime
25. Prison Health and the Health of the Public: Ties That Bind
26. The Global Impact of Gangs

EDUCATION

16. Constructively Challenging Diverse Inner-City Youth's Beliefs About Educational and Career Barriers and Supports
17. The Paradox of Poverty Narratives: Educators Struggling With Children Left Behind
18. Ideological Success, Educational Failure? On the Politics of No Child Left Behind

ENVIRONMENT

27. Nature's Trust: A Legal, Political and Moral Frame for Global Warming
28. Katrina and Power in America
29. Integrating Environmental Justice and the Precautionary Principle in Research and Policy Making: The Case of Ambient Air Toxics Exposures and Health Risks Among Schoolchildren in Los Angeles

GENDER

5. Capitalism, Class, and the Matrix of Domination
11. Reviving Lolita? A Media Literacy Examination of Sexual Portrayals of Girls in Fashion Advertising

17. The Paradox of Poverty Narratives: Educators Struggling With Children Left Behind

21. Welfare Reform in the United States: Gender, Race and Class Matter

GLOBALIZATION

7. Neoliberalism as Creative Destruction
8. Poverty and Inequality in the Global Economy
9. The Making of International Migrants
13. America Transformed
14. 21st Century Slaves
15. "Aqui estamos y no nos vamos!" Global Capital and Immigrant Rights
22. An Understanding of Poverty From Those Who Are Poor
23. Child Labor in Bangladesh: Are Children the Last Economic Resource of the Household?
26. The Global Impact of Gangs

GLOBAL WARMING

27. Nature's Trust: A Legal, Political, and Moral Frame for Global Warming

HEALTH CARE

19. Pills, Power, People: Sociological Understanding of the Pharmaceutical Industry
20. Tango Immigrants in New York City: The Value of Social Reciprocities
25. Prison Health and the Health of the Public: Ties That Bind

INDUSTRY

6. Consumer Culture: An Interview With Juliet Schor
10. The New Media Giants: Changing Industry Structure
19. Pills, Power, People: Sociological Understanding of the Pharmaceutical Industry

IMMIGRATION-IMMIGRANTS

9. The Making of International Migrants
14. 21st Century Slaves
15. "Aqui estamos y no nos vamos!" Global Capital and Immigrant Rights
20. Tango Immigrants in New York City: The Value of Social Reciprocities

INEQUALITY

3. Where Do We Go From Here?
5. Capitalism, Class, and the Matrix of Domination
8. Poverty and Inequality in the Global Economy

MEDIA

10. The New Media Giants: Changing Industry Structure
11. Reviving Lolita? A Media Literacy Examination of Sexual Portrayals of Girls in Fashion Advertising
12. Tripping Up Big Media

Neoliberalism

7. Neoliberalism as Creative Destruction
8. Poverty and Inequality in the Global Economy
15. "Aqui estamos y no nos vamos!" Global Capital and Immigrant Rights
21. Welfare Reform in the United States: Gender, Race and Class Matter

Poverty

8. Poverty and Inequality in the Global Economy
17. The Paradox of Poverty Narratives: Educators Struggling With Children Left Behind
21. Welfare Reform in the United States: Gender, Race and Class Matter
22. An Understanding of Poverty From Those Who Are Poor
23. Child Labor in Bangladesh: Are Children the Last Economic Resource of the Household?
30. Poverty, Inequality, and Youth Violence

Qualitative Data Analysis

11. Reviving Lolita? A Media Literacy Examination of Sexual Portrayals of Girls in Fashion Advertising
17. The Paradox of Poverty Narratives: Educators Struggling With Children Left Behind
20. Tango Immigrants in New York City: The Value of Social Reciprocities
22. An Understanding of Poverty From Those Who Are Poor

Quantitative Data Analysis

23. Child Labor in Bangladesh: Are Children the Last Economic Resource of the Houshold?
32. Combat Casualties and Race: What Can We Learn From the 2003–2004 Iraq Conflict?

Race-Ethnicity

3. Where Do We Go From Here?
5. Capitalism, Class, and the Matrix of Domination
20. Tango Immigrants in New York City: The Value of Social Reciprocities
21. Welfare Reform in the United States: Gender, Race and Class Matter
29. Integrating Environmental Justice and the Precautionary Principle in Research and Policy Making: The Case of Ambient Air Toxics Exposures and Health Risks Among Schoolchildren in Los Angeles
31. Learning War/Learning Race: Fourth-Grade Students in the Aftermath of September 11th in New York City
32. Combat Casualties and Race: What Can We Learn From the 2003–2004 Iraq Conflict?

Social Capital

4. The Fragmentation of Social Life: Some Critical Societal Concerns for the New Millennium
16. Constructively Challenging Diverse Inner-City Youth's Beliefs About Educational and Career Barriers and Supports
20. Tango Immigrants in New York City: The Value of Social Reciprocities

SOCIAL CHANGE

3. Where Do We Go From Here?
12. Tripping Up Big Media
15. "Aqui estamos y no nos vamos!" Global Capital and Immigrant Rights

SOCIAL CLASS

5. Capitalism, Class, and the Matrix of Domination
13. America Transformed
21. Welfare Reform in the United States: Gender, Race and Class Matter

SOCIAL POLICY

17. The Paradox of Poverty Narratives: Educators Struggling With Children Left Behind
18. Ideological Success, Educational Failure? On the Politics of No Child Left Behind
21. Welfare Reform in the United States: Gender, Race and Class Matter
28. Katrina and Power in America

SOCIAL PROBLEMS (GENERAL)

1. The Promise
2. The Art of Savage Discovery: How to Blame the Victim

SOCIAL STRUCTURES

1. The Promise
2. The Art of Savage Discovery: How to Blame the Victim
3. Where Do We Go From Here?
5. Capitalism, Class, and the Matrix of Domination

STEREOTYPES

11. Reviving Lolita? A Media Literacy Examination of Sexual Portrayals of Girls in Fashion Advertising
31. Learning War/Learning Race: Fourth-Grade Students in the Aftermath of September 11th in New York City

URBAN STUDIES

16. Constructively Challenging Diverse Inner-City Youth's Beliefs About Educational and Career Beliefs and Supports
17. The Paradox of Poverty Narratives: Educators Struggling With Children Left Behind
20. Tango Immigrants in New York City: The Value of Social Reciprocities
28. Katrina and Power in America
29. Integrating Environmental Justice and the Precautionary Principle in Research and Policy Making: The Case of Ambient Air Toxics Exposures and Health Risks Among Schoolchildren in Los Angeles

VIOLENCE

   30. Poverty, Inequality, and Youth Violence

WAR

   31. Learning War/Learning Race: Fourth-Grade Students in the Aftermath of September 11th in New York City
   32. Combat Causalities and Race: What Can We Learn From the 2003–2004 Iraq Conflict?

WORK AND LABOR

   13. America Transformed
   14. 21st Century Slaves
   23. Child Labor in Bangladesh: Are Children the Last Economic Resource of the Household?

YOUTH

   11. Reviving Lolita? A Media Literacy Examination of Sexual Portrayals of Girls in Fashion Advertising
   16. Constructively Challenging Inner-City Youth's Beliefs About Educational and Career Barriers and Supports
   23. Child Labor in Bangladesh: Are Children the Last Economic Resource of the Household?
   26. The Global Impact of Gangs
   29. Integrating Environmental Justice and the Precautionary Principle in Research and Policy Making: The Case of Ambient Air Toxics Exposures and Health Risks Among Schoolchildren in Los Angeles
   30. Poverty, Inequality, and Youth Violence
   31. Learning War/Learning Race: Fourth-Grade Students in the Aftermath of September 11th in New York City

ADVISORY BOARD

ABOUT THE EDITORS

Anna Leon-Guerrero is a Professor of Sociology at Pacific Lutheran University, Tacoma, Washington. A recipient of the university's Faculty Excellence Award, she teaches courses on statistics, sociological theory, and social problems. As a social service program evaluator and consultant, her research has focused on welfare reform, employment strategies for the working poor, and program assessment. She is the coauthor of *Social Statistics for a Diverse Society* (with Chava Frankfort-Nachmias).

Kristine Zentgraf is an Associate Professor at California State University, Long Beach. A recipient of the university's 2004–2005 Distinguished Faculty Teaching Award, she teaches courses on sociological theory; social stratification; race, class, and gender; and sociology of immigration. Her research focuses on issues related to gender, family, and immigration, and she is currently working on a project about immigrant family separation. She is the coauthor of *American Transformed: Globalization, Inequality and Power* (with Gary Hytrek).

PREFACE

We live in a time of profound transformations characterized by economic, technological, and social changes. Today the production and distribution of goods and services take place quickly and efficiently across the globe. Technology has made possible immediate and efficient communication with people, and we have access to information and interactions in ways that have never before been possible. Medical research and developments have effectively challenged some of the most threatening diseases of our day.

Despite such progress social problems persist and continue to affect individuals, communities, and societies across the globe. In fact, the economic, social, and political transformations of the past 25 years have come with their own unique set of challenges that have exacerbated "old" social problems and/or contributed to the emergence of "new" social problems. For example, a significant amount of poverty persists in countries all over the world, including the United States. Racial-ethnic and gender inequalities exist in multiple forms and are evident throughout our social institutions. While environmental destruction has long been of concern, the increase in global production has accelerated this problem. An increase in global travel has resulted in diseases being spread more quickly and easily. And currently the threat of global terrorism is always on our minds.

So what do we make of all this? How can we begin to understand social problems? What are the sources of societal problems? Are they inevitable? Why are some people disproportionately affected by social problems? Can we prevent them from happening or take action to eradicate social problems?

These questions are the "stuff" of sociology, and the sociological imagination is a powerful tool that can help us to better understand both the old and new problems that plague our society. Most importantly, a sociological understanding of the world challenges our "taken for granted" notions–especially of the world that we see represented on television and in the written media. We may think we understand contemporary trends and problems, but do we really? Are we asking the critical questions that challenge our assumptions about the world?

This reader was put together with these questions in mind. But it was also informed by the belief that we study social problems so that we can do something about them. We believe that the world can be a better, safer, and more equitable place for all. This said, we recognize that solutions to social problems do not come easily or quickly.

As leaders of the next generation, college and university students will be at the forefront of struggles for the betterment of society, social justice, and human rights. As such, students will not only need to be well informed about contemporary social issues but will need to be able to critically analyze the causes and consequences of social trends and problems. In other words, students will need to learn how to use their sociological imagination. Only then can we begin to create and adopt creative strategies for social change.

The primary message of the articles presented in this reader can be summarized in the following way: social problems are rooted in the macro structures of society—economic, political, and social—and they are maintained and reproduced by social institutions and the daily actions of individuals. This book begins, in Part I, by looking at how the sociological imagination allows us to view social problems in a unique and critical way. Parts II and III examine the role of political, economic, and ideological systems as the basis of contemporary and historical social problems, both in the United States and globally. Parts IV through IX explore the role of social institutions—media, education, work, health, government, and criminal justice—in society. These discussions are complex and multidimensional—social institutions are not only the site of many social problems but they often function in ways that maintain and reproduce societal problems. Finally, in Parts X and XI, we specifically examine social issues and problems related to the topics of the environment and war and safety.

Throughout the book we have included articles that highlight the importance of racial-ethnic, class, and gender inequality. We want students to think specifically about the ways that ideological beliefs and practices that are embedded in the structure of society contribute to the greater vulnerability of some groups over others and the ways that race-ethnicity, class, and gender are structures of group opportunity, power, and privilege. We have also included some articles that offer a global focus on social problems. Not only will this help students begin to understand how social problems in our own society often emerge in a global context, but it will enable students to see how similar issues are experienced by other societies. Although the articles cannot begin to cover every social problems (or even all of the aspects of a particular social problem), our hope is that the articles will draw students' attention to some of the most pressing social problems of our day, engage them in sociological thinking and discussions, and perhaps even move them to social action.

On a final note we have found that when studying social problems it is easy for students to begin to feel overwhelmed. Societal problems and challenges can sometimes feel so huge and out of control that we begin to wonder if there is really anything that an individual or community could do to ever make a difference. To help students think about these feelings, we ask that they do three things. First, pay close attention to those represented in the articles that they will be reading. Everyday individuals and communities are working to address social problems—and they are making a difference. Second, remember that knowledge is not just some abstract thing. If used it can be a powerful and empowering tool that can make a difference in our world. There are consequences to having knowledge that is distorted, wrong, or incomplete, as it leads one to act in ways that are misguided or exclusionary. Thus, we may very well help to maintain and reproduce the social problems that already exist. Finally, the study of social problems is also about people, their values, priorities, and visions. What kind of world will students think is possible? What kind of world will they want to live in today and leave for their loved ones? How do they think that this can be best achieved? What role can they play? We hope that more than anything else, this collection helps to move students down the path of lifelong learning, helps them to learn a little more about themselves, and helps them think about their role in our quickly changing—and sometimes challenging—world.

PART I

THE SOCIOLOGY OF SOCIAL PROBLEMS

CHAPTER 1

The Promise

C. Wright Mills (1959)

In this seminal statement on sociology and the study of social problems, C. Wright Mills advocates for the use of the sociological imagination to understand history, biography, and the intersection between the two. Mills explores the difference between personal troubles and social issues to explain a sociological view of social problems.

"The individual can . . . know his own chances in life only by becoming aware of those of all individuals in his circumstances."

Nowadays men often feel that their private lives are a series of traps. They sense that within their everyday worlds, they cannot overcome their troubles, and in this feeling, they are often quite correct: What ordinary men are directly aware of and what they try to do are bounded by the private orbits in which they live; their visions and their powers are limited to the close-up scenes of job, family, neighborhood; in other milieux, they move vicariously and remain spectators. And the more aware they become, however vaguely, of ambitions and of threats which transcend their immediate locales, the more trapped they seem to feel.

Underlying this sense of being trapped are seemingly impersonal changes in the very structure of continent-wide societies. The facts of contemporary history are also facts about the success and the failure of individual men and women. When a society is industrialized, a peasant becomes a worker; a feudal lord is liquidated or becomes a businessman. When classes rise or fall, a man is employed or unemployed; when the rate of investment goes up or down, a man takes new heart or goes broke. When wars happen, an insurance salesman becomes a rocket launcher; a store clerk, a radar man; a wife lives alone; a child grows up without a father. Neither the life of an individual nor the history of a society can be understood without understanding both.

Yet men do not usually define the troubles they endure in terms of historical change and institutional contradiction. The well-being they enjoy, they do not usually impute to the big ups and downs of the societies in which they live. Seldom aware of the intricate connection between the patterns of their own lives and the course of world history, ordinary men do not usually know what this connection means for the kinds of men they are becoming and for the kinds of history-making in which they might take part. They do not possess the quality of mind essential to grasp the interplay of man and society, of biography and history, of self and world. They cannot cope with their personal troubles in such ways as to control the structural transformations that usually lie behind them.

Surely it is no wonder. In what period have so many men been so totally exposed at so fast a pace to such earthquakes of change? That Americans have not known such catastrophic changes as have the men and women of other societies is due to historical facts that are now quickly becoming "merely history." The history that now affects every man is world history. Within this scene and this period, in the course of a single generation, one-sixth of mankind is transformed from all that is feudal and backward into all that is modern, advanced, and fearful. Political colonies are freed, new and less visible forms of imperialism installed. Revolutions occur; men feel the intimate grip of new kinds of authority. Totalitarian societies rise, and are smashed to bits—or succeed fabulously. After two centuries of ascendancy, capitalism is shown up as only one way to make society into an industrial apparatus. After two centuries of hope, even formal democracy is restricted to a quite small portion of mankind. Everywhere in the underdeveloped world, ancient ways of life are broken up and vague expectations become urgent demands. Everywhere in the overdeveloped world, the means of authority and of violence become total in scope and bureaucratic in form. Humanity itself now lies before us, the supernation at either pole concentrating its most coordinated and massive efforts upon the preparation of World War Three.

The very shaping of history now outpaces the ability of men to orient themselves in accordance with cherished values. And which values? Even when they do not panic, men often sense that older ways of feeling and thinking have collapsed and that newer beginnings are ambiguous to the point of moral stasis. Is it any wonder that ordinary men feel they cannot cope with the larger worlds with which they are so suddenly confronted? That they cannot understand the meaning of their epoch for their own lives? That—in defense of selfhood—they become morally insensible, trying to remain altogether private men? Is it any wonder that they come to be possessed by a sense of the trap?

It is not only information that they need—in this Age of Fact, information often dominates their attention and overwhelms their capacities to assimilate it. It is not only the skills of reason that they need—although their struggles to acquire these often exhaust their limited moral energy.

What they need, and what they feel they need, is a quality of mind that will help them to use information and to develop reason in order to achieve lucid summations of what is going on in the world and of what may be happening within themselves. It is this quality, I am going to contend, that journalists and scholars, artists and publics, scientists and editors are coming to expect of what may be called the sociological imagination.

The sociological imagination enables its possessor to understand the larger historical scene in terms of its meaning for the inner life and the external career of a variety of individuals. It enables him to take into account how individuals, in the welter of their daily experience, often become falsely conscious of their social positions. Within that welter, the framework of modern society is sought, and within that framework the psychologies of a variety of men and women are formulated. By such means the personal uneasiness of individuals is focused upon explicit troubles and the indifference of publics is transformed into involvement with public issues.

The first fruit of this imagination—and the first lesson of the social science that embodies it—is the idea that the individual can understand his own experience and gauge his own fate only by locating himself within his period, that he can know his own chances in life only by becoming aware of those of all individuals in his circumstances. In many ways it is a terrible lesson; in many ways a magnificent one. We do not know the limits of man's capacities for supreme effort or willing degradation, for agony or glee, for pleasurable brutality or the sweetness of reason. But in our time we have come to know that the limits of "human nature" are frighteningly broad. We have come to know that every individual lives, from one generation to the next, in some society; that he lives out a biography, and that he lives it out within some historical sequence. By the fact of his living he contributes, however minutely, to the shaping of this society and to the course of its history, even as he is made by society and by its historical push and shove.

The sociological imagination enables us to grasp history and biography and the relations between the two within society. That is its task and its promise. To recognize this task and this promise is the mark of the classic social analyst. It is characteristic of Herbert Spencer—turgid, polysyllabic, comprehensive; of E. A. Ross—graceful, muckraking, upright; of Auguste Comte and Emile Durkheim; of the intricate and subtle Karl Mannheim. It is the quality of all that is intellectually excellent in Karl Marx; it is the clue to Thorstein Veblen's brilliant and ironic insight, to Joseph Schumpeter's many-sided constructions of reality; it is the basis of the psychological sweep of W. E. H. Lecky no less than of the profundity and clarity of Max Weber. And it is the signal of what is best in contemporary studies of man and society.

No social study that does not come back to the problems of biography, of history, and of their intersections within a society has completed its intellectual journey. Whatever the specific problems of the classic social analysts, however limited or however broad the features of social reality they have examined, those who have been imaginatively aware of the promise of their work have consistently asked three sorts of questions:

1. What is the structure of this particular society as a whole? What are its essential components, and how are they related to one another? How does it differ from other varieties of social order? Within it, what is the meaning of any particular feature for its continuance and for its change?

2. Where does this society stand in human history? What are the mechanics by which it is changing? What is its place within and its meaning for the development of humanity as a whole? How does any particular feature we are examining affect, and how is it affected by, the historical period in which it moves? And this period—what are its essential features? How does it differ from other periods? What are its characteristic ways of history making?

3. What varieties of men and women now prevail in this society and in this period? And what varieties are coming to prevail? In what ways are they selected and formed, liberated and repressed, made sensitive and blunted? What kinds of "human nature" are revealed in the conduct and character we observe in this society in this period? And what is the meaning for "human nature" of each and every feature of the society we are examining?

Whether the point of interest is a great power state or a minor literary mood, a family, a prison, a creed—these are the kinds of questions the best social analysts have asked. They are the intellectual pivots of classic studies of man in society—and they are the questions inevitably raised by any mind possessing the sociological imagination. For that imagination is the capacity to shift from one perspective to another—from the political to the psychological; from examination of a single family to comparative assessment of the national budgets of the world; from the theological school to the military establishment; from considerations of an oil industry to studies of contemporary poetry. It is the capacity to range from the most impersonal and remote transformations to the most intimate features of the human self—and to see the relations between the two. Back of its use there is always the urge to know the social and historical meaning of the individual in the society and in the period in which he has his quality and his being.

That, in brief, is why it is by means of the sociological imagination that men now hope to grasp what is going on in the world, and to understand what is happening in themselves as minute points of the intersections of biography and history within society. In large part, contemporary man's self-conscious view of himself as at least an outsider, if not a permanent stranger, rests upon an absorbed realization of social relativity and of the transformative power of history. The sociological imagination is the most fruitful form of this self-consciousness. By its use men whose mentalities have swept only a series of limited orbits often come to feel as if suddenly awakened in a house with which they had only supposed themselves to be familiar. Correctly or incorrectly, they often come to feel that they can now provide themselves with adequate summations, cohesive assessments, comprehensive orientations. Older decisions that once appeared sound now seem to them products of a mind unaccountably dense. Their capacity for astonishment is made lively again. They acquire a new way of thinking, they experience a transvaluation of values: in a word, by their reflection and by their sensibility, they realize the cultural meaning of the social sciences.

Perhaps the most fruitful distinction with which the sociological imagination works is between "the personal troubles of milieu" and "the public issues of social structure." This distinction is an essential tool of the sociological imagination and a feature of all classic work in social science.

Troubles occur within the character of the individual and within the range of his immediate relations with others; they have to do with his self and with those limited areas of social life of which he is directly and personally aware. Accordingly, the statement and the resolution of troubles properly lie within the individual as a biographical entity and within the scope of his immediate milieu—the social setting that is directly open to his personal experience and to some extent his willful activity. A trouble is a private matter: values cherished by an individual are felt by him to be threatened.

Issues have to do with matters that transcend these local environments of the individual and the range of his inner life. They have to do with the organization of many such milieux into the institutions of an historical society as a whole, with the ways in which various milieux overlap and interpenetrate to form the larger structure of social and historical life. An issue is a public matter; some value cherished by publics is felt to be threatened. Often there is a debate about what that value really is and about what it is that really threatens it. This debate is often without focus if only because it is the very nature of an issue, unlike even widespread trouble, that it cannot very well be defined in terms of the immediate and everyday environments of ordinary men. An issue, in fact, often involves a crisis in institutional arrangements, and often too it involves what Marxists call "contradictions" or "antagonisms."

In these terms, consider unemployment. When, in a city of 100,000, only one man is unemployed, that is his personal trouble, and for its relief we properly look to the character of the man, his skills, and his immediate opportunities. But when in a nation of 50 million employees,

15 million men are unemployed, that is an issue, and we may not hope to find its solution within the range of opportunities open to any one individual. The very structure of opportunities has collapsed. Both the correct statement of the problem and the range of possible solutions require us to consider the economic and political institutions of the society, and not merely the personal situation and character of a scatter of individuals.

Consider war. The personal problem of war, when it occurs, may be how to survive it or how to die in it with honor; how to make money out of it; how to climb into the higher safety of the military apparatus; or how to contribute to the war's termination. In short, according to one's values, to find a set of milieux and within it to survive the war or make one's death in it meaningful. But the structural issues of war have to do with its causes; with what types of men it throws up into command; with its effects upon economic and political, family, and religious institutions, with the unorganized irresponsibility of a world of nation-states.

Consider marriage. Inside a marriage a man and a woman may experience personal troubles, but when the divorce rate during the first four years of marriage is 250 out of every 1,000 attempts, this is an indication of a structural issue having to do with the institutions of marriage and the family and other institutions that bear upon them.

Or consider the metropolis—the horrible, beautiful, ugly, magnificent sprawl of the great city. For many upper-class people, the personal solution to "the problem of the city" is to have an apartment with private garage under it in the heart of the city, and forty miles out, a house by Henry Hill, garden by Garrett Eckbo, on a hundred acres of private land. In these two controlled environments—with a small staff at each end and a private helicopter connection—most people could solve many of the problems of personal milieux caused by the facts of the city. But all this, however splendid, does not solve the public issues that the structural fact of the city poses. What should be done with this wonderful monstrosity? Break it all up into scattered units, combining residence and work? Refurbish it as it stands? Or, after evacuation, dynamite it and build new cities according to new plans in new places? What should those plans be? And who is to decide and to accomplish whatever choice is made? These are structural issues; to confront them and to solve them requires us to consider political and economic issues that affect innumerable milieux.

Insofar as an economy is so arranged that slumps occur, the problem of unemployment becomes incapable of personal solution. Insofar as war is inherent in the nation-state system and in the uneven industrialization of the world, the ordinary individual in his restricted milieu will be powerless—with or without psychiatric aid—to solve the troubles this system or lack of system imposes upon him. Insofar as the family as an institution turns women into darling little slaves and men into their chief providers and unwearied dependents, the problem of a satisfactory marriage remains incapable of purely private solution. Insofar as the overdeveloped megalopolis and the overdeveloped automobile are built-in features of the overdeveloped society, the issues of urban living will not be solved by personal ingenuity and private wealth.

What we experience in various and specific milieux, I have noted, is often caused by structural changes. Accordingly, to understand the changes of many personal milieux we are required to look beyond them. And the number and variety of such structural changes increase as the institutions within which we live become more embracing and more intricately connected with one another. To be aware of the idea of social structure and to use it with sensibility is to be capable of tracing such linkages among a great variety of milieux. To be able to do that is to possess the sociological imagination. . . .

Discussion Questions

1. What is the difference between a personal trouble and a public issue?

   According to Mills, a personal trouble involves the character of an individual and his or her intimate relationships with others. On the other hand, an issue is a public matter, transcending the life of one individual. Mills explains that with a public issue, some public value is being threatened.

2. Does everyone agree on what constitutes a public issue? Why or why not?

   Instructors and students can review several issues, examining if there is agreement on whether these issues qualify as problems. Issues may include the rising price of gas, terrorism, same-sex marriages, or immigration.

Source: From Mills, C. W. (1959). *Sociological imagination.* New York: Oxford University Press. Copyright © 1963. Reprinted with permission from Oxford University Press.

CHAPTER 2

The Art of Savage Discovery

How to Blame the Victim

William Ryan (1971)

Societies tend to blame social problems on their victims, choosing to ignore relevant social and structural inequalities within which social problems are rooted. In this excerpt from *Blaming the Victim* (1971), psychologist William Ryan critically examines the ideological basis of this victim-blaming approach and discusses how such an approach lends itself to the maintenance of the status quo.

I

Twenty years ago, Zero Mostel used to do a sketch in which he impersonated a Dixiecrat Senator conducting an investigation of the origins of World War II. At the climax of the sketch, the Senator boomed out, in an excruciating mixture of triumph and suspicion, "What was Pearl Harbor *doing* in the Pacific?" This is an extreme example of Blaming the Victim.

Twenty years ago, we could laugh at Zero Mostel's caricature. In recent years, however, the same process has been going on every day in the arena of social problems, public health, anti-poverty programs, and social welfare. A philosopher might analyze this process and prove that, technically, it is comic. But it is hardly ever funny.

Consider some victims. One is the miseducated child in the slum school. He is blamed for his own miseducation. He is said to contain within himself the causes of his inability to read and write well. The shorthand phrase is "cultural deprivation," which, to those in the know, conveys what they allege to be inside information: that the poor child carries a scanty pack of intellectual baggage as he enters school. He doesn't know about books and magazines and newspapers, they say. (No books in the home:

the mother fails to subscribe to *Reader's Digest.*) They say that if he talks at all—an unlikely event since slum parents don't talk to their children—he certainly doesn't talk correctly. (Lower-class dialect spoken here, or even—God forbid!—Southern Negro. *Ici on parle nigra.*) If you can manage to get him to sit in a chair, they say, he squirms and looks out the window. (Impulsive-ridden, these kids, motoric rather than verbal.) In a word he is "disadvantaged" and "socially deprived," they say, and this, of course, accounts for his failure (*his* failure, they say) to learn much in school.

Note the similarity to the logic of Zero Mostel's Dixiecrat Senator. What is the culturally deprived child *doing* in the school? What is wrong with the victim? In pursuing this logic, no one remembers to ask questions about the collapsing buildings and torn textbooks; the frightened, insensitive teachers; the six additional desks in the room; the blustering, frightened principals; the relentless segregation; the callous administrator; the irrelevant curriculum; the bigoted or cowardly members of the school board; the insulting history book; the stingy taxpayers; the fairy-tale readers; or the self-serving faculty of the local teachers' college. We are encouraged to confine our attention to the child and to dwell on all his alleged defects. Cultural deprivation becomes an omnibus explanation for the educational disaster area known as the inner-city school. This is Blaming the Victim.

Pointing to the supposedly deviant Negro family as the "fundamental weakness of the Negro community" is another way to blame the victim. Like "cultural deprivation," "Negro family" has become a shorthand phrase with stereotyped connotations of matriarchy, fatherlessness, and pervasive illegitimacy. Growing up in the "crumbling" Negro family is supposed to account for most of the racial evils in America. Insiders have the word, of course, and know that this phrase is supposed to evoke images of growing up with a long-absent or never-present father (replaced from time to time perhaps by a series of transient lovers) and with bossy women ruling the roost, so that the children are irreparably damaged. This refers particularly to the poor, bewildered male children, whose psyches are fatally wounded and who are never, alas, to learn the trick of becoming upright, downright, forthright all-American boys. Is it any wonder the Negroes cannot achieve equality? From such families! And, again, by focusing our attention on the Negro family as the apparent *cause* of racial inequality, our eye is diverted. Racism, discrimination, segregation, and the powerlessness of the ghetto are subtly, but thoroughly, downgraded in importance.

The generic process of Blaming the Victim is applied to almost every American problem. The miserable health care of the poor is explained away on the grounds that the victim has poor motivation and lacks health information. The problems of slum housing are traced to the characteristics of tenants who are labeled as "Southern rural migrants" not yet "acculturated" to life in the big city. The "multiproblem" poor, it is claimed, suffer the psychological effects of impoverishment, the "culture of poverty," and the deviant value system of the lower classes; consequently, though unwittingly, they cause their own troubles. From such a viewpoint, the obvious fact that poverty is primarily an absence of money is easily overlooked or set aside. . . .

The growing number of families receiving welfare are fallaciously linked together with the increased number of illegitimate children as twin results of promiscuity and sexual abandon among members of the lower orders. Every important social problem—crime, mental illness, civil disorder, unemployment—has been analyzed within the framework of the victim-blaming ideology. In the following pages, I shall present in detail nine examples that relate to social problems and human services in urban areas.

It would be possible for me to venture into other areas—one finds a perfect example in literature about the underdeveloped countries of the Third World, in which the lack of prosperity and technological progress is attributed to some aspect of the national character of the people, such as lack of "achievement motivation"—but I plan to stay within the confines of my own personal and professional experience, which is, generally, with racial injustice, social welfare, and human services in the city.

I have been listening to the victim-blamers and pondering their thought processes for a number of years. That process is often very subtle. Victim-blaming is cloaked in kindness and concern, and bears all the trappings and statistical furbelows of scientism; it is obscured by a perfumed haze of humanitarianism. In observing the process of Blaming the Victim, one tends to be confused and disoriented because those who practice this art display a deep concern for the victims that is quite genuine. In this way, the new ideology is very different from the open prejudice and reactionary tactics of the old days. Its adherents include sympathetic social scientists with social consciences in good working order, and liberal politicians with a genuine commitment to reform. They are very careful to dissociate themselves from vulgar Calvinism or crude racism; they indignantly condemn any notions of innate wickedness or genetic defect. "The Negro is *not born* inferior," they shout apoplectically. "Force of circumstance," they explain in reasonable tones, "has *made* him inferior." And they dismiss with self-righteous contempt any claims that the poor man in America is plainly unworthy or shiftless or enamored of idleness. No, they say, he is "caught in the cycle of poverty." He is trained to be poor by his culture and his family life, endowed by his environment (perhaps by his ignorant mother's outdated style of toilet training) with those unfortunately unpleasant characteristics that make him ineligible for a passport into the affluent society.

Blaming the Victim is, of course, quite different from old-fashioned conservative ideologies. The latter simply dismissed victims as inferior, genetically defective, or morally unfit; the emphasis is on the intrinsic, even hereditary, defect. The former shifts its emphasis to the environmental causation. The old-fashioned conservative could hold firmly to the belief that the oppressed and the victimized were born that way—"that way" being defective or inadequate in character or ability. The new ideology attributes defect and inadequacy to the malignant nature of poverty, injustice, slum life, and racial difficulties. The stigma that marks the victim and accounts for his victimization is an acquired stigma, a stigma of social, rather than genetic, origin. But the stigma, the defect, the fatal difference—though derived in the past from environmental forces—is still located *within* the victim, inside his skin. With such an elegant formulation, the humanitarian can have it both ways. He can, all at the same time, concentrate his charitable interest on the defects of the victim, condemn the vague social and environmental stresses that produced the defect (some time ago), and ignore the continuing effect of victimizing social forces (right now). It is a brilliant ideology for justifying a perverse form of social action designed to change, not society, as one might expect, but rather society's victim.

As a result, there is a terrifying sameness in the programs that arise from this kind of analysis. In education, we have programs of "compensatory education" to build up the skills and attitudes of the ghetto child, rather than structural changes in the schools. In race relations, we have social engineers who think up ways of "strengthening" the Negro family, rather than methods of eradicating racism. In health care, we develop new programs to provide health information (to correct the supposed ignorance of the poor) and to reach out and discover cases of untreated illness and disability (to compensate for their supposed unwillingness to seek treatment). Meanwhile, the gross inequities of our medical care delivery systems are left completely unchanged. As we might expect, the logical outcome of analyzing social problems in terms of the deficiencies of the victim is the development of programs aimed at correcting those deficiencies. The formula for action becomes extraordinarily simple: change the victim.

All of this happens so smoothly that it seems downright rational. First, identify a social problem. Second, study those affected by the problem and discover in what ways they are different from the rest of us as a consequence of deprivation and injustice. Third, define the differences as the cause of the social problem itself. Finally, of course, assign a government bureaucrat to invent a humanitarian action program to correct the differences.

Now no one in his right mind would quarrel with the assertion that social problems are present in abundance and are readily identifiable. God knows it is true that when hundreds of thousands of poor children drop out of school—or even graduate from school—they are barely literate. After spending some ten thousand hours in the company of professional educators, these children appear to have learned very little. The fact of failure in their education is undisputed. And the racial situation in America is usually acknowledged to be a number one item on the nation's agenda. Despite years of marches,

commissions, judicial decisions, and endless legislative remedies, we are confronted with unchanging or even widening racial differences in achievement. In addition, despite our assertions that Americans get the best health care in the world, the poor stubbornly remain unhealthy. They lose more work because of illness, have more carious teeth, lose more babies as a result of both miscarriage and infant death, and die considerably younger than the well-to-do.

The problems are there, and there in great quantities. They make us uneasy. Added together, these disturbing signs reflect inequality and a puzzlingly high level of unalleviated distress in America totally inconsistent with our proclaimed ideals and our enormous wealth. This thread—this rope—of inconsistency stands out so visibly in the fabric of American life, that it is jarring to the eye. And this must be explained, to the satisfaction of our conscience as well as our patriotism. Blaming the Victim is an ideal, almost painless, evasion.

The second step in applying this explanation is to look sympathetically at those who "have" the problem in question, to separate them out and define them in some way as a special group, a group that is *different* from the population in general. This is a crucial and essential step in the process, for that difference is in itself hampering and maladaptive. The Different Ones are seen as less competent, less skilled, less knowing—in short, less human. The ancient Greeks deduced from a single characteristic, a difference in language, that the barbarians—that is, the "babblers" who spoke a strange tongue—were wild, uncivilized, dangerous, rapacious, uneducated, lawless, and, indeed, scarcely more than animals. Automatically labeling strangers as savages, weird and inhuman creatures (thus explaining difference by exaggerating difference) not infrequently justifies mistreatment, enslavement, or even extermination of the Different Ones.

Blaming the Victim depends on a very similar process of identification (carried out, to be sure, in the most kindly, philanthropic, and intellectual manner) whereby the victim of social problems is identified as strange, different—in other words, as a barbarian, a savage. Discovering savages, then, is an essential component of, and prerequisite to, Blaming the Victim, and the art of Savage Discovery is a core skill that must be acquired by all aspiring Victim Blamers. They must learn how to demonstrate that the poor, the black, the ill, the jobless, the slum tenants, are different and strange. They must learn to conduct or interpret the research that shows how "these people" think in different forms, act in different patterns, cling to different values, seek different goals, and learn different truths. Which is to say that they are strangers, barbarians, savages. This is how the distressed and disinherited are redefined in order to make it possible for us to look at society's problems and to attribute their causation to the individuals affected.

II

Blaming the Victim is an ideological process, which is to say that it is a set of ideas and concepts deriving from systematically motivated, but *unintended,* distortions of reality. In the sense that Karl Mannheim used the term, an ideology develops from the "collective unconscious" of a group or class and is rooted in a class-based interest in maintaining the *status quo* (as contrasted with what he calls a *utopia,* a set of ideas rooted in a class-based interest in *changing* the *status quo*). An ideology, then, has several components: First, there is the belief system itself, the way of looking at the world, the set of ideas and concepts. Second, there is the systematic distortion of reality reflected in those ideas. Third is the condition that the distortion must not be a conscious, intentional process. Finally, though they are not intentional, the ideas must serve a specific function: maintaining the *status quo* in the interest of a specific group. Blaming the Victim fits this definition of all counts as I will attempt to show in detail in the following chapters. Most particularly, it is important to realize that Blaming the Victim is not a process of *intentional* distortion although it does serve the class interests of those who practice it. And it has a rich ancestry in American thought about social problems and how to deal with them.

Thinking about social problems is especially susceptible to ideological influences since, as John Seeley has pointed out, defining a social problem is not so simple.

"What is a social problem?" may seem an ingenuous question until one turns to confront its opposite: "What human problem is *not* a social problem?" Since any problem in which people are involved is social, why do we reserve the label for some problems in which people are involved and withhold it from others? To use Seeley's example, why is crime called a social problem when university administration is not? The phenomena we look at are bounded by the act of definition. They become social problems only by being so considered. In Seeley's words, *"naming* it as a problem, after naming it as a *problem."*

It is only recently, for example, that we have begun to *name* the rather large quantity of people on earth as the *problem* of overpopulation, or the population explosion. Such phenomena often become proper predicaments for certain solutions, certain treatments. Before the 1930's,

the most anti-Semitic German was unaware that Germany had a "Jewish problem." It took the Nazis to *name* the simple existence of Jews in the Third Reich as a "social problem," and that act of definition helped to shape the final solution.

We have removed "immigration" from our list of social problems (after executing a solution—choking off the flow of immigrants) and have added "urbanization." Nowadays, we define the situation of men out of work as the social problem of "unemployment" rather than, as in Elizabethan times, that of "idleness." (The McCone Commission, investigating the Watts Riot of 1966, showed how hard old ideologies die; it specified both unemployment *and* idleness as causes of the disorder.) In the near future, if we are to credit the prophets of automation, the label "unemployment" will fade away and "idleness," now renamed the "leisure-time problem," will begin again to raise its lazy head. We have been comfortable for years with the "Negro problem," a term that clearly implies that the existence of Negroes is somehow a problematic fact. *Ebony* Magazine turned the tables recently and renamed the phenomenon as "The White Problem in America," which may be a good deal more accurate.

We must particularly ask, "To whom are social problems a problem?" And usually, if truth were to be told, we would have to admit that we mean they are a problem to those of us who are outside the boundaries of what we have defined as the problem. Negroes are a problem to racist whites, welfare is a problem to stingy taxpayers, delinquency is a problem to nervous property owners.

Now, if this is the quality of our assumptions about social problems, we are led unerringly to certain beliefs about the causes of these problems. We cannot comfortably believe that *we* are the cause of that which is problematic to us; therefore, we are almost compelled to believe that *they*—the problematic ones—are the cause and this immediately prompts us to search for deviance. Identification of the deviance as the cause of the problem is a simple step that ordinarily does not even require evidence.

C. Wright Mills analyzed the ideology of those who write about social problems and demonstrated the relationship of their texts to class interest and to the preservation of the existent social order. In sifting the material in thirty-one widely used textbooks in "social problems," "social pathology," and "social disorganization," Mills found a pervasive, coherent ideology with a number of common characteristics.

First, the textbooks present material about these problems, he says, in simple, descriptive terms, with each problem unrelated to the others and none related in any meaningful way to other aspects of the social environment. Second, the problems are selected and described largely according to predetermined norms. Poverty is a problem in that it deviates from the standard of economic self-sufficiency; divorce is a problem because the family is supposed to remain intact; crime and delinquency are problematic insofar as they depart from the accepted moral and legal standards of the community. The norms themselves are taken as givens, and no effort is made to examine them. Nor is there any thought given to the manner in which norms might themselves contribute to the development of the problems. (In a society in which everyone is assumed and expected to be economically self-sufficient, as an example, doesn't economic dependency almost automatically mean poverty? No attention is given to such issues.)

Within such a framework, then, deviation from norms and standards comes to be defined as failed or incomplete socialization—failure to learn the rules or the inability to learn how to keep them. Those with social problems are then viewed as unable or unwilling to adjust to society's standards, which are narrowly conceived by what Mills calls "independent middle class persons verbally living out Protestant ideas in small town America." This obviously, is a precise description of the social origins and status of almost every one of the authors.

In defining social problems in this way, the social pathologists are, of course, ignoring a whole set of factors that ordinarily might be considered relevant—for instance, unequal distribution of income, social stratification, political struggle, ethnic and racial group conflict, and inequality of power. Their ideology concentrates almost exclusively on the failure of the deviant. To the extent that society plays any part in social problems, it is said to have somehow failed to socialize the individual, to teach him how to adjust to circumstances, which, though far from perfect, are gradually changing for the better. Mills' essay provides a solid foundation for understanding the concept of Blaming the Victim.

This way of thinking on the part of "social pathologists," which Mills identified as the predominant tool used in *analyzing* social problems, also saturates the majority of programs that have been developed to *solve* social problems in America. These programs are based on the assumption that *individuals* "have" social problems as a result of some kind of unusual circumstances— accident, illness, personal defect or handicap, character flaw or maladjustment—that exclude them from using the ordinary mechanisms for maintaining and advancing themselves. For example, the prevalent belief in

America is that, under normal circumstances, everyone can obtain sufficient income for the necessities of life. Those who are unable to do so are special deviant cases, persons who for one reason or another are not able to adapt themselves to the generally satisfactory income-producing system. In times gone by these persons were further classified into the worthy poor—the lame, the blind, the young mother whose husband died in an accident, the aged man no longer able to work—and the unworthy poor—the lazy, the unwed mother and her illegitimate children, the malingerer. All were seen, however, as individuals who, for good reasons or bad, were personal failures, unable to adapt themselves to the system.

In America health care, too, has been predominantly a matter of particular remedial attention provided individually to the more or less random group of persons who have become ill, whose bodily functioning has become deviant and abnormal. In the field of mental health, the same approach has been, and continues to be, dominant. The social problem of mental disease has been viewed as a collection of individual cases of deviance, persons who—through unusual hereditary taint, or exceptional distortion of character—have become unfit for normal activities. The solution to these problems was to segregate the deviants, to protect them, to give them *asylum* from the life of the community for which they were no longer competent.

This has been the dominant style in American social welfare and health activities, then: to treat what we call social problems, such as poverty, disease, and mental illness, in terms of the individual deviance of the special, unusual groups of persons who had those problems. There has also been a competing style, however—much less common, not at all congruent with the prevalent ideology, but continually developing parallel to the dominant style.

Adherents of this approach tended to search for defects in the community and the environment rather than in the individual; to emphasize predictability and usualness rather than random deviance; they tried to think about preventing rather than merely repairing or treating—to see social problems, in a word, as social. In the field of disease, this approach was termed public health, and its practitioners sought the cause of disease in such things as the water supply, the sewage system, the density and quality of housing conditions. They set out to prevent disease, not in individuals, but in the total population, through improved sanitation, inoculation against communicable disease, and the policing of housing conditions. In the field of income maintenance, this secondary style of solving social problems focused on poverty as a predictable event, on the regularities of income deficiency. And it concentrated on the development of standard, generalized programs affecting total groups. Rather than trying to fit the aged worker ending his career into some kind of category of special cases, it assumed all sixty-five-year-old men should expect to retire from the world of work and have the security of an old age pension, to be arranged through public social activity. Unemployment insurance was developed as a method whereby all workers could be protected against the effects of the normal ups and downs of the business cycle. A man out of work could then count on an unemployment check rather than endure the agony of pauperizing himself, selling his tools or his car, and finding himself in the special category of those deserving of charity.

These two approaches to the solution of social problems have existed side by side, the former always dominant, but the latter gradually expanding, slowly becoming more and prevalent.

Elsewhere I have proposed the dimension of *exceptionalism-universalism* as the ideological underpinning for these two contrasting approaches to the analysis and solution of social problems. The *exceptionalist* viewpoint is reflected in arrangements that are private, voluntary, remedial, special, local, and exclusive. Such arrangements imply that problems occur to specially defined categories of persons in an unpredictable manner. The problems are unusual, even unique, they are exceptions to the rule, they occur as a result of individual defect, accident, or unfortunate circumstance and must be remedied by means that are particular and, as it were, tailored to the individual case.

The universalistic viewpoint, on the other hand, is reflected in arrangements that are public, legislated, promotive or preventive, general, national, and inclusive. Inherent in such a viewpoint is the idea that social problems are a function of the social arrangements of the community or the society and that, since these social arrangements are quite imperfect and inequitable, such problems are both predictable and, more important, preventable through public action. They are not unique to the individual, and the fact that they encompass individual persons does not imply that those persons are themselves defective or abnormal.

Consider these two contrasting approaches as they are applied to the problem of smallpox. The medical care approach is exceptionalistic; it is designed to provide remedial treatment to the special category of persons who are afflicted with the disease through a private, voluntary arrangement with a local doctor. The universalistic public health approach is designed to provide preventive inoculation to the total population, ordered by

legislation and available through public means if no private arrangements can be made.

A similar contrast can be made between an exceptionalistic assistance program such as Aid to Families with Dependent Children and the proposed universalistic program of family allowances based simply on the number of children in a family. The latter assumes that the size of a family should automatically be a consideration in income supplementation, since it is in no way taken into account in the wage structure, and that it should be dealt with in a routine and universal fashion. The AFDC program, on the other hand, assumes that families need income assistance only as a result of special, impoverishing circumstances.

Fluoridation is universalistic; it is aimed at preventing caries in the total population; oral surgery is exceptionalistic, designed to remedy the special cases of infection or neglect that damage the teeth of an individual. Birth control is univeralistic; abortion exceptionalistic. It has been said that navigational aids have saved far more lives than have rescue devices, no matter how refined they might be. The compass, then, is universalistic, while the lifeboat is exceptionalistic.

The similarity between exceptionalism and what Mills called the "ideology of social pathologists" is readily apparent. Indeed, the ideological potential of the exceptionalist viewpoint is unusually great. If one is inclined to explain all instances of deviance, all social problems, all occasions on which help is provided to others as the result of unusual circumstances, defect, or accident, one is unlikely to inquire about social inequalities.

This is not to devalue valid exceptionalistic services. Despite fluoridation, some instances of caries and gum disease will require attention; despite excellent prenatal care, handicapped children will occasionally be born; husbands will doubtless continue to die unexpectedly at early ages, leaving widows and orphans in need. And at any given moment, the end products of society's malfunctioning—the miseducated teenager, the unskilled adult laborer, the child brain-damaged as a result of prenatal neglect—will require service that is predominantly exceptionalistic in nature.

The danger in the exceptionalistic viewpoint is in its impact on social policy when it becomes the dominant component in social analysis. Blaming the Victim occurs exclusively within an exceptionalistic framework, and it consists of applying exceptionalistic explanations to universalistic problems. This represents an illogical departure from fact, a method, in Mannheim's words, of systematically distorting reality, of developing an ideology.

Blaming the Victim can take its place in a long series of American ideologies that have rationalized cruelty and injustice.

Slavery, for example, was justified—even praised—on the basis of a complex ideology that showed quite conclusively how useful slavery was to society and how uplifting it was for the slaves. Eminent physicians could be relied upon to provide the biological justification for slavery since after all, they said, the slaves were a separate species—as, for example, cattle are a separate species. No one in his right mind would dream of freeing the cows and fighting to abolish the ownership of cattle. In the view of the average American of 1825, it was important to preserve slavery, not simply because it was in accord with his own group interests (he was not fully aware of that), but because reason and logic showed clearly to the reasonable and intelligent man that slavery was good. In order to persuade a good and moral man to *do* evil, then, it is not necessary first to persuade him to *become* evil. It is only necessary to teach him that he is doing good. No one, in the words of a legendary newspaperman, thinks of himself as a son of a bitch.

In late-nineteenth-century America there flowered another ideology of injustice that seemed rational and just to the decent, progressive person. But Richard Hofstadter's analysis of the phenomenon of Social Darwinism shows clearly its functional role in the preservation of the *status quo.* One can scarcely imagine a better fit than the one between this ideology and the purposes and actions of the robber barons, who descended like piranha fish on the America of this era and picked its bones clean. Their extraordinarily unethical operations netted them not only hundreds of millions of dollars but also, perversely, the adoration of the nation. Behavior that would be, in any more rational land (including today's America), more than enough to have landed them all in jail, was praised as the very model of a captain of modern industry. And the philosophy that justified their thievery was such that John D. Rockefeller could actually stand up and preach it in church. Listen as he speaks in, of all places, Sunday school:

> The growth of a large business is merely a survival of the fittest. . . . The American Beauty rose can be produced in the splendor and fragrance which bring cheer to its beholder only by sacrificing the early buds which grow up around it. This is not an evil tendency in business. It is merely the working-out of a law of nature and a law of God.

This was the core of the gospel, adapted analogically from Darwin's writings on evolution. Herbert Spencer and, later, William Graham Sumner and other beginners in the social sciences considered Darwin's work to be directly applicable to social processes: ultimately as a guarantee that life was progressing toward perfection but, in the short run, as a justification for an absolutely uncontrolled laissez-faire economic system. The central concepts of "survival of the fittest," "natural selection," and "gradualism" were exalted in Rockefeller's preaching to the status of laws of God and Nature. Not only did this ideology justify the criminal rapacity of those who rose to the top of the industrial heap, defining them automatically as naturally superior (this was bad enough), but at the same time it also required that those at the bottom of the heap be labeled as patently *unfit*—a label based solely on their position in society. According to the law of natural selection, they should be, in Spencer's judgment, eliminated. "The whole effort of nature is to get rid of such, to clear the world of them and make room for better."

For a generation, Social Darwinism was the orthodox doctrine in the social sciences, such as they were at that time. Opponents of this ideology were shut out of respectable intellectual life. The philosophy that enabled John D. Rockefeller to justify himself self-righteously in front of a class of Sunday school children was not the product of an academic quack or a marginal crackpot philosopher. It came directly from the lectures and books of leading intellectual figures of the time, occupants of professorial chairs at Harvard and Yale. Such is the power of an ideology that so neatly fits the needs of the dominant interests of society.

If one is to think about ideologies in America in 1970, one must be prepared to consider the possibility that a body of ideas that might seem almost self-evident is, in fact, highly distorted and highly selective; one must allow that the inclusion of a specific formulation in every freshman sociology text does not guarantee that the particular formulation represents abstract Truth rather than group interest. It is important not to delude ourselves into thinking that ideological monstrosities were constructed by monsters. They were not; they are not. They are developed through a process that shows every sign of being valid scholarship, complete with tables of numbers, copious footnotes, and scientific terminology. Ideologies are quite often academically and socially respectable and in many instances hold positions of exclusive validity, so that disagreement is considered unrespectable or radical and risks being labeled as irresponsible, unenlightened, or trashy.

Blaming the Victim holds such a position. It is central in the mainstream of contemporary American social thought, and its ideas pervade our most crucial assumptions so thoroughly that they are hardly noticed. Moreover, the fruits of this ideology appear to be fraught with altruism and humanitarianism, so it is hard to believe that it has principally functioned to block social change.

III

A major pharmaceutical manufacturer, as an act of humanitarian concern, has distributed copies of a large poster warning "Lead Paint Can Kill!" The poster, featuring a photograph of the face of a charming little girl, goes on to explain that if children *eat* lead paint, it can poison them, they can develop serious symptoms, suffer permanent brain damage, even die. The health department of a major American city has put out a coloring book that provides the same information. While the poster urges parents to prevent their children from eating paint, the coloring book is more vivid. It labels as neglectful and thoughtless the mother who does not keep her infant under constant surveillance to keep it from eating paint chips.

Now, no one would argue against the idea that it is important to spread knowledge about the danger of eating paint in order that parents might act to forestall their children from doing so. But to campaign against lead paint *only* in these terms is destructive and misleading and, in a sense, an effective way to support and agree with slum landlords—who define the problem of lead poisoning in precisely these terms.

This is an example of applying an exceptionalistic solution to a universalistic problem. It is not accurate to say that lead poisoning results from the actions of individual neglectful mothers. Rather, lead poisoning is a social phenomenon supported by a number of social mechanisms, one of the most tragic by-products of the systematic toleration of slum housing. In New Haven, which has the highest reported rate of lead poisoning in the country, several small children have died and many others have incurred irreparable brain damage as a result of eating peeling paint. In several cases, when the landlord failed to make repairs, poisonings have occurred time and again through a succession of tenancies. And the major reason for the landlord's neglect of this problem was that the city agency responsible for enforcing the housing code did nothing to make him correct this dangerous condition.

The cause of the poisoning is the lead in the paint on the walls of the apartment in which the children live. The presence of the lead is illegal. To use lead paint in a residence is illegal; to permit lead paint to be exposed in a residence is illegal. It is not only illegal, it is potentially criminal since the housing code does provide for criminal penalties. The general problem of lead poisoning, then, is more accurately analyzed as the result of a systematic program of lawbreaking by one interest group in the community, with the toleration and encouragement of the public authority charged with enforcing that law. To ignore these continued and repeated law violations, to ignore the fact that the supposed law enforcer actually cooperates in lawbreaking, and then to load a burden of guilt on the mother of a dead or dangerously-ill child is an egregious distortion of reality. And to do so under the guise of public-spirited and humanitarian service to the community is intolerable.

But this is how Blaming the Victim works. The righteous humanitarian concern displayed by the drug company, with its poster, and the health department, with its coloring book, is a genuine concern, and this is a typical feature of Blaming the Victim. Also typical is the swerving away from the central target that requires systematic change and, instead, focusing in on the individual affected. The ultimate effect is always to distract attention from the basic causes and to leave the primary social injustice untouched. And, most telling, the proposed remedy for the problem is, of course, to work on the victim himself. Prescriptions for cure, as written by the Savage Discovery set, are invariably conceived to revamp and revise the victim, never to change the surrounding circumstances. They want to change his attitudes, alter his values, fill up his cultural deficits, energize his apathetic soul, cure his character defects, train him and polish him and woo him from his savage ways.

Isn't all of this more subtle and sophisticated than such old-fashioned ideologies as Social Darwinism? Doesn't the change from brutal ideas about survival of the fit (and the expiration of the unfit) to kindly concern about characterological defects (brought about by stigmas of social origin) seem like a substantial step forward? Hardly. It is only a substitution of terms. The old, reactionary exceptionalistic formulations are replaced by new progressive, humanitarian exceptionalistic formulations. In education, the outmoded and unacceptable concept of racial or class differences in basic inherited intellectual ability simply gives way to the new notion of cultural deprivation: there is very little functional difference between these two ideas. In taking a look at the phenomenon of poverty, the old concept of unfitness or idleness or laziness is replaced by the newfangled theory of the culture of poverty. In race relations, plain Negro inferiority—which was good enough for old-fashioned conservatives—is pushed aside by fancy conceits about the crumbling Negro family. With regard to illegitimacy, we are not so crass as to concern ourselves with immorality and vice, as in the old days; we settle benignly on the explanation of the "lower-class pattern of sexual behavior," which, no one condemns as evil, but which is, in fact, simply a variation of the old explanatory idea. Mental illness is no longer defined as the result of hereditary taint or congenital character flaw; now we have new causal hypotheses regarding the ego-damaging emotional experiences that are supposed to be the inevitable consequence of the deplorable child-rearing practices of the poor.

In each case, of course, we are persuaded to ignore the obvious: the continued blatant discrimination against the Negro, the gross deprivation of contraceptive and adoption services to the poor, the heavy stresses endemic in the life of the poor. And almost all our make-believe liberal programs aimed at correcting our urban problems are off target; they are designed either to change the poor man or to cool him out.

IV

We come finally to the question, Why? It is much easier to understand the process of Blaming the Victim as a way of thinking than it is to understand the motivation for it. Why do Victim Blamers, who are usually good people, blame the victim? The development and application of this ideology, and of all the mythologies associated with Savage Discovery, are readily exposed by careful analysis as hostile acts—one is almost tempted to say acts of war—directed against the disadvantaged, the distressed, the disinherited. It is class warfare in reverse. Yet those who are most fascinated and enchanted by this ideology tend to be progressive, humanitarian, and, in the best sense of the word, charitable persons. They would usually define themselves as moderates or liberals. Why do they pursue this dreadful war against the poor and the oppressed?

Put briefly, the answer can be formulated best in psychological terms—or, at least, I, as a psychologist, am more comfortable with such a formulation. The highly-charged psychological problem confronting this hypothetical progressive, charitable person I am talking

about is that of reconciling his own self-interest with the promptings of his humanitarian impulses. This psychological process of reconciliation is not worked out in a logical, rational, conscious way; it is a process that takes place far below the level of sharp consciousness, and the solution—Blaming the Victim—is arrived at subconsciously as a compromise that apparently satisfies both his self-interest and his charitable concerns. Let me elaborate.

First, the question of self-interest or, more accurately, class interest. The typical Victim Blamer is a middle class person who is doing reasonably well in a material way; he has a good job, a good income, a good house, a good car. Basically, he likes the social system pretty much the way it is, at least in broad outline. He likes the two-party political system, though he may be highly skilled in finding a thousand minor flaws in its functioning. He heartily approves of the profit motive as the propelling engine of the economic system despite his awareness that there are abuses of that system, negative side effects, and substantial residual inequalities.

On the other hand, he is acutely aware of poverty, racial discrimination, exploitation, and deprivation, and, moreover, he wants to do something concrete to ameliorate the condition of the poor, the black, and the disadvantaged. This is not an extraneous concern; it is central to his value system to insist on the worth of the individual, the equality of men, and the importance of justice.

What is to be done, then? What intellectual position can he take, and what line of action can he follow that will satisfy both of these important motivations? He quickly and self-consciously rejects two obvious alternatives, which he defines as "extremes." He cannot side with an openly reactionary, repressive position that accepts continued oppression and exploitation as the price of a privileged position for his own class. This is incompatible with his own morality and his basic political principles. He finds the extreme conservative position repugnant.

He is, if anything, more allergic to radicals, however, than he is to reactionaries. He rejects the "extreme" solution of radical social change, and this makes sense since such radical social change threatens his own well-being. A more equitable distribution of income might mean that he would have less—a smaller or older house, with fewer yews or no rhododendrons in the yard, a less enjoyable job, or, at the least, a somewhat smaller salary. If black children and poor children were, in fact, reasonably educated and began to get high S.A.T. scores, they would be competing with *his* children for the scarce places in the entering classes of Harvard, Columbia, Bennington, and Antioch.

So our potential Victim Blamers are in a dilemma. In the words of an old Yiddish proverb, they are trying to dance at two weddings. They are old friends of both brides and fond of both kinds of dancing, and they want to accept both invitations. They cannot bring themselves to attack the system that has been so good to them, but they want so badly to be helpful to the victims of racism and economic injustice.

Their solution is a brilliant compromise. They turn their attention to the victim in his post-victimized state. They want to bind up wounds, inject penicillin, administer morphine, and evacuate the wounded for rehabilitation. They explain what's wrong with the victim in terms of social experiences *in the past,* experiences that have left wounds, defects, paralysis, and disability. And they take the cure of these wounds and the reduction of these disabilities as the first order of business. They want to mate the victims less vulnerable, send them back into battle with better weapons, thicker armor, a higher level of morale.

In order to do so effectively, of course, they must analyze the victims carefully, dispassionately, objectively, scientifically, empathetically, mathematically, and hard-headedly, to see what made them so vulnerable in the first place.

What weapons, now, might they have lacked when they went into battle? Job skills? Education?

What armor was lacking that might have warded off their wounds? Better values? Habits of thrift and foresight?

And what might have ravaged their morale? Apathy? Ignorance? Deviant low class cultural patterns?

This is the solution of the dilemma, the solution of Blaming the Victim. And those who buy this solution with a sigh of relief are inevitably blinding themselves to the basic causes of the problems being addressed. They are, most crucially, rejecting the possibility of blaming, not the victims, but themselves. They are all unconsciously passing judgments on themselves and bringing in a unanimous verdict of Not Guilty.

If one comes to believe that the culture of poverty produces persons *fated* to be poor, who can find any fault with our corporation-dominated economy? And if the Negro family produces young men *incapable* of achieving equality, let's deal with that first before we go on to the task of changing the pervasive racism that informs and shapes and distorts our every social institution. And if unsatisfactory resolution of one's Oedipus complex accounts for all emotional distress and mental disorder, then by all means let us attend to that and postpone worrying about the pounding day-to-day stresses of life on the bottom rungs that drive so many to drink, dope, and madness.

That is the ideology of Blaming the Victim, the cunning Art of Savage Discovery. The tragic, frightening truth is that it is a mythology that is winning over the best people of our time, the very people who must resist this ideological temptation if we are to achieve nonviolent change in America.

Discussion Questions

1. According to social pathologists, social problems originate with the individual. From a sociological perspective what is wrong with this view?

   This argument ignores the relationship between social structure and social problems. Sociologists argue that social problems are not based upon individual weaknesses or failures, but rather on inequalities based on class, race and ethnicity, and power.

2. Do you agree with Ryan that as a society, we are likely to blame the victim rather than look to society itself for an understanding of social problems?

   Instructors and students can review several issues, examining if there is agreement on this question. Examples to discuss may include homelessness, violence against women, drug abuse, and crime.

CHAPTER 3

Where Do We Go From Here?

Martin Luther King, Jr. (1967)

In this speech from 1967, Reverend Martin Luther King, Jr. identifies and discusses the structural basis of racism, inequality, and poverty. He argues that to address these problems there must be a massive assertion of "dignity and worth" and that such a movement will help to bring about a "restructuring of the whole of American society."

Dr. Abernathy, our distinguished vice president, fellow delegates to this, the tenth annual session of the Southern Christian Leadership Conference, my brothers and sisters from not only all over the South, but from all over the United States of America: ten years ago during the piercing chill of a January day and on the heels of the year-long Montgomery bus boycott, a group of approximately one hundred Negro leaders from across the South assembled in this church and agreed on the need for an organization to be formed that could serve as a channel through which local protest organizations in the South could coordinate their protest activities. It was this meeting that gave birth to the Southern Christian Leadership Conference.

And when our organization was formed ten years ago, racial segregation was still a structured part of the architecture of southern society. Negroes with the pangs of hunger and the anguish of thirst were denied access to the average lunch counter. The downtown restaurants were still off-limits for the black man. Negroes, burdened with the fatigue of travel, were still barred from the motels of the highways and the hotels of the cities. Negro boys and girls in dire need of recreational activities were not allowed to inhale the fresh air of the big city parks. Negroes in desperate need of allowing their mental buckets to sink deep into the wells of knowledge were confronted with a firm "no" when they sought to use the city libraries. Ten years ago, legislative halls of the South were still ringing loud with such words as "interposition" and "nullification." All types of conniving methods were still being used to keep the Negro from becoming a registered voter. A decade ago, not a single Negro entered the legislative chambers of the South except as a porter or a chauffeur. Ten years ago, all too many Negroes were still harried by day and haunted by night by a corroding sense of fear and a nagging sense of nobody-ness. (Yeah)

But things are different now. In assault after assault, we caused the sagging walls of segregation to come tumbling down. During this era the entire edifice of segregation was profoundly shaken. This is an accomplishment whose consequences are deeply felt by every southern Negro in his daily life. (Oh yeah) It is no longer possible to count the number of public establishments that are open to Negroes. Ten years ago, Negroes seemed almost invisible to the larger society, and the facts of their harsh lives were unknown to the majority of the nation. But today, civil rights is a dominating issue in every state, crowding the pages of the press and the daily conversation of white Americans. In this decade of change, the Negro stood up and confronted his oppressor. He faced the bullies and the guns, and the dogs and the tear gas. He put himself squarely before the vicious mobs and moved with strength and dignity toward them and decisively defeated them. (Yes) And the courage with which he confronted enraged mobs dissolved the stereotype of the grinning, submissive Uncle Tom. (Yes) He came out of his struggle integrated only slightly in the external society, but powerfully integrated within. This was a victory that had to precede all other gains.

In short, over the last ten years the Negro decided to straighten his back up (Yes), realizing that a man cannot ride your back unless it is bent. (Yes, That's right) We made our government write new laws to alter some of the cruelest injustices that affected us. We made an indifferent and unconcerned nation rise from lethargy and subpoenaed its conscience to appear before the judgment seat of morality on the whole question of civil rights. We gained manhood in the nation that had always called us "boy." It would be hypocritical indeed if I allowed modesty to forbid my saying that SCLC stood at the forefront of all of the watershed movements that brought these monumental changes in the South. For this, we can feel a legitimate pride. But in spite of a decade of significant progress, the problem is far from solved. The deep rumbling of discontent in our cities is indicative of the fact that the plant of freedom has grown only a bud and not yet a flower.

And before discussing the awesome responsibilities that we face in the days ahead, let us take an inventory of our programmatic action and activities over the past year. Last year as we met in Jackson, Mississippi, we were painfully aware of the struggle of our brothers in Grenada, Mississippi. After living for a hundred or more years under the yoke of total segregation, the Negro citizens of this northern Delta hamlet banded together in nonviolent warfare against racial discrimination under the leadership of our affiliate chapter and organization there. The fact of this non-destructive rebellion was as spectacular as were its results. In a few short weeks the Grenada County Movement challenged every aspect of the society's exploitative life. Stores which denied employment were boycotted; voter registration increased by thousands. We can never forget the courageous action of the people of Grenada who moved our nation and its federal courts to powerful action in behalf of school integration, giving Grenada one of the most integrated school systems in America. The battle is far from over, but the black people of Grenada have achieved forty of fifty-three demands through their persistent nonviolent efforts.

Slowly but surely, our southern affiliates continued their building and organizing. Seventy-nine counties conducted voter registration drives, while double that number carried on political education and get-out-the-vote efforts.

In spite of press opinions, our staff is still overwhelmingly a southern-based staff. One hundred and five persons have worked across the South under the direction of Hosea Williams. What used to be primarily a voter registration staff is actually a multifaceted program dealing with the total life of the community, from farm cooperatives, business development, tutorials, credit unions, etcetera. Especially to be commended are those ninety-nine communities and their staffs which maintain regular mass meetings throughout the year.

Our Citizenship Education Program continues to lay the solid foundation of adult education and community organization upon which all social change must ultimately rest. This year, five hundred local leaders received training at Dorchester and ten community centers through our Citizenship Education Program. They were trained in literacy, consumer education, planned parenthood, and many other things. And this program, so ably directed by Mrs. Dorothy Cotton, Mrs. Septima Clark, and their staff of eight persons, continues to cover ten southern states. Our auxiliary feature of C.E.P. is the aid which they have given to poor communities, poor counties in receiving and establishing O.E.O. projects. With the competent professional guidance of our marvelous staff member, Miss Mew Soong-Li, Lowndes and Wilcox counties in Alabama have pioneered in developing outstanding poverty programs totally controlled and operated by residents of the area.

Perhaps the area of greatest concentration of my efforts has been in the cities of Chicago and Cleveland. Chicago has been a wonderful proving ground for our work in the North. There have been no earth-shaking victories, but neither has there been failure. Our open housing marches, which finally brought about an agreement which actually calls the power structure of Chicago to capitulate to the civil rights movement, these marches and the agreement have finally begun to pay off. After the season of delay around election periods, the Leadership Conference, organized to meet our demands for an open city, has finally begun to implement the programs agreed to last summer.

But this is not the most important aspect of our work. As a result of our tenant union organizing, we have begun a four million dollar rehabilitation project, which will renovate deteriorating buildings and allow their tenants the opportunity to own their own homes. This pilot project was the inspiration for the new home ownership bill, which Senator Percy introduced in Congress only recently.

The most dramatic success in Chicago has been Operation Breadbasket. Through Operation Breadbasket we have now achieved for the Negro community of

Chicago more than twenty-two hundred new jobs with an income of approximately eighteen million dollars a year, new income to the Negro community. [Applause] But not only have we gotten jobs through Operation Breadbasket in Chicago; there was another area through this economic program, and that was the development of financial institutions which were controlled by Negroes and which were sensitive to problems of economic deprivation of the Negro community. The two banks in Chicago that were interested in helping Negro businessmen were largely unable to loan much because of limited assets. Hi-Lo, one of the chain stores in Chicago, agreed to maintain substantial accounts in the two banks, thus increasing their ability to serve the needs of the Negro community. And I can say to you today that as a result of Operation Breadbasket in Chicago, both of these Negro-operated banks have now more than doubled their assets, and this has been done in less than a year by the work of Operation Breadbasket. [applause]

In addition, the ministers learned that Negro scavengers had been deprived of significant accounts in the ghetto. Whites controlled even the garbage of Negroes. Consequently, the chain stores agreed to contract with Negro scavengers to service at least the stores in Negro areas. Negro insect and rodent exterminators, as well as janitorial services, were likewise excluded from major contracts with chain stores. The chain stores also agreed to utilize these services. It also became apparent that chain stores advertised only rarely in Negro-owned community newspapers. This area of neglect was also negotiated, giving community newspapers regular, substantial accounts. And finally, the ministers found that Negro contractors, from painters to masons, from electricians to excavators, had also been forced to remain small by the monopolies of white contractors. Breadbasket negotiated agreements on new construction and rehabilitation work for the chain stores. These several interrelated aspects of economic development, all based on the power of organized consumers, hold great possibilities for dealing with the problems of Negroes in other northern cities. The kinds of requests made by Breadbasket in Chicago can be made not only of chain stores, but of almost any major industry in any city in the country.

And so Operation Breadbasket has a very simple program, but a powerful one. It simply says, "If you respect my dollar, you must respect my person." It simply says that we will no longer spend our money where we can not get substantial jobs. [applause]

In Cleveland, Ohio, a group of ministers have formed an Operation Breadbasket through our program there and have moved against a major dairy company. Their requests include jobs, advertising in Negro newspapers, and depositing funds in Negro financial institutions. This effort resulted in something marvelous. I went to Cleveland just last week to sign the agreement with Sealtest. We went to get the facts about their employment; we discovered that they had 442 employees and only forty-three were Negroes, yet the Negro population of Cleveland is thirty-five percent of the total population. They refused to give us all of the information that we requested, and we said in substance, "Mr. Sealtest, we're sorry. We aren't going to burn your store down. We aren't going to throw any bricks in the window. But we are going to put picket signs around and we are going to put leaflets out and we are going to our pulpits and tell them not to sell Sealtest products, and not to purchase Sealtest products."

We did that. We went through the churches. Reverend Dr. Hoover, who pastors the largest church in Cleveland, who's here today, and all of the ministers got together and got behind this program. We went to every store in the ghetto and said, "You must take Sealtest products off of your counters. If not, we're going to boycott your whole store." (That's right) A&P refused. We put picket lines around A&P; they have a hundred and some stores in Cleveland, and we picketed A&P and closed down eighteen of them in one day. Nobody went in A&P. [applause] The next day Mr. A&P was calling on us, and Bob Brown, who is here on our board and who is a public relations man representing a number of firms, came in. They called him in because he worked for A&P, also; and they didn't know he worked for us, too. [laughter] Bob Brown sat down with A&P, and he said, they said, "Now, Mr. Brown, what would you advise us to do." He said, "I would advise you to take Sealtest products off of all of your counters." A&P agreed next day not only to take Sealtest products off of the counters in the ghetto, but off of the counters of every A&P store in Cleveland, and they said to Sealtest, "If you don't reach an agreement with SCLC and Operation Breadbasket, we will take Sealtest products off of every A&P store in the state of Ohio."

The next day [applause], the next day the Sealtest people were talking nice [laughter], they were very humble. And I am proud to say that I went to Cleveland just last Tuesday, and I sat down with the Sealtest people and some seventy ministers from Cleveland, and we signed the agreement. This effort resulted in a number of jobs, which will bring almost five hundred thousand dollars of new income to the Negro community a year. [applause] We also said to Sealtest, "The problem that we face is that the ghetto is a domestic colony that's constantly drained without being replenished. And you are always telling us to lift ourselves by our own bootstraps, and yet we are being robbed every day. Put something back in the ghetto." So along with our demand for jobs, we said, "We also demand that you put money in the Negro savings and loan association and that you take ads, advertise, in the Cleveland Call & Post, the Negro newspaper." So along with the new jobs, Sealtest has now deposited thousands of dollars in the Negro bank of Cleveland and has already started taking ads in the Negro newspaper in that city. This is the power of Operation Breadbasket. [applause]

Now, for fear that you may feel that it's limited to Chicago and Cleveland, let me say to you that we've gotten even more than that. In Atlanta, Georgia, Breadbasket has been equally successful in the South. Here the emphasis has been divided between governmental employment and private industry. And while I do not have time to go into the details, I want to commend the men who have been working with it here: the Reverend Bennett, the Reverend Joe Boone, the Reverend J. C. Ward, Reverend Dorsey, Reverend Greer, and I could go on down the line, and they have stood up along with all of the other ministers. But here is the story that's not printed in the newspapers in Atlanta: as a result of Operation Breadbasket, over the last three years, we have added about twenty-five million dollars of new income to the Negro community every year. [applause]

Now as you know, Operation Breadbasket has now gone national in the sense that we had a national conference in Chicago and agreed to launch a nationwide program, which you will hear more about.

Finally, SCLC has entered the field of housing. Under the leadership of attorney James Robinson, we have already contracted to build 152 units of low-income housing with apartments for the elderly on a choice downtown Atlanta site under the sponsorship of Ebenezer Baptist Church. This is the first project [applause], this is the first project of a proposed southwide Housing Development Corporation which we hope to develop in conjunction with SCLC, and through this corporation we hope to build housing from Mississippi to North Carolina using Negro workmen, Negro architects, Negro attorneys, and Negro financial institutions throughout. And it is our feeling that in the next two or three years, we can build right here in the South forty million dollars worth of new housing for Negroes, and with millions and millions of dollars in income coming to the Negro community. [applause]

Now there are many other things that I could tell you, but time is passing. This, in short, is an account of SCLC's work over the last year. It is a record of which we can all be proud.

With all the struggle and all the achievements, we must face the fact, however, that the Negro still lives in the basement of the Great Society. He is still at the bottom, despite the few who have penetrated to slightly higher levels. Even where the door has been forced partially open, mobility for the Negro is still sharply restricted. There is often no bottom at which to start, and when there is there's almost no room at the top. In consequence, Negroes are still impoverished aliens in an affluent society. They are too poor even to rise with the society, too impoverished by the ages to be able to ascend by using their own resources. And the Negro did not do this himself; it was done to him. For more than half of his American history, he was enslaved. Yet, he built the spanning bridges and the grand mansions, the sturdy docks and stout factories of the South. His unpaid labor made cotton "King" and established America as a significant nation in international commerce. Even after his release from chattel slavery, the nation grew over him, submerging him. It became the richest, most powerful society in the history of man, but it left the Negro far behind.

And so we still have a long, long way to go before we reach the promised land of freedom. Yes, we have left the dusty soils of Egypt, and we have crossed a Red Sea that had for years been hardened by a long and piercing winter of massive resistance, but before we reach the majestic shores of the promised land, there will still be gigantic mountains of opposition ahead and prodigious hilltops of injustice. (Yes, That's right) We still need some Paul Revere of conscience to alert every hamlet and every village of America that revolution is still at hand. Yes, we need a chart; we need a compass; indeed, we need some North Star to guide us into a future shrouded with impenetrable uncertainties.

Now, in order to answer the question, "Where do we go from here?" which is our theme, we must first honestly recognize where we are now. When the Constitution was written, a strange formula to determine taxes and representation declared that the Negro was sixty percent of a person. Today another curious formula seems to declare he is fifty percent of a person. Of the good things in life, the Negro has approximately one half those of whites. Of the bad things of life, he has twice those of whites. Thus, half of all Negroes live in substandard housing. And Negroes have half the income of whites. When we turn to the negative experiences of life, the Negro has a double share: There are twice as many unemployed; the rate of infant mortality among Negroes is double that of whites; and there are twice as many Negroes dying in Vietnam as whites in proportion to their size in the population. (Yes) [applause]

In other spheres, the figures are equally alarming. In elementary schools, Negroes lag one to three years behind whites, and their segregated schools (Yeah) receive substantially less money per student than the white schools. (Those schools) One-twentieth as many Negroes as whites attend college. Of employed Negroes, seventy-five percent hold menial jobs. This is where we are.

Where do we go from here? First, we must massively assert our dignity and worth. We must stand up amid a system that still oppresses us and develop an unassailable and majestic sense of values. We must no longer be ashamed of being black. (All right) The job of arousing manhood within a people that have been taught for so many centuries that they are nobody is not easy.

Even semantics have conspired to make that which is black seem ugly and degrading. (Yes) In Roget's Thesaurus there are some 120 synonyms for blackness and at least sixty of them are offensive, such words as blot, soot, grim, devil, and foul. And there are some 134 synonyms for whiteness and all are favorable, expressed in such words as purity, cleanliness, chastity, and innocence. A white lie is better than a black lie. (Yes) The most degenerate member of a family is the "black sheep." (Yes) Ossie Davis has suggested that maybe the English language should be reconstructed so that teachers will not be forced to teach the Negro child sixty ways to despise himself, and thereby perpetuate his false sense of inferiority, and the white child 134 ways to adore himself, and thereby perpetuate his false sense of superiority. [applause] The tendency to ignore the Negro's contribution to American life and strip him of his personhood is as old as the earliest history books and as contemporary as the morning's newspaper. (Yes)

To offset this cultural homicide, the Negro must rise up with an affirmation of his own Olympian manhood. (Yes) Any movement for the Negro's freedom that overlooks this necessity is only waiting to be buried. (Yes) As long as the mind is enslaved, the body can never be free. (Yes) Psychological freedom, a firm sense of self-esteem, is the most powerful weapon against the long night of physical slavery. No Lincolnian Emancipation Proclamation, no Johnsonian civil rights bill can totally bring this kind of freedom. The Negro will only be free when he reaches down to the inner depths of his own being and signs with the pen and ink of assertive manhood his own emancipation proclamation. And with a spirit straining toward true self-esteem, the Negro must boldly throw off the manacles of self-abnegation and say to himself and to the world, "I am somebody. (Oh yeah) I am a person. I am a man with dignity and honor. (Go ahead) I have a rich and noble history, however painful

and exploited that history has been. Yes, I was a slave through my foreparents (That's right), and now I'm not ashamed of that. I'm ashamed of the people who were so sinful to make me a slave." (Yes sir) Yes [applause], yes, we must stand up and say, "I'm black (Yes sir), but I'm black and beautiful." (Yes) This [applause], this self-affirmation is the black man's need, made compelling (All right) by the white man's crimes against him. (Yes)

Now another basic challenge is to discover how to organize our strength in to economic and political power. Now no one can deny that the Negro is in dire need of this kind of legitimate power. Indeed, one of the great problems that the Negro confronts is his lack of power. From the old plantations of the South to the newer ghettos of the North, the Negro has been confined to a life of voicelessness (That's true) and powerlessness. (So true) Stripped of the right to make decisions concerning his life and destiny he has been subject to the authoritarian and sometimes whimsical decisions of the white power structure. The plantation and the ghetto were created by those who had power, both to confine those who had no power and to perpetuate their powerlessness. Now the problem of transforming the ghetto, therefore, is a problem of power, a confrontation between the forces of power demanding change and the forces of power dedicated to the preserving of the status quo. Now, power properly understood is nothing but the ability to achieve purpose. It is the strength required to bring about social, political, and economic change. Walter Reuther defined power one day. He said, "Power is the ability of a labor union like UAW to make the most powerful corporation in the world, General Motors, say, 'Yes' when it wants to say 'No.' That's power." [applause]

Now a lot of us are preachers, and all of us have our moral convictions and concerns, and so often we have problems with power. But there is nothing wrong with power if power is used correctly.

You see, what happened is that some of our philosophers got off base. And one of the great problems of history is that the concepts of love and power have usually been contrasted as opposites, polar opposites, so that love is identified with a resignation of power, and power with a denial of love. It was this misinterpretation that caused the philosopher Nietzsche, who was a philosopher of the will to power, to reject the Christian concept of love. It was this same misinterpretation which induced Christian theologians to reject Nietzsche's philosophy of the will to power in the name of the Christian idea of love.

Now, we got to get this thing right. What is needed is a realization that power without love is reckless and abusive, and that love without power is sentimental and anemic.

(Yes) Power at its best [applause], power at its best is love (Yes) implementing the demands of justice, and justice at its best is love correcting everything that stands against love. (Speak) And this is what we must see as we move on.

Now what has happened is that we've had it wrong and mixed up in our country, and this has led Negro Americans in the past to seek their goals through love and moral suasion devoid of power, and white Americans to seek their goals through power devoid of love and conscience. It is leading a few extremists today to advocate for Negroes the same destructive and conscienceless power that they have justly abhorred in whites. It is precisely this collision of immoral power with powerless morality which constitutes the major crisis of our times. (Yes)

Now we must develop progress, or rather, a program—and I can't stay on this long—that will drive the nation to a guaranteed annual income. Now, early in the century this proposal would have been greeted with ridicule and denunciation as destructive of initiative and responsibility. At that time economic status was considered the measure of the individual's abilities and talents. And in the thinking of that day, the absence of worldly goods indicated a want of industrious habits and moral fiber. We've come a long way in our understanding of human motivation and of the blind operation of our economic system. Now we realize that dislocations in the market operation of our economy and the prevalence of discrimination thrust people into idleness and bind them in constant or frequent unemployment against their will. The poor are less often dismissed, I hope, from our conscience today by being branded as inferior and incompetent. We also know that no matter how dynamically the economy develops and expands, it does not eliminate all poverty.

The problem indicates that our emphasis must be twofold: We must create full employment, or we must create incomes. People must be made consumers by one method or the other. Once they are placed in this position, we need to be concerned that the potential of the individual is not wasted. New forms of work that enhance the social good will have to be devised for those for whom traditional jobs are not available. In 1879 Henry George anticipated this state of affairs when he wrote in Progress and Poverty:

The fact is that the work which improves the condition of mankind, the work which extends knowledge and increases power and enriches literature and elevates thought, is not done to secure a living. It is not the work of slaves driven to their tasks either by the, that of a taskmaster or by animal necessities. It is the work of men who

somehow find a form of work that brings a security for its own sake and a state of society where want is abolished.

Work of this sort could be enormously increased, and we are likely to find that the problems of housing and education, instead of preceding the elimination of poverty, will themselves be affected if poverty is first abolished. The poor, transformed into purchasers, will do a great deal on their own to alter housing decay. Negroes, who have a double disability, will have a greater effect on discrimination when they have the additional weapon of cash to use in their struggle.

Beyond these advantages, a host of positive psychological changes inevitably will result from widespread economic security. The dignity of the individual will flourish when the decisions concerning his life are in his own hands, when he has the assurance that his income is stable and certain, and when he knows that he has the means to seek self-improvement. Personal conflicts between husband, wife, and children will diminish when the unjust measurement of human worth on a scale of dollars is eliminated.

Now, our country can do this. John Kenneth Galbraith said that a guaranteed annual income could be done for about twenty billion dollars a year. And I say to you today, that if our nation can spend thirty-five billion dollars a year to fight an unjust, evil war in Vietnam, and twenty billion dollars to put a man on the moon, it can spend billions of dollars to put God's children on their own two feet right here on earth. [applause]

Now, let me rush on to say we must reaffirm our commitment to nonviolence. And I want to stress this. The futility of violence in the struggle for racial justice has been tragically etched in all the recent Negro riots. Now, yesterday, I tried to analyze the riots and deal with the causes for them. Today I want to give the other side. There is something painfully sad about a riot. One sees screaming youngsters and angry adults fighting hopelessly and aimlessly against impossible odds. (Yeah) And deep down within them, you perceive a desire for self-destruction, a kind of suicidal longing. (Yes)

Occasionally, Negroes contend that the 1965 Watts riot and the other riots in various cities represented effective civil rights action. But those who express this view always end up with stumbling words when asked what concrete gains have been won as a result. At best, the riots have produced a little additional anti-poverty money allotted by frightened government officials and a few water sprinklers to cool the children of the ghettos. It is something like improving the food in the prison while the people remain securely incarcerated behind bars. (That's right) Nowhere have the riots won any concrete improvement such as have the organized protest demonstrations.

And when one tries to pin down advocates of violence as to what acts would be effective, the answers are blatantly illogical. Sometimes they talk of overthrowing racist state and local governments and they talk about guerrilla warfare. They fail to see that no internal revolution has ever succeeded in overthrowing a government by violence unless the government had already lost the allegiance and effective control of its armed forces. Anyone in his right mind knows that this will not happen in the United States. In a violent racial situation, the power structure has the local police, the state troopers, the National Guard, and finally, the army to call on, all of which are predominantly white. (Yes) Furthermore, few, if any, violent revolutions have been successful unless the violent minority had the sympathy and support of the non-resisting majority. Castro may have had only a few Cubans actually fighting with him and up in the hills (Yes), but he would have never overthrown the Batista regime unless he had had the sympathy of the vast majority of Cuban people. It is perfectly clear that a violent revolution on the part of American blacks would find no sympathy and support from the white population and very little from the majority of the Negroes themselves.

This is no time for romantic illusions and empty philosophical debates about freedom. This is a time for action. (All right) What is needed is a strategy for change, a tactical program that will bring the Negro into the mainstream of American life as quickly as possible. So far, this has only been offered by the nonviolent movement. Without recognizing this we will end up with solutions that don't solve, answers that don't answer, and explanations that don't explain. [applause]

And so I say to you today that I still stand by nonviolence. (Yes) And I am still convinced [applause], and I'm still convinced that it is the most potent weapon available to the Negro in his struggle for justice in this country.

And the other thing is, I'm concerned about a better world. I'm concerned about justice; I'm concerned about brotherhood; I'm concerned about truth. (That's right) And when one is concerned about that, he can never advocate violence. For through violence you may murder a murderer, but you can't murder murder. (Yes) Through violence you may murder a liar, but you can't establish truth. (That's right) Through violence you may murder a hater, but you can't murder hate through violence. (All right, That's right) Darkness cannot put out darkness; only light can do that. [applause]

And I say to you, I have also decided to stick with love, for I know that love is ultimately the only answer to mankind's problems. (Yes) And I'm going to talk about it everywhere I go. I know it isn't popular to talk about it in some circles today. (No) And I'm not talking about

emotional bosh when I talk about love; I'm talking about a strong, demanding love. (Yes) For I have seen too much hate. (Yes) I've seen too much hate on the faces of sheriffs in the South. (Yeah) I've seen hate on the faces of too many Klansmen and too many White Citizens Councilors in the South to want to hate, myself, because every time I see it, I know that it does something to their faces and their personalities, and I say to myself that hate is too great a burden to bear. (Yes, That's right) I have decided to love. [applause] If you are seeking the highest good, I think you can find it through love. And the beautiful thing is that we aren't moving wrong when we do it, because John was right, God is love. (Yes) He who hates does not know God, but he who loves has the key that unlocks the door to the meaning of ultimate reality.

And so I say to you today, my friends, that you may be able to speak with the tongues of men and angels (All right); you may have the eloquence of articulate speech; but if you have not love, it means nothing. (That's right) Yes, you may have the gift of prophecy; you may have the gift of scientific prediction (Yes sir) and understand the behavior of molecules (All right); you may break into the storehouse of nature (Yes sir) and bring forth many new insights; yes, you may ascend to the heights of academic achievement (Yes sir) so that you have all knowledge (Yes sir, Yes); and you may boast of your great institutions of learning and the boundless extent of your degrees; but if you have not love, all of these mean absolutely nothing. (Yes) You may even give your goods to feed the poor (Yes sir); you may bestow great gifts to charity (Speak); and you may tower high in philanthropy; but if you have not love, your charity means nothing. (Yes sir) You may even give your body to be burned and die the death of a martyr, and your spilt blood may be a symbol of honor for generations yet unborn, and thousands may praise you as one of history's greatest heroes; but if you have not love (Yes, All right), your blood was spilt in vain. What I'm trying to get you to see this morning is that a man may be self-centered in his self-denial and self-righteous in his self-sacrifice. His generosity may feed his ego, and his piety may feed his pride. (Speak) So without love, benevolence becomes egotism, and martyrdom becomes spiritual pride.

I want to say to you as I move to my conclusion, as we talk about "Where do we go from here?" that we must honestly face the fact that the movement must address itself to the question of restructuring the whole of American society. (Yes) There are forty million poor people here, and one day we must ask the question, "Why are there forty million poor people in America?" And when you begin to ask that question, you are raising a question about the economic system, about a broader distribution of wealth. When you ask that question, you begin to question the capitalistic economy. (Yes) And I'm simply saying that more and more, we've got to begin to ask questions about the whole society. We are called upon to help the discouraged beggars in life's market-place. (Yes) But one day we must come to see that an edifice which produces beggars needs restructuring. (All right) It means that questions must be raised. And you see, my friends, when you deal with this you begin to ask the question, "Who owns the oil?" (Yes) You begin to ask the question, "Who owns the iron ore?" (Yes) You begin to ask the question, "Why is it that people have to pay water bills in a world that's two-thirds water?" (All right) These are words that must be said. (All right)

Now, don't think you have me in a bind today. I'm not talking about communism. What I'm talking about is far beyond communism. (Yeah) My inspiration didn't come from Karl Marx (Speak); my inspiration didn't come from Engels; my inspiration didn't come from Trotsky; my inspiration didn't come from Lenin. Yes, I read Communist Manifesto and Das Kapital a long time ago (Well), and I saw that maybe Marx didn't follow Hegel enough. (All right) He took his dialectics, but he left out his idealism and his spiritualism. And he went over to a German philosopher by the name of Feuerbach, and took his materialism and made it into a system that he called "dialectical materialism." (Speak) I have to reject that.

What I'm saying to you this morning is communism forgets that life is individual. (Yes) Capitalism forgets that life is social. (Yes, Go ahead) And the kingdom of brotherhood is found neither in the thesis of communism nor the antithesis of capitalism, but in a higher synthesis. (Speak) [applause] It is found in a higher synthesis (Come on) that combines the truths of both. (Yes) Now, when I say questioning the whole society, it means ultimately coming to see that the problem of racism, the problem of economic exploitation, and the problem of war are all tied together. (All right) These are the triple evils that are interrelated.

And if you will let me be a preacher just a little bit. (Speak) One day [applause], one night, a juror came to Jesus (Yes sir) and he wanted to know what he could do to be saved. (Yeah) Jesus didn't get bogged down on the kind of isolated approach of what you shouldn't do. Jesus didn't say, "Now Nicodemus, you must stop lying." (Oh yeah) He didn't say, "Nicodemus, now you must not commit adultery." He didn't say, "Now Nicodemus, you must stop cheating if you are doing that." He didn't say, "Nicodemus, you must stop drinking liquor if you are doing that excessively." He said something altogether different, because Jesus realized something basic (Yes): that if a man will lie, he will steal. (Yes) And if a man will steal, he will kill. (Yes) So instead of just getting bogged

down on one thing, Jesus looked at him and said, "Nicodemus, you must be born again." [applause]

In other words, "Your whole structure (Yes) must be changed." [applause] A nation that will keep people in slavery for 244 years will "thingify" them and make them things. (Speak) And therefore, they will exploit them and poor people generally economically. (Yes) And a nation that will exploit economically will have to have foreign investments and everything else, and it will have to use its military might to protect them. All of these problems are tied together. (Yes) [applause]

What I'm saying today is that we must go from this convention and say, "America, you must be born again!" [applause] (Oh yes)

And so, I conclude by saying today that we have a task, and let us go out with a divine dissatisfaction. (Yes)

Let us be dissatisfied until America will no longer have a high blood pressure of creeds and an anemia of deeds. (All right)

Let us be dissatisfied (Yes) until the tragic walls that separate the outer city of wealth and comfort from the inner city of poverty and despair shall be crushed by the battering rams of the forces of justice. (Yes sir)

Let us be dissatisfied (Yes) until those who live on the outskirts of hope are brought into the metropolis of daily security.

Let us be dissatisfied (Yes) until slums are cast into the junk heaps of history (Yes), and every family will live in a decent, sanitary home.

Let us be dissatisfied (Yes) until the dark yesterdays of segregated schools will be transformed into bright tomorrows of quality integrated education.

Let us be dissatisfied until integration is not seen as a problem but as an opportunity to participate in the beauty of diversity.

Let us be dissatisfied (All right) until men and women, however black they may be, will be judged on the basis of the content of their character, not on the basis of the color of their skin. (Yeah) Let us be dissatisfied. [applause]

Let us be dissatisfied (Well) until every state capitol (Yes) will be housed by a governor who will do justly, who will love mercy, and who will walk humbly with his God.

Let us be dissatisfied [applause] until from every city hall, justice will roll down like waters, and righteousness like a mighty stream. (Yes)

Let us be dissatisfied (Yes) until that day when the lion and the lamb shall lie down together (Yes), and every man will sit under his own vine and fig tree, and none shall be afraid.

Let us be dissatisfied (Yes), until men will recognize that out of one blood (Yes) God made all men to dwell upon the face of the earth. (Speak sir)

Let us be dissatisfied until that day when nobody will shout, "White Power!" when nobody will shout, "Black Power!" but everybody will talk about God's power and human power. [applause]

And I must confess, my friends (Yes sir), that the road ahead will not always be smooth. (Yes) There will still be rocky places of frustration (Yes) and meandering points of bewilderment. There will be inevitable setbacks here and there. (Yes) And there will be those moments when the buoyancy of hope will be transformed into the fatigue of despair. (Well) Our dreams will sometimes be shattered and our ethereal hopes blasted. (Yes) We may again, with tear-drenched eyes, have to stand before the bier of some courageous civil rights worker whose life will be snuffed out by the dastardly acts of bloodthirsty mobs. (Well) But difficult and painful as it is (Well), we must walk on in the days ahead with an audacious faith in the future. (Well) And as we continue our charted course, we may gain consolation from the words so nobly left by that great black bard, who was also a great freedom fighter of yesterday, James Weldon Johnson (Yes):

Stony the road we trod (Yes),

Bitter the chastening rod

Felt in the days

When hope unborn had died. (Yes)

Yet with a steady beat,

Have not our weary feet

Come to the place

For which our fathers sighed?

We have come over a way

That with tears has been watered. (Well)

We have come treading our paths

Through the blood of the slaughtered.

Out from the gloomy past,

Till now we stand at last (Yes)

Where the bright gleam

Of our bright star is cast.

Let this affirmation be our ringing cry. (Well) It will give us the courage to face the uncertainties of the future. It will give our tired feet new strength as we continue our forward stride toward the city of freedom. (Yes) When our days become dreary with low-hovering clouds of despair (Well), and when our nights become darker than a thousand midnights (Well), let us remember (Yes) that there is a creative force in this universe working to pull down the gigantic mountains of evil (Well), a power that is able to make a way out of no way (Yes) and transform dark yesterdays into bright tomorrows. (Speak)

Let us realize that the arc of the moral universe is long, but it bends toward justice. Let us realize that William Cullen Bryant is right: "Truth, crushed to earth, will rise again." Let us go out realizing that the Bible is right: "Be not deceived. God is not mocked. (Oh yeah) Whatsoever a man soweth (Yes), that (Yes) shall he also reap." This is our hope for the future, and with this faith we will be able to sing in some not too distant tomorrow, with a cosmic past tense, "We have overcome! (Yes) We have overcome! Deep in my heart, I did believe (Yes) we would overcome." [applause]

Discussion Questions

1. Reverend King's speech was written in 1967. What are some of the problems that he identified? Do you think that these problems are still significant today (more than 40 years later)? Why or why not?

   Instructors should first review Martin Luther King's list of social problems and discuss if any progress has been made. Class discussion may also involve distinguishing between U.S. and global social problems, for example, war and terrorism, AIDS, and global warming.

2. What solutions did Reverend King offer for these problems? Would these solutions be effective today? Why or why not?

   Students should note King's commitment to nonviolence and to the creation of political and economic power among African Americans.

Source: From King, M. L., Jr. (2001). Where do we go from here? In C. Carson & K. Shepard (Eds.), *A call to conscience: The landmark speeches of Martin Luther King, Jr.* New York: Intellectual Properties Management. (Reprinted from Annual Report Delivered at the 11th Convention of the Southern Christian Leadership Conference, Atlanta, Georgia, 1967, August 16). The words of Martin Luther King, Jr. are copyrighted by the King Estate.

PART II

THE FRAGMENTATION OF SOCIAL LIFE

CHAPTER 4

The Fragmentation of Social Life

Some Critical Societal Concerns for the New Millennium

D. Stanley Eitzen (2000)

D. Stanley Eitzen examines the problem of the increasing fragmentation of social life. He identifies four indicators of reduced social cohesion: excessive individualism, heightened personal isolation, the widening income and wealth gap, and the deepening racial, ethnic, religious, and sexuality divide.

For many observers of American society this is the best of times. The current economic expansion is the longest in U.S. history. Unemployment is the lowest in three decades. Inflation is low and under control. The stock market has risen from 3,500 to over 11,000 in eight years. The number of millionaires has more than doubled in the past five years to 7.1 million. The Cold War is over. The United States is the dominant player in the world both militarily and economically. Our society, obviously, is in good shape.

But every silver lining has a cloud. While basking in unprecedented wealth and economic growth, the U.S. has serious domestic problems. Personal bankruptcies are at a record level. The U.S. has the highest poverty rate and the highest child poverty rate in the Western world. We do not have a proper safety net for the disadvantaged that other countries take for granted. Hunger and homelessness are on the rise. Among the Western nations, the U.S. has the highest murder rate as well as the highest incarceration rate. Also, we are the only Western nation without a universal health care system, leaving 44 million Americans without health insurance.

I want to address another crucial problem that our society faces—the fragmentation of social life. Throughout U.S. history, despite a civil war, and actions separating people by religion, class, and race, the nation has somehow held together. Will society continue to cohere or will new crises pull us apart? That is the question of the morning. While there are many indicators of reduced societal cohesion, I will limit my discussion to four: (1) excessive individualism; (2) heightened personal isolation; (3) the widening income and wealth gap; and (4) the deepening racial/ethnic/religious/sexuality divide.

Excessive Individualism

We Americans celebrate individualism. It fits with our economic system of capitalism. We are self-reliant and responsible for our actions. We value individual freedom, including the right to choose our vocations, our mates, when and where to travel, and how to spend our money. At its extreme, the individualistic credo says that it is our duty to be selfish and in doing so, according to Adam Smith's notion of an "invisible hand," society benefits. Conservative radio commentator Rush Limbaugh said as much in his response to an initiative by President Clinton to encourage citizen volunteerism: "Citizen service is a repudiation of the principles upon which our country was based. We are here for ourselves."

While Rush Limbaugh may view rugged individualism as virtuous, I do not. It promotes inequality; it promotes the tolerance of inferior housing, schools, and services for "others"; and it encourages public policies that are punitive to the disadvantaged. For example, this emphasis on the individual has meant that, as a society, the United States has the lowest federal income tax rates in the Western world. Our politicians, especially Republicans, want to lower the rates even more so that individuals will have more and governments, with their presumed interest in the common good, will have less. As a result, the United States devotes relatively few resources to help the disadvantaged and this minimal redistribution system is shrinking.

In effect, our emphasis on individualism keeps us from feeling obligated to others.

Consider the way that we finance schools. Schools are financed primarily by the states through income taxes and local school districts through property taxes. This means that wealthy states and wealthy districts have more money to educate their children than the less advantaged states and districts. The prevailing view is that if my community or state is well-off, why should my taxes go to help children from other communities and other states?

The flaw in the individualistic credo is that we cannot go it alone—our fate depends on others. Paradoxically, it is in our individual interest to have a collective interest. We deny this at our peril for if we disregard those unlike ourselves, in fact doing violence to them, then we invite their hostility and violence, and, ultimately, a fractured society.

Heightened Personal Isolation

There are some disturbing trends that indicate a growing isolation as individuals become increasingly isolated from their neighbors, their co-workers, and even their family members. To begin, because of computers and telecommunications there is a growing trend for workers to work at home. While home-based work allows flexibility and independence not found in most jobs, these workers are separated from social networks. Aside from not realizing the social benefits of personal interaction with colleagues, working from home means being cut off from pooled information and the collective power that might result in higher pay and better fringe benefits.

Our neighborhoods, too, are changing in ways that promote isolation. A recent study indicates that one in three Americans has never spent an evening with a neighbor. This isolation from neighbors is exacerbated in the suburbs. Not only do some people live in gated communities to physically wall themselves off from "others" but they wall themselves off from their neighbors behaviorally and symbolically within gated and nongated neighborhoods alike. Some people exercise on motorized treadmills and other home exercise equipment instead of running through their neighborhoods. Rather than walking to the corner grocery or nearby shop and visiting with the clerks and neighbors, suburbanites have to drive somewhere away from their immediate neighborhood to shop among strangers. Or they may not leave their home at all, shopping and banking by computer. Sociologist Philip Slater says that "a community life exists when one can go daily to a given location at a given time and see many of the people one knows." Suburban neighborhoods in particular are devoid of such meeting places for adults and children. For suburban teenagers almost everything is away—practice fields, music lessons, friends, jobs, school, and the malls. Thus, a disconnect from those nearby. For adults many go through their routines without sharing stories, gossip, and analyses of events with friends on a regular basis at a coffee shop, neighborhood tavern, or at the local grain elevator.

Technology also encourages isolation. There was a major shift toward isolation with the advent of television as people spent more and more time within their homes rather than socializing with friends and neighbors. Now, we are undergoing a communications revolution that creates the illusion of intimacy but the reality is much different. Curt Suplee, science and technology writer for the *Washington Post*, says that we have seen "tenfold increases in 'communication' by electronic means, and tenfold reductions in person-to-person contact." In effect, as we are increasingly isolated before a computer screen, we risk what Warren Christopher has called "social malnutrition." John L. Locke, a professor [of] communications argues in *The De-Voicing of Society* that e-mail, voice mail, fax machines, beepers, and Internet chat rooms are robbing us of ordinary social talking. Talking, he says, like the grooming of apes and monkeys, is the way we build and maintain social relationships. In his view, it is only through intimate conversation that we can know others well enough to trust them and work with them harmoniously. In effect, Locke argues that we are becoming an autistic society, communicating messages electronically but without really connecting. Paradoxically, then, these incredible communication devices that combine to connect us in so many dazzling ways also separate us increasingly from intimate relationships.

Fragmentation is also occurring within many families, where the members are increasingly disconnected from each other. Many parents are either absent altogether or too self-absorbed to pay very much attention to their children or each other. On average, parents today spend 22 fewer hours a week with their children than parents did in the 1960s. Although living in the same house, parents or children may tune out each other by engaging in solitary activities. A survey by the Kaiser Family Foundation found that the average child between 2 and 18 spends 5 and one-half hours a day alone watching television, at a computer, playing video games, on the Internet, or reading. Many families rarely eat together in an actual sit-down meal. All too often material things are substituted for love and attention. Some children even have their own rooms equipped with a telephone, television, VCR, microwave, refrigerator, and computer, which while convenient, isolates them from other family members. Such homes may be full of people but they are really empty.

The consequences of this accelerating isolation of individuals are dire. More and more individuals are lonely, bitter, alienated, anomic, and disconnected. This situation is conducive to alcohol and drug abuse, depression, anxiety, and violence. The lonely and disaffected are ripe candidates for membership in cults, gangs, and militias where they find a sense of belonging and a cause to believe in but in the process they may become more paranoid and, perhaps, even become willing terrorists. At a less extreme level, the alienated will disengage from society by shunning voluntary associations, by home schooling their children, and by not participating in elections. In short, they will become increasingly individualistic, which compounds their problem and society's problem with unity.

The Widening Inequality Gap

There is an increasing gap between the rich and the rest of us, especially between the rich and the poor. Data from 1998 show that there were at least 268 billionaires in the United States, while 35 million were below the government official poverty line.

Timothy Koogle, CEO of Yahoo, made $4.7 million a day in 1999, while the median household income in that year was $110 a day. Bill Gates, CEO of Microsoft is richer than Koogle by far. He is worth, depending on [the] stock market on a given day, around $90 billion or so. Together,

eight Americans—Microsoft billionaires Bill Gates, Paul Allen, and Steve Ballmer plus the five Wal-Mart heirs—have a net worth of $233 billion, which is more than the gross domestic product of the very prosperous nation of Sweden. The Congressional Budget Office reports that in 1999, the richest 2.7 million Americans, the top 1 percent of the population, had as many aftertax dollars to spend as the bottom 100 million put together.

Compared to the other developed nations, the chasm between the rich and the poor in the U.S. is the widest and it is increasing. In 1979, average family income in the top 5 percent of the earnings distribution was 10 times that in the bottom 20 percent. Ten years later it had increased to 16:1, and in 1999 it was 19:1, the biggest gap since the Census Bureau began keeping track in 1947.

The average salary of a CEO in 1999 was 419 times the pay of a typical factory worker. In 1980 the difference was only 42 times as much. This inequality gap in the United States, as measured by the difference in pay between CEOs and workers, is by far the highest in the industrialized world. While ours stands at 419 to 1, the ratio in Japan is 25 to 1, and in France and Germany it is 35 to 1.

At the bottom end of wealth and income, about 35 million Americans live below the government's official poverty line. One out of four of those in poverty are children under the age of 18. Poor Americans are worse off than the poor in other western democracies. The safety net here is weak and getting weaker. We do not have universal health insurance. Funds for Head Start are so inadequate that only one in three poor children who are eligible actually are enrolled in the program. Welfare for single mothers is being abolished, resulting in many impoverished but working mothers being less well-off because their low-wage work is not enough to pay for child care, health care, housing costs, and other living expenses. Although the economy is soaring, a survey of 26 cities released by the U.S. Conference on Mayors shows that the numbers of homeless and hungry in the cities have risen for 15 consecutive years. The demand for emergency food is the highest since 1992 and the demand for emergency shelter is the largest since 1994. According to the U.S. Department of Agriculture, there were about 36 million, including 14 million children living in households afflicted with what they call "food insecurity," which is a euphemism for hunger.

Of the many reasons for the increase in homelessness and hunger amidst increasing affluence, three are crucial. First, the government's welfare system has been shrinking since the Reagan administration with the support of both Republicans and Democrats. Second, the cost of housing has risen dramatically causing many of the poor to spend over 50 percent of their meager incomes for rent. And, third, charitable giving has not filled the void, with less than 10 percent of contributions actually going to programs that help the poor. In effect, 90 percent of philanthropy is funneled to support the institutions of the already advantaged—churches (some of which trickles down to the poor), hospitals, colleges, museums, libraries, orchestras, and the arts.

The data on inequality show clearly, I believe, that we are moving toward a two-tiered society. Rather than "a rising tide lifting all boats," the justification for capitalism as postulated by President John Kennedy, the evidence is that "a rising tide lifts only the yachts." The increasing gap between the haves and the have-nots has crucial implications for our society. First, it divides people into the "deserving" and the "undeserving." If people are undeserving, then we are justified in not providing them with a safety net. As economist James K. Galbraith says: "A high degree of inequality causes the comfortable to disavow the needy. It increases the psychological distance separating these groups, making it easier to imagine that defects of character or differences of culture, rather than an unpleasant turn in the larger schemes of economic history, lie behind the separation." Since politicians represent the monied interests, the wealthy get their way as seen in the continuing decline in welfare programs for the poor and the demise of affirmative action. Most telling, the inequality gap is not part of the political debate in this, or any other, election cycle.

A second implication is that the larger the gap, the more destabilized society becomes.

In this regard economist Lester Thurow asks: "How much inequality can a democracy take? The income gap in America is eroding the social contract. If the promise of a higher standard of living is limited to a few at the top, the rest of the citizenry, as history shows, is likely to grow disaffected, or worse." Former Secretary of Labor, Robert Reich, has put it this way: "At some point, if the trends are not reversed, we cease being a society at all. The stability of the country eventually is threatened. No country can endure a massive gap between people at the top and people at the bottom." Or, as economist Galbraith puts it: "[Equality] is now so wide it threatens, as it did in the Great Depression, the social stability of the country. It has come to undermine our sense of ourselves as a nation of equals. Economic inequality, in this way, challenges the essential unifying myth of American national life."

The Deepening Racial/Ethnic/Religious/Sexuality Divide

The United States has always struggled with diversity. American history is stained by the enslavement of Africans and later the segregated and unequal "Jim Crow" South, the aggression toward native peoples based on the belief in "Manifest Destiny," the internment of Japanese Americans during World War II, episodes of intolerance against religious minorities, gays and lesbians, and immigrants. In each instance, the majority was not only intolerant of those labeled as "others," but they also used the law, religious doctrine, and other institutional forms of discrimination to keep minorities separate and unequal. Despite these ongoing societal wrongs against minorities, there has been progress culminating in the civil rights battles and victories of the 1950s, 1960s, and early 1970s.

But the civil rights gains of the previous generation are in jeopardy as U.S. society becomes more diverse. Currently, the racial composition of the U.S. is 72 percent white and 28 percent nonwhite. In 50 years it will be 50 percent nonwhite. The racial landscape is being transformed as approximately 1 million immigrants annually set up permanent residence in the United States and another 300,000 enter illegally and stay. These new residents are primarily Latino and Asian, not European as was the case of earlier waves of immigration. This "browning of America" has important implications including increased division.

An indicator of fragmentation along racial lines is the "White flight" from high immigration areas, which may lead to what demographer William Frey has called the "Balkanization of America." The trends toward gated neighborhoods, the rise of private schools and home schooling are manifestations of exclusiveness rather than inclusiveness and perhaps they are precursors to this "Balkanization."

Recent state and federal legislation has been aimed at reducing or limiting the civil rights gains of the 1970s. For example, in 1994 California passed Proposition 187 by a 3-to 2-popular vote margin, thereby denying public welfare to undocumented immigrants. Congress in 1996 voted to deny most federal benefits to legal immigrants who were not citizens. A number of states have made English the official state language. In 1997 California passed Proposition 209, which eliminated affirmative action (a policy aimed at leveling the playing field so that minorities would have a fair chance to succeed). Across the nation, Congress and various state legislatures, most recently Florida, have taken measures to weaken or eliminate affirmative action programs.

Without question racial and ethnic minorities in the U.S. are the targets of personal prejudicial acts as well as pervasive institutional racism. What will the situation be like by 2050 when the numbers of Latinos triple from their present population of 31.4 million, and the Asian population more than triples from the current 10.9 million, and the African American population increases 70 percent from their base of 34.9 million now?

Along with increasing racial and ethnic diversity, there is a greater variety of religious belief. Although Christians are the clear majority in the United States, there are also about 7 million Jews, 6 million Muslims (there are more Muslims than Presbyterians), and millions of other non-Christians, including Buddhists, and Hindus, as well as atheists.

While religion often promotes group integration, it also divides. Religious groups tend to emphasize separateness and superiority, thereby defining "others" as infidels, heathens, heretics, or nonbelievers. Strongly held religious ideas sometimes split groups within a denomination or congregation. Progressives and fundamentalists within the same religious tradition have difficulty finding common ground on various issues, resulting in division. This has always been the case to some degree, but this tendency seems to be accelerating now. Not only are there clashes within local congregations and denominational conferences but they spill out into political debates in legislatures and in local elections, most notably school board elections, as religious factions often push their narrow, divisive sectarian policies. These challenges to religious pluralism are increasing, thus promoting fragmentation rather than unity.

There is also widespread intolerance of and discrimination toward those whose sexual orientation differs from the majority. The behaviors of gay men and lesbian women are defined and stigmatized by many members of society as sinful; their activities are judged by the courts as illegal; and their jobs and advancement within those jobs are often restricted because of their being different sexually. As more and more homosexuals become public with their sexuality, their presence and their political agenda are viewed as ever more threatening and must be stopped.

My point is this: diversity and ever increasing diversity are facts of life in our society. If we do not find ways to accept the differences among us, we will fragment into class, race, ethnic, and sexual enclaves.

Two social scientists, John A. Hall and Charles Lindholm, in a recent book entitled *Is America Breaking Apart?* argue that throughout American history there has been remarkable societal unity because of its historically conditioned institutional patterns and shared cultural values. Columnist George Will picked up on this theme in a *Newsweek* essay, postulating that while the U.S. has pockets of problems, "American society is an amazing machine for homogenizing people." That has been the case but will this machine continue to pull us together? I believe, to the contrary, that while the U.S. historically has overcome great obstacles, a number of trends in contemporary society have enormous potential for pulling us apart. Our society is moving toward a two-tiered society with the gap between the haves and the have-nots, a withering bond among those of different social classes, and a growing racial, ethnic, and sexuality divide. The critical question is whether the integrative societal mechanisms that have served us well in the past will save us again or whether we will continue to fragment?

The challenge facing U.S. society as we enter the new millennium is to shift from building walls to building bridges. As our society is becoming more and more diverse, will Americans feel empathy for, and make sacrifices on behalf of, a wide variety of people who they define as different? The answer to this crucial question is negative at the present time. Social justice seems to be an outmoded concept in our individualistic society.

I shall close with a moral argument posed by one of the greatest social thinkers and social activists of the 20th century, the late Michael Harrington. Harrington, borrowing from philosopher John Rawls, provides an intuitive definition of justice. A just society is when I describe it to you and you accept it even if you do not know your place in it. Harrington then asks (I'm paraphrasing here): would you accept a society of 275 million where 44 million people do not have health insurance, where 35 million live in poverty including one-fifth of all children? Would you accept a society as just where discrimination against minorities is commonplace, even by the normal way society works? Would you accept a society where a sizable number of people live blighted lives in neighborhoods with a high concentration of poverty, with inferior schools, with too few good jobs? You'd be crazy to accept such a society but that is what we have. Harrington concludes: "If in your mind you could not accept a society in which we do unto you as we do unto them, then isn't it time for us to change the way we are acting towards them who are a part of us?" If, however, we accept an unjust society, then our society will move inexorably toward a divided and fortress society.

Discussion Questions

1. What social problem does Eitzen identify in his essay?

    He questions what holds us together as a society. Whether it is the result of inequality, diversity, individualism, or isolation, there are greater gaps and divides in society than ever before. Eitzen states that the challenge facing society today is how to shift from building walls to building bridges.

2. Identify each of the indicators of reduced societal cohesion and explain how each contributes to the fragmentation of social life.

    Eitzen identifies four indicators: excessive individualism, heightened personal isolation, the widening inequality gap, and the deepening racial, ethnic, religious, and sexuality divide.

Source: From Eitzen, D. S. (2000, July 1). The fragmentation of social life: Some critical societal concerns for the new millennium: Address by D. Stanley Eitzen, emeritus professor of sociology, Colorado State University delivered to the Life Enrichment Series, Bethel, North Newton, Kansas, April 12, 2000. *Vital speeches of the day*, pp. 563–566. Copyright © 2000 by D. Stanley Eitzen. Used by permission of the author.

CHAPTER 5

Capitalism, Class, and the Matrix of Domination

Allan G. Johnson (2001)

In *Privilege, Power, and Difference* (2001), Allan G. Johnson explores the interconnections among capitalism, privilege, and domination. He argues that rooted in capitalism are not only social class inequalities but also inequalities based on race and gender.

Every year I team-teach a course on race, and there always comes a point in the semester when students start saying things like this: "We don't get it. If race is socially constructed and doesn't exist otherwise, and if human beings aren't bound to be terrified of one another, then where does racism come from? Why all the oppression and hostility and violence over something that's been made up? And why would people make it up this way in the first place? It's stupid."

The answer we give takes us into the history of race, where we find two things that usually startle them as much as they did me when I first became aware of them. First, white racism hasn't been around very long—hardly more than several centuries and certainly not as long as white people have been aware of other races. Second, its appearance in Europe and the Americas occurred right along with the expansion of capitalism as an economic system. This is no coincidence, because capitalism played a major role in the development of white privilege, and still plays a major role in its perpetuation.

This isn't surprising given the importance of economics in social life, which is, after all, how people organize themselves to provide what they need for their material existence—food, shelter, clothing, and the like—and to live what their culture defines as a "good life." Because economic systems are the source of wealth, they are also the basis for every social institution, since

the state and church and universities and the like cannot survive without an economic base. It takes a great deal of material and labor to build a cathedral or a university, for example, or to pay for political campaigns or equip and feed a police force or an army. This means that the central place of economics in social life gives individuals and systems powerful reasons to go along with the dominant economic system. Capitalism has been that system for the last several hundreds years, and today, with the demise of the Soviet Union, it's virtually the only game in town.

What, then, did capitalism have to do with the origins of white racism? In the simplest sense, it was a matter of economics. Understanding why begins with understanding capitalism itself.

How Capitalism Works

The basic goal of modern capitalism is to turn money into more money. Capitalists invest money to buy what it takes to produce goods and services: raw materials, machinery, electricity, buildings, and, of course, human labor. It doesn't matter what they produce so long as they can find a market in which to sell it at a profit—for more than it cost to have it produced—and end up with more money than they started with. Whether the result enhances human life (providing healthy food, affordable housing, health care, and the like) or causes harm (tobacco, alcohol, drugs, weapons, slavery, pollution) may be an issue for individual capitalists who value a clear conscience. But the system itself doesn't depend on such moral or ethical considerations, for profit is profit and there's no way to tell "good" money from "bad." Even the damage done by one enterprise can serve as a source of profit for another. Industrial pollution, for example, creates profitable opportunities for companies that specialize in cleaning it up.

Capitalists employ workers to produce goods and services, paying them wages in exchange for their time. Capitalists then sell the goods and services that workers produce. For capitalists to make a living (since they don't produce anything themselves), they have to get workers to produce goods and services that are worth more than the wages capitalists pay them. The difference is what capitalists live on.

Why, however, would workers accept wages worth less than the value of what they produce? The general answer is that they don't have much choice, because under capitalism the tools and factories used to produce goods aren't owned by the people who actually do the work. Instead, they're owned by capitalists, especially stockholders who invest in companies. So, for most people who want to earn a living, chances are they'll have to work for one capitalist employer or another, which means choosing between working on the capitalist's terms or not working at all. As corporate capitalism has extended its reach into every area of social life, even professionals now have to confront this choice. Physicians, for example, who were once regarded as the model of an independent profession, are increasingly compelled to become what are essentially highly paid employees of health maintenance organizations. As a result, they have recently begun to lobby Congress for the right to engage in collective bargaining with HMOs—in other words, to form a labor union for physicians.

Since capitalists profit from the difference between the cost of producing goods (most of which is people's labor) and what they can sell goods for in markets, the cheaper the labor, the more money left over for them. This is why capitalists are so concerned about increasing "worker productivity"—finding ways for workers to produce more goods for the same or less pay. One way to accomplish this is through the use of technology, especially machines that replace people altogether. Another is to threaten to close down or relocate businesses if workers won't make concessions on wages, health and retirement benefits, job security, and working conditions. A third and increasingly popular strategy in the "new global economy" is to move production to countries where people are willing to work for less than they are in Europe or North America and where authoritarian governments will control workers and discourage the formation of unions and other sources of organized resistance, often with the direct support of the U.S. government.

Capitalism and Class

The dynamics of capitalism produce not only enormous amounts of wealth, but high—and increasing—levels of inequality, both within societies and globally. The richest 10 percent of the U.S. population holds more than two-thirds of all the wealth, including almost 90 percent of cash, almost half the land, more than 90 percent of business assets, and almost all stocks and bonds. In 1998, the richest top 20 percent of all households received almost *half* of all income, and the richest 40 percent received almost *three-quarters,* leaving just a quarter of all income to be divided among the remaining 60 percent of all households.

Such patterns of inequality result from and perpetuate a class system based on widening gaps in income, wealth, and power between those on top and everyone below them. It is a system that produces oppressive consequences. For those at the bottom, the costs are enormous, with living conditions among the rural poor, for example, at or below the level found in many of the world's most impoverished nonindustrial societies. Even among employed members of the working class, as well as many of those in the middle class, the class system offers little security and takes an emotional toll. A great many jobs are boring, mind-numbing, and make use of much less than what most people have to offer. And the vast majority of working people have little if any control over the work they do or whether they keep their jobs.

It also doesn't take much to see that with the bottom 60 percent of the U.S. population having to divide just a quarter of all income among themselves, there isn't going to be enough to go around. While capitalism produces an overall abundance of goods and services, it distributes that wealth so unequally that it also produces conditions of scarcity for most of the population. This makes life for those 150 million or so people an ongoing competition that is full of anxiety and struggle. For a majority of people, it wouldn't take very much—a divorce, perhaps, or a serious illness or being laid off—to substantially lower their standard of living, even to the extent of putting them out of their homes and onto welfare.

The "American Dream" aside, most people also have relatively little power to improve their class position. Much of the increase in household wealth, for example, has been based on a growing mountain of credit card debt, people working two or more jobs, and families relying on two wage earners to support the same standard of living their parents managed with one. Although unemployment is at record low levels, most of the new jobs that have been created over the last several decades have been low-paying and with little chance of advancement. In addition, studies of occupational mobility show most people are as likely to move downward as they are upward in the class system. Because of this and the widening gulf separating the upper class from everyone else, the middle class has actually shrunk. Since 1964, the percentage of people who see themselves as middle class has fallen from 61 to 45, while the percentage seeing themselves as working class has risen from 35 to 44.

In short, in an era of continuing corporate downsizing, the flight of well-paying industrial jobs overseas, and the rapid growth of low-level service occupations, for most people the struggle to move upward rarely gets much beyond hanging on to what they have. There is, of course, upward movement by some, but outside of high-technology fields that are currently in demand, this almost always comes at the expense of others who must move down to make room for them. This creates what economist Lester Thurow calls a "zero-sum" society, adapting a term used to describe games that are designed so that one person's gain is always someone else's loss. This makes it inevitable that at any given moment a substantial proportion of the population will have to live in poverty or close to it. But it also sets the stage for different groups within the "bottom" 60 percent to see one another as competitors and threats to their livelihood.

As we'll see below, such dynamics of capitalism have played a key role in the trouble around difference and privilege, especially in relation to race and gender.

Capitalism, Difference, and Privilege: Race and Gender

Given how capitalism works, it connects to white racism in ways that are both direct and indirect. In the history of the United States, the direct connection is most apparent in the enslavement of millions of Africans as a source of cheap labor on cotton and tobacco plantations in the South. This was done for purely economic reasons, as became dramatically apparent after Eli Whitney's invention of the cotton gin in 1792 made it possible to process many times more cotton than before. Tempted by the potential to multiply cotton production—and profits—many times over, planters chose to minimize labor costs by exploiting slave labor rather than pay free workers a living wage.

As a result, the number of enslaved blacks in the United States jumped from 1 million in 1800 to almost 4 million in 1860, just before the start of the Civil War. The primacy of profit in white thinking was also apparent in the reactions of businesses that relied on paid white workers. They didn't object to slavery on moral grounds. Instead, they complained that slave owners were engaging in unfair competition because their labor costs were so low it was impossible to compete against them. It was common, for example, for construction firms that depended on slave labor to win contracts away from their competition by underbidding them.

Following the Civil War, the capitalist appetite for cheap agricultural labor was no less than before, and freed blacks were held in a new form of bondage by an oppressive system of tenant farming that kept them perpetually in debt. Beyond the South, the profitability of racism showed itself in the widespread use of Chinese immigrant labor to build the Western railways under harsh and demeaning conditions. Even farther west, Japanese immigrants had similar experiences on the sugar and pineapple plantations of Hawaii.

Capitalism's direct connection to white racism has also operated in the acquisition of land and raw materials which, like cheap labor, play a key role in the rapid growth of industry and wealth. In the heyday of capitalist expansion during the eighteenth and nineteenth centuries, Europe and then the United States found an abundance of what they needed in Africa, Asia, and the Americas. To acquire them, they relied on varying combinations of military conquest, political domination, and economic exploitation. They were spectacularly successful at it, especially Great Britain, a small island nation with few natural resources of its own that nonetheless managed to become the world's first true industrial power. Unlike Britain, the United States was already rich in natural resources, but whites could get at them only by taking them away from the Native American tribes who inhabited most of the land as well as from Mexico, which encompassed most of what is now the far western and southwestern United States. Whites managed to take what they wanted through a combination of conquest, genocide, and a complex array of treaties that were routinely ignored.

To justify such direct forms of imperialism and oppression, whites developed the *idea* of whiteness to define a privileged social category elevated above everyone who wasn't included in it. This made it possible to reconcile conquest, treachery, slavery, and genocide with the nation's newly professed ideals of democracy, freedom, and human dignity. If whiteness defined what it meant to be human, then it was seen as less of an offense against the Constitution (not to mention God) to dominate and oppress those who happened to fall outside that definition as the United States marched onward toward what was popularly perceived as its Manifest Destiny.

Other capitalist connections to racism have been less direct. Capitalists, for example, have often used white racism as a strategy to maintain control over white workers and thereby keep wages low and productivity high. This has been done in two main ways. First, beginning early in the nineteenth century, there was a systematic public campaign to encourage white workers to adopt whiteness as a key part of their social identity—something they hadn't done before—and to accept the supposed superiority of whiteness as compensation for their low class position. No matter how badly treated they were by their employers, they could always look in the mirror and comfort themselves with the fact of being white and therefore elevated above people of color, even those who might have a class position higher than their own. With the emancipation of the slaves following the Civil War, however, lower-class whites could no longer point to their freedom as a mark of superiority. Their response to this loss was a period of enormous violence and intimidation directed against blacks, much of which was perpetrated by the newly formed Ku Klux Klan with no serious opposition from government or the larger white population.

Another way for capitalists to control workers is to keep them worried over the possibility of losing their jobs if they demand higher wages or better working conditions. White racism has a long history of being used for this purpose. The oppressed condition of blacks and other racial minorities encourages them to work for wages that are lower than what most whites will accept. Employers have used this to pose an ongoing threat to white workers who have known employers could readily use racial minorities as an inexpensive replacement for them. This has worked most effectively as a way to break strikes and the labor unions that promote them. As unions became more powerful at the turn of the twentieth century, for example, employers often brought in black workers as strikebreakers. The strategy worked to draw the attention of white workers away from issues of capitalism and class to issues of race. It focused their fear and anger on the supposed threat from black workers, which made them less likely to see their common condition

as workers and join together against the capitalists. In this way, racial division and conflict became an effective strategy for dividing different segments of the working class against one another.

Similar dynamics operate today, although perhaps with greater subtlety. The controversy and conflict over affirmative action programs, for example, as well as the influx of immigrant workers from Mexico and Asia reflect an underlying belief that the greatest challenge facing white workers is unfair competition from people of color. This ignores the capitalist system itself, which by its nature increases the wealth of capitalists by controlling workers and keeping wages as low as possible, and allows a small elite to control the vast majority of wealth and income, leaving a relatively small share to be divided among everyone else. This makes for conditions of scarcity that encourage fierce competition, especially in the working and lower classes, but also in many segments of the middle class. Given the historical legacy that encourages whites to feel a sense of superiority and entitlement in relation to people of color, such competition is bound to provoke anger and resentment among whites, which is then directed at people of color rather than at those whose wealth and power lie at the heart of what is essentially an economic problem centering on the distribution of wealth. In this way, dynamics of class privilege fuel continued racism which, in turn, draws attention away from capitalism and the class oppression it produces.

Capitalism also shapes and makes use of gender inequality. The cultural devaluing of women, for example, has long been used as an excuse to pay them less and exploit them as a source of cheap labor, whether in the corporate secretarial pool in New York or garment sweatshops in Los Angeles or electronics industry assembly plants in Asia. Women's supposed inferiority has also been used as a basis for the belief that much of the work that women do isn't work at all and therefore isn't worthy of anything more than emotional compensation. Capitalism couldn't function without the army of women who do the shopping for households (which is how most goods are purchased) and do the labor through which those goods are consumed: cooking the meals, making the bed with the new set of sheets, and so on. On a deeper level, women are, with few exceptions, the ones who nurture and raise each new generation of workers on which capitalism depends, and this vital service is provided without anyone's having to pay wages or provide health and retirement benefits. Women do it for free—even when they also work outside the home—to the benefit of the capitalist system and those who are most privileged by it.

Capitalism, then, provides an important social context for the trouble around privilege and difference. And the class dynamics that arise from capitalism interact with that trouble in powerful ways that both protect capitalism and class privilege and perpetuate privilege and oppression based on difference.

The Matrix of Domination and the Paradox of Being Privileged and Unprivileged at the Same Time

As the dynamics of capitalism and class suggest, systems of privilege are complicated. This is one reason why people can belong to a privileged category and not feel privileged. There are more than one set of categories, which means a person can belong to the privileged category in one set and an unprivileged category in another. So, for example, a middle-class white lesbian's class and race privilege may blind her to issues of race and class, or her experience of gender inequality and heterosexism may foster the illusion that this automatically prepares her to know everything she needs to know about other forms of privilege and oppression. Or a working-class white man may be annoyed by the idea that his whiteness and maleness somehow give him access to privilege. As a member of the working class, he may feel so insecure, pushed around, looked down on, and exploited that the last thing that he feels is privileged.

Part of such feelings comes from the misconception that privilege is something that is just about individuals. From that perspective, either he's privileged or he's not, just like he either has two ears or he doesn't. If he can show that he's not privileged in some way (being working-class), then that would seem to cancel out any claim that he's privileged in another.

But the truth is more complicated than whether *he* is privileged, for in a basic way, privilege isn't really about him, even though he's certainly involved in it. The social categories "white," "male," and "middle-class" are privileged in this society, and he belongs to two of those. Being working-class, however, can set up barriers that make it harder for him to attain the benefits associated with being white and male. If he can't earn a good living, for example, he may have a hard time feeling like a "real man" bonded to other men in their superiority to women. The privileged social category "male" still exists, and he belongs to it, but his social-class position gets in the way of his enjoying the advantages that go with it.

Another complication is that categories that define privilege exist all at once and in relation to one another. People never see me solely in terms of my race, for example, or my gender. Like everyone else's, my place in the social world is a package deal—white male heterosexual (middle-aged, married, father, writer, teacher, middle-class, Anglo, U.S. citizen, and on and on)—and that's the way it is all the time.

Whether, for example, my students perceive me as intelligent, credible, and competent will most likely be affected by their perception of my race. In that sense, no student could look at me simply as professor, for they will also see a person of a certain gender, race, and class. Even if they first meet me on the phone, they'll form impressions of my race if only by assuming I'm white unless I give them reason to think otherwise. In this sense, I don't exist purely as a professor separate from the other social categories I belong to.

Given that reality, it makes no sense to talk about the effect of being in one of these categories—say, white—without also looking at the others and how they're related to it. My experience of being identified as a white person in this society is affected by my also being seen as male and heterosexual and of a certain class. If I apply for a job, for example, white privilege will usually give me an edge over a similarly qualified Latino man. But if the people doing the hiring think I'm gay, my white privilege might lose out to his heterosexual privilege, and he might get the job instead of me.

It's tempting to use such comparisons to try to figure out some kind of net cost or benefit associated with each social category. In other words, you get a point for being white, male, or heterosexual, and you lose a point if you're of color, female, or homosexual. Add up the points and the result is your position in relation to systems of privilege. That would put white male heterosexuals on top (+3) and lesbians of color in some kind of "triple jeopardy" at the bottom (–3). White lesbians (–1) and gay men of color (–1) would fall somewhere in between and presumably on the same "level." This would also be true of gay white men (+1) and heterosexual white women (+1).

Life and privilege aren't that simple, however. It's not as though being male gives you a certain amount of something called "privilege" and being white gives you more of the same, and being gay cancels out half of it. Privilege takes different forms that are connected to one another in ways that aren't obvious. For example, historically one of the ways that white men have justified their domination over black men has been to portray them as sexual predators who pose a threat to white women. At the same time, they've portrayed white women as pure and needing white men's protection, a dependent position that puts them under white men's control. Notice, then, how the dynamics of gender and race are so bound up with each other that it's hard, if not impossible, to tell where one ends and the other begins. How much race or gender "counts" all by itself cannot be determined.

This is why sociologist Patricia Hill Collins describes such systems as a "matrix of domination" or what Estelle Disch calls a "matrix of privilege," and not merely a loose collection of different kinds of inequality that don't have much to do with one another. As Collins and numerous others argue, each particular form of privilege, whether based on race, gender, sexual orientation, class, religion, or ethnicity, exists only as part of a much larger system of privilege.

Looking at privilege and domination in this way simplifies and clarifies things considerably. For example, once we see that each form of privilege exists only in relation to all the rest, we can stop the fruitless habit of comparing them and trying to figure out which is the worst or most oppressive.

We also free ourselves from the trap of thinking that everything is a matter of either/or—either you're oppressed or you're not, privileged or not—because reality is usually a matter of both/and. In other words, we can belong to both privileged and oppressed categories at the same time, and if we're going to make ourselves part of the solution to the problem of privilege, we have to see that. Why? Because we can't make ourselves part of the solution without seeing clearly how we're connected to the problem.

Perhaps most important, the concept of a matrix helps us see how the different dimensions of privilege and domination are connected to one another, how heterosexism is used to support male privilege, for example, or how racism is used to support class privilege. We can also see how subordinate groups are often pitted against one another in ways that draw attention away from the system of privilege that hurts them both. Asian Americans, for example, are often held up as a good example—the "model minority." This makes other racial and ethnic minorities look bad by comparison and encourages them to blame Asian Americans for their disadvantaged status. In this way, Asian Americans serve as a buffer between whites and other peoples of color, as Korean Americans were in Los Angeles after the police who assaulted Rodney King were acquitted and the rage of black people spilled over into Korean neighborhoods, where stores were burned to the ground. Only when the rioting reached the edge of white neighborhoods did police finally respond to pleas for help.

The complexity of the matrix of privilege and domination makes it clear that work for change needs to focus on the idea of privilege itself and all the forms it takes. We won't get rid of racism, in other words, without doing something about sexism and class, because the system that produces the one also produces the others and connects them all together.

Discussion Questions

1. What is the connection between capitalism and racism?

   Johnson identifies direct and indirect connections. An example of a direct connection is the enslavement of Africans as a cheap source of labor on cotton and tobacco plantations in the South. A less direct connection is capitalism's use of white racism to keep (white) workers worried over the possibility of losing their jobs if they demand higher wages or better working conditions. Unions, at the turn of the century, would use black workers as strikebreakers, deflecting the attention of white workers from issues of capitalism and social class inequality to issues of race.

2. What is the relationship between capitalism and gender inequality? How do the two function to support each other?

   The devaluing of women in our society supports existing labor practices to pay women less than men and to continue exploiting them as a source of cheap labor.

Source: From Johnson, A. G. (2001). Capitalism, class, and the matrix of domination. In *Privilege, power, and difference* (pp. 42–56). Boston: McGraw Hill. Used by permission of The McGraw-Hill Companies.

CHAPTER 6

Consumer Culture

An Interview With Juliet Schor

Douglas B. Holt (2005)

In this interview, sociologist Juliet Schor (author of *Born to Buy: The Commercialized Child and the New Consumer Culture*) discusses the significance of the attitude and ideology of consumerism and the emergence of consumer society. Schor identifies and analyzes four major problems associated with consumer society in the United States.

HOLT: A lot of your work has been focused on trying to understand consumerism. What is consumerism from your standpoint? And what is the problem of consumerism that you're trying to unpack in your work?

SCHOR: First, I should define what I mean by the term, in opposition to, for example, consumer society. In my view, consumerism is about an attitude and an ideology, a particular way of relating to consumer goods in which they take on central importance in the construction of culture, identity and social life. Consumer society I define as a situation in which the vast majority of people have a consumerist attitude or are living consumerist lifestyles. I see consumer society as a 20th-century phenomenon because before that you don't have mass consumption. In this I differ from historians, for example, who date the emergence of consumer society in the 17th or 18th centuries. You also asked about the *problem* of consumerism. I see problems with both consumer society and consumerism, but I think the problems of consumerism are derivative of the problems of consumer society. I see four major problems associated with consumer society in the US and, to a lesser extent, other advanced capitalist countries. The first is what I've called the output bias of capitalism, that is the inability to take

productivity in the form of leisure time. This is particularly pronounced in the United States. It involves a very strong orientation from the production side towards maximal levels of consumption. Do you want me to elaborate on that now or shall we come back to it?

HOLT: Yes, let's get into your first point. How does this create a social problem?

SCHOR: It's a serious social problem because what it means is that we have an economy in which it is becoming increasingly difficult to deliver free time to people. Without adequate free time, you suffer the erosion of the social fabric and difficulties reproducing the non-market economy and also an everyday reality of community. I think there's a way in which the market is cannibalizing – this is a strong word, but I think it's a fair one – other parts of social life, especially recently.

HOLT: Can you give an example of cannibalization?

SCHOR: What it means is that there are very strong demands for labor from the market economy, which leaves households with inadequate labor time to reproduce social relations and engage in non-market production. The same goes for community. That's why I say cannibalist. Literally eating up time.

HOLT: So, just like, being able to have dinners together and . . .

SCHOR: Yes.

HOLT: . . . Is that what we're talking about?

SCHOR: Exactly. Labor time for reproducing relationships. So, for example, in the United States, within marriages, spouses are starved for time, particularly in couples with children, because parents try very hard to protect time with children. Instead, they skimp on marital time. Friendships, family connections and communities suffer. I see these effects as a major social problem. Consumerism gets implicated because the dramatic escalation of consumption norms requires that people stay in the labor market at full-time jobs in order to gain full-time incomes. So it's not just a labor market issue.

A second problem which is, I think, extremely serious on a world historical scale is the impact of consumer activity on the planetary ecology.

And, again, this is especially a North American issue because consumption patterns here have such a large environmental impact. Our consumption is a key cause of global warming as well as species extinction, ecosystem degradation and toxic chemical poisoning.

HOLT: Can you give your "hit list" of the worst consumer categories or activities in terms of their environmental impact?

SCHOR: Of course, energy use is paramount because of its effect on climate change. Relevant consumption includes vehicles, which are a salient example, especially with the shift to sport utility vehicles and the decline in average fleet mileage in the US. The tremendous growth in housing size is also important. Residential energy use is now rising in the US after decades of decline. We are building more energy-efficient houses, but that has been more than compensated for by much bigger houses with many more appliances, such as jacuzzis and steam showers and extra freezers and the proliferation of consumer electronics. Air travel is another very, very carbon intensive activity. Meat consumption is also highly environmentally degrading. Shrimp is another good example. We've gone from a world in which shrimp was a luxury, eaten by the wealthy and as a special treat by the middle classes. Now there are "all you can eat" shrimp buffets for $7.99. Shrimp is cheap and the reason is that we have shifted to shrimp cultivation, which is destroying mangroves and coastline ecosystems in many parts of the world and is one of the most environmentally damaging products that we're consuming right now. I've also been thinking a lot about

apparel lately. People tend not to connect clothing with environmental degradation. But there are a variety of degrading effects of apparel production, such as pesticide-intensive cotton cultivation or the synthetic/toxic dyes used in almost all apparel production. Leather is another example of a good which has gone from a luxury to a mass consumer good available at very low prices. Leather tanning is extraordinarily toxic and has enormous health impacts on tannery workers as well as the people dependent on the local water supplies which are polluted by the toxic chemicals used in tanning. Leather tanning has shifted out of Italy and Spain to South Asia, where environmental laws tend not to be followed.

HOLT: Number three?

SCHOR: All private consumption is a substitute for an alternative use of economic resources. And what are those alternatives? Instead of private consumption, one can save money, take leisure or pay for more public consumption. In this country, the excessive orientation to private consumption has squeezed these other things, which I would argue yield more welfare to people once they reach the middle class. More savings, more leisure time and more public consumption would raise well-being more than extra VCRs, cashmere sweaters and shifting from a regular car to an SUV. But the dynamics of production and consumption in the United States are heavily biased in the direction of private consumption.

HOLT: Is this the story of the debt crisis in the country today?

SCHOR: In the United States we have a savings rate that's hovering at about zero, roughly. Large numbers of households live "paycheck to paycheck" (i.e. without financial assets). That introduces levels of stress and insecurity which undermine psychological well-being and put people on the edge financially.

HOLT: Number four.

SCHOR: Number four is a bit more speculative. I have less to contribute in terms of my own research on this, but there's a way in which I believe it is difficult to construct durable community in a highly consumerist society. Some critics of consumer society argue that consumerism has destroyed community. That may not be right. More likely, capitalism destroyed community and consumerism came along later in some ways as a substitute for community. That strikes me as a better account of the destruction of community in the United States than the standard story from the consumer critics. But I think what consumerism has done is to make it more difficult to reconstruct community because it undermines the daily life conditions which true reciprocal bonds require. It keeps people locked into what I've called the cycle of work and spend.

HOLT: That's what I'm trying to understand. Is it a different story than people just don't have time?

SCHOR: Time is a big part of it, but there's also an issue of orientation and goals and what people deem important. So it's a bit derivative.

HOLT: Okay. So, then, is it fair to say that both of your early books and other writings that spin off from them are attempts to explain the macro case of society dominated by consumerism and to try to ameliorate some of these problems?

SCHOR: Yes. The first book is about the production side and how the structure of production makes it difficult to have any outcome other than the consumerist outcome. It's about how workers can't take productivity growth in the form of leisure time.

HOLT: Let's go through this. In *The Overworked American*, you formulate an argument called the work and spend cycle. Why don't you state the thesis and why it was a distinctive thesis versus some of the work that economists were circulating at the time and that you were pushing against.

SCHOR: Sure. But I want to come back to the point that if you want to understand consumption, you have to analyze it in the context of production. I think the linkage between production and consumption is really important and is absent in a lot of other accounts, including both critiques of consumer culture and standard economic analysis. So, the argument of *The Overworked American* was that you have a bias in a labor market, which is that employers refuse to allow a market in hours to operate. They don't let workers choose the number of hours they want to work or give them the opportunity to take productivity growth in the form of shorter hours. Firms set long hours, which go with jobs. If you take a job, you have to work the prescribed hours.

HOLT: This is because there's a fixed cost of benefits to go with the job and so they have a strong economic incentive to push for as many work hours as possible to lower the average (fixed + variable) hourly wage.

SCHOR: There are a couple of different cost structures that employers face and the one you mentioned is the most important. But there are a variety of costs which grow in the post-Fordist era which are paid on a per person basis rather than a per hour basis. Take all types of fringe benefits such as medical, pension, disability, unemployment insurance. Some are purely per person, others level off at a certain level of hours. There are a few other aspects to the cost structures facing the employer, such as the situation of salaried workers. If they're paid on a monthly or yearly basis, then the firm is able to extract extra hours from them because the market in hours isn't functioning. There's also a more esoteric issue, which is actually what got me into this topic, and it involves the scarcity value of the job or what has been called the employment rent. In jobs which are paid by the hour, when hours increase, the worker loses more income when he or she loses the job. So workers are more invested in their jobs when they carry longer hours. They give more effort and are easier to control. Here's an intuitive way of understanding this employer preference for long hours: think about how much you have to give up in terms of pay, promotion and benefits to get a short hours job. For the privilege of working short hours, the employee pays a huge penalty. That's the way firms have structured the labor market.

HOLT: And you see that reflected in gender bias?

SCHOR: Yes, because women have stronger preferences for short hours because of their household responsibilities, they are more likely to make those sacrifices and take those shorter hour jobs.

HOLT: I don't think anybody would argue with you that Americans are working more hours than workers in other countries. And probably one could point to political and historical reasons for these results. But what is the mechanism by which long hours lead to consumer society?

SCHOR: Start with productivity growth occurring at, let's say, an average of 3 percent a year, which means that we could take 3 percent more leisure and produce the same level of output. Alternatively, we could take that extra 3 percent and put it towards more output, which translates into more income for people. What I'm saying is that employers only allow the second option; namely, the translation of all productivity growth into higher output. Of course, they try and keep as much of that income for themselves, but ultimately it gets doled out as income to somebody. Right now, it's going to the upper portion of the income distribution and it's also going into corporate profits. But it's not being used to reduce working hours. It's all going towards higher levels of output. The output is sold and becomes income to the firm, which then disperses it to employees. So then you have a workforce which is getting that additional income. Then the income is virtually all spent on consumer goods and services. That's the core of work and spend. Why is it that people don't save the money or vote to pay it to the government in taxes for more public goods? Why don't they save it up over a number of years and then leave the labor force? Obviously, some of this is happening. But I'm saying there's a bias towards private consumption. The explanation for that is the subject of the second book, *The Overspent American*. One part of the answer related to asymmetries in people's preference for present versus future income. That's where the cycle (in the work and spend cycle) comes in. But we may not want to get into those details.

HOLT: But what is provocative about your thesis is that you are suggesting the causality is from work to spending and that it's because leisure hours are restricted. Is that it or is it because earnings are rising?

SCHOR: It's the same thing. Less leisure means more income. Less income means more leisure. There's a trade-off between income and leisure. What I'm saying is we're always taking the income rather than the leisure. So let's get to where I differ from the standard analyses in sociology, anthropology and cultural studies, which typically locate the drive for consumption elsewhere, and from standard economic analyses which have a very different view of the labor market. Let's start with the economists. The view in economics is that workers choose their hours. If you have a highly consumerist society, it's because people want lots of consumption and they don't want leisure. Workers' preferences determine the outcome. What determines preferences? They're not going to talk about that because that's something that sociologists do or they're attributed to human nature. Preferences are exogenous to the economic analysis. If the US is taking a more consumerist path than in Europe, it's because that's what people prefer. If Americans really wanted more leisure, they would take it. There's no structure in the labor market that makes it difficult or impossible for workers to get more leisure time. And who are you, consumer critic, to beef about the choices that people are making? You're just an elitist academic, looking down on people for wanting to spend their weekends at the mall buying junk. The neoclassical story is that workers get what they want. My story is that workers end up wanting what they have gotten. I believe, as the neoclassical economists

do, that when you ask people, you'll get a relatively high level of satisfaction with the current hours/income trade-off, but that's not because people had preset preferences that got satisfied. It's because people adapt to the level of spending that they've done. In the survey data presented in my book, people are responding that they'd rather have more leisure than more money. But they don't get the leisure. They get the money instead. Once they get the money, they spend it. And when you ask them a year later or two years later how do they feel about their hours/income trade-off, they don't want to revert to their earlier preferences and say now I'm working too many hours, I want to give back some of that money and get more free time. Once they've spent the money, they're acclimatized to it. Their preferences have changed. Year after year, they don't get free time and they adapt to a rising standard of living.

HOLT: So it sounds like, with work and spend, you have a theory of why there is an ultimate lack of leisure in the US society, but you don't have a theory of what leads to consumer spending.

SCHOR: Here my story is more familiar. The arguments I made about the labor market were novel – there was one unpublished paper in economics that made a similar argument. It was written in 1969. My story about why income gets translated into spending is better known, especially in sociology. I argued that people consume [according] to norms which are set socially. It's a story very much in the spirit of Bourdieu and also Jim Duesenberry, who was my colleague at Harvard. In the 1940s, he wrote about keeping up with the Joneses. What's novel in *The Overspent American* is my argument that in the 1980s and 1990s, the United States entered a period of intensified competitive consumption (my term). It also entailed a change in the way the aspirational process for consumption operated, which is in a shift from what I call horizontal to vertical emulation. The idea is that the lifestyles of the top 20 percent became an emulative target for the whole society. The dominant consumption reference group, to use a sociological term, was now the top 20 percent. That was driven mostly by two things. One is the change in the income distribution: the top 20 gained relative to the bottom 80. This, by the way, is why we are different than Northern or even Western Europe. I believe more unequal countries have more intense consumption competitions. The growth of inequality in the last 25 years in the United States has been central to the intensification of status competition in consumption.

HOLT: The US is the most socioeconomically unequal country among the industrialized countries. So, with your argument, would you expect less developed countries with high inequality, such as Brazil, also to have a higher rate of consumerism?

SCHOR: Probably. It also depends on how much social segregation you have. If you have a very large group of people who are very socially marginalized from the top 30 percent, it doesn't necessarily translate into effects across the whole distribution. In the United States, although we have social exclusion, I think that we have more participation in a common consumption culture.

HOLT: That's through the social networks or through the media? What is the mechanism? Is it through the labor force?

SCHOR: I think it's mostly through media and consumer experiences. I don't think it's as much through social networks because there you do have a fair amount of exclusion. But if you look at poor and lower middle-class folks, their consumption aspirations are pretty similar to middle-class and upper middle-class people. They're more modest and they have less of an expectation of being able to succeed in their consumption aspirations, but people across the distribution want the same designer goods and roughly the same bundle of products. I think the media's really key in that. I think one thing that is happening is that as you shift to a more global consumer culture, with a global media, you are getting more convergence in consumption aspirations around the world.

HOLT: Here I think your thesis is more contentious. I think your argument in *The Overworked American* was distinctive, as you say, but probably more widely accepted. This demand-side thesis runs against the grain of a lot of writing about consumption from historians and sociologists. Maybe we can talk about that. So you're saying there was an inflection point in the 1980s that was caused by growing inequality in the US?

SCHOR: Yes. It was also caused by the rise in television viewing time and the decline of social engagement. I believe that, historically, consumption desire has been stimulated in large part through social interaction rather than primarily by media and advertising.

HOLT: That argument certainly runs against what many academics believe. I think most writers and historians who have looked at the rise of consumer culture tie it to the rise of mass media. Magazines are the first instances and the rise of department stores at the turn of the century. Then there's another big inflection point with

television going national in the mid-1950s. Those developments are tightly tied to the formation of a consensus idea of the good life. You need the ranch house in the suburbs with the modern appliances and the big Chevy outside and all the things we see. I think there's compelling evidence that those effects did and do indeed take place. You're saying that there really wasn't that strong an effect until the 1980s?

SCHOR: I don't want to absolutely deny the importance of those things. But my view is that through that period, those effects always got worked out through social processes. Department stores are different because they're not "media." But with magazines and television, their power derived in large part from being embedded in a social process. So you might have the early adopters, who are the first on the block to get the new item or the new style being driven by media, but it's through social interactions that the adoption of products occurs. It's person to person. I just think that's a more forceful mechanism. So you can't completely separate them. But I think advertisers could have gotten out there with all the messages they wanted. They wouldn't work independent of the social networks. The messages had to resonate with those social realities. But what I'm saying about the 1980s and later is that you have the decline of those social networks and the rising importance of media and advertising. The 1980s start an important shift in terms of the decline of the social. The neighborhood, which was the historic site of consumption comparison in the postwar era, becomes very unimportant.

HOLT: So this is Putnamesque? Some people have criticized that thesis as being more of a middle-class kind of story. The middle class became even more socially uprooted and more tied to work. But if you're in a working-class neighborhood, is that holding true as well? I don't know what the evidence is for that.

SCHOR: I think it's pretty much across class. Of course, you never had such a strongly based household comparison among the poor because a lot of competitive consumption took place outside the household, with appearance goods and vehicles. But, in the middle classes, it was more of a household-based dynamic. But I don't want to state this too strongly. I'm not saying there's no more social or interpersonal consumption communication. Of course, that still goes on. But I think you get a shift towards media being more important in setting lifestyle norms and creating reference groups as opposed to day-to-day interpersonal interactions. And certainly the neighborhood declines a lot, which is why you get the vertical emulation. The neighborhood is a very horizontal social space, economically. People in neighborhoods have similar economic situations, and, in workplaces and in the media, it's vertical.

HOLT: Trying to put myself in the community of people who write and think about these things, I'd say that few people would argue with you. They might take you to task on the specifics of . . . was this the inflection point? But not on the increasing power of media spectacle, the mass culture controlled by large companies versus the lifeworld (i.e. the neighborhood community). I don't think anybody would argue that over time there's been a strong movement, especially in the US, in favor of mass culture over community. It's the other piece of the thesis that people might argue with. The more controversial part, I think, that flips around a lot of arguments that have been made by academics and critics that there was an increase in the emulation of luxury. It's almost back to Simmel and Veblen's "trickle down," that all of a sudden, in the 1980s, income inequality went up, richness became more of a good thing, something that regular society valued more.

SCHOR: That the idea of media relative to a lifeworld balance changed. I would say that a lot of the people who write about that do so in a sweeping way that doesn't pay much attention to what's actually happening in people's daily lives. I was trying to give a more empirically grounded argument about why this was happening, which looked at how people are actually spending their time and arguing that that's really important to understanding consumption dynamics, rather than just sort of throwing out these big theories that say, "oh, people shifted from this mindset to this mindset."

HOLT: Hours of television watched . . .

SCHOR: Exactly. And the empirical work in the book shows that the more hours of television people watch, the more money they spend and the less they save. It also refers to the data which show that people are spending less time in conversation with each other or less likely to go into each other's houses and those sorts of things. I think that it's important to understand why the media has become more important. You want to think about the actual social processes that are occurring. I also provided data on what people say about their reference groups. I asked people about who they compare themselves with.

HOLT: But a contrarian might say that among teens, even in the US, there's still tons of social interaction in peer groups. Yet the media effects are startling.

SCHOR: I would agree with that.

HOLT: How do you disentangle that?

SCHOR: I think what's happened there is that the marketing and advertising has been able to insinuate itself into the social contexts of youth and it has become very powerful in driving social dynamics. As teens age and their social interaction declines, I think that the media and consumer effects will probably stay with them. You can have different configurations. You can have active social, non-powerful media. You can have powerful media and active social. You can have neither powerful.

HOLT: Yes, but is it possible to flip the argument around and say that the media and the commodities it produces, whether it be musicians or celebrities or stuff we buy, directs social interaction because they are providing the interactional resources? There could be more social interaction today, but it is around commodities and spectacles. I'm just a little confused why you need the breakdown of community, the Putnam story.

SCHOR: I'm not sure that you do *need* it. I just think that's the way it happened. If you consider television watching, it's a default activity for adults. In countries which have longer hours of work, people watch more television. It's not that you had to have the causal variable of media capturing people's interest and therefore they stopped being civically active. Rising work time pushed out socializing and TV came in to fill the void. The rise of consumer aspirations is a result. That's just an empirical statement.

HOLT: Okay. And so the other part of the story is the upscaling of these desires?

SCHOR: Right. This is the place where I really am very much taking an opposite point of view from the literature, when everybody declared the death of status consumption and lamented that the scholarship had been trapped in a Veblenian vise. It was almost as if Veblen had been a pernicious force, overshadowing all consumer research. People were determined to get out of that box. The place they went was an individualistic model, which saw consumer motivation as emanating from individual identity projects rather than group conformity or people aspiring to social norms. In many ways, this moved the literature to an understanding of consumption which is very close to neoclassical or neoliberal economics. I think it wasn't accidental either because it happened in the 1980s with the rise of Thatcherism and Reaganism, and, although a lot of this literature has a different political veneer to it, I see it as a very similar intellectual point of view to neoliberalism. What are the neoliberals saying? That people have a set of preferences and they satisfy those preferences and get well-being through what they consume. I mean, on some level, can you even debate that statement? It's almost a truism. But – and the word postmodern is not exactly right because if you want to talk about postmodern consumption, there are two very different notions of it in the literature – but the one that I'm talking about is the idea of a postmodern consumer who is creating identity, who has a certain type of preferences and who is into frequent changes in consumer preferences. That story is totally consistent with neoclassical economics. I find it very peculiar that the literature rejects Veblen and Bourdieu just at the moment that we enter a period of intensified status consumption. They're fighting the last war. They forgot to look and see what was happening around them.

HOLT: Coincidence. So your argument is that the 1980s brought this on because these high-end status goods are getting circulated through the media and being presented in the media. That it has a sort of trickledown effect. It heightens the trickle down that had been going and never went away, but because you have more expensive goods and more luxurious lives being portrayed . . . it's not Leave it to Beaver anymore, it's Alice . . .

SCHOR: Okay, but why does it happen? It's because the income distribution changes. That's key and it's mainly absent in these so-called postmodern and other anti-status kinds of accounts. It's perhaps *the* central variable for understanding how the consumption system works. Societies with more egalitarian distributions of income and wealth have much less visible status seeking. Think about the places where you have lots of public consumption and less luxury consumption – Scandinavia, Northern Europe – these are egalitarian countries. In the unequal countries, such as Britain and the US, you've got a lot more status seeking. So it's both the media and the income distribution. I think you can see the evidence in the purchasing patterns around the core status commodities, which are vehicles, housing and what we'll call appearance-related commodities. It also spreads out beyond those. One of the interesting things that happens is that there are many more commodities brought into the competition. Firms are always looking to create more status opportunities because, after all, what is a status good? It's a good that can be branded; that is, a good that people will pay a status or brand premium for. So you do get lots of goods brought into this status system that previously were unbranded and didn't offer status opportunities to the producing companies. The question is, "how much will consumers respond?" and here's a period in

which you have a big expansion in commodities and even a move towards previously privately consumed commodities becoming status goods and therefore coming into public visibility. Take the kitchen, for example. Forty years ago, when people threw dinner parties, they didn't have the guests in their kitchen. Now, of course, with more informality, kitchens have become a huge status good and they are opened to the rest of the house and guests are in them. There's much more social flow through the kitchen.

HOLT: I don't think anybody writing on consumer society would argue that there aren't still status effects. But I think the argument is that the status effects of the postwar period are probably caricatured more than studied carefully. I think, generally, people would agree that there was something more like a Veblen/Simmel sort of effect in that period, where there was kind of a packaged good life that people aspired for. You started out with your Chevy and you moved up to the Oldsmobile and the Cadillac. One version of the postmodern argument is about that kind of single sort of staircase which, when people talk about status competition, I think that's usually what it's referring to. This particular status game has broken down. So it's not that status is gone, in terms of using goods to be admired and respected by others. Rather, I think the argument is that status operates in a more complex way now than the trickledown theories of the modern era suggest. It's no longer, "there's the rich, there's the upper middle class." They set the agenda and, as they are mimicked, they protect their status by inflating their desires for the even bigger house with the even bigger range and even bigger kitchen.

SCHOR: What I agree with in that story is that there are more goods now. So let's say, car. Now you have a range of high-status options. You can get the SUV option, you can get the BMW option, you can have a German luxury car or a Japanese luxury car or an American luxury car. In the 1950s, it was only the American luxury car. There's a proliferation of product options. You've got to be saying more than that.

HOLT: So there's an upper middle class in the United States. This change in income distribution has grown the upper middle class. We've gone from a bulge in the middle to an hourglass, a big bottom-shaped hourglass society where you have the top 15 percent or so of the society working in middle class jobs today. And at the bottom, the rest are not in supervisory salaried jobs. Maybe 20 percent? Roughly that. So you've got a winner-take-all economy. One of the effects is that it has created a luxury market. So if you study retailing, department stores or any class of goods, what you see in most of these is a move upward and downward. So you have Wal-Marts and you have boutiques. Mid-tier department stores struggle to stay in business. In automobiles, the middle tier kind of disappears and you have a proliferation of luxury goods servicing that top 10 percent of the market that can afford them. So I don't think that's a status effect. That's just the market moving to people with money. The status effect would be that for the bottom 80 percent, behavior has changed, as they try and get a piece of that life that the upper class has.

SCHOR: Yes. And that's what I've argued has happened and I have survey data in my book which I think are consistent with that interpretation. But how do you define upper middle class? I define it as the top 20 percent and above. That's about $100,000 a year income and above now. The top of that group is the wealthy, of course. What I'm saying is that in the bottom 80 percent, people want what the top 20 percent have, versus the people at 40 percent wanting what the people at 50 percent have, and people at 50 wanting what people at 60 percent have. That was the horizontal emulation system, where people want just a little more than what they have. Now, that $100,000 a year plus income is an aspiration across the distribution, even for people who have very little or no chance of achieving it.

HOLT: So take a family at the median US income, making perhaps $45,000 per year, what evidence would you bring to demonstrate that their consumer behavior is more emulative of this upper middle class in the 1990s than it was in the 1970s?

SCHOR: There's not a lot of direct evidence on that. I have a little bit of survey data in the book which speak to that, which is about the amount of money people want to make their dreams come true. There's a big increase in the amount of money that people aspire to having in the 1980s and 1990s. The fraction of young people who rate being really rich as their number one aspiration grew dramatically. There's a big increase in people who say that having a lot of money, having a job that pays more than the average, having a really great wardrobe and having a second home are part of their view of the good life. Those are all things that are characteristic of the lifestyles of the top 20 percent. Fewer care now about having a happy marriage, children and a meaningful job. Another factor is the rise of consumer credit, and the place where you see it most is in the $50,000–$100,000 income category. At that level, people can't do very much

in terms of actual behavior to get that high lifestyle because they have very little discretionary income by the time they pay rent and food and transport.

HOLT: That's half the country, right?

SCHOR: Yes. What I'm saying is, you see it in their aspirations. You can't see it in their spending. But that's where you're more likely to see single people who get into credit card debt, buying small luxuries that really they can't afford, but too many of them . . . or college students buying stuff. People early in their earning careers. The $50,000–$100,000 category disproportionately took on consumer credit in the 1980s and 1990s. They're the people struggling to keep up with the rising norms, the so-called new essentials of middle-class life.

HOLT: So where you see your status effect most pronounced is amongst the kind of people who are at the cusp of the new middle class, what you're calling upper middle class? Perhaps they have a college degree, but they don't have the great job that provides the big income. They're still . . .

SCHOR: Aspiring . . . they're the ones who are getting the jacuzzis in their houses or emulating upper middle-class life. I also think this explains the growth of these little luxuries that we've seen a lot of. People who pay for a big status premium percentage-wise, but on a small purchase. Starbucks coffee at $3.50 rather than a generic at 75 cents or bottled water or footwear or lipstick. When they can't afford the big ticket items, they get small ones. It's not just the top 20 percent of the distribution that goes for luxury. They're also striving for the big ticket items when they can. That's why auto leasing became very important, because it allowed many more people to drive luxurious cars than could actually afford to buy them.

HOLT: I think it's important to acknowledge that you work with different kinds of data than the data often used by culturalist researchers, which would look at tastes more closely, and once you get to that level, you see huge differences across class rather than emulation. To take an example from the branding research I've conducted, brands targeted to the lower 60 percent of US society are often sold with brand symbolism that pushes against the upper middle class. It's not emulative at all. For instance, Budweiser makes fun of Heineken and the yuppies who drink it, as a simple example. And that's fairly consistent across the brands that I've studied.

SCHOR: Fair enough for Budweiser. But a very big counter-example is Martha Stewart. Ditto for Ralph Lauren. Look at the whole apparel market. It's been very much along these lines, which is that the designers are marketing all the way down to the bottom.

HOLT: So Martha Stewart is a luxury good?

SCHOR: Absolutely. She starts out with super high cultural capital, very elite, trying to put herself forward at the top of the distribution. Then she markets herself out across the whole society. Eventually she ends up at K-Mart. What she's saying is, I can bring you an elite lifestyle, even if you shop at K-Mart. Do you disagree with that?

HOLT: I don't totally disagree with it. She is selling a version of an American lifestyle that offers up the leisurely moneyed life of the wealthy, in some sense. But the version of it she's selling is the world of homemaking, an anti-consumerist world. Let's take our time, make stuff at home, cook our own stuff, have families together. So I'm not sure that she's upscaling working-class people to luxury consumption.

SCHOR: But it's absolutely very high consumption. It's true it takes a lot of labor time to do it, but that's really the Veblenian world because those were the days when wives weren't in a labor market.

Discussion Questions

1. How does Schor define consumerism and a consumer society?

   Consumerism: An attitude-ideology where consumer goods take on central importance in the construction of culture identity and social life.

   Consumer society: A society where the majority of people have a consumerist attitude or are living consumerist lifestyles.

2. What are the four problems associated with a consumer society?

   The output bias of capitalism (the increasing difficulty of producing free time), impact of consumer activity on the environment, the orientation of private consumption, and the destruction of community.

Source: From Holt, D. B. (2005). Consumer culture—An interview with Juliet Schor. *Journal of Consumer Culture*, 5(1), 5–21. Reprinted by permission of Sage Publications and the author.

PART III

THE GLOBAL FRAGMENTATION OF SOCIAL LIFE

CHAPTER 7

Neoliberalism as Creative Destruction

David Harvey (2007)

David Harvey defines the ideology and impact of neoliberalism and specifically discusses the role of the state institution in creating and maintaining the practices of neoliberalism. Harvey argues that, rather than stimulating economic growth, neoliberal policies have functioned to benefit the dominant classes and richer countries throughout the world. He concludes by discussing forms of resistance and alternatives to the neoliberal ideology.

Neoliberalism is a theory of political economic practices proposing that human well-being can best be advanced by the maximization of entrepreneurial freedoms within an institutional framework characterized by private property rights, individual liberty, unencumbered markets, and free trade. The role of the state is to create and preserve an institutional framework appropriate to such practices. The state has to be concerned, for example, with the quality and integrity of money. It must also set up military, defense, police, and juridical functions required to secure private property rights and to support freely functioning markets. Furthermore, if markets do not exist (in areas such as education, health care, social security, or environmental pollution), then they must be created, by state action if necessary. But beyond these tasks the state should not venture. State interventions in markets (once created) must be kept to a bare minimum because the state cannot possibly possess enough information to second-guess market signals (prices) and because powerful interests will inevitably distort and bias state interventions (particularly in democracies) for their own benefit.

For a variety of reasons, the actual practices of neoliberalism frequently diverge from this template. Nevertheless, there has everywhere been an emphatic turn, ostensibly led by the Thatcher/Reagan revolutions in Britain and the United States, in political-economic practices and thinking since the 1970s. State after state, from the new ones that emerged from the collapse of the Soviet Union to old-style social democracies and welfare states such as New Zealand and Sweden, have embraced, sometimes voluntarily and sometimes in response to coercive pressures, some version of neoliberal theory and adjusted at least some of their policies and practices accordingly. Postapartheid South Africa quickly adopted the neoliberal frame and even contemporary China appears to be headed in that direction. Furthermore, advocates of the neoliberal mindset now occupy positions of considerable influence in education (universities and many "think tanks"), in the media, in corporate board rooms and financial institutions, in key state institutions (treasury departments, central banks), and also in those international institutions such as the International Monetary Fund (IMF) and the World Trade Organization (WTO) that regulate global finance and commerce. Neoliberalism has, in short, become hegemonic as a mode of discourse and has pervasive effects on ways of thought and political-economic practices to the point where it has become incorporated into the commonsense way we interpret, live in, and understand the world.

Neoliberalization has in effect swept across the world like a vast tidal wave of institutional reform and discursive adjustment. While plenty of evidence shows its uneven geographical development, no place can claim total immunity (with the exception of a few states such as North Korea). Furthermore, the rules of engagement now established through the WTO (governing international trade) and by the IMF (governing international finance) instantiate neoliberalism as a global set of rules. All states that sign on to the WTO and the IMF (and who can afford not to?) agree to abide (albeit with a "grace period" to permit smooth adjustment) by these rules or face severe penalties.

The creation of this neoliberal system has entailed much destruction, not only of prior institutional frameworks and powers (such as the supposed prior state sovereignty over political-economic affairs) but also of divisions of labor, social relations, welfare provisions, technological mixes, ways of life, attachments to the land, habits of the heart, ways of thought, and the like. Some assessment of the positives and negatives of this neoliberal revolution is called for. In what follows, therefore, I will sketch in some preliminary arguments as to how to both understand and evaluate this transformation in the way global capitalism is working. This requires that we come to terms with the underlying forces, interests, and agents that have propelled the neoliberal revolution forward with such relentless intensity. To turn the neoliberal rhetoric against itself, we may reasonably ask, In whose particular interests is it that the state takes a neoliberal stance and in what ways have those interests used neoliberalism to benefit themselves rather than, as is claimed, everyone, everywhere?

> *In whose particular interests is it that the state takes a neoliberal stance, and in what ways have those interests used neoliberalism to benefit themselves rather than, as is claimed, everyone, everywhere?*

The "Naturalization" of Neoliberalism

For any system of thought to become dominant, it requires the articulation of fundamental concepts that become so deeply embedded in commonsense understandings that they are taken for granted and beyond

question. For this to occur, not any old concepts will do. A conceptual apparatus has to be constructed that appeals almost naturally to our intuitions and instincts, to our values and our desires, as well as to the possibilities that seem to inhere in the social world we inhabit. The founding figures of neoliberal thought took political ideals of individual liberty and freedom as sacrosanct— as the central values of civilization. And in so doing they chose wisely and well, for these are indeed compelling and greatly appealing concepts. Such values were threatened, they argued, not only by fascism, dictatorships, and communism, but also by all forms of state intervention that substituted collective judgments for those of individuals set free to choose. They then concluded that without "the diffused power and initiative associated with (private property and the competitive market) it is difficult to imagine a society in which freedom may be effectively preserved."[1]

Setting aside the question of whether the final part of the argument necessarily follows from the first, there can be no doubt that the concepts of individual liberty and freedom are powerful in their own right, even beyond those terrains where the liberal tradition has had a strong historical presence. Such ideals empowered the dissident movements in Eastern Europe and the Soviet Union before the end of the cold war as well as the students in Tiananmen Square. The student movement that swept the world in 1968—from Paris and Chicago to Bangkok and Mexico City—was in part animated by the quest for greater freedoms of speech and individual choice. These ideals have proven again and again to be a mighty historical force for change.

It is not surprising, therefore, that appeals to freedom and liberty surround the United States rhetorically at every turn and populate all manner of contemporary political manifestos. This has been particularly true of the United States in recent years. On the first anniversary of the attacks now known as 9/11, President Bush wrote an op-ed piece for the *New York Times* that extracted ideas from a U.S. National Defense Strategy document issued shortly thereafter. "A peaceful world of growing freedom," he wrote, even as his cabinet geared up to go to war with Iraq, "serves American long-term interests, reflects enduring American ideals and unites America's allies." "Humanity," he concluded, "holds in its hands the opportunity to offer freedom's triumph over all its age-old foes," and "the United States welcomes its responsibilities to lead in this great mission." Even more emphatically, he later proclaimed that "freedom is the Almighty's gift to every man and woman in this world" and "as the greatest power on earth [the United States has] an obligation to help the spread of freedom."[2]

So when all of the other reasons for engaging in a preemptive war against Iraq were proven fallacious or at least wanting, the Bush administration increasingly appealed to the idea that the freedom conferred upon Iraq was in and of itself an adequate justification for the war. But what sort of freedom was envisaged here, since, as the cultural critic Matthew Arnold long ago thoughtfully observed, "Freedom is a very good horse to ride, but to ride somewhere."[3] To what destination, then, were the Iraqi people expected to ride the horse of freedom so selflessly conferred to them by force of arms?

The U.S. answer was spelled out on September 19, 2003, when Paul Bremer, head of the Coalition Provisional Authority, promulgated four orders that included "the full privatization of public enterprises, full ownership rights by foreign firms of Iraqi U.S. businesses, full repatriation of foreign profits . . . the opening of Iraq's banks to foreign control, national treatment for foreign companies and . . . the elimination of nearly all trade barriers."[4] The orders were to apply to all areas of the economy, including public services, the media, manufacturing, services, transportation, finance, and construction. Only oil was exempt. A regressive tax system favored by conservatives called a flat tax was also instituted. The right to strike was outlawed and unions banned in key sectors. An Iraqi member of the Coalition Provisional Authority protested the forced imposition of "free market fundamentalism," describing it as "a flawed logic that ignores history."[5] Yet the interim Iraqi government appointed at the end of June 2004 was accorded no power to change or write new laws—it could only confirm the decrees already promulgated.

What the United States evidently sought to impose upon Iraq was a full-fledged neoliberal state apparatus whose fundamental mission was and is to facilitate conditions for profitable capital accumulation for all comers, Iraqis and foreigners alike. The Iraqis were, in short, expected to ride their horse of freedom straight into the corral of neoliberalism. According to neoliberal theory, Bremer's decrees are both necessary and sufficient for the creation of wealth and therefore for the improved well-being of the Iraqi people. They are the proper foundation for an adequate rule of law, individual liberty, and democratic governance. The insurrection that followed can in part be interpreted as Iraqi resistance to being driven into the embrace of free market fundamentalism against their own free will.

It is useful to recall, however, that the first great experiment with neoliberal state formation was Chile after Augusto Pinochet's coup almost thirty years to the day before Bremer's decrees were issued, on the "little September 11th" of 1973. The coup, against the democratically elected and leftist social democratic government of Salvador Allende, was strongly backed by the CIA and supported by U.S. Secretary of State Henry Kissinger. It violently repressed all left-of-center social movements and political organizations and dismantled all forms of popular organization, such as community health centers in poorer neighborhoods. The labor market was "freed" from regulatory or institutional restraints—trade union power, for example. But by 1973, the policies of import substitution that had formerly dominated in Latin American attempts at economic regeneration, and that had succeeded to some degree in Brazil after the military coup of 1964, had fallen into disrepute. With the world economy in the midst of a serious recession, something new was plainly called for. A group of U.S. economists known as "the Chicago boys," because of their attachment to the neoliberal theories of Milton Friedman, then teaching at the University of Chicago, were summoned to help reconstruct the Chilean economy. They did so along free-market lines, privatizing public assets, opening up natural resources to private exploitation, and facilitating foreign direct investment and free trade. The right of foreign companies to repatriate profits from their Chilean operations was guaranteed. Export-led growth was favored over import substitution. The subsequent revival of the Chilean economy in terms of growth, capital accumulation, and high rates of return on foreign investments provided evidence upon which the subsequent turn to more open neoliberal policies in both Britain (under Thatcher) and the United States (under Reagan) could be modeled. Not for the first time, a brutal experiment in creative destruction carried out in the periphery became a model for the formulation of policies in the center.[6]

The fact that two such obviously similar restructurings of the state apparatus occurred at such different times in quite different parts of the world under the coercive influence of the United States might be taken as indicative that the grim reach of U.S. imperial power might lie behind the rapid proliferation of neoliberal state forms throughout the world from the mid-1970s onward. But U.S. power and recklessness do not constitute the whole story. It was not the United States, after all, that forced Margaret Thatcher to take the neoliberal path in 1979. And during the early 1980s, Thatcher was a far more consistent advocate of neoliberalism than Reagan ever proved to be. Nor was it the United States that forced China in 1978 to follow the path that has over time brought it closer and closer to the embrace of neoliberalism.

It would be hard to attribute the moves toward neoliberalism in India and Sweden in 1992 to the imperial reach of the United States. The uneven geographical development of neoliberalism on the world stage has been a very complex process entailing multiple determinations and not a little chaos and confusion. So why, then, did the neoliberal turn occur, and what were the forces compelling it onward to the point where it has now become a hegemonic system within global capitalism?

Why the Neoliberal Turn?

Toward the end of the 1960s, global capitalism was falling into disarray. A significant recession occurred in early 1973—the first since the great slump of the 1930s. The oil embargo and oil price hike that followed later that year in the wake of the Arab-Israeli war exacerbated critical problems. The embedded capitalism of the postwar period, with its heavy emphasis on an uneasy compact between capital and labor brokered by an interventionist state that paid great attention to the social (i.e., welfare programs) and individual wage, was no longer working. The Bretton Woods accord set up to regulate international trade and finance was finally abandoned in favor of floating exchange rates in 1973. That system had delivered high rates of growth in the advanced capitalist countries and generated some spillover benefits—most obviously to Japan but also unevenly across South America and to some other countries of South East Asia—during the "golden age" of capitalism in the 1950s and early 1960s. By the next decade, however, the preexisting arrangements were exhausted and a new alternative was urgently needed to restart the process of capital accumulation.[7] How and why neoliberalism emerged victorious as an answer to that quandary is a complex story. In retrospect, it may seem as if neoliberalism had been inevitable, but at the time no one really knew or understood with any certainty what kind of response would work and how.

The world stumbled toward neoliberalism through a series of gyrations and chaotic motions that eventually converged on the so-called "Washington Consensus" in the 1990s. The uneven geographical development of neoliberalism, and its partial and lopsided application from one country to another, testifies to its tentative character and the complex ways in which political forces, historical traditions, and existing institutional arrangements all shaped why and how the process actually occurred on the ground.

There is, however, one element within this transition that deserves concerted attention. The crisis of capital accumulation of the 1970s affected everyone through the combination of rising unemployment and accelerating inflation. Discontent was widespread, and the conjoining of labor and urban social movements throughout much of the advanced capitalist world augured a socialist alternative to the social compromise between capital and labor that had grounded capital accumulation so successfully in the postwar period. Communist and socialist parties were gaining ground across much of Europe, and even in the United States popular forces were agitating for widespread reforms and state interventions in everything ranging from environmental protection to occupational safety and health and consumer protection from corporate malfeasance. There was, in this, a clear *political* threat to ruling classes everywhere, both in advanced capitalist countries, like Italy and France, and in many developing countries, like Mexico and Argentina.

Beyond political changes, the *economic* threat to the position of ruling classes was now becoming palpable. One condition of the postwar settlement in almost all countries was to restrain the economic power of the upper classes and for labor to be accorded a much larger share of the economic pie. In the United States, for example, the share of the national income taken by the top 1 percent of earners fell from a prewar high of 16 percent to less than 8 percent by the end of the Second World War and stayed close to that level for nearly three decades. While growth was strong such restraints seemed not to matter, but when growth collapsed in the 1970s, even as real interest rates went negative and dividends and profits shrunk, ruling classes felt threatened. They had to move decisively if they were to protect their power from political and economic annihilation.

The coup d'état in Chile and the military takeover in Argentina, both fomented and led internally by ruling elites with U.S. support, provided one kind of solution. But the Chilean experiment with neoliberalism demonstrated that the benefits of revived capital accumulation were highly skewed. The country and its ruling elites along with foreign investors did well enough while the people in general fared poorly. This has been such a persistent effect of neoliberal policies over time as to be regarded a structural component of the whole project. Dumenil and Levy have gone so far as to argue that neoliberalism was from the very beginning an endeavor to restore class power to the richest strata in the population. They showed how from the mid-1980s onwards, the share of the top 1 percent of income earners in the United States soared rapidly to reach 15 percent by the end of the century. Other data show that the top 0.1 percent of income earners increased their share of the national income from 2 percent in 1978 to more than 6 percent by 1999. Yet another measure shows that the ratio of the median compensation of workers to the salaries of chief executive officers increased from just over thirty to one in 1970 to more than four hundred to one by 2000. Almost certainly, with the Bush administration's tax cuts now taking effect, the concentration of income and of wealth in the upper echelons of society is continuing apace.[8]

And the United States is not alone in this: the top 1 percent of income earners in Britain doubled their share of the national income from 6.5 percent to 13 percent over the past twenty years. When we look further afield, we see extraordinary concentrations of wealth and power within a small oligarchy after the application of neoliberal shock therapy in Russia and a staggering surge in income inequalities and wealth in China as it adopts neoliberal practices. While there are exceptions to this trend—several East and Southeast Asian countries have contained income inequalities within modest bounds, as have France and the Scandinavian countries— the evidence suggests that the neoliberal turn is in some way and to some degree associated with attempts to restore or reconstruct upper-class power.

We can, therefore, examine the history of neoliberalism either as a utopian project providing a theoretical template for the reorganization of international capitalism or as a political scheme aimed at reestablishing the conditions for capital accumulation and the restoration of class power. In what follows, I shall argue that the last of these objectives has dominated. Neoliberalism has not proven effective at revitalizing global capital accumulation, but it has succeeded in restoring class power. As a consequence, the theoretical utopianism of the neoliberal argument has worked more as a system of justification and legitimization. The principles of neoliberalism are quickly abandoned whenever they conflict with this class project.

> Neoliberalism has not proven effective at revitalizing global capital accumulation, but it has succeeded in restoring class power.

Toward the Restoration of Class Power

If there were movements to restore class power within global capitalism, then how were they enacted and by whom? The answer to that question in countries such as

Chile and Argentina was simple: a swift, brutal, and self-assured military coup backed by the upper classes and the subsequent fierce repression of all solidarities created within the labor and urban social movements that had so threatened their power. Elsewhere, as in Britain and Mexico in 1976, it took the gentle prodding of a not yet fiercely neoliberal International Monetary Fund to push countries toward practices—although by no means policy commitment—to cut back on social expenditures and welfare programs to reestablish fiscal probity. In Britain, of course, Margaret Thatcher later took up the neoliberal cudgel with a vengeance in 1979 and wielded it to great effect, even though she never fully overcame opposition within her own party and could never effectively challenge such centerpieces of the welfare state as the National Health Service. Interestingly, it was only in 2004 that the Labour Government dared to introduce a fee structure into higher education. The process of neoliberalization has been halting, geographically uneven, and heavily influenced by class structures and other social forces moving for or against its central propositions within particular state formations and even within particular sectors, for example, health or education.[9]

It is informative to look more closely at how the process unfolded in the United States, since this case was pivotal as an influence on other and more recent transformations. Various threads of power intertwined to create a transition that culminated in the mid-1990s with the takeover of Congress by the Republican Party. That feat represented in fact a neoliberal "Contract with America" as a program for domestic action. Before that dramatic denouement, however, many steps were taken, each building upon and reinforcing the other.

To begin with, by 1970 or so, there was a growing sense among the U.S. upper classes that the antibusiness and anti-imperialist climate that had emerged toward the end of the 1960s had gone too far. In a celebrated memo, Lewis Powell (about to be elevated to the Supreme Court by Richard Nixon) urged the American Chamber of Commerce in 1971 to mount a *collective* campaign to demonstrate that what was good for business was good for America. Shortly thereafter, a shadowy but influential Business Round Table was formed that still exists and plays a significant strategic role in Republican Party politics. Corporate political action committees, legalized under the post-Watergate campaign finance laws of 1974, proliferated like wildfire. With their activities protected under the First Amendment as a form of free speech in a 1976 Supreme Court decision, the systematic capture of the Republican Party as a class instrument of *collective* (rather than particular or individual) corporate and financial power began. But the Republican Party needed a popular base, and that proved more problematic to achieve. The incorporation of leaders of the Christian right, depicted as a moral majority, together with the Business Round Table provided the solution to that problem. A large segment of a disaffected, insecure, and largely white working class was persuaded to vote consistently against its own material interests on cultural (antiliberal, antiblack, antifeminist and antigay), nationalist and religious grounds. By the mid-1990s, the Republican Party had lost almost all of its liberal elements and become a homogeneous right-wing machine connecting the financial resources of large corporate capital with a populist base, the Moral Majority, that was particularly strong in the U.S. South.[10]

The second element in the U.S. transition concerned fiscal discipline. The recession of 1973 to 1975 diminished tax revenues at all levels at a time of rising demand for social expenditures. Deficits emerged everywhere as a key problem. Something had to be done about the fiscal crisis of the state; the restoration of monetary discipline was essential. That conviction empowered financial institutions that controlled the lines of credit to government. In 1975, they refused to roll over New York's debt and forced that city to the edge of bankruptcy. A powerful cabal of bankers joined together with the state to tighten control over the city. This meant curbing the aspirations of municipal unions, layoffs in public employment, wage freezes, cutbacks in social provision (education, public health, and transport services), and the imposition of user fees (tuition was introduced in the CUNY university system for the first time). The bailout entailed the construction of new institutions that had first rights to city tax revenues in order to pay off bond holders: whatever was left went into the city budget for essential services. The final indignity was a requirement that municipal unions invest their pension funds in city bonds. This ensured that unions moderate their demands to avoid the danger of losing their pension funds through city bankruptcy.

Such actions amounted to a coup d'état by financial institutions against the democratically elected government of New York City, and they were every bit as effective as the military overtaking that had earlier occurred in Chile. Much of the city's social infrastructure was destroyed, and the physical foundations (e.g., the transit system) deteriorated markedly for lack of investment or even maintenance. The management of New York's fiscal crisis paved the way for neoliberal practices both domestically under Ronald Reagan and internationally through the International Monetary Fund throughout the 1980s.

It established a principle that, in the event of a conflict between the integrity of financial institutions and bond holders on one hand and the well-being of the citizens on the other, the former would be given preference. It hammered home the view that the role of government was to create a good business climate rather than look to the needs and well-being of the population at large. Fiscal redistributions to benefit the upper classes resulted in the midst of a general fiscal crisis.

Whether all the agents involved in producing this compromise in New York understood it at the time as a tactic for the restoration of upper-class power is an open question. The need to maintain fiscal discipline is a matter of deep concern in its own right and does not have to lead to the restitution of class dominance. It is unlikely, therefore, that Felix Rohatyn, the key merchant banker who brokered the deal between the city, the state, and the financial institutions, had the reinstatement of class power in mind. But this objective probably was very much in the thoughts of the investment bankers. It was almost certainly the aim of then–Secretary of the Treasury William Simon who, having watched the progress of events in Chile with approval, refused to give aid to New York and openly stated that he wanted that city to suffer so badly that no other city in the nation would ever dare take on similar social obligations again.[11]

The third element in the U.S. transition entailed an ideological assault upon the media and upon educational institutions. Independent "think tanks" financed by wealthy individuals and corporate donors proliferated—the Heritage Foundation in the lead—to prepare an ideological onslaught aimed at persuading the public of the commonsense character of neoliberal propositions. A flood of policy papers and proposals and a veritable army of well-paid hired lieutenants trained to promote neoliberal ideas coupled with the corporate acquisition of media channels effectively transformed the discursive climate in the United States by the mid-1980s. The project to "get government off the backs of the people" and to shrink government to the point where it could be "drowned in a bathtub" was loudly proclaimed. With respect to this, the promoters of the new gospel found a ready audience in that wing of the 1968 movement whose goal was greater individual liberty and freedom from state power and the manipulations of monopoly capital. The libertarian argument for neoliberalism proved a powerful force for change. To the degree that capitalism reorganized to both open a space for individual entrepreneurship and switch its efforts to satisfy innumerable niche markets, particularly those defined by sexual liberation, that were spawned out of an increasingly individualized consumerism, so it could match words with deeds.

This carrot of individualized entrepreneurship and consumerism was backed by the big stick wielded by the state and financial institutions against that other wing of the 1968 movement whose members had sought social justice through collective negotiation and social solidarities. Reagan's destruction of the air traffic controllers (PATCO) in 1980 and Margaret Thatcher's defeat of the British miners in 1984 were crucial moments in the global turn toward neoliberalism. The assault upon institutions, such as trade unions and welfare rights organizations, that sought to protect and further working-class interests was as broad as it was deep. The savage cutbacks in social expenditures and the welfare state, and the passing of all responsibility for their well-being to individuals and their families proceeded apace. But these practices did not and could not stop at national borders. After 1980, the United States, now firmly committed to neoliberalization and clearly backed by Britain, sought, through a mix of leadership, persuasion—the economics departments of U.S. research universities played a major role in training many of the economists from around the world in neoliberal principles—and coercion to export neoliberalization far and wide. The purge of Keynesian economists and their replacement by neoliberal monetarists in the International Monetary Fund in 1982 transformed the U.S.-dominated IMF into a prime agent of neoliberalization through its structural adjustment programs visited upon any state (and there were many in the 1980s and 1990s) that required its help with debt repayments. The Washington Consensus that was forged in the 1990s and the negotiating rules set up under the World Trade Organization in 1998 confirmed the global turn toward neoliberal practices.[12]

The new international compact also depended upon the reanimation and reconfiguration of the U.S. imperial tradition. That tradition had been forged in Central America in the 1920s, as a form of domination without colonies. Independent republics could be kept under the thumb of the United States and effectively act, in the best of cases, as proxies for U.S. interests through the support of strongmen—like Somoza in Nicaragua, the Shah in Iran, and Pinochet in Chile—and a coterie of followers backed by military assistance and financial aid. Covert aid was available to promote the rise to power of such leaders, but by the 1970s it became clear that something else was needed: the opening of markets, of new spaces for investment, and clear fields where financial powers could operate securely. This entailed a much closer integration of the global economy with a well-defined financial architecture. The creation of new institutional

practices, such as those set out by the IMF and the WTO, provided convenient vehicles through which financial and market power could be exercised. The model required collaboration among the top capitalist powers and the Group of Seven (G7), bringing Europe and Japan into alignment with the United States to shape the global financial and trading system in ways that effectively forced all other nations to submit. "Rogue nations," defined as those that failed to conform to these global rules, could then be dealt with by sanctions or coercive and even military force if necessary. In this way, U.S. neoliberal imperialist strategies were articulated through a global network of power relations, one effect of which was to permit the U.S. upper classes to exact financial tribute and command rents from the rest of the world as a means to augment their already hegemonic control.[13]

Neoliberalism as Creative Destruction

In what ways has neoliberalization resolved the problems of flagging capital accumulation? Its actual record in stimulating economic growth is dismal. Aggregate growth rates stood at 3.5 percent or so in the 1960s and even during the troubled 1970s fell to only 2.4 percent. The subsequent global growth rates of 1.4 percent and 1.1 percent for the 1980s and 1990s, and a rate that barely touches 1 percent since 2000, indicate that neoliberalism has broadly failed to stimulate worldwide growth.[14] Even if we exclude from this calculation the catastrophic effects of the collapse of the Russian and some Central European economies in the wake of the neoliberal shock therapy treatment of the 1990s, global economic performance from the standpoint of restoring the conditions of general capital accumulation has been weak.

Despite their rhetoric about curing sick economies, neither Britain nor the United States achieved high economic performance in the 1980s. That decade belonged to Japan, the East Asian "Tigers," and West Germany as powerhouses of the global economy. Such countries were very successful, but their radically different institutional arrangements make it difficult to pin their achievements on neoliberalism. The West German Bundesbank had taken a strong monetarist line (consistent with neoliberalism) for more than two decades, a fact suggesting that there is no necessary connection between monetarism per se and the quest to restore class power. In West Germany, the unions remained strong and wage levels stayed relatively high alongside the construction of a progressive welfare state. One of the effects of this combination was to stimulate a high rate of technological innovation that kept West Germany well ahead in the field of international competition. Export-led production moved the country forward as a global leader.

In Japan, independent unions were weak or nonexistent, but state investment in technological and organizational change and the tight relationship between corporations and financial institutions (an arrangement that also proved felicitous in West Germany) generated an astonishing export-led growth performance, very much at the expense of other capitalist economies such as the United Kingdom and the United States. Such growth as there was in the 1980s (and the aggregate rate of growth in the world was lower even than that of the troubled 1970s) did not depend, therefore, on neoliberalization. Many European states therefore resisted neoliberal reforms and increasingly found ways to preserve much of their social democratic heritage while moving, in some cases fairly successfully, toward the West German model. In Asia, the Japanese model implanted under authoritarian systems of governance in South Korea, Taiwan, and Singapore also proved viable and consistent with reasonable equality of distribution. It was only in the 1990s that neoliberalization began to pay off for both the United States and Britain. This happened in the midst of a long-drawn-out period of deflation in Japan and relative stagnation in a newly unified Germany. Up for debate is whether the Japanese recession occurred as a simple result of competitive pressures or whether it was engineered by financial agents in the United States to humble the Japanese economy.

So why, then, in the face of this patchy if not dismal record, have so many been persuaded that neoliberalization is a successful solution? Over and beyond the persistent stream of propaganda emanating from the neoliberal think tanks and suffusing the media, two material reasons stand out. First, neoliberalization has been accompanied by increasing volatility within global capitalism. That success was to materialize somewhere obscured the reality that neoliberalism was generally failing. Periodic episodes of growth interspersed with phases of creative destruction, usually registered as severe financial crises. Argentina was opened up to foreign capital and privatization in the 1990s and for several years was the darling of Wall Street, only to collapse into disaster as international capital withdrew at the end of the decade. Financial collapse and social devastation were quickly followed by a long political crisis. Financial turmoil proliferated all over the developing world, and in some instances, such as Brazil and Mexico, repeated waves of structural adjustment and austerity led to economic paralysis.

On the other hand, neoliberalism has been a huge success from the standpoint of the upper classes. It has either restored class position to ruling elites, as in the United States and Britain, or created conditions for capitalist class formation, as in China, India, Russia, and elsewhere. Even countries that have suffered extensively from neoliberalization have seen the massive reordering of class structures internally. The wave of privatization that came to Mexico with the Salinas de Gortari administration in 1992 spawned unprecedented concentrations of wealth in the hands of a few people (Carlos Slim, for example, who took over the state telephone system and became an instant billionaire).

With the media dominated by upper-class interests, the myth could be propagated that certain sectors failed because they were not competitive enough, thereby setting the stage for even more neoliberal reforms. Increased social inequality was necessary to encourage entrepreneurial risk and innovation, and these, in turn, conferred competitive advantage and stimulated growth. If conditions among the lower classes deteriorated, it was because they failed for personal and cultural reasons to enhance their own human capital through education, the acquisition of a Protestant work ethic, and submission to work discipline and flexibility. In short, problems arose because of the lack of competitive strength or because of personal, cultural, and political failings. In a Spencerian world, the argument went, only the fittest should and do survive. Systemic problems were masked under a blizzard of ideological pronouncements and a plethora of localized crises.

If the main effect of neoliberalism has been redistributive rather than generative, then ways had to be found to transfer assets and channel wealth and income either from the mass of the population toward the upper classes or from vulnerable to richer countries. I have elsewhere provided an account of these processes under the rubric of *accumulation by dispossession*.[15] By this, I mean the continuation and proliferation of accretion practices that Marx had designated as "primitive" or "original" during the rise of capitalism. These include (1) the commodification and privatization of land and the forceful expulsion of peasant populations (as in Mexico and India in recent times); (2) conversion of various forms of property rights (common, collective, state, etc.) into exclusively private property rights; (3) suppression of rights to the commons; (4) commodification of labor power and the suppression of alternative (indigenous) forms of production and consumption; (5) colonial, neocolonial, and imperial processes of appropriation of assets (including natural resources); (6) monetization of exchange and taxation, particularly of land; (7) the slave trade (which continues, particularly in the sex industry); and (8) usury, the national debt, and, most devastating of all, the use of the credit system as radical means of primitive accumulation.

The state, with its monopoly of violence and definitions of legality, plays a crucial role in backing and promoting these processes. To this list of mechanisms, we may now add a raft of additional techniques, such as the extraction of rents from patents and intellectual property rights and the diminution or erasure of various forms of communal property rights—such as state pensions, paid vacations, access to education, and health care—won through a generation or more of social democratic struggles. The proposal to privatize all state pension rights (pioneered in Chile under Augusto Pinochet's dictatorship) is, for example, one of the cherished objectives of neoliberals in the United States.

In the cases of China and Russia, it might be reasonable to refer to recent events in "primitive" and "original" terms, but the practices that restored class power to capitalist elites in the United States and elsewhere are best described as an ongoing process of accumulation by dispossession that grew rapidly under neoliberalism. In what follows, I isolate four main elements.

1. PRIVATIZATION

The corporatization, commodification, and privatization of hitherto public assets have been signal features of the neoliberal project. Its primary aim has been to open up new fields for capital accumulation in domains formerly regarded off-limits to the calculus of profitability. Public utilities of all kinds (water, telecommunications, transportation), social welfare provision (public housing, education, health care, pensions), public institutions (such as universities, research laboratories, prisons), and even warfare (as illustrated by the "army" of private contractors operating alongside the armed forces in Iraq) have all been privatized to some degree throughout the capitalist world.

Intellectual property rights established through the so-called TRIPS (Trade-Related Aspects of Intellectual Property Rights) agreement within the WTO defines genetic materials, seed plasmas, and all manner of other products as private property. Rents for use can then be extracted from populations whose practices had played a crucial role in the development of such genetic materials. Bio-piracy is rampant, and the pillaging of the world's stockpile of genetic resources is well under way to the benefit of a few large pharmaceutical companies. The

escalating depletion of the global environmental commons (land, air, water) and proliferating habitat degradations that preclude anything but capital-intensive modes of agricultural production have likewise resulted from the wholesale commodification of nature in all its forms. The commodification (through tourism) of cultural forms, histories, and intellectual creativity entails wholesale dispossessions (the music industry is notorious for the appropriation and exploitation of grassroots culture and creativity). As in the past, the power of the state is frequently used to force such processes through even against popular will. The rolling back of regulatory frameworks designed to protect labor and the environment from degradation has entailed the loss of rights. The reversion of common property rights won through years of hard class struggle (the right to a state pension, to welfare, to national health care) into the private domain has been one of the most egregious of all policies of dispossession pursued in the name of neoliberal orthodoxy.

> *The corporatization, commodification, and privatization of hitherto public assets have been signal features of the neoliberal project.*

All of these processes amount to the transfer of assets from the public and popular realms to the private and class-privileged domains. Privatization, Arundhati Roy argued with respect to the Indian case, entails "the transfer of productive public assets from the state to private companies. Productive assets include natural resources: earth, forest, water, air. These are the assets that the state holds in trust for the people it represents. . . . To snatch these away and sell them as stock to private companies is a process of barbaric dispossession on a scale that has no parallel in history."[16]

2. FINANCIALIZATION

The strong financial wave that set in after 1980 has been marked by its speculative and predatory style. The total daily turnover of financial transactions in international markets that stood at $2.3 billion in 1983 had risen to $130 billion by 2001. This $40 trillion annual turnover in 2001 compares to the estimated $800 billion that would be required to support international trade and productive investment flows.[17] Deregulation allowed the financial system to become one of the main centers of redistributive activity through speculation, predation, fraud, and thievery. Stock promotions; Ponzi schemes; structured asset destruction through inflation; asset stripping through mergers and acquisitions; and the promotion of debt incumbency that reduced whole populations, even in the advanced capitalist countries, to debt peonage—to say nothing of corporate fraud and dispossession of assets, such as the raiding of pension funds and their decimation by stock and corporate collapses through credit and stock manipulations—are all features of the capitalist financial system.

The emphasis on stock values, which arose after bringing together the interests of owners and managers of capital through the remuneration of the latter in stock options, led, as we now know, to manipulations in the market that created immense wealth for a few at the expense of the many. The spectacular collapse of Enron was emblematic of a general process that deprived many of their livelihoods and pension rights. Beyond this, we also must look at the speculative raiding carried out by hedge funds and other major instruments of finance capital that formed the real cutting edge of accumulation by dispossession on the global stage, even as they supposedly conferred the positive benefit to the capitalist class of "spreading risks."

3. The Management and Manipulation of Crises

Beyond the speculative and often fraudulent froth that characterizes much of neoliberal financial manipulation, there lies a deeper process that entails the springing of the debt trap as a primary means of accumulation by dispossession. Crisis creation, management, and manipulation on the world stage have evolved into the fine art of deliberative redistribution of wealth from poor countries to the rich. By suddenly raising interest rates in 1979, Paul Volcker, then chairman of the U.S. Federal Reserve, raised the proportion of foreign earnings that borrowing countries had to put to debt-interest payments. Forced into bankruptcy, countries like Mexico had to agree to structural adjustment. While proclaiming its role as a noble leader organizing bailouts to keep global capital accumulation stable and on track, the United States could also open the way to pillage the Mexican economy through deployment of its superior financial power under conditions of local crisis. This was what the U.S. Treasury/Wall Street/IMF complex became expert at doing everywhere. Volker's successor, Alan Greenspan, resorted to similar tactics several times in the 1990s. Debt crises in individual countries, uncommon

in the 1960s, became frequent during the 1980s and 1990s. Hardly any developing country remained untouched and in some cases, as in Latin America, such crises were frequent enough to be considered endemic. These debt crises were orchestrated, managed, and controlled both to rationalize the system and to redistribute assets during the 1980s and 1990s. Wade and Veneroso captured the essence of this trend when they wrote of the Asian crisis—provoked initially by the operation of U.S.-based hedge funds—of 1997 and 1998:

> Financial crises have always caused transfers of ownership and power to those who keep their own assets intact and who are in a position to create credit, and the Asian crisis is no exception . . . there is no doubt that Western and Japanese corporations are the big winners. . . . The combination of massive devaluations pushed financial liberalization, and IMF-facilitated recovery may even precipitate the biggest peacetime transfer of assets from domestic to foreign owners in the past fifty years anywhere in the world, dwarfing the transfers from domestic to U.S. owners in Latin America in the 1980s or in Mexico after 1994. One recalls the statement attributed to Andrew Mellon: "In a depression assets return to their rightful owners."[18]

The analogy to the deliberate creation of unemployment to produce a pool of low-wage surplus labor convenient for further accumulation is precise. Valuable assets are thrown out of use and lose their value. They lie fallow and dormant until capitalists possessed of liquidity choose to seize upon them and breathe new life into them. The danger, however, is that crises can spin out of control and become generalized, or that revolts will arise against the system that creates them. One of the prime functions of state interventions and of international institutions is to orchestrate crises and devaluations in ways that permit accumulation by dispossession to occur without sparking a general collapse or popular revolt. The structural adjustment program administered by the Wall Street/Treasury/IMF complex takes care of the first function. It is the job of the comprador neoliberal state apparatus (backed by military assistance from the imperial powers) to ensure that insurrections do not occur in whichever country has been raided. Yet signs of popular revolt have emerged, first with the Zapatista uprising in Mexico in 1994 and later in the generalized discontent that informed antiglobalization movements such as the one that culminated in Seattle in 1999.

4. State Redistributions

The state, once transformed into a neoliberal set of institutions, becomes a prime agent of redistributive policies, reversing the flow from upper to lower classes that had been implemented during the preceding social democratic era. It does this in the first instance through privatization schemes and cutbacks in government expenditures meant to support the social wage. Even when privatization appears as beneficial to the lower classes, the long-term effects can be negative. At first blush, for example, Thatcher's program for the privatization of social housing in Britain appeared as a gift to the lower classes whose members could now convert from rental to ownership at a relatively low cost, gain control over a valuable asset, and augment their wealth. But once the transfer was accomplished, housing speculation took over particularly in prime central locations, eventually bribing or forcing low-income populations out to the periphery in cities like London and turning erstwhile working-class housing estates into centers of intense gentrification. The loss of affordable housing in central areas produced homelessness for many and extraordinarily long commutes for those who did have low-paying service jobs. The privatization of the *ejidos* (indigenous common property rights in land under the Mexican constitution) in Mexico, which became a central component of the neoliberal program set up during the 1990s, has had analogous effects on the Mexican peasantry, forcing many rural dwellers into the cities in search of employment. The Chinese state has taken a whole series of draconian measures through which assets have been conferred upon a small elite to the detriment of the masses.

The neoliberal state also seeks redistributions through a variety of other means such as revisions in the tax code to benefit returns on investment rather than incomes and wages, promotion of regressive elements in the tax code (such as sales taxes), displacement of state expenditures and free access to all by user fees (e.g., on higher education), and the provision of a vast array of subsidies and tax breaks to corporations. The welfare programs that now exist in the United States at federal, state, and local levels amount to a vast redirection of public moneys for corporate benefit (directly as in the case of subsidies to agribusiness and indirectly as in the case of the military-industrial sector), in much the same way that the mortgage interest rate tax deduction operates in the United States as a massive subsidy to upper-income home owners and the construction of industry. Heightened surveillance and policing and, in the case of the United States, the incarceration of recalcitrant elements in the population

indicate a more sinister role of intense social control. In developing countries, where opposition to neoliberalism and accumulation by dispossession can be stronger, the role of the neoliberal state quickly assumes that of active repression even to the point of low-level warfare against oppositional movements (many of which can now conveniently be designated as terrorist to garner U.S. military assistance and support) such as the Zapatistas in Mexico or landless peasants in Brazil.

In effect, reported Roy, "India's rural economy, which supports seven hundred million people, is being garroted. Farmers who produce too much are in distress, farmers who produce too little are in distress, and landless agricultural laborers are out of work as big estates and farms lay off their workers. They're all flocking to the cities in search of employment."[19] In China, the estimate is that at least half a billion people will have to be absorbed by urbanization over the next ten years if rural mayhem and revolt are to be avoided. What those migrants will do in the cities remains unclear, though the vast physical infrastructural plans now in the works will go some way to absorbing the labor surpluses released by primitive accumulation.

The redistributive tactics of neoliberalism are wideranging, sophisticated, frequently masked by ideological gambits, but devastating for the dignity and social well-being of vulnerable populations and territories. The wave of creative destruction neoliberalization has visited across the globe is unparalleled in the history of capitalism. Understandably, it has spawned resistance and a search for viable alternatives.

Alternatives

Neoliberalism has spawned a swath of oppositional movements both within and outside of its compass, many of which are radically different from the worker-based movements that dominated before 1980. I say many but not all. Traditional worker-based movements are by no means dead even in the advanced capitalist countries where they have been much weakened by the neoliberal onslaught. In South Korea and South Africa, vigorous labor movements arose during the 1980s, and in much of Latin America working-class parties are flourishing. In Indonesia, a putative labor movement of great potential importance is struggling to be heard. The potential for labor unrest in China is immense though unpredictable.

And it is not clear either that the mass of the working class in the United States, which has over this past generation consistently voted against its own material interests for reasons of cultural nationalism, religion, and opposition to multiple social movements, will forever stay locked into such a politics by the machinations of Republicans and Democrats alike. There is no reason to rule out the resurgence of worker-based politics with a strongly antineoliberal agenda in future years.

But struggles against accumulation by dispossession are fomenting quite different lines of social and political struggle. Partly because of the distinctive conditions that give rise to such movements, their political orientation and modes of organization depart markedly from those typical in social democratic politics. The Zapatista rebellion, for example, did not seek to take over state power or accomplish a political revolution. It sought instead a more inclusive politics to work through the whole of civil society in an open and fluid search for alternatives that would consider the specific needs of different social groups and allow them to improve their lot. Organizationally, it tended to avoid avant-gardism and refused to take on the form of a political party. It preferred instead to remain a social movement within the state, attempting to form a political power bloc in which indigenous cultures would be central rather than peripheral. It sought thereby to accomplish something akin to a passive revolution within the territorial logic of state power.

The effect of such movements has been to shift the terrain of political organization away from traditional political parties and labor organizing into a less focused political dynamic of social action across the whole spectrum of civil society. But what they lost in focus they gained in relevance. They drew their strengths from embeddedness in the nitty-gritty of daily life and struggle but in so doing often found it hard to extract themselves from the local and the particular to understand the macro-politics of what neoliberal accumulation by dispossession was and is all about. The variety of such struggles was and is simply stunning. It is hard to even imagine connections between them. They were and are all part of a volatile mix of protest movements that swept the world and increasingly grabbed the headlines during and after the 1980s.[20] Those movements and revolts were sometimes crushed with ferocious violence, for the most part by state powers acting in the name of order and stability. Elsewhere they produced interethnic violence and civil wars as accumulation by dispossession produced intense social and political rivalries in a world dominated by divide and rule tactics on the part of capitalist forces. Client states supported militarily or in some instances with special forces trained by major military powers (led by the United States with Britain and France playing a minor role) took the lead in a system of repressions and liquidations to ruthlessly check activist movements challenging accumulation by dispossession.

The movements themselves have produced an abundance of ideas regarding alternatives. Some seek to de-link wholly or partially from the overwhelming powers of neoliberalism and neoconservatism. Others seek global social and environmental justice by reform or dissolution of powerful institutions such as the IMF, the WTO, and the World Bank. Still others emphasize a reclaiming of the commons, thereby signaling deep continuities with struggles of long ago as well as with struggles waged throughout the bitter history of colonialism and imperialism. Some envisage a multitude in motion, or a movement within global civil society, to confront the dispersed and de-centered powers of the neoliberal order, while others more modestly look to local experiments with new production and consumption systems animated by different kinds of social relations and ecological practices. There are also those who put their faith in more conventional political party structures with the aim of gaining state power as one step toward global reform of the economic order. Many of these diverse currents now come together at the World Social Forum in an attempt to define their shared mission and build an organizational structure capable of confronting the many variants of neoliberalism and of neoconservatism. There is much here to admire and to inspire.[21]

> *Though it has been effectively disguised, we have lived through a whole generation of sophisticated class struggle on the part of the upper strata to restore or, as in China and Russia, construct class dominance.*

But what sorts of conclusions can be derived from an analysis of the sort here constructed? To begin with, the whole history of the social democratic compromise and the subsequent turn to neoliberalism indicates the crucial role played by class struggle in either checking or restoring class power. Though it has been effectively disguised, we have lived through a whole generation of sophisticated class struggle on the part of the upper strata to restore or, as in China and Russia, construct class dominance. This occurred in decades when many progressives were theoretically persuaded that class was a meaningless category and when those institutions from which struggle had hitherto been waged on behalf of the working classes were under fierce assault. The first lesson we must learn, therefore, is that if it looks like class struggle and acts like class struggle, then we have to name it for what it is. The mass of the population has either to resign itself to the historical and geographical trajectory defined by this overwhelming class power or respond to it in class terms.

To put it this way is not to wax nostalgic for some lost golden age when the proletariat was in motion. Nor does it necessarily mean (if it ever should have) that we can appeal to some simple conception of the proletariat as the primary (let alone exclusive) agent of historical transformation. There is no proletarian field of utopian Marxian fantasy to which we can call. To point to the necessity and inevitability of class struggle is not to say that the way class is constituted is determined or even determinable in advance. Class movements make themselves, though not under conditions of their own choosing. And analysis shows that those conditions are currently bifurcated into movements around expanded reproduction—in which the exploitation of wage labor and conditions defining the social wage are central issues—and movements around accumulation by dispossession—in which everything from classic forms of primitive accumulation through practices destructive of cultures, histories, and environments to the depredations wrought by the contemporary forms of finance capital are the focus of resistance. Finding the organic link between these different class currents is an urgent theoretical and practical task. Analysis also shows that this has to occur in an historical-geographical trajectory of capital accumulation that is based in increasing connectivity across space and time but marked by deepening uneven geographical developments. This unevenness must be understood as something actively produced and sustained by processes of capital accumulation, no matter how important the signs may be of residuals of past configurations set up in the cultural landscape and the social world.

Analysis also points up exploitable contradictions within the neoliberal agenda. The gap between rhetoric (for the benefit of all) and realization (for the benefit of a small ruling class) increases over space and time, and social movements have done much to focus on that gap. The idea that the market is about fair competition is increasingly negated by the facts of extraordinary monopoly, centralization, and internationalization on the part of corporate and financial powers. The startling increase in class and regional inequalities both within states (such as China, Russia, India, Mexico, and in Southern Africa) as well as internationally poses a serious political problem that can no longer be swept under the rug as something transitional on the way to a perfected neoliberal world. The neoliberal emphasis upon individual

rights and the increasingly authoritarian use of state power to sustain the system become a flashpoint of contentiousness. The more neoliberalism is recognized as a failed if not disingenuous and utopian project masking the restoration of class power, the more it lays the basis for a resurgence of mass movements voicing egalitarian political demands, seeking economic justice, fair trade, and greater economic security and democratization.

But it is the profoundly antidemocratic nature of neoliberalism that should surely be the main focus of political struggle. Institutions with enormous leverage, like the Federal Reserve, are outside any democratic control. Internationally, the lack of elementary accountability let alone democratic control over institutions such as the IMF, the WTO, and the World Bank, to say nothing of the great private power of financial institutions, makes a mockery of any credible concern about democratization. To bring back demands for democratic governance and for economic, political, and cultural equality and justice is not to suggest some return to a golden past since the meanings in each instance have to be reinvented to deal with contemporary conditions and potentialities. The meaning of democracy in ancient Athens has little to do with the meanings we must invest it with today in circumstances as diverse as Sao Paulo, Johannesburg, Shanghai, Manila, San Francisco, Leeds, Stockholm, and Lagos. But right across the globe, from China, Brazil, Argentina, Taiwan, and Korea to South Africa, Iran, India, and Egypt, and beyond the struggling nations of Eastern Europe into the heartlands of contemporary capitalism, groups and social movements are rallying to reforms expressive of democratic values. That is a key point of many of the struggles now emerging.

The more clearly oppositional movements recognize that their central objective must be to confront the class power that has been so effectively restored under neoliberalization, the more they will be likely to cohere. Tearing aside the neoliberal mask and exposing its seductive rhetoric, used so aptly to justify and legitimate the restoration of that power, have a significant role to play in contemporary struggles. It took neoliberals many years to set up and accomplish their march through the institutions of contemporary capitalism. We can expect no less of a struggle when pushing in the opposite direction.

Notes

1. See the Web site http://www.montpelerin.org/mpsabout.cfm.

2. G. W. Bush, "Securing Freedom's Triumph," *New York Times,* September 11, 2002, p. A33. *The National Security Strategy of the United State of America* can be found on the Web site www.white house.gov nsc/nss. See also G. W. Bush, "President Addresses the

Nation in Prime Time Press Conference," April 13, 2004, http://www .whitehouse.gov/news/releases/2004/0420040413–20.html.

3. Matthew Arnold is cited in Robin Williams, *Culture and Society, 1780–1850* (London: Chatto and Windus, 1958), 118.

4. Antonia Juhasz, "Ambitions of Empire: The Bush Administration Economic Plan for Iraq (and Beyond)," *Left Turn Magazine* 12 (February/March 2004): 27–32.

5. Thomas Crampton, "Iraqi Official Urges Caution on Imposing Free Market," *New York Times,* October 14, 2003, p. C5.

6. Juan Gabriel Valdez, *Pinochet's Economists: The Chicago School in Chile* (New York: Cambridge University Press, 1995).

7. Philip Armstrong, Andre Glynn, and John Harrison, *Capitalism since World War II: The Making and Breaking of the Long Boom* (Oxford, UK: Basil Blackwell, 1991).

8. Gerard Dumenil and Dominique Levy, "Neoliberal Dynamics: A New Phase?" (Manuscript, 2004), 4. See also Task Force on Inequality and American Democracy, *American Democracy in an Age of Rising Inequality* (Washington, DC: American Political Science Association, 2004), 3.

9. Daniel Yergin and Joseph Stanislaw, *The Commanding Heights: The Battle between Government and Marketplace That Is Remaking the Modern World* (New York: Simon & Schuster, 1998).

10. Thomas Byrne Edsall, *The New Politics of Inequality* (New York: Norton, 1984); Jamie Court, *Corporateering: How Corporate Power Steals Your Personal Freedom* (New York: Tarcher Putnam, 2003); and Thomas Frank, *What's the Matter with Kansas: How Conservatives Won the Heart of America* (New York: Metropolitan Books, 2004).

11. William K. Tabb, *The Long Default: New York City and the Urban Fiscal Crisis* (New York: Monthly Review Press, 1982); and

Roger E. Alcaly and David Mermelstein, *The Fiscal Crisis of American Cities* (New York: Vintage, 1977).

12. Joseph Stiglitz, *Globalization and Its Discontents* (New York: Norton, 2002).

13. David Harvey, *The New Imperialism* (Oxford: Oxford University Press, 2003).

14. World Commission on the Social Dimension of Globalization, *A Fair Globalization: Creating Opportunities for All* (Geneva, Switzerland: International Labor Office, 2004).

15. Harvey, *The New Imperialism,* chap. 4.

16. Arundhati Roy, *Power Politics* (Cambridge, MA: South End Press, 2001).

17. Peter Dicken, *Global Shift: Reshaping the Global Economic Map in the 21st Century,* 4th ed. (New York: Guilford, 2003), chap. 13.

18. Robert Wade and Frank Veneroso, "The Asian Crisis: The High Debt Model versus the Wall Street-Treasury-IMF Complex," *New Left Review* 228 (1998): 3–23.

19. Roy, *Power Politics.*

20. Barry K. Gills, ed., *Globalization and the Politics of Resistance* (New York: Palgrave, 2001); Ton Mertes, ed., *A Movement of Movements* (London: Verso, 2004); Walden Bello, *Deglobalization: Ideas for a New World Economy* (London: Zed Books, 2002); Ponna Wignaraja, ed., *New Social Movements in the South: Empowering the People* (London: Zed Books, 1993); and Jeremy Brecher, Tim Costello, and Brendan Smith, *Globalization from Below: The Power of Solidarity* (Cambridge, MA: South End Press, 2000).

21. Mertes, A Movement of Movements; and Walden Bello, Deglobalization: Ideas for a New World Economy (London: Zed Books, 2002).

Discussion Questions

1. Harvey describes the impact of neoliberalism as "creative destruction." What does he mean by this?

   The creation of a neoliberal system (free market, limited state intervention) has involved the destruction of prior institutional frameworks and powers (e.g., state sovereignty over political-economic affairs), and the destruction of divisions of labor, social relationships, welfare provisions, technological mixes, and ways of life and thought.

2. What alternatives to neoliberalism does Harvey identify?

   Global social and environmental justice by reform or dissolution of powerful institutions, such as the World Bank and increasing oppositional movements addressing inequalities based on class, colonialism, and imperialism.

Source: From Harvey, D. (2007). Neoliberalism as creative destruction. *Annals of the American Academy of Political and Social Science, 610,* 21–44. Reprinted by permission of Sage Publications.

CHAPTER 8

Poverty and Inequality in the Global Economy

Michael D. Yates (2004)

Michael Yates examines the growing problems of poverty and income inequality and examines how these problems, both within and among nations, is inextricably linked to capitalism. Yates argues that no nation, including those with rich capitalist economies like the United States, is immune from these growing problems.

Capitalism is hundreds of years old and today dominates nearly every part of the globe. Its champions claim that it is the greatest engine of production growth the world has ever seen. They also argue that it is unique in its ability to raise the standard of living of every person on earth. Because of capitalism, we are all "slouching toward utopia,"—the phrase coined by University of California at Berkeley economist J. Bradford DeLong—slowly but surely heading toward a world in which everyone will have achieved a U.S.-style middle-class life.[1]

Given the long tenure of capitalism and the unceasing contentions of its adherents, it seems fair to ask if it is true that we are "slouching toward utopia." Let us look at three things: the extent of poverty and inequality in the richest capitalist economy—that of the United States; the extent of poverty and inequality in the poor countries of the world; and the gap between those countries at the top of the capitalist heap and those at the bottom.

The United States is often referred to as a nation dominated by the middle class and one in which it is relatively easy for a poor person to become a person of means. Here, it is said, equality of opportunity rules. It is hard to know what phrases like "middle class" and "equality of opportunity" mean, but it is fair to think that such a society ought not to be one in which there is

widespread poverty and ought to be one in which people do indeed have a great deal of economic mobility.

The data on poverty and inequality of income and wealth do not square very well with this image. In the United States, the federal government had defined a "poverty level of income," one below which families are defined to be poor. It is an income below which families would find it difficult to live without serious problems and which would place them in real danger when faced with any sort of economic crisis, such as a sick child or an injury at work. This official poverty level of income is equal to three times the minimum food budget calculated by the Department of Agriculture, a very modest standard with numerous restrictive and unrealistic assumptions built into it, for example, that poor families will be able to buy food at the lowest unit price and will know how to convert the cheapest food into nutritious meals. In 2002, this was $18,392 for a family of four, or $12.60 per person per day. In 2002, 34.6 million persons lived in poverty, 12.1 percent of the population. The incidence of poverty was 24 percent for blacks and 21.8 percent for Hispanics. In 2001 (I don't have data for 2002), 35.2 percent of black children under six lived in poverty, as did 29.1 percent of Hispanic children under six. These numbers rise and fall over time and while they have been higher in the recent past, they are still remarkably high when we consider the enormous productive capacity of the U.S. economy and the more than 200 years in which this capacity has steadily risen. And if we used a more realistic definition of poverty—such as one-half the median income, a poverty definition typically used to compare the rich capitalist economies—the incidence of poverty would increase dramatically to 17 percent (in 1997), or more than 45 million persons.[2]

What are the chances that this extensive poverty could be eliminated? Not very high, given that this poverty coincides with large and growing inequality of both income and wealth, inequalities ingrained in the laws of motion of capitalism.

In the United States in 2000, income inequality was greater than at any time since the 1920s, with the richest 5 percent of all households receiving six times more income than the poorest 20 percent of households, up from about four times in 1970. A study by economist Paul Krugman (who has been skillfully assailing the Bush administration in his *New York Times* column) estimated that perhaps as much as 70 percent of all of the income growth in the United States during the 1980s went to the richest 1 percent of all families. With respect to wealth, in the United States in 1995, the richest 1 percent of all households owned 42.2 percent of all stocks, 55.7 percent of all bonds, 44.2 percent of all trusts, 71.4 percent of all noncorporate businesses, and 36.9 percent of all non-home real estate. As with income inequality, this inequality has been increasing, at least for the past 20 years.[3]

Great and growing inequality mocks the notion of equality of opportunity. Consider a thought experiment:

In Pittsburgh, Pennsylvania, . . . there is an extraordinarily wealthy family, the Hillman's, with a net worth of several billion dollars. One of their homes, along once fashionable Fifth Avenue, is a gorgeous mansion on a magnificent piece of property. About three miles east of this residence is the Homewood section of the city, whose mean streets have been made famous by the writer, John Edgar Wideman. On North Lang Street there is a row of three connected apartments. One of the end apartments has been abandoned to the elements—to the rodents and the drug users . . . Poverty, deep and grinding, is rampant on this street and in this neighborhood, which has one of the nation's highest infant mortality rates.

Consider two children, one born in the Hillman house and another born in the North Lang Street apartment. In the former, there are two rich and influential parents, and in the latter there is a single mother working nights with three small children. Let us ask some basic questions. Which mother will have the best health care,

with regular visits to the doctor, medicine if needed, and a healthy diet? Which child is more likely to have a normal birth weight? Which child is more likely to get adequate nutrition and have good health care in early childhood? If the poor child does not have these things, who will return to this child the brain cells lost as a consequence? Which child is more likely to suffer the ill effects of lead poisoning? . . . If the two children get ill in the middle of the night, which one will be more likely to make it to the emergency room in time? . . .

As the two children grow up, what sort of people will they meet? Which will be more likely to meet persons who will be useful to them when they are seeking admission to college or looking for a job or trying to find funding for a business venture? . . . Which will go to the better school? Which will have access to books, magazines, newspapers, and computers in the home? . . . Which one will be more likely to have caring teachers who work in well-equipped and safe schools? Which one will be afraid to tell the teacher that he does not have crayons and colored paper at home? . . . When these two children face the labor market [of course, the rich child will never have to face the labor market in the sense the poor child will], which one will be more productive?[4]

We can buttress our thought experiment with empirical evidence. It now appears clear that in the United States—whose politicians and pundits are always touting the myth that "you can be anything you want to be"—it is "increasingly apparent that the secret to success is to have a successful parent." Recent studies tell us that if your parents' income is in the top 20 percent of the distribution of family incomes, you have a 42.3 percent chance of ending up at the top too, but only a 6.3 percent chance of falling into the bottom 20 percent. If your parents' income is in the bottom 20 percent, you have only a 7.3 percent chance of ending up in the top 20 percent. No doubt these correlations would be still stronger if we considered wealth as well as income. If your parents were in the top 1 percent of the income distribution (and therefore certainly had a lot of wealth, something which might not be of true parents at the lower end of the top 20 percent), the chances of you ending up in the top 20 percent would surely be higher than 42.3 percent.[5]

Compounding the unlikelihood of eliminating poverty is the fact that inequality in and of itself generates many socially undesirable outcomes. Inequality research has found that if we consider two states in the United States or two countries, each with the same average income, what we might call "social health" will be poorer in the state or country with the greater income inequality. Put another way, equally poor people will be worse off in terms of many social indicators if they live in the state or country with the greater income inequality. Using as a measure of inequality the share of income going to the poorest 50 percent of households in each U.S. state, researchers found that this share varied inversely (in the opposite direction) with the state's mortality rate. In addition,

> This measure of inequality was also tested against other social conditions besides health. States with greater inequality in the distribution of income also had higher rates of unemployment, higher rates of incarceration, a higher percentage of people receiving income assistance and food stamps, and a greater percentage of people without medical insurance. Again, the gap between rich and poor was the best predictor, not the average income in the state.
>
> Interestingly, states with greater inequality of income distribution also spent less per person on education, had fewer books per person in the schools, and had poorer educational performance, including worse reading skills, worse math skills and lower rates of completion of high school.
>
> States with greater inequality of income also had a greater proportion of babies born with low birth weight; higher rates of homicide; higher rates of violent crime; a greater proportion of the population unable to work because of disabilities; a higher proportion of the population using tobacco; and a higher proportion of the population being sedentary (inactive).[6]

Great and growing inequality saps the political power of those at the bottom, making it more likely that the social welfare programs which help to alleviate the harmful consequences of poverty will be gutted, while at the same time making it more likely that policies which further favor the rich will be put in place. The poor are increasingly filled with hopelessness and despair as they contemplate the yawning gap between them and those at the top.[7]

Although there is great poverty and inequality in the richest capitalist country, this cannot compare to the levels of both of these to be found in the vast majority of the world's economies, which are both capitalist and poor. The World Bank estimates the number of persons in different countries and in the world as a whole who subsist on less than $1 and $2 per day. In Nigeria, for example, in the early 1990s, 90.8 percent of the population lived on $2 per day or less; in India the figure was 86.2 percent in 1997. In a world population of some 6 billion

persons, the World Bank estimates that 2.8 billion survive on $2 per day or less (about 45 percent); 1.2 billion lived on $1 (about 20 percent) per day or less.

The World Bank also uses a number comparable to the U.S. poverty level of income. Remember that the U.S. level for 2002 translates into $12.60 per person per day. The Bank's level for poor countries is now a little more than $1 per day. Using this number, it claims that poverty diminished worldwide over the 1990s. However, this claim is suspect. It is true that $1 per day might go further in a poor country because prices are cheaper, so that while $1 per day in the United States makes a person obviously destitute, such may not be the case in a very poor country. If over time, prices fall in a poor country, then, other things being equal, the number of persons living in poverty will fall. The problem, however, is that when the World Bank speaks of prices in a poor country, it means an index of all prices and not the prices of the things very poor people buy. In general, the prices which are relatively lowest and which have declined most in poor countries are those of services unlikely to be consumed by the poor. As journalist George Monbiot tells us, "[The World Bank's] estimate of the purchasing power of the poor is based on the measure of their ability to buy any of the goods and services an economy has to offer: not only food, water and shelter but also airline tickets, pedicures and personal fitness training. The problem is that while basic goods are often more expensive in poor nations than they are in rich ones, services tend to be much cheaper [reflecting the tremendous pool of surplus labor in poor nations] . . . " He goes on to say, "But the extremely poor, of course, do not purchase the services of cleaners, driver or hairdressers." Two researchers at Columbia University estimated that if corrections were made for the problems in the World Bank's methodology, the number of persons living in absolute poverty would rise by 30 to 40 percent, completely eliminating the alleged decrease in poverty.[8]

It should be noted in connection with the World Bank's poverty level that the World Bank has been instrumental in promoting large-scale export agriculture in poor countries. Many persons living below the World Bank poverty level are subsistence peasants operating outside the money economy. Their economic well-being is often greater than a dollar a day would indicate. As they are in effect dispossessed by Bank-promoted agriculture and move into urban areas, their money income may exceed the World Bank poverty level, but, in fact, they are considerably worse off than they were in the countryside.

Poverty on a global scale is matched by an enormous and growing inequality of incomes, a fact remarked upon in considerable detail in the November 2002 Review of the Month in this magazine. It is worth paraphrasing and supplementing what was said there. In China and India, the world's most populous nations and two of its fastest growing economies, inequality is growing rapidly. In China, once an extremely egalitarian country, income inequality is now barely distinguishable from that in the United States. China has witnessed perhaps the greatest income redistribution in history. In India, "Most of the benefits of . . . rapid economic growth are going to the wealthiest 20% of society." There, "350 million [persons]—more than a third of the population—live in dire poverty . . . In Calcutta alone, an estimated 250,000 children sleep on the sidewalks each night."[9]

World Bank economist Branco Milanovic has overseen the most sophisticated attempt to measure income inequality worldwide. Using a massive household survey covering the entire world, he found that,

> the richest 1 percent of people in the world get as much income as the poorest 57 percent. The richest 5 percent had in 1993 an average income 114 times greater than that of the poorest 5 percent, rising from 78 times in 1988. The poorest 5 percent grew poorer, losing 25 percent of their real income, while the richest 20 percent saw their real incomes grow by 12 percent, more than twice as high as average world income. World inequality grew because inequality grew between and within countries. The rich nations grew richer and the poor nations grew poorer; the rich within each country grew richer at the expense of the poor. Milanovic calculated that the world income gini coefficient [a measure of inequality which increases from zero to one as inequality increases] was between .66 and a staggering .80, depending on the way you converted one currency into another.[10]

Buttressing Milanovic's findings, the United Nation's most recent Human Development Report tells us that the income of the richest 25 million Americans is the equivalent of nearly 2 billion of the world's poorest persons (2 billion is 80 times 25 million). In 1820, per capita income in western Europe was three times that in Africa; by the 1990s it was more than 13 times as high. Adding human meaning to these numbers, the report says, "The statistics today are shaming: more than 13 million children have died through diarrhoeal disease in the past decade. Each year over half a million women, one for every minute of the day, die in pregnancy and childbirth. More than 800 million suffer from malnutrition." In addition, "For many countries the 1990s were a decade of despair.

Some 54 countries are poorer now than in 1990. In 21, a larger proportion is going hungry. In 14, more children are dying before the age of five. In 12, primary school enrollments are shrinking. In 34, life expectancy has fallen. Such reversals in survival were previously rare." Economist James Galbraith tells us that, "Looking at the broad range of developing countries, the University of Texas Inequality Project finds rising inequality in most of them, falling inequality in only a few." In Vietnam, in just two years, between 1999 and 2001, the gap between the richest and the poorest nearly doubled.[11]

Just as capitalism's proponents proclaim the reality of equality of opportunity, so too do they say that today's poor national economies have every chance of someday becoming rich. Can this be so?

The gap between the rich and the poor within countries is paralleled by that among countries. Since countries have widely different populations, a common way to compare countries is by their gross domestic product (GDP) per capita. Such a comparison shows extremely large differences among countries. At the top are what we can call "rich countries"; these are for the most part those capitalist nations which first industrialized and which early on took command, largely through conquest and colonization, of much of the rest of the world, from Latin America to Africa to Southeast Asia. At the bottom are the poorest of "poor countries," those nations on the receiving end of the forced expansion of the rich nations. Countries such as the United States, Norway, Japan, Germany, and France have per capital GDPs 20 to more than 100 times greater than countries like Ethiopia, Malawi, Afghanistan, and Bolivia. It is remarkable to observe that most of the rich countries are those where capitalism first arose, while most of the poor countries have long histories of colonial and imperial domination. In terms of per capita GDP, no Latin American country ranks in the top 35, and no African country ranks in the top 55. More than one-half of the poorest 50 countries are in Africa. Sixty percent of the top 50 are either in Europe or North America.

If we use nonmoney measures of how nations are faring, we see similar differences. In the United States, life expectancy at birth for women is about 80 years, in Switzerland 82; but in Afghanistan it is 46, in Sierra Leone 39. Infant mortality per 1,000 births is 3.98 in Norway, but it is 101 in Ethiopia.[12]

Mainstream economists have argued that the poor nations are simply on a low rung of a "development ladder," and that over time, especially if they adopt "free market" principles (basically the elimination of all barriers to the freedom of employers to try to make money, such as protective trade barriers, protective labor laws, subsidies to the poor, public enterprises, and limitations on the sale of land), they will become rich countries too. This convergence hypothesis is difficult to demonstrate. While a very few formerly poor nations, mostly in Asia, have become relatively rich ones (South Korea, for example), most have remained poor. In fact, Lance Pritchett, a World Bank economist, has persuasively argued that the world's poorest countries diverged in terms of per capita income from 1870 to 1960. The logic underlying Pritchett's methodology is interesting. He compared one of the world's richest nation, the United States, to one of its poorest, Ethiopia. He took the per capita GDP ratio for the United States and Ethiopia for 1960 (U.S. GDP per capita divided by Ethiopia GDP per capita) and noted that there could only have been convergence if the per capita GDP ratio had been larger in 1870. But for this to be true, Ethiopia's per capita GDP in 1870 would have been too low to sustain life! Therefore Pritchett concluded that there must have been divergence.

We also have good evidence that divergence continued after 1960, accelerating after 1980 when "free market" policies were introduced throughout the world on an increasing scale. Between 1980 and 2000, those countries with the highest GDPs per capita grew the most, implying that inequality among nations increased. The British magazine, *The Economist*, citing economists who believe that international inequality has decreased, argued that we need to weight each country's per capital GDP by its population. When we do this, we note that the two most populous countries, India and China, had very high average growth rates over this period, suggesting that in terms of population-weighted growth rates, worldwide inequality decreased. However, what *The Economist* failed to note was that, as we have seen, inequality within India and China rose, most notably in China. China's and India's per capita GDP grew rapidly, but the incomes of the average Chinese and Indian did not. So, in the face of this fact, it is hard to argue that inequality has fallen.

Even if we consider a poor nation that has grown more rapidly than a rich one, this relatively greater growth will have to continue for a very long time for per capita incomes to converge. Pritchett has this to say about India, a country which grew faster than the United States for a while and which is growing rapidly now:

... a few developing countries were actually "converging," that is, they were growing faster than the United States. When are these lucky "convergers" going to overtake the United States? India, for example, registered an annual average growth rate

of 3 percent between 1980 and 1993. If India could sustain this pace for another 100 years, its income would reach the level of high-income countries today. And, if India can sustain this growth differential for 377 years, my great-great-great-great-great-great-great-great-great-great-great-grandchildren will be alive to see India's income level "converge."[13]

Given all of this, it is difficult not to conclude that inequality, both within and among nations, must be endemic to capitalism. It is not very hard to see why. Wealth in a capitalist economy is unevenly divided by definition: Capitalism is an economic system in which the nonhuman means of production (what mainstream economists call "capital") are owned by a small minority of all persons. Wealth inequality in a market economy must, again as a consequence of the nature of the system, generate income inequality. A capitalist system always "builds" on the best, that is, other things equal, those with the most to start with continue to reap the lion's share of the annual income. So, when capitalist economies are not subject to constraints and regulations, inequality will inevitably grow.

In other words, what underlies inequality is the class nature of capitalism. The owning minority has a built-in advantage compared to the nonowning minority, both in terms of economic power inside the workplace and political power in the larger society. Whenever they can, they will press their advantage to secure a still larger share of society's income. Examples are too numerous to mention.

What then sustains the growing inequality both among nations and within nations is the rising power of the owners and the declining power of the workers (and in poor countries, of the peasants, as well). If we look at the world objectively, the income of a nation tends to be more equally divided the more powerful are the workers and peasants. Where they are weak in poor countries, these countries are pulled more tightly into the grip of the rich nations and intercountry inequality rises. Inequality also rises within these nations, while the incomes of the poor sink to levels barely able to sustain life, if that. This is true even when per capita GDP rises at a high rate. Similarly, in the rich countries, the weaker the workers, the greater the inequality, and the less likely it is that workers will reach out in solidarity with their brothers and sisters in the poor nations. It is no accident that the United States has both the weakest labor movement and the most unequal income of any rich country.

Inequality in income and wealth (and all of the social indicators which are linked to these inequalities) are a profound contradiction of the capitalist mode of production. Workers and their employers presumably meet as equals in the labor market, each free to make a bargain. Yet the results of this bargain favor the employers to a striking degree.

In capitalist economies, everyone is free to make money, but it is remarkable how few do. Capitalist economies espouse egalitarian values, but the consequences of their normal operations are extraordinarily inegalitarian. The same contradiction is apparent in relationships among nations. Countries enter into free trade relationships, but the consequences of this trade are enormous disparities in per capita GDP.

A contradiction so blatant requires resolution. On the one hand, workers and peasants have been forming diverse types of organizations to reverse the system-generated inequalities. These have had varying degrees of success, managing sometimes to wring concessions from the owners and on rarer occasions succeeding in making a revolution that transforms the entire system. But on the other hand, capitalists and their multitude of hired guns try to keep the contradiction from generating actions that threaten their existence. Needless to say, force and violence are critical elements in the ruling-class arsenal, especially when revolution threatens. However, there are many other weapons, including cooptation of working-class and peasant leaders, making strategic concessions (best exemplified by the "social pact" between employers and unions in Western Europe and to a lesser degree the United States), and a vast ideological apparatus geared to convincing people that there is no contradiction at all. With respect to the last of these, we are fed a daily diet of procapitalist propaganda, complete with missing or distorted information: workers are really "associates"; the suggestion that the rich benefit in this system at the expense of the poor is denounced as the "politics of hate"; poor nations are falling further behind the rich ones because they have not sufficiently embraced the free market; and on and on.

The glaring and growing inequalities everywhere apparent in the capitalist world have yet to spawn massive resistance. In fact, in the United States, working people often support government policies clearly inimical to their interests, such as the repeal of the estate tax and income tax cuts strongly biased toward the rich.[14] However, there are indications that troubles might be brewing for the rich and powerful. Under the radar screen, a kind of "social war" is being waged in poor neighborhoods around the world. While this war often involves intraclass violence, it has also terrified the elite. Writing in *Le Monde Diplomatique*, Ignacio Ramonet tells us:

Faced with this rising tide of what the media calls insecurity, several countries—including Mexico, Colombia, Nigeria and South Africa—now spend more on fighting this social war than on national defence. Brazil spends 2% of GDP on its armed forces and more than 10.6% on protecting the rich against the despair of the poor.[15]

More publicized have been a wide range of social movements aimed in one way or another at addressing global inequality: armed revolutionary struggles in Colombia and Nepal; peasant movements throughout Latin America, most recently in Bolivia; movements of the poor and unemployed in countries as disparate as Argentina and South Africa; and a far-flung and wide-ranging global justice movement, encompassing campaigns against third world debt, child labor, sweatshops, trade agreements, land theft, and environmental destruction, among others.

It is impossible to tell how all of this "primitive" and more conscious protest will play out. But one gets the feeling that political struggle in the next decades might be intimately tied to the glaring and unconscionable inequality which has become the hallmark of contemporary capitalism. Under these conditions the system is unlikely to be entirely successful at keeping the lid on the boiling discontent underneath.

Notes

1. Details of DeLong's contentions, including draft material for a book, *Slouching Toward Utopia*, can be found at http://econ161.berkeley.edu/TCEH/Slouch_title.html.

2. For details on poverty, see Lawrence Mishel, Jared Bernstein, and Heather Boushey, *The State of Working America*, 2002–2003 (Ithaca, N.Y.: Cornell University Press, 2003), 309–56. For the most recent U.S. Census Bureau data see http://www .census.gov. For international comparisons using the 50 percent of median income definition, see Mishel, State, 416.

3. On income inequality, see Mishel, Berstein, & Boushey, State, 33–112. The income data in the paragraph are taken from http://www.census.gov. The wealth data are from Doug Henwood, "Distributing the Booty," http://www.panix.com/~dhenwood /Wealth_distrib.html. The Krugman data are from Paul Krugman, "The Rich, the Right, and the Facts," *The American Prospect 11* (fall 1992), 19–31.

4. Michael D. Yates, *Naming the System: Inequality and Work in the Global Economy* (New York: Monthly Review Press, 2003), 58–59.

5. Economist Alan B. Krueger reports on the relevant studies in "The Apple Falls Close to the Tree, Even in the Land of Opportunity," *New York Times*, November 14, 2002.

6. The quote is from Yates, Naming, 60. It is taken from Peter Montague, "Economic Inequality and Health," http://www.korpios .org/resurgent/Inequality&Health.htm.

7. See Helen Epstein, "Enough to Make You Sick?," *New York Times Magazine*, October 12, 2003.

8. For World Bank data on poverty, see the Bank's World Development Reports, http://www.worldbank.org. On the inadequacies of the World Bank's methods for calculating poverty rates, see articles available at http://www.columbia.edu~sr793/. The quote is from George Monbiot, "Poor but Pedicured," *The Guardian*, May 6, 2003.

9. Paul Watson, "In India, No Job is Too Small," *Los Angeles Times*, October 25, 2003.

10. The quote is from Yates, Naming, 57–58. The original article is Branko Milanovic, "True World Income Distribution, 1988 and 1993: First Calculations Based on Household Surveys Alone," *The Economic Journal 112* (January 2002), 51–92.

11. For a summary of the UN Report, see Larry Elliot, "The Lost Decade," *The Guardian*, July 9, 2003. The Galbraith quote is from James Galbraith, "Globalisation and Inequality: the Economist Gets it Wrong," http://www.opendemocracy.net/debates/article-7-30-1483.jsp.

On inequality in Vietnam, see "Vietnamese Earn More but Rich-Poor Gap Widens," http://www.globalpolicy.org/socecon/inequal/2003 /0114vietnam.htm.

12. For a wide range of statistics on output, health, life expectancy, labor markets, and other economic indicators, see International Labor Office, Key Indicators of the Labour Market 2001–2002 (Geneva, Switzerland: International Labour Office, 2002).

13. Pritchett's methodology and the quote are in Lance Pritchett, "Forget Convergence: Divergence Past, Present, and Future," http://www.worldbank.org/fandd/english/ 0696/articles/090696.htm. For a discussion of the growth of per capita GDPs, see Galbraith, "Globalisation."

14. For examples, see Alan B. Krueger, "Cloudy Thinking on Tax Cuts," *New York Times*, October 16, 2003.

15. Ignacio Ramonet, "The Social Wars," Le Monde Diplomatique, November 2002, available in English at http:// mondediplo.com/2002/11/.

Discussion Questions

1. Which do you think is the greater problem—poverty or inequality? Define each and explain the reason for your position.

   Students should recognize that poverty and inequality are two different phenomena. Poverty is defined by the federal government as an income level below which families "would find it difficult to live without any serious problems and which would place them in real danger when faced with any sort of economic crisis, such as a sick child or an injury at work." Inequality addresses the range of income and wealth—from the very wealthy to the very poor. Yates presents evidence of the large and growing disparities of both.

2. Why do poverty and inequality exist in capitalist countries?

   Wealth in a capitalist economy is unevenly divided by definition. It is a system where the means of production are owned by a few. The owning minority has a built-in advantage to the nonowning majority, in terms of economic and political power.

CHAPTER 9

The Making of International Migrants

Saskia Sassen (2007)

In this article, Saskia Sassen examines the ways that international migration flows are conditioned by the broader dynamics of globalization. She focuses, in particular, on three types of social conditions that influence and induce individuals to migrate: the structural conditions brought about by "economic internationalization"; the direct recruitment of immigrant workers by employers, governments, or immigrant networks; and the "organized export and trafficking" of men, women, and children.

. . . Cross-border migrations existed long before the current phase of globalization. Thus the task is to understand in what ways and under what conditions today's many migrations are or are not shaped by, grounded in, or merely inflected by globalization. The rich migration scholarship shows us, for instance, that transnational networks between sending and receiving countries were already part of many migration flows centuries ago. The content and modes of communications and transactions in the past may have differed sharply from today's, but the actual social fact was present in the past. Similarly, the scholarship finds that many features of past migrations, such as chain migration and family reunion, are present today . . . .

Building Bridges

We can identify three major patterns among the variety of economic conditions that contribute to migration links between sending and receiving countries: links brought about by economic globalization, links specifically developed to recruit workers, and the legal and illegal organized export of workers. In this section I discuss the first two; in the next section I discuss the third.

ECONOMIC LINKS

Links created by economic internationalization range from the offshoring of production and the establishment of export-oriented agriculture through foreign investment to the weight of multinationals in the consumer markets of labor-exporting countries. For instance, the development of commercial agriculture and export-oriented standardized manufacturing has dislocated traditional economies and eliminated survival opportunities for small producers, who have been forced to become wage laborers. This transition has in turn contributed to the mobilization of displaced smallholders and crafts-based producers in labor migrations, migrations that initially may be internal but eventually can become international. There are numerous examples of this dynamic launching new cross-border migrations. Mahler (1995) found that Salvadoran immigrants in the United States often had prior experience as migrant workers on coffee plantations. Fernandez-Kelly (1982) found that some of the internal migrants in the northern industrialization zone of Mexico eventually immigrated to the United States. Campos and Bonilla (1982) found that the U.S.-sponsored Bootstraps Operation in Puerto Rico had a similar effect in promoting immigration to the United States.

Another type of economic link results from the large-scale development of manufacturing operations in low-wage countries by firms from highly developed countries. The aim here has been, and continues to be, to lower the cost of the production of goods meant for, and reexported to, markets in the home country. This offshoring creates a number of objective and subjective links between the highly developed countries and the low-wage countries. Two migration-inducing conditions are at work here. One is that the better-situated workers may gain access to the contacts for migration, and the second is that the most disadvantaged workers are often "used up" after a few years and then need to find new ways of surviving and helping their families, which may in turn lead to out-migration. Disadvantaged workers are partially in an extended or deterritorialized *local* labor market that connects the two countries involved (see Sassen 1988, 1995, for a full development of these issues). The growing use of offshore production to lower costs also contributes to the creation of conditions in the highly developed countries that may lead to the demand for and recruitment of low-wage immigrant workers, given the growing pressure among firms and countries to lower costs to remain competitive. The internationalization of both manufacturing production and agriculture has contributed to the weakening of unions and has generally led to the search for low-wage workers inside the developed countries.

The case of Japan is of interest here because it allows us to capture the intersection of economic internationalization and immigration in its inception, and to do so in a country whose history, culture, and to a lesser extent, economic organization are radically different from those of other advanced economies. Japan's lack of an immigration history in the high-growth postwar decades—though it had one in the 1800s—provides us with a sharp view of how an immigration can start where there was none before. Furthermore, it started in the 1980s, the start of the current global age. Though its advent was much later than that of most other advanced economies, Japan now has a growing workforce of unauthorized immigrants in low-wage, unskilled jobs, which Japanese workers reject (Tsuzuki 2000; Mori 1997). Why did immigration not occur during the period of extremely rapid economic growth, during the 1950s and 1960s, when Japan experienced very sharp labor shortages? The answer lies partially in the fact that in the 1980s Japan became a major presence in a regional Asian economic system: it became the leading investor, foreign-aid donor, and exporter of consumer goods (including cultural products). In the 1980s, Japanese firms began to set up a large number of manufacturing operations outside Japan, with a heavy concentration in other Asian countries. This expansion

has created legal and illegal networks linking those countries and Japan, and made them into exporters of immigrants to Japan (Morita and Sassen 1994). In its period of rapid growth, Japan lacked the links with potential immigrant-exporting countries that could have facilitated the formation of international migration flows. As Japan internationalized its economy and became a key investor in South and Southeast Asia, it created—wittingly or not—a transnational space for the circulation of its goods, capital, and culture, which in turn created conditions for the circulation of people. A key factor was recruitment by organized crime syndicates and by the government (Sassen 2001, chaps. 8 and 9). We may be seeing the early stages of an international labor market, a market that both labor contractors and unauthorized immigrants can "step into." This space now includes professionals as well (Farrer 2007). The Japanese government also initiated the recruitment of Japanese descendants in Brazil and Peru, adjusting its immigration law to do so. These emergent immigrant communities have now entered the stage of chain migration (Tsuda 1999; Tsuzuki 2000).

Another type of link is shaped by the growing Westernization of advanced education systems (Portes and Walton 1981), which facilitates the movement of highly educated workers into the developed Western countries. This is a process that has been happening for many decades and is usually referred to as the brain drain. Today it assumes specific forms, given the growing interdependence among countries and the formation of global markets and global firms. That is, we are seeing the formation of an increasingly complex and flexible transnational labor market for high-level professionals in advanced corporate services that links a growing number of highly developed and developing countries (Sassen 2001; 2006a, chap. 6; see also Skeldon 1997), including through virtual migration (Aneesh 2006). This development is also occurring in the high-tech sector, where the firms of the highly developed countries ate explicitly recruiting computer and software experts, especially from India. More generally we can capture these and other such dynamics in the strong trend for bimodal immigration in terms of education levels, with concentrations of low-wage, poorly educated workers and concentrations of highly educated workers.

RECRUITMENT AND ETHNIC NETWORKS

The second type of migration link includes a variety of mechanisms for the organized or informal recruitment of workers. This recruitment can operate through governments in the framework of a government-supported initiative by employers, it can operate directly through employers by illegally smuggling workers, or it can operate through kinship and family networks. Some of these mechanisms can also function as more generalized migration channels. Ethnic links established between communities of origin and communities of destination, typically via the formation of transnational households or broader kinship structures, emerge as crucial once a flow has been formed and serve to ensure its reproduction over time (Levitt 2001; Grasmuck and Pessar 1991; Basch, Schiller, and Blanc 1994; Wong 1996; Wallace and Stola 2001; White 1999; Farrer 2007). These recruitment and ethnic links tend to operate within the broader transnational spaces constituted by neocolonial processes and/or economic internationalization.

A key factor in the operation of ethnic and recruitment networks is the existence of an effective demand for immigrant workers in the receiving countries. The effective labor-market absorption of workers coming from different cultures with mostly lower levels of development arose as, and remains, an issue in the context of advanced service economies. Immigrants have a long history of getting hired to do low-wage jobs that require little education and are often situated in the least advanced sectors. Much analysis of postindustrial society and advanced economies generally posits a massive growth in the need for highly educated workers and little need for the types of jobs that a majority of immigrants have tended to hold. It suggests sharply reduced employment opportunities for workers with low levels of education in general and for immigrants in particular. Yet detailed empirical studies of major cities in highly developed countries show an ongoing demand for immigrant workers and a significant supply of old and new jobs requiring little education and paying low wages (Munger 2002; Harris 1995; Pattenas 2001, 2005). One current controversial issue is whether this job supply is merely or largely a residual partly inflated by the large supply of low-wage workers or mostly part of the reconfiguration of the job supply and employment relations that are in fact a feature of advanced service economies—that is, a systemic development that is an integral part of such economies There are no precise measures, and a focus on the jobs by themselves will hardly illuminate the issue. The jobs pay low wages, require little education, are undesirable, with no advancement opportunities and often few if any fringe benefits. There are clearly some aspects of the growth dynamics in advanced service economies that are creating at least part of this job supply (Sassen 2001, chaps. 8 and 9; Munger 2002; Roulleau-Berger 2003), which is a crucial cog in the sets of links used and developed by co-ethnics and recruiters.

One condition in the reproduction of these links is that over the last few decades and, in some cases, over the last century, some countries have become marked as labor exporters. In many ways the labor-exporting country is put in a subordinate position and is continually represented in the media and in political discourse as a labor-exporting country. This was also the case in the last century, when some labor-exporting areas existed in conditions of economic subordination and often quasi-political subordination as well. The former Polish territories partitioned off to Germany constituted such a region, and they generated a significant migration of "ethnic" Poles to western Germany and beyond. It is also the case of the Irish in England.

And it is the case of Italy, which reproduced itself as a supplier of labor to the rest of Europe for over a century.

It does seem—and the history of economic development supports this assertion—that once an area becomes a significant emigration region, it does not easily catch up in terms of development with those areas that emerge as labor-importers. Precisely because the importers have high, or at least relatively high, rates of growth, a cumulative causation effect sets in, which amounts to an accumulation of advantage. Whether immigration contributes to the process of cumulative causation is a complex issue, though much scholarship shows that immigration countries have gained multiple benefits from access to immigrant labor in particular periods of high economic growth (Portes and Rumbaut 2006; Castles and Miller 2003). Furthermore, whether emigration contributes to the negative cumulative causation evident in exporting countries is also a complex matter. The evidence shows that individual households and localities may benefit but national economies do not. History suggests that the accumulation of advantage evident in receiving countries has tended to elude labor-exporting areas because they cannot catch up with, or are structurally excluded from, the actual spatialization of growth, precisely because it is characterized by uneven development. Italy and Ireland for two centuries were labor exporters, a fact that did not turn out to be a macroeconomic advantage. Their current economic dynamism and labor immigration have little to do with their history as emigration countries. Specific economic processes took hold, promoted by specific agents (Ireland's national state and Northern Italy's enterprises) and rapidly expanded each country's economy.

In brief, analytically we could argue that as today's labor-importing countries grew richer and more developed, they kept expanding their zones of recruitment or influence, covering a growing number of countries and including a variety of emigration-immigration dynamics, some rooted in past imperial conditions, others in the newer development asymmetries that underlie much migration today. There is a dynamic of inequality within which labor migrations are embedded that keeps on marking regions as labor exporting or labor importing, though a given country may switch categories, as is the case with Ireland and Italy today.

The Organized Export of Workers

The 1990s saw a sharp growth in the export of workers, both legal and illegal. This growth in exports is not simply the other side of the active recruitment of immigrants described above. It has its own specific features, consisting of operations for profit-making and for enhancing government revenue through the export of workers. In terms of economic conditioning, a crucial matter for research and explanation is what systemic links, if any, exist between the growth of the organized export of workers for private profit or government revenue enhancement, on the one hand, and major economic conditions in poor developing countries, on the other hand. Among these conditions are an increase in unemployment, the closure of a large number of typically small and medium-size enterprises oriented to national rather than export markets, and a large, often increasing government debt. While these economies are frequently grouped under the label of developing, they are in some cases struggling, stagnant, or even shrinking. (For the sake of brevity, we use *developing* here as shorthand for this variety of situations.) The evidence for these conditions is incomplete and partial, yet there is a growing consensus among experts that they are expanding and, furthermore, that women are often a majority of both the legal and illegal exported workers (IOM 2006; World Bank 2006).

The various types of exports of workers have strengthened at a time when major dynamics linked to economic globalization have had significant effects on developing economies. These economies have had to implement a bundle of new policies and accommodate new conditions associated with globalization: structural adjustment programs, the opening up of their economies to foreign firms, the elimination of multiple state subsidies, and, it would seem almost inevitably, financial crises and the prevailing types of programmatic solutions put forth by the IMF. It is now clear that in most of the countries involved, these conditions have created enormous costs for certain sectors of the economy and the population and have not fundamentally reduced government debt. For instance, the debt burden has affected state spending composition. We see this in Zambia, Ghana, and Uganda in the 1990s, when the World Bank saw their governments as cooperative and responsible and as effective in implementing Structural Adjustment Programs (SAPs). Zambia paid US$1.3 billion in debt but only US$37 million for primary education; Ghana paid $375 million in debt service but only $75 million in social expenses; and Uganda paid nine dollars per capita on its debt and only one dollar for health care (Ismi, 1998).

Are there systemic links between these two sets of developments: the growth of organized exports of workers from certain developing economies and the rise in unemployment and debt in their economies? One way of articulating this issue in substantive terms is to posit the growing importance in all these countries of alternative ways of making a living, making a profit, and securing government revenue due to the shrinking opportunities for employment; the shrinking opportunities for more traditional forms of profit making as foreign firms enter an expanding range of economic sectors in these countries; growing pressures to develop export industries; and the decrease in government revenues, partly linked to these conditions and to the burden of debt servicing. Prostitution and labor migration are ways of making a living; the legal and illegal trafficking in workers, including workers for the sex industry, is growing in importance as a way of making a profit; and the remittances sent home by emigrants, as well as the revenues from the organized export of workers, arc increasingly important sources of foreign currency for some governments. Women are by far the majority group in the illegal trafficking for the sex industry and in governments' organized export of workers (see Sassen 2000 for sources on these variables).

The organized export of workers, whether legal or illegal, is facilitated in part by the organizational and technical infrastructure of the global economy: the formation of global markets, the intensification of transnational and translocal networks, the development of communications technologies that easily escape conventional surveillance practices. The strengthening of global networks and, in some of these cases, the formation of new global networks are embedded or made possible by the existence of a global economic system and its associated development of various institutional supports for cross-border money flows and markets. Once there is an institutional infrastructure for globalization, processes that have basically operated at the national level can scale up to the global level even when doing so is not necessary for their operation. Operating globally in such cases contrasts with processes that are by their very features global, such as the network of financial centers underlying the formation of a global capital market.

Debt and debt-servicing problems have become a systemic feature of the developing world since the 1980s and are contributing to the expanded efforts to export workers both legally and illegally. A considerable body of research shows the detrimental effects of such debt on government programs for women and children, notably, programs for education and health care, which are clearly investments necessary to ensure a better future. Furthermore, the increased unemployment typically associated with the austerity and adjustment programs implemented by international agencies to address government debt has been found to have adverse effects on broad sectors of the population. Subsistence food production, informal work, emigration, prostitution— all have grown as survival options. Heavy government debt and high unemployment have brought with them the need to search for alternative sources of government revenue, and the shrinking of regular economic opportunities has brought with it a widened use of illegal profit making by enterprises and organizations. Generally, most countries that became deeply indebted in the 1980s have not been able to solve the problem. And in the 1990s we saw a new set of countries become deeply indebted. Over those two decades many innovations were launched, most importantly by the IMF and the World Bank through their structural adjustment programs and structural adjustment loans, respectively. The latter were tied to economic policy reform rather than the funding of a particular project. The purpose of such programs is to make states more "competitive," which typically means making sharp cuts in various social programs. (For evidence on these various trends, see Ward 1990; Beneria and Feldman 1992; Bradshaw et al. 1993; Cagatay and Ozler 1995; Pyle and Ward 2003; Buechler 2007.)

In the 1990s, thirty-three of the forty-one "heavily indebted poor countries" (HIPCs) paid $3 in debt-service payments to the highly developed countries for every $1 received in development assistance. Debt-service ratios to gross national product (GNP) in many of the HIPCs exceed sustainable limits (United Nations Conference on Trade and Development 1999). Those ratios are far more extreme than what were considered unmanageable levels in the Latin American debt crisis of the 1980s. Debt (including interest)-to-GNP ratios are especially high in Africa, where they stand at 123 percent, compared with 42 percent in Latin America and 28 percent in Asia. The IMF now asks HIPCs to pay 20 to 25 percent of their export earnings toward debt service. In contrast, in 1953 the Allies cancelled 80 percent of Germany's war debt and insisted on a debt service of only 3 to 5 percent of export earnings. The ratio was 8 percent for Central Europe after Communism. This debt burden inevitably has large repercussions for state-spending composition and thus for the population. By 2003 debt service as a share of exports ranged from extremely high levels for Zambia (29.6 percent) and Mauritania (27.7 percent), to significantly lowered levels compared with the 1990s for Uganda (down from 19.8 percent in 1995 to 7.1 percent in 2003) and Mozambique (down from 34.5 percent in 1995 to 6.9 percent in 2003) (World Bank 2005; UNDP 2005). And in 2006 the governments of the leading developed countries cancelled the debt of the eighteen poorest countries, recognizing they would never be able to pay their debts.

A body of research literature on the devastating impact of government debt focused on the implementation of a first generation of structural adjustment programs in several developing countries in the 1980s and on a second generation of such programs, one more directly linked to the implementation of the global economy, in the 1990s. This literature has documented the disproportionate burden that these programs have placed on the lower middle classes, the working poor, and most especially, women (for example, Ward 1990; Bose and Acosta-Belen 1995; Buechler 2007; Tinker 1990; Oxfam 1999; UNDP 2005). These conditions push households and individuals to accept or seek legal or illegal traffickers to take them to any job anywhere.

Yet even under these extreme conditions, in which traffickers often function as recruiters who may initiate the procedure, only a minority of people are emigrating. The participation of traffickers to some extent alters the type of patterning associated with the government and corporate recruitment discussed above, which tends to be embedded in older sets of links connecting the countries involved.

Remittances sent by immigrants represent a major source of foreign exchange reserves for the governments of many developing countries. While the flow of remittances may be minor compared with the massive daily capital flows in various financial markets, it is often very significant for developing or struggling economies. From 1998 to 2005, global remittances sent by immigrants to their home country rose from $70 billion to $230 billion (World Bank 2006). To understand the significance of that figure, it should be related to the GDP and foreign currency reserves in the specific countries involved. For instance, in the Philippines, a key exporter of migrants generally and of women for work in the entertainment industry of several countries, remittances have represented the third largest source of foreign exchange over the last several years. In Bangladesh, a country with a significant number of workers in the Middle East, Japan, and several European countries, remittances represent about one third of foreign exchange.

The illegal exportation of migrants is above all a profitable business for the traffickers, though it can also add to the flow of legal remittances. According to a United Nations report, criminal organizations in the 1990s generated an estimated $3.5 billion per year in profits from trafficking male and female migrants for work. By 2006, trafficking for the sex trades was estimated at US$19 billion by Interpol and US$27 billion by the International Labor Office (Leidholdt 2005:5). Once this trafficking was mostly the trade of petty criminals. Today it is an increasingly organized operation that functions at the global scale. The involvement of organized crime is a recent development in the case of migrant trafficking. There are also reports that organized crime groups are creating intercontinental strategic alliances through networks of co-ethnics throughout several countries; such alliances facilitate transportation, local contacts and distribution, and the provision of false documents.

Men and women are trafficked for work, with women at a greater risk of being diverted to work in the sex trades. Some women know that they are being trafficked for prostitution, but for many the conditions of their recruitment and the extent of abuse and bondage become evident only after they arrive in the receiving country. The conditions of confinement are often extreme, akin to slavery, and so are the conditions of abuse, including rape and other forms of sexual violence, as well as physical punishment. Sex workers are severely underpaid, and their wages are often withheld.

The next two sections focus on two aspects of the organized exportation of workers: government exports and the illegal trafficking in women for the sex industry.

GOVERNMENT-ORGANIZED EXPORTS

The exportation of workers is a means by which governments cope with unemployment and foreign debt. There are two ways in which governments have secured benefits through this strategy. One is highly formalized, and the other is simply a by-product of the migration process itself. Among the strongest examples of the formalized mode are South Korea and the Philippines (Sassen 1988; Parreñas 2001) and now China. In the 1970s, South Korea promoted the export of workers as an integral part of its growing overseas construction industry, initially to the Middle Eastern members of the Organization of Petroleum Exporting Countries (OPEC) and then worldwide. This is the model pursued by China in its current African investments. When South Korea experienced its own economic boom, exports of workers fell and imports began (Seol and Skrentny 2003). In contrast, the Philippine government has expanded and diversified the export of its citizens to deal with unemployment and secure revenue.

The Filipino case illuminates a series of issues concerning a government's exportation of workers (Yamamoto 2006). The government has played an important role in the emigration of Filipino women to the United States, the Middle East, and Japan through the Philippines Overseas Employment Administration (POEA). Established in 1982, POEA organized and oversaw the export of nurses and maids to high-demand areas around the world. High foreign debt and high unemployment combined to make this policy attractive (Sassen 1988). Overseas Filipino workers have sent home almost $1 billion a year on average in the last few years. Labor-importing countries have welcomed this policy for their own reasons. Middle Eastern OPEC members saw the demand for domestic workers grow sharply after the 1973 oil boom. The United States, confronted with an acute shortage of nurses, a profession that demands years of training yet garners rather low wages and little recognition, passed the Immigration Nursing Relief Act in 1989, opposed by the American Nursing Association. About 80 percent of the nurses brought in under that act were from the Philippines. And in the 1980s, when its economy was booming, expendable income was rising, and labor shortages were intensifying, Japan passed legislation that permitted the entry of "entertainment workers," mostly from the Philippines. The government of the Philippines also passed regulations that permitted mail-order-bride agencies to recruit young Filipinas to marry foreign men as a matter of contractual agreement; this was an organized effort by the government. Among the major clients were the United States and Japan. Japan's agricultural communities were a key destination for Filipina brides, given the enormous shortages of people, and especially young women, in the Japanese countryside when the economy was booming and the demand for labor in the large metropolitan areas was extremely high. Municipal governments made it a policy to accept Filipina brides. The largest number of Filipinas going through these government-promoted channels work overseas as maids, particularly in other Asian countries (Parreñas 2001, 2005; Chin 1997; Heyzer 1994). The second largest group, and the fastest growing, comprises entertainers, most of whom work in Japan (Sassen 2001, chap. 9; Yamamoto 2006).

The rapid increase in the number of Filipina migrants working as entertainers is largely due to the "entertainment brokers" in the Philippines, more than five hundred of them, who operate outside the state—even though the government may still benefit from the remittances sent home by these overseas workers. The brokers provide women for the sex industry in Japan, which is basically supported or controlled by organized gangs, rather than going through the government-controlled program for the entry of entertainers. The women are recruited for singing and entertaining, but frequently, perhaps mostly, they are forced into prostitution as well. They are recruited and brought into Japan through both formal legal channels and illegal ones. Either way they have little power to resist once they are in the system. And even though they are paid below minimum wage, they produce significant profits for the brokers and employers. There has recently been an enormous increase in the number of so-called entertainment businesses in Japan (Sassen 2001, chap. 9; Yamamoto 2006).

The government of the Philippines approved most mail-order-bride organizations until 1989. But under the government of Corazon Aquino, the stories of abuse by foreign husbands led to the banning of the business. Nevertheless, it is almost impossible to eliminate these organizations, and they continue to operate in violation of the law.

The Philippines is not the only country to have explored official strategies for the exportation of its workers, although it is perhaps the one with the most developed program. After its 1997–1998 financial crisis, Thailand started a campaign to promote emigration for work and recruitment of Thai workers by overseas firms. The government sought to export workers to the Middle East, the United States, Great Britain, Germany, Australia, and Greece. Sri Lanka's government has tried to export 200,000 workers in addition to the 1 million it already has overseas; Sri Lankan women remitted $880 million in 1998, mostly from their earnings as maids in the Middle East and Far East (Anonymous 1999). By the 1970s, Bangladesh had already organized extensive labor-exporting programs to OPEC members of the Middle East. These programs have continued and—along with individual migration to OPEC nations as well as various other countries, notably the United States and the United Kingdom—are a significant source of foreign exchange. Bangladesh's overseas workers remitted $1.4 billion a year in the late 1990s (David 1999).

TRAFFICKING IN WOMEN

International trafficking in women for the sex industry has grown sharply over the last decade (Lin and Wijers 1997; Shannon 1999; Kyle and Koslowski 2001). The available evidence suggests that it is highly profitable for those running the trade. The United Nations estimates that 4 million people were trafficked in 1998, producing a profit of $7 billion to criminal groups. Those funds include remittances from prostitutes' earnings and payments to organizers and facilitators.

It is estimated that in recent years several million women and girls have been trafficked within and outside Asia and the former Soviet Union, two major trafficking areas. Growth in those areas can be linked to women being pushed into poverty or sold to brokers due to the poverty of their households. High unemployment in the former Soviet republics has been a factor promoting growth of criminal gangs as well as the increase in trafficking in women. For instance, Ukrainian and Russian women, highly prized in the sex market, earn criminal gangs between $500 and $1,000 per woman delivered. The women can be expected to service on average fifteen clients a day and can be expected to make about $215,000 per month for a gang (International Organization for Migration 1996).

Such networks also facilitate the organized circulation of trafficked women among third-party countries. Thus traffickers may move women from Myanmar, Laos, Vietnam, and China to Thailand, whereas Thai women may have been moved to Japan and the United States. There are various reports on the particular cross-border movements in trafficking. Malay brokers sell Malay women into prostitution in Australia. Gangs have sold women from Albania and Kosovo into prostitution in London (Hamzic and Sheehan 1999). European teens from Paris and other cities have been sold to Arab and African customers (Shannon 1999). In the United States the police broke up an international Asian ring that imported women from China, Thailand, Korea, Malaysia, and Vietnam (Booth 1999). The trafficked women were charged between $30,000 and $40,000 in contracts to be paid through their work in the sex or garment trade.

As tourism has grown sharply over the last decade and has become a major development strategy for cities, regions, and whole countries, the entertainment sector has experienced a parallel growth and is seen now as a key aspect of this development strategy. In many places the sex trade is part of the entertainment industry and has similarly grown. At some point it becomes clear that the sex trade itself can become a development strategy in areas with high unemployment, poverty, and a government desperate for revenue and foreign exchange reserves. When local manufacturing and agriculture can no longer function as sources of employment, profits, and government revenue, what was once a marginal source of earnings, profits, and revenue now becomes far more important. The increased importance of tourism in development generates multiplying tie-ins. For instance, when the IMF and the World Bank see tourism as a solution to some of the obstacles to growth in many poor countries and provide loans for its development, they may well be contributing also to the development of a broader institutional setting for the growth of the entertainment industry and, indirectly, the sex trade. This tie-in with development strategies is a signal that trafficking in women may well see a sharp expansion.

The entry of organized crime into the sex trades, the formation of cross-border ethnic networks, and the growing transnationalization in so many aspects of tourism suggest that we are likely to see further development of a global sex industry. This development could mean greater attempts to enter into more and more "markets" and a general expansion of the industry. Given the growing number of women with few if any employment options, the prospects are grim. Women in the sex industry become—in certain kinds of economies—a crucial link supporting the expansion of the entertainment industry, and through that they become a link to tourism as a development strategy, which in turn becomes a source of government revenue. These tie-ins are structural, not a function of conspiracies. Their weight in an economy will be increased by the absence or limitations of other sources for securing a livelihood, profits, and revenues for, respectively, workers, enterprises, and governments.

Conclusion

In this chapter I have sought to specify the ways in which international migration flows are conditioned by broader politico-economic dynamics, even though they cannot be fully explained without introducing more sociological variables. One of the major implications of this type of analysis is that we need to detect the shaping of a migration option and situate the decisions by individual migrants within these broader dynamics.

Three types of social conditions facilitate the decision to migrate and induce individuals to make that decision. A first set of broad structural conditions has to do with the types of links brought about by economic internationalization in its many instantiations: old colonial and more recent neocolonial forms and particular types of links brought about by current forms of economic globalization. A second set of conditions involves the direct recruitment of immigrant workers by employers, by governments on behalf of employers, or through the immigrant network. A third and final set of conditions involves the organized export and trafficking, increasingly illegal, of men, women, and children. These activities create whole new ways of linking labor-export and labor-importing countries, beyond the old colonial or the new global economic connections. . . .

Discussion Questions

1. What are the three major economic conditions, discussed by Sassen, that contribute to migration links between sending and receiving countries?

   Links brought about by economic globalization: The links created by economic internationalization ranging from the offshoring of production and the establishment of export-oriented agriculture through foreign investment to the weight of multinationals in the consumer markets of labor-exporting countries.

   Links specifically developed to recruit workers: This recruitment can operate through the framework of a government-supported initiative by employers, it can operate directly through employers by illegally smuggling workers, or it can operate through kinship and family networks.

   The legal and illegal organized export of workers: Operations that involve the organized export and trafficking of men, women, and children, which is becoming increasingly illegal, for profit-making and for enhancing government revenue.

2. Who benefits from the organized exportation of workers?

   Sassen notes how governments, such as the Philippines, Thailand, and South Korea, export workers in order to cope with growing unemployment and foreign debt. Criminal gangs have expanded and financially profited from the increase in sex trafficking and prostitution. Particularly in countries with high unemployment and poverty, the sex trade industry is linked with the country's entertainment industry. As Sassen writes, "Women in the sex industry become—in certain kinds of economies—a crucial link supporting the expansion of the entertainment industry, and through that they become a link to tourism as a development strategy, which in turn becomes a source of government revenue."

PART IV

MEDIA

CHAPTER 10

The New Media Giants

Changing Industry Structure

David Croteau and William Hoynes (2006, first published in 2001)

In this excerpt from *The Business of Media: Corporate Media and the Public Interest*, sociologists David Croteau and William Hoynes examine the growth and consolidation of the media industry throughout the 1990s. Fueled by what they describe as a "lax regulatory environment," media mergers and buyouts have resulted in the growth of media conglomerates and monopolies.

In September of 1999, Viacom announced its merger with CBS. The huge deal combined CBS's television network, its 15 TV stations, more than 160 radio stations, and several Internet sites with Viacom's well-known cable channels (e.g., MTV, Nickelodeon, Showtime, TNN), 19 television stations, movie and television production (Paramount Pictures, UPN), publishing (Simon & Schuster), theme parks, and more. The $38 billion merger was bigger than any previous deal between two media companies. In fact, it was almost double the size of the previous record. The 1995 record-setting deal in which Disney acquired Capital Cities/ABC had been worth $19 billion [$21.2 billion].

While the size of the Viacom/CBS deal was unprecedented, the basic dynamic underlying the merger was not. Since the mid-1980s, major media companies had been engaged in a feeding frenzy, swallowing up other media firms to form ever larger conglomerates. Including the Viacom/CBS merger, the 1990s alone saw well over $300 billion in major media deals. So rather than being unique, the Viacom/CBS announcement was just another example—and certainly not the last—of the mergers that transformed the industry toward the end of the 20th century.

These deals not only changed the media industry playing field, but also sometimes made it difficult to figure out who, exactly, were the players. While media mergers and acquisitions occurred primarily between media companies, some nonmedia companies also ventured into this lucrative market. In 1985, manufacturing giant General Electric bought RCA—owners of the NBC broadcast network. Westinghouse—producer of everything from household appliances to components for nuclear reactors—bought CBS in 1995. Three years later, the combined company dropped the Westinghouse name in favor of CBS Corporation and then proceeded to sell off the manufacturing parts of the conglomerate—in essence splitting back into two companies. Seagram's, best known for its alcoholic beverages and Tropicana orange juice, became a major media company, buying MCA in 1995 (now Universal Studios), Polygram records in 1998, and others. Microsoft, the software behemoth, also began investing in traditional media companies such as cable company Comcast, as well as Internet sites, and entering into a vast number of other media deals. Most important, traditional telecommunications firms also became central media players. In fact, at the time of the Viacom/CBS merger, the only media deals that had been larger were the ones in which phone company giant AT&T acquired two cable companies, TCI (for $48 billion in 1998) and MediaOne (for $54 billion in 1999), a sign of the coming integration of telephony, cable television, and Internet access.

Making Sense of Mergers

As we saw in the previous chapter, at various points in history antimonopoly concerns have resulted in the dismantling of media conglomerates. In more recent years, facilitated by an increasingly lax regulatory environment, major media companies have been buying and merging with other companies to create ever larger media conglomerates, all of which are now global in their activities. A decade and a half of such mergers have rapidly transformed the organizational structure and ownership pattern of the media industry. In the process, the dilemmas associated with the market and public sphere models of media have been dramatically highlighted.

From a market perspective, industry changes such as the Viacom/ CBS deal can be understood as the rational actions of media corporations attempting to maximize sales, create efficiencies in production, and position themselves strategically to face potential competitors. Despite the growth in media conglomerates, many observers believe the profusion of media outlets made possible by recent technological developments—especially cable and the Internet—makes the threat of monopolistic misbehavior by these media giants highly unlikely. How can we talk about monopolies, they ask, when we have moved from a system of three television networks to one that will soon boast 500+ channels? How can a handful of companies monopolize the decentralized Internet? The media industry as a whole has grown, they also note, and the larger media companies simply reflect the expansion of this field.

But the public sphere perspective directs us to a different set of concerns. Growth in the number of media outlets, for example, does not necessarily ensure content that serves the public interest. Centralized corporate ownership or vast media holdings raise the possibility of stifling diverse expression and raise important questions about the powerful role of media in a democratic society. Even with new media outlets, it is still a handful of media giants that dominate what we see, hear, and read. The expansion of new media technologies has only strengthened, not undermined, the power and influence of new media conglomerates.

To assess the utility of these competing interpretations, we must first familiarize ourselves with the recent changes in the industry. This chapter describes these structural changes.

Structural Trends in the Media Industry

The basic structural trends in the media industry have been characterized in recent years by four broad developments.

1. *Growth*. Mergers and buyouts have made media corporations bigger than ever.

2. *Integration*. The new media giants have integrated either horizontally by moving into multiple forms of media such as film, publishing, radio, and so on, or vertically by owning different stages of production and distribution, or both.

3. *Globalization*. To varying degrees, the major media conglomerates have become global entities, marketing their wares worldwide.

4. *Concentration of Ownership*. As major players acquire more media holdings, the ownership of mainstream media has become increasingly concentrated.

Some of these phenomena are overlapping or interrelated developments. However, to describe the specifics of these developments, we examine each separately.

GROWTH

The last decades of the 20th century will be remembered as ones of expansive media growth. Not only was the number of media outlets available to the public via cable, satellite, and the Internet greater than ever, but the media companies themselves were growing at an unprecedented pace. In 1983, the largest media merger to date had been when the Gannett newspaper chain bought Combined Communications Corporation—owner of billboards, newspapers, and broadcast stations—for $340 million [$581 million]. Even when the value of that deal is adjusted for inflation, 1999's $38 billion Viacom-CBS deal was more than 65 times as big.

This enormous growth in conglomeration was largely fueled by a belief in the various benefits to be had from being big. Larger size meant more available capital to finance increasingly expensive media projects.

Size was also associated with efficiencies of scale. But most important, integrated media conglomerates can exploit the "synergy" created by many outlets in multiple media. *Synergy* refers to the dynamic in which components of a company work together to produce benefits that would be impossible for a single, separately operated unit of the company. In the corporate dreams of media giants, synergy occurs when, for example, a magazine writes about an author, whose book is converted into a movie (the CD soundtrack of which is played on radio stations), which becomes the basis for a television series, which has its own Web site and computer games. Packaging a single idea across all these various media allows corporations to generate multiple revenue streams from a single concept. To do this, however, media companies had to expand to unprecedented size.

Ironically, as the scale of corporate growth increased, concern with regulating potential media monopolies virtually disappeared from mainstream political discourse. As a result, the big media players have—with sometimes stunning frequency—been merging with or buying out other big media players (see Exhibit 10.1).

To better understand these mergers and acquisitions, it is informative to take a closer look at one example, the Viacom/CBS deal mentioned earlier.

The Viacom/CBS Merger

CBS was created in 1928 and has long been a major broadcaster with a strong radio and television presence. Through much of its history, it was popularly associated with its news programming, especially with Edward R. Murrow and Walter Cronkite, who were among the preeminent journalists of their day.

CBS dominated network broadcasting through much of the 1960s. In 1963, CBS owned nine of the top ten prime time shows, and all ten of the top ten daytime shows. In its heyday, it was known as the "Tiffany Network" because of its quality programming. In the mid-1980s, the network went into decline after being taken over by Loew's, which instituted cuts in the CBS news division as one way to increase profits. Ten years after the Loew's takeover, CBS was sold again, this time to the Westinghouse Corporation, an electrical hardware manufacturer that changed its name to CBS Corporation.

Viacom is a much younger company. In 1970, the FCC introduced new regulations requiring networks to purchase their programs from independent producers. The rules meant that networks could not own their new programs and could not sell the rights to air reruns of their old programs—a process known as "syndication."

The goal, according to the FCC, was "to limit network control over television programming and thereby encourage the development of a diversity of programs through diverse sources of program services." This became known as the "financial interest and syndication" rules, or "fin-syn" for short. Viacom was created in 1971 as a spin-off of CBS to comply with these new FCC regulations. To sell the syndication rights to its old programs, such as *I Love Lucy* and *The Andy Griffith Show*, CBS was required to create a new corporate entity, separate from the network. Thus, Viacom was born.

In 1986, National Amusements, a movie theater chain headed by Sumner Redstone, purchased Viacom for $3.4 billion [$5.3 billion], keeping the name for the new company. Viacom grew quickly, purchasing other media enterprises. Most notably, in 1993, it bought Paramount for $8.3 billion [$9.8 billion] and Blockbuster Video for $4.9 billion [$5.8 billion]. From a stepchild of CBS, Viacom had become a media giant in its own right. In 1999 the circle was completed as Viacom returned to purchase its former parent, CBS, for $38 billion, creating a new Viacom that was estimated to be worth over $70 billion.

So what happened? Why was a much smaller media company broken up in 1971 because of fear of monopoly, while a much larger company was allowed to keep growing by acquisitions in 1999? The explanatory equation is something like this; technology + politics = deregulation. It was the combination of changing communications technology, coupled with a conservative shift in national politics, that led to major deregulation of the media industry. This deregulation, in turn, allowed media corporations to expand rapidly, almost exponentially.

Changing Technology

New technology is one key element facilitating industry changes. When CBS was forced to spin off Viacom in 1971, television viewers usually were limited to relatively few options, that is, the national broadcast networks (ABC, CBS, and NBC), public television, and perhaps one or two local independent stations. By the end of the century, there were six national broadcast networks of varying sizes (including Fox, WB, UPN), a virtually countless number of cable channels, and "direct TV" satellite options. Media corporations argued that many ownership regulations were no longer needed in this world of proliferating media outlets.

If television offered abundant choices, critics of regulation contended, then the Internet was virtually limitless in its offerings. In its early days, especially, the

Exhibit 10.1 Select Media Mergers and Acquisitions of $1 Billion (current) or More (1984–2000)

Year	The Deal	Value (in billions $)	
		Current dollars	*Constant 2000 dollars*
1985	Rupert Murdoch's News Corp. (newspapers, television in Australia, Britain, US) buys Metromedia (six television stations) as the launching pad for his new Fox network	$1.6	$2.5
	Turner Broadcasting buys MGM/United Artists (keeping MGM's library of 3,000 films but selling off the rest for $.8 billion)	1.5	2.4
	General Electric buys RCA (owners of NBC network)	6.4	10.1
	Capital Cities (backed by investor Warren Buffett) buys the much larger ABC television network	3.5	5.5
1986	National Amusements (movie theaters) buys Viacom	3.4	5.3
1987	Sony buys CBS Records	2	3
1989	Time Inc. merges with Warner Communications	14.1	19.4
	Sony acquires control of Columbia Pictures and TriStar movie studios	4.8	6.6
1990	Matsushita Electric Industrial Co. buys MCA (Universal Studios, Geffen Records, Motown)	6.6	8.6
1993	US West buys a quarter share of Time Warner	2.5	2.9
	Viacom buys Paramount Communications (Universal Studios, Geffen Records, New York Knicks, publishing)	8.3	9.8
	Viacom buys Blockbuster	4.9	5.8
	TCI re-purchases Liberty Media, which it had spun off earlier (in prelude to failed Bell Atlantic takeover)	3.5	4.1
1994	Cox Cable buys Times Mirror Cable	2.3	2.6
	US West buys Wometco & Georgia Cable TV	1.2	1.4
1995	Telecommunications Act of 1996 introduced in Congress		
	Gannett buys Multimedia Inc.	2.3	2.6
	Time Warner buys Houston Industries	2.5	2.8
	Time Warner buys Cablevision Industries	2.7	3
	Seagram's (beverages) buys 80% of MCA from Matsushita, renames it Universal Studios	5.7	6.4
	MCI buys 10% share of NewsCorp	2	2.2
	Westinghouse Corporation buys CBS (three years later, Westinghouse changes the company name to CBS Corporation)	5.4	6
	Walt Disney Co. buys Capital Cities/ABC	19	21.2
	Time Warner buys Turner Communications	8.5	9.5
	TCI buys Viacom's cable TV system	2.3	2.6
1996	Telecommunications Act of 1996 passed		
	Westinghouse (CBS) buys Infinity Broadcasting (radio stations)	4.9	5.3
	NewsCorp buys New World Communications Group, Inc.	3.6	3.9
	US West buys controlling interest in Continental Cablevision	10.8	11.7
	A. H. Belo Corporation buys Providence Journal Company (16 TV stations plus major newspapers)	1.5	1.6
	Tribune Company buys Renaissance Communications (TV stations)	1.1	1.2

(Continued)

(Continued)

Year	The Deal	Value (in billions $)	
		Current dollars	**Constant 2000 dollars**
1997	Microsoft buys an 11.5% stake in Comcast Corp.	1.1	1.1
	Reed Elsevier and Wolters Kluwer merge (print/electronic publishing/ databases; Lexis/Nexis)	7.8	8.3
	News Corp. buys international Family Entertainment (Family Channel and MTM Entertainment TV production)	1.9	2
	TCI buys one-third of Cablevision Systems	1.1	1.2
	Westinghouse-CBS buys American Radio Systems	2.6	2.8
	Westinghouse-CBS acquires Gaylord, owners of Country Music TV and The Nashville Network	1.6	1.7
1998	AT&T buys TCI (Tele-Communications, Inc)	53.6	56
	Bertelsmann buys Random House/Alfred A. Knopf/Crown Publishing	1.3	1.4
	AOL (America On Line) buys Netscape (Internet browser)	4.2	4.4
	Seagram buys Polygram (music)	15.1	15.8
1999	Direct TV (Hughes Electronics) buys PrimeStar	1.8	1.8
	Charter Communications buys Bresnan Communications (cable)	3.1	3.2
	AT&T buys MediaOne	54	55.2
	@Home Corp. buys Excite (Internet company)	6.7	6.8
	Columbia House (owned by Time Warner and Sony) merges with online retailer CDNow	2	2
	CBS buys King World (syndicated television programs)	2.5	2.6
	Yahoo! buys GeoCities Inc. (Internet company)	4.7	4.8
	Yahoo! buys broadcast.com	5.7	5.8
	VNU (Dutch publisher) acquires Nielsen Media Research	2.7	2.8
	CBS (via subsidiary, infinity Broadcasting) buys Outdoor Systems (billboards)	6.5	6.6
	Viacom announces merger with CBS	38	38.9
	Cox Communications buys cable assets of Gannett Co.	2.7	2.8
	Cox Communications buys TCA Cable TV inc.	3.3	3.4
	Cox Communications buys Media General	1.4	1.4
	Clear Channel Communications buys AMFM Inc.	23	23.5
2000+	America Online (AOL) acquires Time Warner in biggest media deal to date	166	166
	Tribune Company buys Times Mirror Company	6.5	6.5
	Telefonica of Spain acquires Lycos, the Internet portal; as part of deal, Telefonica establishes a partnership with Bertelsmann	12.5	12.5
	Gannett acquires Central Newspapers, owners of six dailies, including the *Arizona Republic* and *The Indianapolis Star*.	2.6	2.6
	Vivendi, a French pay-TV and telecommunication company, buys	34	34
	NewsCorp (Fox), and buys 10 television stations from Chris-Craft Industries	5.4	5.4

Source: Media accounts.

Note: Most dates refer to the announcement of the deal. Many deals were not finalized until the following year. Constant dollar adjustments are based on the Bureau of Labor Statistics' Consumer Price Index and were developed using the American Institute for Economic Research's online cost-of-living calculator (www.aier.org/cgi-aier/colcalculator.cgi).

Constant dollar values should be considered approximate.

Internet was seen even by many critics of mainstream media as an antidote to big media. Because of the apparently low cost of entry and virtually no-cost distribution, it was thought to be a way to level the playing field between large media conglomerates and smaller independent producers. This, too, was a part of the argument against regulation of big media.

But while technology has undoubtedly changed the face of mass media, some of these changes amount to less than they first appear. For example, while changes in television technology are ushering in the era of the 500-channel universe, these new options—unlike traditional broadcast television—are expensive alternatives that many Americans cannot afford. At the end of the century, nearly a third of American households had no cable service at all and another third had only basic cable. Expensive premium channels, pay-per-view selections, and other options remained unaffordable to most families.

Also, more channels have not necessarily meant more diversity. Instead, many of the cable options simply air either reruns of broadcast programs or provide a certain type of previously existing programming (sports, music videos, etc.), 24 hours a day. *More* content does not necessarily mean *different* content.

The Internet, too, has shown signs of becoming dominated by major media giants. For a short period of time, many major media companies were not heavily involved in Internet ventures. As a result, there was a brief window of opportunity for new companies to get established. However, as this first stage of the industry passed, a second consolidation stage took place.

Two major types of players were driving this consolidation stage. First, as successful new Internet companies saw the value of their stock rise, they often tried to solidify that value by buying something tangible with the money—often other media firms. That way, when stock prices on overvalued Internet companies fell—as they inevitably did—these companies still had valuable, although more traditional, media assets. Second, after small ventures began showing how the Internet might be used for commerce, major media players stepped in and either bought smaller companies or forced them to merge to remain in business. Thus, established companies used their resources to buy their way into the expanding Internet market. In the first half of 1999 alone, there were more than 650 Internet mergers and acquisitions valued at over $37 billion. This number was more than three times greater than the number of deals made in the first six months of 1998.

These large-scale companies make it difficult for new companies to compete independently. The once relatively low startup costs of running a significant World Wide Web site—originally touted as a central reason for the Internet's revolutionary character—now routinely exceeds $1 million. As a result, media companies with major capital to invest now dominate the most popular sites on the World Wide Web.

THE POLITICS OF DEREGULATION

If technology provided the tracks upon which deregulation was able to ride, then conservative, pro-business politics was the engine that propelled it along. The relaxation of key regulations was absolutely essential for the rapid expansion of media conglomerates.

Earlier antimonopoly regulation sometimes prevented the growth of major media conglomerates—or even required their dismantling. As we saw in chapter 2, the Justice Department's breakup of the Hollywood studios was one example of reaction to a single media company owning the means of producing, distributing, and exhibiting media products. The "fin-syn" regulations, too, were implemented to prevent control of production and distribution from resting in the hands of a single company.

In recent years, however, overall growth in media outlets and a more conservative, pro-business political environment have contributed to the significant relaxation of ownership regulations.

The 1980s was a period of deregulation that affected many different industries, including the media. Regulatory agencies—in this case the FCC—became staffed by appointees who shared many of the basic pro-business and antiregulatory sentiments of the Reagan administration. This shift gave a green light to the first round of media mergers in the mid-1980s. In 1988, Time Inc.'s annual report to stockholders stated flatly that "by the mid-1990s, the media entertainment industry will consist of a handful of vertically integrated worldwide giants. Time Inc. will be one of them."

Simultaneously, with the growth of larger media companies, the number of media outlets expanded, especially in the areas of cable and satellite television. These new technologies were a key reason that, in 1993, a U.S. District Court ruled that broadcast networks should no longer be subject to many of the fin-syn regulations. Previously, television networks acquired programming from outside producers who continued to own the programs. However, with the elimination of "fin-syn" rules, networks were now free to air their own programming. Increased vertical integration of production and exhibition resulted. For example, in the summer of 1999, Disney formalized its vertical integration in television by merging its television production studios with its ABC network operations. The shift was aimed at controlling costs by encouraging the in-house development and production of programs by Disney/ABC for broadcast on the ABC network. Such integration would have been impossible without changes in the fin-syn regulations.

The shifting regulatory environment encouraged more mergers as companies with production facilities went shopping to buy a broadcast network to air their programs. For example, in its 1999 deal, Viacom—a company with production facilities but not a major network—merged with CBS—a major network without production facilities. Changing regulations were widely seen as encouraging this type of merger. By the beginning of 2000, NBC was the last remaining network not owned by a company with major production facilities. Many analysts believe this makes the network a prime target for a takeover.

The antiregulatory sentiment in government that had escalated under the Republican Reagan and Bush administrations continued into Democrat Bill Clinton's administration. Nowhere was this more clear than in the passage of the wide-ranging 1996 Telecommunications Act. The act had been heavily promoted by the media and telecommunications industries, leading even the *New York Times* to editorialize, "Forty million dollars' worth of lobbying bought telecommunications companies a piece of Senate legislation they could relish. But consumers have less to celebrate." The *Times* went on to argue that the bill's "antiregulatory zeal goes too far, endangering the very competition the bill is supposed to create."

But antiregulation ruled the day and among the many provisions of the Act were those that relaxed the rules governing the number of media outlets a single company may own. (See Exhibit 10.2.) While the Telecommunications Act was promoted using a market approach that emphasized more competition, the changes actually helped to fuel a new wave of media mergers and acquisitions.

Patricia Aufderheide notes that "in the months following the act, mergers and buyouts multiplied. In 1997 alone, $154 billion [$163 billion] in media and telecommunication deals was recorded in the following categories, according to Paul Kagan Associates research, telephone, $90 [b]illion; radio, $8.3 billion; TV station deals, $9.3 billion; and entertainment and media networks, $22 billion."

One of the act's provisions called for a review of certain ownership restrictions and, as a result, the FCC announced another round of deregulation in the summer of 1999. This time, the FCC eased restrictions on the number of local radio and television stations a single company could own. The FCC eliminated regulations restricting companies to one local TV station in a market. Now companies are allowed to own two stations, as long as at least eight other competitors are in the same market and one of the company's two stations is not among the market's top four. Other conditions too, such as a failing station, can be used to justify multiple station ownership. In a reflection of the convergence of media forms, another regulatory change now allows for a single company to own two TV stations and six radio stations in a market as long as there are at least 20 competitors among all media—cable, newspapers, and other broadcast stations. Consumer advocates bemoaned the changes, arguing that they once again would lead to more media outlets in fewer hands. But media executives had something to cheer about. Lowell "Bud" Paxon, owner of PAX TV, greeted the changes by saying, "I can't wait to have a glass of champagne and toast the FCC!" Barry Diller, chairman and CEO of USA Networks observed, "This is a real significant step. . . . This is going to change things."

He was right. Less than a month after these new FCC regulatory changes, Viacom and CBS announced their plans to merge—a deal that would have been impossible before the relaxation of FCC regulations. Even with the new rules, the new Viacom would violate existing regulations. For example, its television stations could reach into 41% of American households, but the FCC cap was 35%. In addition, it owned both the CBS network and had a 50% stake in the UPN network, but FCC regulations prevent a network owner from having an ownership interest in another network. Finally, Viacom's ownership of numerous radio and television stations violated ownership limitation rules in a half-dozen markets. Upon approval of the deal, the FCC gave Viacom time to comply with such regulations. Some observers, however, believed that the FCC might change some of these limits by the time the compliance period expired.

So the growth in media conglomerates has been fueled, in part, by the changing regulatory environment. In the years when public interest concerns about monopolies were preeminent, media companies were constrained in their ability to grow unchecked. However, with the rise of more media outlets via new technology, the conservative shift toward business deregulation starting in the Reagan administration, and the media industry's lobbying clout, media corporations have been relatively unencumbered in their ability to grow.

Thus, as the 20th century came to a close, a loose regulatory environment allowed Viacom and CBS to create a new media giant. As announced, the 1999 merger created a Viacom that

Exhibit 10.2 Select Ownership Rules Changes in the 1996 Telecommunications Act

The 1996 Telecommunications Act eased restrictions on media ownership, leading to larger media companies and more concentration of ownership.	
Previous Rules	**New Rule Changes**
National television A single entity: Can own up to 12 stations nationwide or Can own stations reaching up to 25% of U.S. TV households	No limit on number of stations Station reach increased to 35% of U.S. TV households
Local television A single entity: Can own only one station in a market	Telecom Act called for review. In 1999, FCC announced it would allow multiple station ownership in a single market under certain circumstances
National radio A single entity: Can own up to 20 FM and 20 AM stations	No limit on station ownership
Local radio A single entity: Cannot own, operate, or control more than two AM and two FM stations in a market Audience share of co-owned stations cannot exceed 25%	Ownership adjusted by market size: In markets with 45+ stations, a single entity cannot own more than 8 stations total and no more than 5 in the same service (AM or FM) . . . with 30 to 44 stations; 7 total, 5 same service . . . with 15–29 stations; 6 total, 3 same service (but no more than 50% of the stations in the market) . . . with 14 or fewer; 5 total, 3 same service (but no more than 50% of the stations in the market) Limits may be waived if the FCC rules it will increase the total number of stations in operation

- was the nation's largest owner of TV stations,
- was the nation's largest owner of radio stations,
- controlled the nation's largest cable network group,
- controlled the nation's largest billboard company,
- was the world's largest seller of advertising with estimated sales of $11 billion—nearly twice that of second-place News Corp. ($5.8 billion), and more than double its next two competitors (Disney's $5.1 billion and Time Warner's $3.8 billion).

In an earlier era, such concentrated market power would likely have been met by regulatory roadblocks. In this new era of deregulation, it is likely that the deal will be followed in the coming years by further industry consolidation and even larger deals.

INTEGRATION

Media empires are nothing new. William Randolph Hearst built a powerful newspaper empire that wielded considerable political clout. However, the scale of the contemporary conglomerates is unprecedented. The pinnacle of the Hearst empire during his lifetime would be just a small part of today's megamedia corporations. In fact, the

Hearst empire lives on in the form of a multimedia conglomerate many times the size of anything that existed when Hearst was alive. The Hearst Corporation Web site now touts the company as "one of the world's largest diversified communications companies, with interests in newspaper, magazine, book, and business publishing; television and radio broadcasting; cable network programming; newspaper features distribution; television production and distribution; and new media activities." Having long outgrown the newspaper empire of its founder, the company's holdings by early 2000 included 7 radio stations, 26 television stations, nearly two dozen magazines and magazine distributors, and 16 business-to-business publications, in addition to more than 30 daily or weekly newspapers.

Beyond sheer scale, one of the key differences in today's media companies is the wide variety of media they comprise. Hearst owned newspapers. Today's media giants are likely to be involved in almost all aspects of the media: publishing, television, film, music, the Internet, and more. Again, turning to our case of Viacom, we can easily see the extensive integration that is a part of such a media company. A simplified listing of Viacom holdings is presented in Exhibit 10.3. These holdings are separated into two columns to show the assets that Viacom and CBS each brought to their 1999 merger. Of course, with the exceptions noted above resulting from FCC restrictions, most assets in both columns became part of the new, post-merger Viacom.

Even a simplified profile, such as Viacom's in Exhibit 10.3, may at first seem like a tangled maze of companies. A conglomerate by definition consists of many diverse companies. But we can better understand the relationships among individual companies by considering the idea of horizontal and vertical integration.

Horizontal Integration

A media corporation that is horizontally integrated owns many different types of media products. Viacom is clearly a horizontally integrated conglomerate because it owns, among other things, properties in broadcast and cable television, film, radio, and the Internet—all different types of media.

Companies integrate horizontally for two general reasons. First, as we will see in more detail in the next chapter, some companies believe that they can use their diverse holdings to better market and promote their media products. Owning properties across media allows one type of media (e.g., CBS Sports) to promote and work with another type of media (e.g., CBSSports Line.com). Viacom's ownership of the *Star Trek* franchise, to use another example, has allowed it to develop and promote a variety of products that cut across media, including several television series, films, books, computer games, and even a theme park. The result of such efforts, corporate executives hope, is a company that exploits its synergy potential by becoming greater than the sum of its parts.

This sort of integration can be seen every time Hollywood releases a major summer blockbuster. The movie is usually accompanied by a soundtrack CD and music video, related publishing ventures (books, calendars, etc.), an Internet site (often with audio or video clips of the film), and television specials exploring the "making of" the movie, not to mention the countless movie T-shirts, paraphernalia, and fast-food chain promotional tie-ins. In the hands or an integrated media conglomerate, what was once a film release now becomes an integrated media campaign of enormous proportions.

The second development encouraging integration has involved technological change. It used to be that each medium was a distinct entity. Text-based products were distributed on paper (magazines, books, newspapers). Music and other audio products were available on vinyl records or magnetic tapes (reel-to-reel, cassette, 8-tracks). Video products were either shown as films in a theater or were available on videocassettes for home use. The radio and television broadcast media used analog signals to make audio and video widely available without actually physically distributing their media products. Each medium, therefore, had its own distinct format and media companies tended to focus on their one specific media specialty.

All that has changed with the coming of the digital age. Digital data—the 1s and 0s that make up binary code—are the backbone of contemporary media products. With the transformation of text, audio, and visual media into digital data, the technological platforms that underlie different media forms have converged, blurring the lines between once-distinct media.

One visible example of convergence is the compact disk. This single digital data storage device can be used for text, audio, video, or all three simultaneously. Its introduction—along with other types of digital data storage devices—has changed the nature of media. The personal computer is another symbol of change. It can be

Exhibit 10.3   Simplified Listing of Viacom Holdings (After Merger with CBS[a])

Original Viacom Holdings	CBS Holdings
Television Broadcast Networks and Stations	
UPN (United Paramount Network), a joint venture with BHC Communications Paramount Stations Group (19 television stations)	CBS Television (15 television stations, 212 affiliates)
Cable Television	

MTV (Music Television)
Nickelodeon
TV Land
VH1
Comedy Central (joint venture with Time Warner)
    Showtime Networks
    SET Pay-per-view
    Showtime
    Showtime en Espanol
    Showtime Extreme
    Sundance Channel (joint venture with Robert Redford and Polygram)
    The Movie Channel
    FLIX
 	
All News Channel (joint venture with Hubbard Broadcasting)
The Paramount Channel (United Kingdom)
Viacom Interactive Services
	TNN (The Nashville Network)
	CMT (Country Music Television)
	CBS Eye on People
	CBS TeleNoticias—Spanish-language news
	Home Team Sports Channel (majority owner)—regional sports network
	Midwest Sports Channel (majority owner)—Minneapolis area sports network
	Group W Network Services—technology services for the cable and broadcast industries

Radio	
	Infinity Broadcasting—160+ radio stations Westwood One (equity interest)—radio network syndicated program/ producer Metro Networks
Film and Television Production/Distribution	
Paramount Pictures (2,5000+ film library) Paramount Television Paramount Home Video CIC Video (joint venture) Viacom Productions	CBS Productions EYEMARK—marketing and production of syndicated programming King World Productions—first-run television syndication (e.g., *Jeopardy, Wheel of Fortune*)

(Continued)

(Continued)

MTV Films	
MTV Productions	
Nickelodeon Studios	
Nickelodeon Movies	
Wilshire Court Productions	
Spelling Entertainment Group (80% ownership)	
Spelling Films	
Spelling Television	
Republic Entertainment	
Big Ticket Television	
Worldvision Enterprises	
Hamilton Projects	
United International Pictures (joint venture with Universal)	
Publishing	
Anne Schwartz Books	
Archway Paperbacks and Minstrel Books	
Lisa Drew Books	
Fireside	
The Free Press	
MTV Books	
Nickelodeon Books	
Simon & Schuster—including Consumer Group, Audio Books, Children's Publishing, Interaction, Libros en Español	
Pocket Books	
Scribner	
Star Trek	
Touchstone	
Washington Square Press	
Music	
Famous Music (copyright holders of more than 100,000 songs)	
Internet	
	CBS.com
	CBSSportsLine.com
	CBSMarketWatch.com (joint venture with Data Broadcasting Corporation) Third Age
Theaters	
Paramount Theaters	
Famous Players (Canada)	
United Cinemas International (joint venture with Universal) —more than 90 theaters in Asia, Europe, and South America	

(Continued)

(Continued)

Retail, Theme Parks, Other	
Blockbuster Video	TDI Worldwide—outdoor advertising
Blockbuster Music	Outdoor Systems
Viacom Entertainment Stores	
Paramount Theme Parks: Carowinds (Charlotte, NC), Great America (Santa Clara, CA), Kings Dominion (Richmond, VA), Kings Island (Cincinnati, OH), Canada's Wonderland (Toronto, ON), Raging Waters (San Jose, CA), Star Trek: The Experience (Las Vegas, NV)	
Viacom Consumer Products	
Famous Music	
Star Trek Franchise	

Source: Company web sites (www.viacom.com and www.cbs.com), *Columbia Journalism Review* (www.cjr.org/owners), and media accounts.

a. This merger was approved in May, 2000. Viacom is required to sell some of its assets within one year to comply with FCC rules. However, it is likely that some of these rules will be revised, allowing Viacom to retain almost all of the pieces of the company in this exhibit.

used to create and read text documents; show static and animated graphics; listen to audio CDs or digital music files; play CD computer games that combine audio, video, and text; watch digital videos; access and print photos taken with a digital camera; and surf the Internet, among other things. All this is possible because of the common digital foundation now available for various media.

But the significance of digital data extends way beyond CDs and computers. Now, the digital platform encompasses all forms of media. Television and radio broadcast signals are being digitized and analog signals phased out. Newspapers exist in digital form on the Internet, and their paper versions are often printed in plants that download the paper's content in digital form from satellites. This allows for simultaneous publication in many cities of national papers such as *USA Today*. Filmless digital movie theaters are beginning to appear, where movies, digitally downloaded via the Internet, are shown on a sophisticated computerized projector.

The convergence of media products has meant that media businesses have also converged. The common digital foundation of contemporary media has made it easier for companies to create products in different media. For example, it was a relatively small step for newspapers—with content already produced on computers in digital form—to develop online World Wide Web sites and upload newspaper articles to it. Thus, newspaper publishers have become Internet companies. In fact, many media have embraced the Internet as a close digital cousin of what they already do. The music industry, to use another example, has responded to the proliferation of boot-legged digital music files (MP3, Napster, etc.) by developing its own systems to deliver music via the Web to consumers—for a fee, of course

Furthermore, convergence has eroded the walls between what used to be three distinct industries: media, telecommunications, and computers. Recently, major cable TV companies began entering the phone service business and offering cable-based Internet access. "Baby Bells" and long-distance phone companies are getting involved in video delivery and Internet access. Computer software firms are teaming up with cable companies to create various "smart boxes" that facilitate delivery of cable-based media and communications services. Integration, therefore, involves even companies outside of the traditional media industry, making it more difficult than ever to mark clear boundaries.

Vertical Integration

While horizontal integration involves owning and offering different types of media products, vertical integration involves owning assets involved in the production, distribution, exhibition, and sale of a single type of media product. In the media industry, vertical integration tends to be more limited than horizontal integration, but it can still play a significant role. For some time, there has been a widespread belief that "content is king." That is, the rise of the Internet and cable television in particular, has led to an explosion in outlets available to deliver media products. Consequently, owning the media content that is to be distributed via these channels is widely believed to be more valuable than owning the channels themselves. However, with the elimination of most fin-syn rules, interest in vertical integration has resurfaced, enabling broadcast networks to once again produce and exhibit their own programs.

Viacom's vertical integration can be seen, for example, in the fact that it owns film production and distribution companies (e.g., Paramount Pictures) and multiple venues to exhibit these films. These venues include theater chains to show first-run films (e.g., Famous Players and United Cinemas International theater chains) and a video store chain to distribute the movie once it is available on videocassette for rental (Blockbuster Video). Viacom also owns premium cable channels (e.g., Showtime, The Movie Channel), basic cable channels (e.g., Comedy Central), and a broadcast network (CBS), all to air a film after its rental life is over. Thus, when Viacom produces a movie, it is assured of multiple venues for exhibition.

By understanding the basic idea of integration, we can see why many industry observers saw the Viacom/CBS deal as a logical one. First, CBS was the owner of one of the premier exhibition spaces: the CBS network, one of the "Big Four" television networks. However, it did not have major program production facilities, nor was it positioned to take advantage of the elimination of most "fin-syn" regulations. Viacom, however, was very strong in production but owned only a 50% stake in a very small broadcast network, UPN. It did not, therefore, have a premier venue for broadcasting. Bringing Viacom and CBS together created a new company with much better vertical integration.

The merger also dramatically enhanced the company's horizontal integration. In many ways, the strengths of one company complemented the weakness of the other. CBS's primary strengths in television broadcasting, radio, outdoor advertising, and the Internet were all areas of weakness for Viacom. In turn, Viacom's strengths in film, cable television, and publishing filled gaps in the CBS holdings. Mergers and acquisitions, therefore, are often carried out to bolster a company's holdings in an attempt to become more strongly integrated, either horizontally, vertically, or both. The numerous mergers that have left an industry dominated by large companies have also produced an industry where the major players are highly integrated.

At first glance, the average person may be unaware of these trends that have reshaped the media industry. It is usually difficult to discern that apparently diverse media products are, in fact, all owned by a single company. Take television, for example. If you surf the television universe, you might come across a local CBS affiliate, MTV, Comedy Central, Nickelodeon, Showtime, a UPN affiliate, VH-1, The Movie Channel, The Nashville Network, and your local team on Home Team Sports. It is virtually impossible for the casual viewer to realize that all of these are actually owned—wholly or in part—by Viacom. It is even less likely that average viewers connect the owner of all these stations with the owner of their local theme park, movie theater, and radio stations. But again, one company could own them all: Viacom. However, Viacom is not unique in this regard. The same phenomenon is true of other collections of disparate media outlets that are owned by the other media giants.

GLOBALIZATION

Growth in the size and integration of companies has been accompanied by another development: the globalization of media conglomerates. More and more, major media players are targeting the global marketplace to sell their products.

There are three basic reasons for this strategy. First, domestic markets are saturated with media products, so many media companies see international markets as the key to future growth. Media corporations want to be well positioned to tap these developing markets.

Second, media giants are often in a position to effectively compete with—and even dominate—the local media in other countries. These corporations can draw on their enormous capital resources to produce expensive media products, such as Hollywood blockbuster movies, which are beyond the capability of local media. Media giants can also adapt already successful products for new markets, again reaping the rewards of expanding markets in these areas.

Third, by distributing existing media products to foreign markets, media companies are able to tap a lucrative source of revenue at virtually no additional cost. For example, a movie shown in just one country costs the same to make as a movie distributed globally. Once the tens of millions of dollars involved in producing a major motion picture are spent, successful foreign distribution of the resulting film can spell the difference between profit and loss. As a result, current decision making as to whether a script becomes a major film routinely includes considerations of its potential for success in foreign markets. Action and adventure films translate well, for example, because they have limited dialogue, simple plots, and rely heavily on special effects and action sequences. Sexy stars, explosions, and violence travel easily to other cultures. Comedies, however, are often risky because humor does not always translate well across cultural boundaries.

We can see examples of globalization strategies in the case of Viacom. In our listing of Viacom's holdings (Exhibit 10.3) we greatly simplified the chart for clarity. However, hidden behind some of those assets are what amount to mini-global empires. For example, MTV is a popular Viacom cable channel reaching over 70 million U.S. households. It originated as a venue for record companies to show music videos to advertise their artists' latest releases. Over time, MTV has added a stable of regular series (e.g., *The Real World, Road Rules, Beavis and Butthead*), specials (e.g., *MTV's House of Style*) and events (e.g., *MTV Video Music Awards, MTV's Spring Break*), all aimed at the lucrative teen and young adult market.

MTV describes itself in publicity material as having an environment that is "unpredictable and irreverent, reflecting the cutting edge spirit of rock n' roll that is the heart of its programming." In reality, MTV is a well-developed commercial formula that Viacom has exported globally, by making small adjustments to account for local tastes. In fact, MTV is really a global collection of MTVs (see Exhibit 10.4). Together, these MTV channels are available in more than 300 million households in 82 countries. That, Viacom says, makes MTV the most widely distributed network. In the world. More than three-quarters of the households that receive MTV are *outside* of the United States.

Viacom's global ventures do not end with MTV. Virtually every aspect of its media business has a global component. Examples include the following specifics.

- Major motion pictures are routinely distributed internationally and many, such as Paramount's *Forrest Gump* and *Mission Impossible*, earn more money for Viacom internationally than they do in the United States.
- Famous Players Theatres Canada operates more than 660 screens in more than 100 locations. United Cinemas International—a joint venture with Universal—operates more than 90 theaters in Asia, Europe, and South America.
- Paramount International Television distributes more than 2,600 series and movies internationally.
- Blockbuster Video operates 6,000 stores in 27 different countries.

- Publisher Simon & Schuster has international operations in both the United Kingdom and Australia and sells books in dozens of countries.
- Nickelodeon distributes its children's programming in more than 100 countries and, much like MTV, operates its own cable channels across the globe. These include Nickelodeon Latin America, Nickelodeon in the Nordic Region, Nickelodeon Turkey, Nickelodeon U.K., Nickelodeon Australia, and the Nickelodeon Global Network. Nickelodeon even has theme parks in Australia and other locations.
- Viacom's production companies license and coproduce programs based on U.S. hits to be sold in international markets. These include *Entertainment Tonight/China*, a 50-minute Mandarin-language series produced in cooperation with the Chinese government, and other national versions of the *Entertainment Tonight* series that appear in the United Kingdom, Germany, and other countries.

International revenues are making up an increasingly large percentage of the income of such companies as Viacom, Disney, Time Warner, and News Corp. As a result, all major media conglomerates are now global players, representing a major shift in industry structure.

CONCENTRATION OF OWNERSHIP

While individual media companies grow, integrate, and pursue global strategies, ownership in the media industry as a whole becomes more concentrated in the hands of these new media giants. There is considerable debate about the significance of this trend but the trend itself is clear.

The concentration of media ownership is a phenomenon that applies to the industry as a whole, rather than to a single media conglomerate. The fact that media conglomerates are getting larger does not necessarily mean that ownership is becoming more concentrated. Growth in media companies may just be a sign that the industry as a whole is expanding—as it certainly has in recent years. The real question is whether the revenues of the industry as a whole are being channeled to just a handful of companies.

When researchers analyze ownership patterns in any industry, they often measure concentration by determining the percentage of total revenue in an industry segment going to the top four and the top eight companies. These numbers are referred to as the "concentration

Exhibit 10.4   The Global Reach of MTV (Music Television)

Company	Territory	Language
MTV Networks Asia		
MTV India	India, Sri Lanka, Bangladesh, Nepal, Pakistan	English, Hindi
MTV Japan (licensing agreement)	Japan	Japanese
MTV Mandarin (joint venture with Polygram)	Brunei, certain provinces in China, South Korea, Philippines, Singapore, Taiwan	Mandarin
MTV Southeast Asia (joint venture with Polygram)	Brunei, Thailand, Singapore, Philippines, Indonesia, Malaysia, Vietnam, Hong Kong, South Korea, Papua New Guinea	English
MTV Australia (licensing agreement)	Australia	English
MTV Brasil (joint venture with Abril S.A.)	Brazil	Portuguese
MTV Networks Europe		
MTV	United Kingdom, Ireland	English
MTV Central	Austria, Germany, Switzerland	German
MTV Europe	Belgium, France. Greece, Israel, Romania and 30 other territories, including some in the former Soviet Union, the Middle East, Egypt, Faroe Islands, Liechtenstein, Malta, Moldova	English
MTV Nordic	Sweden, Denmark, Norway, Finland	English
MTV Southern	Italy	Italian
MTV Networks Latin America		
Northern Feed	Bolivia, Caribbean, Central America, Colombia, Ecuador, Mexico, United States (select Hispanic markets), Venezuela	Spanish
Southern Feed	Argentina, Brazil, Chile, Paraguay, Peru, Uruguay	Spanish
MTV Russia	Russia (select cities)	Russian

Source: http://www.viacom.com (accessed September 27, 1999) and Viacom 1998 Annual Report.

Note: Viacom's international MTV ventures are summarized by company name, territories where each is available, and the languages in which they are broadcast.

ratio," or "CR," of an industry. CR4, then, refers to the ratio of revenue going to the top four companies in an industry. CR8 is a calculation of the same ratio for the top eight companies. A common threshold for declaring an industry highly concentrated is if the top four companies control 50% or more of the industry's revenue or if the top eight companies control 75% or more.

One such analysis of media industries by Albarran and Dimmick found that, using the CR4 ratio, every segment of the media industry in 1994 was highly concentrated except for newspapers, book publishers, consumer magazines, and a residual category referred to as "miscellaneous communications." On the CR8 scale, cable systems joined these four market segments in being the only ones not considered highly concentrated.

Ben Bagdikian is another researcher whose work on the ownership of media has revealed increased concentration. In various editions of his *The Media Monopoly*,

Bagdikian has tracked the number of firms that control the majority of all media products. This number has been declining dramatically in the last 15 years. He notes that in recent years, "a small number of the country's largest industrial corporations has acquired more public communications power—including ownership of the news—than any private businesses have ever before possessed in world history." In the fifth edition of his book, he reports that in 1996, just 10 media companies dominated the entire mass communication industry. With recent high profile mergers, this figure continues to decline.

Within each sector of the industry, a few large companies dominate smaller competitors.

- Two companies—Borders/Walden and Barnes & Noble—account for one-third of all retail book sales in the United States.
- Five movie companies—Disney's Buena Vista, News Corporation's Fox, Time Warner's Warner Bros., Viacom's Paramount, and Sony—dominate that industry, accounting for more than 75% of the domestic box office in the summer of 1998.
- Five companies—Seagram's Universal, Sony, Time Warner, Bertelsmann, and EMI—distribute 95% of all music carried by record stores in the United States.
- Television continues to be dominated by four major networks—Disney's ABC, Viacom's CBS, News Corporation's Fox, and General Electric's NBC. Several new fledgling networks have entered the field but are not yet major competitors—WB (Time Warner), UPN (Viacom), USA, and PAX.

Even in the newspaper industry, which has historically been considered among the least concentrated of media segments on the national level, Bagdikian notes that "At the end of World War II . . . 80 percent of the daily newspapers in the United States were independently owned, but by 1989 the proportion was reversed, with 80 percent owned by corporate chains." And, on the local level, the newspaper industry consists mostly of local monopolies, with only a handful of cities maintaining more than one daily paper in 2000.

The highly concentrated nature of the media industry exists, in large part, because of the relaxation of ownership regulations discussed earlier in this chapter. The 1996 Telecommunications Act not only allowed companies to get bigger, it also allowed companies to dominate a larger share of the industry, thus increasing ownership concentration. Patricia Aufderheide writes that with the introduction and passage of the law,

Total TV and station sales almost doubled between 1995 and 1996. The biggest short-range prize was radio, where national concentration limits had been lifted entirely. Virtually overnight, an industry marked by relative diversity or ownership and formats, and low advertising races, became highly concentrated. Within a year and a half, more than a quarter of U.S. radio stations had been sold at least once. Radio stock prices rose 80 percent in 1997, reflecting the new market power of group owners. The FCC calculated that two years after the Act the number of owners of radio stations had declined nearly 12 percent, while the number of commercial radio stations had increased 2.5 percent.

Radio ownership went the way of other media outlets and became concentrated in the hands of major corporate chains.

It is clear that some forms of media are more concentrated than others and that the level of ownership concentration can change. For example, in the 1970s, the three major television networks collectively had more than a 90% share of all television viewers—and thus, the associated advertising revenue. Television was enormously concentrated. (A program's "rating" is basically the percent of *all* television households that are watching a program. Its "share" is the percentage of television sets *in use* that are tuned to the program.) By 1999, the share of prime time television viewers who tuned in to the four major networks usually hovered just above 50%. Networks still dominate, but the playing field has changed considerably, Cable television has become—collectively—a major competitor for the networks, even though no single cable channel comes anywhere near generating the ratings that even the lowest rated of the four major broadcast networks receives. A modestly rated program on network television often gets twice the audience that the very highest rated cable programs receive.

One of the reasons for variable concentration between media segments is the cost of entry. Publishing a magazine requires considerably less funding than launching a television network, to take just one example. As a result, large, big-budget media such as movies and television tend to be much more concentrated than lower-cost media, such as various forms of publishing and radio.

However, as Aufderheide's observations about radio ownership suggest, low entry cost is not always a deterrent to concentrated ownership. One reason is that some forms of media still face conditions of scarcity. While there is no limit to the number of newspapers that might compete in a city, there is a practical limit on the number of broadcast television and radio stations that a location can accommodate because of the narrowness of the electromagnetic spectrum used to send broadcast signals. The FCC regulates broadcast licenses and assigns a spot on the radio or television dial to licensed broadcasters to prevent interference from overlapping signals. While digital broadcasting compresses the amount of space needed to send a signal, and thus allows for more signals in the same electromagnetic spectrum, populated areas still do not have enough space to meet interest and demand. The bottom line is that there are not enough broadcast slots to go around. Industry segments without this limitation are less likely to be concentrated.

Interpreting Structural Changes

The media industry, then, has been undergoing significant changes in recent decades as companies have grown, integrated, and become global players. There is little debate about these basic trends. However, the significance of these trends is a subject of intense debate. Market advocates see these structural changes as the normal evolution of a growing and maturing industry. But the public sphere framework reminds us that media cannot be treated simply as any other industry. Furthermore, it raises serious questions about what these structural changes mean for diversity and independence in content and for the power of newly emerging media corporations.

THE MARKET PERSPECTIVE

From the perspective of the market model, the media industry is one that has enjoyed enormous growth in recent years. With that growth has come a repositioning of major players, the introduction of some significant new players, and an evolution in the basic terrain of the industry. This perspective tends to see this growth as a logical outcome in an industry that has become more integrated across media and more global in scope. To operate effectively in such a new environment, media corporations must develop new business strategies (to be discussed in the next chapter) and draw on the large capital resources available only to major global corporations. The structural changes of growth, integration, and globalization are merely the signs of companies positioning themselves to operate in this new media world. The concentration of media ownership, on the other hand, is the natural byproduct of a maturing industry, as young startups and older, underperforming firms are consolidated

into the business plans of mature but innovative companies.

The rapid growth in media outlets, the constant shifts in consumer tastes, and the ever-changing terrain of the industry itself make any apparent domination of the industry by a few companies an illusion. No one can control such a vast and constantly evolving industry. Companies such as America Online (AOL), which have become major players in the industry, did not exist a few years ago, while old media standards, such as ABC, were long ago incorporated into newly consolidated media companies. Change is built into the market and no company can really dominate the marketplace.

Market advocates note that we should not be nostalgic about the media era gone by. In reality, as recently as the mid-1970s, the media landscape was much more sparsely populated than it is today and consumers had far fewer choices, on the whole. Compared with this earlier period, market advocates point out, we have a cornucopia of media outlets and products available to us.

It is true that more communities had competing daily newspapers than today, but often the quality of those smaller local papers was mediocre at best. In contrast, today's papers may be local monopolies and part of larger chains, but by drawing on the resources of their owners, they are able to produce a higher-quality product. Also, consumers have many more options for news—especially with cable television and the Internet—than they ever did in the days of more competing daily papers, making local newspaper monopolies less significant.

In the 1970s, many communities had only small local bookstores with very limited inventory and choice. Today, more and more communities have "superstore" booksellers with thousands of diverse selections of books and magazines. Rather than killing the old print medium, the Internet has been a shot in the arm for book sales as online retailers such as Amazon.com offer hundreds of thousands of titles for sale at the click of a mouse. This has made books and other media products more widely available than ever.

In the 1970s, local movie theaters were beginning to feature more multiscreen offerings, but these were limited compared to what is available today. Video rentals were not readily available because VCRs were still primitive in those days. Today, more multiplex theaters bring more options to moviegoers, while VCRs are in 85% of homes and a wide array of videos are readily available for low-cost renting. DVDs, too, have entered the media landscape.

Radio was admittedly more diverse in terms of regional preferences years ago, but it is not clear whether a broader range of music was readily available to listeners then. Today, radio has become largely a chain-owned affair with new standards of professionalism and high production values. In addition, online streaming offers the potential of greater musical variety to listeners.

Most striking, 90% of the prime-time television audience in the mid-1970s was watching just three television networks. Cable television was not really an alternative because it was largely used to transmit the "big three" broadcast networks to homes where reception was difficult. Satellite television, of course, was unheard of. Today, three new broadcast networks have joined the older "big three." Nearly three-quarters of U.S. homes have cable, delivering an average of almost 60 channels. Satellite television, with hundreds of channels, is expanding and by 2000, was in more than 10% of homes. Finally, the vast universe of the Internet is becoming available to more and more people at work and home, opening up unprecedented avenues for news, entertainment, and commerce via the printed word or streaming audio-video.

In light of these rapid changes, as we have seen, market advocates have called for more deregulation of the industry to spur increased competition. Because of digitization, companies in fields that were previously separate can now compete with each other if regulations are lifted. On the delivery side, telephone companies, for example, can now offer Internet access as well, while cable companies can enter the telephone and Internet businesses. On the content side, companies that had traditionally been focused in one medium can now branch out to work in films, television, print, Internet, and other media. All of this, market advocates contend, means more choices and better media for the consumer; a regulatory system created in a far different era is obsolete in this new dynamic media environment.

QUESTIONING THE MARKET: REVISITING THE PUBLIC SPHERE APPROACH

Although the market approach may celebrate the new media environment, there are questions that this focus on markets and profits effectively obscures. The public sphere perspective suggests that the technological change and growth in the number of media outlets should not be accepted as an unequivocal benefit, especially if these outlets are linked to a growing concentration in media ownership.

The introduction of new media has never ensured quality content. History has shown that the great potential of new media forms has often been subverted for purely commercial purposes. Both radio and television, at various points, were touted as having profound educational and civic potential. That potential was never reached. Cable television has, in many ways, simply reproduced the formats and formulas of broadcast television. Because it is not covered by the same content rules that regulate broadcast television, cable has had more leeway to air raunchy, violent, and sensational entertainment. This type of entertainment could be seen in everything from adult oriented cable movies to the funny, but foul-mouthed, animated prepubescent offerings of *South Park*. Cable's vast wasteland was perhaps epitomized by its most highly rated programs in the late 1990s: professional wrestling. The popularity of such cable programming pressured broadcast television to seek increasingly wild and aggressive programs, leading many parents to despair about the lack of appropriate entertainment and educational television for their children.

More wasted potential seems to have plagued the growth of the Internet. Early discussion of the "information superhighway" was quickly supplanted by a focus on e-commerce. Here, too, adult oriented sites proved to be very popular. While there may be more media outlets, we need to examine what these channels are delivering.

A concern for the health of the public sphere leads us to argue that media outlets are only truly beneficial if they serve the public interest by delivering content that is genuinely diverse and substantive. Early indications were that, to the contrary, much of cable television was delivering more of the same commercial fare that characterized broadcast television. Why could not some of these many channels be used to deliver innovative, diverse, and inclusive public affairs programming? Or alternative visions from independent filmmakers and other artists? Or programming that specifically spoke to the common challenges we face as a society? Instead, the fragmentary nature of the cable television world might even be exacerbating cultural divisions in society, as segregated programming targets separate demographic groups based on age, gender, class, and race. The Internet, too, has been used by major media companies primarily to sell products to consumers and to promote other media ventures, little of which added significantly to a vibrant public sphere.

Finally, the blurring of boundaries between media coupled with calls for deregulation raises the specter of fully integrated, multinational media giants that can simultaneously dominate multiple media. Old monopoly criteria seem incapable of dealing with this new market reality. Despite the fact that it was promoted as a means of increasing competition, the 1996 Telecommunications Act has resulted in renewed consolidation in the media industry. Despite this continuing consolidation, market advocates still talk about the new "competition," and policymakers seem unwilling to examine the significance of an emerging media monopoly owned by a few giant firms.

Part of the problem is that the recent waves of media mergers have often brought together companies that have not been direct competitors in the past. So, for example, a phone company buys a cable company or an Internet provider buys a multimedia conglomerate. Using traditional market theory, antitrust law has had to show that a proposed merger would substantially reduce competition and that this reduced competition would enable combined companies to increase prices. But as one *Wall Street Journal* reporter put it, "It is tough to show that rivalry could suffer where none exists, as with a merger between companies that have never competed against each other." Recent mergers were often across forms of media, but they nonetheless raise troubling questions. While it was difficult for such deals to be challenged based on the traditional criteria of monopolies, who was to say that the blurring lines between cable, telephone, and Internet, for example, could not be exploited by just a few companies who would dominate all three?

On the content side, market theory promised diversity from an unregulated market, but the reality seems to be quite different, as the same old media content is being sold in new packaging and underserved communities continue to be marginalized. Little that is fresh or independent seems to come from the new media giants. This, coupled with the growth in the sheer size of these corporations, raises the disturbing specter of concentrated corporate power capable of stifling diverse expression and exerting significant political power.

Thus, while the structural changes in the media industry are apparent, what these changes mean is not at all settled. Advocates of a market approach to media, the most visible perspectives in the public debate, see growth as positive evidence of a vibrant industry. But from a public sphere perspective, it is clear that we need to look beyond economic criteria to assess the new media giants. Instead, we need to ask, what have the media corporations done with their newly acquired resources? What strategies have they pursued in this new media environment?

Discussion Questions

1. How has the structure of the media industry changed over the past 2 decades? Why has this happened?

   Major media companies have been buying and merging with other companies, all of which are global in their reach. This has rapidly transformed the organizational structure and ownership pattern of the media industry, consolidating ownership among select media giants. The growth in mergers is fueled by the belief that there are economic and market benefits from being big. Size was associated with efficiencies of scale. Conglomerates are also able to exploit the synergy created by having many outlets in multiple media.

2. In what ways is this restructuring problematic?

   Although the industry contends that restructuring leads to more choices and better media for the consumer, critics worry about the homogenization of media (more choices, but little diversity in media messages). As Croteau and Hoynes state, "Even with new media outlets, it is still a handful of media giants who dominate what we see, hear, and read."

Source: From Croteau, D., & Hoynes, W. (2006). The new media giants: Changing industry structure. In *The business of media: Corporate media and public interest* (pp. 71–107). Thousand Oaks, CA: Sage. Copyright © 2006. Reprinted by permission of Sage Publications.

CHAPTER 11

Reviving Lolita?

A Media Literacy Examination of Sexual Portrayals of Girls in Fashion Advertising

Debra Merskin (2004)

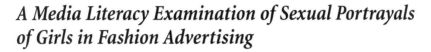

Using a media literacy framework, sociologist Debra Merskin examines the portrayal of "girls as women" and "women as girls" in four fashion advertisements. She argues that the continued sexualization of young girls in popular culture has significant implications for their psychological and physical well-being.

Lolita, light of my life, fire of my loins. My sin, my soul. Lo-lee-ta.

—Nabokov (1958, p. 1)

First, there was the book. Then there was the 1962 film followed by yet another filmic version in 1997 of Nabokov's (1958) infamous best seller *Lolita*. Simultaneously repulsive and fascinating mediated portrayals of young girls as inviting and willing participants in their own sexual exploitation have fueled many a male fantasy. Sexualized images of girls are not only found between the covers of books. Rather, "under-aged sexualized 'nymphets'" have provocatively posed in television programs, movies, magazine stories, and even more so, in advertising (Albright, 2002, para. 4). Even consumer products are named after the literary vixen and celluloid coquette: Lolita Lempicka fragrance, Lolita leggings in a recent Nordstrom catalogue, or playing on words, Nolita hair care products with the subheading "no limits, no boundaries." Although not necessarily named after sexy stars, sexually alluring clothing has reached the prepubescent crowd as well. Abercrombie & Fitch, for example, faced criticism over marketing thong underwear, with

the words "eye candy" and "wink wink," to the age 7- to 14-year-old crowd. A spokesperson for the company said, "The underwear for young girls was created with the intent to be lighthearted and cute" (Odell, 2002, para. 6). Similarly, a Fetish perfume advertisement raised a stink with the image of a young-looking girl with blackened eyes and the copy "so he can smell it when you say no."

The message from advertisers and the mass media to girls (as eventual women) is they should always be sexually available, always have sex on their minds, be willing to be dominated and even sexually aggressed against, and they will be gazed on as sexual objects. The increasing sexualization of children, in particular girls, in fashion advertising is a disturbing phenomenon (Kilbourne, 1999a). To examine this inclination, I apply Galician's (2004) seven-step media literacy analysis framework to illustrative magazine fashion advertisements. My central concern is fetishization of young girls' innocence and their vulnerability to physical and emotional violence as possible outcomes of sexualized representations in the media (Kincaid, 1998). Images cannot say "no." Just as "eroticized gazes at the child-woman" are everywhere (Walkerdine, 1997, p. 166), so too are sexualized portrayals of women as child-like. In the media in general and fashion advertising in particular, the "merchandising of children as sexual commodities is ubiquitous and big business" (Rich, 1997, p. 23). Accumulation theory (DeFleur & Dennis, 1994) predicts that if messages are seen and heard consistently across media forms, corroborated between those forms, and persistently presented, they will have long-term, powerful effects on audiences. Hence, the accumulation process normalizes looking at images of and thinking about preadolescent and adolescent girls and adult women as sexually available.

In the following sections, I briefly discuss the sociological and cultural context within which girls are sexualized, explore ideas about the use of adolescent girls' bodies in fashion advertising, apply Galician's (2004) seven-part media analysis framework, and reflect on the potential consequences of sexual images of girls in the advertisements. As a method of analysis and pedagogy, a media literacy perspective such as Galician's provides the mechanism through which this issue can be explored and functions as a tool to educate parents, teachers, and young people about the existence of and problems with this type of representation. The findings are important to scholars, parents, and policy makers who, when armed with knowledge and skills of media literacy, can work to disillusion the sexualized images of girls in popular culture.

Ideology of the Sexualized Child

In contemporary culture, the name Lolita has become synonymous with forbidden lust and love of preadolescent, and by extension, adolescent girls. Looking at sexualized portrayals of girls appropriates them for male consumption. Defined as "the voyeuristic way men look at women" (Evans & Gamman, 1995, p. 13), the male gaze appeals to the scopophilic desire of seeing what is prohibited in relation to the female body and "projects its phantasy on to the female figure which is styled accordingly" (Mulvey, 1992, p. 27). An image "orchestrates a gaze and its pleasurable transgression. The woman's beauty, her very desirability, becomes a function of certain practices of imagining—framing, lighting, camera movement, angle" (Berger, 1972, p. 43). This "fusion of sexual and ideological issues" supports men as "active, thinking subjects and women as passive, receptive objects" (Caputi, 1994, p. 16). Specifically, Walkerdine (1997) posited, "There is a hidden and covered-over eroticization of little girls in the everyday gaze at them" (p. 162). The girl model's return of the gaze offers the simultaneous appeal of the vampish and virginal, the forbidden and accessible.

The "pornographication of the American girl" (Junod, 2001, p. 133) is found in television programs, movies, video games, music videos, magazines, and popular culture. A plethora of "erotically coded" images of adolescent girls pervades American popular culture (Walkerdine, 1997, p. 3). Mohr (1996) described society as saturated with "pedophilic images" that are "surprisingly common" considering how we "careen from hysteria to hysteria over the possible sexiness of children" (p. 64). Before directing Britney Spears's videos, Gregory Dark directed pornographic films. Dark described the transition of pornographic presentations from traditional sources into mainstream popular culture as "not so much anomalous as inevitable" with an appeal based, at least in part, on what he refers to as 'the lure of jail bait'" (Junod, 2001, p. 133).

Hollywood had and has a bevy of beguiling underage beauties. Mary Pickford, Deanna Durbin, Carroll Baker, Tuesday Weld, Hayley Mills, and Sue Lyon, all teens when their careers began, became known for portrayals of under-age nymphets "who enjoyed the attentions of men but made a game of arousing them" (Sinclair, 1988, p. 92). Adding to the mystique, Tuesday Weld declared, "I didn't have to play Lolita, I *was* Lolita" (Sinclair, 1988, p. 108). In the 1970s, 20-something actor Pia Zadora looked like a child and played "jail bait" roles (Burchill, 1986, p. 122). In the 1980s, Brooke Shields was "sold as a fully-fashioned grown up sex child" at age 12 in *Pretty Baby,* as was 12-year-old Jody Foster in *Taxi Driver* (Burchill, 1986, p. 123). Both played characters who were not only sexualized preadolescents but also prostitutes, adding a layer of invitation, accessibility, and possibility to the gaze. In the 1990s, in *Interview with the Vampire,* 9-year-old Kirsten Dunst played a woman trapped in a child's body. Drew Barrymore is the eternal cinematic wild child described in *Esquire* (Hirschorn, 1994) as "thespian, pinup, recovering addict, teenager" and 10 years later in *Elle* as "28, which technically is pushing 30, but she looks 16" (Glock, 2004, p. 122). Sinclair (1988, p. 5) called these portrayals the "nymphet syndrome" in movies.

Magazines also have a version of the teenage tart in cultivating a climate of acceptability and not only in the advertising contained within them. In an extensive study of images of children, crime, and violence in *Playboy, Penthouse,* and *Hustler* magazines, Reisman (1990) found during the period from 1954 to 1984, 6,004 images of children (in cartoons and advertising) that accounted for 24% of all representations containing children. It is important to note that depictions of child sexual abuse showed the child unharmed or having benefited from the activity (Reisman, 1990, p. 156). In 2001, Dark art-directed a

Rolling Stone cover featuring Christina Aguilera with shorts unzipped and her "athletic tongue licking her lascivious lips" (Junod, 2001, p. 133). Other examples include the cover of the June 1997 issue of *Spy* magazine with Christina Ricci, Alicia Silverstone, and Liv Tyler dressed in their pajamas with the word *jailbait*. The feature, which declared the state of "the new Lolitocracy," also included other teen girl stars such as Anna Paquin, Neve Campbell, Natalie Portman, Claire Danes, and Brandi. The March 1996 issue of *Playboy* showed a "knock-kneed adolescent in a parochial school uniform depicted as the 'stripper next door'" (Smith, 1996, p. 11). Used in this manner, "pornography can be considered mainstream" (Kilbourne, 1999a, p. 271). Today, Britney Spears, Christina Aguilera, Destiny's Child, and Beyoncé are "just adult enough to be available, just young enough to be non-threatening" (Asher, 2002, p. 23).

Throughout the 1980s and 1990s, advertising became the domain of sexual symbolism and seduction where adolescent girls are continually "marketed as highly sexualized beings, ready to cater to the whims of men" (Asher, 2002, p. 23). In the early 1990s, a *New York Times* magazine fashion spread, "Lolita is a Come Back Kid," showcased grown women as adolescent girls, infantilized and powerless, standing around in baby doll-style dresses that reached only to the upper thigh, hair arranged in bows and barrettes (Kilbourne, 1999b, p. 141). The 14-year-old-and-under emporium Delia's sells thongs with slogans such as "feeling lucky?" and tiny T-shirts proclaiming their wearer as a "porn star" (Pollet & Hurwitz, 2004, para. 7). This "beauty pornography" artificially connects commodified beauty "directly and explicitly to sexuality" (Wolf, 1991, p. 11).

Fashion advertising imagery is replete with photographs in which women are "dressed down" like little girls and conversely, young girls are "dressed up" as grown women, offering a veritable visual feast based on pedophiliac fantasy (Cortese, 1999). In 1980, 14-year-old Brooke Shields informed us that nothing came between her and her Calvins. As the Calvin Klein label grew, so did opportunities for creating controversy. Were the models in the campaign older than 18? What about the little boys and girls bouncing on beds dressed only in their underwear? Calvin Klein spokespeople stated these advertisements were intended "to capture the same warmth and spontaneity that you find in a family snapshot" (Media Awareness Network, n.d.). In the March/April 2004 issue of *American Photo,* 10 young women are presented as the "faces and figures that define beauty now" (Sterling, 2004). One model is described as "barely 15," a

16-year-old as "the girl the industry wants with abiding passion," a 17-year-old as having "faunlike [sic] beauty and impossibly long limbs," and another lambent girl as a "feline Canadian" (Sterling, 2004, p. 64).

The strategy behind these advertisements goes beyond the sexualization of adolescent girls but supports an ideology of lower regard and class status for women and children (Goffman, 1976). *Ideology* is defined as "those images, concepts and premises which provide the framework through which we represent, interpret, understand, and 'make sense' of some aspect of social existence" (Hall, 2003, p. 89). Althusser (1969) suggested ideology provides "a representation of the imaginary relation of individuals to the real condition of existence" (p. 233). Through the social construction of sexuality, society shapes sexual desire, and the appropriate or inappropriate targets of that desire, through the controlled production of cultural images (Henslen, 1993). Eventually, beliefs supporting certain behaviors and images become reified or, drawing on Hall (2003), they are articulated in ways that make them appear natural, normal, and hence, unremarkable. Thus, sexualized representations of girls in advertising fuel the "ideology of girl as sexual agent in the imaginary relations between men and girls provided by these images" (Albright, 2002, para. 4). The willingness, passivity, and availability suggested by these images have the potential to fuel pedophilic desires.

Reading Sexualized Images

Silverblatt's (1995) five elements of media literacy inform this article: (a) "awareness of the impact of the media," (b) recognizing media content as a "resource for cultural insight," (c) understanding the process of mass communication, (d) "developing strategies to analyze and discuss media messages" and as a result, (e) increased enjoyment and appreciation of media content (pp. 2–3). Galician's (2004) model extends the inquiry by adding redesign of media content, discussion of the effects of the message, and steps for change. In the following section, Galician's "seven-step *dis*-illusioning" model is applied to four fashion advertisements to unveil the façade of implied sexual innocence. The user of this model goes further into the analysis and initiates change by incorporating elements of reflection and action—"action learning's empowerment spiral (awareness, analysis, reflection, and action)"—an essential aspect of the present study (Galician, 2004, p. 107).

Dis-Illusioning Girl Images in Fashion Advertisements

Step 1: Detection (finding/identifying). Four fashion advertisements that contain sexualized representations are examined to illustrate my concern about what appear to be underage girls. These advertisements appear in current mainstream American print publications (*Vogue, Elle, Cosmopolitan,* and *The New York Times*).[1] Although all models are conceivably older than 18 years of age, three advertisements display girls positioned and made up to look older (La Perla, Baby Phat, and Gucci) and the fourth is of a woman made to look like a little girl (Marc Jacobs).

Step 2: Description. La Perla is a high-end Italian-based, international lingerie company that has global retail affiliations. In *The New York Times* (February 12, 2004), the company ran an advertisement featuring a young woman who appears to be a preteen girl. Although the advertisement is in black and white, a visit to the Web site (http://www.laperla.com) reveals her to be a blonde girl/woman wearing a pale blue lace demi and matching G-string type bikini panties, leaning against a shadowy cream-colored wall. Her hands reach down and behind her bottom. Her gaze is somnolent and she looks directly at the viewer.

The second advertisement is for Baby Phat, a clothing company owned, until recently, by rapper Russell Simmons and his wife, supermodel Kimora Lee. Not only do the advertisements seem to be peopled by young girls but the models are posed, positioned, and prepared in ways that border on pornographic as well. On the company Web site (http://www.babyphat.com), celebrities who wear Baby Phat clothing are listed and range in age from Alicia Keys (20) to Madonna (46). An advertisement from the Summer/Spring 2002 collection displays an African American girl seated on a bright lemon-yellow chair. Her legs are spread eagled across the seat, she is leaning on her right elbow, head turned sidewise revealing her pink glossy lips wrapped around her thumb. She wears a bright emerald green satin jacket that is unzipped to below her cleavage. The jacket is short enough to reveal her bare stomach, and her sky blue silk short shorts (they come to the crease between top of thigh and hip area) are emblazoned with huge emerald green cat eyes, one on each side of her hips, in a way that draws the spectator's eyes to her crotch area. She stares directly at the spectator with a seductive, come-and-get-me kind of look that communicates, "When I look like this I always get what I want, and I know it's what you want. Look at me, what are you waiting for?"

The third advertisement is for a Gucci swimming suit. The image is of a very thin, pubescent-bodied blond White model posed floating on her back with her right arm positioned behind her head. She is seen directly from above, affirming her availability and vulnerability. Her black-and-red string bikini slides up to the inside of her inner thighs just enough to reveal her tan lines and what appears to be shadows or a hint of pubic hair. Her lips are slightly parted and her gaze is directly at the spectator, with a slightly defiant and yet accessible look. Her gaze conveys a longing and waiting; she invites the viewer to watch and implies, "Look at me as long as you want, I am not going anywhere."

In the fourth advertisement for Marc Jacobs clothing, the model, who is photographed from above, reclines on her left elbow, wears a tiny strapped cream-colored tank and bright orange short shorts that end at the thigh/hip crease. The shorts have a V pattern, with the vortex leading to the 1-to-2-inch wide crotch of the shorts. Her legs are parted; one is straight and the other bent, forming a V shape between them. She has candy-type plastic baubles attached to one strap of her top and the MJ monogram on the other. She is very thin, boyish in appearance. Her blondish brown hair is cut very short, in a boy style reminiscent of early Mia Farrow haircuts. She gazes up to and directly at the viewer. Her peach-colored lips are slightly parted.

Step 3: Deconstruction. Sexuality is an essential component of adolescent curiosity and, based on media representations, a clear path to popularity with peers and most importantly, with boys. It is a time of conflicting demands—she should appeal to boys, but not too much; appear vampish, but be virginal. While her "parts"—breasts, hips—are developing, she is also learning what those parts do, are expected to do, and what behaviors accompany becoming feminine in American society. Thus, she learns to fashion, adopt, and present a false self (Goffman, 1976). On the inside, she might be shy, innocent, and insecure. However, as shown in the La Perla advertisement, for example, the self she shows to the world might be seductively posed, use seductive language, and her appearance might be suggestive. Kate Moss (and all things Calvin) was frequently portrayed as child-like and exploitable—frolicking in her underpants or lying naked on a sofa. Lederer (1995) pointed out that "use of the pseudo-child technique—adults dressing and acting like children—is standard fare in pornography" (p. 139). In the Baby Phat and Gucci advertisements, the "serious facial expressions, the absence of clothing, the adult hairstyles and makeup, and body gestures and postures" all contribute to making the girl models appear older (Cortese, 1999, p. 65). Conversely, the Marc Jacobs advertisement reverses the younger-to-older-looking technique by applying childlike cosmetics and presentation methods to a model who is clearly not a child.

Step 4: Diagnosis. Myths are recurring stories "that determine a society's perspectives about the world, about themselves, about what behaviors and approaches have meaning or value *beyond* the real" (Galician, 2004, p. 34). They are the mainstay of media content and communicate a version of reality or truth. Using images of prepubescent and pubescent girls (or grown women made to look that way) in advertising activates and facilitates voyeuristic fantasies about what is appropriate, inappropriate, possessable, and safe. Although there are some variations, taboos against sexual predation on children are nearly universal. Yet there remains a level of curiosity about children as sexual beings, even if that thought is simultaneously expunged.

Step 5: Design. What would be a realistic reframing of these advertisements? I suggest using girls in advertisements targeted toward girls and portraying them in healthy and realistic ways that have relevance to their lives. If the advertised product or brand is an article of clothing or fashion line, then it logically follows to show that item in a realistic way on realistic-looking examples of the intended target of the advertisement. For example, if the product is a swimsuit, why not show the model swimming? How likely is this? Not very. Despite research that suggests otherwise, sex is still thought to sell, even if what is being sold is not the product per se but rather the idea of a sexual connection between consumer and product.

Step 6: Debriefing. An oppositional reading of these advertisements reveals that what is really for sale goes beyond the product (if the product is even shown in the advertisements). As a site of power, the body is "conceived in terms of being inscribed, constituted or rendered meaningful in representation and culture" (Lewis, 2002, p. 302). In the Gucci advertisement, for example, the model's body is displayed in ways that communicate availability and willingness. The body as text is written on in a way that is decipherable through use of sexual referents defined as "message elements (visual or verbal) that serve to elicit or educe sexual thoughts" (Reichert, 2003, p. 23).

According to Foucault, as described by Lewis (2002), sex is discussed and presented by social institutions to control it, which by extension also can "incite and facilitate modes of sexual experience" (p. 302). A symbolic reading of adolescent girl bodies in fashion advertisements reveals that what is being procured, offered, and sold is a point of view that supports an ideology that sexualizes girls and infantilizes women to control them and to legitimize that control.

The implications, discussed further in the conclusion, of these representations are serious and far reaching. Three stand out: (a) soft porn portrayals encourage the sexual exploitation of girls, (b) sexual portrayals contribute to the fetishization of girls and women in the media, and (c) passive and eroticized images foster an overall climate that does not value girls' and women's voices or contributions to society.

Step 7: Dissemination. This approach to media analysis speaks to the need for knowledge followed by action. Fortunately, several media literacy groups challenge stereotypical portrayals of girls and women. The Internet provides fertile ground for planting the seeds of online activism. Activist Web sites, such as About-face.org and adiosbarbie.com, teach and use media literacy skills in analyses of images and offer suggestions for taking action, such as writing to companies, boycotting products, organizing local protests, and forming positive images.

Conclusion

I don't want to be part of someone's Lolita thing.

—Britney Spears

This brief study uses media literacy as a framework to explore portrayals of girls as women and women as girls in fashion advertising. The Lolita look is not only found in fashion advertisements; rather, it is a multimedia phenomenon, the negative effects of which (high teen pregnancy rates, sex slavery, sexually transmitted diseases among teens and preteens, eating disorders, and suicide) are predicted by accumulation theory (DeFleur & Dennis, 1994). Steed (1994) found, for example, that as adult sex offenders "got older, they found their predilections reinforced by mainstream culture, movies and rock videos that glorify violent males who dominate younger, weaker sex objects" (p. 138).

Several questions need to be examined in future work. These include (a) What message(s) do images like these send to young girls about sex? (b) What message(s) do images like these send to young boys about sex? (c) What do images like these suggest to older men about girls? (d) In what ways might this be dangerous? (e) Are there connections between how young models are portrayed in fashion magazines and child pornography? and (f) What are the political economics of adolescent erotics? As parents, siblings, aunts, uncles, citizens, and scholars, we should be concerned about this.

In 1997, the dead body of 6-year-old beauty queen JonBenet Ramsey was found in the basement of her parent's Boulder, Colorado, home. She had been beaten, and most reports say she had been sexually assaulted (Cottle, 1997, p. 21). Although the perpetrator of the crime remains unknown, media coverage of the investigation featured repeated displays of beauty-contest and promotional photographs that came "from the deceased's pageant portfolio, professional glossies showing the petite six-year-old dolled up to look twice her age" (Cottle, 1997, p. 21). Some speculate it was this glamorized, sexualized look that motivated her assault and murder. According to Cottle (1997), "despite JonBenet's youth, [she] embodied the dual nature of Woman as The Virgin and The Whore, that nebulous combination of innocence and sexuality that has long titillated Man" (p. 21). Thus, "girls packaged to sell products or ideas to an adult market-place are not making active choices to be sexual" (Asher, 2002, p. 22). Returning to JonBenet, she "was turned into a fashion plate before she could even dress herself" (Cottle, 1997, p. 24).

Similar to content that is regarded as "kiddie porn," sexualized images of girls in advertisements have the potential to contribute to the ongoing and increasing problem of child sexual abuse. These kinds of representations indirectly condone use of children in inappropriate sexual contexts and "not only focus and allow desire but also erase various social and political complications" (Kincaid, 1998, p. 20). The display of children as sexual objects, as sites of spectacle where "pleasure, desire, and commodification intersect" (Giroux, 1996, p. 16), works to desensitize and thus, sets new standards for what is acceptable. The ubiquity of sexual representations in advertising also communicates to children that this is something adults condone and the glamorization of which celebrates girls as sexual objects. Even more alarming is the "myth that children want to be sexually used by adults—paralleling the age-old myth women want to be raped" thereby supporting the concatenation of pedophiles that children are asking for "it" (Davidson, 1997, p. 61). Similarly, the "double-dealing that dresses the erotic woman as a child" (Kincaid, 1995, p. 105) reinforces the powerlessness of women and children in American society. Has Lolita been revived? Some argue she never went to sleep; rather, that by continuously representing her in media, "the sexualized girl-child 'Lolita' has become a cultural icon" (Albright, 2002, para. 1). What is important to note is the lack of agency little girls have in the process of becoming desirable.

Note

1. Three of the advertisements can be viewed at the following Web sites: (a) http://www.laperla.com, (b) http://www.babyphat.com, and (c) http://www.about-face.org (Gucci).

References

Albright, J. M. (2002, February 17). *Smoking fetishization and the sexualization of under-aged females.* Retrieved February 27, 2004, from http://www-rcf.usc.edu/~albright/lolitashort.htm

Althusser, L. (1969). *For Marx.* London: New Left.

Asher, T. (2002, May/June). Girls, sexuality, and popular culture. *Off our backs,* 22–26.

Berger, J. (1972). *Ways of seeing.* London: British Broadcasting Corporation.

Burchill, J. (1986). *Girls on film.* New York: Pantheon.

Caputi, M. (1994). *Voluptuous yearnings: A feminist theory of the obscene.* London: Rowman & Littlefield.

Cortese, A. J. (1999). *Provocateur.* New York: Rowman & Littlefield.

Cottle, M. (1997, November). You've come a long way, maybe. *The Washington Monthly, 29*(11), 20–24.

Davidson, M. (1997, September). Is the media to blame for child sex victims? *USA Today Magazine, 126,* 60–63.

DeFleur, M. L., & Dennis, E. E. (1994). *Understanding mass communication: A liberal arts perspective.* Boston: Houghton Mifflin.

Evans, C., & Gamman, L. (1995). The gaze revisited, or reviewing queer viewing. In P. Burston & C. Richardson (Eds.), *A queer romance: Lesbians, gay men and popular culture* (pp. 13–56). London: Routledge.

Galician, M. L. (2004). *Sex, love, and romance in the mass media.* Mahwah, NJ: Lawrence Erlbaum.

Giroux, H. A. (1996, February). What comes between kids and their Calvins. *The New Art Examiner, 23,* 16–21.

Glock, A. (2004, January). Miss congeniality. *Elle, 19*(221), 118–126.

Goffman, E. (1976). *Gender advertisements.* Cambridge, MA: Harvard University Press.

Hall, S. (2003). The whites of their eyes: Racist ideologies and the media. In G. Dines & J. M. Humez (Eds.), *Gender, race, and class in media: A text-reader* (2nd ed., pp. 89–93). Thousand Oaks, CA: Sage.

Henslen, J. M. (1993). *Sociology: A down-to-earth approach* (6th edition). Boston: Allyn & Bacon.

Hirschorn, M. (1994, February). Drew Barrymore is. *Esquire, 121,* 69.

Junod, T. (2001, February). The devil Greg Dark. *Esquire, 135*(2), 130–135.

Kilbourne, J. (1999a). *Can't buy my love: How advertising changes the way we think and feel.* New York: Simon & Schuster.

Kilbourne, J. (1999b). *Deadly persuasion: Why women and girls must fight the addictive power of advertising.* New York: Free Press.

Kincaid, J. R. (1998). *Erotic innocence: The culture of child molesting.* Durham, NC: Duke University Press.

Lederer, L. J. (1995). The price we pay: The case against racist speech, hate propaganda, and pornography. In L. J. Lederer & R. Delgado (Eds.), *The price we pay: The case against racist speech, hate propaganda, and pornography* (pp. 131–140). New York: Hill and Wang.

Lewis, J. (2002). *Cultural studies: The basics.* London: Sage.

Media Awareness Network. (n.d.). *Calvin Klein: A case study.* Retrieved from http://www.media-awareness.ca/english/reso urces/educational/handouts/ethics/calvin_klein_case_ study.cfm

Mohr, R. D. (1996, June 24). The pedophilia of everyday life. *Newsweek, 127*(26), 64–65.

Mulvey, L. (1992). Visual pleasure and narrative cinema. In M. Merck (Ed.), *The sexual subject: A screen reader in sexuality* (pp. 22–33). New York: Routledge.

Nabokov, V. (1958). *Lolita.* New York: Putnam.

Odell, P. (2002). Abercrombie markets children's thongs, riles critics. *Direct Marketing Business Intelligence.* Retrieved February 27, 2004, at http://www.directmag.com/ar/marketing_ abercrom bie_markets_childrens/

Pollet, A., & Hurwitz, P. (2004, January 6). Strip till you drop. *The Nation.* Retrieved February 19, 2004, from http://www.alternet.org

Reichert, T. (2003). What is sex in advertising? Perspectives from consumer behavior and social science research. In T. Reichert & J. Lambiase (Eds.), *Sex in advertising: Perspectives on the erotic appeal* (pp. 11–38). Mahwah, NJ: Lawrence Erlbaum.

Reisman, J. A. (1990). *Images of children, crime and violence in Playboy, Penthouse, and Hustler* (Report supported by the Office of Juvenile and Delinquency Prevention Program, U.S. Department of Justice). Lafayette, LA: Huntington House.

Rich, F. (1997, January 18). Let me entertain you. *The New York Times,* Sect. 1, p. 23.

Silverblatt, A. (1995). *Media literacy: Keys to interpreting media messages.* Westport, CT: Praeger.

Sinclair, M. (1988). *Hollywood Lolitas: The nymphet syndrome in the movies.* New York: Henry Holt.

Smith, L. (1996). *Playboy:* R & R for pedophiles. *Action Agenda: Challenging Sexist and Violent Media Through Education and Action, 2,* 11.

Steed, J. (1994). *Our little secret: Confronting child sexual abuse in Canada.* Toronto, Canada: Random House.

Sterling, W. (2004, March/April). The top ten models. *American Photo, XV*(2), 64–67.

Walkerdine, V. (1997). *Daddy's girl: Young girls and popular culture.* Cambridge, MA: Harvard University Press.

Wolf, N. (1991). *The beauty myth.* New York: William Morrow.

Discussion Questions

1. What is the "Lolita" image?

   Definition: The image of young girls as inviting and willing participants in their own sexual exploitation. The image is a multimedia phenomenon, popular in television programs, movies, magazine stories, and particularly in fashion advertising. In advertising, the sexualized representations of girls fuel the "ideology of girl as sexual agent in the imaginary relations between men and girls provided by these images."

2. Which four fashion advertisements are analyzed in this research? How is Galican's dis-illusioning model applied to these advertisements?

   Magazine fashion advertisements for La Perla, Baby Phat, Gucci, and Marc Jacobs.

   Merskin relies on Galican's model to deconstruct and analyze the content of the four advertisements but adds the redesign of media content, discussion of the effects of the message, and steps for change.

3. What future research is suggested by Merskin? Can you think of other applications of her research?

   Merskin raises the following questions:

   What messages do images like these send to young girls and boys about sex?

   What do images like these suggest to older men about girls? In what ways might these be dangerous?

   Are there connections between how young models are portrayed in fashion magazines and child pornography?

   What is the political economics of "adolescent erotics"?

Source: From Merskin, D. (2004). Reviving Lolita? A media examination of sexual portrayals of girls in fashion advertising. *American Behavioral Scientist, 48:* 119–129. Reprinted by permission of Sage Publications.

CHAPTER 12

Tripping Up Big Media

Gal Beckerman (2003)

In 2003, when FCC Commissioner Michael Powell proposed relaxing media ownership rules, a coalition of liberal and conservative organizations responded in force. This diverse group, including representatives from Code Pink, Parents Television Council, National Rifle Association, and the National Organization for Women, were united by their belief that a further consolidation of media ownership would lead to singular programming and homogenized news and entertainment. Journalist Gal Beckerman chronicles the efforts of one of these groups—Code Pink—and their role in helping to ultimately defeat Powell.

One of the strangest Left-Right coalitions in recent memory has challenged a free-market FCC. What's the glue that holds it together?

The angels of the public interest, with large pink wings and glittering halos, descended on Michael Powell this fall, five years after he had, somewhat sarcastically, first invoked them. That was back in April 1998, when Powell was speaking to a Las Vegas gathering of lawyers. Only a few months had passed since his appointment to one of the five spots on the Federal Communications Commission, and the new commissioner had been invited to speak about a longstanding and contentious issue: Was it the FCC's responsibility to keep the media working toward the public good?

Powell made clear that he placed his faith in the invisible hand of the market: the business of the FCC, he said, was to resolve "matters that predominantly involve the competing interests of industry" and not some vague "public interest." The FCC had no role in deciding whether to give free airtime to presidential candidates, for example, or in forcing television channels to carry educational or children's programming. "Even if what is portrayed on television encourages or perpetuates some

societal problem, we must be careful in invoking our regulatory powers," Powell insisted.

The angels of public interest arrived in hot pink and wings, demanding repeal of the new FCC rules.

To highlight the point, Powell used biblical imagery. "The night after I was sworn in, I waited for a visit from the angel of the public interest," Powell said. "I waited all night but she did not come. And, in fact, five months into this job, I still have had no divine awakening."

This September 4 the angels finally arrived.

Fifteen women dressed entirely in fluorescent pink and spreading frilly wings emblazoned with the words "Free Speech" stood on the sidewalk outside the large glass doors of the FCC. They banged on bongos and shouted chants, unfurling a large pink scroll containing their demands: full repeal of the new rules that Michael Powell had just shepherded into existence.

By this time, Powell had become FCC chairman and had overseen the biggest relaxation of media ownership rules in over thirty years (see "Powell's Rules," below). But the day before, a federal appeals court in Philadelphia had granted an emergency stay barring the FCC from putting his new rules into effect. The court gave as one of its reasons "the magnitude of this matter and the public's interest in reaching the proper resolution." So the angels were celebrating, and they were not alone.

The massive public response to the rule changes, in fact, had been unprecedented. For months before and after the new rules were announced on June 2, opposition had been loud, passionate, and active. Hundreds of thousands of comments were sent to the FCC, almost all in opposition. It was the heaviest outpouring of public sentiment the commission had ever experienced.

Even more striking was the makeup of this opposition, what *The New York Times* called "an unusual alliance of liberal and conservative organizations." Together in the mix, along with Code Pink, the activists in angel wings, were the National Rifle Association, the National Organization for Women, the Parents Television Council (a conservative group focused on indecency in television), every major journalism association, labor groups like the Writers and Screen Actors Guilds, and a collection of liberal nonprofit organizations that had been focused on media issues for decades.

It is not every day that the ideological lines get redrawn over an issue, let alone an issue that had been destined to remain obscure and complex for all but telecommunications experts to debate. What's the glue that has held this unlikely coalition together?

Victoria Cunningham is the twenty-four-year-old national coordinator of Code Pink, a grass-roots women's organization that engages in wacky direct action. Code Pink has sung Christmas carols outside Donald Rumsfeld's home and arrived at Hillary Clinton's Senate office wearing underwear over their clothing to deliver her a "pink slip" of disapproval for her early support of the war in Iraq. I met with her a month after her group's boisterous visit to the FCC. Code Pink's office is little more than a broom closet on the fifth floor of a building a few blocks from the White House. Pink beads and rainbow flags cram the walls. Cunningham was wearing— what else?—a very pink shirt.

Why were her members, who number in the thousands, so interested in this issue? "Our people are informed enough that they understand what happens when there are only one or three or four companies that are controlling the information we get," Cunningham said. "A lot of our people would love to turn on the evening news and see a variety of opinions coming out."

Like everyone I talked to who was involved in the opposition to the FCC rules, Cunningham spoke of the intuitive understanding most people had of an issue that seems complex on the surface. Over and over, as I attempted to understand what it was that was holding

together this diverse coalition, I heard the same phrase: "People just get it." And I heard this from groups both left and right. The oddest invitation Cunningham said she had received in the last few months was to appear on Oliver North's conservative radio talk show to debate the FCC issue. "And when we talked about that," she said, "we just couldn't say anything bad to each other."

Next, I made my way to a rather different scene, the headquarters of the United States Conference of Catholic Bishops, to talk with Monsignor Francis J. Maniscalco, its director of communications. No broom closet, the conference's home is in a giant modern Washington building behind a large sculpture of Jesus pointing to the sky.

Monsignor Maniscalco, a clerical collar under his soft, round face, spoke like a weathered telecommunications professional about his opposition to the FCC's new rules. The bishops are concerned about the loss of religious shows, like Catholic mass on television—but also the loss of a time when, he says, in order for broadcasters to keep their licenses they had to "prove they were being responsive to the local community." The further consolidation of the media that would be spurred by the new FCC rules, he said, would only increase the lack of responsiveness to community needs. "We see the media as being very formational of people, formational of a culture, formational of people's attitudes," he said, "and if certain strains of community life are not on television they are, by that very reason, considered less important, less vital to society."

Even though he and the conference had always opposed media consolidation, Maniscalco said, until recently they felt they were working in a vacuum. When the monsignor began talking about the current effort, though, he visibly brightened. His eyebrows, which are red, lifted, and he rolled forward in his chair. "The consumption of media is a passive consumption, it is a passive act in itself," he said. "And it is a passive audience that has said, 'We just have to take what they give us.' But interestingly enough, this seems to be something that has finally caught people's imagination, that they could make a difference in terms of turning back these rules and saying no, we don't see that as being very helpful to our situation."

At countless public hearings over the last half-year, the bishop sat next to the gun lobbyist who sat next to a woman from NOW, all united around some common denominator.

Media industry insiders were taken by surprise at how fast these groups managed to come together and exercise political influence. In addition to the emergency stay issued by the Philadelphia federal appeals court on the day before Powell's six new rules were to go into effect, Congress has responded with zeal to their demands. Consider: on July 23, only a month after the rules were approved, the House of Representatives voted 400 to 21 to roll back the ownership cap to 35 percent. Then, on September 16, the coalition had an even greater success. The Senate used a parliamentary procedure, called a resolution of disapproval—used only once before in history—to pass a bill repealing all the new regulations. It passed 55 to 40, and was supported by twelve Republicans, and cosponsored, astonishingly, by none other than Trent Lott. Such quick legislative action has generated excitement, but it is unlikely that the coalition will find such easy victory in the future. The Senate bill must now face House Republican leaders who have vowed to prevent the measure from going to a vote, partly to keep this political hot potato away from the president during an election year. The court case that has put the new rules on hold, meanwhile, promises a complicated legal contest when it takes place next year.

But these challenges don't take away from what has been achieved. Such ideologically disparate groups rarely find common cause. As Powell himself has pointed out, the reasons behind most of these groups' opposition are parochial and narrow. The unions are worried that more consolidation will lead to fewer jobs; the left-leaning groups are still shivering from what they saw as nationalistic coverage of the war; groups like the Parents Television Council want less Buffy the Vampire Slayer and more Little House on the Prairie. Yet there they were, at countless public hearings over the last half-year, the bishop sitting next to the gun lobbyist sitting next to a woman from NOW, all united around some common denominator.

To get a better idea of what that common denominator might be, I went to visit Andrew Schwartzman, the fifty-seven-year-old president of the Media Access Project, a small public-interest law firm that has been fighting big media and the FCC for more than three decades. Schwartzman was the lead lawyer in the case that led to the September 4 emergency stay.

A week after that triumph, he looked exhausted, his bloodshot eyes contrasting with his white hair and bushy moustache. He looked a little like Mark Twain—a very tired Mark Twain. He spoke slowly and deliberately. "Michael Powell has significantly misunderstood what this is about, to his detriment," Schwartzman said. "He repeatedly says, somewhat disdainfully, that all the disparate organizations are unhappy about what they see on the air. The right-wingers think the media is liberal and the left-wingers think the media is a corporate conspiracy, and they all can't be right. This is a way of dismissing

and trivializing their position. For me, what these groups have in common is that they represent people who are within the relatively small group of Americans who choose to be active participants in the political process, the people who exercise their First Amendment rights aggressively. And even where their principal areas of interest may be the Second Amendment or other things, they understand the importance of the electronic mass media in the democratic process. And Michael Powell hasn't understood that."

What unites these groups, he told me, is that they all generally believe that the media are limited, and that this limitation comes from the fact that there is too much control in too few hands. This leads to a lack of diversity of voices, to programming that is out of touch with local concerns, to increasingly commercial and homogenized news and entertainment. And this is what has triggered people's passions. It is not the fear that their own voice won't echo loud enough, he said, but that further consolidation will produce media in which only the powerful few will be heard at all.

But why now? Neither Schwartzman nor anyone else I talked to could explain why, coming from so many different directions, all these groups landed in the same place at the same time. After all, this is not the first time that free-market enthusiasts have smashed up against the defenders of the public interest.

The 1980s saw a major crack in the idea that the public interest was the top priority for the FCC. President Reagan's FCC chairman, Mark Fowler, presided over the death of the Fairness Doctrine, which required broadcast stations to provide airtime for opposing voices in controversial matters of public importance. Then in 1996 Congress passed, and President Clinton signed, a major overhaul of U.S. telecommunications law, permitting greater media concentration. Radio was significantly deregulated, leading to the growth of companies such as Clear Channel, which now operates more than 1,200 stations in more than 300 markets. It was in that period that the national ownership cap for television stations went from 25 percent to 35 percent.

Such developments happened away from the public eye, in a place where only members of Congress and lobbyists roam. According to Celia Wexler, director and researcher for Common Cause, the nonpartisan citizens' lobby, those past fights were "very much inside the Beltway. It was very complicated, and there were no groups able to tell the story in a way that really made people understand what was at stake. There were media reformers who understood, who wanted a discussion of the public-interest obligations of broadcasters. But it didn't really catch fire."

At a morning session on media issues at a Common Cause conference, I saw how dramatically the situation had changed. Seats to the event were in hot demand. Next to me an elderly couple sat clutching newspaper clippings, one of which was headlined new FCC rules sap diversity in media owners.

Wexler, a small woman with the air of a librarian, was sitting on stage in a panel that included Gloria Tristani, a former FCC commissioner, who said of Michael Powell at one point: "I think he has lost touch with people or maybe never had touch with people in this country." The star of the morning, though, was John Nichols, a Nation Washington correspondent, who, together with Robert McChesney, another media reformer, this year started an organization called Free Press. Nichols has a professorial air, but he started his talk so dramatically that the couple next to me started nodding furiously.

He contended that, in the wake of September 11 and in the buildup to the war in Iraq, Americans had come to realize how shallow and narrow were their media. "People said maybe I support this war, maybe I oppose it, but I would like to know a little more about who we're going to bomb," Nichols said. "And I would like to know more about what came before and how this works—not just cheerleading. And all of that churned, combined, to have a profound impact."

This was an explanation I had heard from other liberal groups involved in the media movement. But it still didn't explain why conservatives had chosen this particular moment to join this coalition. As with the liberals, there have always been conservative groups that have opposed media deregulation, most notably the Catholic Church, but the message never resonated widely.

That, too, has changed. Take, for example, the Parents Television Council, an organization with 800,000 members that monitors indecency. The group regularly sends letters to the FCC when a show contains what they call "foul language" or racy subject matter. In August, L. Brent Bozell, the council's president, joined Gene Kimmelman of Consumers Union, a longtime advocate of media reform, in an editorial that was published in the *New York Daily News*, writing that in spite of their ideological differences they "agree that by opening the door to more media and newspaper consolidation, the FCC has endangered something that reaches far beyond traditional politics: It has undermined the community-oriented communications critical to our democracy."

Conservatives see a link between the growth of big media and the amount of blood and skin they see on television. The smaller and more local that media are, the

argument goes, the more attuned to community standards of decency. If local stations could preempt what was being fed from New York and Los Angeles, then programming could be more reflective of family values. Here again, the sense is that media have become too large and all-encompassing and lost touch with their audience.

Melissa Caldwell, director of research at the council, points out that the new ownership rules were a way for big media companies to buy up even more local stations. This is worrisome, she explained, because locally owned broadcast affiliates tend to be more responsive to community standards of decency. The council's surveys, Caldwell says, show that network-owned stations almost never preempt network shows, "whereas locally owned and operated stations were more likely to do so. We don't want to see the networks become even less responsive to community concerns than they already are."

By the end of September, with his rules in deep freeze, Powell, speaking to *The New York Times*, expressed exasperation with the effectiveness of the opposition. "Basically, people ran an outside political campaign against the commission," Powell was quoted as saying. "I've never seen that in six years."

At the core of this "campaign" were four groups—Consumers Union, led by Kimmelman, and the Consumer's Federation of America, represented by Mark Cooper, as well as Andrew Schwartzman's Media Access Project and the Center for Digital Democracy, run by Jeffrey Chester. The four men (who often referred to themselves as the "four Jewish horsemen of the apocalypse") played the central role in translating the growing anger and frustration of the Left and the Right into a cohesive movement.

Early on, these groups realized that to fight the FCC they would need more political power than their dependable but small progressive base could offer. One of their first steps, in addition to beginning a conversation with conservative groups like Parents Television Council, was to call on labor organizations like the Writers Guild and AFTRA, which could provide the resources and the manpower to get the message out.

By the beginning of 2003, a loose coalition was in place. And at that point, Powell's personality, of all things, began to play a galvanizing role. In pronouncement after pronouncement, he trumpeted the importance of these new rules—highlighted by his decision to vote on all of them in one shot. He insisted that their rewriting would be based purely on a scientific examination of the current broadcasting world.

It was true, as Powell claimed, that reexamining the rules was not his idea. The District of Columbia Court of

Appeals, interpreting the 1996 Telecommunications Act, had ordered him to conduct a biennial assessment. But Powell had many chances to include the public in this review, and he did not. No public hearings were necessary, he said; the facts would do the talking, and would point to the rightness of his free-market convictions. "Michael Powell deserves a public-interest medal because he practically single-handedly created this enormous opposition," said Jeffrey Chester.

In December, Powell announced a single public hearing, to be held in what one opponent jokingly referred to as "the media capital" of Richmond, Virginia. Soon, groups that had been only peripherally involved in the loose coalition became increasingly angered by Powell's intransigence. One story often invoked to illustrate the unifying power of Powell's stubbornness involves a meeting that took place between members of the Hollywood creative community and labor groups, including producers and writers, and Kenneth Ferree, the chief of the media bureau at the FCC. According to several people present at the gathering, when a request for public hearings was made, Ferree was dismissive and rude, saying he was only interested in "facts," not "foot-stomping." "The sense of helplessness and anger that he generated by that meeting was enormous," said Mona Mangan, executive director of Writers Guild East.

If Powell's refusal to hold public hearings galvanized the opposition in one direction, the desire of another commissioner, Michael J. Copps, to engage with the public on this issue also played a key role. Copps, one of the two Democrats on the FCC, was unhappy with Powell's insistence on keeping the issue within the Beltway. When Powell finally announced that the number of public hearings would be limited to one, Copps issued a statement that read like the complaints of the growing grass-roots opposition. "At stake in this proceeding are our core values of localism, diversity, competition, and maintaining the multiplicity of voices and choices that undergird our marketplace of ideas and that sustain American democracy," he said.

"The idea that you are changing the basic framework for media ownership and you don't really want to make this a public debate was a reflection of Powell's own sort of arrogant, narrow mind-set," said Chester. "He didn't understand that this is about journalism, this is about media. No matter what the outcome, you have to go the extra mile to encourage a serious national debate."

Through the winter and early spring, Copps organized unofficial hearings around the country in collaboration with groups like the Writers Guild, earning the nickname Paul Revere in some quarters. As media reform groups searched for a wide range of witnesses to speak at these hearings, the coalition grew to include groups like the National Rifle Association and the National Organization for Woman. Out of the meetings came the first sense that this issue could resonate.

In the spring, after Powell refused to delay the June vote for further discussion, the FCC was flooded with calls and letters. Petitions were signed with hundreds of thousands of names and comments. Something was happening. Despite the scant press coverage, citizens were responding. The Internet helped to make this response immediate and numerous, mostly through an Internet-based public interest group called MoveOn.org, which had been an organizing force against the Iraq war, capable of turning out thousands upon thousands of signatures and donations in a matter of days. Now it turned its attention to media reform, and the result surprised even its organizers.

"We thought it was just kind of a weird issue because it's this wonky regulatory thing, it's not a typical MoveOn issue like stopping the drilling in the Arctic," said Eli Pariser, MoveOn's young national campaigns director. "After we heard from a critical mass of people we decided to pursue it and see what happened. And when we went out with our petition we got this amazing response."

A few days before the September 16 Senate vote on the resolution of disapproval, I accompanied lobbyists from Consumers Union and Free Press as they delivered a huge MoveOn petition. Lining one of the halls in the Hart Senate Office Building were stacks upon stacks of paper, 340,000 names in all. It was the quickest and largest turnover MoveOn had ever experienced, including its antiwar effort.

As the activists, young and in rumpled, ill-fitting suits, delivered these petitions to Senate aides, everyone was struck by the fact that they were more than just names printed on paper, more than a rubber-stamp petition drive. Many of the statements seemed heartfelt. Sometimes they were only a line, "I want more diversity and freedom of speech," and sometimes long letters, taking up whole pages. People expressed their personal dissatisfaction with what they saw when they turned on the TV. But mostly, they expressed passion. It popped off the page. People in Batesville, Arkansas, and Tekamah, Nebraska, were angry. Media had become a political issue, as deeply felt as the economy, health care, or education. Senate Republicans and Democrats alike understood this. A few days later, they voted to repeal all the new regulations.

When I asked the coalition partners how long their alliance could last beyond the battle over the ownership rules, their answers were uniform: not long. If the Parents Television Council and the Writers Guild ever sat down and tried to figure out rules for TV, the decency monitors would demand stricter limits on sex and violence, and the screenwriters who make up the guild would recoil in horror, shouting about the First Amendment.

But on the question of what these groups' larger and long-term objectives were for the media, I did get some kind of consensus. At the most fundamental level, there is a demand for a forum, for a place where diverse ideas can be heard and contrasted. The ideal seemed to be media that better reflect America, with its diversity, its ideological contentiousness, its multitude of values and standards.

When I asked Monsignor Maniscalco how he would want broadcasters to act in an ideal world, I assumed he would posit some narrow vision of an all-Catholic twenty-four-hour news channel, but he didn't.

"We would like them to take a chance on things that are noncommercial, that are simply not on television," the monsignor said. "Not for the sake of how much money they can make, but because they represent significant aspects of the community. We would really like to see the concept of broadcasting in the public interest be recognized by these people as a legitimate aspect of their work."

When I posed the problem of whether he could eventually agree to share airtime with all the groups in this coalition, groups like NOW with which he had fundamental and deep disagreements, Monsignor Maniscalco had a simple answer: "You could say that the goal is for the media to give us access so we can finally have a space to argue amongst ourselves."

Discussion Questions

1. Why were Michael Powell, the FCC, and media industry insiders surprised by this coalition's response?

   They were surprised by several things. First, how quickly these groups managed to come together and exercise political influence. The government and industry leaders did not see what held these disparate groups together—assuming that right- and left-wing groups would have nothing in common. In the end, what united these groups is the belief that the media are limited, which would lead to a lack of diverse messages.

2. Despite differences between individual groups, how did the coalition act strategically in their response to Powell's proposed legislation?

   Powell describes that they ran an "outside political campaign against the commission." Early on, members from the core group—Consumers Union, Consumer's Federation of American, Media Access Project, and the Center for Digital Democracy—realized that they needed more political power. They initiated conversations with conservative groups, expanding their membership. Petitions, unofficial hearings and meetings, and the internet helped spread the message and expand support against Powell's proposal.

PART V

WORK

CHAPTER 13

America Transformed

Gary Hytrek and Kristine Zentgraf (2008)

In this excerpt from their book, *America Transformed: Globalization, Inequality and Power* (2007), sociologists Gary Hytrek and Kristine Zentgraf examine how globalization has transformed the U.S. economy and its labor markets. They argue that globalization has led to greater economic insecurity and has increased income and wealth inequality in the United States.

- An individual with a college education in 1979 started his or her work life making 25 percent more than a typical high school graduate; in 2000, the difference was almost 70 percent.
- Everyday in the United States, 85,444 people lose their jobs and are forced to compete for jobs that pay 21 percent less than the job they lost.
- In the past 3 years, 2.9 million well-paying U.S. manufacturing jobs have disappeared.
- Experts estimate that 14 million white-collar jobs in the United States will be shipped *permanently* overseas in the next few years.
- After losing a job, the average time a person spends out of work increased from 13 weeks in 2003 to 18 weeks in 2005 because of changes in technology and the fact that there are three job seekers for every one job.

Contemplating what to do after high school or college or whether or not to change jobs is a daunting task. As the above data from Mishel, Bernstein, and Allegreto (2005) and the AFL-CIO (n.d.c., 2004a) suggest, we are truly living and working in a new age. Analyzing such changes led the authors of the 2001 Economic Report to the President (2001, 19) to conclude that "over the last eight years the American economy has transformed itself so radically that many believe we have witnessed the creation of a New Economy." Gone is the predictability of the fixed Keynesian model; flexibility, innovation, and risk rule the day. In the twenty-first century, we must be well educated and we must be flexible enough to change where we live, where we work, and what work we do at the drop of a hat. What happened?

Economic globalization and the attendant political policies accelerated competition, which along the way restructured and transformed the U.S. economy and the occupational structures. At the dawn of the twenty-first century, we are more individualized, more educated, more competitive, and more unequal than ever before. In this chapter, we examine the way in which globalization has altered the workplace and intensified class inequality (income, wealth, and poverty) in the period since the Second World War.

The Context: Fordism to Flexibility

The three decades after World War II were hopeful times for many in the United States. When the war ended, soldiers came home anxious to return to their jobs and resume their daily lives. Factories that had been producing war-related products were retooled to produce commodities for domestic consumption (e.g., cars, household appliances, etc.) and export. Jobs that paid living wages were relatively plentiful, and labor unions were active; poverty rates declined, and income distribution became more equal. For many—mainly the white working and middle classes—the "Ozzie and Harriet" image of the family was an attainable goal. Our present notion of the traditional family emerged in this period: living in the suburbs with a car in the driveway and a balance of work and personal life that included being home for dinner at five, taking yearly family vacations, and saving for the children's college education.

As the competitive environment changed in the 1970s and U.S. firms went "global," the restructuring of the U.S. economy created a more flexible and uncertain job market. New workers were no longer entering predictable work settings; rather, they, along with displaced workers from declining industries, were confronting more intense global and national competition for jobs that either paid too little or required specialized training and education. The globalization of the U.S. economy was altering the location of production as well as the mix of jobs *between* and *within* the U.S. manufacturing and services sectors. Over time, the U.S. occupational structure shifted from one resembling a diamond, with a large middle sector, to one in the shape of an hourglass, with cognitive-intensive jobs at one end and low-wage jobs at the other. The way in which globalization transformed the blue- and white-collar sectors is central to explaining the shifting patterns of inequality and stratification in the United States.

U.S. Workers in the Globalized Economy

Flexibility, as we have noted, is a fundamental aspect of globalization. From the position of the corporation, firms must be flexible in order to react quickly to market changes and remain competitive. Technology is a central factor in the globalization process, functioning as the mechanism that coordinates the flexible global production process, replaces human labor, and creates new forms of technology–human collaboration. Research shows that computers can *substitute* for human labor or they can *complement* human labor (see Levy and Murnane 2004). Because computers excel at processing information through the application of rules, computers will complement humans working in jobs characterized by complex perceptual problems and requiring contextual knowledge.

For example, a cardiologist complements her experience and her patient's medical history with an echocardiogram to arrive at an accurate diagnosis; without the aid of the echocardiogram, her task would be much more difficult.

New information technology can also complement human labor and enhance competitiveness by speeding up and adding flexibility to the production process. Boeing, for instance, launched its 727 passenger plane in 1962 after an 81-month development process. In 1994, Boeing used a computer aided design (CAD) system developed by Dassault, a French engineering company, to complete its new 777 passenger plane in only *52 months* (Levy and Murnane 2004, 31–32). Even in labor-intensive industries, such as textiles, CAD systems can reduce the design time for a garment from weeks to minutes. Already by the late 1980s, Nike could specify a shoe design in Oregon and send these plans by satellite to a CAD firm in Taiwan, which in turn could fax the plans to engineers in South Korea. In other words, information technology and CAD systems allow firms to easily and quickly change designs to "tailor-make" products and meet rapidly changing individual consumer demand.

By contrast, computers will substitute for humans in jobs governed by rule-based logic. Jobs that can be fully and easily described by rules, such as many blue-collar and clerical jobs, are the most likely candidates for substitution by a robot or computer. Assembly line jobs and those involving tax preparation or financial bond trading are good examples of jobs where human beings have been replaced (substituted) by robots and computers (Levy and Murnane 2004, Chapter 3).

For positions in which technology cannot easily substitute for human labor, such as security guards or janitors, a large pool of available workers keeps wages low. For other non-rule-based jobs, such as textiles and electronics, technology facilitates a different type of substitution through outsourcing and subcontracting. Take the example of the textile industry. The sewing of garments remains labor-intensive, but information technology allows the repositioning of these jobs in the global production line through outsourcing and subcontracting (see Chapter 4 [of *America Transformed: Globalization, Inequality and Power*]). The creation of the global production process enhances flexibility by allowing the substitution of U.S. jobs for ones (outside of the United States) that are nonunionized, cheaper, and highly mobile.

Yet, not all corporations are moving offshore, and thus, there are alternative strategies that corporations use in an effort to cut costs and increase flexibility. Manufacturers, for example, routinely rely on **just-in-time production** strategies, whereby goods are ordered via computer direct from the factory (which is often located in another country) and shipped immediately to retail establishments (located in yet another country). This eliminates the need to warehouse goods and the second-guessing associated with product supply and demand. Firms are also creating a **just-in-time labor force** based on nonstandard part-time, temporary, or **contingent labor** that allows firms to meet increased demand or to finish specialized projects—just in time—without the costs and long-term commitments that come with full-time or permanent workers.

The shift to **nonstandard work arrangements** throughout the 1980s and 1990s not only enhanced flexibility but also reduced labor costs (by decreasing healthcare benefits, vacation, sick pay, and pensions). The average part-time worker, for example, gets paid 60 percent of the average wage rate of a full-time worker. And 25 percent of part-time workers earn minimum wage compared to 5 percent of full-time workers (Williams 2000). Over the 1980s and 1990s, temporary work doubled each decade (Mishel, Bernstein, and Boushey 2003), with low-wage workers hit the hardest by these changes (Belous 1997). Of the 2.4 million workers employed by temporary help agencies in 1996, six out of ten did work on the lowest end of the corporate job ladder (Belous 1997). By the late 1990s, however, nonstandard arrangements had spread throughout the occupational ladder to include white-collar professional occupations (e.g., lawyers, accountants, physicians, technicians, college and university professors, among others) and firms known for their long-term employment policies (e.g., IBM, AT&T).

Thinking about these kinds of changes in the context of our discussion in the previous chapters, what are the effects on working women and men in the United States? Recall that neoliberals argued that these changes would create a new economy with virtually endless growth potential and increasing wealth through the generation of high-skilled and high-wage jobs. Let's look more closely at labor market changes and, more specifically, at what Schumpeter calls the "creative destruction process."

Changing Mixture of Employment Opportunities: The Manufacturing Sector

Manufacturing, we noted in the previous chapter, has been hardest hit by globalization. Between 1979 and 2001, employment in goods-producing industries declined from 29.5 to 19.0 percent (Mishel, Bernstein, and Schmitt 2001); in manufacturing, the U.S. industry lost more than 3 million jobs from 1998 to 2003, reducing this sector to its pre-1958 size (Bivens 2004). During this period, 14 states lost more than 10 percent of their manufacturing workforce—with ten states losing at least 65,000 manufacturing jobs—which accounts for more than half of the total U.S. job losses. Five states—California, New York, Pennsylvania, Texas, and Ohio—accounted for 30 percent of the loss (AFL-CIO n.d.a).

Significantly, corporations did not fire employees "here and there"; rather, they instituted **mass layoffs** in the process of restructuring their operations by adding technology or moving offshore. The transportation equipment, primary metals (e.g., steel), apparel, computer and electronic products, and food manufacturing industries were the hardest hit by mass layoffs and plant closures. For example, 33 steel companies filed for bankruptcy and/or ceased operations between 2000 and 2002, affecting more than 73,000 steelworker jobs. Similarly, the textile industry saw 150 textile plants close since 2000—116 during 2001 alone—with North Carolina, South Carolina, and Georgia accounting for two-thirds of the losses (AFL-CIO n.d.a). These trends continued in 2002 and 2003 with 39,240 mass layoff events that prompted 4.1 million people to file for unemployment benefits (Brown 2004).

The way globalization is shaping the job mix in the manufacturing sector is illustrated by the U.S. automobile sector. Several trends are apparent. First, the sector has eliminated most entry-level, labor-intensive, assembly line jobs in the United States and increased job growth in the parts sector, jobs that assemble modules such as seats and climate control systems for final assembly elsewhere. Since the early 1980s, the parts sector has added over 220,900 jobs versus 25,300 assembly sector jobs. Hourly wages in the parts sector average $17.91, or 75 percent of the $24.25/hour pay in the assembly sector, declining from rough parity as late as 1978 (Sturgeon and Florida 2004, 55). Second, following the parts sector in job growth have been positions in research and design, engineering, and administration. Finally, while jobs in the parts sector are located throughout the world, the research and design, engineering, and administrative jobs typically remain in the United States.

The employment outlook for high-tech workers is no less problematic; in this industry, the number of jobs shrank by 18.8 percent to 1.7 million positions from mid-2001 to mid-2004 (Srivastava and Theodore 2004). Again, we find research and development jobs maintained in the United States while assembly jobs are relocated offshore.

In the hard disk drive sector, for instance, U.S. firms produced 80 percent of the world's hard drives in 1999 but assembled fewer than 1 percent in the United States, with 70 percent assembled in Southeast Asia (McKendrick 2004, 145). As late as 1985, 55 percent of hard drives were assembled in the United States; in 1995, over half of those working for U.S. firms in this sector were employed in Southeast Asia (McKendrick 2004, 145).

Jobs in software occupations within the manufacturing sector shrank even faster than overall manufacturing jobs. Between 2000 and 2002, total manufacturing jobs fell by 12 percent, while software jobs within manufacturing dropped by 19 percent. From mid-2001 to mid-2004, while the U.S. manufacturing sector shed 15 percent of its jobs, the software-producing industries lost 16 percent (Economic Policy Institute 2003).

Where did these manufacturing and high-tech jobs go? Figure 13.1 provides a partial picture. The software sector, one of the key sectors in the global economy, exemplifies the process by which U.S. jobs are outsourced to other places (in this case, India) in the global economy . . . Other jobs have been casualties of technology. In 1980, U.S. Steel employed 120,000 workers; by 1990, the firm had cut 100,000 jobs yet maintained the same output of steel. On Ford assembly lines, robots do 98 percent of the spot welds on such cars as the Taurus. In addition, the advent of certain technologies, such as CAD, has changed the skill requirements for numerous jobs. As the motor vehicle industry suggests, the typical assembly line worker was more likely sitting at a computer than at the line by the new millennium. The point here is that technology not only accelerates the pace of job change; it also raises the value of verbal and quantitative literacy.

Changing Mixture of Employment Opportunities: The Service Sector

Reflecting the general structural transition of the U.S. economy, the service sector accounted for over 80 percent of the jobs at the end of the twentieth century (increasing from 70 percent in 1979 to 81 percent in 2001). Between 1969 and 1999, the fastest-growing service sector occupations were the low-paying categories (those non-rule-based, difficult to outsource jobs, such as janitors, cafeteria workers, and security guards). In this same period, high-paying professional, managerial, and technical sectors and middle-range service jobs (e.g., administrative support workers) showed the greatest *decline* (Levy and Murnane 2004, 42, Figure 3.2). Other service sector jobs experiencing decline include the geographic information systems services for insurance companies, stock market research for financial firms, medical transcription services, legal online database research, customer-service call centers, and payroll and other back office-related activities, to name a few.

The forces at work in the service sector are the same ones shaping the manufacturing, high-tech, and software production jobs—specifically, advances in the information infrastructure, the emergence of a global "24/7" economy capable of operating in real time, as well as institutional convergence as many parts of the world adopt common accounting and legal systems. Still, outsourcing these service jobs would be difficult without the presence of another global process—cultural globalization. Increasingly, English is the accepted medium of communication and business throughout the world, and

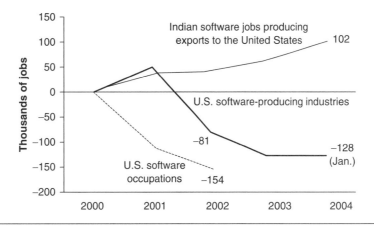

Figure 13.1   Changes in Software-Related Jobs Since 2000

Source: Mishel, Bernstein, and Allegreto (2005).

there is a steady and copious supply of technically savvy graduates, many of whom leave their native countries to study in the United States and later return home to work in globalized firms (see Bardhan and Kroll 2003).

These transformations are aptly illustrated by trends in the software sector. The transfer of service activities in this sector to offshore locations has created a critical mass of expertise and resources in concentrated locales (e.g., the city of Bangalore in India…). Firms involved with software services outsourcing and **business processing outsourcing** (BPO) are rapidly gaining ground in places such as the Philippines and Malaysia (call centers and other back-office BPO), China (embedded software, financial firms, back-office BPO, some application development), Russia and Israel (high-end customized software and expert systems), and Ireland (packaged software and product development). At the same time, the higher value-added, better-paying jobs in management, finance, marketing, and research and development have been retained in the United States, as we found within the manufacturing sector. Estimates suggest these outsourcing trends will continue. Forrester Research predicts that $151.2 billion in wages will be shifted from the United States to lower-wage countries by 2015, while Dobbs (2004a) argues that this trend will affect some 3.4 million white-collar service jobs in 550 of the 700 service job categories in the United States in the coming decade.

The changes in the software industry are consistent with the arguments of neoliberals and Marxists alike: that the United States will shed low-wage jobs and retain the higher-end, more profitable ones. For the neoliberals, the transition is a temporary one that will eventually lead to better jobs and higher income; for the Marxists, the results are not so benign. We might even ask how much it matters if those bearing the majority of the costs today will be better off in the *long run*. When confronted with a similar situation many years ago, J. M. Keynes replied that in the long run no one benefits. With this in mind, what are the ramifications of all these changes for class inequality in the United States?

PATTERNS IN CLASS INEQUALITY

Income

As we mentioned in Chapter 5, differences in income, wealth, and poverty are central indicators of class stratification. How, then, have the structural shifts—from manufacturing to services and changes within the manufacturing and service sectors—affected class stratification in the United States? In general, the nature of these shifts has

contributed to a widening in the income gap in the United States, which many suggest is wider today than at any time since the Great Depression. Data from the Center on Budget and Policy Priorities and the Economic Policy Institute, for instance, indicate that the income gaps have widened in 45 states over the past 20 years (Bernstein et al. 2002). But not all have experienced declines in income. Professional, administrative, and technical workers have experienced the greatest returns for their labor as shown in Table 13.1.

While these data are consistent with the occupational shifts described above, they likely underestimate the earnings of professional workers, which often include bonuses and stock options. For instance, those in the top 5 percent of income earners saw their income increase the most after the 1970s. Part of this story is the often ignored issue of CEO compensation. During the 1990s, CEO compensation soared to unprecedented heights. Data from United for a Fair Economy (2001, 10) show that "if the minimum wage, which stood at $3.80 an hour in 1990, had grown at the same rate as CEO pay over the decade, it would now be $25.50 an hour [2001], rather than the current $5.15 an hour." According to *Business Week* (2004a), the pay gap between an average blue-collar salary and the CEO of a large company was 531-to-1 in 2000 and remained more than 300-to-1 in 2003 compared to 42-to-1 in 1982 (also Gill 2001). For the average blue-collar worker, wages did not keep up with inflation after the 1980s, which supports another finding: the severing of the historical link between rising productivity and rising median family income. Historically, the two tended to rise together, but from 1973 to 2003 median family income grew less than one-third as fast as productivity (Mishel, Bernstein, and Allegreto 2005).

Thus, it is not surprising that the median annual real income per worker *fell* from $25,896 in 1979 to $24,700 in 1995 (Table 13.1). By 2003, the average worker

Table 13.1 Changes in Hourly Wages by Selected Occupation (Males), 1973–2001 (2001 Dollars)

	1973	2001
White-collar occupations		
Managers	$22.08	$27.53
Professional	$22.12	$26.31
Technical	$18.80	$21.38
Other services	$12.49	$11.42
Blue-collar occupations		
Craft	$17.18	$16.21
Operatives	$13.47	$13.05
Laborers	$12.34	$10.75

Source: Mishel, Bernstein, and Schmitt (2001, 125).

was taking home $517 in the weekly paycheck; the average CEO collected $155,769 weekly. We might note that the average worker probably makes less than these figures suggest. According to the Economic Policy Institute, the hourly wage for (male) blue-collar workers as a group declined from $15.02 per hour in 1973 to $14.32 per hour (2001 dollars) in 2001 (Mishel, Bernstein, and Schmitt 2001, 125). Yet, for (male) laborers—a subcategory of blue-collar workers—the hourly wage declined from $12.34 to $10.75 (2001 dollars) during the same period. The hourly wage decline was even greater for those working at minimum wage (7 million adult workers in 2000), as Figure 13.2 shows.

The changes are reflected in the fact that by the year 2000 the average income for the top 1 percent of the population was 88.5 times that of the lowest 20 percent, an increase from 33 times since 1979 (Mishel, Bernstein, and Allegretto 2005).

The sum of these changes is reflected in income trends since the 1950s. To begin, data in Figure 13.3 indicate that as a nation we are much richer in terms of household income since the late 1960s. Compared with 1967, the first year for which household income statistics are available, real median household income is up 30 percent. Median income peaked in 1999, was unchanged in 2000, and declined over the next 2 years (Mishel, Bernstein, and Allegretto 2005).

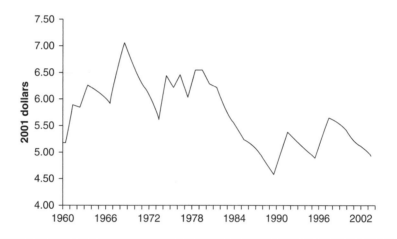

Figure 13.2   Real Value of the Minimum Wage (2001 Dollars), 1960–2002

Source: Mishel, Bernstein, and Boushey (2003, 197).

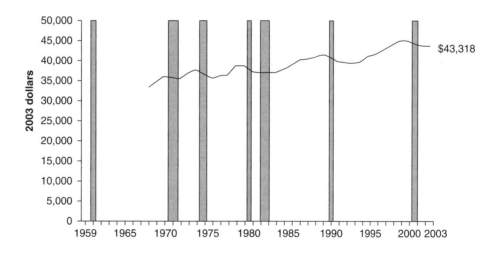

Figure 13.3   Changes in Real Median Household Income, 1967–2005

Source: DeNavas-Walt, Proctor, and Lee (2005, 3).

Note: The data points are placed at the midpoints of the respective years. Median household income data are not available before 1967.

If we look at changes within the aggregate data, a different picture emerges. Data in Tables 13.2 and 13.3 reveal a stark difference in the trends before 1970 and those after 1980—precisely the point at which the United States became more integrated into the global economy. Leading up to the 1970s, the data indicate a growing *equality* as the share of total income grew more rapidly for the lower and middle quintiles than for the top quintile. After 1979, however, the trend reversed itself as the share of total income going to the top quintile accelerated and growth dramatically slowed for the lower and middle quintiles. Overall, U.S. society has become *more unequal* since the late 1970s. In other words, the distribution of income reflects the polarization in the occupational structure—or the hourglass phenomenon—with growth in the low- and high-income quintiles and a shrinking in the middle.

Wealth

Wealth is a better indicator of inequality for the reasons we mentioned in Chapter 5 (e.g., links to power, opportunities to generate additional income, greater life chances, among others), Existing data on wealth reveal trends that are not unexpected. Recall that by *net worth* we are talking about total assets less any liabilities. Data in Table 13.4 and Figure 13.4 indicate the trend since the early 1980s. Note that in 1989 the bottom 20 percent of the U.S. population

actually had a *negative* net worth! Overall, however, we can see that by the late 1990s the top 1 percent of the U.S. population controlled almost 40 percent of the total assets of the United States, while 90 percent of the population shared 29 percent of the total assets. Has this changed since 1983? Yes: The top 1 percent has *increased* its control to 34 percent, while the bottom 90 percent of the population has *lost* 2.8 percent. Overall, the bottom 40 percent of the population suffered the greatest decline, which is precisely what we would expect given the changes in the U.S. economy since the end of the 1970s (see Domhoff 1998, 2002).

Finally, the data on income and wealth are suggestive of another, more hidden trend: the rapid growth of millionaires and billionaires in the United States. Between 1997 and 2005, the number of millionaires grew from 1,800,000 to 7,500,000, while in the 10 years after 1996, the number of billionaires increased from 179 to over 400 (Lynch Capgemini Consulting 2000, Figure 3; 2001; Christie 2005; *Forbes* 2006).

Poverty

As the number of millionaires and billionaires increased, so too did the number of children in poverty: up from 3.4 million in 1979 to 13 million in 2004 (Eitzen and Baca Zinn 2003, 182–183; Children's Defense Fund 2004). And 8.9 million of these children are in working families—an

Table 13.2 Change in Family Income by Quintile and the Top 5 Percent, 1947–1979

	Bottom 20%	Second 20%	Middle 20%	Fourth 20%	Top 20%	Top 20%
1979 Income range	Up to $9,861	$9,861-$16,215	$16,215–$22,972	$22,972–$31,632	$31,632 and up	$50,746 and up
1947-1979 Income change	+116%	+100%	+111%	+114%	+99%	+86%

Table 13.3 Change in Family Income by Quintile and the Top 5 Percent, 1979–2001

	Bottom 20%	Second 20%	Middle 20%	Fourth 20%	Top 20%	Top 5%
2001 Income range	Up to $24,000	$24,000-$41,127	$41,127–$62,500	$62,500–$94,150	$94,150 and up	$164,104 and up
1979-2001 Income change	+3%	+11%	+17%	+26%	+53%	+81%

Sources: Data for Tables 13.2 and 13.3 are from United for a Fair Economy, n.d.

Table 13.4   Distribution of Net Worth (by Population Segments—Quintiles)

Wealth Class	1983	1989	1992	1995	1998
Top 1%	33.8	37.4	37.2	38.5	38.1
Next 4%	22.3	21.6	22.8	21.8	21.3
Next 5%	12.1	11.6	11.8	11.5	11.5
Next 10%	13.1	13.0	12.0	12.1	12.5
Next 20%	12.6	12.3	11.5	11.4	11.9
Middle 20%	5.2	4.8	4.4	4.5	4.5
Bottom 40%	0.9	−0.7	0.4	0.2	0.2

Source: Wolff (2000).

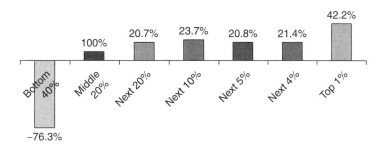

Figure 13.4   Change in Average Household Net Worth by Wealth Class, 1983–1998

Source: Wolff (2000: Table 3).

increase of 623,000 since 2001 (Children's Defense Fund 2004). Today, people under the age of 18 have the highest **poverty rate** of any age group, with one in six children in the United States living in poverty (DeNavas, Proctor, and Mills 2004). The point? When we discuss wealth and the rich, we imply that there are individuals who are not rich—the poor. The most common indicator of the *lack of wealth* is poverty.

What do we mean by poverty? We can think of poverty in two ways: relative and absolute. By **relative poverty**, we mean an individual's economic position relative to the prevailing living standards of the society. From this perspective, an individual may be able to buy her or his basic necessities (e.g., food, shelter, and clothing) but unable to maintain the *average standard of living* for members of that society. By **absolute poverty**, we mean that an individual lacks the minimal requirements to sustain a healthy existence (e.g., the basic necessities of food, clothing, and shelter). To reduce relative poverty, the gap between the wealthy and the poor must be reduced (the distributional question); to reduce absolute poverty, the income of the poorest needs to be raised above the poverty line—or the annual amount of income a family requires to meet its basic needs. Thus, it is

possible to have no absolute poverty with an extremely unequal distribution of income or high relative poverty.

In the United States, we use the absolute method, with the poverty line determined by the government and adjusted to reflect family size and annual inflations. We included data for the years 2000 and 2004 in Table 13.5 to give you an idea of what the poverty line looks like in the United States. By using the poverty line, we can identify the percentage of the population that is "officially" poor, or the poverty rate. Trend data for the poverty rate and the number of poor in the United States are provided in Figure 13.5. The data suggest two points. First, the trends in the poverty rate reflect changes in the distribution of income: poverty declined through the mid-1970s, began to increase until the mid-1990s, and once more began to increase after 2000. Second, the trend is consistent with the overall transformation of the U.S. economy within the context of globalization.

INEQUALITY AND POVERTY BY RACE AND ETHNICITY

How do race and ethnicity fit in here? In general, the data suggest patterns quite similar to the polarizing trends in the economy as a whole. Data on income in

Table 13.5 U.S. Poverty Thresholds by Family Size and Year

2000		*2004*	
Family Size (Persons)	*Poverty Threshold ($)*	*Family Size (Persons)*	*Poverty Threshold ($)*
1	8,794	1	9,645
2	11,239	2	12,334
3	13,739	3	15,067
4	17,603	4	19,307
5	20,819	5	22,831
6	23,528	6	25,788
7	26,754	7	29,236
8	29,701	8	32,641
9 or more	35,060	9 or more	39,048

Note: Poverty thresholds are used to calculate the poverty rate, while the Department of Health and Human Service's poverty guidelines are used to determine financial eligibility for certain programs. To compare the two, see the data at http://aspe.hhs.gov/poverty/04poverty.shtml.

Source: U.S. Bureau of the Census (2000; 2004).

Table 13.6 show that the income gap has increased across all racial groups relative to whites since 1983. Moreover, the gap grows even wider when we adjust income for wealth. The data for African Americans show a wealth gap with whites that is larger than the income gap; since 1983, both the mean wealth-adjusted income and income gaps have grown wider. Looking at the data for Latinos, there was a steep drop in wealth-adjusted income and income relative to whites from 1983 to 2001 (e.g., median wealth-adjusted income dropped from 0.61 to 0.50 and median income declined from 0.67 to 0.59). This may reflect the characteristics of Latino immigration during the 1980s and 1990s that, as we discuss in the next chapter, was driven by an insatiable need for low-wage labor. The outlier, at least initially, was the Asian population, which had a virtual parity with whites in wealth-adjusted income and money income in 1983. By 2001, however, the ratios slipped, with wealth-adjusted income declining to three-quarters and income dropping to 0.80 (median) and 0.85 (mean) compared to whites. Similar to the Latino population, one possible factor is the large Asian immigration and expansion of the Asian population in the intervening years.

Other evidence supports the data in Table 13.6. According to Mishel, Bernstein, and Allegreto (2005) and United for a Fair Economy (2006), the average income for white families has risen 34 percent since 1995 while

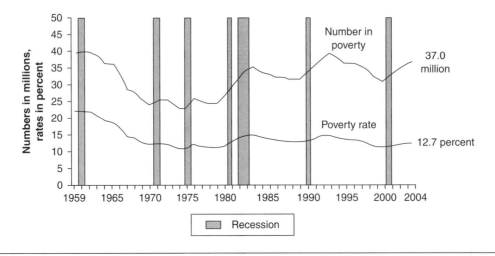

Figure 13.5 Number in Poverty and Poverty Rate, 1959–2004

Source: DeNavas-Walt, Proctor, and Lee (2005:13).

Note: The data points are placed at the midpoints of the respective years.

Table 13.6 Family Income by Racial and Ethnic Groups

	1983		1983 Ratio to whites		2001		2001 Ratio to whites	
	Median	*Mean*	*Median*	*Mean*	*Median*	*Mean*	*Median*	*Mean*
Non-Hispanic whites								
Income	38,540	51,658	1.00	1.00	43,586	72,860	1.00	1.00
Wealth-adjusted income[a]	42,243	62,013	1.00	1.00	52,591	97,108	1.00	1.00
African Americans								
Income	21,474	29,231	0.56	0.57	24,683	36,321	0.57	0.50
Wealth-adjusted income	22,324	31,093	0.53	0.50	25,714	39,356	0.49	0.41
Latinos								
Income	25,693	32,912	0.67	0.64	25,711	39,494	0.59	0.54
Wealth-adjusted income	25,719	34,523	0.61	0.56	26,365	41,709	0.50	0.43
Asian and other races								
Income	38,356	51,619	1.00	1.00	34,967	61,544	0.80	0.85
Wealth-adjusted income	40,156	55,303	0.95	0.89	38,508	75,514	0.73	0.78

Source: Wolff and Zacharias (2006).

[a] Money income minus property income (sum of dividends, interest, and rent) plus income from home and non-home wealth.

African American and Latino family income has risen 25 percent. Still, this masks the fact that African American and Latino families *lost* income between 2001 and 2003 at a rate faster than did white families: a negative 1.5 percent for African Americans and a negative 2.3 percent for Latinos compared to a negative 0.5 percent for whites. In terms of wealth, the median African American family saw no growth in net worth from 2001 to 2004; yet, mean African American net worth grew sharply, up 37 percent, reflecting growing inequality among African American families. In fact, income growth among the top 5 percent of African American families increased by 61 percent from 1979 to 2001, while the bottom 20 percent saw an increase of only 1 percent. Finally, poverty rates for African American and Latino families have remained roughly twice that of white families since the 1970s (in 2003 the rates were 24 percent, 22 percent, and 13.2 percent, respectively, according to U.S. Bureau of the Census data). For Asian families, poverty levels have been roughly on par with white families.

WORKING HOURS

Given the nature of the changes in the U.S. economy, inequality and poverty rates might have been even higher had the average U.S. worker not increased his or her working hours. By the year 1997, U.S. workers were logging the greatest number of hours of all industrialized nations, averaging 1,966 hours per year, *up* from 1,942 hours in

1990 (it was 1,978 in 2000). In comparison, the average Japanese worker—long known for working the longest hours—put in 1,899 hours per year in 1997, *down* from 2,031 in 1992, Comparative 1997 figures for Norway and Sweden are 1,399 and 1,522, respectively (ILO 2001).

Although U.S. Bureau of the Census interviews show that the average male worked 43.5 hours a week in 1970 and 43.1 hours a week in 2000 and the average female worked 37.1 hours in 1970 and 37.0 hours in 2000, these averages are misleading (Gerson and Jacobs 2004, 30). To begin, more workers are putting in over 50 hours per week and more workers are logging fewer than 30 hours per week. Additionally, today, when the dual-income family is the norm, we find that 60 percent of couples (parents and nonparents alike) work more than *80 hours* per week—compared to 71 hours in the United Kingdom and 69 hours in Sweden—and 12 percent of U.S. families work in excess of *100 hours* per week (Gerson and Jacobs 2004).

There are several immediate explanations for the changes in work hours. First, when faced with declining wages and insecure employment, workers must put in more hours (sometimes at multiple jobs) in order to survive economically. Second, while the average workweek for individuals has decreased, it has increased for couples as more women are working. For instance, in 1970, one-third of all married-couple families had two wage earners; by 2000, this had increased to two-thirds (Gerson and Jacobs 2004, 33). A third factor is that increasingly employers are expecting more hours, which is particularly true in the white-collar sector of the economy.

Average work hours in the professional service sector have steadily increased over time to the point that currently over 25 million Americans work more than 49 hours each week and some log a good deal more. Nearly 12 percent of the workforce (about 15 million people) report spending 49–59 hours weekly at the office, and 8.5 percent (11 million) spend 60 or more hours there (Fraser 2001). Here, we need to keep in mind the reorganization of the workplace we mentioned earlier, which has increased the workload and job spill for millions of workers. Most of these people are white-collar professionals—corporate managers, marketing staffers, investment bankers, office administrators, software designers, lawyers, editors, engineers, accountants, business consultants, and the secretaries, word processors, computer programmers, and back-office clerks who support their activities (Fraser 2001). Fraser (2001) argues that in some industries, among them the technology and financial services sectors, the norms—everyday expectations about just how much time people should spend at the office each day—have become so extreme that a 12-hour workday can seem "positively lightweight."

The Working and the New Poor

The trends in the income, wealth, and poverty data are consistent with what we would expect given the structural changes induced by globalization: the shedding of traditional manufacturing jobs, the growing numbers of both high-wage professional jobs and low-wage service and industrial jobs, and the reorganization of jobs and changes in requirements in both the service and industrial sectors. As firms continue to outsource, downsize, and introduce technology, they *directly* affect the number and type of jobs available in the United States and create a more polarized labor force. This is reflected in a growing number of working and **new poor** (Barrington 2000; Thurow 1987; Harrison and Bluestone 1988; Mishel and Bernstein 1993; Mishel, Bernstein, and Schmitt 2001).

Data, for instance, show that jobs in expanding occupations pay 21 percent less per year than jobs in contracting ones, suggesting links between globalization and the **working poor** (see Dobbs 2004a, Ettinger and Chapman 2004). The official definition of *working poor* is anyone working 27 weeks per year who falls below the poverty line. Moreover, 22 percent of jobs in the United States were in occupations that paid below the poverty level in 2000 (U.S. Department of Labor 2004). In the states of Alabama, Arkansas, Florida, Louisiana, Mississippi, Montana, New Mexico, North Dakota, Oklahoma, South Dakota, West

Virginia, and Wyoming, more than 30 percent of the jobs were in occupations that paid below the poverty level in 2002 (AECF 2004). Not surprisingly, 7.4 million of the 34.6 million persons officially defined as poor in 2002 were classified as the working poor (about 560,000 more than in 2001), according to the U.S. Department of Labor (2004). Of these 7.4 million workers, 29.3 percent worked in the service sector; yet, only 2 percent of those in such service occupations as managers and professionals were classified as working poor. Even more troubling is the fact that 11.5 percent of the poor worked *full time and year round* in 2004—9.4 million compared to 7.7 percent in 1978 (U.S. Bureau of the Census 2006).

If we break down these numbers by race and ethnicity, we find that 30.4 percent of black workers and 39.8 percent of Hispanic workers earned poverty-level wages in 2003 (Mishel, Bernstein, and Allegreto 2005). As a result, we find that African Americans and Latinos are heavily represented among the working poor: 10.5 percent of African Americans and 10.4 percent of Latinos were classified as working poor compared to 4.5 percent of whites and 4.6 percent of Asians (U.S. Bureau of Labor Statistics 2004). Consistent with the overall changes in the economy—and leaving aside issues of discrimination—we find fewer African American and Latino workers among the poor and working poor as we move up the educational ladder or into managerial, professional, and related occupations (U.S. Bureau of Labor Statistics, 2004).

Many of these workers are also categorized as part of the new poor—or those people displaced by new technologies or mass layoffs and plant closings who have difficulty moving out of poverty. The poor of previous generations had hopes and opportunities to experience upward social mobility, but the new poor are not so fortunate. About 15 percent of the "tens of millions of Americans" who have lost their jobs in the past two decades because of these changes could not find employment (Eitzen and Baca Zinn 2003, 188). A related category of the working and new poor are displaced older workers (see Helyar 2005). Between 1970 and 1998, for instance, the **labor-force participation** of men aged 55–65 declined from about 79 percent to roughly 70 percent (Carnoy 2000, 28). More recent evidence suggests that globalization via increasing competition and the use of technology is also rapidly affecting younger workers—those over 40 (Fraser 2001; Helyar 2005).

Looking once more at the software industry, 5 years after finishing college, about 60 percent of computer science graduates are working as programmers; at 15 years, the figure drops to 34 percent, and at 20 years—when most are still only age 42 or so—it is down to 19 percent (Fraser 2001, 139). "Older" workers in the software industry suffer longer bouts of unemployment when laid off, where each additional year of a "mid-career" programmer (mid-forties) seeking a new job translates to three additional weeks of unemployment (Fraser 2001, 137). The employment trend is toward new and recent college graduates who command less salary, cost less in terms of benefits, and are more likely to work large amounts of unpaid overtime. Changing technology raises skill requirements, which younger workers are more likely to have; and because training and retraining costs are high, employers tend to shun poorly educated workers, especially older workers. Although this argument is not new, a study by William Baumol and Edward Wolff (quoted in Koretz 1999) shows a positive correlation between the lengthening of jobless spells and research and development outlays and spending on computers per employee. The most significant factor for longer jobless spells for older workers is the increase in computer outlays (Koretz 1999).

A VIEW FROM THE BOTTOM: INSECURITY AND VULNERABILITY

The direct effects of globalization are clearly evident in increased income and wealth inequality, which alter the well-being of individuals and families in the United States and across the globe. We need to keep in mind that the consequences of our class position, as Beth Shulman (2003) argues, are "about more than money" and affect our life chances—where we live, what we eat, the type of health care and schools we can afford for our children, and our access to transportation. Within the context of tighter, more competitive global labor markets, U.S. workers find themselves in jobs that are increasingly competitive, demanding, and insecure.

The need for employer flexibility, as we noted, is closely connected to these outcomes. Yet, in what might be called the "workplace paradox," most employees work in jobs characterized by *inflexibility*; employers want the flexibility to determine when, where, and how their employees will work, without the state or labor unions regulating employee-employer relations. Yet, among low-wage workers, only 13 percent are able to adjust their start and finish time at work when necessary (Galinsky and Bond, forthcoming). In these cases, any delay in getting to work—even 5 minutes—can result in disciplinary action, a cut in pay, or dismissal. Employers typically do not hesitate to rid themselves of workers in such cases, especially those in low-wage jobs in which

employers have invested little time or money in such things as worker training. In 1996, for instance, 53.5 million workers—40 percent of the total labor force—worked in jobs that required only short-term on-the-job training (Silvestri 1997). Similarly, if jobs require little skill and workers are quickly and easily available, employers will not think twice about replacing workers.

Moreover, the impact of declining union power on workers, their families, and communities cannot be overstated, especially for those at the lower end of the wage spectrum (Card 1998). Some estimate, for instance, that unions increase wages for workers at the lower-wage sectors of the economy as much as 30 percent and a unionized high school graduate earns 21 percent more than the equivalent nonunion worker. When other types of compensation ensured by unions are considered, however, the total compensation is much higher (Mishel, Bernstein, and Schmitt 2001). Health-care insurance coverage, for example, is 35 percent higher in union than nonunion establishments (Belman and Heywood 1991, Fosu 1993).

These data are particularly meaningful when analyzed within the changing context of work. Unionized employees are also more likely to have retirement plans and to gain access to worker protections such as wage and work-hour guarantees, promotional procedures, due process in firings and layoffs, and unemployment insurance (Freeman 1980, Belman and Heywood 1991, Fosu 1993, Budd and McCall 2004, U.S. GAO 2000). Such benefits provide short- and long-term security for workers and their families. Without such benefits, the prolonged illness (or injury) of a family member, a bout of unemployment (even a temporary one), or the reduction of work hours can be devastating.

Particularly vulnerable are those who have little savings or economic assets (wealth) to fall back on. Personal savings in the United States have declined drastically from 10 percent of personal disposable income in 1980 to 2 percent in 2003 (U.S. Bureau of Economic Analysis 2004). A Gallup survey conducted in 2003 reported that four in ten Americans say they could survive without a job for only about a month before "experiencing significant financial hardship" (Jacobe 2005). For families of color the savings rate is even more problematic, with more than twice as many African American households (30.9 percent) as white households (13.1 percent) having zero or negative net worth in 2001. In fact, while nearly three-quarters of whites owned their homes, less than half of African American or Latinos were homeowners in 2003—white, 72 percent; African American, 48 percent; Latino, 46.7 percent (Mishel, Bernstein, and Allegretto 2005).

Related to this, consumer debt has been steadily rising since 1970 (Board of Governors of the Federal Reserve System 2003). As one might expect, the debt burden is highest for those at the lower end of the income hierarchy. In 1998, for example, the debt burden was highest for those families earning less than $10,000 a year and the next highest debt burden was typically carried by families with incomes between $25,000 and $49,999. This growing burden of debt means increasing financial insecurity for most households, particularly families of color (Mishel, Bernstein, and Allegreto 2005). Personal bankruptcies shot up from 330,000 in 1980 to 1.4 million in 1990 (Henwood 1999) and in 2002 hit a record of over 1.5 million (Redmond 2003).

As more and more working individuals and families struggle to balance their responsibilities on the job and at home, people are working longer hours and multiple jobs to offset what have been reductions in pay and benefits. The effects of these changes on the family are particularly ominous. Carnoy (2000) argues that these changes are a major reason that young adults are increasingly unwilling to enter serious relationships until late in their twenties. Marriage remains a goal of most young adults, but they are waiting to get married and, once married, delay having children (Carnoy 2000). One result is an increasing number of families that care for not only young children (and young adults) but older parents or relatives as well. Yet, these may be the fortunate families; families lacking "built-in child care" must often patch together child care in ways that leave parents anxious and may potentially put their children in jeopardy (Presser 2003, Han 2005).

Faced with such challenges, parents adopt a variety of strategies to ensure economic survival and to provide for the health and well-being of their families. As we noted above, there has been a steady increase not only in the average number of individual work hours but also in the number of hours worked by all family members since the 1970s (Bernstein and Kornbluh 2004, Gerson and Jacobs 2004). While such strategies increase family wages, the day-to-day lives of individuals and their families often suffer. More than one-quarter of working women, including mothers, for example, spend at least some of their nights and weekends at work, and nearly half of all women who are married or living with someone work different schedules from their spouses or partners (AFL-CIO n.d.b).

The stress effects of such work arrangements on marital relationships can undermine otherwise healthy relationships (Rubin 1995). As couples struggle to juggle money, time, and child care, they have less quality time together, less leisure time, fewer meaningful conversations, and engage in fewer, if any, social or community activities. Combine this with the finding that 40 percent of U.S. workers describe their jobs as "very" or "extremely" stressful and we have a recipe for disaster. Living under these conditions takes a toll on workers' health and day-to-day family lives. The National Institute for Occupational Safety and Health, for instance, records that self-reported "stressed" employees incur health-care costs that are 46 percent higher—an average of $600 more per person per year—than employees who are not stressed (Healy 2005). For children, rising stress levels are even more hazardous. According to research from the Children's Defense Fund (2005), children who live in families with annual incomes less than $15,000 are 22 times more likely to be abused or neglected than children living in families with annual incomes of $30,000 or more. The culprit, according to the research? Stress. There is a great deal more stress in lower-income families.

What does this mean for the family? Clearly, the family is changing, and trying to manage a complex matrix of work, personal, and family lives can have devastating effects on mental and physical health. As market forces unleashed by the policies that have been instituted since the crisis of the 1970s continue to individualize and atomize our society, workers and families increasingly confront these market forces alone. How we respond to the heightened vulnerability and insecurity will determine the future health of our families as well as that of our communities.

Conclusion

In this chapter, we have examined how the economic changes in the United States have affected class stratification. As the global economic environment becomes more competitive and unions become less central to the lives of U.S. workers, the U.S. economy and occupational categories have been dramatically transformed. Contrary to the predictions of neoliberal globalists, however, globalization has *increased* the share of lower-wage employment in the United States, not decreased it. Globalization has created conditions of *greater* insecurity, not less. Globalization has *widened* the margin of inequality, not narrowed it. African American, Latino, and white families structurally located in the blue-collar sector have been particularly hard hit by the transformations, which involved the outsourcing of good-paying manufacturing jobs and a corresponding decline in wages. Still, few workers have been immune to these changes. Middle-class and professional workers also saw many of their jobs disappear or take on qualities that left less money and time for themselves and their families. For the poor and working poor, globalization has transformed them into our society's major philanthropists, greasing the wheels of economic growth by cleaning the rooms of the globe-trotting capitalists, delivering the food to the Wall Streeters burning the midnight oil, and neglecting their own children to care for the children of others (see Ehrenreich 2001).

Globalization has not created the conditions for widespread upward social mobility (or even those needed to get out of debt!). Not only have U.S. workers been increasingly *substituted* with low-paid labor in developing countries (outsourcing) and/or by technological advancements but the jobs that remain in the United States require workers to be flexible, competitive, and educated. The irony is that the demand for a *flexible* labor force has resulted in a tremendous *inflexibility and insecurity* for workers at all levels of the occupational hierarchy.

In the end, all workers are confronting heavier demands on their time, their money, and their other resources (medical care, unemployment benefits, etc.). What does this mean for the future of our communities and our society when we have less time for our families and communities and fewer opportunities to acquire the requisite skills to improve our positions in the global labor market? What does it mean for our society when the middle and upper classes ignore or are too economically insecure to care about the poor and working poor? How might we reverse these trends? These questions have taken on a renewed sense of urgency as the globalization of the U.S. economy continues under a political and ideological framework that deifies individualism and markets.

Discussion Questions

1. Explain the impact of globalization on U.S. manufacturing and service sectors.

   Manufacturing: Hardest hit by globalization, employment has declined, workers experienced mass layoffs (the result of operational restructuring, outsourcing).

   Service: Increase in the number of low paying jobs; decrease in high paying professional, managerial, and technical sectors and middle range service jobs; offshore outsourcing.

2. How have these labor and occupational shifts affected class stratification? Review the evidence in the following areas: income, wealth, and poverty. How does this vary among racial and ethnic groups?

   Overall, globalization has not delivered on its promise to increase income and wealth across the board. Income and wealth are increasingly concentrated among a small proportion of the population. While the number of millionaires and billionaires has increased, so too has the number of children in poverty. In the United States, the income gap across all racial groups relative to whites has increased; poverty rates for African Americans and Latinos have remained roughly twice the rate of white families.

CHAPTER 14

21st Century Slaves

Andrew Cockburn (2003)

Though we tend to think of slavery as a thing of the past, Andrew Cockburn documents the extent of "debt slavery" that exists throughout the world today. Many are lured into debt slavery with the expectation of a better life, leaving them exposed to victimization and cruelty at the hands of slave traffickers and employers. Cockburn analyzes the reasons for the upsurge in this increasingly profitable industry.

The headline below is not a metaphor. This story is about slaves. Not people 200 years ago. It's about 27 million people worldwide who are bought and sold, held captive, brutalized, exploited for profit. It's about 21ST CENTURY SLAVES.

Sherwood Castle, headquarters to Milorad Milakovic, the former railway official who rose to become a notorious slave trafficker in Bosnia, looms beside the main road just outside the northwest Bosnian town of Prijedor. Under stucco battlements, the entrance is guarded by well-muscled, heavily tattooed young men, while off to one side Milakovic's trio of pet Siberian tigers prowl their caged compound.

I arrived there alone one gray spring morning—alone because no local guide or translator dared accompany me—and found my burly 54-year-old host waiting for me at a table set for lunch beside a glassed-in aquamarine swimming pool.

The master of Sherwood has never been shy about his business. He once asked a dauntless human rights activist who has publicly detailed his record of buying women for his brothels in Prijedor: "Is it a crime to sell women? They sell footballers, don't they?"

Milakovic threatened to kill the activist for her outspokenness, but to me he sang a softer tune. Over a poolside luncheon of seafood salad and steak, we discussed the stream of young women fleeing the shattered economies of their home countries in the former Soviet bloc. Milakovic said he was eager to promote his scheme to legalize prostitution in Bosnia—"to stop the selling of people, because each of those girls is someone's child."

One such child is a nearsighted, chain-smoking blonde named Victoria, at 20 a veteran of the international slave trade. For three years of her life she was among the estimated 27 million men, women, and children in the world who are enslaved—physically confined or restrained and forced to work, or controlled through violence, or in some way treated as property.

Victoria's odyssey began when she was 17, fresh out of school in Chisinau, the decayed capital of the former Soviet republic of Moldova. "There was no work, no money," she explained simply. So when a friend—"at least I thought he was a friend"—suggested he could help her get a job in a factory in Turkey, she jumped at the idea and took up his offer to drive her there, through Romania. "But when I realized we had driven west, to the border with Serbia, I knew something was wrong."

It was too late. At the border she was handed over to a group of Serb men, who produced a new passport saying she was 18. They led her on foot into Serbia and raped her, telling her that she would be killed if she resisted. Then they sent her under guard to Bosnia, the

Balkan republic being rebuilt under a torrent of international aid after its years of genocidal civil war.

Victoria was now a piece of property and, as such, was bought and sold by different brothel owners ten times over the next two years for an average price of $1,500. Finally, four months pregnant and fearful of a forced abortion, she escaped. I found her hiding in the Bosnian city of Mostar, sheltered by a group of Bosnian women.

In a soft monotone she recited the names of clubs and bars in various towns where she had to dance semi-naked, look cheerful, and have sex with any customer who wanted her for the price of a few packs of cigarettes. "The clubs were all awful, although the Artemdia, in Banja Luka, was the worst—all the customers were cops," she recalled.

Victoria was a debt slave. Payment for her services went straight to her owner of the moment to cover her "debt"—the amount he had paid to buy her from her previous owner. She was held in servitude unless or until the money she owed to whomever controlled her had been recovered, at which point she would be sold again and would begin to work off the purchase price paid by her new owner. Although slavery in its traditional form survives in many parts of the world, debt slavery of this kind, with variations, is the most common form of servitude today.

According to Milorad Milakovic, such a system is perfectly aboveboard. "There is the problem of expense in bringing a girl here," he had explained to me. "The plane, transport, hotels along the way, as well as food. That girl must work to get that money back."

In November 2000 the UN-sponsored International Police Task Force (IPTF) raided Milakovic's nightclub-brothels in Prijedor, liberating 34 young women who told stories of servitude similar to Victoria's. "We had to dance, drink a lot, and go to our rooms with anyone," said one. "We were eating once a day and sleeping five to six hours. If we would not do what we were told, guards would beat us."

Following the IPTF raids, Milakovic complained to the press that the now liberated women had cost a lot of money to buy, that he would have to buy more, and that he wanted compensation. He also spoke openly about the cozy relations he had enjoyed with the IPTF peacekeepers, many of whom had been his customers.

But there were no influential friends to protect him in May this year, when local police finally raided Sherwood Castle and arrested Milakovic for trafficking in humans and possessing slaves.

We think of slavery as something that is over and done with, and our images of it tend to be grounded in the 19th century: black field hands in chains. "In those days slavery thrived on a shortage of person power," explains Mike Dottridge, former director of Anti-Slavery International, founded in 1839 to carry on the campaign that had already abolished slavery in the British Empire. The average slave in 1850, according to the research of slavery expert Kevin Bales, sold for around $40,000 in today's money.

I visited Dottridge at the organization's headquarters in a small building in Stockwell, a non-descript district in south London. "Back then," said Dottridge, "black people were kidnapped and forced to work as slaves. Today vulnerable people are lured into debt slavery in the expectation of a better life. There are so many of them because there are so many desperate people in the world."

The offices are festooned with images of contemporary slavery—forced labor in West Africa, five- and six-year-old Pakistani children delivered to the Persian Gulf to serve as jockeys on racing camels, Thai child prostitutes. File cabinets bulge with reports: Brazilian slave gangs hacking at the Amazon rain forest to make charcoal for the steel industry, farm laborers in India bound to landlords by debt they have inherited from their parents and will pass on to their children.

The buying and selling of people is a profitable business because, while globalization has made it easier to move goods and money around the world, people who want to move to where jobs are face ever more stringent restrictions on legal migration.

Almost invariably those who cannot migrate legally or pay fees up front to be smuggled across borders end up in the hands of trafficking mafias. "Alien smuggling [bringing in illegal aliens who then find paying jobs] and human trafficking [where people end up enslaved or sold by the traffickers] operate exactly the same way, using the same routes," said a veteran field agent from the U.S. Immigration and Naturalization Service (INS). "The only difference is what happens to people at the other end." As the fees people must pay for transport rise in step with tightening border controls, illegal immigrants are ever more likely to end up in debt to the traffickers who have moved them—and are forced to work off their obligations as slaves.

It's dangerous for outsiders to show too close an interest in how these trafficking mafias work (a point that had occurred to me at Sherwood Castle), but in Athens I found a man who has made the study of slave trafficking his specialty and lives to tell the tale.

In 1990 Grigoris Lazos, a sociology professor at Panteion University, embarked on what he thought would be straightforward research on prostitution in Greece. Bright and intense, he resolved to go straight to the source, the prostitutes themselves. Through them he eventually made contact with the people who had enslaved them. Over the course of a decade—and in the face of intense disapproval from his professional colleagues—Lazos gained access to trafficking operations from the inside and was able to paint a clear picture of the interplay between prostitution and slavery in his country.

"You should note the difference between a small trafficking gang and a large network, which uses the Internet and bank accounts," he said. "Any bar owner or group of bar owners in Greece can send someone up to southern Bulgaria to buy women for cash. The cost of a girl in that area is $1,000, or, if you negotiate, you might be able to get two for $1,000. Best to try on a Monday for cheap prices, because most trafficking happens at the weekends. Mondays are slow, so you can get the leftovers."

"A network on the other hand," he continued, "has the ability to bargain and complete financial transactions from a distance. Simply call Moscow, ask for women, and they will be sent to Romania and from there on through Bulgaria to Greece. The parties don't even have to know each other. The importer simply says, 'I want so-and-so many first quality women, so-and-so many second quality, so-and-so many third quality.'"

Flicking through his exhaustive files, the professor rattled off the cold data of human trade. "Between 1990 and 2000 the total amount earned in Greece from trafficked women, that is to say those who were forced into this kind of prostitution, was 5.5 billion dollars. Voluntary prostitutes, those who were working of their own accord and are mostly Greek women, earned 1.5 billion dollars."

The efficiency and scope of the Greek traffickers' operations studied by Lazos are by no means unique. In Trieste, the gateway from the Balkans into northern Italy, investigators from the local anti-mafia commission tracked the activities of Josip Loncaric, a former taxi driver from Zagreb, Croatia.

By the time Loncaric was finally arrested in 2000 he owned airlines in Albania and Macedonia and was involved in moving thousands of people destined for work not only in prostitution but in any menial task requiring cheap labor in the prosperous world of the European Union. His Chinese wife, who was also his business partner, provided a link to criminal Chinese triads with which Loncaric did profitable business smuggling Chinese as well as Kurds, Iraqis, Iranians, and any other afflicted people willing to mortgage themselves in hopes of a better future. Many of Loncaric's Chinese victims found themselves locked up and forced to work 18 hours a day in restaurants or in the famous Italian leather workshops.

Trafficking mafias and smugglers, in the last decade of the 20th century, brought 35,000 people a year into Western Europe through the Trieste area, guiding them at night through the rugged mountains and forests straddling the border with Slovenia. But this is only one of many funnels between poor worlds and rich ones. Thousands of miles away I found another flood of migrants fleeing Central America on their way to El Norte, the United States, where they could ultimately become slaves.

These migrants' homes were ravaged by the wars of the 1980s and '90s and reduced to further ruin by a succession of natural and manmade disasters. Hurricane Mitch pounded Honduras and Nicaragua in 1998; afterward the number of homeless street children in Central America jumped by 20 percent. El Salvador was hit by a 7.6 earthquake in 2001. Large parts of the region have been without rain for the past three years, and the world price of coffee has crashed, ruining the Central American coffee industry and leaving 600,000 workers unemployed. In Guatemala more than half a million coffee workers face starvation.

Many economists argue that the North American Free Trade Agreement has made its own contribution to the flood of people trying to move north, maintaining that cheap U.S. corn imported into Mexico has effectively driven millions of Mexican peasant corn farmers out of business and off the land. They suggest that for every ton of corn imported into Mexico, two Mexicans migrate to the U.S.

The tiny Guatemalan town of Tecún Umán lies on the bank of the Suchiate River. Here migrants from Central America gather to cross into Mexico on their way north. Those with valid travel documents for Mexico cross the bridge over the river; those without them pay a few cents to be ferried across on rafts made from tractor inner tubes.

No matter where they come from, a great majority of migrants arrive in Tecún Umán penniless, easy prey for the local hoteliers, bar owners, and people smugglers—known as coyotes—who live off the flow of humanity. It is a town where, in the words of one former resident, "everything and everyone is for sale."

Some of the luckier migrants find a temporary safe haven at Casa del Migrante, a walled compound just a few yards from the muddy riverbank. "Every day, morning and night, I give a speech here," says the Casa's director, Father Ademar Barilli, a Brazilian Jesuit who remains surprisingly buoyant despite the surrounding misery. "I talk about the dangers of the trip north and urge them to go back. It's a bad choice to go home, but a worse one to try to go on to the U.S."

Barilli warns migrants about the bosses in Mexico who may take their precious documents and force them into slavery on remote plantations. He tells them about the brothels in Tapachula, the Mexican town across the river, where girls are forced into prostitution. Most, remembering the misery they have left behind, disregard his warnings. As Adriana, a 14-year-old prostitute in a Tapachula bar, exclaimed when asked if she would consider going home to Honduras: "No, there you die of hunger!"

Despite Barilli and Casa del Migrante, Tecún Umán itself is hardly safe. The week before I arrived, a dead coyote had been dumped just outside the gates of the compound with a hundred bullets in his body. "People are killed here because of the traffic in people and babies. There are many mafias involved in the business of this town. Aquí uno no sale en la noche—Here you don't go out at night," Barilli said.

As I calculated the amount of daylight left, Barilli explained what local bar owners say to girls from the buses that roll in every day from the south. "They talk about a job working in a restaurant. But the job is in a bar. After the girl has worked for a while just serving drinks, the owner denounces her to the police and gets her arrested because she has no documents. She is jailed; he bails her out. Then he tells her she is in his debt and must work as a prostitute. The debt never ends, so the girl is a slave."

Barilli cited a recent case involving a bar named La Taverna on the highway out of town. The owner, a woman, had duped six girls in this fashion. "Some of them got pregnant, and she sold the babies," he said. Thanks partly to the efforts of a Casa del Migrante lay worker (who afterward went into hiding in response to a flood of very credible death threats), the bar owner was finally arrested and jailed.

Stepped-up security in the wake of 9/11 has made the major obstacle on the road from the south, the border between Mexico and the U.S., more difficult than ever to clear. With heightened control has come a commensurate increase in the price charged by smuggling gangs to take people across: up from an average of about $1,000 a person to $2,000. Survivors of the journey arrive deeply indebted and vulnerable to slavers.

In Immokalee, Florida, I sat in a room full of men and women with the same Maya features I had last seen on the faces of the people in Tecún Umán. Almost all of them were farm laborers, toiling on Florida's vast plantations to pick fruit and vegetables consumed all over the U.S. They were meeting at the headquarters of a farm-worker organization, the Coalition of Immokalee Workers (CIW), to discuss ways of improving conditions in their ill-paid occupation. When the rapid-fire Spanish conversation died away, an elderly man picked up a guitar and began to sing about Juan Munoz, who left Campeche, Mexico, "to seek his fortune in the U.S." but ended up in Lake Placid, Florida, working "as a slave" for a cruel boss who stole all his money.

Blues singers composed similar laments about the miseries of plantation life in the Old South, and we think of those songs as part of our heritage. But this song was not about the past. Juan Muñoz is a real person, a 32-year-old who left his small farm in Campeche because he couldn't earn enough money to feed his family. He made his way across the border to Marana, Arizona, where a coyote promised him a ride all the way to a job picking oranges in Florida. The ride cost $1,000, which Muñoz was told he could pay off over time. On arrival he found he had in fact joined the modern slave economy.

Highway 27 runs through citrus country in the heart of Florida, which supplies 80 percent of U.S. orange juice. The pickers in the fields that line the highway are overwhelmingly immigrants, many undocumented and all poor. They earn an average $7,500 a year for work that is hard and unhealthy, toiling for bosses who contract with growers to supply crews to pick crops. The law generally leaves these people alone so long as they stick to low-paid but necessary work in the fields.

Sweatshop conditions in the fields are almost inevitable, since the corporations that buy the crops have the power to keep the prices they pay low, thus ensuring that wages paid by harvesting companies to pickers stay low too. These conditions lead to a high turnover in the workforce, since anyone with a prospect of alternative work swiftly moves on. Hence the appeal to crew bosses of debt-slave crews, whose stability and docility are assured. That is how Juan Muñoz found himself held captive along with at least 700 others in the well-guarded camps operated by the Ramos family in and around the little town of Lake Placid.

"They had almost all been picked up in Arizona by coyotes who offered to take them to Florida and then sold them to the crew bosses," says Romeo Ramirez, a 21-year-old Guatemalan who went undercover to investigate the Ramoses' operation on behalf of the CIW.

Captives in eight camps in and around Lake Placid were living "four to a room, which stank, sleeping on box springs." Not surprisingly, the workers were terrified of their bosses. "People knew they would be beaten for trying to get away," said Ramirez, citing the rumor about one would-be escapee who "had his knees busted with a hammer and then was thrown out of a car moving 60 miles an hour."

"The workers were paid by the growers every Friday," Ramirez continued, "but then they would all be herded to the Ramoses' stores in Lake Placid and forced to sign over their checks. By the time they had paid for rent and food, their debt was as high as ever." One such store, Natalie's Boutique, is a block from the police station.

In April 2001 a team from the CIW helped four of the captive laborers, including Muñoz, to make a break. Spurred to action by the unequivocal testimony of the escapees, the FBI and INS mounted a raid—although the prominent "INS Deportation Service" sign on the side of the bus accompanying the raiding party gave the crew bosses enough warning to send the workers out into the orange groves around Lake Placid to hide. Nevertheless, the brothers Ramiro and Juan Ramos, along with their cousin José Luis Ramos, were eventually charged with trafficking in slaves, extortion, and possession of firearms. In June 2002 the three Ramoses were convicted on all counts and received prison sentences totaling 34 years and 9 months.

This 21st-century slave operation may have been ignored by the Ramoses' corporate clients; and federal agencies may have been slow to react to prodding by the CIW. But the slave crews were hardly out of sight. The main camp in which the Ramoses confined their victims was just on the edge of town right beside a Ramada Inn. On the other side of the compound a gated community, Lakefront Estates, offered a restful environment for seniors.

"The slaves in Lake Placid were invisible, part of our economy that exists in a parallel universe," points out Laura Germino of the CIW. "People were playing golf at the retirement community, and right behind them was a slave camp. Two worlds, speaking different languages."

The Ramos case was in fact the fifth case of agricultural slavery exposed in Florida in the past six years. All came to light thanks to the CIW, which is currently promoting a boycott of fast-food giant Taco Bell on behalf of tomato pickers. The corporation boasts of its efforts to protect animal welfare in its suppliers' operations. Corporate officials also say they demand compliance with labor laws, but point out that since they cannot monitor suppliers' labor practices continually they rely on law enforcement to ensure compliance.

Slavery and slave trafficking in the U.S. today extend far beyond farm country into almost every area of the economy where cheap labor is at a premium. In 1995 more than 70 Thai women were rescued after laboring for years behind barbed wire in the Los Angeles suburb of El Monte, making clothes for major retailers while federal and state law enforcement repeatedly failed to obtain a proper warrant to search the premises. In June 2001

federal agents in Yakima, Washington, arrested the owners of an ice-cream vending company and charged them with using Mexican slaves, working to pay off transportation debts, to sell ice cream on city streets. According to Kevin Bales, there are between 100,000 and 150,000 slaves in the U.S. today.

The Department of State puts the number of people trafficked into the U.S. every year at close to 20,000. Many end up as prostitutes or farm laborers. Some work in nursing homes. Others suffer their servitude alone, domestic slaves confined to private homes.

The passage by Congress in 2000 of the Victims of Trafficking and Violence Protection Act, which protects such slaves against deportation if they testify against their former owners, perhaps has helped dispel some fearfulness. The growth of organizations ready to give help, like the CIW or the Coalition to Abolish Slavery and Trafficking, a southern California group that has assisted more than 200 trafficked people, means that victims are not alone. Public scrutiny in general is rising.

Still, such captives the world over are mostly helpless. They are threatened; they live in fear of deportation; they are cut off from any source of advice or support because they cannot communicate with the outside world. And the harsh fact remains that this parallel universe, as Laura Germino called it, can be a very profitable place to do business. Before sentencing the Ramoses, U.S. District Court Judge K. Michael Moore ordered the confiscation of three million dollars the brothers had earned from their operation, as well as extensive real estate and other property.

Moore also pointed a finger at the agribusiness corporations that hired the Ramoses' picking crews. "It seems," he said, "that there are others at another level in this system of fruit picking—at a higher level—that to some extent are complicit in one way or another in how these activities occur."

A former slave named Julia Gabriel, now a landscape gardener in Florida and a member of CIW, remembers her arrival in the U.S. from Guatemala at the age of 19. She picked cucumbers under armed guard in South Carolina for 12 to 14 hours a day; she saw fellow captives pistol-whipped into unconsciousness. "Maybe this is normal in the U.S.," she thought. Then a friend told her, "no, this is not normal here," so Gabriel found the courage to escape.

"This is meant to be the country to which people come fleeing servitude, not to be cast into servitude when they are here," says Attorney General John Ashcroft. But some historians argue that the infamous trans-Atlantic slave trade that shipped millions of Africans to the New World was abolished only when it had outlived its economic usefulness. Now slave traders from Sherwood Castle to sunny Florida—and at hundreds of points in between—have rediscovered the profitability of buying and selling human beings. Which means that, in the 21st century, slavery is far from gone.

Discussion Questions

1. What are the differences between 19th and 21st century slavery?

   In the 19th century, people were kidnapped and forced to work as slaves. In the 21st century, people are lured into slavery with the expectation of a better life. There is no shortage of slaves, as "there are so many desperate people in the world."

2. What has contributed to the increase in human trafficking? What has been done to reduce it?

   Although globalization has made it easier to move goods and money around the globe, moving people has been made more difficult under increasing governmental regulations and restrictions. Those who are unable to migrate legally or pay fees to border smugglers end up indebted to trafficking mafias. In 2000, the U.S. Congress passed the Victims of Trafficking and Violence Prevention Act, which protects slaves against deportation if they testify again their former owners.

Source: From Cockburn, A. (2003, September). 21st century slaves. *National Geographic, 204*(3), 2. Reprinted by permission of National Geographic Society.

CHAPTER 15

"Aqui estamos y no nos vamos!"

Global Capital and Immigrant Rights

William Robinson (2006)

> Many argue that the recent mass demonstrations by Latino immigrants and their supporters represent a "new civil rights movement." William Robinson, however, argues that these demonstrations move far beyond this by challenging the structural changes bound up with global capitalism. He discusses how such demonstrations represent one of the many ways that the "global working class" is beginning to fight back against capitalist globalization.

A spectre is haunting global capitalism—the spectre of a transnational immigrant workers' uprising. An immigrant rights movement is spreading around the world, spearheaded by Latino immigrants in the US, who have launched an all-out fight-back against the repression, exploitation and racism they routinely face with a series of unparalleled strikes and demonstrations. The immediate message of immigrants and their allies in the United States is clear, with marchers shouting: *"aqui estamos y no nos vamos!"* (we're here and we're not leaving!). However, beyond immediate demands, the emerging movement challenges the very structural changes bound up with capitalist globalisation that have generated an upsurge in global labour migration, thrown up a new global working class, and placed that working class in increasingly direct confrontation with transnational capital.

The US mobilisations began when over half a million immigrants and their supporters took to the streets in Chicago on 10 March 2006. It was the largest single protest in that city's history. Following the Chicago action, rolling strikes and protests spread to other cities, large and small, organised through expanding networks of churches, immigrant clubs and rights groups, community associations, Spanish-language and progressive media,

trade unions and social justice organisations. Millions came out on 25 March for a "national day of action." Between one and two million people demonstrated in Los Angeles—the single biggest public protest in the city's history—and millions more followed suit in Chicago, New York, Atlanta, Washington DC, Phoenix, Dallas, Houston, Tucson, Denver and dozens of other cities. Again, on 10 April, millions heeded the call for another day of protest. In addition, hundreds of thousands of high school students in Los Angeles and around the country staged walk-outs in support of their families and communities, braving police repression and legal sanctions.

Then on the first of May, International Workers' Day, trade unionists and social justice activists joined immigrants in "The Great American Boycott 2006/A Day Without an Immigrant." Millions—perhaps tens of millions—in over 200 cities from across the country skipped work and school, commercial activity and daily routines in order to participate in a national boycott, general strike, rallies and symbolic actions. The May 1 action was a resounding success. Hundreds of local communities in the south, midwest, north-west and elsewhere, far away from the "gateway cities" where Latino populations are concentrated, experienced mass public mobilisations that placed them on the political map. Agribusiness in the California and Florida heartlands—nearly 100 per cent dependent on immigrant labour—came to a standstill, leaving supermarket produce shelves empty for the next several days. In the landscaping industry, nine out of ten workers boycotted work, according to the American Nursery and Landscape Association. The construction industry suffered major disruptions. Latino truckers who move 70 per cent of the goods in Los Angeles ports did not work. Care-giver referral agencies in major cities saw a sharp increase in calls from parents who needed last-minute nannies or baby-sitters. In order to avoid a total shutdown of the casino mecca in Las Vegas—highly dependent on immigrant labour—casino owners were forced to set up tables in employee lunch-rooms and hold meetings to allow their workers to circulate petitions in favour of immigrant demands. International commerce between Mexico and the United States ground to a temporary halt as protesters closed Tijuana, Juarez-El Paso and several other crossings along the 2,000-mile border.[1]

These protests have no precedent in the history of the US. The immediate trigger was the passage in mid-March by the House of Representatives of HR4437, a bill introduced by Republican representative James Sensenbrenner with broad support from the anti-immigrant lobby. This draconian bill would criminalise undocumented immigrants by making it a felony to be in the US without documentation. It also stipulated the construction of the first 700 miles of a militarised wall between Mexico and the US and would double the size of the US border patrol. And it would apply criminal sanctions against anyone who provided assistance to undocumented immigrants, including churches, humanitarian groups and social service agencies.

Following its passage by the House, bill HR4437 became stalled in the Senate. Democrat Ted Kennedy and Republican John McCain co-sponsored a "compromise" bill that would have removed the criminalisation clause in HR4437 and provided a limited plan for amnesty for some of the undocumented. It would have allowed those who could prove they have resided in the US for at least five years to apply for residency and later citizenship. Those residing in the US for two to five years would have been required to return home and then apply through US embassies for temporary "guest worker" permits. Those who could not demonstrate that they had been in the US for two years would be deported. Even this "compromise" bill would have resulted in massive deportations and heightened control over all immigrants. Yet it was eventually jettisoned because of Republican opposition, so that by late April the whole legislative process had

become stalled. In May, the Senate renewed debate on the matter and seemed to be moving towards consensus based on tougher enforcement and limited legalisation, although at the time of writing (late May 2006) it appeared the legislative process could drag on until after the November 2006 congressional elections.

However, the wave of protest goes well beyond HR4437. It represents the unleashing of pent-up anger and repudiation of what has been deepening exploitation and an escalation of anti-immigrant repression and racism. Immigrants have been subject to every imaginable abuse in recent years. Twice in the state of California they have been denied the right to acquire drivers' licences. This means that they must rely on inadequate or non-existent public transportation or risk driving illegally; more significantly, the drivers' licence is often the only form of legal documentation for such essential transactions as cashing cheques or renting an apartment. The US-Mexico border has been increasingly militarised and thousands of immigrants have died crossing the frontier. Anti-immigrant hate groups are on the rise. The FBI has reported more than 2,500 hate crimes against Latinos in the US since 2000. Blatantly racist public discourse that, only a few years ago, would have been considered extreme has become increasingly mainstreamed and aired in the mass media.

More ominously, the paramilitary organisation Minutemen, a modern day Latino-hating version of the Ku Klux Klan, has spread from its place of origin along the US-Mexican border in Arizona and California to other parts of the country. Minutemen claim they must "secure the border" in the face of inadequate state-sponsored control. Their discourse, beyond racist, is neo-fascist. Some have even been filmed sporting T-shirts with the emblem "Kill a Mexican Today?" and others have organised for-profit "human safaris" in the desert. One video game discovered recently circulating on the internet, "Border Patrol," lets players shoot at Mexican immigrants as they try to cross the border into the US. Players are told to target one of three immigrant groups, all portrayed in a negative, stereotypical way, as the figures rush past a sign that reads "Welcome to the United States." The immigrants are caricatured as bandolier-wearing "Mexican nationalists," tattooed "drug smugglers" and pregnant "breeders" who spring across with their children in tow.

Minutemen clubs have been sponsored by right-wing organisers, wealthy ranchers, businessmen and politicians. But their social base is drawn from those formerly privileged sectors of the white working class that have been "flexibilised" and displaced by economic restructuring, the deregulation of labour and global capital flight. These sectors now scapegoat immigrants—with official encouragement—as the source of their insecurity and downward mobility.

The immigrant mobilisations have seriously threatened ruling groups. In the wake of the recent mobilisations, the Bush administration stepped up raids, deportations and other enforcement measures in a series of highly publicised mass arrests of undocumented immigrants and their employers, intended to intimidate the movement. In April 2006 it was revealed that KBR, a subsidiary of Halliburton—Vice-President Dick Cheney's former company, which has close ties to the Pentagon and is a major contractor in the Iraq war—won a $385 million contract to build large-scale immigrant detention centres in case of an "emergency influx" of immigrants.

Latino immigration to the US is part of a worldwide upsurge in transnational migration generated by the forces of capitalist globalisation. Immigrant labour worldwide is conservatively estimated at over 200 million, according to UN data.[2] Some 30 million are in the US, with at least 20 million of them from Latin America. Of these 20 million, some 11–12 million are undocumented (south and east Asia are also significant contributors to the undocumented population), although it must be stressed that these figures are low-end estimates.[3] The US is by far the largest immigrant-importing country, but the phenomenon is global. Racist attacks, scapegoating and state-sponsored repressive controls over immigrants are rising in many countries around the world, as is the fightback among immigrant workers wherever they are found. Parallel to the US events, for instance, the French government introduced a bill that would apply tough new controls over immigrants and roll back their rights. In response, some 30,000 immigrants and their supporters took to the streets in Paris on 13 May 2006 to demand the bill's repeal.

The Global Circulation of Immigrant Labour

The age of globalisation is also an age of unprecedented transnational migration.[4] The corollary to an integrated global economy is the rise of a truly global—although highly segmented—labour market. It is a global labour market because, despite formal nation state restrictions on the free worldwide movement of labour, surplus labour in any part of the world is now recruited and redeployed through numerous mechanisms to where capital is in need of it and because workers themselves undertake worldwide migration, even in the face of the adverse migratory conditions.

Central to capitalism is securing a politically and economically suitable labour supply, and at the core of all class societies is the control over labour and disposal of the products of labour. But the linkage between the securing of labour and territoriality is changing under globalisation. As labour becomes "free" in every corner of the globe, capital has vast new opportunities for mobilising labour power where and when required. National labour pools are merging into a single global labour pool that services global capitalism. The transnational circulation of capital induces the transnational circulation of labour. This circulation of labour becomes incorporated into the process of restructuring the world economy. It is a mechanism for the provision of labour to transnationalised circuits of accumulation and constitutes a structural feature of the global system.

While the need to mix labour with capital at diverse points along global production chains induces population movements, there are sub-processes that shape the character and direction of such migration. At the structural level, the uprooting of communities by the capitalist break-up of local economies creates surplus populations and is a powerful push factor in outmigration, while labour shortages in more economically advanced areas is a pull factor that attracts displaced peoples. At a behavioural level, migration and wage remittances become a family survival strategy (see below), made *possible* by the demand for labour abroad and made increasingly *viable* by the fluid conditions and integrated infrastructures of globalisation.

In one sense, the South penetrates the North with the dramatic expansion of immigrant labour. But transnational migratory flows are not unidirectional from South to North and the phenomenon is best seen in global capitalist rather than North-South terms. Migrant workers are becoming a general category of super-exploitable labour drawn from globally dispersed labour reserves into similarly globally dispersed nodes of accumulation. To the extent that these nodes experience labour shortages—skilled or unskilled—they become magnets for transnational labour flows, often encouraged or even organised by both sending and receiving countries and regions.

Labour-short Middle Eastern countries, for instance, have programmes for the importation (and careful control) of labour from throughout south and east Asia and north Africa. The Philippine state has become a veritable labour recruitment agency for the global economy, organising the export of its citizens to over a hundred countries in Asia, the Middle East, Europe, North America and elsewhere. Greeks migrate to

Germany and the US, while Albanians migrate to Greece. South Africans move to Australia and England, while Malawians, Mozambicans and Zimbabweans work in South African mines and the service industry. Malaysia imports Indonesian labour, while Thailand imports workers from Laos and Myanmar and, in turn, sends labour to Malaysia, Singapore, Japan and elsewhere. In Latin America, Costa Rica is a major importer of Nicaraguan labour, Venezuela has historically imported large amounts of Colombian labour, the Southern Cone draws on several million emigrant Andean workers and an estimated 500,000 to 800,000 Haitians live in the Dominican Republic, where they cut sugar cane, harvest crops and work in the *maquiladoras* under the same labour market segmentation, political disenfranchisement and repression that immigrant workers face in the United States and in most labour-importing countries.

The division of the global working class into "citizen" and "non-citizen" labour is a major new axis of inequality worldwide, further complicating the well-known gendered and racialised hierarchies among labour, and facilitating new forms of repressive and authoritarian social control over working classes. In an *apparent* contradiction, capital and goods move freely across national borders in the new global economy but labour cannot and its movement is subject to heightened state controls. The global labour supply is, in the main, no longer coerced (subject to extra-economic compulsion) due to the ability of the universalised market to exercise strictly economic discipline, but its movement is juridically controlled. This control is a central determinant in the worldwide correlation of forces between global capital and global labour.

The immigrant is a juridical creation inserted into real social relations. States create "immigrant labour" as distinct categories of labour in relation to capital. While the generalisation of the labour market emerging from the consolidation of the global capitalist economy creates the conditions for global migrations as a world-level labour supply system, the maintenance and strengthening of state controls over transnational labour create the conditions for immigrant labour as a distinct category of labour. The creation of these distinct categories ("immigrant labour") becomes central to the global capitalist economy, replacing earlier direct colonial and racial caste controls over labour worldwide.

But why is this juridical category of "immigrant labour" reproduced under globalisation? Labour migration and geographic shifts in production are alternative forms for capitalists to achieve an optimal mix of their capital with labour. State controls are often intended *not to prevent* but to *control* the transnational movement of

labour. A *free* flow of labour would exert an equalising influence on wages across borders whereas state controls help reproduce such differentials. Eliminating the wage differential between regions would cancel the advantages that capital accrues from disposing of labour pools worldwide subject to different wage levels and would strengthen labour worldwide in relation to capital. In addition, the use of immigrant labour allows receiving countries to separate reproduction and maintenance of labour, and therefore to "externalise" the costs of social reproduction. In other words, the new transnational migration helps capital to dispose of the need to pay for the reproduction of labour power. The inter-state system thus acts as a condition for the structural power of globally mobile transnational capital over labour that is transnational in actual content and character but subjected to different institutional arrangements under the direct control of national states.

The migrant labour phenomenon will continue to expand along with global capitalism. Just as capitalism has no control over its implacable expansion as a system, it cannot do away in its new globalist stage with transnational labour. But if global capital needs the labour power of transnational migrants, this labour power belongs to human beings who must be tightly controlled, given the special oppression and dehumanization involved in extracting their labour power as non-citizen immigrant labour. To return to the situation in the US, the immigrant issue presents a contradiction for political and economic elites: from the vantage points of dominant group interests, the dilemma is how to deal with the new "barbarians" at Rome's door.

Latino immigrants have massively swelled the lower rungs of the US workforce. They provide almost all farm labour and much of the labour for hotels, restaurants, construction, janitorial and house cleaning, child care, gardening and landscaping, delivery, meat and poultry packing, retail, and so on. Yet dominant groups fear a rising tide of Latino immigrants will lead to a loss of cultural and political control, becoming a source of counterhegemony and instability, as immigrant labour in Paris showed itself to be in the late 2005 uprising there against racism and marginality.

Employers do not want to do away with Latino immigration. To the contrary, they want to sustain a vast exploitable labour pool that exists under precarious conditions, that does not enjoy the civil, political and labour rights of citizens and that is disposable through deportation. It is the *condition of deportability* that they wish to create or preserve, since that condition assures the ability to super-exploit with impunity and to dispose of this labour without consequences should it become unruly or unnecessary. The Bush administration opposed HR4437 not because it was in favour of immigrant rights but because it had to play a balancing act by finding a formula for a stable supply of cheap labour to employers with, at the same time, greater state control over immigrants.

The Bush White House proposed a "guest worker" programme that would rule out legalisation for undocumented immigrants, force them to return to their home countries and apply for temporary work visas, and implement tough new border security measures. There is a long history of such "guest worker" schemes going back to the *bracero* programme, which brought millions of Mexican workers to the US during the labour shortages of the Second World War, only to deport them once native workers had become available again. Similar "guest worker" programmes are in effect in several European countries and other labour-importing states around the world.

The contradictions of "immigrant policy reform" became apparent in the days leading up to the May 1 action, when major capitalist groups dependent on immigrant labour—especially in the agricultural, food processing, landscaping, construction, and other service sectors—came out in support of legalisation for the undocumented. Such transnational agro-industrial giants as Cargill, Swift and Co, Perdue Farms, Tyson Foods and Goya Foods, for instance, closed down many of their meat-packing and food processing plants and gave workers the day off.

Neoliberalism in Latin America

If capital's need for cheap, malleable and deportable labour in the centres of the global economy is the main "pull factor" inducing Latino immigration to the US, the "push factor" is the devastation left by two decades of neoliberalism in Latin America. Capitalist globalisation—structural adjustment, free trade agreements, privatisations, the contraction of public employment and credits, the break-up of communal lands and so forth, along with the political crises these measures have generated—has imploded thousands of communities in Latin America and unleashed a wave of migration, from rural to urban areas and to other countries, that can only be analogous to the mass uprooting and migration that generally take place in the wake of war.

Just as capital does not stay put in the place it accumulates, neither do wages stay put. The flip side of the intense upsurge in transnational migration is the reverse flow of remittances by migrant workers in the global economy to their country and region of origin. Officially recorded international remittances increased astonishingly, from a mere $57 million in 1970 to $216 billion in 2005, according to World Bank data. This amount was higher than capital market flows and official development assistance combined, and nearly equalled the total amount of world FDI (foreign direct investment) in 2004. Close to one billion people, or one in every six on the planet, may receive some support from the global flow of remittances, according to senior World Bank economist Dilip Ratha.[5] Remittances have become an economic mainstay for an increasing number of countries. Most of the world's regions, including Africa, Asia, Latin America and southern and eastern Europe, report major remittance inflows.

Remittances redistribute income worldwide in a literal or geographic sense but not in the actual sense of *redistribution,* meaning a transfer of some added portion of the surplus from capital to labour, since they constitute not additional earnings but the separation of the site where wages are earned from the site of wage-generated consumption. What is taking place is a historically unprecedented separation of the point of production from the point of social reproduction. The former can take place in one part of the world and generate the value—then remitted—for social reproduction of labour in another part of the world. This is an emergent structural feature of the global system, in which the site of labour power and of its reproduction have been transnationally dispersed.

Transnational Latino migration has led to an enormous increase in remittances from Latino ethnic labour abroad to extended kinship networks in Latin America. Latin American workers abroad sent home some $57 billion in 2005, according to the Inter-American Development Bank.[6] These remittances were the number one source of foreign exchange for the Dominican Republic, El Salvador, Guatemala, Guyana, Haiti, Honduras, Jamaica and Nicaragua, and the second most important source for Belize, Bolivia, Colombia, Ecuador, Paraguay and Surinam, according to the Bank. The $20 billion sent back in 2005 by an estimated 10 million Mexicans in the US was more than the country's tourism receipts and was surpassed only by oil and *maquiladora* exports.

These remittances allow millions of Latin American families to survive by purchasing goods either imported from the world market or produced locally or by transnational capital. They allow for family survival at a time of crisis and adjustment, especially for the poorest sectors—safety nets that replace governments and fixed employment in the provision of economic security. Emigration and remittances also serve the political objective of pacification. The dramatic expansion of Latin American emigration to the US from the 1980s onwards helped to dissipate social tensions and undermine labour and political opposition to prevailing regimes and institutions. Remittances help to offset macroeconomic imbalances, in some cases averting economic collapse, thereby shoring up the political conditions for an environment congenial to transnational capital.

Therefore, bound up with the immigrant debate in the US is the entire political economy of global capitalism in the western hemisphere—the same political economy that is now being sharply contested throughout Latin America with the surge in mass popular struggles and the turn to the Left. The struggle for immigrant rights in the US is thus part and parcel of this resistance to neoliberalism, intimately connected to the larger Latin American—and worldwide—struggle for social justice.

No wonder protests and boycotts took place throughout Latin America on May 1 in solidarity with Latino immigrants in the US. But these actions were linked to local labour rights struggles and social movement demands. In Tijuana, Mexico, for example, *maquiladora* workers in that border city's in-bond industry marched on May 1 to demand higher wages, eight-hour shifts, an end to "abuses and despotism" in the *maquila* plants and an end to sexual harassment, the use of poison chemicals and company unions. The workers also called for solidarity with the "Great American Boycott of 2006 on the other side of the border" and participated in a protest at the US consulate in the city and at the main crossing, which shut down cross-border traffic for most of the day.

The Nature of Immigrant Struggles

Labour market transformations driven by capitalist globalisation unleash what McMichael calls "the politics of global labor circulation"[7] and fuel, in labour-importing countries, new nativisms, waves of xenophobia and racism against immigrants. Shifting political coalitions scapegoat immigrants by promoting ethnic-based solidarities among middle classes, representatives of distinct fractions of capital and formerly privileged sectors among working classes (such as white ethnic workers in the US and Europe) threatened by job loss, declining income and the other insecurities of economic restructuring. The long-term tendency seems to be towards a generalisation of labour market conditions across borders, characterised by segmented structures under a regime of labour deregulation and racial, ethnic and gender hierarchies.

In this regard, a major challenge confronting the movement in the US is relations between the Latino and the Black communities. Historically, African Americans have swelled the lower rungs in the US caste system. But, as African Americans fought for their civil and human rights in the 1960s and 1970s, they became organised, politicised and radicalised. Black workers led trade union militancy. All this made them undesirable labour for capital—"undisciplined" and "noncompliant."

Starting in the 1980s, employers began to push out Black workers and massively recruit Latino immigrants, a move that coincided with deindustrialisation and restructuring. Blacks moved from super-exploited to marginalized—subject to unemployment, cuts in social services, mass incarceration and heightened state repression—while Latino immigrant labour has become the new super-exploited sector. Employers and political elites in New Orleans, for instance, have apparently decided in the wake of Hurricane Katrina to replace that city's historically black working class with Latino immigrant labour. Whereas fifteen years ago no one saw a single Latino face in places such as Iowa or Tennessee, now Mexican, Central American and other Latino workers are visible everywhere. If some African Americans have misdirected their anger over marginality at Latino immigrants, the Black community has a legitimate grievance over the anti-Black racism of many Latinos themselves, who often lack sensitivity to the historic plight and contemporary experience of Blacks with racism, and are reticent to see them as natural allies. (Latinos often bring with them particular sets of racialised relations from their home countries.)[8]

White labour that historically enjoyed caste privileges within racially segmented labour markets has experienced downward mobility and heightened insecurity. These sectors of the working class feel the pinch of capitalist globalisation and the transnationalisation of formerly insulated local labour markets. Studies in the early 1990s, for example, found that, in addition to concentrations in "traditional" areas such as Los Angeles, Miami, Washington DC, Virginia and Houston, Central American immigrants had formed clusters in the formal and informal service sectors in areas where, in the process of downward mobility, they had replaced "white ethnics," such as in suburban Long Island, the small towns of Iowa and North Carolina, in Silicon Valley and in the northern and eastern suburbs of the San Francisco Bay Area.[9]

The loss of caste privileges for white sectors of the working class is problematic for political elites and state managers in the US, since legitimation and domination have historically been constructed through a white racial hegemonic bloc. Can such a bloc be sustained or renewed through a scapegoating of immigrant communities? In attempting to shape public discourse, the anti-immigrant lobby argues that immigrants "are a drain on the US economy." Yet, as the National Immigrant Solidarity Network points out, immigrants contribute $7 billion in Social Security a year. They earn $240 billion, report $90 billion, and are only reimbursed $5 billion in tax returns. They also contribute $25 billion more to the US economy than they receive in health-care and social services.[10] But this is a limited line of argument, since the larger issue is the incalculable trillions of dollars that immigrant labour generates in profits and revenue for capital, only a tiny proportion of which goes back to them in the form of wages.

Moreover, it has been demonstrated that there is no correlation between the unemployment rate among US citizens and the rate of immigration. In fact, the unemployment rate has moved in cycles over the past twenty-five years and exhibits a comparatively lower rate during the most recent (2000–2005) influx of undocumented workers. Similarly, wage stagnation in the United States appeared, starting with the economic crisis of 1973, and has continued its steady march ever since, with no correlation to increases or decreases in the inflow of undocumented workers. Instead, downward mobility for most US workers is positively correlated with the decline in union participation, the decline in labour conditions and the polarisation of income and wealth that began with the restructuring crisis of the 1970s and accelerated the following decade as Reaganomics launched the neo-liberal counterrevolution.[11]

The larger backdrop here is transnational capital's attempt to forge post-Fordist, post-Keynesian capital-labour relations worldwide, based on flexibilisation, deregulation and deunionisation. From the 1970s onwards, capital began to abandon earlier reciprocities with labour, forged in the epoch of national corporate capitalism, precisely because the process of globalisation allowed to it break free of nation state constraints. There has been a vast acceleration of the primitive accumulation of capital worldwide through globalisation, a process in which millions have been wrenched from the means of production, proletarianised and thrown into a global labour market that transnational capital has been able to shape.[12] As capital assumed new power relative to labour with the onset of globalisation, states shifted from reproducing Keynesian social structures of accumulation to servicing the general needs of the new patterns of global accumulation.

At the core of the emerging global social structure of accumulation is a new capital-labour relation based on alternative systems of labour control and diverse contingent categories of devalued labour—sub-contracted,

outsourced, casualised, informal, part-time, temp work, home-work, and so on—the essence of which is cheapening and disciplining labour, making it "flexible" and readily available for transnational capital in worldwide labour reserves. Workers in the global economy are themselves, under these flexible arrangements, increasingly treated as a sub-contracted component rather than a fixture internal to employer organisations. These new class relations of global capitalism dissolve the notion of responsibility, however minimal, that governments have for their citizens or that employers have towards their employees.

Immigrant workers become the archetype of these new global class relations. They are a naked commodity, no longer embedded in relations of reciprocity rooted in social and political communities that have, historically, been institutionalised in nation states. Immigrant labour pools that can be super-exploited economically, marginalised and disenfranchised politically, driven into the shadows and deported when necessary are the very epitome of capital's naked domination in the age of global capitalism.

The immigrant rights movement in the US is demanding full rights for all immigrants, including amnesty, worker protections, family reunification measures, a path to citizenship or permanent residency rather than a temporary "guest worker" programme, an end to all attacks against immigrants and to the criminalisation of immigrant communities. While some observers have billed the recent events as the birth of a new civil rights movement, clearly much more is at stake. In the larger picture, this goes beyond immediate demands; it challenges the class relations that are at the very core of global capitalism. The significance of the May 1 immigrant rights mobilisation taking place on international workers' day—which has not been celebrated in the US for nearly a century—was lost on no one.

In the age of globalisation, the only hope of accumulating the social and political forces necessary to confront the global capitalist system is by transnationalising popular, labour and democratic struggles. The immigrant rights movement is all of these—popular, pro-worker and democratic—and it is by definition transnational. In sum, the struggle for immigrant rights is at the cutting edge of the global working-class fightback against capitalist globalisation.

Notes

1. For these details, and more, see, inter alia, summaries of press reports from around the US compiled by *CIS-DC Info Digest* (Vol. 41, no. 17), "Tally of plant closings and demonstrations," available by request at <http://www.mutualaid.org>.

2. Manuel Orozco, "Worker remittances in an international scope," *Working Paper* (Washington, DC, Inter-American Dialogue and Multilateral Investment Fund of the Inter-American Development Bank, March 2003), p. 1.

3. For this and more data and links to different academic and foundation reports and government census agencies, see the University of California at Santa Barbara web site <http://aad .english.ucsb.edu>.

4. On migration and globalisation, and more generally on capitalism and migration, see, among others, Peter Stalker, *Workers Without Frontiers* (Boulder, CO, Lynne Riener, 2000); Robin Cohen, *The New Helots: migrants in the international division of labour* (Aldershot, Ashgate, 1987); Nigel Harris, *The New Untouchables: immigration and the new world worker* (London, I. B. Tauris, 1995); Stephen Castles and Mark J. Miller, *The Age of Migration: international population movements in the modern world* (New York, Palgrave Macmillan, 1993); Lydia Potts, *The World Labor Market: a history of migration* (London, Zed, 1990). For discussion of current topics and new directions in the sociology of migration, see Alejandro Portes, "Immigrant theory for a new century: some problems and opportunities," *International Migration Review* (Vol. 3, no. 4, 1997), p. 799–825. See also Alejandro Portes and Jozsef Borocz, "Contemporary immigration: theoretical perspectives on its determinants and modes of incorporation," *International Migration Review* (Vol. XXIII, no. 3, 1990), pp. 606–30.

5. For these details, see Richard Boudreaux, "The new foreign aid: the seeds of promise," *Los Angeles Times* (14 April 2006), p. 1A.

6. Inter-American Development Bank, *Remittances 2005: promoting financial democracy* (Washington DC, IDB, 2006).

7. Philip McMichael, *Development and Social Change: a global perspective,* (Thousand Oaks, CA, Pine Forge Press, 1986), p. 189.

8. In a commentary observing that mainstream Black political leaders have been notably lukewarm to the immigrant rights movement, Keeanga-Yamahtta Taylor writes: "The displacement of Black workers is a real problem—but not a problem caused by displaced Mexican workers . . . if the state is allowed to criminalize the existence [of] immigrant workers this will only fan the flames of racism eventually consuming Blacks in a back draft of discrimination. How exactly does one tell the difference between a citizen and a non-citizen? Through a massive campaign of racial profiling, that's how . . . In fact, the entire working class has a stake in the success of the movement." She goes on to recall how California building owners and labour contractors replaced Black janitors with largely undocumented Latino immigrants in the 1980s. But after a successful Service Employees International Union drive in the "Justice for janitors" campaign of the late 1980s and 1990s, wages and benefits went up and the union's largely Latino members sought contractual language guaranteeing African Americans a percentage of work slots. See Taylor, "Life ain't been no crystal stair: Blacks, Latinos and the new civil rights movement," *Counterpunch* (9 May 2006), downloaded 18 May 2006 <http://www.counterpunch.org/taylor0508 2006.html>.

9. See the special issue of *NACLA Report on the Americas,* "On the line: Latinos on labor's cutting edge" (Vol. 30, no. 3, November/December 1996).

10. For this data, further information and links, see the Network's website at <http:// www.immigrantsolidarity.org >.

11. For these details see <http://aad.english.ucsb.edu/econimpacts.html>.

12. In drawing on migrant workers, dominant groups are able to take advantage of a global reserve army of labour that has experienced historically unprecedented growth in recent years. For instance, the entry of China, India and the former Soviet bloc into the global economy led to a doubling of the global labour market, from 1.46 to near 3 billion workers by 2000, which resulted in a decline in the global capital/labour ratio to just 55–60 per cent of what it otherwise would have been. See Richard Freeman, "China, India and the doubling of the global labor force: who pays the price of globalization," The Globalist (3 June 2005), posted at Japan Focus, 26 August and downloaded on 13 October 2005, < http://www.japanfocus. org/ article.asp?id = 377 >

Discussion Questions

1. Examine the relationship between migrant labor and global capitalism. Can one exist without the other?

   As Robinson describes, the corollary to an integrated global economy is the rise of the global (migrant) labor market. Surplus labor is recruited throughout the world and redeployed where it is needed. Migrant labor will continue to expand along with global capitalism.

2. How is the immigrants' rights movement affected by U.S. ethnic relations (between white, Latino, and black communities)?

   According to Robinson, "a major challenge confronting the movement in the US is relations between the Latino and Black communities." Black workers in some locations and economic sectors have been replaced by Latino immigrants since the 1980s. Blacks moved from "super-exploited to marginalized—subject to unemployment, cuts in social services, mass incarceration and heightened state repression—while Latino immigrant labour has become the new super-exploited sector." In addition, white labour has experienced downward mobility and heightened insecurity.

Source: From Robinson, W. (2006). "Aqui estamos y no nos vamos!" Global capital and immigrant rights. *Race and Class, 48*(2), 77–91. Reprinted by permission of Institute of Race Relations.

PART VI

EDUCATION

CHAPTER 16

Constructively Challenging Diverse Inner-City Youth's Beliefs About Educational and Career Barriers and Supports

Margo A. Jackson, Jaclyn Mendelsohn Kacanski, Jonathan P. Rust, and Sarah E. Beck (2006)

The researchers examine school and work "barrier beliefs" about the limitations of education for future career rewards and perceived supports for attaining educational and career aspirations of low-income, inner-city, African American, Hispanic/Latino(a), and Caribbean immigrant youth. Higher levels of school and work barrier beliefs are related to lower aspirations among students. In their evaluation of a school-based educational and career enrichment program, they conclude that students responded best to contextual supports (relational and community support) and personal resources (psychological assets within the individual, e.g., positive work habits).

Youth in low-income, culturally diverse, inner-city schools are at risk for low educational attainment, limited future career options, and severely reduced earnings potential (Education Trust, 2000; Turner & Lapan, 2003; U.S. Department of Education, 1996). Particularly at risk may be minority youth who are not recent U.S. immigrants and thus are more vulnerable to believe in the permanence of the effects of continuing systemic racial discrimination in access to educational and vocational opportunities (Ogbu, 1990, 2003). High school students from various ethnic and socioeconomic groups understand that a good education leads to good jobs (Steinberg, Dornbusch, & Brown, 1992). However, faced with limited access to educational attainment and occupational choice, many low-income and African American and Hispanic students develop compensatory beliefs about the value of academic effort and performance; they believe that academic effort and achievement will not pay off for them (Graham, Taylor, & Hudley, 1998; Ogbu, 1989). These beliefs may further constrain (beyond the systemic barriers that do exist) their educational and career achievement (Arbona, 2000; Constantine, Erickson, Banks, & Timberlake, 1998).

One potential career barrier perception for at-risk urban minority youth, one that has seldom been addressed in the current literature, may be their understandable but maladaptive beliefs in the limited value of education for future career rewards. Krumboltz (1996) proposed that the role of career counseling is to help clients expand their learning and clarify beliefs that hinder and facilitate their career development. Jackson and Nutini's (2002) interviews with at-risk diverse urban youth revealed both barriers and resources (supports) for their learning about potential educational and career development opportunities. From the perspective of social learning theory (Krumboltz, 1996), career counselors might constructively challenge urban minority youth's beliefs in the limited value of education (i.e., perceptions of barriers) by expanding their learning about accessible sources of support (i.e., perceptions of support) for their school, work, and life goals.

Kenny, Blustein, Chaves, Grossman, and Gallagher (2003) conducted two studies with a sample of urban minority ninth graders (predominantly African American, Hispanic/Latino(a), and Black/Caribbean). They found that students who perceived lower levels of barriers and higher levels of relational support, from family members and others, also reported higher levels of engagement with school and more positive attitudes about and higher aspirations for their future careers. Kenny et al. (2003) noted implications for career counseling interventions in schools, such as helping urban youth to identify their perceived barriers and develop counteractive strategies to build relational supports (e.g., Kenny, Waldo, Warter, & Barton, 2002; Solberg, Howard, Blustein, & Close, 2002).

From learning experiences, Krumboltz (1991) proposes that individuals develop career beliefs (some helpful and others unhelpful) about themselves and their relation to the environment that facilitate or hinder them from taking constructive action in their career and educational development. In light of Kenny et al.'s (2003) findings, urban minority youth's perceptions of contextual supports may be conceptualized in social learning theory as helpful career beliefs in relation to facilitative environmental conditions (Mitchell & Krumboltz, 1996). In addition to perceived environmental supports, Jackson and Nutini (2002) found that urban minority youth identified psychological resources (e.g., positive motivational beliefs, resilient personality characteristics, personal skills, and constructive problem-solving approaches) as sources of support for their educational and career development. We propose that such personal resources may be a second type of support and may be conceptualized from social learning theory as task approach skills; that is, through "inferences about how they might apply their skills in the real world, [individuals] develop work habits and problem-solving skills for coping with the world" (Krumboltz, 1994, p. 18).

Purpose of the Study and Hypotheses

One purpose of this exploratory study was to investigate the relationships between perceived barriers (beliefs about the limitations of education for future economic rewards) and supports to progress toward achieving the school, work, and life aspirations of low-income, inner-city, African American, Hispanic/Latino(a), and Caribbean immigrant youth. We further sought to empirically examine Ogbu's (1989, 1990, 2003) contention that

minority youth who are less recent immigrants are more likely to believe that education will not pay off for them and have lower educational and career aspirations. Based on the literature, we hypothesized the following: (1) Higher levels of beliefs in the limitations of education are associated with lower educational and career aspirations, (2) less recent immigration status is associated with (a) higher beliefs in the limitations of education and (b) lower educational and career aspirations, and (3) higher levels of supports are associated with (a) lower beliefs in the limitations of education and (b) higher educational and career aspirations.

A second purpose of the study was to describe differences in the frequency and types of support sources identified at the start and end of a career learning intervention for urban minority youth. Two workshops were designed to help participants not only expand their knowledge of self and educational and career options but also constructively challenge potentially unhelpful beliefs about the value of education for achieving educational and career aspirations. Grounded in social learning theory (Krumboltz, 1996), one learning objective of the workshops was to expand the number of support sources from pre to post that participants might identify as accessible toward realizing their school, work, and life goals. Finally, we were interested to learn if two types of support sources (contextual supports and personal resources) would be endorsed and, if so, if support types vary from pre to post.

Method

PARTICIPANTS

The participants were low-income, inner-city, African American, Hispanic/ Latino(a), and Caribbean immigrant youth involved in a larger, multiple-year, school-university-community partnership project with the U.S. Department of Education, GEAR UP (Gaining Early Awareness and Readiness for Undergraduate Programs). The participants' home community was culturally diverse (in 50% of families, a language other than English was spoken at home) and of low socioeconomic status (greater than 80% of the school district's students in middle school at the start of the project were eligible for free lunch, and 48% of families lived below the poverty level).

At the start of the study, 83% of the participants were in ninth grade, and 17% were in eighth grade. Their average grades in academic subjects (math, English, social studies, and science) were Bs ($M = 3.12$, $SD = 0.51$) and ranged from 1.38 to 4.00 (Ds to As). Most participants were 14- or 15-year-olds ($M = 14.21$, $SD = 1.28$), and 71% were female. Participants primarily identified their ethnicity as Black or African American (49%), Hispanic or Latino/Latina (42%), or biracial, multiracial, or multicultural (9%). Many were from families of recent immigrants to the U.S. mainland (64% were first- or second-generation immigrants), and 53% came from Caribbean countries (including 23% from the Dominican Republic).

PROCEDURE

The proposal for this research was approved by the human subjects review board of the researchers' university, the GEAR UP administrators and staff, and the college sites. Two 2-hr career learning workshops, titled "Learning About Occupations of Interest, How Education Relates, and Sources of Support for Career/Life Goals," were offered to approximately 150 students as part of the weekly GEAR UP Saturday academic enrichment programs held at two local college campuses in 2003 and 2004. The workshop series was promoted as a research study to better inform us regarding how to assist students such as themselves. Informed consent forms and flyers describing the study and workshops were mailed to potential student participants and their parents as well as promoted through a GEAR UP newsletter. A total of 66 GEAR UP students voluntarily participated in the first 2-hr workshop, and (in response to reminder invitations by mail, phone, and e-mail) a subsample of 33 participants returned for the follow-up 2-hr workshop.

Briefly, the content of the career learning workshops included four of the five critical components of effective career choice interventions suggested by the results of meta-analyses (Brown & Ryan Krane, 2000): committing their career goals and plans to writing; individualized interpretations and feedback regarding career self-assessment; up-to-date information on interests, skills, and education required for pursuing different career paths; and identifying sources of support and means to access support for their career development. Consistent with Krumboltz's (1996) theory, the workshops included activities for participants to (a) expand their learning about occupations of interest through career self-assessment tools (e.g., considering occupations at three levels of educational requirements as well as one unfamiliar occupation), (b) explore their career beliefs (about the value of education for future career rewards), and (c) expand their learning about accessible sources of

support (environmental and personal resources) for their educational and career goals and aspirations.

The first author (a university faculty member in counseling psychology) trained and supervised research assistants (graduate students in counseling and school psychology) to serve as workshop facilitators with small groups (of one to five participants). A fluent Spanish-speaking facilitator was available at the workshops if needed or preferred by participants. Participants completed questionnaires, career self-assessment surveys, and interactive exercises; they received written material on occupations of interest; and they processed this information in individual and small-group discussions with workshop facilitators. For example, to explore personally relevant supports with participants, facilitators led discussions using a handout outlining "Possible Sources of Help for Doing Well in School, Work, and Life" that was developed from the sources of support identified by GEAR UP students in previous interviews (Jackson & Nutini, 2002). At the end of the follow-up workshop, participants anonymously completed evaluations of the workshops. A detailed outline of the content and procedures of the workshops is available from the first author on request.

MEASURES

School and work beliefs. At the first workshop, participants completed the 15-item Economic Value of Education Questionnaire (Murdock, 1999; Murdock, Anderman, & Hodge, 2000), which is designed to assess adolescents' perceptions of the relevance of education to their future economic success in work and life. One subscale, Limitations of Education, has 10 items to assess views of the limitations of education in attaining financial rewards (e.g., "I can make good money someday without an education"). The other subscale, Benefits of Education, has five items to assess beliefs that education will result in economic rewards (e.g., "I will make more money someday if I do well in school"). Respondents rate the degree to which they agree or disagree with each statement on a 5-point Likert-type scale ranging from *disagree* (1) to *agree* (5), with higher scores reflecting stronger endorsement of the school and work beliefs on each subscale.

Scores on the measure have been found to predict school engagement and discipline problems among low-income, African American, middle school students (Murdock, 1999) and to predict student motivation and behavior from middle to high school (Murdock et al., 2000). Internal consistency estimates reported were .70 for the Limitations of Education and .65 for the Benefits of Education subscales (Murdock et al., 2000). Cronbach's alphas for the current sample were .77 for Limitations of Education and .50 for Benefits of Education, suggesting adequate reliability for the former but not the latter subscale. Therefore, we used only Limitations of Education (and not Benefits of Education) subscale scores in our analysis.

Sources of support. At the beginning of the first workshop (pre) and at the end of the follow-up workshop (post), participants wrote responses to the following open-ended item: "*List as many ways as you can think of* for getting help and support in the process of working toward your future work and life goals." After all data were collected, graduate student research assistants coded the frequency of support sources listed by participants at pre and post, and they discussed and revised coding discrepancies to reach 100% agreement. Then, the first and fourth authors independently coded each support source as either a contextual support (1) or personal resource (2) (see the appendix for coding protocol). The intraclass correlation coefficient (interrater reliability) for support sources identified at pre was .85 ($n = 117$) and at post was .68 ($n = 268$). A third independent coder (professional colleague) subsequently met with the first author to review all coding discrepancies and to reach 100% agreement.

Educational and career aspirations. In the second workshop, after reviewing information on six occupations of interest requiring a range of education levels that participants had identified during the first workshop, they were instructed to indicate their top occupation of interest and the level of education required. Workshop facilitators had the participants use occupational information printouts to check the accuracy of their responses regarding education level required and consistency with individual participants' educational aspirations. After data collection, participants' responses were coded (by a graduate student research assistant and checked by the first author) with one of the five education levels for each first choice occupation as listed in Holland's (1996) *The Occupations Finder*: 2 = *elementary school or no special training*; 3 = *high school*; 4 = *some college, technical, or business training*; 5 = *college*; and 6 = *advanced degree*.

Results

Preliminary analyses revealed no significant differences between the sample and subsample on the variables of gender, average grades, school and work beliefs, and frequency of supports identified at the first workshop. Following are descriptive statistics for the sample ($n = 66$) and subsample ($n = 33$). The mean score on beliefs in the limitations of education was 2.29 ($SD = 0.75$) for the sample and 2.19 ($SD = 0.70$) for the subsample, suggesting that overall participants somewhat disagreed that school effort would not pay off in future economic rewards. Mean frequency of supports at the first workshop was 3.27 ($SD = 1.74$) for the sample and 3.55 ($SD = 2.00$) for the subsample. At the end of the second workshop, the mean number of supports listed by subsample participants was 8.12 ($SD = 3.12$), showing an increase from pre to post. At the second workshop, the education levels of subsample participants' first choice occupations (45.5% college and 45.5% advanced degree) indicated high educational and career aspirations.

Table 16.1 presents Pearson intercorrelations between beliefs in limitations of education, supports (pre), and generation since immigration. Consistent with Hypothesis 2a, higher beliefs in the limitations of education were significantly and positively associated with a higher number of generations since U.S. immigration ($r = .35, p < .01, n = 61$). In other words, minority youth from less recent immigrant groups (fourth and fifth generation) more strongly doubted the value of education for attaining career and life goals. However, supports frequency did not significantly correlate with school and work barrier beliefs; contrary to Hypothesis 3a, higher supports were not associated with lower beliefs in the limitations of education for attaining future economic goals.

Also presented in Table 16.1 are Spearman's rho intercorrelations between beliefs in limitations of education, supports pre and post, educational and career aspirations, and generation since immigration of the subsample (participants who completed both workshops). Transformations were applied to the data for the positively skewed variable of supports, post (log 10), and negatively skewed variables of educational and career aspirations (inverse) to approximate normal distributions. As hypothesized (Hypothesis 1), higher beliefs in the limitations of education were significantly associated with lower educational and career aspirations ($r = -.38, p < .05, n = 32$). Again, consistent with Hypothesis 2a, minority youth from less recent immigrant groups (fourth and fifth generation) had higher beliefs in the limitations of education for attaining future economic rewards ($r = .48, p < .01, n = 32$). Minority youth from fourth- and fifth-generation immigrant groups also had significantly lower educational and career aspirations ($r = -.35, p < .05, n = 33$), suggesting support for

Table 16.1 Intercorrelations Between Beliefs in Limitations of Education, Supports Pre and Post, Educational and Career Aspirations, and Generation Since Immigration for Urban Minority Youth

	1	2	3	4	5
1. Beliefs in limitations of education					
Pearson correlation		-0.11^a	0.35^{a**}		
Spearman correlation	1.00	1.43^b	0.13^b	-0.38^{b*}	0.48^{b**}
2. Supports, pre					
Pearson correlation	-0.11^a		-0.09^a		
Spearman correlation	1.43^b	1.00	0.01^b	0.02^b	-0.19^b
3. Supports, post					
Spearman correlation	0.13^b	0.01^b	1.00	-0.05^b	-0.09^b
4. Educational and career aspirations					
Spearman correlations	-0.38^{b*}	0.02^b	-0.05^b	1.00	-0.35^{b*}
5. Generation since immigration					
Pearson correlation	0.35^{a**}	-0.09^a			
Spearman correlation	0.48^{b**}	-0.19^b	-0.09^b	-0.35^{b*}	1.00

Note: Pearson correlations are used for samples, and Spearman correlations are used for subsamples.

a. Sample ($n = 66$; except for beliefs in limitations of education, $n = 61$).

b. Subsample ($n = 33$; except for beliefs in limitations of education, $n = 32$).

$*p < .05. **p < .01.$

Hypothesis 2b. Again, contrary to Hypothesis 3a, no significant correlations were found between levels of support, pre or post, and school and work barrier beliefs. Also contrary to Hypothesis 3b, no significant correlations were found between levels of support, pre or post, and educational and career aspirations.

Finally, we investigated whether two types of support sources—contextual supports and personal resources—would be endorsed by participants and, if so, if support types vary from pre to post. A total of 117 supports were endorsed by subsample participants at the first workshop; 26.5% were coded as contextual supports and 73.5% as personal resources. A greater number of supports (268) were endorsed by these participants at the end of the second workshop; 66% were coded as contextual supports and 34% as personal resources. In other words, there were more personal resources listed by participants at pre and more contextual supports at post.

Many examples of contextual supports endorsed were similar from pre to post (e.g., relational sources). However at post, participants endorsed more specifically named individual social and kin supports (e.g., listing the GEAR UP coordinators, specific teachers, and particular friends and family members by name or relation). At post compared to pre, participants listed additional sources of contextual or social support, such as pastor, church, school guidance counselor, and after-school and community programs (all sources of support reviewed during the second workshop). Also at post, consistent with learning objectives of the workshops, participants listed more contextual supports for seeking information (e.g., Internet) and contact with role models relevant to their occupations of interest.

Regarding personal resources at both pre and post, participants endorsed facilitative task approach skills regarding work habits (e.g., maintaining motivation to do one's best). More often at pre than at post, however, participants listed educational and career subgoals (more short-range goals toward future work and life goals), such as getting good grades and finishing high school. Although at post participants listed proportionately more contextual supports, the personal resources they endorsed at post slightly outnumbered those listed at pre (90 compared to 86). The personal resource supports that participants listed at post included additional examples of facilitative task approach skills (e.g., "determination," "self-discipline," "expressing yourself creatively," "living a healthy balanced life"). Participants also listed personal assets, abilities, or characteristics (e.g., "myself," creativity, bicultural, religious faith).

Workshop evaluations were completed by 31 of 33 participants at post. On a 5-point Likert-type scale, participants rated to what extent they agree (5) or disagree (1) with 16 statements of the learning objectives of the workshops. Participants' mean workshops evaluation rating on the four items on learning about sources of support was 4.68 ($SD = 0.47$), suggesting that they somewhat agreed or agreed that they learned about school and work supports relevant to their life and career goals.

Discussion

Congruent with our first hypothesis, we found that a higher level of beliefs in the limitations of education (school and work barrier beliefs) was significantly associated with lower educational and career aspirations in our sample of low-income, inner-city, African American, Hispanic/Latino(a), and Caribbean immigrant youth. This result was consistent with Kenny et al.'s (2003) finding that urban minority youth who perceived higher levels of barriers reported lower aspirations for their future careers. This result also supports Constantine et al.'s (1998) assertion that educational and career barriers encountered by urban minority youth may become internalized into their belief systems, thereby limiting their educational and career aspirations. On one hand, Steinberg et al. (1992) found that low-income minority youth understand that higher educational achievement generally leads to higher future economic rewards in career attainment. On the other hand, as our finding suggests, in the face of racism, cultural discrimination, economic deprivation, and inadequate schooling, many low-income minority youth believe that high educational and career aspirations are not attainable for them (Arbona, 2000; Graham et al., 1998; Murdock, 1999; Ogbu, 1989). Although such beliefs may be understandable responses to these barriers, these beliefs may reduce their aspirations, undermine their effort and persistence in educational and career development, and further constrain their future achievement.

Our results supported the second hypothesis. Low-income urban minority youth who were less recent immigrants had higher beliefs in the limitations of education for attaining future economic rewards and lower educational and career aspirations. These results support Ogbu's (1989, 1990, 2003) contention that compared to recent immigrants who still believe in the U.S. ideal of equal opportunity, minority youth who are not recent immigrants and have a history of experience contrary to this ideal may be particularly at risk for doubting the future economic value of education for them.

Contrary to our third hypothesis, we did not find that a higher level of perceived supports was associated with lower beliefs in the limitations of education or higher educational and career aspirations. In contrast, Kenny et al. (2003) found that urban minority youth who perceived higher levels of support from family and others within their environments endorsed more positive attitudes about the value of education and their future careers. Although our finding of no association may suggest that these influences function independently, an alternative explanation may be in the limitations of the measures of supports and aspirations used in this study. Problems with our measure of educational and career aspirations included a restricted range and the negatively skewed distribution of the data (for which we applied an inverse transformation to approximate normality). Future studies may help address this limitation by obtaining larger sample sizes and including urban minority youth with a broader range of educational and career aspirations. Also, our method of assessing the simple frequency of supports listed by participants has not been established as a robust measure. Future research is needed to develop sound methods for assessing the frequency and types of supports most relevant to facilitating the educational and career development of low-income urban minority youth.

The social learning theory of career development (Krumboltz, 1996) informed our design to pilot two workshops that might constructively challenge low-income urban minority youth's counterproductive school and work barrier beliefs by expanding their learning about accessible sources of support for attaining their career goals. One objective of the workshops was to help participants expand the number and types of support sources they might identify as accessible to them toward realizing their goals. We found that the mean number of support sources identified by participants did increase from pre to post. However, because we had no control or comparison group in this study, we cannot determine if the increase was a significant effect of the workshops. Yet participants reported high ratings on their evaluation of the workshops regarding the extent to which they learned about sources of support for their school, work, and life goals.

We found that participants who completed both career learning workshops did endorse two types of support sources: contextual supports (accessible in their environments) and personal resources (psychological assets within the individual). Contextual supports, particularly relational support from family and others (Blustein, 2001), have been shown to be critical factors in promoting academic success (Dryfoos, 1995; Paavola et al., 1995; Schorr, 1997) and, among minority youth in particular, higher levels of school engagement (Murdock, 1999) and career aspirations (Kenny et al., 2003). At both pre and post, participants in our study endorsed many of the same examples of relational and community contextual supports (e.g., parents, family, friends, coaches, and GEAR UP). At post, consistent with one purpose of the career learning workshops, participants listed more contextual supports for seeking information and contact with role models relevant to their occupations of interest. From the perspective of low-income urban minority youth, these findings affirmed the importance they attributed in the process of working toward their future educational and career goals to contextual support and helpful information from their family and other people, services, and institutions in their community.

Constantine et al. (1998) noted the need for empirical research to assess how both personal and external factors influence the career development of urban racial and ethnic minority youth. Jackson and Nutini's (2002) interviews with at-risk diverse urban youth revealed both internal (psychological) and external (contextual) supports for their educational and career development. We proposed that personal resources within the individual is a type of support that may be conceptualized from social learning theory (Krumboltz, 1994) as facilitative task approach skills (e.g., positive work habits and effective problem-solving skills). Our results affirmed this proposition. At both workshops, participants endorsed facilitative task approach skills regarding work habits (e.g., working hard and maintaining motivation to do one's best). More frequently at pre than at post, the personal resources listed by participants were academic achievement subgoals toward attaining future career and life goals (e.g., getting good grades, finishing high school). One explanation may be that participants were influenced by GEAR UP, which promoted these cognitive processes of educational and career planning and promoted forming short-range goals toward long-range goals. At post, consistent with the learning objectives of

the workshops, participants identified as personal resources additional examples of facilitative task approach skills, such as productive work habits (self-discipline), learning-oriented performance expectations (e.g., "willingness to learn," seeking opportunities to develop skills and knowledge in a career-related academic subject or athletic or artistic pursuit), helpful cognitive processes (e.g., "talking about my goals with others"), beneficial problem orientations (e.g., "listening skills," "constructive ways for dealing with problems"), self-regulated emotional responses (e.g., patience, sense of humor), and other personal assets (e.g., strong cultural identity, bilingual, skills in math, science, music). Many of the examples of personal resources endorsed by our participants are similar to protective factors or internal assets that have been shown to promote resilience in the face of adversity (e.g., positive identity, social competencies, and commitment to learning [Benson, Galbraith, & Espeland, 1998] and the ability to self-regulate emotion, attention, and behavior [Masten & Coatsworth, 1998]). Our results suggest that personal resources as well as contextual supports may be helpful targets in promoting educational and career development among low-income, urban minority youth who are at risk of low educational and career achievement.

LIMITATIONS AND FUTURE RESEARCH

Future studies might address generalizability questions raised concerning the small sample size in our study, large proportion of female to male participants, and predominance of Dominican Republican immigrants (perhaps culturally specific factors might offer alternative explanations for our results). Furthermore, our sample is not representative of the most disenfranchised among low-income urban minority youth, as our participants had the benefits of involvement with GEAR UP and the level of motivation to voluntarily attend on Saturdays the educational and career enrichment programs through which this study was conducted. Further research is needed to develop and examine the utility of the preliminary conceptualization of and coding scheme for personal resources proposed in this study. Furthermore, we used descriptive and correlational analyses, so causality cannot be assumed. Future studies using quasi-experimental designs are needed to examine the effectiveness of educational and career development interventions to constructively challenge unhelpful barrier beliefs and promote relevant supports with low-income, inner-city, culturally diverse youth.

APPENDIX

Coding Protocol for Sources of Support and Examples

1 = contextual supports

- Accessible in the participant's environment
- Helpful people, places, or services to facilitate one's educational and vocational development
  - Family
  - Friends
  - Teachers
  - Coaches
  - Internet
  - Library
  - Community people, places, services, programs
  - GEAR UP cohort coordinators
  - School guidance counselors
  - College office at school
  - *Occupational Outlook Handbook*

2 = personal resources

- Accessible within oneself to develop toward one's educational, vocational, and life goals
- Positive, constructive, or adaptive "task approach skills"—skills that individuals bring to a task—such as
  - Work habits
    - Studying
    - Practicing self-discipline
    - Working hard
  - Performance expectations
    - Good grades
    - Learning goals
    - Seeking opportunities to develop skills and knowledge in a career-related academic subject or athletic or artistic pursuit
  - Cognitive processes
    - Planning ahead
    - Positive beliefs about the value of education
    - Forming subgoals toward more long-range goals
    - Maintaining motivation to do one's best
    - Recognizing transferable skills
  - Problem orientations
    - Striving to learn from errors
    - Persisting in the face of obstacles
    - Using listening and empathy skills to understand multiple perspectives
    - Flexibility in considering and trying out options
  - Emotional responses
    - Effectively dealing with stress, conflict, or discrimination through positive emotional regulation
  - Personal assets, abilities, or characteristics to develop or apply
    - Religious faith
    - Relationship skills
    - Bicultural or multicultural experience and competence
    - Strong racial, ethnic, or cultural identity
    - Belief in oneself and one's abilities to learn and grow
    - Second language communication ability
    - Sense of humor
    - Service to one's community

References

Arbona, C. (2000). The development of academic achievement in school aged children: Precursors to career development. In S. D. Brown & R. W. Lent (Eds.), *Handbook of counseling psychology* (pp. 270–309). New York: Wiley.

Benson, P. L., Galbraith, J., & Espeland, P. (1998). *What kids need to succeed: Proven, practical ways to raise good kids.* Minneapolis, MN: Free Spirit.

Blustein, D. L. (2001). The interface of work and relationships: A critical knowledge base for 21st century psychology. *The Counseling Psychologist, 29,* 179–192.

Brown, S. D., & Ryan Krane, N. E. (2000). Four (or five) sessions and a cloud of dust: Old assumptions and new observations about career counseling. In S. D. Brown & R. W. Lent (Eds.), *Handbook of counseling psychology* (3rd ed., pp. 740–766). New York: Wiley.

Constantine, M. G., Erickson, C. D., Banks, R. W., & Timberlake, T. L. (1998). Challenges to the career development of urban racial and ethnic minority youth: Implications for vocational intervention. *Journal of Multicultural Counseling & Development, 26,* 82–95.

Dryfoos, J. G. (1995). Full service schools. Revolution or fad? *Journal of Research on Adolescence, 5,* 147–172.

Education Trust. (2000). *Achievement in America: GEAR UP.* Washington, DC: Author.

Graham, S., Taylor, A. Z., & Hudley, C. (1998). Exploring achievement values among ethnic minority early adolescents. *Journal of Educational Psychology, 90,* 606–620.

Holland, J. L. (1996). *The occupations finder* (SDS, Self-Directed Search, Form R, 4th ed.). Lutz, FL: Psychological Assessment Resources.

Jackson, M. A., & Nutini, C. D. (2002). Hidden resources and barriers in career learning assessment with adolescents vulnerable to discrimination. *The Career Development Quarterly, 51,* 56–77.

Kenny, M. E., Blustein, D. L., Chaves, A., Grossman, J. M., & Gallagher, L. A. (2003). The role of perceived barriers and relational support in the educational and vocational lives of urban high school students. *Journal of Counseling Psychology, 50,* 142–155.

Kenny, M. E., Waldo, M., Warter, E., & Barton, K. (2002). School-linked prevention: Theory, science and practice for enhancing the lives of children and youth. *The Counseling Psychologist, 30,* 726–748.

Krumboltz, J. D. (1991). *Manual for the Career Beliefs Inventory.* Palo Alto, CA: Consulting Psychologists Press.

Krumboltz, J. D. (1994). Improving career development theory from a social learning perspective. In M. L. Savickas & R. W. Lent (Eds.), *Convergence in career development theories* (pp. 9–31). Palo Alto, CA: Consulting Psychologists Press.

Krumboltz, J. D. (1996). A learning theory of career counseling. In M. L. Savickas & W. B. Walsh (Eds.), *Handbook of career counseling theory and practice* (pp. 55–80). Palo Alto, CA: Davies-Black.

Masten, A. S., & Coatsworth, J. D. (1998). The development of competence in favorable and unfavorable environments: Lessons from research on successful children. *American Psychologist, 53,* 205–220.

Mitchell, L. K., & Krumboltz, K. D. (1996). Krumboltz's learning theory of career choice and counseling. In D. Brown & L. Brooks (Eds.), *Career choice and development* (3rd ed., pp. 233–280). San Francisco: Jossey-Bass.

Murdock, T. B. (1999). The social context of risk: Status and motivational predictors of alienation in middle school. *Journal of Educational Psychology, 91,* 62–75.

Murdock, T. B., Anderman, L., & Hodge, S. (2000). Middle-grades predictors of student motivation and behavior in high school. *Journal of Adolescent Research, 15,* 327–351.

Ogbu, J. U. (1989). Cultural boundaries and minority youth orientation toward work preparation. In D. Stern & D. Eichorn (Eds.), *Adolescence and work: Influences of social structure, labor markets, and culture* (pp. 101–140). Mahwah, NJ: Lawrence Erlbaum.

Ogbu, J. U. (1990). Minority education in comparative perspective. *Journal of Negro Education, 59,* 45–57.

Ogbu, J. U. (2003). *Black American students in an affluent suburb: A study of academic disengagement.* Mahwah, NJ: Lawrence Erlbaum.

Paavola, J. C., Cobb, C., Illback, R. J., Joseph, H. M., Torruellaa, A., & Talley, R. C. (1995). *Comprehensive and coordinated psychological services for children: A call for service integration.* Washington, DC: American Psychological Association.

Schorr, L. B. (1997). *Common purpose: Strengthening families and neighborhoods to rebuild America.* New York: Anchor.

Solberg, V. S., Howard, K., Blustein, D. L., & Close, W. (2002). Career development in the schools: Connecting school-to-work-to-life. *The Counseling Psychologist, 30,* 705–725.

Steinberg, L., Dornbusch, S. M., & Brown, B. B. (1992). Ethnic differences in adolescent achievement: An ecological perspective. *American Psychologist, 47,* 723–729.

Turner, S. L., & Lapan, R. T. (2003). The measurement of career interests among at-risk inner-city and middle-class suburban adolescents. *Journal of Career Assessment, 11,* 405–420.

U.S. Department of Education. (1996). *Urban schools: The challenge of location and poverty* (NCES Publication No. 96–184r). Washington, DC: Government Printing Office.

Discussion Questions

1. Why is it important to study immigrant students' barrier beliefs about work and education?

   These questions are not addressed directly in the article. Students should consider the alternatives for inner-city youth with no perceived future educational and/or work goals. What impact will this have on society? And on the quality of life for these youth?

2. What three hypotheses were tested in this study, with what results?

   a. *Higher levels of beliefs in the limitations of education are associated with lower educational and career aspirations.*

   b. *Less recent immigrant status is associated with higher beliefs in limitations of education and lower educational and career aspirations.*

   c. *Higher levels of supports are associated with lower beliefs in the limitations of education and higher educational and career aspirations.*

   All hypotheses were confirmed.

Source: From Jackson, M. A., Mendelsohn Kacanski, J., Rust, J. P., & Beck, S. E. (2006). Constructively challenging diverse inner-city youth's beliefs about educational and career barriers and supports. *Journal of Career Development, 32(3),* 203–218. Reprinted by permission of Sage Publications.

CHAPTER 17

The Paradox of Poverty Narratives

Educators Struggling With Children Left Behind

Cynthia I. Gerstl-Pepin (2006)

Cynthia I. Gerstl-Pepin explores the relationship between the No Child Left Behind legislation and class inequality. Based on qualitative research, she concludes that policymakers must acknowledge and value the challenges faced by teachers and staff who work with students and families living in poverty.

An equal society begins with equally excellent schools, but we know our schools today are not equal. The failure of many urban schools is a great and continuing scandal. Rarely in American history have we faced a problem so serious and destructive on which change has come so slowly. (Bush, 2001a, §12)

There's a perception that people living in poverty are not working hard enough. We live in a culture that blames victims. It blames poor people and the teaching profession, but as a society, we need to look at the big picture. Most employers of low-income parents do not let them take a half day to come to a school conference. They would lose pay and have to ride the bus back and forth just to get here. We need to look at what families are up against trying to get affordable housing, transportation, and a job with healthcare that pays a livable wage. It's stressful enough to raise children when you have the resources. (Westover Elementary school teacher, personal communication, May 19, 2005)

George W. Bush's comments on education, aired on *CNN*, might have been chilling if they had not been so familiar. Since the publication of *A Nation at Risk* in 1983 (National Commission on Excellence in Education,

1983), U.S. politicians and media commentators have intermittently raised the specter of failing schools, each time lamenting the glacial pace of change. Rarely, however, do policymakers do what the teacher quoted does—set school inequities in a context of social inequities. Powerful stories, such as the one President Bush promulgates, are used to justify policymaking: "Because of their simplicity and transparency, narratives can crystallize and mobilize public opinion, and force an issue to the top of the political agenda" (Hyman, 2000, p. 1149).

The far-reaching reauthorization of the Title I component of the Elementary and Secondary Education Act (ESEA, 1965) entitled the *No Child Left Behind Act* (NCLB, 2002) is one such policy. It reflects a long held belief that the public education system alone is responsible for achievement gaps between children living in poverty and children from more affluent families.

Educators are often assumed to be primarily responsible for these gaps. Research highlights the importance of an effective teacher for student success (Haberman, 1995). However, these public assumptions and representations often present a narrow view of education and do not acknowledge the very real contextual disparities in which different teachers find themselves. The social justice narrative embedded in NCLB suggests student success should not be determined by a student's economic circumstances. Although this is a noble sentiment, it misses the deeper social justice challenges that children and parents from impoverished backgrounds and their teachers face every day. In the past few years, research has highlighted the importance of early childhood education, nutrition, health care, and the well-being of parents and caregivers for a child's success in school and society (Meyers, Rosenbaum, Ruhm, & Waldfogel, 2004; Pebley & Sastry, 2004). For example, Evans (2004) notes, "Low-income children in comparison to middle-income children are exposed to greater levels of violence, family disruption, and separation from their family" (p. 78). Furthermore, many of the traditional safety nets that low-income families have counted on—such as company pension plans, health insurance, and welfare supports—have dwindled significantly during the past few decades (Gordon, 1994; Piven & Cloward, 1993; Weiss, 2004).

Class inequities are also embedded in the norms that shape schooling. Middle-class families are often able to maneuver their children through public schooling in a way that results in higher achievement (Brantliner, 2003). Schools as institutions are embedded with the same economic inequities that permeate society (Apple, 2004). It is no surprise that wealthier students are more successful in schools because school curricula reflect middle-class norms about what counts as knowledge (Apple, 2004).

Yet for some reason, the public, and more importantly policymakers, assume that the individuals who inhabit schools are somehow not working hard enough. They minimize the social justice implications of poverty, such as the complex interrelated issues of improper health care, early childhood care, nutrition, literacy, and livable wages that are important factors in a child's readiness for school (McLaren, 2005). This alternative narrative is not included in the dominant stories that frame educational policymaking. Moreover, a natural human response to this social crisis is to care, which carries an additional burden for educators who seek to make a difference in the lives of their students. To examine this paradox, this article uses narrative policy analysis to examine the social justice narrative embedded in No Child Left Behind, specifically with respect to the economic inequities, and compares it to the narratives of educators working within a school that serves an economically challenged community.

Examining Poverty via Narrative Policy Analysis

Narrative policy analysis builds on literary theory that highlights the ways in which power is embedded in language (Roe, 1994). To understand policy stories, it is important to understand power—the ability of a group, individual, or structure to exercise control or authority. Collins (2000) suggests that power relations are unequal and operate on an array of levels. These power relations include overt and covert exertions of control and domination, including individual experiences of prejudice and bias and structural forms of power (such as policies, organizational structures, or legislation). Policies are a form of power that operate through a "constellation of organized practices in employment, government, education, law, business, and housing that work to maintain an unequal and unjust distribution of resources" (Collins, 2000, p. 301). When policy issues are highly complex and uncertain, such as the achievement gap, narrative policy analysis provides a way of examining how policy stories shape policymaking. "Sometimes what we are left to deal with are not the facts but the different stories that people tell as a way of articulating and making sense of the uncertainties and complexities that matter to them" (Roe, 1994, p. IX). Focusing on policy narratives provides a way of exploring how stories are used to shape policy issues. Through examination of these stories, narrative policy analysis seeks to build a more comprehensive and complex picture of policy issues.

Roe (1994) articulates three key components of narrative policy analysis; dominant policy narratives, nonstories and counterstories, and metanarratives. Primary policy narratives are those used to establish and stabilize policy assumptions when an issue involves a great deal of complexity, ambiguity, or divisiveness. Nonstories are stories that do not conform to the primary policy narratives, whereas counterstories are stories that contradict the primary policy narratives. Once the primary narratives and nonstories have been identified, Roe suggests that the policy analyst can synthesize the narratives together to develop a metanarrative. The term *metanarrative* used here is different from the term described by postmodernists (e.g., Lyotard, 1984). Postmodernists are wary of "big M" metanarratives such as deterministic social theories that seek to homogenize experience. Policy narrative analysis, in contrast, uses the notion of "little m" metanarratives that seek to complicate our understanding of policy issues by integrating seemingly conflicting policy stories together. The purpose of the metanarrative, then, is to transform these polarized narratives into "another story altogether" (Roe, 1994, p. 4).

In this analysis, I focus on uncovering the interaction between dominant narratives, nonstories, and metanarratives to examine how poverty complicates teaching. Because of the polarized nature of educational reform, this approach provides a way of examining the nonstory of poverty embedded in the NCLB policy. Narrative policy analysis provides one way of expanding our understanding of school reform and NCLB by encompassing alternative school reform stories and narratives that have not been included in the dominant school reform policy narratives.

Methods

At both the federal and local level, stories were collected via a qualitative approach to narrative policy analysis. To capture the dominant policy narrative at the federal level, semistructured interviews were conducted with three key political informants on Capitol Hill who were knowledgeable about NCLB. Additionally, a document review was conducted on federal policy legislation, public documents, and media documents such as newspaper articles and television transcripts. These documents provided a way of capturing the official stories used to promote and justify NCLB for public consumption.

These initial data were expanded with case study data (Merriam, 1992) designed to capture narrative stories within a high-poverty school. Semistructured interviews were conducted with seven teachers, the principal, and an outside reading consultant. The school is one of the poorest elementary schools in New England with 100% of the students qualifying for the free and reduced lunch program. The school was selected because it represents a unique case sample (Patton, 2002). Although the school serves an impoverished community, it significantly increased test scores in reading and was considered a state and national success story. Narrative policy analysis was used to analyze the data. First, dominant stories were identified, then nonstories. These two sets of stories were then woven together into a combined metanarrative. The next section explores the dominant policy narratives used to justify NCLB and is followed by a section on the nonstories of poverty. Then, a final section intertwines the themes from the two previous sections into a combined metanarrative.

Dominant Policy Narratives Shaping NCLB

Dominant narratives around NCLB reveal themselves in the public speeches, documents, legislation, and media reporting surrounding the reauthorization of ESEA. Similar to the Reagan administration of the 1980s,

George W. Bush's administration has relied heavily on the use of what the press term the *bully pulpit* (Wirt & Kirst, 1992, p. 252): public speeches and public relations documents serve as avenues for perpetuating stories that seek to validate NCLB on moral grounds. There is a strong sense in Washington that President Bush was the force behind the creation and passage of NCLB. As one Washington insider noted, "The bill was Bush's idea and without him it would have never gotten bi-partisan support." Although on the surface, NCLB seems to be about ensuring that all children are successful, the words used to justify the legislation focus more on describing the policy problem as holding failing educational systems accountable.

The aphorism, *No Child Left Behind,* serves as a policy narrative in itself, powerful in its social justice content but also misleading. On one hand, the idea implies that the needs of each child will be addressed; yet at the same time, it assumes that if schools only changed their assumptions about students, the achievement gap would cease to exist. Interestingly, during Bush's initial bid for the White House, he originally referred to his reform package as "Leave No Child Behind": that was the slogan that Marion Wright Edelman and the Children's Defense Fund used to focus on the holistic needs of children and encompassed a need to address housing, food, child care, health care, clothing, transportation, and livable wages ("Children Left Behind," 2001; Children's Defense Fund, 2004).

For Bush, though, the central justification for the legislation is the notion that schools and teachers are leaving children behind.

> When we find failure we're going to do something about it. We're going to take corrective action in society. But if a school can't change, if a school can't show the parents and the community leaders that they can teach the basics, something else has to take place. In order for there to be accountability, there has to be consequences. (Bush, 2002, §79)

For Bush, no other factors (such as economic inequities or the geographical segregation of high-poverty communities) intrude on his narrative: failure is a result of not being held accountable. The failure is contained entirely within the schools themselves, as if they existed in a separate dimension completely independent of the other obstacles children face when they leave the school grounds.

An additional troubling aspect of the stories used to justify NCLB is that race is emphasized to the point that poverty almost disappears. The achievement gap is often referred to almost exclusively as a racial issue, but this story minimizes the central role that poverty plays in achievement inequities. Although the percentages of students of color living in poverty are higher than White students, the reality is that low-income White students are also failing in high numbers in rural and suburban areas (Books, 2004), as this quote from Bush reveals:

> And then you'll hear people say it's racist to test. Folks, it's racist not to test, because guess who gets shuffled through the system oftentimes? Children whose parents don't speak English as a first language. Inner-city kids. It's so much easier to quit on somebody than to . . . remediate. (Bush, 2001b, §30–31)

Bush's use of the term *inner city* in this quote is a codeword for students of color. In deploying the phrase, Bush perpetuates dominant stories that identify race as the central issue in school achievement differentials.

Although addressing the cultural construct of racism is critically important to understanding achievement inequities, economic factors are also critical (Books, 2004; Rothstein, 2004). The historical legacy of racism embodied in slavery and the cultural imperialism that immigrants endure have been acknowledged as important factors in school achievement (Anderson, 1988; Rothstein, 2004; Valenzuela, 1999). When cultural and economic factors are conflated, however, the racial gap dominates, minimizing the very real economic inequities that cross racial boundaries.

Untangling the Complexity of Poverty

Poverty, as a concept, is at once well researched and yet poorly understood from a policy perspective. Federal guidelines for defining poverty have been criticized for being too low, inadequate to cover basic needs such as housing, food, and clothing (Citro & Michael, 1995; National Center for Children in Poverty [NCCP], 2005). The term *low income* describes an income level that would cover basic needs, an amount twice the poverty level. In 2004, the federal poverty level was designated as $18,850 for a family of four, so $37,700 is the amount a family of four on average would need to make ends meet (Institutes for Research on Poverty, 2005). Under these guidelines, 38% of children younger than the age of 18 (almost 27 million) live in low-income families, whereas 17% (more than 11 million) live in poor families (NCCP, 2005). Additionally, poverty rates vary greatly between states (NCCP, 2004). On average between 2001 and 2003, the poverty rates were lowest in New Hampshire,

Connecticut, Delaware, Maryland, and Minnesota (all less than 8%), whereas Arkansas and New Mexico had the highest poverty rates (18% or more) (Institutes for Research on Poverty, 2005).

Poverty is considered to be an important factor in school failure (Orfield & Lee, 2005; Phillips & Chin, 2004; Rothstein, 2004). High school dropout rates are higher for low income students, and male students who drop out are 5 to 20 times more likely to be incarcerated than men who attend college (Western, Kleykamp, & Rosenfeld, 2004). There is also a documented relationship between inadequate child care (because of the high cost of quality care) and the likelihood that a student will drop out of school and eventually end up in prison (Masse & Barnett, 2002). Although there is an awareness that economics matter, the assumption of equality of opportunity serves as the justification for looking exclusively at schools rather than wider contextual factors. Equality of opportunity assumes that schools can serve as great equalizers despite social inequities (Books, 2004).

Nonstories of Serving a High-Poverty Community

This section discusses the nonstories that emerged out of interviews with teachers, educators, and staff at Westover Elementary School (a pseudonym), a high-poverty school that increased reading scores through a comprehensive reform model. The stories gleaned from a narrative analysis suggest a more complex story of school change. Before NCLB was passed, Westover had already transformed itself through the adoption of a whole school reform model that targeted literacy. In 1998, only 44% of students met standards in reading that led to the school being identified as one of the lowest performing schools in the state. Starting in 2000, the school applied for and received a comprehensive school reform grant that allowed the school to hire a literacy consultant, purchase materials, and add additional staff. Not only did the school undergo substantial professional development, but as a staff, they made a schoolwide commitment to change. The change process generated a dramatic turnaround in reading test scores with 83% of students exceeding or meeting state reading standards.

Westover is situated in a high-poverty community with 100% of its students qualifying for a free or reduced lunch. Additionally, the school's student population is diverse with 20% of students designated as limited English proficiency, 20% qualifying for special education services, and 28.2% representing racial minorities. Westover also has a student transience rate of 20% and has five times the state average of children in foster care or protective custody. There is no racial gap in testing; consequently the influence of poverty is pronounced at the school.

CREATING A CARING COMMUNITY BY UNDERSTANDING POVERTY

Rather than assuming that poverty should not matter in student achievement, as the dominant NCLB narrative seems to suggest, the teachers at Westover viewed understanding poverty as central to helping students learn. The leadership team at the school focused initially on changing the school culture. As one teacher noted, "We looked at really trying to create a caring community." Work with the literacy specialist helped them see that much of classroom instruction was focused on controlling the students rather than teaching them. Their awareness of this was fostered by visiting a school in New York City that served a similar community. Although many teachers expected the school to be very structured and controlled, they discovered a very different school culture. As a staff member noted,

> When we went to see schools in NYC . . . we assumed there would be a lot of rules, consequences and suspensions. It was not like that. The school was really about good instruction and meeting kids' needs where they were at. The teachers didn't say, "Oh, a child has to leave the room when they act out and they are not allowed back: "[I]nstead, they said "We want kids in our room and we do everything we can to keep them learning and we know it might be really hard." So, I think . . . that really changed our thinking to focus on creating a caring community.

Creating a positive environment where students felt cared for became important. They began to realize that they had made assumptions about what their students needed because of their community and economic background.

With the leadership of the principal, the school as a whole began to look at how economic inequities might be hindering student success. Specifically, they began to try and understand what was causing students to be disruptive. One of the professional development activities targeted by the principal was helping the faculty understand how poverty shapes their student's lives. Teachers participated in workshops on poverty and read Payne's

(2001) *A Framework for Understanding Poverty* to become aware of how middle-class norms shape classroom environments. As one teacher noted,

> We started to read things, like *A Framework for Understanding Poverty,* just to raise our awareness of class expectations. It helped me realize that our school was operating through a middle-class lens and that our kids didn't necessarily recognize that lens. So, we started to unpack those sorts of things.

Educators at Westover recognized that they could not assume that students understood middle-class norms around behavior and attitude, so in addition to teaching reading, they were careful to educate students on expected classroom behavior. Then they also examined their own instruction and why they had been so focused on controlling students.

> I think when you have kids who misbehave you tend to react by making the classroom more like prison. I think there is a human tendency to want to punish, punish, punish, and research says it doesn't work, but you know, you kind of get caught in that mode sometimes. So we started to ask questions like, "How do we provide instruction so that kids feel confident?"

This shift not only created a more positive environment for students but also created a more supportive environment for teachers and staff. By working together as a staff to address student issues through common meeting times and professional development activities, the school became more cohesive. Student behavior became more positive as did the school culture that created a more positive learning and working environment for students, teachers, and staff.

They began to realize that many of the behavioral problems in their classrooms were related to student insecurities.

> I think it was pretty clear that students acted out because they assumed that it was better to be bad than stupid. They thought that if they acted out, then teachers wouldn't know they couldn't read. And I really think they were thinking, "Get me out of this classroom; it's way too hard. If I misbehave, I'll get pulled out, and then I don't have to worry that I don't understand." So, there was a lot of that going on when we started our work.

Additionally, the staff at the school worked together to develop literacy assessments to gauge student ability levels in reading. The periodic assessments provided a way to document student skills to systematically measure student progress in reading throughout the year. As this teacher noted, "The assessments helped us identify students who were most in need of attention. What we found is that our students are really good at looking good, even if they don't understand. They are good at faking it, so you wouldn't necessarily know that they were in such deficit mode."

Educators at the school also developed an innovative approach for helping students who might ordinarily be lost. These were not students who were designated special education; rather, they were students that teachers and staff felt were in danger of failing. The team involved the classroom teacher, principal, and other educators who brainstorm ways to meet student needs and ensure they would make progress.

Westover educators have made significant progress in creating a welcoming and caring environment for students.

> For a lot of our kids, they don't want the summer. They don't want school to end. They are scared. School is a stable, safe place for them. This is where they get food; they don't eat at home; they come to school dirty. It's not as easy in our school as it is in a middle-class school. Not that middle-class students are easier to teach; rather, our students come with a lot more to work on.

The teachers realize that school is an important place for students whose home lives are challenging and unstable.

Seeing Literacy as Empowerment and Enjoyment

In addition to tackling assumptions around poverty, school staff reframed their work in social justice terms. Specifically, they saw supporting literacy as a way to empower students. They did not just want to teach students how to read but they also wanted them to enjoy reading and to engage texts that resonated with their interests.

> I knew in my heart that if we were going to make a difference in the lives of these children, we needed to literally enrich their lives and not just treat reading as a task. The model that we choose is very much a model that is child centered . . . It also works at matching kid's reading lives with their real lives, so that they're not separate. They can find characters in the books that resemble themselves and their

circumstances. . . . This way of teaching reading is really a form of social action and can really open the world to a child.

These teachers viewed literacy as a form of social justice in that engagement with literature can empower students to become lifelong learners. Consequently, reading is not just a skill that is taught, as NCLB implies; rather, the focus is on encouraging students to enjoy reading and books.

At Westover, they are aware of the class inequities that add a unique complexity to the act of teaching. When teaching is reduced to NCLB's technocratic narratives such as needing to employ scientifically based instruction, dominant policy narratives can miss the passionate reasons why teachers want to teach. One aspect that can aid in teacher retention is a supportive work environment and pride in their work (Metz, 1988), as this educator notes:

> For me, the greatest reward I've had so far is visiting classrooms, hearing kids talk about reading aloud and their reading plans, and knowing that they are indeed readers. When the governor visited, they asked him questions like, "What books have you been reading lately?" and "What's the book that changed your life or touched your heart?" These kids carry books around; they are part of their lives and they are reading them.

The degree of engagement of the students is apparent in how comfortable they felt questioning the governor about his own reading habits.

Teaching is a caring profession similar to nursing and social work. Teachers, who work in economically challenged communities, often do not go into teaching because they want to test students. Many have become teachers because they have a social justice interest in making the world a better place for children (Casey, 1993) For children in need, teachers often have to cross boundaries and help with the issues that can get in the way of teaching, as this educator notes:

> We often have to deal with crises that do not relate to what you traditionally think school is about. We deal with issues like drugs, health, housing, or what have you. We really have to support the kids and their families. Many of our teachers make home visits. They pick kids up just to make sure they get to school. They make those kinds of extraordinary efforts all of the time. Their heart is certainly there;

they want to serve this population. All of the teachers were given the opportunity to leave with no strings attached and to transfer to other schools but they decided to stay. So to me, working in this school requires a huge commitment and personal sacrifice.

These personal sacrifices often go unacknowledged by policymakers. Instead, the cult of efficiency model dominates, which places a high value on standardization in the United States (Bracey, 2002; Callahan, 1962). The stories woven together to support NCLB are frequently laced with discussions of the need for punitive measures and consequences for failing schools and their employers.

NCLB's dominant policy narrative asserts that if teachers just worked hard enough and had high expectations of their students, there would be no achievement gap. However, this story oversimplifies the very real context of schools. Equally important are the narratives about the need for passionate and skilled teachers who are willing to make personal sacrifices for their students.

The work by scholars such as Anyon (1997), illustrates a different story. They suggest that it is difficult to truly change the life chances of a child unless you also work on the community context in which children live. Anyon does not suggest that a quality education is not possible for children living in poverty; rather that quality schooling alone will not necessarily transform the child's home life, health, or their parents' job prospects. Some children face such a challenging home situation that schools serve only part of their needs. The teachers at Westover Elementary paint a different picture. They have made a significant difference in the lives of the children they serve in terms of opening the world of literacy to them and in creating a safe, caring, and supportive environment for learning. What is different though is the emotional toll serving children with so many needs can take:

The personal sacrifice you make is immense, and that is not really recognized by the public and policymakers. The reward is certainly the difference you make in kids' lives. There is a real trade-off in terms of stress and trying to address so many needs. When you care about kids, it really hurts when you know they lack basic necessities like warm clothes, food, health care, or a stable home. It breaks your heart.

Making a difference in the lives of children is not the easy task that dominant NCLB narratives seem to imply. It is hard work to teach children who have multiple needs and sometimes it is emotionally devastating.

Acknowledging this challenge rather than minimizing it would place more of a value on the teaching profession.

The teachers and staff at Westover work hard to create a supportive environment for students but sometimes, after encountering the inequities their students face, educators themselves need support.

I have to constantly challenge myself not to become numb to poverty and the challenges these kids face every day. Just the other day, I was about to drive out of the parking lot when I noticed a child standing in the rain without a jacket. It was cold. I almost just drove off, I was tired, and I see those inequities every day. I had to stop myself and say, "Hey, wait a minute; this is not okay." I had to remind myself that in middle-class communities, this would be unacceptable. So I stopped the car and went over to take care of the child. The gross inequities you see everyday are heartbreaking.

This is one of the nonstories that are ignored by the public justifications of NCLB, namely the very real and painful aspects of serving children living in poverty. Teacher turnover in high-poverty schools is much higher (Books, 2004). When a community faces so many challenges, these seep into the school. They are part of the context in which the school and students are situated. Collectively, teachers, staff, and administrators confront a myriad of nonschool emergencies including medical, criminal justice, and human services. Distressing situations often have to be dealt with on a daily basis. For example, one teacher at Westover observed,

The other thing that stands in the way of improvement in a school like this is just the complexity of it. It's the daily trauma of a community in crisis . . . and people don't realize this is happening and that it tends to make people feel powerless, like you can't make a difference and slowly your belief in your own abilities and . . . your students starts to erode. You don't mean for it happen but it is just such a powerful force, the poverty, the complexity, the kids in crisis, the trauma. The school starts to resemble an emergency room. You're just responding, so you can't feel proactive and you don't feel confident in your responses.

Acknowledging the potentially traumatic side of the work that teachers engage in is important. Teachers need a supportive and caring environment just as much as students.

Although policymakers suggest that schools in general are failing (Berliner & Biddle, 1997; Gerstl-Pepin, 2002), the reality for the teachers at Westover is that their job is stressful and at times their work is challenged by crises that occur around students' lives outside of school, as this educator notes:

> I think when we started this work teachers thought that . . . the work would get easier. But they realize now that it's never going to be easy teaching here. You always have to be well planned; you always have to be on top of things. I don't mean that teachers aren't always working hard, but you can't stay up late or have down time in the evening. I was talking to a former colleague who used to work in a similar school, and she said, "You know, now I can go to a movie on Thursday night!" You would never do that working here because you have to be ready for anything that happens.

It is in many cases much easier for a teacher who primarily teaches in communities that are less corrosive. This is not to suggest that middle-and upper-class students do not also face challenges around academic achievement, but rather that lower income children have a much greater likelihood of not succeeding in school because of economic and resource inequities.

Implications: The Poverty Dilemma as a Metanarrative

> The emergence of any problem may divert public attention from a different one that can be more threatening. Such covert masking of more ominous conditions is a property of discourse about public issues and often an explanation for the willingness of a large public to accept an issue as legitimate even if they have no particular interest in remedying it. (Edelman, 1988, p. 27)

The above quote by Edelman raises an important point about how policy problems are defined. Shifting blame to schools and away from economic disparities allows social inequalities to remain firmly entrenched. Because the dominant narrative on NCLB defines teachers and schools as the heart of educational ills, the harsh realities of poverty remain hidden. Bringing together the dominant narratives around NCLB and the nonstories of teachers and staff as Westover Elementary

involves taking a step back and trying to see both stories as important. Disaggregating test scores by race and class is an important outcome of the NCLB legislation, and one agreed on by the president and lawmakers of all political persuasions. Clearly, in the stories that Westover educators tell, it is also important to recognize the particular challenges that educators face who work in high-poverty schools and to acknowledge that the neighborhoods struggling with poverty contribute significantly to a child's chances. Furthermore, these narratives suggest that it is also critical to see poverty as a distinct factor in a child's life that should not be conflated with race. Although educators, such as the ones at Westover, have made significant gains, school reform is only one of a multiplicity of factors that need to be addressed.

Policymakers suggest that the crux of the argument is that educators claim these kids are too hard to teach. It is time, policymakers argue, to stop making excuses. What this narrative ignores is that lower income children and those living in poverty are the ones who are most likely to come to school unprepared, and this adds a layer of complexity to the work that teachers do. Their students are also more likely to live in communities that are dangerous and inequitable. We also know that investing in early childhood education can reap significant benefits and has even been correlated with keeping kids out of prison.

For schools such as Westover, sustaining the change process is always challenging (Berman & McLaughlin, 1978; Shields & Knapp, 1997). Since the initial data collection, they no longer have the literacy consultant or the comprehensive school reform grant. Although they successfully won a Reading First grant under NCLB to assist with literacy, the federal focus on scientifically based reading instruction meant that they had to forego their successful program in favor of an NCLB-approved program. The new focus on the science of reading further minimized the importance of creating a caring learning community for children who may be emotionally fragile (Gerstl-Pepin & Woodside-Jiron, 2005). Emphasizing the science of education more than emotional connection has the potential to reinforce the institutional aspects of schooling, thus, equating schools more with prisons (Foucault, 1979) rather than a supportive learning environment where students make connections and feel cared for (Noddings, 2002).

Although plenty of schools and teachers have served children living in poverty and helped them become literate, we also know that a startling number of children receive inadequate preschool preparation and have parents who were not successful in school themselves (Meyers et al., 2004; Shonkoff & Phillips, 2000), as this educator at Westover also noted:

> I've certainly always been an advocate for early child programs for kids going into really good early childhood settings. Having childcare programs where all of the people involved are trained and understand the importance of early literacy is really important. I mean, we can certainly do far more with a child who has been engaged with 1,000 books than we can with child who has had only 25. . . . I think if we could prepare children entering school by making sure that all of our childcare programs nationwide had good resources and well-trained staff, we would be a lot farther along in this whole literacy business.

What is most troubling is that we have research that highlights the importance of devastating external factors such as the challenges of single parenting, lack of affordable housing, inadequate childhood education, violence, inaccessible health care, or even lack of books, clothing, toys, or food (Books, 2004; Diener, Nievar, & Wright, 2003; Okin, 2003; Pebley & Sastry, 2004; Rothstein, 2004; Shonkop & Phillips, 2000). Scholars (Hewlett, Rankin, & West, 2002; Hewlett & West, 1998) have also highlighted the plight of parents in today's society and the many challenges they face with the cost of child care and employers that are not supportive of time off to care for sick children or involvement in their child's school, particularly in the service industry. Single parents face an even bigger challenge in making ends meet and rearing children (Ellwood & Jencks, 2004), which is an important consideration because 50% of children living in low income families live in single parent households (NCCP, 2004).

In the high-stress situation that many schools serving economically depressed communities find themselves, it is challenging to sustain the level of work required to help students. This is not only in terms of personnel but also resources, as a larger portion of funding for high-poverty schools is now provided through grants for which these schools must continually apply. It is also important to acknowledge the emotional aspects of working in high-poverty schools. When educators care about their students, the impact of child abuse, violence, transience, nutrition, and constant emergencies can take their toll, as Liston and Garrison (2004) assert:

> Seeing the students before us as whole human beings in search of meaning is the kind of understanding that a loving perspective affords teachers. Seeing the hurt and the pain that inevitably arise from daily life is another such recognition. Love makes us vulnerable and that vulnerability invites loss and grief. (p. 2)

When you care about a student, then the gross inequities of the child's situation can be painful and challenging. It is therefore important for policymakers to celebrate the work of teachers who are making a difference, as this teacher noted:

> You can take all of the scientifically based research in the world and you can have teachers who know every little move to make, but if they don't have the heart to work in a place like this, it won't make any difference. Every child will be left behind if that heart isn't there. And that's something that's really, really hard to mandate.

The NCLB narrative of accountability claims to focus on not leaving children behind, but this ignores the critical issue of early childhood education (via quality child care) and the often toxic environments in which these children live. Focusing on school reform without also elevating the stature of teachers and early childhood educators—and acknowledging the challenges they face—is a gross injustice and flawed policy.

If as a society we truly want to address the issue of children being left behind, we need to expand how inequities are described and acknowledge that the reason many children come to school unprepared is related to economic and cultural inequities. Additionally, conflating race with poverty ignores the very real impact that economic disparities have on children and the communities that they inhabit. The narratives of Westover educators show how challenging working in high-poverty communities can be. When educators transform a school into a caring environment, they open themselves to the trauma of their students' lives. This is not to say that teachers who work in high-poverty schools should not care but rather that the honorable work that they do needs to be acknowledged and supported.

References

Anderson, J. D. (1988). *The education of Blacks in the South, 1860–1935.* Chapel Hill: University of North Carolina Press.

Anyon, J. (1997). *Ghetto schooling: A political economy of urban educational reform.* New York: Teachers College Press.

Apple, M. W. (2004). *Ideology and curriculum.* New York: Routledge.

Berliner, D. C. & Biddle, B. J. (1997). *The manufactured crisis: Myths, fraud, and the attack on America's public schools.* White Plains, NY: Longman.

Berman, P., & McLaughlin, M. (1978). *Federal programs supporting educational changes, Vol. VIII: Implementing and sustaining innovation.* Santa Monica, CA: RAND.

Books, S. (2004). *Poverty and schooling in the U.S.: Contexts and consequences.* Mahwah, NJ: Lawrence Erlbaum.

Bracey, G. W. (2002). *The war against America's public schools: Privatizing schools, commercializing education.* Boston, MA: Allyn & Bacon.

Brantliner, E. (2003). *Dividing classes: How the middle class negotiates and rationalizes school advantage.* New York: Routledge/Falmer.

Bush, G. W. (2001a, August 1). *White House Briefing: Remarks by President George W. Bush to the National Urban League Conference.* The Washington Convention Center. Washington, D.C. Federal News Service.

Bush, G. W. (2001b, August 21). *Remarks by President George W. Bush.* Harry S. Truman High School. Independence, Missouri: Federal News Service.

Bush, G. W. (2002, January 8). *George W. Bush delivers remarks on education.* Durham, NH: Federal News Service.

Callahan, R. E. (1962). *Education and the cult of efficiency: A study of the social forces that have shaped the administration of the public schools.* Chicago: University of Chicago Press.

Casey, K. (1993). *I answer with my life: Life histories of women teachers working for social change.* New York: Routledge.

Children left behind [Editorial]. (2001, December 17). *Boston Globe* (3rd ed.), p. A20.

Children's Defense Fund. (2004, August). *Defining poverty and why it matters for children.* Washington, DC: Author.

Citro, C. F., & Michael, R.T. (Eds.). (1995). *Measuring poverty: A new approach, Commission on Behavioral and Social Sciences and Education.* Washington, DC: National Academy.

Collins, P. H. (2000). *Black feminist thought: Knowledge, consciousness, and the politics of empowerment.* New York: Routeledge.

Diener, M. L., Nievar, M. A., & Wright, C. (2003). Attachment security among mothers and their young children living in poverty: Associations with maternal, child, and contextual characteristics. *Merrill-Palmer Quarterly, 49*(2), 154–182.

Edelman, M. (1988). *Constructing the political spectacle.* Chicago: University of Chicago Press.

Elementary and Secondary Education Act. (1965). Pub. L. No. 89–10, 79 Stat. 27, 20 U.S.C. §§6301 et seq.

Ellwood, D. T. & Jencks, C. (2004). The uneven spread of single-parent families: What do we know? Where do we look for answers. In K. M. Neckerman (Ed.), *Social inequality* (p. 3–77). New York: Russell Sage.

Evans, G. W. (2004). The environment of childhood poverty. *American Psychologist, 59*(2), 77–92.

Foucault, M. (1979). *Discipline and punish: The birth of the prison* (A. Sheridan, Trans.). New York: Vintage Books.

Gerstl-Pepin, C. I. (2002). Media (mis)representations of education in the 2000 presidential election. *Educational Policy, 16,* 37–55.

Gerstl-Pepin, C. I., & Woodside-Jiron, H. (2005). Tensions between the "science" of reading and a "love of learning": One high poverty school's struggle with NCLB. *Equity & Excellence in Education,* 38(3), 232–241.

Gordon, L. (1994). *Pitied but not entitled: Single mothers and the history of welfare.* New York: Free Press.

Haberman, M. (1995). *Star teachers of children living in poverty.* West Lafayette, IN: Kappa Delta Pi.

Hewlett, S. A., Rankin, N., & West, C. (Eds.). (2002). *Taking parenting public: The case for a new social movement.* Lanham, MD: Rowman & Littlefield.

Hewlett, S. A., & West, C. (1998). *The war against parents: What we can do for America's beleaguered moms and dads.* Boston, MA: Houghton Mifflin.

Hyman, D. A. (2000). Do stories make for good policy? *Journal of Health Politics, 25*(6), 1149–1155.

Institutes for Research on Poverty. (2005). *Who was poor in 2003?* Retrieved April 25, 2005, from http://www.irp.wisc.edu/faqs/faq3.htm

Liston, D., & Garrison, J. (2004). Introduction: Love revived & examined. In D. Liston & J. Garrison (Eds.), *Teaching, learning, and loving: Reclaiming passion in educational practice* (pp. 1–19). New York: Routledge.

Lyotard, J. (1984). *The postmodern condition: A report on knowledge.* (G. Bennington & B. Massumi, Trans.). Minneapolis: University of Minnesota Press.

Masse, L. N. & Barnett, W. S. (2002). A benefit-cost analysis of the Abecedarian early childhood intervention. In H. M. Levin & P. J. McEwan (Eds.), *Cost-effectiveness and educational policy: 2002 yearbook of the American Educational Finance Association* (pp. 157–176). Larchmont: Eye On Education.

McLaren, P. (2005). Capitalists and conquerors: An introduction. In P. McLaren, (Ed.), *Capitalists and conquerors: A critical pedagogy against empire* (pp. 1–15). Lanham, MD: Rowman & Littlefield.

Merriam, S. (1992). *Qualitative research and case study applications in education.* San Francisco, CA: Jossey-Bass.

Metz, M. H. (1988). Teachers' pride in craft, school subcultures, and societal pressures. *Journal of Educational Policy, 1*(1), 115–134.

Meyers, M. K., Rosenbaum, D., Ruhm, C., & Waldfogel, J. (2004). Inequality in early childhood education and care: What do we know? In K. M. Neckerman (Ed.), *Social inequality* (p. 223–269). New York: Russell Sage.

National Center for Children in Poverty. (2004, September). *Rate of children in low-income families varies widely by state.* New York: Author.

National Center for Children in Poverty. (2005, February). *Basic facts about low-income children in the United States.* New York: Author. Retrieved on April, 25, 2005, from http://nccp.org/pub_lic05.html

National Commission on Excellence in Education. (1983). *A nation at risk: The imperative for educational reform.* Washington, DC: Government Printing Office.

No Child Left Behind Act of 2001. (2002). Pub. L. No. 107–110, 115 Stat. 1425, 20 U.S.C. §§6301 et seq.

Noddings, N. (2002). *Starting at home: Caring and social policy.* Berkeley: University of California Press.

Okin, S. M. (2003). Poverty, well-being, and gender: What counts, who's heard? *Poverty & Public Affairs, 31*(3), 280–316.

Orfield, G., & Lee, C. (2005). *Why segregation matters: Poverty and educational inequality.* Cambridge, MA: The Civil Rights Project at Harvard University.

Patton, M. Q. (2002). *Qualitative research methods* (3rd ed.). Thousand Oaks, CA: Sage.

Payne, R. (2001). *A framework for understanding poverty.* Highland, TX: Aha! Process.

Pebley, A. R., & Sastry, N. (2004). Neighborhoods, poverty, and children's well-being. In K. M. Neckerman (Ed.), *Social inequality* (pp. 119–145). New York: Russell Sage.

Phillips, M., & Chin, T. (2004). School inequality: What do we know? In K. M. Neckerman (Ed.), *Social inequality* (p. 467–519). New York: Russell Sage.

Piven, F. F., & Cloward, R. A. (1993). *Regulating the poor: The functions of public welfare.* New York: Vintage Books.

Roe, E. (1994). *Narrative policy analysis: Theory and practice.* Durham, NC: Duke University Press.

Rothstein, R. (2004). *Class and schools: Using social, economic, and educational reform to close the Black-White achievement gap.* Washington, DC: Economic Policy Institute.

Shields, P., & Knapp, M. (1997). The promise and limits of school-based reform. *Phi Delta Kappan, 79*(4), 288–294.

Shonkoff, J. P., & Phillips, D. A. (Eds.). (2000). *From neurons to neighborhoods: The science of early childhood development, A Report by the Committee on Integrating the science of early childhood development.* Washington, DC: National Academy.

Valenzuela, A. (1999). *Subtractive schooling: U.S.-Mexican youth and the politics of caring.* Albany: State University of New York Press.

Weiss, L. (2004). *Class reunion: The remaking of the American White working class.* New York: Routledge/Falmer.

Western, B., Kleykamp, M., & Rosenfeld, J. (2004). Crime, punishment, and American inequality. In K. M. Neckerman (Ed.), *Social inequality* (pp. 771–796). New York: Russell Sage.

Wirt, F., & Kirst, M. (1992). *The politics of education: Schools in conflict* (3rd ed.). Berkeley, CA: McCutchan.

Discussion Questions

1. What paradox is Gerstl-Pepin referring to in the title of her article?

   Based on her analysis of policy and educator narratives, she notes how policymakers assume that poverty has no impact on educational outcomes. As she describes, "poverty almost disappears" from their narratives; instead, racial-ethnic disparities are emphasized. From the set of educator narratives, she learns how "understanding poverty is central to helping students learn."

2. What is the consequence of policy narrative? How is NCLB flawed?

   As policymakers shift blame to individual schools and teachers, social-structural inequalities remain unaddressed by the legislation. The realities of poverty and the impact of economic disparities on learning remain hidden.

Source: From Gerstl-Pepin, C. I. (2006). The paradox of poverty narratives: Educators struggling with children left behind. *Educational Policy, 20*(1), 143–162. Reprinted by permission of Sage Publications.

CHAPTER 18

Ideological Success, Educational Failure?

On the Politics of No Child Left Behind

Michael W. Apple (2007)

Based on a critical review of literature on the No Child Left Behind legislation, educator Michael Apple examines the pros and cons of the assumptions behind the legislation and identifies a number of key negative implications for educational policy and practice.

This article was more difficult to write than one might expect. This is not because I have ambivalent feelings about the topic itself. Indeed, I am strongly opposed to most of the logics and practices embodied in "reforms" such as No Child Left Behind (NCLB). Nor is it because this is the first opportunity I have had to state these educational, political, and conceptual concerns publicly. Rather, the difficulty lies in exactly these things. There is so much that needs to be said, so many areas that need to be focused on, that one hardly knows where to begin. And, because I have made these criticisms publicly in considerably more detailed ways in a series of books and articles, in particular in the new and enlarged second edition of *Educating the "Right" Way: Markets, Standards, God, and Inequality* (Apple, 2006; see also, Apple, 2000), there is a real risk of repetition.

Thus, what I have chosen to do is to state in broad outline some of the arguments I have made more extensively elsewhere and to connect the books under review here to these concerns and arguments. Because of this, I need to be somewhat self-referential, referring the reader to more detailed analyses that I and a number of others have made before. In the process, I first show how the books compare to each other. I then detail some of the serious issues that have been raised about NCLB itself.

Finally I critically examine the ways in which the logics behind the more conservative of these books—and NCLB as well—participate in a worrisome attempt to change our common sense by connecting markets to strict regimes of accountability.

The books considered here represent different tendencies and different educational and political affiliations. Their very similar titles, then, are deceptive. *Many Children Left Behind* (Meier & Wood, 2004) speaks back to NCLB and, like myself and a considerable number of other people throughout the nation, is deeply and justifiably critical of its assumptions and effects on real schools, real educators, and real communities. *No Child Left Behind?* (Peterson & West, 2003) and *Leaving No Child Behind?* (Hess & Finn, 2004) are not uncritical of some aspects of how the legislation has worked at the level of policy and practice but support its overall commitments. By and large, the book edited by Meier and Wood (2004) contains the voices of well-known educational activists, many of whom have worked in schools for years, and thus has a more realistic and less distant feel to it. The voices of educators who have devoted their lives to building alternatives that actually work in urban and rural schools are hard to ignore, even amid the din of the constant call for more testing more often—or as some might say a situation in which "the tail of test wags the dog of the teacher."

The books edited by Hess and Finn and Peterson and West are in general more distant from the realities of schools and are, again in general, written by academics who are well known for their more conservative leanings and credentials. For the latter, their bête noir is most often teachers unions, an antipathy that is more than a little evident in their discussions of what is needed to reform schools, teaching, and increasingly now teacher education. One of the more pronounced characteristics of their discussions is their thinly veiled mistrust of teachers, the voices of whom almost never appear. Teachers are simply there as embodied in teachers unions. And the unions themselves by and large are simply represented as impediments to "what we all know" are needed reforms, impediments that are shared by the widely accepted ways we educate teachers. If we were to change the language of these authors just a bit, it might echo the ways in which business leaders blame their economic woes on paid workers and their unions, at the very same time that they are making decisions that destroy the lives and hopes of so many of these very same people. The fact that part of the funding for the Peterson and West volume comes from the Olin Foundation, one of the most conservative foundations in the country and well known for its commitments to rightist policies in the economy and elsewhere, speaks to its ideological tendencies.

As a former union leader myself, I have had enough experience with unions to know that their decisions are not always totally wise, especially when it comes to dealing with oppressed communities of color who are demanding a voice in educational decisions. This is one of the reasons that some African American activists have not totally rejected the idea of vouchers for example (Apple & Pedroni, 2005). This said, however, anti-union sentiment, at a time when so much of the organized business community is bent on destroying the collective bodies of as many workers as possible, is one of the least attractive positions I can imagine right now. The language of "producer capture"—that is, schools are organized around the needs of teachers and other educators, not "consumers," a position that underlies a good deal of the assumptions in these two books—positions teachers who wish to defend their hard-won autonomy and skills in their schools and in colleges of education in ways that are often simply disrespectful. This shouldn't surprise us because this too is a characteristic of NCLB.

Ignoring Complexity

Most educators in the United States, and an increasing number of government official and educators in many other nations, are of course now familiar with the key elements of the federal reauthorization of the Elementary and Secondary Education Act, commonly known as No Child Left Behind, passed by Congress in 2001 and signed by President Bush in January 2002. This represents a set of initiatives that can radically transform the federal role in policing and controlling core aspects of education. The major components of the legislation center on testing and accountability but also provide inroads toward a larger agenda of privatization and marketization.

There are of course other important elements included in the NCLB legislation. It should be immediately clear that the proposals incorporate a number of progressive-sounding issues and are couched in seemingly progressive language. As a number of the chapters in the Peterson and West volume indicate, this is partly a result of the compromises made to get the legislation passed with bipartisan support in Congress. However, it also continues an established tradition of the conservative production of discourse that incorporates progressive language while advancing key elements of the neo-liberal and neo-conservative agendas. It in essence creates what Smith and others have called a "political spectacle," one in which proposals that seemingly lead to reforms that are wanted by the least powerful actors in society are instead largely used to gain legitimacy for very different kinds of agendas and policies (Smith, with Miller-Kahn, Heinecke, & Jarvis, 2004).

Indeed, NCLB is one of the best examples I can think of that documents Nancy Fraser's (1987) claims about the politics of needs and needs discourses. Fraser argued that dominant groups often listen very carefully to the worries and demands that come from below. They then attempt to capture the discourse in which such concerns are voiced. This discourse is then redefined so that the words mean different things. Reforms are then instituted that do not threaten dominant groups' agendas. Rather they respond not to the original meanings inherent in key concepts within the discourse but to policies that create the conditions that dominant groups are able to control or that extend the influence of such groups in the sector of society out of which the concerns come.

Because of the history of such political spectacles and the realities of inequalities in our society, many of the provisions of NCLB, and their hidden effects and connections to other aspects of the conservative agenda, are—and should be—controversial. Controversies continue to swirl and intensify around such things as its redefinition of *literacy and reading instruction* and its emphasis on only one set of strategies for teaching such things. There are major questions as well about its budget priorities and about whether the supposed increase in funding is "real" or not. To these, others can be added. Its redefinition of *accountability* as reducible to scores on standardized achievement tests, and used inappropriately for comparative purposes, is more than a little problematic, although this agenda is pushed forward by the majority of authors in the Peterson and West book. The manner in which NCLB defines success and failure, and the shaming practices associated with these processes, has caused numerous complaints and even rebellions in some states and districts that are continuing to this day. The accompanying loss of local control has also been a consistent worry, as have its less well known linkages with the militarization of schools and the larger society.

There has been little thought about its effect as well on the ways in which the constant stress on "failing public schools" can act to make such things as home schooling— one of the fastest growing transformations in education today, with many more children and parents involved than in charter schools or voucher programs—that much more attractive. With little accountability at all in home schooling, the stress on reductive forms of accountability in NCLB and its emphasis not on improvement (moving a child from, say, a score of 20 to a score of 60) but on an arbitrary definition of *adequate yearly progress* on these same tests, can have the paradoxical effect of actually creating a situation in which ever more children are educated in institutions that have minimal if any forms of public accountability (Apple, 2006; Apple & Buras, 2006). The implications here for teacher education are serious. Anyone can teach anything, thereby undercutting the rhetorical commitment in NCLB to having "fully qualified" teachers throughout the schools of the nation.

Furthermore, the clear implication that what counts as good teaching as well is to be evaluated only on improvements in students' scores on these tests is less than satisfactory and shows a profound misunderstanding of the complexity of the teaching act. The ways in which it tacitly defines what counts as legitimate knowledge as only that which can be included on such reductive tests flies in the face of decades of struggle over the politics of official knowledge and over the inclusion of the cultures, languages, histories, and values of a country made of cultures from all over the world (Apple, 2000).

Not least, as Valenzuela and her colleagues have so clearly demonstrated in places such as Texas, this assemblage of "reforms" has had truly damaging consequences for a large number of our most dispossessed peoples, with race and/or ethnicity being a prime marker of these negative consequences (Valenzuela, 2005; see also Lipman, 2004; McNeil, 2000). All of these concerns are made public in the essays included in Meier and Wood's collection, *Many Children Left Behind*. Although this volume is less seemingly "academic" than the other two books, it does succeed in providing powerful voices of protest, often from the ground up rather than the top down.

All of these issues are crucial, and as I noted I have talked about a number of them elsewhere (Apple, 2006). As I note there, one of the key areas of contention has been the way in which, while (temporarily) limiting some aspects of the pressure to expand voucher and privatization initiatives, the underlying logic of NCLB sutures together the requirements of strong accountability measures with an even further opening toward funding for private education and marketization. The connections between strong accountability measures and a (largely uncritical) faith in marketization are more than a little evident in the Hess and Finn and Peterson and West volumes. Indeed, although there are a few dissenting voices in them that raise questions about such things, much of each of these volumes is grounded in a faith in the efficacy of strong testing regimes and/or a commitment to market logics and processes. Each of these two books is technically sophisticated. Yet this is coupled with a less-than-satisfactory political sensibility about the complexities and social and cultural effects of the thin democracy and thin morality associated with markets and privatization.

Furthermore, and again as I showed in *Educating the "Right" Way* (2006), each is less than knowledgeable about what has happened in other nations when the combination of "audit cultures" and markets has been instituted. The results have often not been salutary. The near-total absence of international perspectives—and the failure to recognize that we may have a large amount to learn from the experiences of other nations that have tried this combination of neo-liberal, neo-conservative, and new managerial impulses—is worrisome. It signifies what is dangerously close to arrogance.

It is important to understand the connections between these dual emphases on markets and the regulatory state. Even though many conservative members of Congress had to back away from their original plan to include federal support for vouchers in the legislation, it would be a grave mistake to not see the connection between privatization and increased federal control and intervention through testing. As Valenzuela (2005) documented in Texas, for example, these connections are often very overt in the political actions of conservative advocates.

Elsewhere I have argued that there is no contradiction between supposedly decentralized market-based models of education and centralization through strong regimes of curricular control, testing, and accountability (Apple, 2006). Indeed, the movement toward marketization and "choice" requires the production of standardized data based on standardized processes and "products" so that comparisons can be made and so that "consumers" have relevant information to make choices on a market.

I and many others have documented the negative effects of such "reforms." Because of this, we need to focus on the logics that underpin interventions such as NCLB and similar initiatives, on the creative ideological and/or political work that has gone on to make them acceptable, and on the complicated class and raced dynamics that created them and are the effects of them. To do this, I need to say a few things about the general context and shifting logics in which NCLB operates, logics that work to place strong state models of accountability in close contact with marketization. NCLB does not stand alone and appears on a terrain on which crucial ideological work has already been done.

Changing Common Sense

NCLB represents what has been called the politics of "conservative modernization"—the complicated alliance behind the wave after wave of educational reforms that have centered on neo-liberal commitments to the market and a supposedly weak state, neo-conservative emphases on stronger control over curricula and values, and "new managerial" proposals to install rigorous forms of accountability in schooling at all levels (Apple, 2006). The first set of reforms has not demonstrated much improvement in education and has marked a dangerous shift in our very idea of democracy—always a contested concept (Foner, 1998)—from "thick" collective forms to "thin" consumer-driven and overly individualistic forms. As I noted earlier, the second misconstrues and then basically ignores the intense debates over whose knowledge should be taught in schools and universities and establishes a false consensus on what is supposedly common in the United States. The third takes the position that "only that which is measurable is important"

and has caused some of the most creative and critical practices that have been developed through concerted efforts in some of the most difficult settings to be threatened (Apple & Beane, 2007; Lipman, 2004; McNeil, 2000). Unfortunately, all too many of the actual effects of this assemblage of reforms have either been negligible or negative, or they have been largely rhetorical. This is unfortunate, especially given all of the work that well-intentioned educators have devoted to some of these efforts. However, reality must be faced if we are to go beyond what is currently fashionable.

The odd combination of marketization on one hand and centralization of control on the other is not only occurring in education through things such as NCLB, nor is it only going on in the United States. This is a worldwide phenomenon. And although there are very real, and often successful, efforts to counter it (Apple et al., 2003; Apple & Buras, 2006), this has not meant that the basic assumptions that lie behind neo-liberal, neo-conservative, and new managerial forms have not had a major impact on our institutions throughout society and even on our common sense.

In a significant article analyzing the dangers to thick democracy associated with neo-liberal policies, Olssen (1996) made the important point that neo-liberalism requires the constant production of evidence that you are doing things "efficiently" and in the "correct" way. He critically examines the effects of the suturing together of the seemingly contradictory tendencies of neo-liberal and neo-conservative discourses and practices, and publicly worries that these effects may be very damaging to our sense of the importance of our public institutions. Yet bringing together seemingly disparate tendencies is exactly what is happening at all levels of education and is strikingly visible in NCLB. This is occurring at the same time as the state itself becomes increasingly subject to commercialization. This situation has given rise to what might best be called an *audit culture*. To get a sense of the widespread nature of such practices, it is useful here to quote from Leys (2003), one of the most perceptive analysts of this growth:

> [There is a] proliferation of *auditing,* i.e., the use of business derived concepts of independent supervision to measure and evaluate performance by public agencies and public employees, from civil servants and school teachers to university [faculty] and doctors: environmental audit, value for money audit, management audit, forensic audit, data audit, intellectual property audit, medical audit, teaching audit and technology audit emerged and, to varying

degrees of institutional stability and acceptance, very few people have been left untouched by these developments. (p. 70)

The widespread nature of these evaluative and measurement pressures and their ability to become parts of our common sense crowd out other conceptions of effectiveness and democracy.

In place of a society of citizens with the democratic power to ensure effectiveness and proper use of collective resources, and relying in large measure on trust in the public sector, there emerged a society of "auditees," anxiously preparing for audits and inspections. A punitive culture of "league tables" developed (purporting to show the relative efficiency and inefficiency of universities or schools or hospitals). Inspection agencies were charged with "naming and shaming" "failing" individual teachers, schools, social work departments, and so on; private firms were invited to take over and run "failing" institutions. (Leys, 2003, p. 70)

The ultimate result of an auditing culture of this kind is not the promised decentralization that plays such a significant role rhetorically in most neo-liberal self-understandings but also what seems to be a massive recentralization and what is best seen as a process of dedemocratization. Making the state more "business friendly" and importing business models directly into the core functions of the state such as hospitals and education—in combination with a rigorous and unforgiving ideology of individual accountability—these are the hallmarks of life today. The blame-and-shame policies embodied in NCLB, the growth of for-profit ventures such as Edison Schools and the rapid growth of the supplementary services industries associated with NCLB that are discussed in the Hess and Finn volume, the increasing standardization and technicization of content within teacher education programs so that social reflexivity and critical understanding are nearly evacuated from courses (Apple, 2001), the constant pressure to "perform" according to imposed and often-reductive standards in our institutions of education, and similar kinds of things are the footprints that these constantly escalating pressures have left on the terrain of education.

A key to all of this is the devaluing of public goods and services. It takes long-term and creative ideological work; however, people must be made to see anything that is public as "bad" and anything that is private as "good," a very real cause and effect of NCLB's emphasis on failure.

And anyone who works in these public institutions must be seen as inefficient and in need of the sobering facts of competition so that they work longer and harder. When the people who work in public institutions fight back, as in the case of the authors included in Meier and Wood's book, and argue for more respectful treatment and for a greater realization that simplistic solutions do not deal with the complexities that they face everyday in the real world of schools, universities, and communities, they are labeled as recalcitrant and selfish and as uncaring. Sometimes, as in the case of former U.S. Secretary of Education Page's public comments to what he thought was a sympathetic audience, they are even called "terrorists." And these "recalcitrant, selfish, and uncaring" employees—teachers, academics, administrators, social workers, and almost all other public employees—can then have their labor externally controlled and intensified by people who criticize them mercilessly, often as in the case of major corporations while these same businesses are shedding their own social responsibilities by paying little or no taxes.

I noted earlier that it is not just the labor of state employees that is radically altered; so too is the labor of "consumers." When services such as hospitals and schools are commodified, a good deal of the work that was formerly done by state employees is shifted onto those using the service. Examples of labor being shifted to the "consumer" include online banking, airline ticketing and check-in, supermarket self-checkouts, and similar things. Each of these is advertised as enhancing "choice" and each comes with a system of incentives and disincentives. Thus, one can get airline miles for checking in on one's computer. Or as some banks are now doing, there is an extra charge if you want to see a real live bank teller rather than using an ATM machine (which itself often now has an extra charge for using it).

The effects of such changes may be hidden; however, that does not make them any less real. Some of these are clearly economic: the closing of bank branches; the laying off of large numbers of workers, including in elementary, middle, and secondary schools and in higher education; the intensification of the workload of the fewer workers who remain. Some are hidden in their effects on consumers: exporting all of the work and the necessary commitment of time onto those people who are now purchasing the service; searching for information that was once given by the government; doing one's banking and airline work oneself; bagging and checking out at supermarkets. The classed and raced specificities of this are crucial because the ability to do such electronic searching and education, for example, is dependent on the availability of computers and especially time to engage in such actions. It requires resources—temporal and financial, to say nothing of emotional—that are differentially distributed. Even the Peterson and West and Hess and Finn books recognize that this is not an inconsequential problem.

This all may seem so trivial. However, when each "trivial" instance is added up, the massiveness of the transformation in which labor is transferred to the consumer is striking. For it to be successful, our common sense must be changed so that we see the world only as individual consumers, and we see ourselves as surrounded by a world in which everything is potentially a commodity for sale. To speak more theoretically, the subject position on offer is the deraced, declassed, and degendered "possessive individual," an economically rational actor who is constructed by and constructs a reality in which democracy is no longer a political concept but is reduced to an economic one (Apple, 2006).

Mark Fowler, Ronald Reagan's chair of the Federal Communications Commission, once publicly stated that television is simply a toaster with pictures. A conservative media mogul in England seemed to agree when he said that there is no difference between a television program and a cigarette lighter (Leys, 2003, p. 108). Both positions are based on an assumption that cultural form and content and the processes of distribution are indeed commodities. There are few more important mechanisms of cultural selection and distribution than schools and universities. And under this kind of logic, one might say that educational institutions are simply toasters with students. There is something deeply disturbing about this position not only in its vision of education but also profoundly in its understanding of the lives of the people who actually work in such institutions and in the often underfunded, understaffed, and difficult conditions now being experienced there. Although it would be too reductive to see educational work merely in labor process terms, the intensification that has resulted from the conditions associated with this assemblage of assumptions has become rather pronounced (Apple, 1995, 2000). Yet, like so much else, this is one of the things so clearly missed by the authors included in the Peterson and West and Hess and Finn volumes.

Of course, many of us may be apt to see such things as relatively humorous or innocuous. Aren't proposals that combine audit cultures and markets for such things as schools, universities, health care, and so much more just another, but supposedly more efficient, way of making services available. However, not only are these ideologically driven "reforms" not all that efficient, but also

the process of privatization is strikingly different from public ownership and control. For example, to market something such as education, it must first be transformed into a commodity, a "product." The product is then there to serve different ends. Thus, rather than schooling being aimed at creating critically democratic citizenship as its ultimate goal (although we should never romanticize an Edenic past when this was actually the case; schooling has always been a site of struggle over what its functions would actually be, with the working class and many women and people of color being constructed as "not quite citizens"), the entire process can slowly become aimed instead at the generation of profit for shareholders or a site whose hidden purpose is to document the efficiency of newly empowered managerial forms within the now supposedly more business-like state.

The fact that such things as the for-profit Edison Schools have not generated the significant profits that their investors had dreamed of means that the process of commodification is at least partly being rejected. For many people in all walks of life, the idea of "selling" our schools and our children is somehow disturbing, as the continuing controversy over Channel One, the for-profit television station with advertising now being broadcast in 43% of all public and private middle and secondary schools in the United States, amply demonstrates (Apple, 2000). These intuitions demonstrate that in our everyday lives there remains a sense that there is something very wrong with our current and still too uncritical fascination with markets and audits.

David Marquand (2000) summarized the worrisome tendencies I have been describing in the following way:

> The public domain of citizenship and service should be safeguarded from incursions by the market domain of buying and selling. . . . The goods of the public domain—health care, crime prevention, and education—should not be treated as commodities or proxy commodities. The language of buyer and seller, producer and consumer, does not belong in the public domain; nor do the relationships which that language implies. Doctors and nurses do not "sell" medical services; students are not "customers" of their teachers. . . . The attempt to force these relationships into a market model undermines the service ethic, degrades the institutions that embody it and robs the notion of common citizenship of part of its meaning. (pp. 212–213)

I agree. In my mind, public institutions are the defining features of a caring and democratic society. The market relations that are sponsored by our economy should exist to pay for these institutions, not the other way around. Thus, markets are to be subordinate to the aim of producing a fuller and thicker participatory democratic polity and daily life. It should be clear by now that a cynical conception of democracy that is "on sale" to voters and manipulated and marketed by political and economic elites does not adequately provide for goods such as general and higher education, objective information, media and new forms of communication that are universally accessible, well-maintained public libraries for all, public health, and universal health care. At best, markets provide these things in radically unequal ways, with class, gender, and especially race being extremely powerful markers of these inequalities. If that is the case—even if the definitions of the "public" were and often still are based on the construction of gendered and raced spaces (Fraser, 1987)—the very idea of public institutions is under concerted attack. They need to be provided—and defended—collectively. Such things are anything but secondary. They are the defining characteristics of what it means to be a just society.

Unfortunately, as the books by Hess and Finn and Peterson and West demonstrate, the language of privatization, marketization, and constant evaluation has increasingly saturated public discourse in almost all of our institutions, including as I showed in much greater detail in an earlier essay in this journal (Apple, 2001), institutions involved in teacher education. In many ways, it has become common sense—and the critical intuitions that something may be wrong with all of this may slowly wither. Yet, in many nations where conditions are even worse, this has not necessarily happened—and this is a crucial point. The growth of participatory budgeting, "Citizen Schools," and close relations among teachers, teacher education programs, and building more socially responsive and critical curricular and pedagogical initiatives in Porto Alegre, Brazil, and elsewhere documents that there are indeed powerful alternatives to the logics embodied in reforms such as NCLB, if we but look for them (Apple et al., 2003; Apple & Buras, 2006). We can learn from these nations' experiences, and we can relearn what it means to reconstitute the civic in our lives.

When combined with the experiences of building more critically democratic schools and curricula that are found in such things as the journal *Rethinking Schools* and in descriptions of the growing democratic schools movement in the United States (Apple & Beane, 2007), we can continue to demonstrate that education, rightly conceived, has a fundamental role to play in doing exactly that reconstitution. However, as the authors included in

Many Children Left Behind eloquently argue, education and teacher education can only do so if they are protected from those who see them as one more set of products to be consumed as we measure them and who interpret the intellectual and emotional labor of those who are engaged in educational work though the lenses of standardization, rationalization, and auditing. With its combination of aggressive blame and shame policies and its opening toward marketization, NCLB doesn't come close to enabling an education worth its name.

References

Apple, M. W. (1995). *Education and power* (2nd ed.). New York: Routledge.

Apple, M. W. (2000). *Official knowledge: Democratic education in a conservative age* (2nd ed.). New York: Routledge.

Apple, M. W. (2001). Markets, standards, teaching, and teacher education. *Journal of Teacher Education, 52*(3), 182–196.

Apple, M. W. (2006). *Educating the "right" way: Markets, standards, God, and inequality* (2nd ed.). New York: Routledge.

Apple, M. W., Aasen, P., Cho, M. K., Gandin, L., Oliver, A., Sung, Y. K., et al. (2003). *The state and the politics of knowledge.* New York: Routledge.

Apple, M. W., & Beane, J. A. (Eds.). (2007). *Democratic schools: Lessons for a powerful education* (2nd ed.). Portsmouth, NH: Heinemann.

Apple, M. W., & Buras, K. L. (Eds.). (2006). *The subaltern speak: Curriculum, power, and educational struggles.* New York: Routledge.

Apple, M. W., & Pedroni, T. (2005). Conservative alliance building and African American support for voucher plans. *Teachers College Record, 107*(9), 2068–2105.

Foner, E. (1998). *The story of American freedom.* New York: Norton.

Fraser, N. (1987). *Unruly practices.* Minneapolis: University of Minnesota Press.

Hess, F. M., & Finn, C. E. (2004). *Leaving no child behind? Options for kids in failing schools.* New York: Palgrave Macmillan.

Leys, C. (2003). *Market-driven politics: Neoliberal democracy and the public interest.* New York: Verso.

Lipman, P. (2004). *High stakes education.* New York: Routledge.

Marquand, D. (2000). *The progressive dilemma.* London: Phoenix Books.

McNeil, L. (2000). *The contradictions of school reform.* New York: Routledge.

Meier, D., & Wood, G. (Eds.). (2004). *Many children left behind: How the No Child Left Behind Act is damaging our children and our schools.* Boston: Beacon.

Olssen, M. (1996). In defense of the welfare state and of publicly provided education. *Journal of Education Policy, 11*(3), 337–362.

Peterson, P. E., & West, M. R. (Eds.). (2003). *No Child Left Behind? The politics and practice of school accountability.* Washington, DC: Brookings Institution Press.

Smith, M. L., with Miller-Kahn, L., Heinecke, W., & Jarvis, P. (2004). *Political spectacle and the fate of American schools.* New York: Routledge.

Valenzuela, A. (Ed.). (2005). *Leaving children behind: How "Texas-style" accountability fails Latino youth.* Albany: State University of New York Press.

Discussion Questions

1. How does NCLB represent the politics of "conservative modernization"?

   Apple argues that conservative modernization is behind NCLB reforms. Conservative modernization represents three elements: neo-liberal commitments to free market and a supposedly weak state, neo-conservative emphases on curricula and values, and the management priority of accountability in schooling.

2. What contradictions are inherent in NCLB?

   While encouraging stronger accountability standards for public schools, NCLB also encourages the funding for private education and increased "marketization" of education. Schools may be held accountable, but parents are able to "opt out" of failing schools. While NCLB encourages decentralization of educational oversight, a regular system of standardized testing (for accountability) actually increases centralization and oversight.

Source: From Apple, M. W. (2007). Ideological success, educational failure? On the politics of no child left behind. *Journal of Teacher Education, 58*(3), 108–116. Reprinted by permission of Sage Publications.

PART VII

HEALTH CARE

CHAPTER 19

Pills, Power, People

Sociological Understandings of the Pharmaceutical Industry

Joan Busfield (2006)

Joan Busfield examines the work, power, and impact of the pharmaceutical industry. She examines the scientific "fact making" involved in the industry's drug evaluation process, both at pre- and post-approval. Busfield concludes that with this process unchecked, drug manufacturers have been able to increase the public's dependency and reliance on pills.

The pharmaceutical industry is now a major global industry dominated by multinational companies selling their products across the world. Sales of pharmaceutical products in 2003 amounted to just over $466 billion (IMS Health, 2004a), more than the GNP of many developing countries, and the consumption of prescribed medicines in advanced industrial societies is high and increasing. In England, for instance, the number of prescriptions issued by the National Health Service (excluding hospital prescriptions) has increased from an average of eight per person in 1989 to 12.5 in 2002—an increase of 56 percent (Department of Health, 2000, 2003). This is more than one prescription per month on average for every year of a person's life.

The leading pharmaceutical companies all have head offices in advanced industrial societies, and their hold on the world market is increasing. Whereas in 1992 the top 10 companies accounted for roughly one-third of global pharmaceutical revenue (Tarabusi and Vickery, 1998), after a period of consolidation, by 2001 the top 10 accounted for nearly half (ABPI, 2003). Most of their revenue comes from patented drugs, the standard patent now lasting 20 years, although under certain circumstances patents can be extended.[1] The US is the largest

market for pharmaceuticals, accounting for just under half of world revenue in 2003 (IMS Health, 2004a), and in 2004 six of the top 10 companies were based in the US: Pfizer, Merck & Co, Johnson & Johnson, Bristol-Myers Squibb, Abbott and Wyeth (IMS Health, 2004b). The other four had European headquarters: GlaxoSmithKline and AstraZeneca based in Britain; Novartis in Switzerland; and Aventis, based in France. Aventis merged with Sanofi-Synthelabo in 2004, which made the combined company the sixth largest (IMS Health, 2006) and give the top 10 over half the global revenue. All 10 are highly commercial companies, have high profit levels (Moncrieff, 2002), and are major contributors to their national economies in terms of employment and export income (Harrison, 2003), although their manufacturing is more widely distributed than their research and development (R&D) (Busfield, 2003). In order to protect the flow of new drugs crucial to profitability, the companies are also entering into alliances with the smaller biotechnology companies, which now contribute to the research that leads to marketable drugs.

In addition, there are pharmaceutical companies in developing countries; the most important are located in India, Brazil and China. These countries are increasingly being pressured to accept World Trade Organization requirements on intellectual property and the companies largely concentrate on the production of "generic" drugs that are out of patent. Generic pharmaceutical companies are less profitable than those producing patented medicines, but can still be important to a national economy. Moreover generic drugs are of increasing importance in world markets in terms of sales *volume* (IMS Health, 2004c), partly as a result of service funders' pressure on doctors to prescribe them where possible, and their use potentially poses a threat to leading companies' profits. Consequently some have entered into partnerships with generic companies or, in some cases, taken them over.

Yet despite the importance of the industry as a productive activity to national economies and international markets and its role in patterns of consumption, it has received surprisingly little sociological attention. Sociologists of health and illness have done some research on pharmaceutical regulation (e.g. Abraham, 1995; Abraham and Lewis, 2000), on the controversies around specific preparations that draw on the sociology of science (e.g. Brown and Funk, 1986; Bury and Gabe, 1996), and rather more on medical prescribing (e.g. Britten, 2001; Weiss and Fitzpatrick, 1997), but the industry is rarely mentioned in key textbooks in the field.[2] The lack of interest in the industry (but see Conrad, 2005) may spring from the field's origins as a sociology of medicine and, in Britain, from the focus on the experience of illness, itself perhaps a reflection of the sociological tendency to focus on the powerless rather than the powerful. Yet even if the omission of work on the industry within this field is explicable, one might expect it to feature in other sociological areas.

Rather surprisingly, notwithstanding the industry's importance to the global economy, standard sociological discussions of globalization have not used the industry as a case study (Busfield, 2003). Nor do sociological analyses of consumption discuss medicines as a major consumer good, even though they are open to many of the analyses of the construction of desires and wants as other goods. Perhaps this is because the medical prescribing that mediates between the industry and consumers makes medicines seem less obviously governed by consumer choice. Pills also belong to the category of "inconspicuous consumption" (Warde and Shove, 1998), items that are not part of any visible display and have received less sociological examination. Nor does the use of psychotropic medication feature in Giddens' (1991) discussion of anxiety and risk and the "reflexive project"

of the self, which he sees as key features of late modernity, even though the widespread use of psychotropics could be regarded as a marker of that anxiety. Significantly, sociologists and historians of science have paid more attention to medical technologies in the form of machines such as x-rays (Howell, 1995) and newer imaging devices (Blume, 1992) than to drugs.[3]

Greater attention to the industry is crucial for several reasons. First, as I have indicated, the industry is a major power within the global economy and some national economies. In Britain, for instance, the two global pharmaceutical companies, GlaxoSmithKline and AstraZeneca, ranked fourth and sixth in the FTSE top-100 companies in terms of market capitalization in 2004 (*Observer* 1.8 04).[4] Second, the industry is a major force shaping health care in many societies, with the prescribing of medicines a dominant feature of medical care. Third and related to this, there has been a significant cultural shift in which people increasingly see medicines as a way of solving a wide range of problems, which are transformed into illnesses, instead of seeing them as a possible solution for a narrower range of physical sicknesses.[5] Pill taking has become a key feature of life in late modern society that looks set to continue into the future, even though the health of populations in such societies has generally improved—improvements that cannot largely be accounted for by the greater use of medicines (Colgrove, 2002; Lichtenberg, 2003; McKeown, 1976).[6]

I seek in this article to consider how certain sociological ideas and understandings can inform discussions of the increasing power and influence of the pharmaceutical industry. I approach the industry with a degree of scepticism, not just the usual scepticism about the industry's relation to developing countries—its reluctance to focus on their health problems and its unwillingness to sell them vital drugs at affordable prices—but a scepticism about the very widespread, and I suggest sometimes excessive, use of pharmaceuticals in advanced industrial societies. This scepticism is not grounded in any general claim that modern therapeutic drugs have little value. Many are invaluable, especially in the treatment of severe illnesses. However, to recognize this is not incompatible with the claim that drugs are frequently used indiscriminately—antibiotics are an obvious example.

There are three aspects to this indiscriminate use. First, pills are frequently taken by those whose problems would be better dealt with by other means and for whom they have little or no benefit and may lead to unwanted side effects—an example would be the very extensive use of psychotropic medication. Second, pills are frequently produced and prescribed in dosages that are far too high. And third, even if initially necessary, pills are often prescribed for too long a period of time. My argument is that an industry in the business of meeting health needs in fact creates a culture in which the use of drugs is encouraged even when this is unhelpful, counterproductive and even harmful. This is not just a matter of the industry's promotional activities but also arises because of its contribution to the science on which judgements of the safety and effectiveness of drugs are made. Drawing on the work of sociologists of science, this article examines the science underpinning drug evaluation.

Many sociologists will be familiar with Latour's influential book, *Science in Action,* first published in 1987, in which he develops an interesting analysis of how scientific facts are constructed. Whilst the notion of social construction is now commonplace in sociology, theoretical understandings of construction vary enormously. What is important about Latour's study is that he provides an analysis of the social processes involved in the construction of facts—fact making—that goes beyond those of other writers, and is informed by empirical studies of work in scientific laboratories. His concern is not with the products of science: "a computer, a nuclear plant, a cosmological theory, the shape of a double helix, a box of contraceptive pills, a model of the economy" (1987: 21). These are the accepted facts of science—the "black boxes" that have been closed.[7] Instead, his concern is with examining the black boxes before they were closed: "science in the making." This he sees as involving a whole series of uncertainties, controversies and alliances between actors—a term he uses to embrace things as well as people. These activities include research in the laboratory, the development of networks and the production of scientific papers. He identifies a range of devices and procedures involved in fact creation, skilfully analysing the rhetorical devices used in academic papers, the use of citation, the creation of allies, as well as the "trials of strength" between the different protagonists that can lead to the closure of a black box. He also argues that whether the box remains closed depends on the activities of others—its fate is in users' (in the broadest sense) hands: "Buying a machine without question or believing a fact without question has the same consequence: it strengthens the case of whatever is bought or believed" (1987: 29).

Viewing pharmaceutical products as new technologies, we can draw on certain aspects of Latour's analysis to examine how the industry contributes to the construction of scientific facts about new drugs; how it helps to ensure they are judged safe and effective by drug approval agencies, so closing the black box for many people; and consequently, how once launched onto the market, companies are in a relatively powerful position to keep the box closed and to encourage a drug's use, often well beyond its useful boundaries.

A common criticism of writers such as Latour is that they do not pay enough attention to issues of power. The point is not that power has no part in the analysis; indeed, Latour's language is redolent of power with his reference to trials of strength, actors' interests and so forth. But, as with symbolic interactionism, we are not offered much in the way of a structural analysis of power. This is essential in any consideration of the pharmaceutical industry and is not, in my view, incompatible with Latour's approach. In this article I draw on two sets of ideas about power: first, Light's (1995) notion, adapted from Galbraith (1956), of countervailing powers; and second, Mann's (1993) discussion of sources of power. The force of Light's analysis is the observation that powers stand in dynamic relation to one another: power is not monolithic and the power of one body may lead to resistance and the reassertion of power by another. In the case of health services, the focus of his work, the key powers are the state (government), commercial companies, service users, and the medical profession. The sociological question pertinent here is how the balance of power operates between these groups at the different stages of the development and use of a drug. We also need to consider the sources of power in the industry. Following Mann's analysis, we can see the industry as potentially exercising three of the four sources of power he outlines: ideological, economic and political (but not military).

Applying Latour's analysis to the development of pharmaceuticals, it is helpful to consider two stages in the making of scientific facts about drugs. The first, pre-approval stage, is that leading up to, and including, the formal approval necessary for a drug's release onto the market. The second is that of post-approval evaluation. The first aims to establish a drug's safety and effectiveness in order to secure approval; the second involves a refinement of the assessment, relating to questions such as: For what conditions more precisely is it useful? What are its side effects if used long term? What is its value in treating less serious cases? I look at fact making during both stages and, moving beyond Latour's analysis, at the operation of power during each.

Stage I: Pre-Approval Drug Development

As Latour observes, much R&D in the scientific arena is carried out in industrial contexts—his overall figure is 70 percent (1987: 170). A similar percentage of pre-approval R&D is paid for and controlled by the pharmaceutical industry (Bodenheimer, 2000), leading companies spending around 15 to 16 percent of revenue on R&D (PhRMA, 2004a). Typically, initial development is carried out by laboratory scientists, particularly pharmacologists, but also medical researchers, employed either by the pharmaceutical companies or the newer biotechnology companies. The subsequent pre-approval testing is carried out either by the pharmaceutical companies themselves or is contracted out to the new breed of commercial companies specializing in testing. The industry's control over R&D means that it plays the dominant role in fact making in the pre-approval period, which puts it at a major advantage when seeking approval for new drugs, including the power to select information to support their case and to withhold information that might undermine it (Harrison, 2003).[8] Using Mann's framework, we can see that the industry's fact-making activities constitute a form of ideological power, grounded in the industry's economic power; power that derives from the size of the companies, the profits they make and the resources they control, which enable them to fund the expensive R&D work. Consequently the industry's economic and ideological power are intertwined, economic power underpinning ideological power and ideological power in turn contributing to economic power.

Pharmaceutical companies' control over research is clearly manifest in the selection of the substances they seek to develop and test. Commercially the ideal product is one that can be patented, is used by a large number of people over lengthy periods, and can be priced quite highly in relation to production costs. This means that leading companies' R&D typically focuses on substances that could be used to treat the health problems faced by richer countries rather than on infectious diseases in developing countries. In 2003 the best sellers globally by revenue were two cholesterol-lowering statins, an anti-psychotic and a drug to reduce blood pressure (IMS Health, 2004d).[9] The competitive environment of the industry also means that companies frequently concentrate on finding a similar product to a competitor's, but one that is sufficiently different that it can be patented—so

called "me-toos." A study of approvals by the US Food and Drug Administration (FDA) between 1989 and 2000 showed that approvals for new drugs constituted only a relatively small proportion of all approvals, with only 35 percent of applications related to new chemical entities. The remainder involved active ingredients already available in marketed products (NIHCM, 2002).

Once the early development of a new preparation has been carried out, testing is necessary to establish its safety and effectiveness in order to secure the necessary approval for release onto the market. The FDA is the most important regulatory body for the world market, both because of the size of the US market and because approval in the US can affect the decisions of other regulatory bodies. The agency requires four types of testing for new drugs. These constitute the requirements for the scientific evaluation of a drug prior to licensing, which in effect takes the form of a cost (the side effects)—benefit (the health improvements) analysis. The first, pre-clinical testing, involves testing on animals "to determine if the product is reasonably safe for humans, and if the compound exhibits pharmacological activity that justifies commercial development" (FDA, 2004). The focus is on toxicity, testing ranging from six months to a year. In addition carcinogenicity tests are carried out with rodents. Human testing involves three phases. Phase 1 involves testing the drug on around 20 to 80 *healthy* volunteers, to examine its metabolic and pharmacological actions, obvious side effects, and some data on effectiveness. Phase 2 consists of the first controlled trials of the drug on patients, usually several hundred with the specific condition it is intended to treat. Finally, Phase 3 involves randomized controlled trials using the drug and a comparator or placebo. These clinical trials involve several hundred to several thousand patients and are designed to provide additional data about effectiveness and safety in a way that can be extrapolated to the general population and used in information given to doctors. Developing a new drug is a lengthy process and the time between the first identification of an active agent with therapeutic potential and formal approval is now around 10 to 15 years (PhRMA, 2004a). Since patents are secured well before approval, the industry has been keen to speed up testing and approval so that the time between approval and patent expiry is maximized, and the FDA approval time for new priority drugs declined during the 1990s with most approved within one year instead of two.

Following Latour, we can see the requirements outlined above as constituting the procedures necessary for the acceptance of the first scientific facts about a drug, and regulatory approval as providing the first point of closure in which the initial facts about safety and effectiveness are established. Once approved, the details of the testing become for many clinicians and the lay public the black box of complexity that no longer needs to be opened. The necessary scientific evaluation has been carried out, the drug's safety and effectiveness are accepted and it can be used in routine clinical practice: a cognitive closure results. This closure is most obviously evidenced by the very rapid uptake of many new drugs and from the off-license prescribing that frequently occurs. Many clinicians feel free to prescribe new drugs very widely—a tendency often exacerbated by patients who learn about a drug and are keen to use it.[10]

However, although for many people the black box is firmly closed once a drug is officially licensed, it needs to be noted that pre-approval testing is limited and the scientific facts contained in the black box are not well established. First, the animal testing to determine toxicity and carcinogenicity is restricted in scope, and there is evidence that with attempts to harmonize requirements internationally, testing standards are being lowered (Abraham and Reed, 2002). Second, companies select certain dosage levels to test and there may be little systematic effort to identify the lowest effective dosage (Cohen, 2001). Third, the length of testing involved is usually no more than a year, and often considerably less (the FDA does not specify the necessary length of testing). The short duration of trials is a double problem: some side effects may take time to emerge, and some may arise only as a result of longer-term use. When the tranquillizer, Halcion, was submitted for approval in Britain, the longest testing was on 60 patients who used the drug for only 91 days (Abraham and Sheppard, 1999: 29). Fourth, the drug is only tested on selected groups—normally adult men. There are good reasons for this (the thalidomide tragedy highlighted the dangers of some drugs for pregnant women), but the absence of trials on women, children and the elderly is a problem since their metabolisms usually differ—a point of particular relevance to dosage levels. The lack of pre-approval testing on the elderly is an especial problem since typically they make more extensive use of drugs. And fifth, testing relates only to the condition specified in the approval application. This is reasonable, but it means that the drug is not tested for a broader range of patients, often with less clearly defined conditions for which it may actually be used in clinical practice. The restricted nature of clinical trials is the reason why some commentators have argued that pre-approval trials test a drug's efficacy—whether it has an effect in ideal conditions—rather than its effectiveness—whether it works under real-world conditions (Streiner, 2002).

There is a further, more fundamental problem with the testing: the freedom given to companies to demonstrate a preparation's value by carrying out the studies, selecting the tests and presenting the data in ways they choose. Assessing effectiveness involves comparison. A drug is more or less effective than something else and the selection of the comparator, the strength of the tested drug, and the measures of effectiveness, are crucial to the evaluation. Yet regulatory agencies do not specify the required comparisons, do not set standards for the necessary minimal clinical difference to demonstrate effectiveness, nor the indicators to be used. The chosen comparator can be a placebo with no active ingredient, an attractive strategy to highlight a drug's effectiveness, and small differences may be heralded as showing superior effectiveness even if they only make a minimal difference to a patient's condition.[11] Where the aim is to show that the new treatment is more effective than alternatives, the company may compare the new preparation with another available drug. Decisions have to be made as to which drug serves as the comparator and about the relevant dosage levels since this affects the trial results. Choice of a low dosage of the comparator can help to make the tested preparation look more effective. Equally, selection of a high dosage of the tested drug can make it appear more effective than comparators. Cohen (2001) has argued that the pressure to demonstrate effectiveness encourages the selection and subsequent licensing of high dosage pills where frequently a lower dosage would be almost as effective and have fewer side effects. Dosage selection is also crucial to assessments of safety. Since higher dosage products are likely to generate more side effects, this might suggest the biases cancel each other out: that the pressure to select high dosages of the tested drug to show its effectiveness is counterbalanced by the need to show its side effects are not too extensive. However, a drug's effectiveness often shows up quite quickly, whereas side effects may take time to appear. Consequently, given the relatively short length of pre-approval trials, the two pressures are not likely to be balanced.

As with effectiveness there are no absolute standards of safety. Whilst a drug known to produce fatalities would not normally be deemed safe, it may be acceptable for it to produce quite severe side effects in a very small proportion of patients, on the grounds that if these emerge treatment can be stopped. This is especially the case if the benefits may be considerable as with drugs for severe, potentially fatal, illnesses.[12] The task for the company is to show that a drug is just as effective as (or preferably more effective than) alternatives but has no worse, or fewer, side effects. Here companies are considerably advantaged by the fact that they are permitted to obtain their own data and construct their own scientific case and have not been required to include data from all the studies that have been carried out.[13] This is despite the fact that various studies show that the results of industry-funded trials tend to be more favourable to a drug than independent studies (Davidson, 1986; Kjaegard and Als-Nielson, 2002). Companies can also decide how trial withdrawals are presented, which can affect test outcomes. Yet in other contexts, scientific work carried out under these conditions is seen as suspect, as when research on the MMR vaccine and autism was criticized as "poor science" when it emerged it had been funded by a patient group to provide evidence of a link between the two, *The Lancet's* editor stating that had he known of this interest he would not have published the paper (*Guardian* 21.2.04).

How important are these limitations, some of which are recognized by the regulatory bodies, which qualify their approval, licensing a drug for specified dosages for particular categories of patients with specific conditions, and which recognize that its safety is not adequately established and that a fuller evaluation will occur through further post-approval testing? I suggest that the limitations are serious. First, there is a risk that licensed drugs will prove either to be less effective or have more severe, sometimes life threatening, side effects than initially assessed. This has high costs for any patient who suffers these effects. For instance, the anti-inflammatory, Vioxx, licensed in 1999, was withdrawn in 2004 after a study showed an increased risk of heart attacks and strokes (some fatal) with longer-term use. Moreover, even if the side effects are not severe, it can mean that resources are wasted on relatively ineffective medicines.

Second and related to this, because drug approval provides an initial point of closure in establishing the facts about a drug's safety and effectiveness, the qualifications about a drug's use may be forgotten, notwithstanding the very limited nature of the pre-approval evaluation. It may thus be prescribed quite freely, including beyond the boundaries of the established facts, thereby changing the risk—benefit equation: potentially reducing the benefits but not the risks. Most clinicians do not have the resources, not least in terms of time, to open the scientific black box that underpins approval, particularly now there are so many drugs on the market. Moreover, they tend not to note the freedom companies

have to choose the comparisons they make in seeking to establish safety and effectiveness, nor the frequently limited nature of the demonstrated differences in effectiveness. Here companies' control of the science is crucial. They make the facts and select the data that are reviewed by the approval agencies. Yet licensing serves as a badge of effectiveness and safety that colours subsequent perceptions and affects practice.

Given the limitations of pre-approval drug testing, we need to consider the extent to which drug approval agencies are independent of the industry. Do the agencies adequately protect patients' interests? In theory they act on behalf of government to mediate between the conflicting interests of public and industry. The industry is keen to ensure that approval is speedy and successful, and the public has an interest in getting some new drugs onto the market quickly.

Against this pressure for speed and successful approval, patients have to be protected from unsafe or ineffective drugs and the approval process needs to be adequate to achieve this. Approval processes reflect a compromise between these conflicting interests, and governments, on whose behalf regulatory bodies act, are open to the same conflicts. They have a clear interest in protecting the public. Yet they are usually anxious to support the industry whether because of its value to the economy, or because of their desire as health care providers or funders to have access to drugs at reasonable prices.[14] The aim is to balance the conflicting interests without fear or favour.

In practice, achieving an appropriate degree of independence is difficult and there is a real danger of "regulatory capture" (Abraham, 1995: 22–3): that the industry manages to ensure that its concerns and ways of seeing issues shape decision making and the agencies do not serve as a countervailing power. In countries where major companies are located, capture is made more likely by the industry's control over the science submitted to the regulatory body—a control that governments have permitted. The independence of the FDA is particularly crucial, since companies outside the US often seek its approval for their products because of the global importance of the US market. Abraham (1995) argued that the FDA had managed to maintain more independence from the industry than British regulatory agencies. But there is evidence that US administrations in the 1990s and since have been particularly sympathetic to the industry and that the FDA's regulatory regime was loosened.[15] However, the withdrawal of Vioxx in 2004 has led to adverse publicity about the agency and calls for tighter regulation.

The industry's political power at the pre-approval stage lies therefore in the influence it can exert, partly by virtue of its ideological and economic power, over the regulatory processes, such as its power and influence over the licensing of new drugs. It is hard to escape the conclusion that the industry's power during this stage is currently very extensive, though the adequacy of regulation is now under discussion in the US and Europe.

Stage 2: Post-Approval Evaluation

Approval by a regulatory authority is a turning point for a drug; it gives factual status to claims about safety and effectiveness, claims that tend to be accepted by many ordinary clinicians and the public without much in the way of further questioning. Latour argues, however, that although we can identify moments when a particular claim is accepted as a scientific fact and the data supporting the claim are no longer explored, this does not mean it is necessarily treated as a scientific fact for all time: that depends on the subsequent actions of others. Whilst many clinicians and patients in the post-approval stage treat the initial approval as establishing for practical purposes the safety and effectiveness of a drug, further research does take place and this, along with patients' and clinicians' experiences of the drug, can lead to questioning of the facts about a drug, a reopening of the scientific black box and the overthrow of earlier conclusions. There are many other examples, apart from Vioxx, of licensed and widely used drugs later withdrawn on safety grounds. These include the sleeping pill, Halcion, the arthritis drug, Opren, and the statin, Baycol.

A number of factors generate further testing and create possibilities that the black box is reopened. First, the company itself may be keen to obtain data that shows the drug is useful for a wider range of conditions than those for which it is licensed and so fund further tests (though equally it may encourage wider use without further testing). Such testing is not so much designed to reopen the black box as to extend its scope. Second, since another company may be working on a competitor product and seeking to establish its superiority, the first may need to engage in further defensive testing. The aim of the competitor is to supplant the existing black box with a new one, whereas the first tries to make sure that the black box is strengthened. Third, senior doctors, especially those with academic posts alongside clinical responsibilities, may be keen to carry out research to generate further facts about a drug. For precisely which

groups of patients is it useful? What are the most suitable dosage levels? Are there side effects from long-term use? If therefore they can secure funding from the industry or elsewhere, they may carry out more extensive clinical trials that may either strengthen a box's defences or threaten to undermine it. And fourth, while many ordinary clinicians and patients accept claims about safety and effectiveness relatively uncritically, they may notice problems once a drug is in use, though often they only raise questions if fairly clear-cut problems emerge. The reporting of side effects observed in clinical practice to the regulatory authorities is not mandatory. However, in Britain, as elsewhere, there is an official, non-compulsory reporting system—the yellow card system. This does not generate systematic data and there is evidence that side effects are massively underreported (Cohen, 2001: 5). It can, nonetheless, lead to major concerns about a product. If these are raised, the industry needs, if possible, to try and rebut them and may engage in further testing in an effort to do so. Post-approval testing, referred to as Phase IV research, is therefore a very different process from pre-approval testing in terms of its initiation, extent and purposes. In 2002 it amounted to only around 12.4 per-cent of all R&D expenditure by the leading pharmaceutical companies (PhRMA, 2004a).

Often the debates about a drug continue over many years. Currently a highly contested re-evaluation of hormone-replacement therapy is underway, especially of its value as a long-term treatment following the results of several studies indicating higher breast cancer levels for long-term users (Beral, 2003). In other cases, studies show clearly that the initial assessment needs to be more qualified and that the facts in the original black box must be modified. Nonetheless, the industry may do relatively little to publicize the new facts. There may be regulatory requirements about changing packaging leaflets, but such changes often occur slowly and revised information may not be read very carefully either by doctors or patients. Consequently, given the cognitive closure that often results from initial approval, the additional advice may have little impact on clinical practice.

Post-approval evaluation is therefore a lengthy process—indeed, unless a drug is withdrawn, it is potentially unending—and is made more difficult by the changes introduced to the chemical composition of certain drugs as new findings emerge. The contraceptive pill, introduced in Britain in 1963, has under-gone a number of changes in composition and even now, over 40 years later, its side effects are still debated.

The pharmaceutical industry's power in the post-approval stage is extensive though arguably always at risk in relation to specific preparations. Companies start with the ideological advantage that the drug in question has been approved as safe and effective, and although approval is qualified, these qualifications do not feature very heavily in the perceptions of most clinicians and patients. This ideological advantage is then backed up by major marketing activities that are dependent on the companies' economic power but strengthen the ideological impact of the scientific work. Spending on marketing by leading companies is considerable (GAO, 2002). The broad features are well known. Much is directed at doctors who are inundated with pens, pads and mugs embellished with brand names. Companies also have extensive sales forces and company reps make visits to doctors' surgeries and hospitals with product leaflets. They also fund medical conferences both large and small. And even when direct-to-consumer advertising is not permitted, press releases can be used to spread knowledge of, and demand for, a drug. These may report a drug's approval, studies of its effectiveness, or epidemiological work that emphasizes the prevalence of the illness, potentially broadening its boundaries and expanding the market for treatments.[16]

The industry's ideological advantage is compounded by the fact that doctors are often willing allies of the industry. Instead of acting as a countervailing power, as potentially they could, most doctors have a shared interest in prescribing the industry's products and not challenging its claims. Clinicians typically want to "do something" to help their patients, and drugs provide a solution to the diverse problems they encounter. Drugs also help to maintain the aura of science crucial to medicine's professional power, are easy to prescribe, and reduce the time needed with patients (Weiss and Fitzpatrick, 1997; Wilkin et al., 1987). Indeed, the industry and profession largely stand in a symbiotic relation. The industry needs doctors to prescribe its products, and practising doctors need the industry's products to help to maintain their professional standing and power, a situation enhanced by their near monopoly over prescribing.[17] Of course doctors try to represent patients' interests, but they often share the belief that medications provide the best, easiest or most readily available solution for patients' problems. As a result they only tend to challenge the industry's claims about a preparation if they encounter marked side effects. If and when they do decide that the black box must be reopened they can be a powerful force, using adverse publicity to strengthen their hand and posing a real threat to a particular product. Yet, faced with an individual patient, it can be difficult to determine whether the reported problem can be blamed on a specific drug since it might result from the illness. Moreover,

ordinary doctors rarely challenge medicine's general reliance on the industry's products, though they may be concerned about the value of a specific drug and report side effects. Consequently, while the profession is powerful, and could use its power to challenge the activities of the industry, it only rarely acts as a countervailing power.

Although patients often value the medicines they are given, they do not have the same interest in supporting the pharmaceutical industry as many doctors and could collectively be an important countervailing power. Certainly their reporting of side effects can lead to a radical questioning of specific products. But patients have typically been deferential towards medical authority, accepting medical advice on trust and lacking the expertise to question it (though there are signs of change in this respect). Patients often, therefore, accept the culture in which drugs are viewed as the appropriate remedy for a range of ills and may be slow to identify side effects as arising from a drug they are using. Some patients and their families do become vocal about side effects, transforming themselves into user groups and deploying the media to publicize their concerns. Campaigns about the addictive properties of tranquillizers are one example. Such campaigns can be influential, though the impact is often slow, and many suffer ill-effects before a treatment is withdrawn or prescribing advice changed.

Once a drug is approved, the agencies tend not to play a very active part in considering whether a license should be revoked. If evidence is brought to them they may consider withdrawing approval but this is relatively rare. And if they request further Phase IV trials, they do not always ensure these are carried out (Cohen, 2001). Where health care is state funded, other government bodies may play a part in controlling which medicines can be prescribed and how much is paid for them, and the same role can be played by commercial health companies keen to keep costs down. In Britain, for instance, the government negotiates with the industry over drug prices, and decides whether doctors can prescribe particular patented drugs or must use generic versions. These strategies help to keep drug prices down but profit margins are arguably still quite generous to the industry (Harrison, 2003). The National Institute for Clinical Excellence (NICE) also assesses a range of medical interventions in the post-approval phase. However, such bodies are also open to capture by the industry. A recent World Health Organization report (2003) was critical of the industry's influence on NICE recommending that, while manufacturers should be able to put their views to the Appraisal Committee, they should no longer be members.

Conclusion

Whilst the boundaries of sociological endeavour are potentially extensive, the discipline has always been selective in its concerns. The absence of attention to the pharmaceutical industry is regrettable, not least because, in alliance with medicine, the industry is shaping the ways in which society responds to a very broad range of problems. It is contributing to an extension of the territory of medical problems and the tendency to respond to problems by pill taking, as if the problem will be solved by magic. This response often fails to grapple with the sources of these problems. As many writers have noted (see Conrad and Schneider, 1992), drugs provide an individualized solution to problems that often have social and structural origins, which are not tackled by pharmaceutical remedies, as for instance, where pills are used to treat obesity. Whilst the industry's power is not unregulated, an important source of its power is the control it exerts over the scientific fact making that underpins a drug's evaluation. Given that once licensed these facts tend to be accepted, and given that the potential challenges to the drug companies face a struggle in which the cards are not equally stacked, the industry has a major advantage.

It is true that with time a fuller evaluation of a drug takes place. Yet there is little sign that this is leading to a more cautious approach to pharmaceutical use. Moreover, relying on time to produce a fuller picture of the value of particular preparations means that many people suffer adverse, sometimes even fatal, side effects that might have been avoided. Instead, what is needed is to ensure that more independent research is carried out, both pre- and post-approval, and that the uncertainties about safety and effectiveness are well publicized. Such research could be funded by the industry with companies required by government to pay a compulsory levy to fund independent, non-commercial research institutes to evaluate drugs, which would hire the researchers and control the research.[18] There is also a need for far greater openness and transparency in the availability of all trial data, whether favourable to a drug or not; an issue now receiving some publicity. Regulatory agencies also need to strengthen testing requirements, including ensuring that, where possible, drugs are tested against competitors and that data on differences in effectiveness are presented in more meaningful ways. A system of provisional licensing would also be desirable with a requirement for more extensive and lengthier testing before a full license were confirmed.

This article has focused on the producers of medicines rather than the consumers. Pharmaceutical producers use their ideological, economic and political power to play on the anxieties and discontents of life in late modern society, creating a market for their products that extends well beyond obvious health needs. Health services, which are supposedly based on considerations of welfare and professionalism and a commitment to patients' interests, become the means of generating large profits for a highly commercial industry that uses scientific fact making as a tool to serve its own interests as much, if not more, than the interests of health service users.

Notes

1. A patent can be obtained if the invention is new, involves an "inventive step" and is capable of industrial application.

2. There has been considerable interest from economists, policy analysts and journalists.

3. See Berg's (1997) work on electronic records in medicine.

4. Their market capitalizations were £65.98 and £41.16 billion (*Observer* 1.8.04).

5. Such medicalization may reduce stigma.

6. Lichtenberg (2003) found 40 percent of improvements in longevity between 1986 and 2000 were due to new chemical entities, though his findings have been contested.

7. "The word black box is used by cyberneticians whenever a piece of machinery or a set of commands is too complex. In its place they draw a little box about which they need to know nothing but its input and output" (Latour, 1987: 2–3).

8. Companies are talking of a new code of practice on transparency (PhRMA, 2004b).

9. This list changes quite rapidly.

10. Some drugs reach blockbuster status (sales of more than $1 billion a year) within a year of release (IMS Health, 2002).

11. This was highlighted in relation to Donepezil, a drug for Alzheimer's. This improved performance on a simple memory test but had little impact on clinical deterioration or the chances of hospitalization (AD2000 Collaborative Group, 2004).

12. An example would be the hair loss associated with cancer drugs.

13. When the possible suicidal impact of Seroxat on children became a public issue it emerged that GlaxoSmithKline, which secured a license for the drug for adults, had not revealed data that showed suicidal tendencies in some children taking the drug.

14. The French government was strongly opposed to Aventis being taken over by the Swiss Novartis rather than the French Sanofi.

15. For example, the reduction in the time taken to secure FDA approval for which the industry pressed (Cohen, 2001).

16. Drug companies funded a Global Initiative for Asthma, publicizing an apparent worldwide increase and the need for greater awareness of the condition and treatments (*Guardian* 17.2.04).

17. In Britain, nurses' powers to prescribe are being increased.

18. Strenuous efforts would be needed to ensure the research was independent.

References

Abraham, J. (1995). *Science, Politics and the Pharmaceutical Industry.* London: UCL Press.

Abraham, J. and G. Lewis (2000). *Regulating Medicines in Europe.* London: Routledge.

Abraham, J. and T. Reed (2002). "Progress, Innovation and Regulatory Science in Drug Development," *Social Studies of Science* 32(3): 337–69.

Abraham, J. and J. Sheppard (1999). *The Therapeutic Nightmare.* London: Earthscan.

ABPI (2003) *Facts & Statistics from the Pharmaceutical Industry,* URL (consulted Aug. 2004): www.abpi.org.uk?statistics/section.asp?sect=1

AD2000 Collaborative Group (2004). "Long-term Donepezil Treatment in 565 Patients with Alzheimer's Disease (AD2000)," *Lancet* 363(9427): 2105–15.

Beral, V. (2003). "Breast Cancer and Hormone-replacement Therapy in the Million Women Study," *Lancet* 362(9382): 419–27.

Berg, M. (1997). *Rationalizing Medical Work.* Cambridge, MA: MIT Press.

Blume, S.C. (1992). *Insight and Industry.* Cambridge, MA: MIT Press.

Bodenheimer, T. (2000). "Uneasy Alliance–Clinical Investigators and the Pharmaceutical Industry," *New England Journal of Medicine* 342(20): 1539–44.

Britten, N. (2001). "'Prescribing and the Defence of Clinical Autonomy," *Sociology of Health and Illness* 23(4): 478–96.

Brown, P. and S.C. Funk (1986). "Tardive Dyskinesia: Barriers to the Professional Recognition of Iatrogenic Disease," *Journal of Health and Social Behavior* 27: 116–32.

Bury, M. and J. Gabe (1996). "Halcion Nights: A Sociological Account of a Medical Controversy," *Sociology* 30(3): 447–69.

Busfield, J. (2003). "Globalization and the Pharmaceutical Industry Revisited," *International Journal of Health Services* 33(3): 581–605.

Cohen, J. (2001). *Over Dose.* New York: Putnam.

Colgrove, J. (2002) "The McKeown Thesis," *American Journal of Public Health* 92(5): 725–29.

Conrad, P. (2005). "The Shifting Engines of Medicalization," *Journal of Health and Social Behavior* 46: 3–14.

Conrad, P. and J.W. Schneider (1992) *Deviance and Medicalization.* Missouri: Mosby.

Davidson, R.A. (1986). "Sources of Funding and Outcome of Clinical Trials," *Journal of General Internal Medicine* 1: 155–8.

Department of Health (2000). *Prescriptions Dispensed in the Community, 1989 to 1999: England.* London: Department of Health.

Department of Health (2003). *Prescriptions Dispensed in the Community, 1992 to 2002: England.* London: Department of Health.

FDA (2004) URL (consulted Jun. 2004): www.fda.gov/cder/about/smallbiz/faq/htm

Galbraith, J.K. (1956). *American Capitalism.* Boston, MA: Houghton Mifflin.

GAO (General Accounting Office) (2002). *Prescription Drugs: FDA Oversight of Direct-to-consumer Advertising Has Limitations.* Washington: US General Accounting Office.

Giddens, A. (1991). *Modernity and Self-Identity.* London: Polity.

Harrison, A. (2003). *Getting the Right Medicine?* London: King's Fund.

Howell, J.D. (1995). *Technology in the Hospital.* Baltimore, MD: John Hopkins University Press.

IMS Health (2002). "Blockbusters Blast a Highway through Pharma Sales," URL (consulted Nov. 2005): www.ims-global.com/insight/news_story/0203/ news_story_020317.htm

IMS Health (2004a). "2003 Global Pharma Sale by Region," URL (consulted Jul. 2004): www.ims-global.com/insight/news_story_040316.htm

IMS Health (2004b). "Top Companies, November 2004," URL (consulted Nov. 2004): http://open.imshealth.com/dept.asp/dept%5Fid=2

IMS Health (2004c). "Generics Flourish as Innovation Stalls," URL (consulted Jul. 2004): www.ims-global.com/insight/news_story_0406/news_story_ 040614a.htm

IMS Health (2004d). "Lipitor Leads the Way in 2003," URL (consulted Jul. 2004): www.ims-global.com/insight/news_story/0403/news_story_040316.htm

IMS Health (2006). "Top Companies, November 2005," URL (consulted Feb. 2006): http://www.imshealth.com/dept.asp?dept%5fid=2

Kjaegard, L.L. and B. Als-Nielson (2002). "Association between Competing Interests and Authors" Conclusions," *British Medical Journal* 325(7358): 249–52.

Latour, B. (1987). *Science in Action.* Cambridge, MA: Harvard University Press.

Lichtenberg, F.R. (2003). *The Impact of New Drug Launches on Longevity: 1982–2001.* Cambridge, MA: National Bureau of Economic Research.

Light, D. (1995). "Countervailing Powers," in T. Johnson, G. Larkin and M. Saks (eds) *Health Professions and the State in Europe,* pp. 25–41. London: Routledge.

McKeown, T. (1976). *The Modern Rise of Population.* London: Edward Arnold.

Mann, M. (1993) *The Sources of Social Power,* Vol II. Cambridge: Cambridge University Press.

Moncrieff, J. (2002). *Is Psychiatry for Sale?* London: Institute of Psychiatry.

Moynihan, R., I. Heath and D. Henry (2002). "Selling Sickness: The Pharmaceutical Industry and Disease Mongering," *British Medical Journal* 324: 886–91.

NIHCM (2002). *Changing Patterns of Pharmaceutical Innovation.* Washington: National Institute for Health Care Management Foundation.

PhRMA (2004a). *Pharmaceutical Industry Profile 2004.* Washington: Pharmaceutical Research and Manufacturers Association.

PhRMA (2004b). *Principles on Conduct of Clinical Trials and Communication of Clinical Trial Results.* Washington: Pharmaceutical Research and Manufacturers Association.

Streiner, D. (2002). "The 2 'Es' of Research Efficacy and Effectiveness," *Canadian Journal of Psychiatry* 47: 552–6.

Tarabusi, C. and G. Vickery (1998). "Globalization in the Pharmaceutical Industry, part I," *International Journal of Health Services* 28(1): 67–105.

Warde, A. and E. Shove (1998). "Inconspicuous Consumption," URL (consulted Aug. 2004): www.comp.lancs.ac.uk/sociology/soc001aw.html

Weiss, M. and R. Fitzpatrick (1997). "Challenges to Medicine: The Case of Prescribing," *Sociology of Health and* Illness 19: 297–327.

Wilkin, D., L. Hallam, R. Leavey and D. Metcalfe (1987). *Anatomy of Urban General Practice.* London: Tavistock.

World Health Organization (2003). *Technology Appraisal Programme of the National Institute for Clinical Excellence.* Geneva: WHO.

Discussion Questions

1. How has the pharmaceutical industry influenced society's reliance on pills and medicines?

    Busfield argues that an industry in the business of meeting health needs must first create the need itself. It does this by creating a culture in which the use of drugs is encouraged. It is encouraged not just by marketing or promotional materials, but also in how drug research and development is deemed as part of a "scientific" process, irrefutable and accepted as "fact."

2. What "power" does the industry have during the two drug development stages: pre-approval drug development and post-approval evaluation?

    Three types of power are identified: ideological, economic, and political. For example, the decision on which set of drugs to pursue is not made randomly. Commercially, the ideal product to develop is the one that can be patented. As a result, not all diseases or illnesses are addressed. Often, companies will respond to a popular drug manufactured by a competitor—not motivated by the need to help people, but by achieving a competitive, economic edge on their competition.

Source: From Busfield, J. (2006). Pills, power, people: Sociological understanding of the pharmaceutical industry. *Sociology, 40*(2), 297–314. Reprinted by permission of the author.

CHAPTER 20

Tango Immigrants in New York City

The Value of Social Reciprocities

Anahí Viladrich (2005)

Building upon social capital theory, sociologist Anahí Viladrich examines the importance of New York City tango groups as a source of social resources. The "tango" immigrants informally access health care through the assistance of health care practitioners belonging to their tango network. The network, according to Viladrich, is an invaluable source of health information, as well as job contacts and referrals.

"'You can find all the resources you need in the tango world.' (Cristal, thirty-year-old tango dancer)"

The tango's centennial existence, as both a dancing and a musical form, has been marked by periods of uprising and decline in the Río de la Plata region, including Buenos Aires and Uruguay, as well as abroad. Created as the bastard child of a blend of African and European rhythms, the tango's international prominence in the early twentieth century was soon followed by its rising as the symbol of the emergent Argentine urban middle classes of European descent (see Archetti 1997; Corradi 1997; Castro 1991; Guy 1991). In following decades, the tango's fate suffered from uneven periods of stardom and progressive decline, encouraged by periods of military censorship and the rise of folklore music and foreign rhythms, which relegated the tango to secluded social enclaves (Vila 1991; Viladrich 2004; Viladrich, forthcoming a). Since the mid-1980s, however, tango dancing has become the epitome of a lofty dancing trend supported by an eclectic community of tango fans around the globe, which has led its grasp to geographical, commercial, and symbolic areas where it had never been seen before. Despite the fact that the tango has become a global

artistic form that resists local adscription to a particular social group or geography, the promotion of Argentine tango has encouraged the demand for professional and amateur tango artists of Argentine origin. In addition, the tango renaissance has helped reactivate a thriving domestic tango industry in Argentina while encouraging the migratory paths abroad of both reputed and amateur Argentine tango artists.

In the midst of its global renaissance, the tango has become the object of growing interest by both the academic and the popular literature, spanning from its conceptualization as an exotic merchandise within the globalized economy of feelings (Savigliano 1995, 2003) to the analysis of its hybridization as an evolving artistic form (see Pelinski 2000; Steingress 2002). Scholars have also explored the tango's social history vis-à-vis the sociopolitical changes that have occurred in Argentina for the past one hundred years (see Viladrich 2003, 2004; Guy 1991; Vila 1991; Castro 1991). Rather than exploring the transnational character of the tango as an artistic form, which has been so well done by colleagues in the field, this article follows an alternative theoretical standpoint. Researchers interested in the novel formation of immigrant communities have somehow overlooked the importance of social entertainment forms as ethnic spaces for social reproduction. In particular, a paucity of research exists regarding the contributions of the tango, as well as other artistic forms, in the creation of social niches that allow the circulation of resources among its members. This article will address this issue by building on the theory of social capital (defined as access to resources via social relationships) to conceptualize the tango's social reproduction as a social field that provides access to precious social assets to its practitioners. It will be argued that the Manhattan tango world, instituted on tango *milongas* (dancing halls), constitutes a point of intersection of Argentines from different social origins who exchange favors and services on the basis of sharing a common tango passion.

The article begins with the presentation of social capital categories and is followed by a detailed description of my participatory role in Manhattan milongas, which allowed me to grasp the subtle nuances of tango immigrants' social exchanges. The article's narrative will continue by revealing the role of the Manhattan tango world as an ethnic hub and a social field of power that facilitates the exchange of social capital among its members in the form of contacts, jobs, and free access to health care. The latter topic will be further explored by describing tango immigrants' hardships and their access to informal assistance and health resources in the hands of their tango brokers, represented by doctors that provide health resources on the basis of belonging to the same ethnic field. Finally, the article will underscore the contributions of this ethnographic enterprise to our understanding of the importance, as well as the caveats, of social capital categories to our understanding of the role of artistic fields for immigrants' access to informal resources to address their unmet needs.

Social Capital: Access to Resources via Social Relationships

The literature on social capital has been prolific in recent years, particularly regarding social inequalities in health (e.g., poverty and social exclusion) and the relationship between morbidity and mortality indicators and socioeconomic status (see Hawe and Shiell 2000; Kawachi et al. 1997; Rose 2000). Bourdieu (1985) emphasizes the notion of social capital as the access to scarce goods via social relationships embedded in specific fields of power, which complements other forms of capital such as economic or symbolic. Within this notion, social capital is unevenly distributed across social classes and can be converted into other types

(e.g., economic, human, and symbolic). Contrary to other forms, social capital depends on social webs to be created, circulated, and accumulated (Portes 1998; Fernández Kelly 1995).

Despite its heuristic power, some authors suggest caution with the enthusiastic use of social capital (Cattell 2001; Wall, Ferrazi, and Schryer 1998) because of its dissimilar definitions and operationalizations. Still, some value more its metaphoric power than its practical use (Hawe and Shiell 2000). Furthermore, social capital is often mingled with other forms, such as human or cultural, particularly because of the close relationship among all these types. For example, social capital influences the extent to which individuals expand (or diminish) their human capital (e.g., skills, education, job training; see Coleman 1988), while investments in human and cultural assets also provide opportunities to expand social capital, as in the case of credentials that entitle membership in exclusive professional clubs (see Bourdieu and Passeron 1979).

In spite of its different conceptualizations, social capital generally refers to the nontangible values exchanged through social relationships that require some kind of reciprocity and trust. As Portes (1998) argues, there is an increasing agreement on the notion of social capital as the ability to obtain valuable resources on the basis of belonging to particular social networks. Contrary to the positive effects commonly associated with the accumulation of social capital, this author also points out some of its negative consequences, such as the exclusion of outsiders and the excessive control and social pressure exerted on networks' members.

In addition, social capital's indicators stem from an array of concepts and vocabulary, including those from the social network and social support literature. Nevertheless, while studies on social networks tend to focus on the quantitative structure of social relationships and those on social support on the qualitative impact of social webs, the notion of social capital emphasizes the access and availability of resources (material and symbolic) by way of social relationships. Furthermore, social capital is invested neither in the individuals themselves nor in the goods provided and received, but in people's social relationships. As other authors have noted (Berkman et al. 2000), although social networks are the source of social capital, the effect of their use is a specific gain (e.g., material or symbolic power).

With regard to social capital's reach and impact, it is not only important to estimate the number of relationships (and their frequency) but also the specific *kind* of social ties able to provide essential resources in time of need. As Fernández Kelly (1995) observes, social networks are not just characterized by the quantity or type of contacts or their strength but by the resources they entitle to their members. Granovetter's (1974) notion of "the strength of weak ties," which emphasizes the importance of indirect relationships in the access to status and power, suggests that strong ties and homogeneous networks are not necessarily considered more convenient for the circulation of social capital than weak and loose webs. The latter may allow access to a wider and richer array of resources via a greater number of contacts. For example, individuals with strong social network resources living in impoverished neighborhoods tend to have less social capital than those with weaker social networks residing in better areas (Cattell 2001; Fernández Kelly 1994). In addition, while social capital is produced and distributed through social relationships, the number or density of relationships does not guarantee, per se, capital accumulation.

For the purpose of this article, *social capital* will be defined as relationships of reciprocity in the provision and reception of social resources (e.g., health advice, referrals, and prescriptions drugs) among immigrants sharing the tango floor. In the following pages, this essay will examine some relevant categories of social capital that will contribute to our understanding of the tango world as a social field, including their members' reliance on *trust* as the basic currency for their interpersonal exchanges, the preeminence of rules of inclusion and exclusion, and bounded solidarity, defined as expectations of interpersonal assistance among those belonging to the same community of interest. *Multiplexiality* is probably one of the most relevant concepts related to the accumulation and circulation of social capital, as it suggests its uneven appropriation within and across social webs joined by members belonging to different social strata. As Fernández Kelly (1995, 220) observes, multiplexity refers to the degree to which networks "may be composed of persons with differing social status linked in a variety of ways, who play multiple roles in several fields of activity." Multiplexity expands the possibilities for the circulation of valuable resources (such as housing, jobs, and skills) among those belonging to the same social networks.

In this article, I will argue that Manhattan tango halls constitute a unique multiplexial social field as they gather individuals belonging to different social and cultural worlds on the basis of dancing and listening to tango. This article will also examine the disadvantages of obtaining resources via social webs such as unspecified obligations among parties, which may lead to

misunderstandings and disappointments, uncertain time horizons in reciprocity terms, and the potential violation of exchange norms (Portes 1998; Bourdieu 1985).

Entering the Tango World

As an Argentine immigrant myself, my incursions into the tango field began a few years ago when as a newcomer in New York City (NYC), I felt compelled to find traces of my own Argentine identity within the façade of an idiosyncratic Argentine milieu. At the time, I had occasionally attended tango events for the purpose of chatting with friends, while listening to the same old tango tunes that my relatives used to hum and sing when I was growing up in Buenos Aires. With the guidance of Argentine comrades, I discovered early on the nomadic milongas that began mushrooming in the mid-1990s, along with the underground social world that was attracting both Argentine and international regulars alike. Although in the following years I continued being in touch with some of the tango acquaintances I had met during those early outings, I neither joined the troupe of tango practitioners nor included tango lessons as part of my cosmopolitan social routine (Viladrich, forthcoming b, forthcoming c).

The tango world was again brought up to my attention some years later when as a PhD candidate at Columbia University, I began conducting research on Argentine immigrants' social networks and was attempting to understand the importance of entertainment forms as social reservoirs for social webs to be activated and reproduced. At that time, tango dancing in Manhattan had already become a unique entertainment field attracting an eclectic cluster of Argentine artists and entrepreneurs, along with a multinational crowd. This also took place at a time when ballroom dancing (e.g., salsa, swing, rumba) was becoming popular not only on the East Coast but also on the West Coast (Finnegan 1992), following a renewed global interest in eclectic ethnic trends and world music. The latter led a growing number of aficionados into taking dancing lessons in Latin American and Caribbean tunes, attracted by their exotic hints, the physicality of coupling dancing, and its dramatic composition (Dunning 1997; Hood 1994).

By the turn of the twenty-first century, the former timid presence of tango in NYC dancing academies had been replaced by burgeoning tango venues where teaching and dancing tango (and tango only) had become a cornerstone of the Manhattan entertainment world.

Suddenly, the tango world revealed itself as the visible façade of the Argentine minority that until recently had remained as a hidden immigrant group in NYC. On this realization, I decided to focus on the tango world as a specific case study where Argentines, along with an international crowd of *milongueros* (tango dancers), congregate to dance and exchange valuable resources, from visa information to free prescription of drugs.

For two years (1999–2001), I conducted formal fieldwork for this study, which in practice continued after the data collection was completed. The ethnographic methods implemented mostly relied on participant observation and informal interviews held with tango artists and patrons. In addition, I conducted fifteen interviews with Argentine tango artists and entrepreneurs, following a semistructured guideline that addressed their sociodemographic characteristics and migratory story, their health status, and the resources (both informal and formal) through which they attempted to solve their health problems in NYC. I also inquired about their perceived obstacles in obtaining affordable care in the United States and the strategies they implemented to overcome them. Systematic field notes were written throughout the research process. During fieldwork, I also jotted down quotes and accounts of conversations with immigrants in the field (field cases) whose remarks were illuminating on some of the main aspects described in this article. Although the project included tango venues in other NYC boroughs, I mostly focused on Manhattan milongas, given their relevance as unique social resorts for Argentine immigrants as well as an international audience of practitioners.

For months, I followed my tango informants through their social and artistic troupes, often waiting for them at dancing academies and milongas doorsteps during cold winter evenings. I visited nightclubs and restaurants where my tango comrades worked (as hostesses, waiters and occasionally as dancers or singers), and I listened to their life stories over *mate* (an herbal drink) and Argentine pastries at the coffee shops of Little Argentina in Queens. I also chaperoned them to different institutions and job venues, which provided me with an acute sense of the resources they had (and did not have), along with witnessing the display of their diverse social personas.

As a female Argentine immigrant myself, most of my interviewees felt that "I was one of them" even though I am not a tango artist and do not publicly practice tango. In fact, my nondancing participatory role ended up becoming the most conspicuous unanticipated decision I

made during fieldwork, as it provided me with a unique opportunity to talk with all sorts of tango artists and enthusiasts who would join me at the side of the dancing floor in between tango tunes to rest, drink, and eat (Viladrich, forthcoming c). In between sets, tango musicians, dancers, and their friends would gather around a table to chat, sharing stories and complaints. During my incursions to milongas salons, it was common to witness milongueros exchange information and resources regarding housing facilities, visa applications, and cheap access to health care. As many of us would see each other on a regular basis, our encounters on the tango floor would seem like an expected rendezvous that lengthened the thematic thread of previous exchanges. Much of my understanding of the informal transactions taking place at the milongas arose from my participation in these informal gatherings that often preceded and followed my formal interviews with tango immigrants. On those occasions, my informants would spontaneously engage in discussing their everyday tribulations and other issues on which I would eventually provide my expertise. Sharing information often involved seeking help for physical complaints such as sore muscles, a common issue given tango immigrants' reliance on their physical strength to both teach and perform.[1]

As I was studying social capital, I did not immediately realize that my encounters in the field would be tainted with the same limitations that characterize social capital exchanges (Viladrich, forthcoming b). Social reciprocity in the tango field, although not limited to those sharing the same nationality, translates into subtle rights and obligations in which the terms of the transactions are not always clearly delimited, and my case was no exception. As I did not pay my interviewees for their participation in this study, we typically subscribed to informal agreements of reciprocity. As part of a discreet code of interpersonal trade, most of my tango friends would generously share their stories with me in exchange for my services as translator, shopping guide, and unconditional listener to their everyday tribulations. Our regular conversations included accounts of their disenchantments with compatriots who had unreliably promised some help to solve a myriad of problems, from filling forms for health insurance applications to getting new visas after their previous ones had expired. Although for the most part, I was able to satisfy my informants' open (and often understated) requests for assistance in exchange for their volunteering information, I also experienced a few frustrated social encounters tainted by our often blurred and unspoken contractual terms.

The Manhattan Tango World: A Social Niche for Argentine Artists

Argentines dance with a natural passion, while Americans dance with a borrowed one.

(American tango fan)

For the purpose of this article, the most significant aspect characterizing the NYC's tango world relates to the emergence of a Manhattan tango niche fed by an international community of well-off customers, tango amateurs, and struggling artists from different nationalities. In only a few years, Manhattan milongas and other tango settings have become glamorous events readily available to an international clientele with enough economic capital, time to spare, and loneliness to share. Manhattan tango venues are unique multiplexial social fields (rich in social capital) that attract a variety of customers from diverse social origins and professions. They provide a wide range of tango products: ballroom lessons catering to the international middle and upper-middle class, milongas with restaurant and bar services, seminars and workshops to explore diverse sexual possibilities, and tango lessons for the gay community. In Manhattan alone, on any day of the week, there are at least three tango milongas to choose from. During the spring and the summer, tango is also being danced outdoors in Central Park, the Sea Port, and at the Lincoln Center under the sponsorship of the Lincoln Center Outdoor Festival, which usually includes two outdoor tango nights.

Manhattan milongas typically follow a complex routine that usually begins with a class (for apprentices and those who want to enhance their skills for a moderate fee), followed by ballroom dancing that usually extends until late hours at night. For a given fee (usually between ten and fifteen dollars) some milongas offer some food and soft drinks, while others have a full bar and restaurant available on the premises. Dancing sets are organized according to different pieces interpreted by either an ensemble of tango musicians or recorded tunes from old-time Argentine tango orchestras. On regular intervals, dancers usually stop to switch partners, rest, converse, and eat or drink, particularly in between musical sets.

In spite of the participation of amateurs from all nationalities in the tango's social reproduction, the predominance of the Argentine style in the ballroom floor (with all its variances) has contributed to placing Argentine artists in the spotlight. Internationally, the promotion and practice of "Argentine tango" have captured a loyal audience of customers and fans who, particularly in NYC, are eager to learn from those who embody the know-how of the tango's technical and emotional reservoir. Therefore, tango performance has become a vehicle for Argentines to become ambassadors of the genre and a passport to leave their country in search for better opportunities abroad. As a result, growing numbers of Argentine artists have arrived in NYC in recent years eager to satisfy the demand arising from the offerings of new tango products, including the opening of new milongas and the presence of new and recycled tango shows. According to Windhausen (2001), the search for tango professors in the early 1990s stimulated the "importation" of both tango instructors and dancers from Argentina. Many Argentines, descendants of those European immigrants who held tango as their personal rubric a century ago, are currently the ones in charge of bringing it abroad.

As with other immigrant groups (see Waldinger 1999, 2001) network recruitment has become the main strategy to bring compatriots into the tango field, which has reassured the Argentine presence in both the local and the international market. Argentine tango artists, both in New York and other global cities, have taken advantage of the international demand for the tango's sublimated passion that implies the circulation of emotional capital (see Savigliano 1995) by stressing their reputation as the *authentic* interpreters of the genre and the *legitimate holders* of the tango spirit. Therefore, being Argentine and being able to teach/dance tango have become a precious combination, a social warranty to reassure that passionate tango will emanate from its original reservoirs. In the words of one tango artist,

> Being Argentine and teaching tango is a plus; we are expected to know about it, and it gives us an advantage over other tango teachers since tango is our national product.

Although from a technical point of view, it would be difficult to distinguish among tango instructors and dancers from different nationalities, Argentine tango dancers rely on the status ascribed to their national origin, as well as to their extensive experience in tango practice, to consider themselves as the natural translators of the tango's emotional philosophy over their non-Argentine competitors. For many, the tango can be taught, interpreted, and danced by an international crowd around the world, but it is mostly through its

Argentine carriers that it develops its "true character." Milongas run by Argentines not only draw the presence of the Argentine community at large but also sponsor the itinerant visits of reputed Argentine artists who come to NYC on a regular basis to perform and teach tango workshops. In NYC, not all milongas are run by Argentines, but those hosted by them hold a touch of legitimacy as unique social resorts where dancing and listening to tango tunes go along with socializing, drinking, and eating, as will be discussed next.

Uncovering the Social World of Manhattan Milongas

Although the main stated purpose of tango practitioners and artists is to practice complicated steps with others, there is much more at stake among those who regularly meet at the Manhattan milongas. Participant observation allowed me to grasp the relevance of the tango field as a community of interest among worldwide tango artists and patrons, supported by relational dynamics often marked by spontaneous social negotiations instituted by subtle power hierarchies. Following Bourdieu's conceptualization (Bourdieu 1984; Bourdieu and Passeron 1979), tango milongas can be considered as unique social fields in which relationships of power are dynamic and relational and supported by actors' shared rules of the game.

As stated earlier, multiplexial social networks are characterized by their members' diversity in terms of social statuses, skills (human capital), and fields of activity. Although Manhattan milongas mostly recruit a middle-class clientele (e.g., professionals, entrepreneurs, and business people), they also welcome a heterogeneous crowd of Argentines from diverse social origins, including impoverished tango newcomers and representatives of the old tango guard. In spite of the fact that Manhattan milongas are for-profit enterprises, they constitute splendid social venues for Argentines to interact and exchange favors and services.

Paradoxically, accumulation of social capital among tango practitioners also requires other sources of capital (Bourdieu 1985; Hawe and Shiell 2000), particularly as its investment is a money-spending, energy-costing, and time-consuming endeavor. For example, in order to diversify their pool of potential students, as well as to be in tune with the latest dancing venues, tango immigrants must spend more resources (e.g., expensive dresses, commuting time, money to pay for transportation and meals) than they would if remaining isolated and indoors or as

members of narrower social niches. For reputed and aspiring tango artists (even if dancing part-time), attending different milongas on regular basis is a condition *sin equanon* and an investment that must be taken seriously to make their careers flourish. As noted earlier, capital accumulation relies on the importance of relying on social connections to achieve goals and resources (see Lin 2001; Willer 1999). The urge for tango immigrants to be "on the spot" also relates to social capital's *reverse depreciation* through which the more it is used, the larger it becomes. In the words of an informant: "you have to be seen, you have to get there and practice with your students, talk to your peers and show that you are serious about it, even if you are exhausted by the end of the day."

Indeed, the time and energy spent at the milonga also mean social investment (in the form of contacts, relationships, and referrals) that can potentially turn into meaningful leads during the daytime. By sharing the tango floor, tango immigrants get embedded in subtle power games in which they try to impress each other and gain access to scarce resources, such as invitations to participate in upscale dancing shows and contacts to get entry into prestigious dancing auditions. Dancing couples will display their skills in front of others not just to enhance their reputation but also to woo potential students, and tango amateurs will attempt to enchant respected tango artists, secretly hoping to become tango performers themselves. In almost all cases, tango habitués interact with each other over and over by attending different tango venues every week, even before or after the milongas have closed their doors. Tango immigrants and their customers get involved in more than one "game" at the same time (in Bourdieu's [1984] terms), as they perform as professors-students during tango classes, as partners during the tango practice, and even as friends who may go out for a bite late at night once dancing is over.

Within its diversity, the tango field operates within a particular hierarchy of professional authority and prestige that does not necessarily follow mainstream status markers. Those who are more experienced and have built their careers as well-known milongueros may not be the most successful in mainstream society, and vice versa. As a chain of alternate hierarchies, the superiority of the expert dancer and musician on the tango floor becomes the ground for leveraged power with those belonging to higher status positions in the outer world. The same well-off tango devotee, who will celebrate the opportunity to dance and take lessons from one of the many expert female dancers in an evening milonga, will be the one who will hire her as a part-time secretary or as a waitress during the daytime. And vice versa, the young

Argentine male tango practitioner who arrives late in the milonga, just after having finished his chores as a busboy at a nearby restaurant, will benefit from the contacts, treats, and generous friendship offered by the affluent professional women to whom he has become a steady tango companion.

As informed by social exchange theorists (see Zafirovski 2001), the interpersonal transactions taking place in the tango world provide revenues to those located at strategic sites, closer to those well connected with both the job and the artistic market. Above all, if milongas welcome a variety of tango immigrants, adherents, and entrepreneurs, then those who get closer to the decision-making nodes benefit from their tango connections the most. In sum, what happens at the dancing floor is transferred to the wider world, particularly among those for whom the tango field constitutes a nurturing social hub that provides specific responses to their everyday needs.

Even when the trade of resources would not appear to be based on reciprocal obligations, some kind of return will be expected in the medium and long run. Quite often, I heard my informants say "te hago la gauchada," which literally means "I'll be a good gaucho," a slang phrase that refers to helping others without expecting specific goods in exchange. Nevertheless, intangible returns in the form of moral obligation and personal gratitude will be expected, or will be sanctioned with open or subtle criticism otherwise. As Portes notes (1998), what characterizes the provision and reception of social capital is that reciprocity terms are neither univocal nor scheduled in advance. Although in some cases, it may seem that no payment is involved, exchanges may be delayed in time and specification of mutual benefits may not be explicit, aspects that will be explored next.

Social Reciprocity and Tango Brokers

You can find all the resources you need in the tango world.

(Cristal, thirty-year-old tango dancer)

In spite of the glamour that characterizes the internationalization of tango dancing, the lives of most tango artists are not as flamboyant as their external personas might suggest. Quite often, the tango's apparent lavishness has led observers to overlook the hardships experienced by many artists, who become prey of the job market's uncertainties. Several of the tango artists

I met in the field were forced to perform a dual life by combining their roles as "glamorous artists" with low-skilled occupations to make ends meet (see Viladrich 2005).

Indeed, many tango immigrants endure everyday lives that are far from the fairy tales imagined by many of their compatriots back home. To a certain extent, tango artists have problems similar to the ones experienced by other immigrants, including holding undocumented statuses and facing obstacles to obtaining affordable health care. In some cases, they are forced to work as part-time contractors or as freelancers by being "on call" at different tango venues that may need them on last-minute notice. Tango artists are especially vulnerable to the high costs of living in NYC, expenses that are much more predictable than their changing, and often erratic, job opportunities. Surely, the expensive prices of basic goods (such as food, transportation, and housing) are problems affecting tango immigrants the most, as they must invest considerable time and money in the production of their tango personas.[2] In the young female dancer Carmin's words,

> People in Argentina think that this is a glamorous life and that it is easy to make money here, but they don't realize how tough it is. New York is a very competitive place, which in part is good because it forces you to continue learning, but it is also difficult and expensive to live here. There are so many out there trying to make it in the city.

Most tango immigrants do not count on health insurance in the United States, despite having to rely on their physical ability to make ends meet. Curiously, health issues among artists in general, and among tango artists in particular, have been mostly unstudied, although performers (musicians and dancers) depend on their bodies to excel in their artistic skills, which also demand continuous investments (e.g., time, practice, rehearsals, and rest), to keep their careers ongoing. Physical injuries of arms and legs were among the most frequent problems reported by the participants in this study, problems that if not properly attended to could impair their ability to teach, play, sing, and dance. Unquestionably, good physical health is a prerequisite in a tight job market where professors and artists compete for students and sponsors. Roman (a tango newcomer in his sixties who plays the *bandoneón*) summarized the fears he shared with his colleagues regarding health issues in the following way:

Here, one becomes a doctor for oneself. You have to be okay since there is no insurance and everything is expensive. I would like to insure my hands just in case something happens and I can't play anymore. The problem of [a lack of] coverage is one of the big issues for immigrants like us.

It is precisely because of tango immigrants' exposure to unexpected changes of luck and fate (e.g., not having a visa, losing their tango patrons) that the tango field has become such a resourceful hub where they get exposure and have access to different resources to satisfy their diverse needs. Contrary to the emphasis placed on social networks' size and density, social capital theory highlights the quality of social webs in terms of allowing their members to access valued resources rather than their frequency or number of their social contacts. Argentine artists rely on their ingenious talents to make ends meet other than the practice of tango, and milongas are ideal hubs to advertise their services. For example, a young apprentice of oriental therapies may provide her services for free to her tango clients eager to play as guinea pigs for their in-residence therapist. On the basis of "bartering" services, some tango artists are eager to teach lessons for free in exchange for help finding cheap housing or affordable health care.

As noted before, the amount of social capital is relatively independent of the size and density of social networks. For example, my informants' opportunities to obtain useful assistance regarding health issues were not a matter of how many individuals they were connected with but rather who they were related to and what sort of relationships they developed with each other (e.g., through mutual obligations). As summarized by one of my interviewees who paraphrased a popular saying, "Dime con quien andas y te dire quien eres ("Tell me who you are with and I will tell you who you are"). This issue became even more conspicuous when examining tango immigrants' resolution of their health problems and their need to find accessible and affordable medical care in NYC.

Many tango artists solved their more immediate health problems through the direct help of medical doctors and alternative health practitioners (often from Argentina or of Latino origin) who either belonged to their tango networks or were directly referred by them. Particularly in the case of newcomers, the obstacles to obtaining health services through formal channels were a main reason for them to seek the assistance of their tango comrades to solve their health needs. I have coined the term *tango brokers* to refer to physicians who facilitate

immigrants' access to and use of the U.S. health system by virtue of their sharing ethnic and social interests with their clients that transcend the clinical setting. The social capital exchanges involved in this kind of brokerage are at the core of understanding its meaning.

Tango brokers' performance can clearly be witnessed at Manhattan milongas, where health professionals and their clients exchange social resources of different natures (e.g., prescription drugs for social company and tango practice) as members of the same social domain. Tango brokers often become trustful health consultants for their tango pals while charging them lower fees or no fees at all in exchange for opportunities to dance and interact with talented artists and amateur tango fans. While tango artists obtain medical services for low fees or for free, doctors are rewarded, both inside and outside the tango field, in the form of status recognition and potential clientele. Doctors, lawyers, undocumented tango artists, and business entrepreneurs who might not be able to socialize in other social fields will get together in the tango salon to exchange transpiration, embraces, and informal social transactions. In this way, health brokers and tango immigrants subscribe to a paralleled power hierarchy that somehow challenges their status differences in the real world. For most Argentine tango immigrants and tango fans, both uninsured and insured, health brokers constitute the best antidote against the barriers they face to access the U.S. health system, as they speak Spanish, are easily reachable, and treat them as members of the same group. Nevertheless, to find trustful and inexpensive biomedical practitioners is not an easy task, particularly for those who are undocumented and count on few (if any) social connections. Even so, relying on a tango broker does not imply exclusivity or loyalty on their clients' part, as many tango practitioners negotiate different sorts of assistance over time, depending on their specific life circumstances.

In addition, health problems are an additive to the many issues tango immigrants have to deal with in NYC. By following some of my informants through time, I was able to witness the flexibility and vulnerability of tango immigrants' legal careers (changes in their legal status), which in some cases forced them to obtain jobs in less attractive fields. Some tango artists ended up undocumented in the United States mostly because of the increasing restrictions to obtain visa-sponsored jobs, as well as their difficulties in renewing nonpermanent U.S. visas. Even if legally in the United States, tango artists are exposed to the flexibility (and variability) of show business, which often makes them vulnerable to unfair contractual obligations on the part of their employers.

Carmin had begun working as a tango instructor in one of the many dancing studios in Manhattan in exchange for a working visa. Nonetheless, her dream of coming to America seemed crushed. Not only was she forced to teach for uncountable hours in exchange for a minimal wage, but she also had to learn the "American way" to tango as a requirement for her to be able to teach.

I was hired by this academy to teach tango full-time, but they did all sorts of illegal things. For example, I was supposed to sign blank receipts, and they exploited me since they only paid me for a few hours of teaching, although I was there all day. But because they gave me the visa [a working visa], I could not go anywhere. I was trapped and they did not keep their promises.

Nonetheless, thanks to her regular attendance at different Manhattan milongas, Carmin was finally able to meet many other Argentines who ultimately helped her find alternative solutions to both her legal and working tribulations. One of her social connections was Dr. L., an Argentine tango fan who offered her a visa sponsorship in exchange for participating in common professional projects. Through time, this doctor turned out to be Carmin's legal sponsor and dancing friend, as well as her main medical counselor during critical health episodes, since she was suffering from stress, bodily fatigue, and stomach problems. The following excerpts illustrate Carmin's combination of diverse healing practices recruited via her tango connections:

I have called my sponsor [Dr. L.] in all cases to ask for his opinion, and then I have self-referred myself to alternative medicine. If I have a problem, he is the first person I will call because he is a physician; he helps me with most of my medical needs. If I cannot find him because he is traveling, I will go to the hospital or to an alternative doctor.

Although Carmin considered herself lucky, she did not regard Dr. L.'s help as an exemption but as a token of the solidarity exchange taking place among compatriots, which implies that those in better positions should help those in more susceptible ones. Following Carmin's reasoning (also shared by other study participants), these kinds of interactions are not supported by an altruistic nature but by a shared code of reciprocal favors in which the circulation of social capital is nurtured by the exchange of people's singular skills (human capital) within specific social fields. Without knowing it, Carmin

was referring to what has been called "bounded solidarity" (Portes 1998; Coleman 1990), which implies actors' provision of valuable resources, without expecting direct retribution, based on their belonging to the same community of interests.

Teo, a tango entrepreneur in his fifties, was an enthusiastic dancer who had limited health coverage that he paid for out-of-pocket. Through his tango activities, Teo had met not only professionals of various disciplines but also a female doctor (Doctor M.) who had become his informal primary care practitioner and with whom he routinely danced tango at weekly milongas. In exchange, Teo would help his friend improve her expertise with tango steps by rehearsing together choreographed tango routines. Teo called this doctor any time he had a health problem, and she would either briefly check his condition at the tango practice or recommend him prescriptions over the phone. Just before our first interview, Teo had experienced continuous coughing and fever and decided to visit the emergency room where he got X rays, after which he remained in bed for several days. Nevertheless, instead of continuing his care through the hospital's doctors (who were not covered by his insurance), Teo asked another tango dancer who was staying in his place at that time to bring the X rays to his doctor friend. After examining the X rays, Doctor M. concluded that he had caught pneumonia (a similar diagnosis to what he got in the hospital) and prescribed him medicines over the phone.

In return for their services, Doctor L. and Doctor M., as many professional tango enthusiasts I met during fieldwork, found in the tango world an ethnic niche where they could dance and practice with skillful artists, as well as develop social relationships with other Argentines. As noted earlier, the tango field constitutes a fertile area for professionals' recruitment of clients, who contribute to building up (and maintaining) their good reputation as well as to increasing their clientele. As Portes (1998) observes, social capital's returns come back not necessarily from recipients but from the community at large in terms of prestige, approval, and potential referrals. While immigrants obtain medical services for either low fees or for free, doctors benefit from social company and approval in the form of social recognition both inside and outside the tango field. In fact, since the reputation of healers is greatly supported by public acknowledgment and recommendations, their participation in ethnic social fields constitutes an ideal marketing arena from where to collect social capital's returns.

Reciprocity is one of the most conspicuous characteristics of social capital which, contrary to economic or financial returns, requires agents to be involved in inter-personal exchanges of products that are not easily mea-sured in economic terms. By belonging to the same community (in this case the tango field, with its sanctions and rules), donors and recipients of social capital guaran-tee that favors will be returned in one way or another. In Carmin's words, "Una mano lava la otra" ("One hand washes the other hand"), which means that the exchange of favors is embedded in shared codes of retribution. Nonetheless, as noted by Portes (1998), the absence of a priori rules regarding the principles commanding social capital's transactions often provides fertile ground for misunderstanding, disappointment, and loss of trust. During fieldwork, I had the opportunity to witness the breakage of such sanctioned codes through gossip, hidden or overt attacks to the parties' reputation, and even the exclusion from the tango field, as will be described next.

The Loss of Trust: Social Capital and Unmet Expectations

Many of the tango practitioners I met during fieldwork had built unique reputations as tango masters, which often mismatched the often low-skill occupations they would hold otherwise. In fact, among tango habitués, those belonging to a lower socioeconomic status were often the ones enjoying the highest prestige in the tango ballroom, particularly by holding a distinctive tango expertise that they displayed and shared with others. Social differences that would be irreconcilable in the light of day vanish under the lure of tango dancing, where power hierarchies are measured under the canons of artistic cachet and skillful performance. By sharing the same social fields (tango milongas in this case), some of my informants held the illusion that the tango's social hierarchy would be extended beyond, and above, the tango salon's doors.

Violeta's case illustrates this point. She was one of the tango's grandmothers, as she was older, more trained, and held a reputation as a long-term *milonguera* (*milonguera vieja*). Although she belonged to a working-class family and had been a housewife most of her life, she had built up a tango career for herself and for some members of her fictitious tango family, as she and her husband were considered mentors for younger genera-tions of Argentine tango fans. Violeta knew more about tango than many of the tango amateurs she had met, including an Argentine practitioner, Dr. F., who for a while had become her main medical practitioner. On one occasion, Violeta was complaining about Dr. F., saying,

You see, I used to see this doctor, Mr. F., whom I met in the milongas. I actually taught him how to dance his first steps, and I believed we were friends, always teas-ing and talking to each other in the milongas. I was having problems [emotional], so he told me that he could help me; so I began to see him on regular basis . . . for a year. . . . But he did not like the fact that I was not taking the medicines he gave me because these were bad for me, and even when I took them, I always did it in lower doses. Also, he canceled my appointments many times. And the thing that hurt me the most was that one day, I had to cancel the appoint-ment because I was going to get the American citizen-ship. So I called him up and he told me that I had to pay half of the consultation. After that day, I stopped seeing him because it hurt me so much what he did.

If he had not told me that [to pay for that day's consultation], I would have probably offered to pay, but now I've been hurt. . . . My husband tells me to go back, and he [the doctor] also tells me that since I continue seeing him in the milongas. . . . I thought we were friends, you see *tango friends*, since we danced together, made jokes, gave each other kisses and hugs. But now I have lost *trust* in him, because there was a kind of friendship between us. . . . He knew all the problems of my life.

Immigrants' social webs are not quiescent and may suffer from exaggerated expectations, misunderstand-ings, and overwhelming demands (see Menjívar 2000). As illustrated in the excerpts above, unmet reciprocal expectations may lead to misunderstandings and the eventual rupture of trust when individual expectations are not met. Exchanges based on social capital transac-tions, although holding the promise of being supported by unselfish motivations, provide fertile ground for dis-appointments and misunderstandings, particularly when individual expectations are not met. Violeta felt betrayed by her doctor's behavior, as she had expected to be able to extend to the medical field the same codes of semiequal-ity she shared with him in the tango field. For Violeta, the message she had received from Dr. F. could be decodified as, "We can be almost equals in the tango milonga, but in my office I am the doctor and you become my patient." As such, Violeta was expected to follow the doctor's prescrip-tions "palabra por palabra" ("word for word"), even if this implied taking the prescription drugs as provided and waiting a long time in the office to be seen.

As unique social fields supported by social capital exchanges, Manhattan milongas have the property of "camouflaging" social differences by bringing together individuals belonging to different social strata, occupations, and ages. Violeta's disappointments emerged from an illusion of social equality that was broken by her doctor's reminder of their actual status differences. Immigrants who would have probably never met otherwise (e.g., doctors, psychologists, veteran housewives, and mechanics) are brought together at particular points in time on the basis of sharing similar interests. Social hierarchies that would be irreducible in other scenarios temporarily vanish in the tango world under the umbrella of belonging to the same entertainment community. To a certain extent, the wonders of the tango world's social diversity also become its Achilles heel because of the informal nature of the social exchanges it nurtures, which also leave room for unmet expectations, and the eventual rupture of trust among artists and clients belonging to different social worlds.

Epilogue: Beyond Social Capital

This article has revealed some of the characteristics of NYC's tango world in the context of the tango's broader circulation, in which customers and Argentine tango artists are shareholders of the same entertainment market. For years, I have been at the milongas to examine how tango (or even better, its *tangoified* relationships) has become a socialized metaphor for something else: for relationships to be created, for social and economic transactions to take place, and for interpersonal reciprocity to be instituted.[3] In the end, I found the ritualized performance metalanguage of Argentines' social solidarities and conflicts is exposed, dramatized, shared, and occasionally solved.

This study has provided a window of opportunity to examine the contribution of social capital categories to our understanding of the Manhattan tango field as a unique reservoir for social resources to be circulated on the basis of individuals belonging to the same community of interest. The tango world has revealed itself as an ideal place from which to understand how entertainment fields provide alternative venues for their members' provision and reception of material and symbolic and emotional assistance on the bases of social capital exchanges. As we have seen, by sharing the same entertainment niche, Argentine tango artists and some doctors are linked (through favors and sublet obligations) to a double form of bounded solidarity in which they share membership in the same "artistic community" (tango milongas) and a common ethnic allegiance as Argentine or Latino practitioners.

In spite of the barriers to health care experienced by tango artists, this study has shown that the tango world,

as a community of interest for Argentine immigrants, provides unique resources for the resolution of their health problems. The analytical approach developed here could be useful for the study of other cosmopolitan dancing fields also sponsored by ethnic minorities' social webs, as in the case of the salsa world also supported by nationals from Caribbean countries in the United States.

Some caveats regarding the buoyant possibilities of social capital categories deserve further consideration. In recent years, the literature has addressed (and questioned) the importance of social capital as a resource for social integration and community empowerment, as well as an enhancement of health and social indicators (Cattell 2001; Kawachi et al. 1997). Those interested in fomenting social capital at the local level have raised concerns about the disruption of community bonds and the pervasive loss of America's social fabric represented in the image of the individual "bowling alone" (Putnam 1995). Although this study has concluded that Argentine tango artists do not bowl alone, their richest sources of social capital are mostly drawn from informal links of trust and reciprocity emerging from their participation in itinerant social fields—in this case, the tango world.

In addition, returns from social capital are not the panacea for immigrants' needs. If at the individual level, access to its benefits depends on social networks' diversity (multiplexity), there exist specific limits at the macro level (based on class, ethnic differences, and physical location) to immigrants' participation in rich social fields, particularly among disenfranchised individuals who need them the most. As we have seen in this article, social capital is dependent on norms of exclusion and inclusion that follow belonging criteria, such as national origin, ethnicity, and shared interests. Most ethnic fields are not as diverse as Manhattan milongas where only a selected pool, including struggling immigrants, are recruited from among its members. Among newcomers in particular, counting on tango brokers is not an easy task unless they rely on diversified social networks where people with different skills, professions, and interests interact on the basis of sharing common goals and activities. To a certain extent, access to the U.S. health system via health brokers is a symptom of the hidden demand for health care among immigrants, which would probably remain otherwise unattended. As we have seen, reciprocity exchanges between providers and recipients of social capital are not always clear, leaving room for exaggerated demands that may jeopardize the expectations of trust between parties. In addition, since the health broker model is based on informal codes of reciprocity, immigrants may lose their health brokers if their social exchanges are modified or if they stop sharing common social fields. Finally, in many cases, the private (and informal) nature of the medical encounter exceeds the supervision of health institutions over medical practice.

Furthermore, not all the benefits deriving from immigrants' participation in social fields are reproduced beyond its reach. As previously noted, ethnic solidarity (mostly in the form of bounded solidarity) will coexist in the tango domain as long as participants' exchanges do not challenge their unequal locations in mainstream society. Rich ethnic fields, such as the tango world, are not enduring substitutions for formal channels (e.g., job insurance's comprehensive health benefits or government programs) that should provide access to basic resources, disregarding immigrants' involvement with informal social webs. The fact that informal networks are doing (even if partially) what other formal channels are not, tells us something important about immigrants' unmet needs. More studies are needed to expand the theory subjacent to the access of scarce social resources via social relationships within specific fields of power. Finally, we need more information on which networks facilitate the circulation, access to, and provision of social capital, including information concerning who is accounted for and excluded from the networks' benefits on the basis of social participation.

Notes

1. My nondancing role as a tango aficionado also protected me from the subtle competition for male dancing partners and from playing within the tango's unspoken hierarchical structure where performers measure their talents vis-à-vis others (Viladrich, forthcoming c).

2. Tango performers in New York City (NYC) are not exempt from the lure of sophisticated representations that characterize the tango's public imagery and are quite aware of the need to create specific characters, which require not only the mastering of tango techniques but also the personification of elaborate "tango selves." The latter implies assuming particular attitudes (e.g., the male seductive, the femme fatale, the gracious performer) both on the stage and the ballroom floor.

3. My search for the ways through which Argentines have access to social resources became the catalyst that sent me back to the original social relationships that had welcomed me in NYC at the beginning of my own, and still inconclusive, migratory journey.

References

Archetti, Eduardo P. (1997). Multiple masculinities: The worlds of tango and football in Argentina. In *Sex and sexuality in Latin America,* edited by Daniel Balderston and D. J. Guy, 200–16. New York: New York University Press.

Berkman, Lisa, Thomas Glass, Ian Brissettec, and Teresa E. Seeman. (2000). From social integration to health: Durkheim in the new millennium. *Social Science & Medicine* 51 (6): 843–57.

Bourdieu, Pierre. 1984. *Distinction: A social critique of the judgement of taste.* Cambridge, MA: Harvard University Press.

———. (1985). The forms of capital. In *Handbook of theory and research for the sociology of education,* edited by J. G. Richardson, 241–58. New York: Greenwood.

Bourdieu, Pierre, and Jean-Claude Passeron. (1979). *The inheritors: French students and their relation to culture.* Trans. Richard Nice. Chicago: University of Chicago Press.

Castro, Donald S. (1991). *The Argentine tango as social history, 1880–1955.* Latin American Series, vol. 3. Queenston, UK: Edwin Mellen.

Cattell, Vicky. (2001). Poor people, poor places, and poor health: The mediating role of social networks and social capital. *Social Science & Medicine* 52 (10): 1501–16.

Coleman, J. S. (1990). Social capital in the creation of human capital. *American Journal of Sociology* 94 (suppl.): S95–S121.

Corradi, Juan E. (1997). How many did it take to tango? Voyages of urban culture in the early 1900s. In *Outsider art: Contesting boundaries in contemporary culture,* edited by Vera L. Zolberg and J. Maya Cherbo, 194–214. London: Cambridge University Press.

Dunning, Jennifer. (1997). When folkways point the way to innovation: Ethnic dance in New York City. *The New York Times,* June 1, B10.

Fernández Kelly, M. Patricia. (1994). Towanda's triumph: Social and cultural capital in the transition to adulthood in the urban ghetto. *Journal of Urban Research* 18:88–111.

———. (1995). Social and cultural capital in the urban ghetto: Implications for the economic sociology of immigration. In *The economic sociology of immigration: Essays on networks, ethnicity and entrepreneurship,* edited by A. Porte, 213–47. New York: Russell Sage.

Finnegan, Lora J. (1992). Ballroom dancing is back: San Francisco Bay Area clubs. *Sunset* 188:40.

Granovetter, M. S. (1974). *Getting a job: A study of contacts and careers.* Cambridge, MA: Harvard University Press.

Guy, Donna J. (1991). *Sex and danger in Buenos Aires: Prostitution, family, and nation in Argentina.* Engendering Latin America Series, vol. 1. Lincoln: University of Nebraska Press.

Hawe, Penelope, and Alan Shiell. (2000). Social capital and health promotion: A review. *Social Science & Medicine* 51 (6): 871–85.

Hood, Lucy. (1994). Warming up to Latin rhythms. *Américas* 46:14–19.

Kawachi, I., B. Kennedy, K. Lochner, and D. Prothrow-Stith. (1997). Social capital, income inequality, and mortality. *American Journal of Public Health* 87:1491–98.

Lin, Nan. (2001). *Social capital: A theory of social structure and action.* Structural Analysis in the Social Sciences Series, vol. 19. New York: Cambridge University Press.

Menjívar, Cecilia. (2000). *Fragmented ties: Salvadoran immigrant networks in America.* Berkeley: University of California Press.

Pelinski, Ramón, ed. (2000). *El tango nómade: Ensayos sobre la diáspora del tango.* Buenos Aires, Argentina: Corregidor.

Portes, Alejandro. 1998. Social capital: Its origins and applications in modern sociology. *Annual Review of Sociology* 24:1–24.

Putnam, R. D. (1995). Bowling alone: America's declining social capital. *Journal of Democracy* 6:65–78.

Rose, Richard. (2000). How much does social capital add to individual health? A survey study of Russians. *Social Science & Medicine* 51 (9): 1421–35.

Savigliano, Marta E. (1995). *Tango and the political economy of passion.* Boulder, CO: Westview.

———. *Angora matta: Fatal acts of north-south translation.* Middletown, CT: Wesleyan University Press.

Steingress, Gerhard, ed. (2002). *Songs of the minotaur: Hybridity and popular music in the era of globalization: A comparative analysis of rebetika, tango, rai, flamenco, sardana, and English urban folk.* Münster: Lit.

Vila, Pablo. (1991). Tango to folk: Hegemony construction and popular identities in Argentina. *Studies in Latin American Popular Culture* 10:107–39.

Viladrich, Anahí. (2003). Social careers, social capital, and immigrants' access barriers to health care: The case of the Argentine minority in New York City (NYC). PhD diss., Columbia University.

———. (2004). From the brothel to the salon: The tango's social history as an evolving artistic trend. *The Lost Notebook* 2. http://www.lostnotebook.org.

———. (2005). Performing the tango's dual life: Immigrant tales from the field. *Women and Performance.* 24 (28): 105–10.

———. Forthcoming a. Neither virgins nor whores: Tango lyrics and gender representations in the tango world. *Journal of Popular Culture* 39 (2).

———. Forthcoming b. You just belong to us: Tales of identity and difference with populations to which the ethnographer belongs. *Cultural Studies, Critical Methodologies* 5 (3).

———. Forthcoming c. More than two to tango: Ethnographic rendezvous in the Manhattan tango world. In *Ethnographic objectivity revisited: From rigor to vigor.* Lincoln: University of Nebraska Press.

Waldinger, Roger. (1999). *Still the promised city? African-Americans and new immigrants in postindustrial New York.* Cambridge, MA: Harvard University Press.

———. (2001). *Strangers at the gates: New immigrants in urban America.* Berkeley: University of California Press.

Wall, E., G. Ferrazi, and F. Schryer. (1998). Getting the goods on social capital. *Rural Sociology* 63:300–22.

Willer, David, ed. (1999). *Network exchange theory.* Westport, CT: Praeger.

———. (2001). El fenómeno del tango en Nueva York. *La Gaceta,* February 28.

Zafirovski, Milan. (2001). *Exchange, action, and social structure: Elements of economic sociology.* Westport, CT: Greenwood.

Discussion Questions

1. What is meant by the term *social capital* and why is it important? How is the New York tango world an example of social capital?

   Social capital defined: "relationships of reciprocity in the provision and reception of social resources." Social capital is particularly important if individuals do not have access to scarce resources, as is the case with the tango artists studied by Viladrich. The social relationships that were part of the tango networks provided these artists with access to health care. The tango artists studied by Viladrich were particularly vulnerable: residing in an area with a high cost of living, working part-time to support themselves (but without health care coverage), and some also having undocumented immigration status.

2. Assess your own social capital. What social networks do you rely upon and for what resources?

   Students may reflect on their own "relationships of reciprocity" such as familial relationships, friendships, relationships with coworkers, team members, club members, and so on.

3. How did Viladrich conduct her research?

   She relied on ethnographic methods—participant observation, informal interviews, and semistructured interviews. She focused on tango venues in Manhattan, New York.

Source: Viladrich, A. (2005). Tango immigrants in New York City: The value of social reciprocities. *Journal of Contemporary Ethnography,* 34(5), 533–559. Reprinted by permission of Sage Publications.

PART VIII

POVERTY AND SOCIAL WELFARE POLICY

CHAPTER 21

Welfare Reform in the United States

Gender, Race and Class Matter

Mimi Abramovitz (2006)

Mimi Abramovitz attempts to explain why gender, race, and class matter in welfare reform. In this excerpt, she provides an overview of U.S. social welfare policies, describing the main provisions of welfare reform and its impact on women and children. She concludes that welfare reform is part of a neoliberal effort to reduce the welfare state.

In a 1972 article in *MS Magazine,* Johnnie Tillmon, president of the National Welfare Rights Organization, presented her thoughts about welfare. Back then she declared:

> There are lots of lies that male society tells about welfare mothers: that welfare mothers are immoral, that welfare mothers are lazy, misuse their welfare checks, spend it all on booze and are stupid and incompetent. If people are willing to believe these lies, it's partly because they are just special versions of the lies that society tells about all women. (Tillmon, 1972)

Speaking at the height of the women's movement in the United States Tillmon, an African American, single mother on welfare, saw that the treatment of women on welfare reflected public anxieties about ALL women's preference for economic independence, personal autonomy, and social justice. Unfortunately few policy-makers, politicians, or advocates heeded her warnings that gender, race and class matter. Nor did they remember her words in the early 1990s—when women and welfare once again became the target of reform. If they had, maybe welfare in the U.S. would help rather than punish women, support rather than undermine their care-giving work.

Almost everyone has an opinion about today's welfare reform. Most policy-makers and politicians celebrated when the welfare caseload dropped by half in four years, falling from 4,159,369 families in December 1996 to 2,264,806 in 2000 and then reached 1,974,751 families in December 2004 (U.S. Department of Health and Human Services, 2004c). If cutting the welfare rolls was the main goal of the reform—their applause was justified. But if welfare reform set out to improve the lives of women, something has gone dangerously awry. As Tillmon predicted, the reformers built public support for cutting the rolls by playing to gender and racial stereotypes and demonizing big government (MacDonald, 1997, 1998; Mead, 1992; Murray, 1984). They stigmatized single mothers for failing to comply with prescribed wife and mother roles; depicted women of colour as matriarchal, hypersexed, and promiscuous; and blamed single motherhood for most of society's woes. Despite opposition to big government and contrary to existing data, they produced a programme that still uses the strong arm of the state to regulate the lives of women (Abramovitz, 1996, 2000; Delgado and Gordon, 2002; Hays, 2003: ch. 3; Mink, 1998).

The following analysis seeks to explain why gender, race and class matter in welfare reform. It provides a brief overview of the U.S. welfare programme for single mothers, describes the main provisions of welfare reform and identifies its impact on women and children. It concludes by suggesting that welfare reform was neither accidental nor simply mean-spirited. Rather it is best understood as part of the neo-liberal effort to downsize the state.

Overview of Welfare Reform

Welfare reform is the name given in 1996 to changes made in the U.S. public assistance programme designed to provide cash benefits just to single mothers (U.S. Congress, 1996). From 1908 to 1935 many, but not all, of the states provided a cash grant to single mothers. Referred to as the 'Widow's Pension,' the programme wrongly implied that all recipients had been married. In the early 1900s, the progressive era reformers feared that to acknowledge other types of single motherhood would cause them to lose public support for the programme they had fought so hard to enact—so they spotlighted those viewed as deserving of public aid (Abramovitz, 1996; Gordon, 1994) (Table 21.1).

In 1935, the U.S. Congress enacted the Social Security Act which included both universal social insurance and means-tested public assistance programmes. Widely regarded as the foundation of the U.S. welfare state, the landmark legislation transferred legal responsibility for social welfare from the states to the federal government and created an entitlement to income support. The historic shift in social policy was legitimized in the late 1930s by two important events. The Supreme Court declared the constitutionality of federal responsibility for the general welfare and officialdom accepted the economic theory of the British economist, John Maynard Keynes who had called for greater government spending to increase aggregate demand and otherwise stimulate economic growth. In 1962, following the post-war expansion of the welfare state, Congress liberalized welfare and changed its name from Aid to Dependent Children (ADC) to Aid to *Families* with Dependent Children (AFDC). But it maintained the image of single mothers as less deserving of aid than married women. In 1996, with the rise of neo-liberalism, Congress transformed welfare from a programme to help single mothers stay home with their children into a restrictive transitional work programme called Temporary Aid to Needy Families or TANF (Abramovitz, 1997).

Key Provisions of Welfare Reform

The Personal Responsibility and Work Opportunity Reconciliation Act (PRWORA) (U.S. Congress, 1996) was part of an agenda that had three main goals: work enforcement, marriage promotion, and a smaller welfare state. All three focused on changing the behaviour of women, the majority of welfare state clients and workers.

WORK ENFORCEMENT

The best-known provision of welfare reform, popularly known as "work first," targeted women's work behaviour. To move women off welfare the 1996 law intensified the programme's already stiff work requirements. The reform added more and stricter work rules, expanded workfare which requires that women on welfare without a job work-off their benefits by raking leaves in city parks, filing papers in municipal offices, or performing other unskilled tasks at non-profit human service agencies; and limited access to most of the educational opportunities that had been allowed under prior welfare reform (i.e. the 1988 Family Support Act). Work-first enforced these rules with punishment and deterrence.

Table 21.1   Historical Overview of the U.S. Programme for Single Mothers

Name of programme	Date	Programme
Widows' Pensions	1908–35	State programmes, variously implemented
Aid to Dependent Children (ADC)	1935	Title IV of the 1935 Social Security Act; federal/state partnership
Aid to Families with Dependent Children (AFDC)	1962	Liberalization of Title IV
Family Support Act	1988	Moves toward mandatory work program with various supports for working mothers
Temporary Aid to Needy Families (TANF) (i.e. "welfare reform")	1996	The Personal Responsibility and Work Opportunity Act

Women faced benefit reductions (e.g. sanctions) for minor rule violations and local welfare offices deterred applications with long waits, complicated forms, and unresponsive case managers (Hays, 2003: ch. 4; Abramovitz, 2002; Fox, 2000). Most dramatically, for the first time in the history of welfare, Congress imposed a five-year lifetime limit on the receipt of benefits regardless of need. When women reach the limit they have no choice but to take any job regardless of wages, working conditions, or family needs.

Congress adopted the work-first approach despite data showing that most women stayed on welfare for only two years and/or cycled on and off in response to changed labour market conditions or personal crises (Spalter-Roth et al., 1992). Many women forced off welfare in the late 1990s found work due to the booming economy. Even so, large numbers of former recipients could not make ends meet owing to low wages, part-time work, and the high cost of both childcare and transportation (Boushey, 2001; Cancian et al., 1999; Chapman and Bernstein, 2003; Loprest, 2003b). Many women lost Food Stamps, Medicaid, and subsidized housing; and food pantries and homeless shelters often reported that they had to turn people away (Dion and Pavetti, 2000). This grim picture does not include the presumably worse-off women whom the researchers never found or the women who returned to the rolls. Many of the women receiving welfare today are not highly employable owing to lack of work experience, few employment skills, poor physical or mental health, disabilities and the shortage of childcare services (Loprest, 2002, 2003a). Yet the nation's leaders plan to tighten the work requirements by 1) raising the number of adults that must be at work if the state is not to lose federal funding from 50 per cent to 70 per cent of the caseload; and by 2) increasing from 20 to 35 or 40 the number of hours a recipient must be at work if the state is to receive federal credit on which other funding is based (Center on Budget and Policy Priorities, 2005).

MARRIAGE PROMOTION

The second goal of welfare reform was to promote marriage as the foundation of society (U.S. Congress, 1996). The initial pro-marriage strategy relied on demonizing single motherhood. During the welfare reform debate the reformers evoked gender and racial stereotypes to portray single motherhood as the nation's number one social problem (MacDonald, 1997, 1998; Mead, 1992; Murray, 1984). They implied that crime, drug use, school dropouts, teenage pregnancies, and drive-by shootings were

transmitted from one generation to the next by husbandless women (read women of colour) heading their own families. They added that women on welfare prefer welfare to work, live the good life, cheat the government, and have kids for money. They called for regulating the child bearing, marital, and parenting choices of single mothers (MacDonald, 1997, 1998; Mead, 1992; Murray, 1984).

Three welfare reform provisions reflected this goal: the child exclusion, the abstinence-only grants, and the "illegitimacy" bonus.

The child exclusion (also called the family cap). Welfare reform presumed that poor women had large families and were having children in order to obtain or increase their cash benefits (Murray, 1984). Designed to limit non-marital births, the child exclusion allowed states to deny aid forever to children born while their mother is receiving welfare. Opponents countered that women on welfare did not have extra-large families and that the average welfare family was a mother and two kids, the same as the rest of the nation (National Governors' Association, 1999). Despite considerable evidence that family caps did not work, 25 states adopted the optional provision of PRWORA.

The "illegitimacy" bonus. Welfare reform also included an "illegitimacy" bonus for the five states that had achieved the greatest decrease in non-marital births statewide, while reducing their abortions below the 1995 rate. Beginning in 1999, the winning five states each received a $20 million supplement. The controversial measure reflected the belief that women on welfare had more "kids for money" despite government data showing that the increase in benefits that accompanied a birth was too small to be a factor in a woman's decision to have another child (National Governors' Association, 1999). It was also meant to send a message to all women, since the non-marital birth rate and abortion counts were not limited to women on welfare.

The abstinence-only provision initially earmarked $250 million for school sex education programmes that taught all children attending the school to postpone sex until marriage and prohibited teaching anything about contraception or safe sex (NOW Legal Defense and Education Fund, 1999; Sawhill, 2000). Yet by the early 1990s, government data revealed that 60 per cent of all births to never-married women in the United States were unintended, suggesting the need for birth control (U.S. Department of Health and Human Services, 1995). It also showed that the non-marital birth rate had started its steady decline long before 1996, especially among teens—the icon of welfare reform (Ventura et al., 2003; University of Michigan, 1994) (Table 21.2).

The exposure to abstinence-only sex education classes goes beyond the children of welfare recipients since all children attending public schools with abstinence-only programmes must attend these classes.

In 1999, nearly one-third of the nation's high schools—more than 10 per cent at faith-based programmes—were offering abstinence-only sex education (Landry et al., 1999). In 2001 alone, 53 of 59 States and Territories received $43.5 million in federal funds to provide abstinence education, mentoring, and counselling (U.S. Department of Health and Human Services, 2003b). Since 1997, Congress has allocated well over half a billion dollars to abstinence-only programmes which also censor other information about sexual activity and no funds for comprehensive sexual education programmes that teach both abstinence and contraceptive use (American Civil Liberties Union, 2005).

Demonizing parenting by single mothers. Welfare reform also encouraged marriage by demonizing the parenting practices of single mothers (Abramovitz, 2000; Roberts, 1993; Fineman, 1995). On the basis of the untested belief that financial deprivation motivates "responsible" parenting, welfare reduced the welfare cheque of unmarried mothers viewed as bad parents. For example "Learnfare" docked the cheques of single mothers with truant children and "Healthfare" lowered the grant of single mothers whose children did not get their immunization shots on time or missed a paediatric appointment (U.S. Government Accounting Office, 2000; Grossman, 1999; Abt Associates, 2000). But little or nothing was done to improve community conditions such as the lack of local doctors, deteriorating public schools, the shortage of childcare services, high priced grocery stores, substandard housing, and other features common to poor neighbourhoods which undermine effective parenting (Jennings, 2003).

Dead beat dads. Welfare reform also demonized the fathers of children receiving welfare calling them "dead beat dads" if they did not pay child support. One week before signing the 1996 welfare bill, President Clinton declared that non-payment of child support was a serious crime, comparing it to robbing a bank or a 7-Eleven store. He warned "[I]f you owe child support, you better pay it. If you deliberately refuse to pay it, you can find your face posted in the Post Office. We'll track you down with computers. We'll track you down with law enforcement. We'll find you through the Internet." He added: "If every parent paid the child support they could move 800,000 women and children off welfare immediately" (Hansen, 1999). Welfare reform requires that welfare mothers establish the identity of their children's father(s) and work with child support enforcement officials in demanding that fathers provide financial support or risk loss of benefits. This aggressive approach often ignores the reasons why non-custodial fathers may not be supporting their children. While some men shirk their responsibility and others are not asked, for many others the problem is due to lack of work, too little income, or a second family to support (Sorensen, 1995; Sorensen and Zibman, 2000). Furthermore, increased pressure for child support can lead the father to disappear from the scene and deprive the family of the benefits of paternal visitation. The lost benefits may include a) a reduction in anger, depression and role discontinuity for the father, b) intermittent relief from full-time responsibility for parenting for the mother, and c) an ongoing relationship with both parents for the child (Leger, 2003; Seltzer, 1991).

Healthy marriages. More recently, rather than just demonizing single mothers and dead beat dads, the U.S. government has taken to promoting "healthy" (that is heterosexual) marriages. Once the work-first approach had exhausted its potential to reduce the rolls, the "reformers" began to argue that welfare reform had failed to live up to its promise to promote marriage as the foundation of society (Rector and Pardue, 2004; White House, 2002).

Table 21.2 Teenage Pregnancy and Birth Rates, 1990–2000

Year	Pregnancy rates: teens aged 15–19	Birth rates: teens aged 15–19
1990	116.3 per 1000	59.5 per 1000
1996	97.9 per 1000	53.5 per 1000
2000	85.5 per 1000*	42.9 per 1000

*The lowest ever reported since pregnancy estimates began in 1976.

Source: United States National Vital Statistics Reports 52(7), p. 3. [http://www.cdc.gov/nchs/data/nvsr/nvsr52/nvsr52_07.pdf].

Since then the Bush administration has proposed the Healthy Marriage Initiative (HMI). It funds the states to provide premarital counselling, school-based marriage education, fatherhood initiatives, and special services for married couples. In sharp contrast to its opposition to same sex marriages, Congress is poised to spend $200 million a year in "healthy" marriage promotion grants as well as $100 million on marriage-related research and demonstration projects—and not just for those on welfare (U.S. Department of Health and Human Services, n.d.).

There is consensus that two incomes are better than one. But critics of marriage promotion policies argue that poverty rather than welfare breaks up families. Women's advocates charge that marriage promotion infringes on family privacy, may encourage battered women to remain in abusive relationships, and may push teens prematurely into unstable marriages. By focusing on individual choices, the marriage promotion drive also deflects attention away from the real causes of women's poverty: too few jobs, low wages, childcare shortages, male violence, and the lack of economic recognition for care work (Dailard, 2005; Jones-DeWeever, 2002; Hartmann and Talley, 2002).

What about the children? Despite the emphasis on family values and welfare's intent to benefit children, most welfare policy is directed at adults. The main concern about the fate of children was the provision of temporary subsidies for childcare. But this was marred by a shortage of slots, a complex application process, long waiting lists, the privatization of the services, and often substandard care. According to the National Study of Child Care for Low Income Families (Collins et al., 2000), in 1999 despite a large increase in the number of children receiving childcare subsidies, states on average served only 15 to 20 per cent of federally eligible children and 12 of the 17 states had a waiting list. From 1997 to 1999 most of the growth in childcare subsidies reflected children in families who had left TANF or who had never received it. The Administration for Children and Families reported a six per cent increase in the number of children receiving subsidies in 2000 (U.S. Department of Health and Human Services, 2003a). Even so, since January 2001, policy changes in 23 states have decreased the availability of childcare and 26 states give lowest priority to families leaving or who have already exited TANF (U.S. Government Accounting Office, 2003). The National Women's Law Center (2004) reported that many states have reduced income eligibility cut-off points for childcare programmes, increased family co-payments, continued their waiting lists and reimbursed providers at substandard rates.

Beyond childcare, welfare reform paid scant attention to the impact of the law's time-limited access to benefits, tough work mandates, and harsh sanctions (benefit reduction) on the lives of children in welfare households. The same welfare reformers who called upon middle class mothers to stay home with their children, insisted that poor women on welfare work outside the home. This double standard of womanhood based on marital status is built into the welfare-to-work programmes. It downplays the value of poor single mothers' care work and implies that poor children are better off if their mothers are not in the home. The tough work rules also ignore the difficulties that women, even middle class women with resources, have in balancing work and family responsibilities. Wealthy women solve the problem by hiring other women, often women of colour, to care for their children and clean their house. When asked by researchers, women on welfare talked about the financial and psychological benefits of work. But they also worried about access to affordable quality childcare, the need for time to guide their children, and the impact of leaving their kids for long periods of time without parental supervision (Scott et al., 2001).

Only a few of the official evaluations of welfare-to-work programmes focused on the outcomes of the welfare overhaul for children. Those that did reported mixed results about the complicated dynamics of work, welfare, parenting, and child well being. However, the most positive impact of welfare-to-work programmes on children was related to the programme's ability to improve family's finances. Programmes that improved the family's economic status or maternal education had favourable outcomes especially for children under five. But even these improvements did not bring children to the level of national norms for positive child development. Unfavourable outcomes for children resulted when families showed no economic progress, when their economic situation worsened, and when the children were adolescents (Zaslow et al., 2003). Economic well being also made a difference in a study of health outcomes involving 2,700 households. The rates of hospitalization and food insecurity rose for children under age three in households whose income from benefits fell due to sanctions or other reductions (Cook et al., 2002).

Inadequate income undermined the well being of children in other ways as well. When the loss of welfare benefits (owing to sanctions or reaching the new 60-month lifetime limit) compounded the well-known negative effects of grinding poverty, some poor women found that they could not protect their children from illness, malnutrition, delinquency, or poor school performance (Boushey et al., 2001). A national children's advocacy group reported that, as families reached welfare reform's five-year lifetime limit, the resultant chaos and increase in poverty placed children at greater risk for abuse and neglect (Firestein, 2000). Some mothers lost custody of their children. Unable to provide for their family, others voluntarily relinquished the care of their children to relatives or to the state, at great emotional cost to themselves. But the already strained child welfare system could not always deliver the supports needed to keep the families together or provide adequate foster care (Firestein, 2000). The 1997 Adoption and Safe Families Act (ASFA) accelerated the break-up of families (Roberts, 1999). ASFA required social workers to terminate the custodial rights of the biological parent if the parent could not "shape-up" within 12 to 15 months. The law also promotes adoption as the means for reducing the exploding foster care population. Signed by President Clinton, to foster the safety of children, this child welfare law along with many other systemic forces such as the lack of jobs, income, and housing tends to disadvantage women as they try to regain custody of their children (Child Welfare League of America, n.d.; Abramovitz, 2002).

Reduced Federal Responsibility for Social Welfare

The third major goal of welfare reform was to reduce federal responsibility for the programme—or in the words of Bill Clinton, "to end welfare as we know it." President Clinton, a Democrat seeking to pull his party to the centre of the American political spectrum, was a major architect of welfare reform (Klinker, 1999). While his initial welfare proposal was less harsh than the version eventually passed by the Republican-controlled Congress, it is widely believed that Clinton supported welfare reform to burnish his own conservative credentials while campaigning against the first President Bush (Deacon, 2003).

Clinton's support for welfare reform played to the well-known racial tensions that U.S. politicians often evoke to win elections (Reed, 1999). The politicians are typically aided and abetted by a media that has forged an invidious link between race, welfare, and poverty, often putting a "black face" on poverty (Gilens, 1999). When the media paints poverty as black and does not discuss the related issues of racial discrimination or structural racism, it tends to confirm false racial stereotypes and inevitably blames the victim (Neubeck and Casenave, 2001; Gilens, 1999).

This was most recently evident in the media coverage of Hurricane Katrina in the United States. The television pictures of crowded shelters and the high concentration of African Americans left behind were frequently overshadowed by the ongoing, and racially coded, news reports of looting and shooting, reports which have since been proven to be highly inflated. Only this time around the hurricane's uneven racial impact stripped away the veil that typically covers both racial and class divides in the United States. Many Americans were forced to ask why the federal government took so long to respond, why so many more black and Latino than white people lived in neighbourhoods that were below sea level, and why so many did not have the means to evacuate.

The inept federal response to Hurricane Katrina further highlights what happens when the government sheds its responsibility for general welfare. Welfare reform weakened federal responsibility for public assistance by stripping the welfare programme of its entitlement status and converting it into a state-administered block grant. This change ended the guaranteed federal funding for welfare, placed a cap on total spending for the programme, and subjected it to the political risks of annual Congressional budget review. Funding for TANF expired in September 2002. Since then Congress has passed ten short-term extensions with no change in the law. Fearing a more punitive outcome from an administration that does not believe in an active state, most advocates now favour a "clean extension," that is, no change in the programme that they initially opposed and continue to see as seriously flawed (Swan, 2004; Mink, 2004).

As with the low-lying flooded neighbourhoods in New Orleans, the poor, women, and persons-of-colour are disproportionately represented among the victims of governmental aloofness about poverty. In welfare reform, like so many U.S. public policies, class, race and gender clearly matter!

Why Welfare Reform? Welfare Reform and Neo-Liberalism

In the final analysis, the drive to reform welfare was neither accidental nor simply mean-spirited. Rather it is best understood as part of the economic recovery strategy launched by President Reagan in the 1980s, and continued by every U.S. President since then, to stimulate economic growth by redistributing income upwards and downsizing the state.

From 1935 to 1975 the role of the U.S. government expanded steadily. The expansion began in the early

1930s following the first major economic crisis of 20th century America, the collapse of the economy. At this time, however reluctantly, the nation's leaders blamed the crisis on the failure of the market and saw massive federal spending as the solution. The resulting New Deal programmes included the foundation of the U.S. welfare state.

From the New Deal to the Great Society (1970s) the post-war welfare state expanded in response to prosperity, population growth, the emergence of new needs, and the demands made by the increasingly militant trade union, civil rights, women's liberation and other popular movements (Abramovitz, 1992). The programmes lifted people out of poverty, trained youth for new jobs, increased access to health, mental health and social services as well as childcare, food and housing, and corrected long-standing laws that had tolerated discrimination. The government also collected the taxes needed to pay for these programmes, allowed a mild deficit to stimulate economic growth, and slowly, if only minimally, reduced the large gap between the rich and the poor.

By the mid 1970s, de-industrialization, globalization, and other changes in the domestic and global economy had seriously slowed both capital formation and economic growth. Faced with the second major economic crisis of the 20th century, this time business and government concluded that "big government," and especially the welfare state, was part of the problem rather than part of the solution. The resulting economic recovery plan variously known as Reaganomics, trickle down economics, supply side economics, or neo-liberalism sought to undo the New Deal. To this end it called for: limiting the (domestic) role of the federal government; shrinking the welfare state; and lowering the cost of labour and weakening the political influence of social movements best positioned to fight back. At the same time the Right gained a firm grip on U.S. public policy and called for the restoration of patriarchal "family values" and for race neutral social policy. Welfare reform helped to advance each of these goals.

LIMITING THE ROLE OF THE FEDERAL GOVERNMENT

The first neo-liberal goal is to limit the role of the federal government—or to paraphrase Bill Clinton, "the era of big government is over." The means to these ends include now familiar tactics, nearly all of which applied to welfare reform. 1) *Tax cuts* for the rich which have contributed to a massive federal budget deficit, a mounting national debt, and deep cuts in most social programmes except for homeland security and military programmes. 2) *Devolution* or the shift of social welfare responsibility from the federal government to the states—the centre-piece of welfare reform—relies on increased use of block grants which channel limited federal dollars to the states to run programmes while adding to the state's responsibilities. 3) *Privatization*—another feature of welfare reform—shrinks the welfare state by transferring public responsibility for social welfare from the public to the private sector. 4) Finally, *deregulation* weakens federal oversight and/or eliminates regulations that protect the rights of workers, consumers, and the health of the environment.

Government data on federal tax and spending trends document how neo-liberalism downsized the state. It shows that the post-war expansion of federal revenues and spending slowed down in the late 1960s, 1970s or early 1980s (varies by programme), declined thereafter, and reached new lows in the early 2000s.

The overall *federal revenues* rose from 17.5 per cent of the gross domestic product (GDP) in 1962, to a high of 19.7 per cent in 1969 and then fell to a low of 16.3 per cent in 2004 (Table 21.3). The new low reflected the declining progressivity of the U.S. tax code and the deep tax cuts in 2001 and 2003 which favoured the wealthy over the middle class and the poor.

Lower revenues meant less *total federal spending* which grew from 17.2 per cent of the GDP in 1965 to a high of 23.5 per cent in 1982, only to fall to 18.4 per cent in 2000, below that of 1950, indeed before the U.S. had Medicare, Medicaid, and the interstate highway. The percentage climbed to 19.8 per cent in 2004 due to the war in

Table 21.3 Federal Income Tax Revenues (% Of GDP)

Year	ALL federal taxes	Year	Individual and corporate taxes
1962	17.5%	1950	9.6%
1969	19.7% (peak)	1970	13.2% (peak)
1996	18.9%	1990	9.5%
2004	16.3%	2004	9.2%

Source: Office of the President of the United States (2006).

Iraq, the rising costs of homeland security, and the costs of reconstruction in Afghanistan and Iraq (Table 21.4).

SHRINKING THE WELFARE STATE

The second neo-liberal strategy calls for shrinking the welfare state.

Total domestic discretionary spending (non-military, non-international) rose from 2.5 per cent of the GDP (1962) to a high of 4.8 per cent (1978) and then declined to a low of 3.0 in 1999 (Table 21.5). Despite increasing to 3.5 per cent of the GDP in 2004, the growth rate had slowed significantly, dropping from 12.3 per cent a year in 2002 to 4.9 per cent in 2004 (U.S. Congress, 2005).

Even outlays for the popular, non-means-tested programmes serving the middle class as well as the poor have fallen. This includes both Social Security (U.S. House of Representatives, 2004b) and Unemployment Insurance (U.S. House of Representatives, 2004a; Um'rani and Lovell, 1999). Both programmes help women—who represent 60 per cent of all Social Security recipients and 40 per cent of Unemployment Insurance claimants—to sustain their families and themselves. Social Security spending rose from 2.5 per cent of the GDP in 1962, to a

high of 4.9 per cent in 1983, but sagged to 4.3 per cent in 2004 (Table 21.6). Only spending for Medicare (for the elderly) and Medicaid (for the poor)—two other entitlement programmes—grew, reflecting the high cost of health care, especially the high cost of prescription drugs (U.S. Congress, 2005). The Bush administration seeks to retrench these health care programmes by privatizing or otherwise shifting the cost from the government to seniors and to the poor—that is to the consumers of health care services (Ku, 2005; Park et al., 2003).

The programmes for the poor, especially income security programmes, were particularly hard hit. TANF, the programme for single mothers, became a convenient target for neo-liberalism because it serves a vulnerable and unpopular group, not known for high voter turnout. Spending for *means-tested income security programmes* for the poor (including AFDC/TANF) rose from 1.1 per cent of the GDP in 1962 to a high of 2.2 per cent in 1976 but then fell to 1.4 per cent in 2001 (Table 21.7). With higher poverty rates the caseload grew larger, leading costs to climb back to 1.7 per cent in 2004 (U.S. Congress, 2005).

The welfare reformers built support for the programme by highlighting the growth of the total AFDC/TANF caseload until the mid 1990s. But, they neglected to add that despite higher absolute numbers, with the exception of 1993, the number of recipients had been falling since the mid 1970s as a percentage of the *total* U.S. population and as a percentage of the *poverty*

Table 21.4 Total Federal Spending

Year	Amount (in billions)	% of GDP
1962	$106.8	18.8
1965	$118.2	17.2
1968	$178.1	20.5
1982	$745.7	23.5
1996	$1560.5	20.4
2000	$1788.8	18.4
2004	$2292.2	19.8

Source: U.S. Congress (2005: 138–9).

Table 21.5 Total Domestic Discretionary (Non-Defence, Non-International) Spending

Year	Amount (in billions)	% of GDP
1962	$14.0	2.5
1965	$22.2	3.0
1968	$31.0	3.6
1978	$105.5	4.8 (peak)
1996	$248.4	3.2
1999	$277.0	3.0
2004	$407.1	3.5

Source: U.S. Congress (2005: 140–1).

Table 21.6 Federal Spending on the Social Security Program

Year	Amount (in billions)	% of GDP
1962	$14.0	2.5
1965	$17.1	2.5
1983	$168.5	4.9 (peak)
1996	$347.1	4.5
2004	$491.5	4.3

Source: U.S. Congress (2005: 142–3).

Table 21.7 Federal Spending on Income Security Program (Means-Tested)

Year	Amount (in billions)	% of GDP
1962	$6.1	1.1
1976	$37.6	2.2 (peak)
1996	$121.0	1.6
2001	$142.7	1.4
2004	$190.7	1.7

Source: U.S. Congress (2005: 142–3).

Table 21.8   AFDC/TANF Caseload

Absolute numbers		% of total population		% of poverty population	
Year	In millions	Year	Per cent	Year	Per cent
1970	8.3	1970	4.1	1970	32.7
1973	10.7	1973	5.1	1973	46.7 (peak)
1975	11.1	1975	5.2 (peak)	1975	43.0
1985	10.8	1985	4.5	1985	32.3
1993	14.0 (peak)	1993	5.4	1993	35.7
1996	12.1	1996	4.5	1996	33.3
2002	5.5	2002	1.9	2002	16.0

Source: U.S. Department of Health and Human Services (2004b).

population. The caseload dropped from a high of 5.2 per cent (1975) of the *total* U.S. population to 4.5 per cent (1996), the year Congress enacted welfare reform (Table 21.8). During the same period, the caseload dropped from a high of 46.7 per cent (1973) of the *poverty* population to 33.3 per cent (1996) (U.S. Department of Health and Human Services, 2004b). In 2002, six years after the enactment of welfare reform, welfare recipients, most of whom are women and children, represented only 1.9 per cent of the total population and 16 per cent of those living in poverty. However, in 2002 although the poverty rate inched up, only 48 per cent of the families who were eligible for welfare benefits received help, down from 80.2 per cent in the 1980s (U.S. Department of Health and Human Services, 2004a). The use of other neo-liberal tactics, such as the devolution of welfare responsibility to the states via block grants and the privatization of many welfare-to-work pro- grammes, has also helped to shrink the federal role in social welfare provision. The retrenchment of the wel- fare state has also cost many women (and men) the public sector jobs that had once lifted them into the middle class.

Lower Labour Costs

The third neo-liberal goal seeks to reduce the cost of labour to business and industry. Along with de- industrialization, globalization, and the well-documented attack on organized labour, welfare reform has helped to press wages down for both poor and working class women (and men). Caseload reductions and welfare's tough work rules have flooded the labour market with thousands of new and increasingly desperate workers in search of employment. The increased competition for jobs has made

it easier for employers to keep wages low and harder for unions to negotiate good contracts (Table 21.9).

The New York Times recently reported that the large influx of women into low wage jobs owing to the welfare overhaul had depressed the median wage of women as a whole, not just welfare recipients (Utichelle, 2004). Alan Greenspan, chair of the U.S. Federal Reserve Board, clarified the link between welfare and low wages when he explained that the economy's "extraordinary" and "exceptional" performance during the late 1990s was, in part, due to "a heightened sense of job insecu- rity" which helps to subdue wage gains (Piven, 1999). Taking women off welfare contributed to this goal. Like a strike fund, welfare (but also Unemployment Insurance and Social Security) acts as an alternative source of income. By reducing fears of unemployment, access to this increases women's leverage on the job.

It also makes it easier for unions to negotiate good contracts and harder for employers to increase profits by pressing wages down.

Table 21.9   Wage Rates

Year	Falling wages
1979–99	9.3% drop in wages for the bottom 10 per cent of the workforce
2002	About 40% of low wage workers lived in families with incomes below 200 per cent of the poverty line (less than $29,000 for a family of three)
2005	Due in part to welfare overhaul, large influx of women into low wage jobs depressed median wage of women as a whole

FAMILY VALUES

A fourth item on the neo-liberal agenda is the Right's call for family values and race neutral social policy. The Right argues that the welfare state has created a crisis in the family by undermining "personal responsibility," usurping parental authority, and generally weakening so-called "family values." The family values component of welfare reform, described earlier, exploits poor women's dire financial situation, forcing them to trade their marital, child bearing, and parenting independence for a welfare cheque. It also continues the deep distrust of parenting by single mothers, especially women of colour, found in most U.S. social welfare policies. These policies blame single mothers for their children's behaviour while, as noted earlier, blatantly ignoring the social and economic conditions that undermine effective parenting. Few supporters of welfare reform knew, or even asked, how women forced to leave welfare coped with sickness, unpaid bills, kids wanting brand name sneakers, men who do not pay child support, or the shame of having to repeatedly ask friends and relatives for time and money.

Critics of welfare on the Right also say that access to government aid induces "*dependency.*" But their real concern may be that access to income outside of marriage, through employment or government aid, actually has the potential to increase women's economic *independence.*

This, in turn, can strengthen women's bargaining power with male partners as well as with employers, enable women to raise children on their own, and otherwise challenge patriarchal structures.

RACE NEUTRAL SOCIAL POLICY

Neo-liberalism also calls for a race neutral social policy and a colour-blind society. But even before this period the U.S. welfare state contained what some call "welfare racism" (Neubeck and Casenave, 2001). From the start the welfare state favoured assisting white households, especially married couples. Its early programmes excluded African American and Latino families and, over the years, provided them with lower benefits, reinforced discriminatory labour market policies, and otherwise deprived families of colour of the resources needed to adequately care for themselves (Neubeck and Casenave, 2001; Brown, 1999). Pressed by the civil rights movement, some welfare state programmes began to protect persons-of-colour and compensate them for the harsh impact of racial discrimination. These changes helped to mediate the contradiction between ongoing racial inequality and the "democratic promise" of equal opportunity for all. Although the changes did not eliminate institutionalized racism or even racial discrimination in the United States, the threats they posed to white privilege and white domination launched a racially coded backlash against welfare for the poor.

That advocates of welfare reform capitalized on racialized fears among white voters to build support for the programme is evident in the racialized rhetoric that tainted the entire reform process from the initial debate over the proposed programme, to its implementation, and its outcomes. As noted earlier, the welfare reform debate evoked invidious racial as well as gender stereotypes even though the majority of clients at the time were white. The discourse was fuelled by a media that regularly linked poverty and welfare to race (Gilens, 1999). Many white people turned against welfare thinking (wrongly) that they had nothing to lose.

The implementation of welfare reform also reflected racism. During the 1980s the federal government waived federal rules and allowed the states to experiment with many of the highly restrictive welfare measures that were later incorporated in the 1996 law. The most consistent predictor of which states applied for these waivers was the racial composition of its welfare programme (Fording, 2003).

Similarly, the states with larger black populations and larger welfare caseloads were more likely to provide lower benefits, to cut welfare programmes (Johnson, 2003), and to adopt the strictest reforms (Soss et al., 2003).

Discrimination appears in the front office as well. Gooden (1998, 1999) reports that both welfare department case managers and local employers treated recipients differently by race. Despite similar personal backgrounds, work experience, and welfare histories, case managers were more likely to offer white than black clients educational opportunities and work-related supports (i.e. childcare and transportation expenses), while employers were more likely to hire white over black applicants despite similar profiles. As a result, since welfare reform, more white than black women have exited welfare. Between 1996 and 2001, the number of white families fell from 35.5 per cent of the welfare caseload to 30.1 per cent, while the number of black families rose from 36.9 to 39.0 per cent and Hispanics from 20.8 to 26.0 per cent (U.S. Department of Health and Human Services, 2001).

SOCIAL MOVEMENTS

The fifth neo-liberal strategy is to reduce the power of social movements that are best positioned to resist the attack on the welfare state. It is no secret that U.S. social movements contributed to the strength of the welfare state during the post-war period (Abramovitz, 1992; Piven and Cloward, 1977; Sitkoff, 1981) and that since 1980 they have been on the defensive. One administration after another has taken back some of the hard-won gains made by the trade union, civil rights, gay rights, welfare rights and women's movements as well as weakened workplace, consumer, and environmental protections.

However, the targets of the neo-liberal assaults have resisted. Not always visible on the national front and not always victorious, poor women and their allies have frequently disrupted the status quo, in the voting booth, in legislative halls, and in the streets (Abramovitz, 2000: ch. 4). Hundreds of local community organizations have joined forces around a wide range of issues to defend their gains and advance new ones. Following in the footsteps of Johnnie Tillmon, the welfare rights leader quoted at the beginning of this paper, they are part of a long 20th-century tradition of activism among poor and working class women. The women's demands prefigured what the welfare state would have to provide (1900–35), contributed to its expansion after the Second World War (1945–75), and since the mid 1970s have defended the safety net against the repeated assaults (1975–present) (Abramovitz, 2000: ch. 4). The activists have given voice to the needs of all women for jobs and a living wage, to the rights of motherhood and womanhood, and government support for care work. Their activism shows still another way in which race, class, and gender matter in welfare reform.

References

Abramovitz, M. (1992). "The Reagan Legacy: Undoing the Class, Race and Gender Accords," *Journal of Sociology and Social Welfare* 19(1): 91–110.

Abramovitz, M. (1996). *Regulating the Lives of Women: Social Welfare Policy from Colonial Times to the Present*. Boston: South End Press.

Abramovitz, M. (1997). "Temporary Aid To Needy Families," pp. 311–30 in *19th Encyclopedia of Social Work, 1997 Supplement*. Washington, DC: National Association of Social Workers.

Abramovitz, M. (2000). *Under Attack, Fighting Back: Women and Welfare in the United States*. New York: Monthly Review Press.

Abramovitz, M. (2002). "In Jeopardy: The Impact of Welfare Reform on Non-Profit Human Service Agencies in New York City," United Way of New York City [http://www.uwnyc.org].

Abt Associates (2000). "Abt Associates Finds Welfare Children Missing More School," Press release, 1 March [http://www.abtassociates.com/Page.cfm?PageID = 16132].

American Civil Liberties Union (2005). "ACLU Letter to Senate Opposing Abstinence-Only Until Marriage Programs" [http://www.aclu.org/ReproductiveRights/ReproductiveRights.cfm?ID = 18853&c = 147].

Boushey, H. (2001). "Last Hired, First Fired, Job Losses Plague Former TANF Recipients," Issue Brief £171, 12 December. Washington, DC: Economic Policy Institute.

Boushey, H., Gunderson, G., Brocht, C. and Bernstein, J. (2001) *Hardships in America: The Real Story of Working Families*. Washington, DC: Economic Policy Institute.

Brown, M. (1999). *Race, Money and the Welfare State*. Ithaca: Cornell University Press.

Cancian, M., Haveman, R., Meyer, D. R. and Wolfe, B. (1999) *Before and After TANF: The Economic Well-Being of Women Leaving Welfare*. Madison, WI: Institute for Research on Poverty, University of Wisconsin, Madison.

Center on Budget and Policy Priorities (2005) "TANF Reauthorization in 2005: A Brief Guide to the Issues," September [http://www.cbpp.org/4-21-05tanf.pdf].

Chapman, J. and Bernstein, J. (2003) "Falling Through the Safety Net: Low Income Single Mothers in the Jobless Recovery," Issue Brief £191, 11 April. Washington, DC: Economic Policy Institute [http:// www.epi.org].

Child Welfare League of America (n.d.) "Summary of the Adoption and Safe Families Act of 1997 (PL: 105–89)" [http://www.cwla.org/advocacy/asfap1105–89summary.htm].

Collins, A., Layzer, J., Kreader, J. L., Werner, A. and Glantz, F. (2000) *National Study of Child Care for Low-Income Families State and Community Substudy*, Interim Report, 2 November, p. 36 [http://www.abtassoc.com/reports/NSCCLIF.pdf].

Cook, J. T., Frank, D. A., Berkowitz, C., Black, M. M., Casey, P. H., Cutts, D. B., Meyers, A. F., Zadivar, F., Skalicky, A., Levenson, S. and Hereen, T. (2002) "Welfare Reform and the Health of Young Children: A Sentinel Survey in Six United States Cities," *Archives of Pediatric and Adolescent Medicine* 156(7): 678–84.

Dailard, C. (2005). "Reproductive Health Advocates and Marriage Promotion: Asserting a Stake in the Debate," *The Guttmacher Report on Public Policy* [http://www.guttmacher.org/pubs/ tgr/08/1/gr080101.pdf].

Deacon, A. (2003). "Ending Consensus as We Began to Know It: Welfare Reform and the Republicans After 2002," *Social Policy and Society* 2(2): 171–5.

Delgado, G. and Gordon, R. (2002). "From Social Contract to Social Control: Welfare Policy and Race," pp. 25–52 in G. Delgado (ed.) *From Poverty to Punishment: How Welfare Reform Punishes the Poor*. Oakland, CA: Applied Research Center.

Dion, R. M. and Pavetti, L. (2000). *Access to and Participation in Medicaid and the Food Stamp Program: A Review of the Literature*, Final Report to the U.S. Department of Health and Human Services, Administration for Children and Families, Washington, DC, 7 March.

Fineman, M. (1995). *The Neutered Mother, the Sexual Family and Other Twentieth Century Tragedies*. New York: Routledge.

Firestein, R. (2000). "Working Without a Net: Children, Welfare Reform and the Child Welfare System," *Children's Rights* January [http://www.childrensrights.org/PDF/01-25-00.pdf].

Fording, R. C. (2003). "Laboratories of Democracy or Symbolic Politics," pp. 72–100 in S. F. Schram, J. Soss and R. C. Fording (eds) *Race and the Politics of Welfare Reform*. Ann Arbor, MI: University of Michigan Press.

Fox, C. (2000). *Hunger Is No Accident: New York and Federal Welfare Rules Violate the Human Right to Food*. New York: New York City

Welfare Reform and Human Rights Documentation Project, Urban Justice Center.

Gilens, M. (1999). *Why Americans Hate Welfare: Race, Media, and the Politics of Anti-Poverty Policy.* Chicago: University of Chicago Press.

Gooden, S. (1998). "All Things Not Being Equal: Difference in Caseworker Support Toward Black and White Welfare Clients," *Harvard Journal of African American Public Policy* 4: 23–33.

Gooden, S. (1999). "The Hidden Third Party: Welfare Recipients' Experiences with Employers," *Journal of Public Management and Social Policy* 5(1): 69–83.

Gordon, L. (1994). *Pitied But Not Entitled: Single Mothers and the History of Welfare 1890–1935.* New York: The Free Press.

Grossman, J. (1999) "The New Math," *City Limits.org* December [http://www.citylimits.org/content/articles/articleView.cfm?articlenumber = 468].

Hansen, D. D. (1999). "The American Invention of Child Support: Dependency and Punishment in Early American Child Support Law," *Yale Law Journal* 108(5): 1123–53 [http://www.ancpr.org/american_invention_of_child_supp.htm].

Hartmann, H. and Talley, M. K. (2002) "Welfare, Poverty and Marriage: What Does the Research Say?," *Quarterly Newsletter* Winter/Spring: 1, 4–5. Washington, DC: Institute for Women's Policy Research.

Hays, S. (2003). *Promoting Family Values.* New York: Oxford University Press.

Jennings, J. (2003). *Welfare Reform and the Revitalization of Inner City Neighborhoods.* East Lansing, MI: Michigan State University Press.

Johnson, M. (2003). "Racial Context, Public Attitudes, and Welfare Effort," pp. 151–70 in S. F. Schram, J. Soss and R. C. Fording (eds) *Race and the Politics of Welfare Reform.* Ann Arbor, MI: University of Michigan Press.

Jones-DeWeever, A. (2002). *Marriage Promotion and Low Income Communities: An Examination of Real Needs and Real Solutions,* Briefing Paper, June. Washington, DC: Institute for Women's Policy Research.

Klinkner, P. A. (1999). "Bill Clinton and the Politics of the New Liberalism," pp. 11–28 in A. Reed, Jr. (ed.) *Without Justice for All: The New Liberalism and Our Retreat from Racial Equality.* Boulder, CO: Westview Press.

Ku, L. (2005). "New Research Sheds Light on Risks from Increasing Medicaid Cost-Sharing and Reducing Medicaid Benefits," Center on Budget and Policy Priorities, 18 July [http://www.cbpp.org/7–18–05health.htm].

Landry, D. J., Kaeser, L. and Richards, C. L. (1999). "Abstinence Promotion and the Provision of Information About Contraception in Public School District Sexuality Education Policies," *Family Planning Perspectives* 31(6) [http://www.guttmacher.org/archive/searchPSRH.jsp].

Leger, P. (2003). "Low Income Fathers and Child Support: Starting Off on the Right Foot," Annie E. Casey Foundation, 30 January [http://www.aecf.org/publications/data/right_track.pdf].

Loprest, P. (2002). "Who Returns to Welfare," Urban Institute, 1 September [http://www.urban.org/url.cfm?ID = 310548].

Loprest, P. (2003a). "Disconnected Welfare Families Face Serious Risks," *Snapshots of America's Families* 3(7). Urban Institute [http://www.urban.org/url.cfm?ID = 310839].

Loprest, P. (2003b). "Fewer Welfare Leavers Employed in Weak Economy," *Snapshots of America's Families* 3(7). Urban Institute, 31 August [http://www.urban.org/url.cfm?ID = 310837].

MacDonald, H. (1997). "Welfare Reform Discoveries," *The City Journal* Winter [http://www.city-journal.org/html/7_1_welfare.html\].

MacDonald, H. (1998). "The Real Welfare Problem is Illegitimacy," *The City Journal* Winter [http://www.city-journal.org/html/8_1_a1.html].

Mead, L. (1992). *The New Politics of Poverty.* New York: Basic Books.

Mink, G. (1998). *Welfare's End.* New York: Cornell University Press.

Mink, G. (2004). "Proceedings, TANF Briefing," National Council of Women's Organizations, Washington, 24 June [http://www.womensorganizations.org/pages.cfm?ID = 39].

Murray, C. (1984). *Losing Ground: American Social Policy 1950–1984.* New York: Basic Books.

National Governors' Association Center for Best Practices (1999). "Round Two: Summary of Selected Elements of State Programs for Temporary Assistance for Needy Families," 14 March [http://www.nga.org/CBP/Activities/WelfareReform.asp].

National Women's Law Center (2004). "Child Care Assistance Policies 2001–2004: Families Struggling to Move Forward, States Going Backward," Issue Brief, September [http://www.nwlc.org/pdf/childcaresubsidyfinalreport.pdf].

Neubeck, K. and Casenave, N. (2001). *Welfare Racism: Play the Race Card Against America's Poor.* New York: Routledge.

NOW Legal Defense and Education Fund (1999) "What the States Didn't Tell You: A State by State Guide to the Welfare Law's Reproductive Rights Agenda," p. 1. NOW Legal Defense and Education Fund.

Office of the President of the United States (2006). *Budget of the United States Government, Fiscal Year 2006,* Historical tables, T. 3–1: 45–52 [http://www.whitehouse.gov/omb/budget/fy2006/pdf/hist.pdf].

Park, E., Friedman, J. and Lee, A. (2003). "Health Savings Security Accounts: A Costly Tax Cut that Could Weaken Employer-based Health Insurance," Center on Budget and Policy Priorities, 8 July [http://www.cbpp.org/6–25–03tax.htm].

Piven, F. Fox (1999). "The Welfare State as Work Enforcer," *Dollars and Sense* September/October: 34.

Piven, F. Fox and Cloward, R. (1977). *Poor People's Movements.* New York: Vintage.

Rector, R. and Pardue, M. G. (2004). "Understanding the President's Healthy Marriage Initiative," Backgrounders, The Heritage Foundation, 24 March [http://www.heritage.org/Research/Family/bg1741.cfm].

Reed, A. A. Jr. (1999). "Introduction: The New Liberal Orthodoxy on Race and Inequality," pp. 1–8 in A. Reed, Jr. (ed.) *Without Justice for All: The New Liberalism and Our Retreat from Racial Equality.* Boulder CO: Westview Press.

Roberts, D. (1993). "Racism and Patriarchy in the Meaning of Motherhood," *The American University Journal of Gender and the Law* 1(1): 1–38.

Roberts, D. (1999). "Is there Justice in Children's Rights? A Critique of Federal Family Preservation Policy," *University of Pennsylvania Journal of Constitutional Law* December: 1–17.

Sawhill, I. (2000). "Welfare Reform and Reducing Teen Pregnancy," *The Public Interest* Winter [http://www.brookings.edu/views/articles/Sawhill/Winter 2000.htm].

Scott, E. K., Edin, K., London, A. S. and Mazellis, J. M. (2001). "My Children Come First: Welfare-Reliant Women's Post TANF View of Work-Family Trade-Offs and Marriage," pp. 132–53 in

G. Duncan and P. L. Chase-Lansdale (eds) *For Better and For Worse: Welfare Reform and the Well-Being of Children and Families.* New York: Russell Sage Foundation.

Seltzer, J. (1991). "Relationships Between Fathers and Children Who Live Apart: The Father's Role After Separation," *Journal of Marriage and the Family* 52(1): 79–101.

Sitkoff, H. (1981). *The Struggle for Black Equality 1954–1980.* New York: Hill & Wang.

Sorensen, E. (1995). "Noncustodial Fathers: Can They Afford to Pay More Child Support?," Urban Institute, February [http://www.aspe.os.dhhs.gov/hsp/isp/13xsum.htm].

Sorensen, E. and Zibman, C. (2000). "A Look at Poor Dads Who Don't Pay Child Support," Urban Institute Discussion Paper 00–07, September.

Soss, J., Schram, S. F., Vartanian, T. P. and O'Brien, E. (2003). "The Hard Line and the Color Line," pp. 225–53 in S. F. Schram, J. Soss and R. C. Fording (eds) *Race and the Politics of Welfare Reform.* Ann Arbor, MI: University of Michigan Press.

Spalter-Roth, R., Hartmann, H. and Andrews, L. (1992). *Combining Work and Welfare: An Alternative Anti-Poverty Strategy.* Washington, DC: Institute for Women's Policy Research.

Swan, C. D. (2004). "Mayors Call for 'Clean' Extension of Welfare Program," United States Conference of Mayors, 15 March [http://www.usmayors.org/uscm/us_mayor_newspaper/documents/03_15_04/clean_welfare.asp].

Tillmon, J. (1972). "Welfare is a Women's Issue," *Liberation News Service* No. 415 (26 February), reprinted in R. Baxandall and L. Gordon, eds (1976) *American Working Women: A Documentary History 1600 to the Present*, pp. 354–8. New York: Vintage Books.

Um'rani, A. and Lovell, V. (1999). "Women and Unemployment Insurance," *Research In Brief*, £A122, November. Washington, DC: Institute for Women's Policy Research.

University of Michigan. (1994). "Researchers Dispute Contention that Welfare is Major Cause of Out-of-Wedlock Births," Press release, School of Social Work, 23 June.

U.S. Congress. (1996). "Personal Responsibility and Work Opportunity Reconciliation Act of 1996," 104th Cong. 2nd Sess, reprinted in G. Mink and R. Solinger, eds (2003). *Welfare: A Documentary History of U.S. Policy and Politics*, pp. 647–54. New York: New York University Press. [http://www.thomas.loc.gov]

U.S. Congress. (2005). *The Budget and Economic Outlook: Fiscal Years 2006 to 2016,* January, p. 139. Washington, DC: Congressional Budget Office. [http://www.cbo.gov/ftpdocs/60xx/doc6060/01-25-BudgetOutlook.pdf]

U.S. Department of Health and Human Services. (1995). *Report to Congress on Out-of-Wedlock Childbearing, Executive Summary,* September, pp. 2–4. Washington, DC.

U.S. Department of Health and Human Services. (2001). "Characteristics and Financial Circumstances of TANF Recipients" [http://www.acf.dhhs.gov/programs/ofa/character/FY2001/characteristics.htm£_Toc25546989].

U.S. Department of Health and Human Services. (2003a). *Child Care Development Fund Report to Congress,* January, Administration for Children, Child Care Bureau [http://www.acf.hhs.gov/programs/ccb/policy1/congressreport/CCDFreport.pdf].

U.S. Department of Health and Human Services. (2003b). *Women's Health USA 2003, Health Services Utilization, Title V: Abstinence Education,* Health Resources and Services Administration, Maternal and Child Health Bureau [http://mchb.hrsa.gov/pages/page_68.htm].

U.S. Department of Health and Human Services. (2004a). Administration for Children and Families, Office of Family Assistance, Monthly Caseload Data, 1996, 2004 [http://www.acf.hhs.gov/programs/ofa/caseload/2004/1204tanf.htm].

U.S. Department of Health and Human Services. (2004b). *Indicators of Welfare Dependence,* Annual Report to Congress 2004, Appendix A, Table IND 4 [http://www.aspe.hhs.gov/hsp/indicators04/ ch2.htm£IND4].

U.S. Department of Health and Human Services. (2004c). Administration for Children and Families, Office of Family Assistance, Monthly Caseload Data, 1996, 2000, 2004 [http://www.acf.hhs.gov/programs/ofa/caseload/2004/1204tanf.htm].

U.S. Department of Health and Human Services. (n.d.) "Healthy Marriage Initiative" [http://www.acf.hhs.gov/healthymarriage/index.html].

U.S. Government Accounting Office. (2000). "Welfare Reform: State Sanctions Policies and the Number of Families Affected," March [http://www.gao.gov/new.items/he00044.pdf].

U.S. Government Accounting Office. (2003). "Child Care: Recent State Policy Changes Affecting the Availability of Assistance to Low Income Families," May [http://www.gao.gov/new.items/d03588.pdf].

U.S. House of Representatives. (2004a). *Committee on Ways and Means, Overview of Entitlement Programs, 2004 Green Book,* Unemployment Insurance Table 4-A. Washington, DC: Government Printing Office. [http://waysandmeans.house.gov/ media/pdf/greenbook2003/Section4.pdf]

U.S. House of Representatives. (2004b). *Committee on Ways and Means, Overview of Entitlement Programs, 2004 Green Book,* Social Security, Legislative History, pp. 35, 1–39 and Tables 1–17, 1–18. Washington, DC: Government Printing Office. [http://waysandmeans.house.gov/media/pdf/greenbook2003/section1.pdf]

Utichelle, L. (2004). "Gaining Ground on the Wage Front," *The New York Times* 31 December: 1.

Ventura, S., Abma, J. C. and Mosher, W. D. (2003). "Revised Pregnancy Rates 1990–1997, and New Rates for 1998–1999, United States," *National Vital Statistics Reports* 52(7) [http://www.cdc.gov/nchs/data/nvsr/nvsr52/nvsr52_07.pdf].

White House. (2002). "Working Toward Independence. Policy in Focus: Welfare Reform," February [http://www.whitehouse.gov/news/releases/2002/02/welfare-reform-announcement-book.html].

Zaslow M. J., Moore, K. A., Brooks, J. L., Morris, P. A., Tout, K., Redd, Z. A. and Emig, C. A. (2003). "Experimental Studies of Welfare Reform and Children," *Future of Children* 12(1): 80–95 [www.futureofchildren.org].

Discussion Questions

1. How did the first U.S. social welfare policies treat single mothers?

    From 1908 to 1935 many states provided a cash grant to single mothers. The program was called Widow's Pension, which implied that all recipients had been married. In fact, the progressive era reformers were concerned that to acknowledge other types of single motherhood would cause the loss of public support for the program and chose to focus on women whom they thought the public would consider more deserving. In 1935, the social welfare system was changed to Aid to Dependent Children (eventually to Aid to Families with Dependent Children in 1962), maintaining that the image of single mothers as still less deserving of aid than married women.

2. What are the key provisions of the 1996 welfare reform law?

    Students should review the three provisions: work enforcement, marriage promotion, and a smaller welfare state.

3. What is the relationship between a neoliberal ideology and U.S. welfare reform?

    Abramovitz explains that welfare reform has helped to advance neoliberal goals: limiting the role of the federal government, lowering the cost of labor, and weakening the political influence of social movements. Conservative politicians and groups encourage the restoration of family values and race-neutral social policy.

Source: From Abramovitz, M. (2006). Welfare reform in the United States: Gender, race and class matter. *Critical Social Policy*, *26*, 336–364. Reprinted by permission of Sage Publications and the author.

CHAPTER 22

An Understanding of Poverty From Those Who Are Poor

Stephanie Baker Collins (2003)

Featured in this article by Stephanie Baker Collins are women who tell their own stories about living in poverty. Based on data collected from a group of Canadian women, Baker Collins identifies four themes that characterize their experiences of poverty: an emphasis on social relationships, the impact of pervasive scrutiny of the social assistance bureaucracy, the importance of community goodwill, and the possibilities for community action.

Introduction

The participatory research project described in this article began with a commitment to include the experiences of persons who are poor in an analysis of poverty. Listening to the voices of households who are poor can provide a deeper understanding of the multiple dimensions of poverty as well as the activities people undertake to make a living and the choices they make when assets are inadequate. Participants in poverty assessments teach others about their daily lives. In order to honour the knowledge and wisdom of those living in difficult circumstances, a participatory poverty assessment was facilitated among a small group of women living on a social assistance income in Niagara Falls, Ontario.

The Participatory Poverty Assessment (PPA) undertaken in Niagara Falls was one component of a doctoral research project.[1] The doctoral project integrated an analysis of the structural and institutional contexts of poverty with an analysis of the everyday livelihood strategies used by households who are poor. The structural and institutional context was explored using the sustainable livelihoods framework, drawing particularly on the concepts of assets and vulnerability. Everyday livelihood strategies were explored through the Participatory

Poverty Assessment. The goal of this integrated project is to contribute to a fuller understanding of poverty than that achieved by conventional income poverty measures.

Official definitions of poverty are usually compiled by "experts" who are not themselves poor. Definitions are derived based on decisions about the best proxy (income or consumption) for material deprivation. A certain abstract statistical precision is required since the purpose of such measures is to count the number of poor persons in a particular geographic space to determine the proportion of households who are poor in that society.

Income poverty measures are useful because income data is readily available and they allow for comparisons over time and between nations. At the same time, they suffer from important weaknesses which have been well documented (Chambers, 1995; Kabeer, 1996; Rahnema, 1992). An income poverty line represents an abstraction from lived experience in which important contextual factors are not taken into account (Max-Neef, 1991). For example, the ability to translate income into well-being is shaped by gender inequalities (Kabeer, 1996). Other contextual factors which are missing include: access to local resources (Sachs, 1992); livelihood contexts (Rahnema, 1992); the role of social networks (Appadurai, 1990); and a lack of power (Room, 1995).

Participation in Poverty Assessments

The opportunity to explore these contextual factors is one of the benefits of the introduction of participatory methods to poverty research. Participation in research, whereby persons become subjects and not objects in the pursuit of knowledge, serves a number of important goals. Participation includes the voices of those who are usually excluded. Participation honours local knowledge about life circumstances and coping strategies (Chambers, 1995). Participation changes the role of the researcher from one of "expert" to listener and provides a "view from below" (Mies, 1996, p. 13). Participation can also be a catalyst to working for social justice (Carniol, 2000). And lastly, participation is itself a basic human need. The capability approach to poverty and inequality developed by Sen recognizes that in assessing human capabilities and the resources required to exercise those capabilities, choice and participation are important (Alkire, 1999).

There are also a number of caveats regarding participatory research in general and in this project specifically that should be acknowledged at the outset. Participation in development and poverty assessments has become mainstream and widespread (Botes & van Rensburg, 2000; Holland and Blackburn, 1998; Pratt, 2001; Robb, 1999), with rapid expansion of new participatory methods (participatory poverty assessments, participatory learning and action, appreciative inquiry, open space). It is possible, however, to use the tools of participation without a commitment to the principles which underlie the development of the tools (Attwood & May, 1998). As Ashley and Carney (1999) point out, participatory poverty methods may be used as a set of *tools* for research, as an *objective* (participation by poor households) or as a set of *principles*. Participation as a research tool or technique could remain exclusively within an interpretive or positivist framework, without addressing critical issues such as the structural and institutional forces and power relationships that operate in the lives of households that are poor. In that situation, participatory processes "are approached as technical, management solutions to what are basically political issues" (Guijt & Kaul Shah, 1998, p. 3).

If participation can be used in service to a variety of goals (not all of them beneficial) what did participation mean for this study? The goal in this study was for participation to be a principle of research rather than a technique, with participation tied to advocacy and action taken to improve the livelihoods of households who are poor. Ideally participatory research means participation both in

knowledge generation and knowledge utilization (Park, 1993). A partnership is formed between ordinary people and the researcher for the purpose of learning and taking collective action on a particular problem as it is defined by those who are affected. According to Park, the participants should be involved at each stage of the research: problem identification; research design and methods; dialogue; data gathering and analysis; and utilization.

Engaging in participatory research as part of a doctoral dissertation brings with it a specific limitation regarding participation at each stage of the research (Maguire, 1993). The limitation is that the initial goals and plan for the research topics have already been outlined by the researcher as part of the requirements for a dissertation. This limitation, however, did not need to remain in place for the life of the project. One of the goals of this project was to work towards group participation in setting the agenda for the Participatory Poverty Assessment.

There were also several advantages to undertaking a PPA as part of doctoral research. One significant advantage is that the project was not bound by time constraints. The researcher was able to take six months to become familiar with the organization and the members as a volunteer prior to facilitating a PPA. Another advantage is that the project was not bound by the demands of a funding body regarding expected outcomes. The PPA could unfold according to an agenda derived from discussions among the participants.

Procedures and Methodology

The methodology used in this study was adapted from Participatory Poverty Assessments, part of a family of participatory methodologies which have had a long association with international development work (Ros & Craig, 1997).[2] Participatory Poverty Assessments (PPA) use participatory tools to engage households who are poor in an assessment of their own living conditions. The methodology is deliberately non-technical and accessible. Visual methods are used such as mapping exercises, seasonality diagrams, time lines, and ranking exercises. Focus groups and semi-structured interviews are undertaken to draw out perceptions of well-being. The purpose of drawing on the expertise of households who are poor is not just to improve understanding, but to demonstrate the micro-effects of macro-policy (Booth, 1998). An additional purpose is to enable local people to analyse their own situation and develop the confidence to make decisions and take action to improve their circumstances.

A Participatory Poverty Assessment was conducted from June to December 2000 with a small group of women who are members of a food co-operative in Niagara Falls, Ontario. The food co-operative is sponsored by Project SHARE (Support, Housing, Awareness, Resources and Emergency), a multi-service centre in Niagara Falls which serves urban poor households. The Food Co-operative Program has been described as "a self help model that has been a positive solution to hunger, lack of information and self-esteem issues for those who are isolated due to lack of income" (Project SHARE, 2001, p. 6). Members of the co-op contribute a minimum of three hours a month to Project SHARE (usually in the food warehouse, helping with the semi-annual food drives or with the Christmas basket program). In return, co-op members receive a food pick-up once a month for each household. Co-op members also receive special donations that come in such as linens from local hotels or surplus clothing from tourist shops. Members attend co-op meetings which are scheduled bi-monthly and elect an executive once a year at the co-op annual meeting. The co-operative holds social events such as a barbecue in September and a Christmas party in November at which member households receive toys for their children. Fund raising events are held throughout the year to help pay for the Christmas toy baskets.

From the extensive inventory of tools available for participatory assessment (Attwood et al., 1998; Holland & Blackburn, 1998; Pretty, Guijt, Thompson & Scoones, 1995), those tools were chosen that could be adapted to an urban setting and could meet the following goals: to learn about the daily living experiences of those on low-income; to analyse the role of institutions in people's lives; to have agenda setting become a shared task; and to provide the opportunity for setting local priorities in working for change. Participatory topics were sequenced from the general to the more personal so as to begin with the least threatening topics. Topics were presented in such a way that the discussion/findings could be recorded in charts, visual maps, pictures or notes on flip charts. In this way the recording was a group effort, not the interpretation of an individual or of the researcher.

Recruiting Participants

Recruiting participants for the participatory project began with establishing a connection with co-op members through volunteering at Project SHARE and attending several monthly co-op food pick-ups. The researcher met with the executive of the co-op and the co-op support worker to receive permission to present the project to co-op members. Executive members made suggestions for the presentation itself and for meeting arrangements with those who agreed to participate. The co-op support worker offered to consider participation in the project as fulfilling the requirements for monthly co-op work hours.

The invitation to participate in the project was extended in a presentation given at a monthly meeting of the food co-op members. The researcher introduced the project by explaining that the intent of the research was to have people speak for themselves rather than someone else speaking for them. Examples were given of some of the topics that might be discussed and several questions were answered. The co-op members voted to allow the PPA to be conducted among co-op members, with the understanding that a vote to approve was not a commitment to personally participate. Although the co-op approved the project, when interested participants were asked to sign up (name and phone number) at the end of the meeting only a small number responded. The women who indicated an interest in participating became long-term participants in the project.

The Participatory Poverty Assessment was primarily conducted with the small group of women who signed up to participate. There was one additional invitation to co-op members to join the PPA two months later. The group presented the results to date of their discussion at a co-op membership meeting and invited co-op members to take part in a participatory exercise around defining a good quality of life. An invitation for additional participants was extended at this time. This invitation did not result in new participants.

The process of recruiting participants raised a number of issues about the nature of the urban community that existed in the Project SHARE food co-op. Some of these issues were identified in conversations with co-op members during volunteer shifts. Others were identified in discussions within the small group itself. The consensus was that an atmosphere of trust did not exist among the members of the co-op. For example, when the co-op members were invited to participate in the quality of life exercise at the meeting, members were described as reluctant to post any information they had written on a sticky note onto a larger broadsheet because someone might see what they had written. Their concerns about confidentiality were not primarily in relation to the researcher but in relation to each other. The severe cuts to social assistance incomes several years earlier accompanied by the introduction of fraud lines where recipients were encouraged to report on each other contributed to the atmosphere of fear and mistrust.[3]

In selecting Project SHARE as a site for this research project, one of the most important features was the presence of a food co-operative where a Participatory Poverty Assessment might be undertaken. The reluctance to participate and the mistrust among co-op members are important reminders of the dangers of an assumption of solidarity among the members of a community group or geographical location. An assumption of an idealized community can take several forms including an assumption of homogeneity (Norton, 1998) or an assumption of harmony (Guijt & Kaul Shah, 1998). Assuming homogeneity can lead to a masking of the differences that exist within communities based on gender, age, ethnicity or some other factor. Assuming harmony can lead to a failure to take into account intra-communal differences.

The lack of cohesion and trust within the food co-op at Project SHARE seemed to be based more on a lack of harmony than a lack of homogeneity. Discussions with co-op members did not reveal internal hierarchies based on differences of gender, ethnicity or economic class. All the members of the co-op are part of a marginalized group. But the common characteristics of co-op membership, urban location and income levels did not necessarily in and of themselves provide meaningful coherence (or harmony) to the population of the food co-op (Demers & White, 1997). When the members of the small group that did develop were asked to comment on the distrust in the co-op some months later, they suggested several reasons. People join for the extra food and don't necessarily desire a social connection. People are ashamed; they don't want others to know their situation. Finally, for some people, it isn't distrust but a desire to be by themselves.

It needs to be recognized that participation by its very nature must be an invitation, not a requirement. It must meet the needs of those who are asked to participate. For most members of the co-op what had been an anticipated benefit of participation, an alternative way to meet co-op work requirements that involved informal and closer social interaction with other co-op members, was not perceived as a benefit. Participatory research has a tendency to stress the solidarity of communities and to picture community as a natural social entity (Cleaver, 2000). In reality, communities often embody "both solidarity and conflict, shifting alliances, power and social structures" (Cleaver, 2000, p. 45.) It is important not to deny the presence of conflict, but to make both the forces of inclusion and exclusion part of the analysis.

Moving From Functional to Interactive Participation

The general atmosphere of mistrust within the co-op was contrasted by the atmosphere of trust and enthusiastic participation that developed among the women who participated in the small group. After spending some time getting acquainted, the group began by talking about what makes for a good quality of life. From among a number of examples from other PPAs, the group chose to portray their characteristics of a good quality of life as a sun diagram with a house in the centre. One of the women who had been praised for her handwriting agreed to draw the pictures that emerged from group discussions. As the group became used to using the tools of word pictures and visual representations, there was a growing comfort level with this method of recording the discussion. The early discussions centered around topics introduced by the researcher, but one of the goals of the project was to work towards group participation in setting the agenda.

Functional participation is characterized by predetermined objectives while interactive participation is characterized by joint analysis with the group taking control over local decision making (Pretty et al., 1995). The format of the small group meetings gradually began to move from a functional format to an interactive format. In the first several meetings, the small group followed an agenda which had been introduced by the researcher. This format began to change, as the group gained confidence in their own voice and their familiarity with each other. In the second meeting, for example, concerns about the changes to the education system were raised in the discussion about assets and time was spent drawing out specific concerns around education. The third meeting took place after a co-op membership meeting in which further changes to the administration of social assistance had been announced. When the group was asked what topics they wanted to discuss they identified the changes reviewed at the co-op membership meeting and the cutbacks to social assistance. This led to a general and wide-ranging discussion of life on social assistance. Several personal stories were shared about cutbacks, overpayment rulings and subsequent deductions, and fear of losing an asset such as an inherited house. This was the first of numerous discussions about life on social assistance. By the fourth meeting, the group set the agenda together at the beginning of the meeting or in planning for the next meeting.

The women expanded the agenda for the meetings by expressing and implementing a desire to include a social and celebrative aspect to their time together. This included planning a potluck meal together after one of the meetings and planning a Christmas party for the group. The women also stated a desire to continue meeting after the discussions of PPA topics had been completed. Time was spent at a fall meeting evaluating the discussion sessions and the women stated that they enjoyed the meetings, and that it was helpful to learn they were not alone in their situation. The women expressed a unanimous desire to continue meeting. (The group has continued meeting now for the past three years.)

Lessons From a Participatory Poverty Assessment in Niagara Falls

The participants gave the title "Welcome to the Real World" to the report of their work, a title they chose because it expresses what life in poverty and on social assistance is like and it expresses the view that for someone else to understand that life, they would need to live it themselves. A number of important findings from that report are presented below. The drawings were made by the women themselves. The findings were initially summarized by the researcher and then reviewed by the women in the group who made changes and additions and decided on the title for the report. Except where noted the following summaries of the drawings reflect the findings as reviewed and edited by the women.

A Good Quality of Life

The Participatory Poverty Assessment began with a discussion of well-being. Definitions of poverty reflect and illustrate definitions of well-being, of a good quality of life. The group answered the question, "What is a good life?" by first making a list of items that make for a good quality of life.[4] Then each person voted on the list, designating items into three categories: very important, somewhat important, and not as important. The women developed a key for this drawing in which those items which had the most "very important" votes were surrounded with a heart, those with the most "somewhat important" votes surrounded with a circle and those with the most "not as important" votes surrounded with a square. The diagram of a good quality of life is shown as Figure 22.1. The numbers in Figure 22.1 refer to the number of votes received for that item.

In the drawing of a good quality of life, relationships with friends and with family and children are rated as the most important factors in a good life. Factors that relate to the quality of relationships are also listed as very important, such as love, happiness, and self-esteem.

A number of qualities of a good life point to the need for a cushion: enough to live without stress; to have full cupboards; to have a savings account; to be debt free; to take a vacation; to pursue dreams; and to help others in need. One theme alluded to here is the presence of savings which would mean that emergencies can be weathered with less stress. Another theme is the possibility for celebration, the possibility to treat oneself, and the possibility of rest.

Figure 22.1   Good Quality of Life

There are a number of tangible assets that are mentioned as part of a good quality of life including an automobile, fresh water, a good place to live, health, a good job, and full cupboards. More prominent, however, are intangible qualities such as love, happiness, religion, success, no stress, understanding one another, self esteem and courage. Well-being for this group is not defined primarily in material terms or as material abundance. Money is not even mentioned directly, only indirectly in terms of the material goods that create a good quality of life and that require money. The fulfilling of human needs is portrayed as a means to human functioning, not as an end in itself. A good quality of life is fully embedded in a community of family and friends.

A Poor Quality of Life

The women also drew a picture of a poor quality of life. The heavily drawn caption of this picture is the word, STRESS (see Figure 22.2.) A poor quality of life is a life lived in the context of stress and worry. One of the causes of stress is expressed in the term "giant microscope." The women described life on social assistance as "living under a giant microscope." This feeling of being watched adds to the stress of living on an inadequate income. (The arbitrary and punitive nature of the social assistance system in the province of Ontario was often a topic of conversation.)

While the good quality of life drawings (Figure 22.1) drew extensively on intangible qualities and on the importance of relationships, the poor quality of life drawing (Figure 22.2) is more tangible. It mentions the lack of money and termination of income directly and outlines the consequences of not having enough money.

The lack of income leads to not enough food to eat, to poor quality of housing and to poor health and illness. There are also consequences for relationships as shown in "can't afford to help" and "kids on the wrong path." The researcher interprets the intangible nature of the good quality of life drawing to reflect a life in which there is sufficient income that the intangible qualities of life can have a rightful place. And the poor quality of life drawing may reflect a life in which the lack of money looms so large that it colours also the intangible qualities of life.

Seasonality

The relationship between stress and a poor quality of life is further explained in a drawing describing the seasonality of life on social assistance. Seasonality is an important dimension to the experience of poverty in the Southern hemisphere. The seasonality usually referred to and studied in Participatory Poverty Assessments in the South is the seasonality of weather, of the dry and wet season. Weather seasons affect almost every aspect of life including workload, availability of food, level of income and agricultural activities (Attwood et al., 1998).

One of the topics for discussion in the small group was whether there is a seasonality in the Northern hemisphere. This question was pursued by asking what variations are important over the course of a year and what variations are important over the course of a month. Those items which vary by the time of year were identified as changes in the cost of several main expenditure items such as clothing, utilities, medicine, food and school supplies. For some items this is due to an increase in use (utilities, medicine,

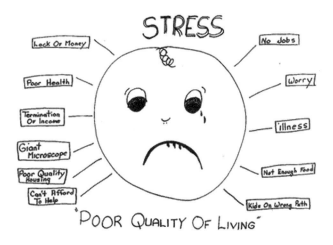

Figure 22.2   Poor Quality of Life

clothing); for others it was due to an increase in price (food). Important dimensions which vary over the course of a month were identified as the amount of stress, the amount of food, the amount of pocket money and the level of indebtedness. The members of the small group were unanimous in identifying the monthly variations as those which have the greatest impact on their lives. A simple chart outlining each of the identified monthly variations was drawn. It appears as Figure 22.3.

The relationship between stress and a poor quality of life is clearly visible in this chart. The end of the month is described as "you've lost it, not enough to buy bread and milk, nerves are gone." In addition, the notices are coming in from bill collectors with possible threats of utility cut-offs. There is clearly a cyclical pattern to the stress. The beginning of the month sees the stress gone, some bills are paid, the cupboards are full and there is even a bit of pocket money. The end of the month looks very different.

INCOME GROUP DESCRIPTIONS

The exploration of what constitutes a good quality of life includes within it an exploration of the relationship between wealth and well-being. This relationship was explored more specifically by asking the question: what distinguishes rich and poor households; how do people compare in terms of income and lifestyle? This question was answered by developing a chart which defined and compared various income groups. The women first talked about how many income groups exist. It was easiest to begin with the two extremes, the rich and those who are very poor. When other categories were filled in, the group identified five income groups. Each income group was described on

a separate sheet of paper. When the descriptions were compared it was discovered that each income group description commented on the level of debt, the level of income, the attitude to others and the level of personal contentment. These four categories were then used to develop a chart which compared the five income groups. This chart appears as Figure 22.4.

The *rich* and *above average* in Figure 22.4 are described as those who have "lots of money" and are "living in luxury," but their high income is accompanied by numerous problems. They are described as having high levels of debt and living beyond their means. In their attitude to others they are tight-fisted and competitive. In addition, both income groups experience high levels of stress and the extreme stress of the rich leads them to resort to drugs and alcohol. Ironically, this image of the rich is a mirror image of the stereotypes of the poor, especially with regard to the level of indebtedness and the use of drugs and alcohol. These results parallel the results of a Participatory Poverty Assessment conducted in the Shinyanga region of Tanzania, where, "Wealthy people were seen as those with access to material wealth, but they did not necessarily use this wealth to ensure their well-being" (Attwood et al., 1998, p. 59).

The *average* income group has the most positive description and appears to be the ideal income group in the eyes of the women. This group has enough income to live comfortably. They are not in debt, but "live within their means." They have "good relations" with other income groups and are content though there is some stress in their lives. The *low income* group, which the women in the small group belong to, is pictured as being in debt and living with stress, but they are happy, and

MONTHLY SEASONAL VARIATION

	Start of month	Middle of month	End of month
Stress	Fine/stress is gone	Starting to come	At end of month, you've lost it, not enough to buy bread and milk, nerves are gone
Food	Cupboards are full	Little bit low	Run out of meat, milk, bread, butter, eggs, potatoes, veggies, fruit, and toilet paper
Bills	Some bills paid, some not; borrowing from Peter to pay Paul	Same as start of month	Notices coming, pay interest, threat of disconnection, notice from collection agency
Pocket money	Might have $5.00	Some months may have extra from GST or Baby Bonus, other months nothing	Zero

Figure 22.3   Monthly Seasonal Variation

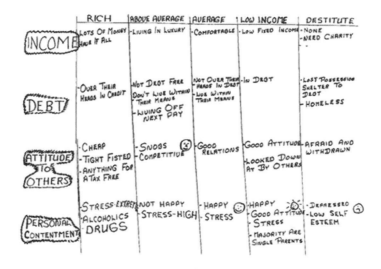

Figure 22.4   Description of Income Groups

have a good attitude toward others. They, themselves, however are looked down on by others. The *destitute* income group is without money or shelter and have lost most of their possessions. They are afraid and withdrawn, with low self-esteem. This group includes the long-term homeless.

There are several comparisons across income groups that surface in this diagram. One comparison is that levels of debt correspond to low income for the two lowest income groups, but debt appears to correspond with lifestyle for the two upper income groups. They do not manage their wealth responsibly. They have enough income to live without debt, but are portrayed as heavily indebted. In addition, there is an undercurrent of tight-fistedness in the description of the upper income groups which suggests that their level of generosity does not correspond to their level of income. Their wealth has not made them generous. One of the recorded comments during the discussion of income groups emphasizes this lack of generosity of those with more income, "People with a lot of money can also be tight with their money."

A cross-income comparison of the comments on *attitudes towards others* suggests that they are essentially a description of the attitudes of other income groups towards those in the low income group. Except for the *destitute,* who are withdrawn and isolated, the diagram suggests that the lower the income group, the better the attitude towards those on low incomes. It may be that the attitude towards others is seen as a function of one's own

experience of need or that too much income distances one from those in need. The often repeated comment that for someone to really understand the situation of the low income group they would need to live on a welfare income for several months reinforces this interpretation. In addition, one of the comments recorded during the discussion of income groups suggests that this sharing of experiences ought to go both ways. The comment "I would love to have one cheque to spend how I want," suggests that the low income group would also like to share in the experience of being able to spend freely, without having to worry about making ends meet.

The overall relationship between wealth and well-being in this diagram of income groups appears to be one of diminishing returns. There is a desire for enough to live comfortably, but without all the stress and indebtedness that are seen to accompany the higher income groups. Personal contentment and an understanding attitude toward others are highly valued and they also are seen to exist at their highest levels in the lower and middle income groups.

"Living Under a Giant Microscope":
Life on Social Assistance

The power of the social assistance system to shape the lives of the women in the group began to emerge in both the Poor Quality of Life diagram (Figure 22.2) and the Seasonality diagram (Figure 22.3). The nature of life on social assistance became the focus of a number of discussions among the women, particularly as they began to set the agenda for group discussion topics.

The following statements by the women in the group illustrate a key theme in the discussions about life on social assistance, the feeling of being under constant surveillance:

It's not right to get into your personal life. You don't feel like a human being.

Even if you know yourself to be honest, you wonder, who's watching me?

The feeling of being watched has at least two consequences identified by the women. The first consequence is "feeling guilty for every little thing you do." The second consequence is that living on social assistance requires giving up enough personal privacy that human dignity is diminished. There is a feeling that the surveillance is pervasive, not just applied to the determination of eligibility or conformity to the rules. For example, recipients must sign a waiver granting access to one's bank account. The bank account is examined not just to determine whether assets are within allowable limits; rather, case workers consider any transaction fair game for questions. Rather than facing specific questions around conformity to specific rules, the women experience a culture of surveillance.

This experience of surveillance is not unique to this group of women, but has been a theme in other explorations of life on social assistance in Ontario after the 1995 reforms. The Interfaith Social Assistance Reform Coalition [ISARC] (1998) held hearings across Ontario during 1997 at which persons who are poor were invited to tell their stories. Participants referred to the "daily humiliations from government agencies" (ISARC, 1998, p. 19) and one participant spoke of being "treated like I'm guilty until proven innocent" (1998, p. 32). In addition, a study of the new regulatory system put in place for determining and maintaining eligibility for social assistance speaks of the "micro-regulation of the lives of poor people" (Herd & Mitchell, 2003, p. 2). "What is new," state Herd and Mitchell, "is the intensity of surveillance and the technologies employed . . ." (2003, p. 3). The means used for regulation include inordinate requests for information, complicated application and appeals processes, "deliberately confusing" language and processes, and restricted times for the appeal of decisions (Herd & Mitchell, 2003, p. 2).

The World Bank's 47 country Participatory Poverty Assessment reveals that negative experiences with state institutions is a common theme when poor households are asked about their own definition of poverty (Narayan, Patel, Schafft, Rademacher & Koch-Schulte, 1999). The dimensions of humiliation and bureaucratic barriers were commonplace in the country PPAs and included such factors as unreasonable requests for documentation, complicated regulations, corruption, and lack of knowledge about entitlements.

The group discussion of the culture of rules set for social assistance was summarized in a web chart drawing documenting what the women see themselves as giving up in order to receive assistance (see Figure 22.5).[5] The central theme of this diagram is the loss of freedom that accompanies life on social assistance. Freedom to spend, freedom to have a good time, freedom to voice an opinion, freedom to work and freedom to make sensible decisions ("sometimes have to go against good budgeting sense to follow the rules") are all identified as part of the price that is paid. The interaction in the social assistance regimen of rules is seen as one-way. There is no opportunity for input on the part of recipients. Their views are not significant.

In addition to paying a price in terms of freedom there is also a cost in lowered self-esteem. Feeling looked down upon by others was expressed in other discussions with the women, and was strongly represented in the diagram of various income groups. In addition, the reference in Figure 22.5 to "Maple Street School" refers to an incident where neighbourhood protests prevented Project SHARE from moving to a new facility, a school donated by the city. This lack of community goodwill translates into approval of or at least indifference to the public service cutbacks, restricted eligibility, reduced assistance and increased surveillance which characterized the recent political environment in Ontario. The experience of the harsh judgement of the community on people living on welfare is as painful for the women as not having their basic necessities met.

Expressions by the poor of powerlessness, an inability to make themselves heard and a lack of influence with politicians were also common themes in the country PPAs conducted for the World Bank Participatory Poverty Assessment. Participants in qualitative interviews conducted in Georgia (Dudwick, 1997) associated poverty with a "lack of freedom" (1997, p. 19) in words that echo those of the women in Niagara Falls. The summary report of the World Bank PPA (Narayan et al., 1999) noted that these "psychological dimensions of poverty are central to poor people's definitions of poverty" (1999, p. 217):

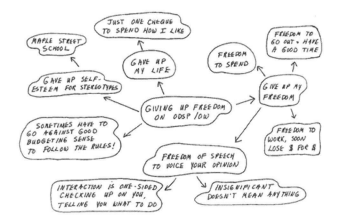

Figure 22.5   Giving Up Freedom

The adverse psychological impact of negotiating their way through the corruption and rude treatment endemic in state institutions can leave poor respondents feeling powerless, voiceless and excluded from state services to which they are entitled. (Narayan et al., 1999, p. 76)

The loss of freedom portrayed in Figure 22.5 speaks strongly to the denial of human agency in the administration of social assistance. The women in the small group do not accept the situation of surveillance without challenge and their resistance takes on two forms. The first form is to resist rules that seem unfair and petty. Winning at bingo is seen as personal good fortune that helps ease the stress of poverty, and therefore should not be subject to the scrutiny of social assistance caseworkers, nor should winnings be deducted from one's cheque.

The second form is a resistance to the pervasiveness of the scrutiny. Having every bank transaction subject to the perusal of caseworkers is seen as unnecessarily intrusive. Because their financial transactions are scrutinized well before they reach allowable asset limits, the women may put their savings under another bank account. To avoid questions about purchases, bills for the purchase of furniture, for example, are put under someone else's name. There is an agreement that some reporting requirements are appropriate, such as major changes in income. But as far as is possible, this will be done on terms set by the women, not by having all of their personal finances an open book. As one woman stated, "I want to feel like a person. I want to have part of my life for myself."

The resistance to the pervasive scrutiny of social assistance caseworkers can be seen as an attempt to recapture human agency, to carve out a piece of life that is free from the gaze of caseworkers. At the same time, it

carries the significant risk of being cut off social assistance on a permanent basis. When the women were asked how they distinguish between what they may report and what they may not report, the reply was, "It's a gut feeling. You get to know what you'll tell them and what you won't." When asked whether the distinction was based on the level of risk, the answer was no, "Nothing is petty to them. It's a risk no matter what you do."

Although the women are trying to recapture human agency it is important not to valorize their efforts as if taking action against the social assistance system is one of a number of strategies from which they can freely choose. Refusing to comply with a set of regulations about which there is no negotiation is not the same as being in a position where one can opt out of a punitive system or take part in negotiations around the demands of that system (Feldman, 1992; Johnson, 1997). Refusing to comply may simply mean that the women "equate adherence with unbearable costs, either for themselves or for those with whom they share interests" (Johnson, 1997, p. 15). The women in the food co-op identified these costs as pervasive surveillance and being forced to act against their own best interests in terms of budgeting decisions. The women are engaged in a risky balance between agency and access to income support.

One of the positive benefits of participation in poverty assessments is that respondents have an opportunity to express the full range of their experiences of poverty including the problematic relationship to state institutions. Participation has the benefit of legitimating the knowledge claims of ordinary people, who can teach others about the impact of social policies on daily life (Cornwall & Gaventa, 2001). For example, when an opportunity was given for evaluating the discussion sessions, the women said that talking about the cutbacks and social assistance had relieved tension in their lives. It was also important to them that the researcher had listened, and had not tried to defend social assistance or to take sides. (The provision of information about social policies does not in and of itself lead to changes in those policies, a dilemma which is taken up in the concluding discussion.)

Working for Change

For the women in the group, the Participatory Poverty Assessment became a catalyst for working for change in the food co-operative of which they are members. The group moved from analysing their own poverty to talking about the food co-operative and the meaningful role it could play as a supportive organization in their lives. The severe cutbacks to social assistance and the increased surveillance had created an atmosphere of mistrust in the food co-op. The women brainstormed about the positive changes that could make the food co-op a place of social support. They took their suggestions to the executive of the co-op and the ideas began to be implemented. Subsequently two of the women ran for the executive of the co-op and were elected. One has since been elected president. They have implemented changes such as: reviewing suggestions and answering questions from members at membership meetings; producing an annual co-op cookbook; holding parties for the children in the co-op; planning an opening fall barbecue; and creating more autonomy for the co-op from Project SHARE as an organization. Membership in the food co-operative has grown from 40 households to almost 70 households. The women also produced, with the researcher, a report of their work. This report was shared in a presentation to the Niagara Social Assistance Reform Committee, a local group that works for improvements to the social assistance system. The report was also made available to the Social Assistance Advisory Committee, an advisory committee to the Regional Municipality of Niagara, which administers social assistance in the region.

The participation of the Niagara Falls women in an analysis of their own poverty contributed some important insights into the importance of social relationships, the stress of an inadequate monthly income and social assistance surveillance, and the deep desire to be treated with goodwill and respect. Participation also made

possible the confidence to plan for and implement changes in the food co-operative that made it a more positive place of support in the lives of the members.

Participation and Power

One of the hallmarks of good participatory research is a commitment to reflect on one's own practice (Pratt, 2001). Reflecting on the Participatory Poverty Assessment in Niagara Falls raises some important dilemmas about power and participation in research that has the goal of working for social change. The purpose of participatory research is to give voice, and beyond giving voice, to mobilize for social change. Participatory research by its very nature, however, is communal research. Working for social change must be a communal goal. Local priorities may not reflect a desire to challenge dimensions of the institutional framework that have been identified by participants as problematic for their lives (Maguire, 1993).

One important consideration may be that local priorities reflect local perceptions of what is possible. Participants may choose not to work for social change at the level of state social policy because they do not believe it is within their power to do so. The question which researchers need to ask is what kind of power does participation give? The capacity to describe what's wrong with a system that has a powerful hold on one's life does not necessarily translate into the capacity to change that system. Cornwall and Gaventa report on the work of an NGO which develops alliances with grassroots organizations in India: "SPARC's approach has been to work to use what spaces were available to develop solutions for themselves, rather than to engage directly against state policies" (2001, p. 14). In analysing decisions around working for change, it is important to recognize that not all points of power (particularly state power) are local points of power (Mohan, 2001). Participation in Niagara Falls enabled the women in the group to think about what they would like to be different in their lives and to work for change in the food co-op so that it would be a place of social solidarity. But participation in and of itself did not confer on them the power to change provincial welfare policy.

Households who are poor do not generally have political power. In fact, it is their lack of political power that motivates a desire to make room for them to participate. Researchers must be alert to the possibility of unfair expectations around mobilization for social change and the possibility of an unfair shifting of responsibility for change to those who lack political power. Participation as a tool for mobilization must be in the context of "the extent and conditions under which social movements can effectively make claims on the state" (Cornwall & Gaventa, 2001, p. 15). Cornwall and Gaventa note that recent work suggests the differences in the nature of the state (which in turn affects the nature and extent of social movements) are more important than differences in the mobilization capacity of poor people.

It is important, therefore, to evaluate participatory research tools and opportunities for citizen participation in terms of their potential to effect change and the nature of the change that is possible. Participation in analysis, such as the Participatory Poverty Assessment in this study, can offer legitimacy to the expertise of people whose lives are impacted by social policies and the administration of social assistance. Changes in policy, however, require participation that goes beyond the sharing of expertise and includes direct engagement with policy makers and implementers. This participation can take many forms, from participation in a user committee to direct engagement in policy making, such as the participatory budgeting process at the municipal level in Brazil (Cornwall & Gaventa, 2001). In the former, citizens can participate in deliberations on the delivery of services, while in the latter they can participate in deliberations on the nature of the services to be delivered.

It is important, then, for academic researchers to share their own power and points of access to the policy process. In this study, for example, the researcher had links to a local social assistance reform committee and facilitated the presentation to that committee by the women of their work. The presentation of the Participatory Poverty Assessment has since led to a proposal for a community based research project in which social assistance recipients will be trained to interview other recipients about their experiences. This research will involve partnerships with community agencies who serve households who are poor and is being sponsored by the local community advisory committee to the regional department which administers social assistance.

This discussion about the limitations of participation in research should not detract from the important principle behind participation, that those who are generally objects of study become subjects and participants in the analysis of their own situation. The knowledge of households who are poor about the complex negotiation between means and ends and the stressful impact of a scrutinizing social assistance system has much to teach those who write and speak about poverty but who do not experience it themselves.

Notes

1. This article is based on research conducted for my PhD thesis, Vulnerability and assets in urban poverty: Bringing together participatory methods and a sustainable livelihoods framework, 2002, University of Toronto. I would like to acknowledge the support of the Social Sciences and Humanities Research Council of Canada through a doctoral fellowship.

2. Participatory poverty approaches have their roots in several sources. Among the most important are the following: the activist participatory research inspired by Paulo Freire, which contributed a recognition of the capability of poor people and the goal of empowerment; field research which contributed farmers' participation in the analysis of systems and informal mapping techniques; and applied anthropology which contributed the benefits of participatory observation and the validity of rural peoples' knowledge (Cornwall, Guijt & Welbourn, 1993 and Chambers, 1992, both cited in Pretty et al., 1995). There are a number of versions of participatory methods, but they share similar principles: reversal of learning (learning from local people), multiple perspectives, group learning process, context specific flexibility, facilitating role for experts, and research that leads to change (Chambers, 1992; Pretty et al., 1995).

3. A new provincial government cut social assistance rates by 21.6 percent in October 1995. In addition, significant restructuring of the social assistance system took place in 1997/1998 and embodied the view that social assistance should be a system of last resort after all other assets have been used up and that the extent of fraud in the system warranted punitive measures such as snitch lines, where recipients were encouraged to report suspected fraud on the part of other recipients to a toll free number.

4. While all of the other drawings were made by the small group, the quality of life drawing was made by the co-op membership at a meeting of the food co-op. This was the meeting at which the women presented the preliminary results of their work and invited the co-op members to take part in defining a good quality of life. The participants in the PPA presented their quality of life drawing which was then enlarged upon and each item ranked by co-op members.

5. The references to OW and ODSP in Figure 22.5 refers to two kinds of social assistance, Ontario Work and Ontario Disability Supports Program.

References

Alkire, S. (1999). Operationalizing Amartya Sen's capability approach to human development: A framework for identifying "valuable capabilities." Unpublished doctoral dissertation, Magdalen College, University of Oxford.

Appadurai, A. (1990). Technology and the reproduction of values in rural Western India. In F. Apffel Marglin & S. Marglin (Eds.),

Dominating knowledge: Development, culture and resistance (pp. 185–216). Oxford: Clarendon Press.

Ashley, C., & Carney, D. (1999). *Sustainable livelihoods: Lessons from early experience.* London: Department for International Development.

Attwood, H., & May, J. (1998). Kicking down doors and lighting fires: the South African PPA. In J. Holland & J. Blackburn (Eds.), *Whose voice? Participatory research and policy change* (pp. 119–130). London: Intermediate Technology Publications.

Attwood, H., Jamhuri, W., Lugusha, E., Lukondo, M., Madenge, R., Masaiganah, M., Mtani, M., Mwaruke, T., & Shilogile, E. (1998). *Participatory poverty assessment: Shinyanga region, Tanzania.* United Nations Development Programme, Shinyanga, Tanzania: Shinyanga Regional Government.

Baker Collins, S. (2002). Vulnerability and assets in urban poverty: Bringing together participatory methods and a sustainable livelihoods framework, Unpublished doctoral dissertation, University of Toronto.

Booth, D. (1998). Coping with cost recovery in Zambia: A sectoral policy study. In J. Holland & J. Blackburn (Eds.), *Whose voice? Participatory research and policy change* (pp. 28–30). London: Intermediate Technology Publications.

Botes, L., & van Rensburg, D. (2000). Community participation in development: Nine plagues and twelve commandments. *Community Development Journal, 35*(1), 41–58.

Carniol, B. (2000). *Case critical: Challenging social services in Canada.* (4th Ed.) Toronto, ON: Between the Lines.

Chambers, R. (1992). *Rural appraisal: Rapid, relaxed and participatory,* IDS Discussion Paper 311, Brighton, Institute of Development Studies.

Chambers, R. (1995). *Poverty and livelihoods: Whose reality counts?* IDS Discussion Paper 347, Brighton, Institute of Development Studies.

Cleaver, F. (2000). Institutions, agency and the limitations of participatory approaches to development. In B. Cooke & U. Kothari (Eds.), *Participation: The new tyranny?* (pp. 36–55). London: Zed Books.

Cornwall, A., & Gaventa, J. (2001). *From users and choosers to makers and shapers: Repositioning participation in social policy,* IDS Working Paper 127, Brighton, Institute of Development Studies.

Cornwall, A., Gujit, I., & Welbourn, A. (1993). Acknowledging process: Challenges for agricultural research and extension methodology. In J. N. Pretty, I. Gujit, J. Thompson and P. Scoones (Eds.), *Beyond Farmer First.* London: Intermediate Technology Publications.

Demers, A., & White, D. (1997). The community approach to prevention: Colonization of the community? *Canadian Review of Social Policy, 39,* 1–19.

Dudwick, N. (1997). *Georgia: A qualitative study of impoverishment and coping strategies.* Washington, DC: World Bank, Europe and Central Asia Region.

Feldman, S. (1992). Crises, poverty, and gender inequality: Current themes and issues. In L. Beneria & S. Feldman (Eds.), *Unequal burden: Economic crises, persistent poverty and women's work* (pp. 1–25). Boulder, CO: Westview Press.

Guijt, I., &Kaul Shah, M. (1998). Waking up to power, conflict and process. In I. Guijt & M. Kaul Shah (Eds.), *The myth of community: Gender issues in participatory development* (pp. 1–23). London: Intermediate Technology Publications.

Herd, D., & Mitchell, A. (2003). *Discouraged, diverted and disentitled: Ontario works new service delivery model.* Community Social Planning Council of Toronto.

Holland, J., & Blackburn, J. (1998). Introduction: Participatory poverty assessments. In J. Holland & J. Blackburn (Eds.), *Whose voice? Participatory research and policy change* (pp. 91–96). London: Intermediate Technology Publications.

Interfaith Social Assistance Reform Coalition. (1998). *Our neighbours' voices: Will we listen?* Toronto: James Lorimer.

Johnson, C. (1997). *Rules, norms and the pursuit of sustainable livelihoods,* IDS Working Paper 52, Brighton, Institute of Development Studies

Kabeer, N. (1996). Agency, well-being and inequality: Reflections on the gender dimensions of poverty. *IDS Bulletin, 27*(1), 11–21.

Maguire, P. (1993). Challenges, contradictions, and celebrations: Attempting participatory research as a doctoral student. In P. Park, M. Brydon-Miller, B. Hall & T. Jackson (Eds.), *Voices of change: Participatory research in the United States and Canada* (pp. 157–176). Toronto, ON: OISE Press.

Max-Neef, M. (1991). *Human scale development: Conception, application and further reflections.* New York: Apex Press.

Mies, M. (1996). Liberating women, liberating knowledge: Reflections on two decades of feminist action research. *Atlantis, 21*(1), 10–24.

Mohan, G. (2001). Beyond participation: Strategies for deeper empowerment. In B. Cooke & U. Kothari (Eds.), *Participation: The new tyranny?* (pp. 153–167). London: Zed Books.

Narayan, D., Patel, R., Schafft, K., Rademacher, A., & Koch-Schulte, S. (1999). *Can anyone hear us? Voices from 47 countries.* Washington, DC: World Bank, Poverty Group, PREM.

Norton, A. (1998). Analysing participatory research for policy change. In J. Holland & J. Blackburn (Eds.), *Whose voice? Participatory research and policy change* (pp. 179–191). London: Intermediate Technology Publications.

Park, P. (1993). What is participatory research? A theoretical and methodological perspective. In P. Park, M. Brydon-Miller, B. Hall, & T. Jackson (Eds.), *Voices of change; Participatory research in the United States and Canada* (pp. 1–19). Toronto, ON: OISE Press.

Pratt, G. (2001). *Practitioners' critical reflections on PRA and participation in Nepal,* IDS Working Paper 122, Brighton, Institute for Development Studies.

Pretty, J. N., Guijt, I., Thompson, J., & Scoones, I. (1995). *Participatory learning and action; A trainer's guide.* London: International Institute for Environment and Development.

Project SHARE of Niagara Falls, Inc. (2001, June 7). *Annual report 2000.* Niagara Falls: Project SHARE of Niagara Falls, Inc.

Rahnema, M. (1992). Poverty. In W. Sachs (Ed.), *The development dictionary: A guide to knowledge as power* (pp. 158–176). London: Zed Books.

Robb, C. (1999). *Can the poor influence policy? Participatory poverty assessments in the developing world.* Washington, DC: The World Bank.

Room, G. (1995). Poverty and social exclusion: The new European agenda for policy and research. In G. Room (Ed.), *Beyond the threshold: The measurement and analysis of social exclusion* (pp. 1–9). Bristol: The Policy Press.

Ros, D., & Craig, Y. (1997). Participation begins at home. *Gender and Development, 5*(3), 35–44.

Sachs, W. (1992). The discovery of poverty. *New Internationalist, June,* 7–9.

Discussion Questions

1. Explain Baker Collins' research methodology.

   Baker Collins utilized a participatory methodology to engage households who are poor in an assessment of their own living conditions. It relies on different data collection methods—visual methods (such as mapping exercises, diagrams, timelines), focus groups, and semistructured interviews. In addition to utilizing the methodology for data collection, the process also enables subjects to analyze their own situation and "develop the confidence to make decisions and take action to improve their circumstances."

2. Summarize Baker Collins' study findings.

   Students should review the following themes: a good quality life, a poor quality life, seasonality, and life on social assistance.

Source: From Baker Collins, S. (2003). An understanding of poverty from those who are poor. *Action Research*, *3*(1), 9–31 (2003). Reprinted by permission of Sage Publications and the author.

CHAPTER 23

Child Labor in Bangladesh

Are Children the Last Economic Resource of the Household?

Claire Salmon (2005)

Claire Salmon explores the relationship between poverty and child labor in Bangladesh in this article. In 2000, about one-fifth of all Bangladeshi children between the ages of 5–14 years were classified as child workers. Based on her analysis, Salmon confirms how children serve as the last economic resource in Bangladeshi households and are more likely to work when they live in a household where the potential of income generation is low and where this potential has already been used up.

1. Introduction

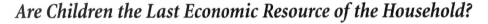

In recent years, child labor has increasingly drawn the attention of policymakers, governments, nongovernmental organizations, and international agencies. There is also a rich literature—both theoretical and empirical—analyzing this important issue and proposing policy measures to deal with it. In the case of Bangladesh, the issue of child labor is important for at least two reasons. First, the scale of child labor in Bangladesh is substantial. In 2000, child labor constituted 9–11 percent of the total labor force. Nearly a fifth of all children aged 5–14 years, or 5.4 to 7.9 million children, work actively in the labor market. Second, the child labor issue has been extensively debated in Bangladesh after the adoption of the Harkin Bill (Child Labor Deterrence Act, 1993) in the United States. The threat of American trade sanctions against countries employing child workers has led to thousands of Bangladeshi children losing their jobs, particularly in the garment industry. Some have argued that these retrenchments have often pushed children to more hazardous jobs (Rahman et al., 1999; Bissell, 2001). In this context, it is important to understand the context and determinants of child labor in Bangladesh.

Several articles have already studied the issue of child labor in Bangladesh. Among the more recent studies, Amin et al. (2004), using the 1996 Household Expenditure Survey (HES), find household poverty as one of the main predictors of child labor. Ravallion and Wodon (2000) focused on the effect of a targeted school subsidy on child labor and school attendance in the rural areas of the country. Their results, also based on the 1996 HES data set, indicate that the enrollment subsidy has significantly reduced the incidence of child labor. Using data collected from Dhaka slums in 1996, Delap (2001) finds that girls are more likely than boys to be the last economic resource of the household. According to Delap, this finding is likely to be explained by cultural norms, such as the importance of *purdah*. The possible impact of Harkin's Bill on Bangladesh is discussed in Rahman et al. (1999) and Bissell (2001).

In this article, we try to contribute to the empirical literature on child labor in Bangladesh by analyzing the 2000 Labor Force Survey data.[1] The first section of the article describes the main features of child labor in Bangladesh, including the scale of the problem. Following the hypothesis suggested by Delap (2001), we explore if children are driven to work when the household's full potential of income generation has already been used. The second section presents the characteristics of children's work—the age, gender and rural/urban composition of child labor. This section describes the sectoral distribution of child labor, the duration of work, and the typical contribution of children to the total income of the household. The third section presents how working children—and their households—differ from non-working children in terms of poverty and adult employment patterns. The usual determinants of children's work are discussed in the fourth section, while the results of the econometric estimation are presented in the fifth section. Finally, the research findings are summarized in the concluding section.

2. Scale of the Child Labor Problem

According to the Bangladesh Bureau of Statistics, child workers are defined as children in the age group of 5–14 years who were found to be working during the survey reference period. Theoretically, it means that a child is said to work if he or she was found working one or more hours for pay or profit in an establishment or for no pay in a family farm or enterprise during the reference period.[2] Moreover, for all persons aged 10 years and over, two definitions of what counts as labor can be adopted. The *extended* definition of labor contains all economic activities, paid or unpaid, including own household economic activities, such as care of poultry and livestock, threshing, boiling,

drying, and processing and preservation of food. The *usual* definition excludes these own household activities. Of course, the first definition leads to inclusion in the labor force a large proportion of women or girls who would be excluded from the definition of the active population otherwise. In this article, we have adopted the extended definition of child labor in order to capture unpaid household activities. The latter are often poorly observed in many studies on child labor, and this leads to an underestimation of the participation of girls in the labor market.

Table 23.1 shows that, in 2000, the number of child laborers in Bangladesh numbered 5.4 million or 7.9 million, depending on the definition of the labor force that is adopted. Of these, around 1.1 million were under the age of 10 years. Given that the 2000 LFS questionnaire does not enable a distinction between the usual and extended definitions of the labor force for children under 10, these figures must be taken as the upper bound of child labor estimates. In other words, it means that, at the most, 21 percent of the child population aged 5–14 is economically active according to the extended definition and around 15 percent according to the usual definition of the labor force. According to these estimates, child workers represented between 9 and 13 percent of the total labor force of the country, which is almost the same share as that computed from the previous surveys.[3]

As shown in Figure 23.1, the labor force participation rate varies by age and gender. Fewer than 6 percent of very

Table 23.1 Number of Child Workers, by Age and by Gender (LFS 2000)

	Millions		Labor force participation (%)	
	Extended definition	*Usual definition*	*Extended definition*	*Usual definition*
Child workers aged 5–9	**1.12**	**1.12**	**5.8%**	**5.8%**
Boys	0.65	0.65	6.4%	6.4%
Girls	0.47	0.47	5.1%	5.1%
Rural	0.95	0.95	6.1%	6.1%
Urban	0.16	0.16	4.5%	4.5%
Child workers aged 10–14	**6.77**	**4.31**	**38.5%**	**24.5%**
Boys	4.02	2.85	43.1%	30.6%
Girls	2.74	1.46	33.2%	17.6%
Rural	5.54	3.27	41.0%	24.2%
Urban	1.22	1.04	30.8%	26.2%
All child workers aged 5–14	**7.89**	**5.43**	**21.4%**	**14.7%**
Share of 5–9 year olds	15.1%	20.6%	–	–
Share 10–14 year olds	84.9%	79.4%	–	–
Total	100%	100%	–	–

Source: Author's calculations based on LFS 2000 data.

Notes: The 2000 LFS questionnaire does not permit distinguishing between the usual and extended definitions of the labor force for children aged 5–9 years.

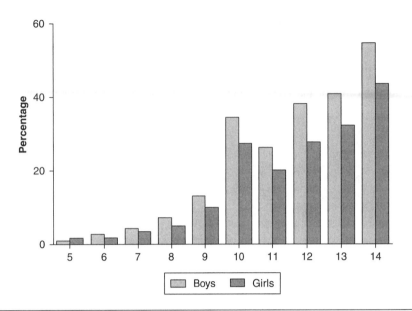

Figure 23.1. Labor Force Participation of Children Aged 5–14, by Age and by Sex

Source: Author's calculations based on LFS 2000 data. Extended definition of the labor force.

young children—those under 10—are observed to work, against 24–38 percent (depending on definition) of the children older than 10 years of age. At every age, the labor force participation of girls is lower than that of boys.

It is noteworthy that these results are considerably different from those reported in the analysis based upon the Household Expenditure Surveys. According to the analysis of the 2000 HES, only 5 percent of all children aged 5–14 years were employed and 15 percent were either employed or looking for employment. As mentioned earlier, this large discrepancy in participation rates may be due to differences in definitions of labor force participation in the two data sets.[4] The LFS adopted a more extended definition of the labor force than the HES, which allows the former to count as workers a larger number of children. According to Ravallion and Wodon (2000: c165), the HES may "understate the extent of child labor either because of deliberate under-reporting, or because relatively small amounts of part time work are not deemed to constitute the child's normal activity." In contrast, our calculations of participation rate of children in the labor market based upon the 2000 LFS are lower than those reported by Delap (2001). In her study on child labor in Dhaka, the definition of what constitutes work is also extended, but the age group she considers is wider than ours (5–16 years). In her survey, 30 percent of children were found to be engaged in income-generating work.

3. Characteristics of Child Labor in Bangladesh

A. Sectoral Distribution by Gender, Age and Location

Among the very young children, differences of participation between girls and boys and between rural and urban areas are negligible. Table A1, in the Appendix, reveals that the majority of the child workers under 10 are employed in the agricultural sector. The remainder are found in the different services sectors. The great majority of these children work as helpers or non-salary earners. A quarter of the service-sector child workers are salary earners and 10 percent are employed by the government's Food-For-Work program.

Boys constitute 58 percent of all employed child workers aged 10 and over, while girls account for the remaining 42 percent. After agriculture, it is the services sector that employs the largest share of child workers. As for adults, the findings reveal clear gender divisions in the child workforce, particularly in the urban areas. Given gender norms, girls, like their mothers, are almost totally excluded from sectors and occupations which do not enable maintenance of a certain degree of *purdah* (Delap, 2001).[5] Hence, in the urban areas, boys are mainly found in trade, hotel and restaurant sectors (37 percent) and girls in household services (32 percent). Even though the manufacturing sector employs both (urban) boys and girls, there is segmentation *within* that sector. Boys have more options, while girls are almost exclusively employed in the garment sector. In 2000, this sector employed around 8 percent of all child laborers and 15 percent of all child workers living in the urban areas. Interestingly, 70 percent of all child workers employed in the garment sector were girls.[6]

B. DURATION OF WORK AND SCHOOL ATTENDANCE

The average duration of work of the older child workers is longer than that of the younger ones. Tables A3 and A4 in the Appendix show that child workers aged 10 and over work around 26 hours per week, while those aged 5–9 years work 18 hours per week on average. Working hours are particularly long (more than 40 hours per week) in the construction, manufacturing and household service sectors. Figure 2 shows that, on average, the working hours of girls are lower that of boys— 23 hours per week versus 29 hours per week. However, further analysis of data also reveals that the proportion of children who work more than 50 hours per week is higher among urban girls than among urban boys (respectively 27% versus 20%).[7]

Figure 23.2 also shows that the duration of work is correlated with the initial level (i.e. exclusive of the financial contribution of children) of income of the household. Child workers residing in the poorest households tend to work longer hours than child workers in all other households excepting the richest ones. At first glance, it may seem paradoxical that the working hours of child laborers who live in the richest quintile of households are so large (about 30–3 hours weekly). In fact, this is explained by the fact that the great majority of child laborers who belong to the richest quintile are domestic servants who live with their employer. They are counted as "members" of their employer's household. Given the construction of the LFS data set, the characteristics of their own household cannot be observed. As documented in other studies (Ward et al., 2004), most of these domestic servants probably come from the poorest families.

For the children who work only a few hours a week, one could suppose that they also attend school. Unfortunately, the LFS data set reports very limited information on the school attendance of the children aged 10 and over. But for the younger children—under age 10—the data reveal a very strong correlation between child work and school non-attendance. While 80 percent of all children under 10 attended school in Bangladesh in 2000, only 21 percent of child workers of the same age could attend school in the same period.[8] A

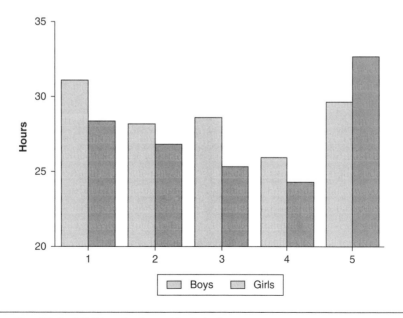

Figure 23.2.   Average Time Work of Children, by Sex and by Quintile

Source: Author's calculations based on LFS 2000 data.

Notes: Extended definition of the labor force is used. Quintiles are calculated on the basis of per capita income without the financial contribution of children.

detailed analysis of interactions between school attendance and child labor in rural Bangladesh is available in Ravallion and Wodon (2000).

C. CONTRIBUTION OF CHILDREN TO THE EARNINGS OF THE HOUSEHOLD

According to the 2000 LFS, children engaged in income-generating work earned, on average, 43 takas per day when they are daily laborers. In comparison, daily laborers aged over 15 years old were found to earn 62 takas per day in the survey. Table A5 in Appendix reports the different child wages and salaries by status, gender, age and location.

What is the relative contribution of children to household income? In fact, only 3 percent of incomes in Bangladesh are earned by children—somewhat lower than the 5 percent contribution of their mothers. Of course, these figures hide large disparities depending on the level of income of the household and the engagement of children in income-generating work. If only households receiving some child income are counted, the earnings of children represent one-third of the total income of these households (see Figure 3). These findings are very similar to those reported by Rahman et al. (1999).

4. Poverty, Employment of Adults and Child Labor: Preliminary Analysis

Who are the working children and how do they differ from the non-working children? What are the main characteristics of the households which provide child labor? The following two tables describe both the characteristics of households with or without child laborers and the characteristics of child workers and non-workers. They also compare the characteristics of working girls and working boys and the characteristics of households which supply only boys' work versus boys' and/or girls' work. Tables 23.2a and 23.2b focus on the characteristics of adult employment in the household and the level of income.[9]

As expected, we find that working children come from poorer households. The average household income per capita of children who do not work is 943 taka versus 871 taka for child workers. The gap between child workers and non-workers is even larger if we exclude the children who are unrelated members of the household (those working as domestic servants) (see Table 23.2a). The comparison of means across the different sub-samples reveals that the proportion of adults who work—as paid or unpaid workers—is significantly greater in the households where a child is observed to work.[10] At the same

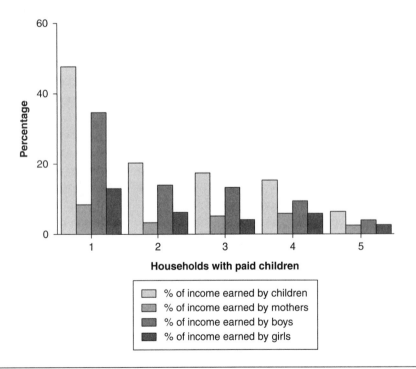

Figure 23.3   Contribution of Children and Mothers to Income, by Quintile

Source: Author's calculations based on LFS 2000 data.

Notes: Extended definition of the labor force is used. Quintiles are calculated on per capita income without the financial contribution of children. Contributions are calculated on the total income of all households with and without child workers.

Table 23.2a   Comparison of Means—Child Workers Versus Child Non-Workers and Working Boys Versus Working Girls

	Sample 1 S1	Sample 2 S2	Sample 3 S3	Sample 4 S4	Test H0	Test H0
	Child non-worker	Child worker	Working boy	Working girl		
Characteristics of the child's household	Mean	Mean	Mean	Mean	S1 = S2	S3 = S4
Income per capita, without children's contribution						
Sons, daughters, and non-biological children	943	871	790	962		
	2654	*2849*	*1936*	*3783*	***	***
Sons, daughters	939	700	690	716	***	**
	2654	*1760*	*1892*	*1540*		
% of adult workers among all adults	0.710	0.774	0.772	0.776	***	ns
	0.268	*0.257*	*0.252*	*0.263*		
% of adult paid workers among all adults	0.505	0.533	0.532	0.536	***	ns
	0.229	*0.242*	*0.235*	*0.252*		
% of males over the age of 15	0.244	0.249	0.247	0.251	ns	ns
	0.111	*0.124*	*0.120*	*0.129*		
% of females aged 15–60	0.229	0.231	0.232	0.228	ns	ns
	0.089	*0.095*	*0.092*	*0.099*		
Dummy: 1 if mother works	0.496	0.569	0.559	0.583	***	ns
	0.500	*0.495*	*0.497*	*0.493*		
Dummy: 1 if mother is a paid worker	0.137	0.147	0.138	0.161	ns	***
	0.344	*0.355*	*0.345*	*0.368*		
Dummy: 1 if all adults work	0.395	0.500	0.492	0.512	***	ns
	0.488	*0.500*	*0.500*	*0.500*		
Dummy: 1 if single-parent household	0.077	0.099	0.090	0.112	***	*
	0.264	*0.299*	*0.285*	*0.316*		
Number of observations	10,751	2755	1617	1138		

Source: Author's calculations based on LFS 2000 data.

Notes: Standard deviations in italics. Test of Mann-Whitney: the two samples are significantly different if *** H0 is rejected at 1% level, ** H0 is rejected at 5% level, * H0 is rejected at 10% level.

time, Table 23.2b shows that the share of adults—male or female—within the household is lower in the households where children work. Mothers are much more likely to work in households with child workers than in households without child workers (56 percent versus 44 percent). One-half of all child workers live in a household where all the adults work. Further, child workers are more often found in single-parent than in two-parent households. In short,

the evidence suggests that child labor is more common among households where the potential for further income generation from adult members is low—either because of the absence of a parent or because all the adult members in the household are already fully employed.

There are some interesting differences in the characteristics of households that supply girls' labor and those that supply only boys' labor. In the former, the share of

Table 23. 2b　Comparison of Means—Households With Child Worker(s) Versus Households Without Child Workers and Households With Boy Worker(s) Versus Household With Boy and/or Girl Worker(s)

	Sample 1' S1' Households without child workers	Sample 2' S2' Households with out child worker(s)	Sample 3' S3' Households with only boy worker(s)	Sample 4' S4' Households with girl and/or boy worker(s)	Test H0	Test H0
Characteristics of the household	Mean	Mean	Mean	Mean	S1' = S2'	S3' = S4'
Income per capita, without children's contribution	1141	871	790	962	***	***
	2244	3182	2247	3979		
% of adult workers among all adults	0.682	0.768	0.770	0.774	***	ns
	0.280	0.259	0.253	0.265		
% of adult paid workers among all adults	0.505	0.530	0.528	0.536	***	ns
	0.245	0.241	0.233	0.252		
% of males over the age of 15	0.332	0.257	0.251	0.256	***	ns
	0.172	0.127	0.121	0.129		
% of females aged 15–60 in the household	0.307	0.238	0.237	0.232	***	***
	0.153	0.098	0.093	0.100		
Dummy: 1 if mother works	0.448	0.563	0.556	0.583	*	*
	0.497	0.496	0.497	0.493		
Dummy: 1 if mother is a paid worker	0.147	0.144	0.133	0.161	ns	**
	0.354	0.352	0.339	0.368		
Dummy: 1 if all adults work	0.365	0.491	0.474	0.510	***	*
	0.481	0.500	0.499	0.500		
Dummy: 1 if single-parent household	0.115	0.102	0.090	0.115	*	**
	0.319	0.303	0.287	0.319		
Number of observations	7606	2181	1155	1026		

Source: Author's calculations based on LFS 2000 data.

Notes: Standard deviations in italics. Test of Mann-Whitney: the two samples are significantly different if *** H0 is rejected at 1% level, ** H0 is rejected at 5% level, * H0 is rejected at 10% level.

female members in household size is lower, the mother is more likely to be working, and the mother is more likely to be engaged in wage employment. Further, households which supply girls' labor are more likely to be single-parent households or households where the entire potential of adult work is already exhausted. This in turn suggests that girls are sent to work in households that are severely constrained. These results seem to be consistent with those found by Delap (2001) on urban child workers in Dhaka.

5. Determinants of Child Labor in the Empirical Literature

The empirical literature on child labor has identified at least four types of factors that are likely to influence a household's decision to allocate their children's time to work. The first set of factors are child-specific: age, gender, and the child's level of schooling. As noted by Grootaert

(1998) the magnitude and the direction of these effects are largely country-specific, depending on the cultural context, labor market opportunities, cost of schooling, and wage patterns. The second set of factors are related to parental characteristics. There is ample empirical evidence that the schooling of parents and the nature of their employment—whether regular or irregular, formal or informal, agricultural or non-agricultural—affect the allocation of child labor. After controlling for household income, the regularity and security of income often appear as significant determinants of child labor. Most previous studies have shown that children are less likely to work when parents are better schooled (Grootaert, 1998; Diallo, 2001). The third set of factors to influence child labor includes household characteristics. Besides the level of income and other wealth variables—for instance, owned land and livestock—the demographic composition of a household can have an impact on child labor. Numerous studies have shown that the number and the gender of siblings, the presence or absence of a parent, and the sex of the household head have significant influences on the intra-household allocation of time (Patrinos and Pascharopoulos, 1997; Grootaert, 1998; Delap, 2001). Fourth and finally, community-level factors, such as the cost of schooling, labor market opportunities, cultural norms, and child wage rates, can have an important bearing on the incidence of child labor (Siddiqui and Patrinos, 1995).

The recent empirical literature on child labor has focused largely on the effects of household income—known as the "luxury axiom"[11] of Basu and Van (1998)—and of parental employment. Canagarajah and Coulombe (1997) observed an inverted U-shaped relationship between child labor and household consumption expenditure per capita expenditure in Ghana. Using Peruvian and Pakistani data sets, Ray (2000) found that child labor was influenced by household poverty in Pakistan but not in Peru. Bhalotra (2003) and Bhalotra and Heady (2003) found that income had a negative impact on boys' work in Pakistan but no significant impact on girls' work. Many studies, however, support the more traditional view that poverty pushes children into the labor market (Psacharopoulos, 1997; Blunch and Verner, 2000; Diallo, 2001; Delap, 2001; Amin et al., 2004).

The influence of adult employment on child labor has been tested in different ways. Ray (2000) found that children living in households with a working adult woman worked longer hours on average than children in households without a working woman. Jensen and Nielsen (1997) found that the proportion of other family members who worked had a strong positive influence on the incidence of child labor. Delap (2001) found that in urban Bangladesh girls are more likely to enter the labor market

when all other household members, including adult women, are working.

The strong positive correlation between adult employment—especially of women—and child labor is generally treated as reflecting complementarity between adult and child labor markets (Canagarajah and Coulombe, 1997; Grootaert, 1998; Ray, 2000). While this may be true of agricultural employment (especially self employment), it is not clear why there would be complementarily between adult and child labor in other forms of (non-agricultural) employment. Another interpretation of the positive correlation between adult employment and child labor is that children are the last economic resource of the household (Walters and Briggs, 1993; Jensen and Nielsen, 1997; Delap 2001). They enter the labor market when all the potential of income generation has already been used in a household (i.e. when all the other members are already working full time).

6. Determinants of Child Labor in Bangladesh: Empirical Results

To investigate the determinants of child labor in Bangladesh, we have used unit record data from the 2000 Labor Force Survey to estimate the probability of a child working using the maximum-likelihood probit method. The parameter estimates are reported in Tables A6 and A7 in the Appendix.

Given the gender segmentation of the Bangladeshi labor market, the model has been estimated separately for boys and girls and for urban and rural areas. Only the sons and the daughters of the household head were retained in the sample, since most of the "non-biological" children in a household are typically domestic servants who are unrelated to the household.

As noted earlier, we particularly focus on the influence of poverty and adult employment on the probability of child labor in a household. We try to examine if poverty compels children to enter the labor market. Further, we also test the hypothesis that children are pushed into work because the household has completely used up its potential of income-generating work. This potential is captured by several different variables, such as the share of adults in the household who are employed, the labor force participation of the mother, and the entry of all adults in the labor market. If children are really the last economic resource of the household, the probability of child labor should rise when the share of adult employment reaches its peak and should decrease when there is a potential of income generation remaining in the household.

234 PART VIII POVERTY AND SOCIAL WELFARE POLICY

A. Impact of Poverty on Child Labor

To test the effect of poverty on child labor, we have included dichotomous variables for per capita income quintiles (calculated obviously *without* the contribution of children). As expected, children from the poorest two quintiles of households are observed to be significantly more likely to work than those from better-off households. This result corroborates the "luxury axiom" of Basu and Van (1998). It is also consistent with the results obtained by Ravallion and Wodon (2000), Delap (2001) and Amin et al. (2004). Contrary to the findings of Bhalotra and Heady (2003) on Pakistan, the income of the household plays a significant role in explaining the tendency of both boys *and* girls to work.

Two other variables are also likely to capture the effect of wealth on child labor: the amount of owned land and home ownership. The latter variable has an expected negative association with the probability of child labor. Surprisingly, land ownership is not a significant determinant of child labor. The same result has been observed by Bhalotra and Heady (2003) for Pakistan and Ghana, who argue that, in addition to being a proxy for household wealth, land constitutes an opportunity for productive employment of children, especially in a context where family and hired labor are imperfect substitutes for each other (see also Deolalikar and Vijverberg, 1987).

B. Potential of Work, Adult Employment and Child Labor

The empirical results suggest two interesting conclusions. First, without controlling for the level of work in the household, Regression 1 shows that children are less likely to work when adults—male or female—constitute a large share of household size. At first glance, this might suggest that adult and child labor are substitutes, with the presence of adults liberating children from the need to work. But, when variables relating to adult employment are included in the regression, the results change. Regression 2 shows that children are more likely to work when they live in a household where all the adults (i.e. those members who are older than 15 years of age) are working. Similarly, the share of adults working for a wage is highly significant in explaining the probability of child labor (Regression 3). Thus, children are more likely to work when all adult members in a household work and when a larger proportion of these adults are paid workers. This can be seen as an indication of the household's need for additional resources; in other words, children are sent to work to increase the income potential of the household. These results generally tend to support the hypothesis of

child labor being the "last economic resource" of households.

Second, the type of activity in which the mother is engaged has an influence on the probability of child labor. The empirical results indicate that, after controlling for wealth and other (i.e. other than the mother) adult employment, children are more likely to work when their mother is also working. But contrary to the effect of other adults, children are less likely to work when the mother is working in the paid labor market than when she does not work or is an unpaid family worker. This result seems to suggest that children and mothers may be substitutes for each in the paid labor market. But the relationship is more complex as it also depends on the gender of the child. Regressions 5 and 6 show that boys are more likely to work when the mother is unpaid but less likely to work when the mother is a paid employee. In contrast, girls are more likely to enter the labor market when the mother works whether as an unpaid worker or a wage employee. It thus appears that when the mother works outside the home, her daughters are likely to take her place in the home as unpaid family workers. In contrast, sons and mothers appear to be substitutes for each other in income-generating (paid) activities.

C. Effects of Other Variables

The results also highlight the importance of child characteristics in determining the probability of their entry into the labor market. First, as expected of an Islamic country, girls are less likely to enter the labor market than boys. Second, older children are more likely to work than younger ones. Third, illiterate children are more likely to work than literate ones. Fourth and finally, the presence of very young children—those under 5 years of age—reduces the probability of other children in the household being sent to work. The latter probably occurs because the older children are needed to take care of their younger siblings.

Community variables are also found to be significant in explaining the incidence of child work. Other things equal, children living in a rural area or in Dhaka city are more likely to work than those living in other urban areas. The effect of the overall unemployment rate in a community on child labor differs across locations. In rural areas, children are less likely to work when they live in a district with a high unemployment rate, but the reverse is true in urban areas. These effects are difficult to interpret as they require strong assumptions on the nature of the relationship between adult and child labor markets (see Gupta, 1997; Basu, 1999, 2000 for theoretical models linking adult unemployment with child labor). If these labor markets are complementary, a high level of the overall unemployment rate will diminish employment opportunities for children. Under this simplistic explanation, child and adult labor might be complements in rural areas and substitutes in urban areas. However, this interpretation does not take into account the possible impact of child labor on the unemployment rate of adults as well as the level of adult wage rates.[12] A further exploration of this relationship is needed.

The empirical estimates reveal that there are substantial differences in the determinants of work across boys and girls. First, we have already noted the finding that girls (unlike boys) are more likely to work even when their mother is a paid employee. Second, we find that the nature of employment of the household head matters for the work status of boys but not of girls. Boys (but not girls) are less likely to work when the head of the household is an employee. Third, the level of parental schooling plays a significant role in explaining child labor among boys but not among girls. Finally, the availability of schools in a community has a stronger negative effect on the work status of boys than on the work status of girls.[13]

All of these gender-differentiated results need further exploration. Nevertheless, they support the findings of the large literature on Bangladesh and on other South Asian countries on intra-household discrimination against girls and women in the allocation of food, medical care, and access to schooling (Behrman, 1988; Fauveau et al., 1990; Behrman and Deolalikar, 1993; Quisumbing and de la Brière, 2000).

7. Conclusion

This article uses data from the 2000 Labor Force Survey to analyze the scale, nature and determinants of child labor in Bangladesh. The main empirical findings of the article are as follows. First, around one-fifth of all Bangladeshi children between the ages of 5 and 14 years were "child workers" in 2000. There were a total of 5.4–7.9 million child workers in the country (depending upon the definition of the labor force), constituting 9–11 percent of the national labor force. Although a large proportion of these young workers are found in the agricultural sector, the data revealed clear gender divisions in the child workforce in the urban areas. The findings also revealed that the contribution of boys to household income is greater than that of girls. While, overall, the income earned by children is a small share of total household income, the share is large among households that supply positive amounts of child labor. In the

poorest quintile of such households, the share of child income in total household income reaches almost 50 percent. Thus, the poorest households in the country very much depend upon their children's earnings to pull themselves out of poverty.

Second, the empirical results confirm earlier findings that children from the poorest households are much more likely to enter the labor force than children from better-off households. In this sense, there is support for the widely-held assumption that poverty compels children to work.

Third, the analysis of links between adult employment and child labor lends support to the hypothesis that children are the last economic resource of the household. Children are much more likely to work when they live in a household where the potential of income generation is low and where this potential has already been used up. In other words, children are more likely to work when all the adults in the household, including the mother, are already employed. However, there are some variations across gender. Boys, unlike girls, are less likely to enter the labor market when their mother is engaged in paid labor activities. A possible explanation is that girls and mothers substitute for each other in performing household chores, while boys and mothers are substitutes for each other in paid (wage) employment. In Bangladesh, girls mostly work in unpaid family work.

The finding that there are significant gender differences in the scale, nature and determinants of child labor suggests the importance of adopting a gender-specific approach to addressing the child labor problem in Bangladesh.

Notes

1. This is a nationally-representative survey which collected data on income and employment from 41,404 individuals residing in 9787 households. The full sample consists of 13,506 children aged 5–14 years (7115 boys and 6391 girls). The survey was carried out by the Bangladesh Bureau of Statistics (BBS) in 1999 and 2000.

2. Children who were found not working but had a job or business from which he or she was temporarily absent during the reference period are also considered as child laborers. In reality, very few children reported to have worked less than 7 hours in the preceding week.

3. According to the Child Labor Survey, 1995–6, the number of children in the labor force was 6.58 million out of the 34.45 million children aged 5–14 years old. At this time, children constituted 12 percent of the total labor force of Bangladesh.

4. The LFS adopted a more extended definition of the labor force than the HES, which allows definition of a larger number of children as workers.

5. Salway et al. (2003) underlined that, in Dhaka, women's work opportunities are comparatively much more severely constrained than their male counterparts. Women are totally excluded

from a large part of the occupational options: transport sector, service industry and trade.

6. Bissell (2001) reported that while there is sex segregation in this industry among the adults, this was not true for children: boys and girls have similar conditions of work and earnings.

7. The working time is really high for the children living with their employer as they were found to work, on average, 58 hours per week. A great majority of these workers are girls employed as domestic servants.

8. The main reason given for the non-attendance at school of the young children is "financial crisis" rather than the involvement of the child in a work. Nevertheless, this financial crisis is likely to explain both the inability of parents to pay the school expenditures and the necessity for the child to work. Moreover, parents may be reluctant to admit that child labor is a reason for the absence from school (Ravallion and Wodon, 2000).

9. The other characteristics of these sub-samples—household size, number and proportion of siblings, etc.—are available from the author on request.

10. An adult is defined in this article as an individual aged 15 years and over.

11. According to this axiom, "a family will send the children to the labor market only if the family's income from non-child-labor sources drops very low" (Basu and Van, 1998).

12. The average level of wages—adult or child—in the district was not significant to explain the probability of child labor.

13. The school availability has been proxied by the school attendance rate of children aged 5–9 in the district.

References

Amin, S., Quayes, M.S. and Rives, J.M. (2004). "Poverty and Other Determinants of Child Labor in Bangladesh," *Southern Economic Journal* 70(4): 876–92.

Basu, K. (1999). "Child Labor: Cause, Consequence, and Cure, with Remarks on International Labor Standards," *Journal of Economic Literature* 37: 1083–119.

Basu, K. (2000). "The Intriguing Relation Between Adult Minimum Wage and Child Labour," *The Economic Journal* 110: C50–C61.

Basu, K. and Van, P.H. (1998). "The Economics of Child Labor," *The American Economic Review* 88(3): 412–27.

Behrman, J.R. (1988). "Allocation of Nutrients in Rural India: Are Boys Favored? Do Parents Exhibit Inequality Aversion?" *Oxford Economic Papers* 40: 32–54.

Behrman, J.R. and Deolalikar, A.B. (1993). "The Intrahousehold Distribution of Market Labour Supply in Rural South India," *Oxford Bulletin of Economics and Statistics* 55(4): 409–20.

Behrman, J.R. and Knowles, J.C. (1999). "Household Income and Child Schooling in Vietnam," *The World Bank Economic Review* 13(2): 211–56.

Bhalotra, S. (2003). "Is Child Work Necessary," working paper, University of Bristol. Discussion Paper no. 3/554.

Bhalotra, S. and Heady, C. (2003). "Child Farm Labour: The Wealth Paradox," *World Bank Economic Review* 17(2): 197–227.

Blunch, N.H. and Verner, D. (2000). "Revisiting the Link between Poverty and Child Labor: The Ghanaian Experience," World Bank, Policy Research Working Paper, no. 2488.

Bissell, S. (2001). "Young Garment Workers in Bangladesh: Raising the Rights Question," *Development* 44(2): 75–80.

Canagarajah, S. and Coulombe, H. (1997). "Child Labor and Schooling in Ghana," World Bank, Policy Research Working Paper, no. 1844.

Delap, E. (2001). "Economic and Cultural Forces in the Child Labour Debate: Evidence from Urban Bangladesh," *The Journal of Development Studies* 37(4): 1–22.

Deolalikar, A.B. and Vijverberg, W.P. (1987). "A Test of Heterogeneity of Family and Hired Labour in Asian Agriculture," *Oxford Bulletin of Economics and Statistics* 49(3): 291–303.

Diallo, Y. (2001). "Les déterminants du travail des enfants en Côte d'Ivoire," document de travail n°DT/55/2001, Centre d'économie du Développement, Université Montesquieu-Bordeaux IV.

Fauveau, V., Briend, A. Chakraborty, J. and Sarder, A.M. (1990). "The Contribution of Severe Child Mortality in Bangladesh: Implications for Targeting Nutritional Interventions," *Food Nutrition Bulletin* 12: 215–19.

Grootaert, C. (1995). *Child Labor: A Review*. Washington, DC: World Bank, Office of the Vice President, Development Economics.

Grootaert, C. (1998). "Child Labor in Côte d'Ivoire: Incidence and Determinants," Policy Research Working Paper no. 1905, World Bank.

Gupta, M.R. (1997). "Unemployment of Adult Labour and the Supply of Child Labour: A Theoretical Analysis," mimeo, Jadavpur University, Calcutta.

HIES-2000 (2001). "Employment and Earnings in Bangladesh: Evidence for the 2000 Household Income and Expenditure Survey," draft, Poverty Reduction and Economic Management Unit, South Asia Region, World Bank.

Jensen, P. and Nielsen, H.S. (1997). "Child Labour or School Attendance? Evidence from Zambia," *Journal of Population Economics* 10: 407–24.

Patrinos, H.A. and Psacharopoulos, G. (1997). "Family Size, Schooling and Child Labor in Peru—An Empirical Analysis," *Journal of Population Economics* 10: 387–405.

Psacharopoulos, G. (1997). "Child Labour versus Educational Attainment: Some Evidence from Latin America," *Journal of Population Economics* 10: 377–86.

Quisumbing, A.R. and de la Brière, B. (2000). "Women's Assets and Intrahousehold Allocation in Rural Bangladesh: Testing Measures of Bargaining Power," FCND Discussion Paper No. 86. Washington, DC, International Food Policy Research Institute.

Rahman, M.M., Khanam, R. and Nur Uddin, A. (1999). "Child Labor in Bangladesh: A Critical Appraisal of Harkin's Bill and the MOU-Type Schooling Program," *Journal of Economic Issues* 33(4): 985–1003.

Ravallion, M. and Wodon, Q. (2000). "Does Child Labour Displace Schooling? Evidence on Behavioural Responses to an Enrollment Subsidy," *The Economic Journal* 110: c158–c75.

Ray, R. (2000). "Child Labor, Child Schooling, and their Interaction with Adult Labor: Empirical Evidence for Peru and Pakistan," *The World Bank Economic Review* 14(2): 347–67.

Salway, S., Rahman, S. and Jesmin, S. (2003). "A Profile of Women's Work Participation Among the Urban Poor of Dhaka," *World Development* 31(5): 881–901.

Siddiqui, F. and Patrinos, H.A. (1995). "Child Labor Issues, Causes and Interventions," HR and Operations Policy working paper, World Bank.

Walters, P.B. and Briggs, C.M. (1993). "The Family Economy, Child Labor, and Schooling: Evidence from the Early Twentieth-Century South," *American Sociological Review* 58(2): 163–81.

Ward, K., Rahman, F. et al. (2004). "The Effects of Global Economics Restructuring on Urban Women's Work and Income-Generating Strategies in Dhaka, Bangladesh," *Critical Sociology* 30(1): 63–102.

Table A1   Employed Children Aged 5–9 by Sector, LFS 2000 (in %)

	Total	Rural	Urban	Boys	Girls	Rural boys	Rural girls	Urban boys	Urban girls
Agriculture	43.1	45.7	28.8	46.1	38.8	50	39.6	25	34.6
Manufacturing	2.7	2.3	5.3	2.6	3	2.3	2.2	3.8	7.7
Trade, hotel, restaurant	10.3	6.4	32.6	15.3	3.3	9.4	2.2	47.5	9.6
Transport	3.9	3.7	0	5.3	0	4.7	2.2	8.8	0
Community services	14.2	15.5	6.8	10.9	19	11.7	20.9	6.3	7.7
Household services	14.4	13.7	18.2	8.4	22.9	8.6	20.9	7.5	34.6
Miscellaneous	11.3	12.7	3.1	11.4	10.3	13.3	12.1	1.3	5.7
Total	100	100	100	100	100	100	100	100	100
Self-employed	4.2	2.7	12.7	7	0.3	4.7	0	20	1.9
Salary earner	23	24	17.2	27	17.5	29.5	16.7	13.8	22.2
Unpaid family worker	59.2	60	54.5	51.3	69.9	50.4	72.9	56.3	51.9
Day laborer	3.6	3.6	3.7	4	2.9	3.9	3.1	5	1.9
FFW	9.7	9.3	11.9	9.9	9.4	10.9	7.3	5	22.2
Apprentice	0.4	0.4	0	0.7	0	0.8	0	0	0
Total	100	100	100	100	100	100	100	100	100

Source: Author's calculations based on LFS 2000 data.

Note: FFW: Food for Work program.

Table A2   Employed Children Aged 10–14 by Sector, LFS 2000 (in %)

	Total	Rural	Urban	Male	Female	Rural boys	Rural girls	Urban boys	Urban girls
Agriculture	64.0	72.7	24.6	62.3	66.7	71.2	75.1	19.4	31.5
Manufacturing	8.1	5.0	22.1	7.0	9.7	4.5	5.8	19.3	25.9
Trade, hotel, restaurant	12.3	10.2	22.0	19.7	1.4	16.1	1.2	36.9	2.4
Transport	2.6	2.1	5.0	4.2	0.2	3.3	0.2	8.5	0.2
Community services	3.4	2.7	6.4	2.7	4.3	2.0	3.8	6.5	6.3
Household services	7.4	5.1	17.6	2.3	15.0	1.4	10.8	6.3	32.4
Misc.	2.2	2.2	2.3	1.8	2.8	1.6	3.2	3.2	1.2
Total	100	100	100	100	100	100	100	100	100
Self employed	9.2	8.2	13.8	11.4	6.0	9.7	6	19.4	6.3
Employer	0.1	0.1	0.1	0.1	0	0.1	0	0.2	0
Employee	18.8	13.2	44.2	17.4	20.9	13.1	13.3	37.9	52.4
Unpaid family worker	60.3	65.7	35.4	55	68.1	59.5	75.3	33.3	38.3
Day laborer	11.6	12.7	6.4	16.1	4.9	17.5	5.4	9.1	2.9
Total	100	100	100	100	100	100	100	100	100

Source: Author's calculations based on LFS 2000 data. Extended definition of the labor force.

Table A3   Employed Children 5–9 Years, by Working Hours (in %)

Weekly hours worked	Total	Rural	Urban	Boys	Girls
<15	52.2	53.5	44.8	43.4	64.3
15–19	12.9	12.4	15.7	14.8	10.3
20–9	16.4	15.5	21.6	20.8	10.4
30–9	8.3	8.4	7.5	10.7	4.9
>40	10.2	10.2	10.4	10.3	10.1
Total	100.0	100.0	100.0	100.0	100.0
Mean weekly hours worked	18	18	19	19	14

Source: Author's calculations based on LFS 2000 data.

Table A4   Employed Children 10–14 Years, by Working Hours, LFS 2000 (Extended Definition) (in %)

Weekly hours worked	Total	Rural	Urban	Boys	Girls	Rural boys	Rural girls	Urban boys	Urban girls
<15	27.1	28.7	19.5	21	36.0	22.1	38.6	15.4	24.8
15–19	12.5	13.9	5.8	10.7	15.0	12	16.9	4.9	7.0
20–9	21.3	22.2	17.2	20.5	22.4	21.0	23.9	18.0	16.0
30–9	15.4	15.1	16.6	18.4	10.9	17.9	10.8	20.8	11.0
40–9	11.7	10.4	17.6	15.4	6.3	14.3	4.6	20.6	13.8
50–9	6.1	5.5	9.0	8.0	3.3	7.8	2.0	9.1	9.0
60–9	3.5	2.3	8.7	3.7	3.2	2.9	1.4	7.4	10.4
>70	2.2	1.6	5.2	2.0	2.6	1.7	1.4	3.4	7.6
Total	100	100	100	100	100	100	100	100	100
Mean weekly hours worked	26	25	34	29	23	28	20	34	33

Source: Author's calculations based on LFS 2000 data.

Table A5   Average Income of Child Workers, 2000 LFS (in Taka)

	Child workers aged under 10	Child workers aged 10–14			
		Day laborers	Regular employee		Self-employer
	Weekly pay	Daily pay in cash	Daily pay in kind	Monthly pay	Monthly net income
All child workers	48	43	27[a]	599	1076
Urban child workers	50	53	33[a]	811	1425
Rural child workers	48	42	26[a]	452	958
Boys, child workers	55	42	29[a]	653	1676
Girls, child workers	34	46[a]	19[a]	532	799

Source: Author's calculations based on LFS 2000 data.

[a] Fewer than 50 cases.

Note: Extended definition of the labor force used.

Table A6 Estimation Results of Probit Models: Marginal Effects of the Probability of a Child Working (Full Sample)

Independent variable	Reg.1		Reg. 2		Reg. 3		Reg. 4	
Girl = 1	−0.049***	0.007	−0.050***	0.007	−0.050***	0.007	−0.050***	0.007
Age	0.125***	0.010	0.124***	0.010	0.122***	0.010	0.122***	0.010
Age^2	−0.003***	0.000	−0.003***	0.000	−0.003***	0.000	−0.003***	0.000
Literate	−0.075***	0.007	−0.075***	0.007	−0.073***	0.007	−0.074***	0.007
Presence of children under 5	−0.270***	0.014	−0.260***	0.014	−0.263***	0.014	−0.263***	0.014
% of boys aged 5–9	−0.028	0.037	−0.034	0.037	−0.026	0.037	−0.026	0.037
% of boys aged 10–14	0.065*	0.035	0.057	0.035	0.067*	0.035	0.065*	0.035
% of girls aged 5–9	0.020	0.040	0.014	0.039	0.021	0.039	0.020	0.039
% of girls aged 10–14	0.049	0.035	0.042	0.035	0.050*	0.035	0.049	0.035
% of male adults	−0.078**	0.034	−0.041	0.034	−0.061*	0.034	−0.062*	0.033
% of women aged 15–60	−0.099**	0.040	−0.053	0.040	−0.064	0.040	−0.060	0.040
% of women over 60	−0.199**	0.096	−0.065	0.096	−0.110	0.096	−0.102	0.095
% of adult paid workers			0.011	0.015	0.078***	0.020	0.088***	0.017
All adults work			0.052***	0.008				
Mother works					0.052***	0.007		
Mother paid					−0.037***	0.010		
Mother employee							0.001	0.017
Mother unpaid							0.050***	0.008
Mother day laborer							0.0004	0.016
Head employee					−0.044***	0.014	−0.047***	0.013
Head employer					−0.050	0.030	−0.054	0.028
Head day laborer					−0.006	0.017	−0.010	0.016
Head self employed					−0.015	0.016	−0.020	0.015
Single parent household	0.036	0.025	0.032*	0.018	0.047***	0.022	0.040**	0.020
Household headed by a woman	−0.004	0.021						
Quintile 1	0.116***	0.015	0.120***	0.015	0.116***	0.015	0.116***	0.015
Quintile 2	0.045***	0.009	0.045***	0.009	0.044***	0.009	0.044***	0.009
Household owns its house	−0.016*	0.009	−0.018**	0.009	−0.023**	0.010	−0.022**	0.010
Main activity is agriculture	0.017***	0.007	0.014*	0.007	0.007	0.007	0.008	0.007
Land size	0.000006	0.00001	0.000006	0.00001	0.000005	0.00001	0.000003	0.00001
Mother has no education	0.046***	0.011	0.046***	0.011	0.038***	0.011	0.038***	0.011
Mother has a basic education level	0.041***	0.013	0.041***	0.013	0.035***	0.013	0.034***	0.013
The head has no education	0.007	0.010	0.002	0.010	−0.003	0.010	−0.003	0.010
The head has basic education level	0.013	0.010	0.009	0.009	0.006	0.009	0.006	0.009
Unemployment rate	−0.012	0.132	0.064	0.132	0.101	0.132	0.101	0.133
Rural area	0.037***	0.009	0.027***	0.009	0.023**	0.009	0.023***	0.009
% school attendance of children aged 5–9 in the district	−0.192***	0.032	−0.191***	0.032	−0.189***	0.032	−0.188***	0.032
Dhaka city	0.025**	0.013	0.022*	0.013	0.022*	0.013	0.022*	0.013
Chittagong city	0.018	0.013	0.015	0.013	0.011	0.013	0.011	0.013
Rajshahi city	−0.001	0.017	−0.007	0.017	−0.005	0.017	−0.004	0.017
Khulna city	0.010	0.018	0.011	0.018	0.014	0.018	0.014	0.018
Number of observations	12,374		12,374		12,374		12,374	

Notes: * significant at 10% level. ** significant at 5% level. *** significant at 1% level.

Robust Standard Error in italics. The basic education level is class 1 to 5.

Table A7 Estimation Results of Probit Models: Marginal Effects of the Probability of a Child Working (Different Sub-Samples)

Independent variable	Sons Reg. 5		Daughters Reg. 6		Rural area Reg. 7		Urban area Reg. 8	
Girl					−0.055***	0.011	−0.042***	0.009
Age	0.142***	0.014	0.089***	0.013	0.158***	0.015	0.081***	0.012
Age²	−0.004***	0.001	−0.002***	0.001	−0.004***	0.001	−0.002***	0.001
Literate	−0.092***	0.010	−0.056***	0.009	−0.089***	0.010	−0.055***	0.009
Presence of children under 5	−0.304***	0.019	−0.219***	0.019	−0.283***	0.018	−0.246***	0.021
% of boys aged 5–9	0.002	0.056	−0.018	0.048	−0.001	0.056	−0.038	0.045
% of boys aged 10–14	0.129**	0.053	−0.022	0.046	0.111**	0.054	0.027	0.043
% of girls aged 5–9	0.098	0.063	−0.073	0.049	0.050	0.059	−0.004	0.049
% of girls aged 10–14	0.052	0.056	0.043	0.045	0.111**	0.055	0.006	0.043
% of male adults	−0.058	0.052	−0.063	0.042	−0.015	0.052	−0.092**	0.041
% of women aged 15–60	−0.103***	0.060	−0.023	0.052	−0.109*	0.063	−0.027	0.047
% of women over 60	−0.125	0.142	−0.053	0.125	−0.070	0.141	−0.130	0.126
% of adult paid workers	0.108***	0.025	0.066***	0.022	0.114***	0.027	0.063***	0.020
Single-parent household	0.030	0.028	0.051**	0.028	0.019	0.030	0.032	0.023
Mother employee	−0.046*	0.020	0.051**	0.028	0.004**	0.045	0.003	0.017
Mother unpaid	0.028**	0.011	0.074***	0.011	0.047***	0.011	0.054***	0.013
Mother day laborer	−0.025	0.022	0.031	0.024	−0.006	0.023	0.003	0.023
Head employee	−0.068***	0.019	−0.029	0.018	−0.065**	0.021	−0.029*	0.016
Head employer	−0.076	0.036	−0.042	0.036			−0.019	0.033
Head day laborer	−0.014	0.023	−0.007	0.020	−0.013	0.026	−0.009	0.017
Head self-employed	−0.028	0.023	−0.016	0.020	−0.041***	0.026	−0.006	0.017
Quintile 1	0.129***	0.022	0.103***	0.020	0.079***	0.021	0.149***	0.023
Quintile 2	0.043***	0.014	0.045***	0.012	0.031*	0.016	0.038***	0.010
The household owns its house	−0.023*	0.015	−0.022*	0.013	−0.058**	0.028	−0.010	0.009
Main activity is agriculture	0.012	0.011	0.004	0.009	0.009	0.010	0.011	0.013
Land size	0.00002	0.00001	0.00002	0.00003	0.00002	0.00003	0.00002	0.000
Mother has no education	0.058***	0.017	0.018	0.014	0.031	0.019	0.026**	0.013
Mother has a basic education level	0.050***	0.019	0.020	0.016	0.006	0.020	0.038***	0.014
The head has no education	0.002***	0.015	−0.008	0.012	−0.016	0.015	0.012	0.012
The head has basic education level	−0.001	0.014	0.015	0.012	0.007	0.015	0.009	0.011
Unemployment rate	0.084	0.208	0.134	0.167	−0.442**	0.190	1.155***	0.202
Rural area	0.010	0.013	0.033***	0.012				
% school attendance of children aged 5–9 in the district	−0.213***	0.049	−0.162***	0.041	−0.193***	0.041	−0.356***	0.062
Dhaka city	0.004	0.019	0.040**	0.019			0.011	0.010
Chittagong city	−0.009	0.017	0.032*	0.019			0.021*	0.012
Rajshahi city	−0.004	0.025	−0.010	0.022			−0.020	0.012
Khulna city	−0.017	0.023	0.040*	0.027			0.050***	0.020
Number of observations	6601		5773		6565		5807	

Notes: * significant at 10% level. ** significant at 5% level. *** significant at 1% level.

Robust Standard Error in italics. The basic education level is class 1 to 5.

Discussion Questions

1. Who are the working children described by Salmon? Discuss their demographic background and work characteristics.

   Boys constitute the majority of children workers in the country (58%). The majority of child workers under 10 are employed in agriculture, working as helpers or non-salary earners. As with adult workers, there are gendered divisions in the workforce—among industrial sectors girls are more likely to be employed in the garment sector. Child workers aged 10 and over work 26 hours per week; those aged 5–9 years work 18 hours per week.

2. What are the reasons that some children work and others do not?

   Salmon identifies several relationships; the following is a selected list:

   First, children are more likely to work when all adult members in the household work and when a larger proportion of these adults are paid workers. Children are perceived as the "last economic resource" of households, sent to work to increase the income potential of the household.

   Second, children are less likely to work when the mother is working in the paid labor market than when she does not work or is an unpaid family worker. This relationship varies by the gender of the child. Girls are more likely to enter the labor market when the mother works whether as an unpaid worker or wage employee. Boys are more likely to work when the mother is unpaid but less likely to work when the mother is a paid employee.

   Third, children living in a rural area or in Dhaka city are more likely to work than those living in other urban areas. In rural areas, children are less likely to work when they live in a district with a high unemployment rate, but the reverse is true in urban areas.

Source: From Salmon, C. (2005). Child labor in Bangladesh: Are children the last economic resource of the household? *Journal of Developing Societies,* 21(1–2), 33–54. Reprinted by permission of Sage Publications India Pvt. Ltd.

PART IX

CRIMINAL JUSTICE

CHAPTER 24

Crime

Michael Tonry (2005)

In this article, Michael Tonry challenges us to think about crime, not simply as a series of "bad acts" committed by "bad people," but from a holistic, sociological perspective. He examines four of the many complex dimensions of crime: criminal harms, fear, victimization, and collateral costs.

Crime is a congeries of social problems that are best thought of together but generally are not. A short list would include criminal harms, fear of crime, victimization, and collateral effects. The meanings of the first three are self-evident. By "collateral effects," I mean the unintended or incidental effects of crime and punishment on offenders, victims, and their families; their immediate communities; and the larger community.

The crime-preventive effects of punishment are a good thing, but they are purchased at a high cost in state resources and human suffering and have many unintended and undesirable consequences. Many are collateral, such as the psychological effects on children of having their mothers sent to prison or the living-standard effects of the family's loss of an imprisoned parent's income. Some are direct, such as the multiple harms done to people sent to prison and to the people who work in them as guards and in other roles. Some are indirect, such as public goods foregone when, for example, a state spends money on prison operations rather than on higher education.

This is a handbook of "social problems." It may be useful if I spell out what I mean by that term. Among many possibilities, two primary conceptions contend. The first, top-down, latches on to "social" and focuses on the processes and meanings that cause some phenomena to be characterized as problems. This is not nonsensical. Homosexuality, drug use, prostitution, or heresy are in one

sense "problems" only if that is how they are conceived, and whether and to what extent they are varies with time and place. However, that a practice such as prostitution is lawful or widely accepted as socially acceptable does not mean that it does not cause social harm. Alcohol use is an example of a lawful and socially accepted practice that nonetheless has behavioral, health, and economic consequences that are widely seen as harmful.

The second, bottom-up, conception focuses on "problems" and looks at harms or social disadvantages associated with social practices. It tries to measure them, understand their causes, and look for ways they can be eliminated, reduced, or ameliorated.

This top-down/bottom-up difference in conceptions can easily be overstated. Social problems necessarily are socially constructed. Nonetheless, for crime, at least, the bottom-up conception that begins with harms and disadvantages suffered by human beings is the more useful. Many forms of violence and takings of others' property are regarded as crimes in most societies. Focusing on them empirically and building understanding upwards sheds more light than does focusing on how and why particular behaviors come to be seen as problems.

This does not mean that the flowering of a set of harms into a "social problem" is not an important occurrence. Until recognition and description by doctors of the abused-child syndrome in the 1960s or the emergence of

244

heightened concern about violence against women in the 1970s, child and spousal abuse were regarded as small-scale problems but quickly came to be seen as vastly bigger. Whether they did become vastly bigger is an open question. Heightened attention led to creation of new reporting and data-recording systems, to changes in laws and practices in the criminal justice and social welfare systems, and to increases in the number and influence of advocacy groups.

These developments, among many other effects, led to vastly greater reporting and recording of information about possible or alleged incidents of abuse. Whether the steep increase in the 1980s and 1990s in official estimates of the number of incidents of child abuse resulted wholly from increased reporting is unknowable, but there is wide agreement that most of it did. Likewise for domestic violence. No one doubts that much of the apparent increase in the 1980s and 1990s shown by police data resulted from changes in citizen reporting and police recording of incidents.

The social construction of phenomena into social problems has important consequences. Whether or not child and spouse abuse became more common in the 1980s and 1990s, characterizing them that way led to enormous increases in political attention and investment of public resources in efforts to address them.

Nonetheless, to understand the dimensions of phenomena that are constructed into social problems, we need first to understand their prevalence and incidence. To understand crime-writ-large as a social problem, we need to see the subject whole—as criminal harms, fear, victimization, collateral effects, and state responses. Otherwise, a complicated set of interrelated harms and disadvantages disappears from view.

In the contemporary United States, for example, crime is conceived of primarily as criminal harms. This has had a number of unfortunate effects. First, crime is seen primarily as a problem caused by criminals who deliberately choose to harm others. So seen, it seems natural to focus policy responses on criminals' bad motives or characters and to punish them, and to base prevention approaches primarily on efforts to incapacitate and deter offenders. As a result, the severity of penalties and the prison population in the United States ratcheted up continuously for 30 years beginning in 1972. In most Western countries, imprisonment rates were broadly stable or grew a little during most of that period, followed by modest increases in a number of countries in the late 1990s. By 2000, the number of people in American prisons per 100,000 population (the rate was around 700 per 100,000) was 5 to 12 times higher than in other Western countries.

Second, if the crime problem is understood primarily as the immoral behavior of individuals, there is little reason to invest heavily in treatment programs. Criminals don't deserve to have their immoral behavior rewarded. And in any case, there's no reason to suppose that treatment programs will prevent crime any better than do deterrent and incapacitative strategies. As a result, rehabilitation programs withered away in prison and community settings beginning in the mid-1970s, and probation and parole redefined their core missions from treatment and support to control and surveillance. Many Western governments, especially in Germany, the Netherlands, and Scandinavia, make much larger investments in treatment and educational programs for offenders than occurs in the United States. There is ample evidence that many well-run programs can reduce future offending so the American failure to invest in them means that less crime is prevented that at reasonable expense could be and that victims and offenders both suffer unnecessarily.

Third, if crime is primarily the result of criminals' immoral choices, there's little reason to invest in crime prevention efforts outside the criminal justice system. Most Western countries, including notably Belgium, Denmark, England, France, the Netherlands, and Sweden, have established major crime prevention agencies that develop programs of developmental, community, and situational prevention. There is no comparable American agency.

Failure to invest more money and energy in prevention is unfortunate because there is substantial evidence that many developmental and situational crime prevention programs are effective. Developmental prevention programs identify factors in children's lives that put them at particular risk of becoming involved in crime, drug use, or other forms of antisocial behavior, and attempt to reduce the influence of those factors. Situational prevention programs attempt to redesign products, buildings, and processes to make them less vulnerable to crime. Cost-benefit analyses show that developmental programs in particular are considerably more cost-effective crime preventatives than are harsher punishments.

Fourth, if policymakers focus primarily on offenders, there is little reason to think about victims or others who are affected by crime and responses to it. Victims' rights and interests, for example, received little attention in the United States until the 1980s, and even today, the principal programs for victims are funded not from general government revenues, but from fines and other financial penalties paid by offenders. And programs remain much less comprehensive than in other countries. In England, for example, a state-funded program

PART IX CRIMINAL JUSTICE

called Victim Support has since the 1960s organized visits and support from volunteers for most victims of nontrivial crimes.

But other people who are affected by crime and its consequences have also been overlooked. These include offenders, who are stigmatized when they are convicted or sent to prison. Offenders sent to prison may lose their jobs or families, become socialized into deviant values, and emerge from prison with a shorter life expectancy and lower annual and lifetime earnings than other people. If a large proportion of young men are sent to prison, they aren't available as partners for young women or as workers. Partners and children are affected by what happens to offenders, and if offenders are concentrated, as they are, in particular neighborhoods, then the neighborhood will be damaged as a functioning social organism.

So, those are some reasons why, if we want to understand crime as a social problem, we need to look at it as a whole and not simply in terms of bad acts of bad people. This is not a new idea. More than 200 years ago, Jeremy Bentham, the utilitarian theorist, argued that the only justifiable policies for dealing with crime were those that minimized human suffering or maximized human satisfaction, taking everybody, including offenders, into account. He concluded that punishments cannot be justified if on balance they cause more harm than they prevent.

Criminal Harms

Crime is a pervasive phenomenon in industrialized Western societies. A core set of behaviors—killings (murders and manslaughters), inflicting significant injuries (various kinds of assaults), forcible or abusive sexual relations (rape), stealing (theft or larceny, and if by force or threat of force, robbery), serious cheating (fraud), entering property with bad motive (burglary)—is everywhere counted as serious crime. Drug dealing and trafficking are regarded as serious crimes in most places, as is procuring for prostitution. Behaviors commonly regarded as less serious crimes include shoplifting, drug use and possession, gambling, prostitution, and driving under the influence of drugs or alcohol (DUI). In this chapter, I attend almost exclusively to the core set of commonly recognized serious crimes, and I don't discuss organized crime, transnational crime, or gangs. What distinguishes these groups is not the kinds of crimes they commit—garden variety violent, property, and drug crimes mostly—but the threats that their organizations present. I also don't discuss white-collar crime or political crime.

In most Western countries, violent and property crime rates have been falling or stable from the early 1990s through the beginning of the new century. Figure 25.1 illustrates this for the United States. It is based on data collected from police departments and published by the Federal Bureau of Investigation (FBI) in the Uniform Crime Reports (UCR). It shows reported crime rates for 1960 through 2000 for murder, rape, robbery, burglary, and motor vehicle theft. Because my interest here is in crime trends rather than in absolute levels, some rates have been multiplied or divided by 10 so that they can all be shown in one figure. Rates for all offenses peaked around 1980 and again in 1990, and since then have fallen steadily.

A similar pattern, though typically with the peak slightly later, characterizes most Western countries. This can be shown using official police data from individual countries, but it is difficult to make cross-national comparisons. That is because offenses are defined differently in different countries and statistical recording systems vary substantially. Consequently, when official data from two countries are compared, it is very difficult to know whether the same things are being measured in both. To remedy this, the International Crime Victims Survey (ICVS) is administered approximately every 4 years in a sizeable and increasing number of countries. Because the ICVS uses the same questions, the same definitions of crimes, and the same data collection method in each country, it is the most credible source of comparative knowledge of victimization trends.

This section discusses the harms caused by major categories of crime and recent trends in their occurrence. Harms vary from clear and unambiguous to unclear and disputed.

The harms caused by violent crimes, and therefore why they are everywhere taken seriously, are self-evident. They cause or threaten death, pain, or sexual violation and attendant adverse consequences to their victims, and vicarious suffering for victims' loved ones.

The harms caused by property crimes are sometimes more uncertain. Many losses suffered by businesses from shoplifting or other thefts are regarded as costs of doing business and are taken into account in setting prices. A business that experiences less theft than it expected will, in a sense, receive a windfall. It has made customers pay more than they otherwise would have had theft losses not been overestimated. An insured private citizen may benefit from losing property in a theft. Many insurance policies provide "replacement cost coverage," which means that theft of a two-year-old television will result in purchase of a new one. This may provide a collateral benefit to the economy since it provides demand

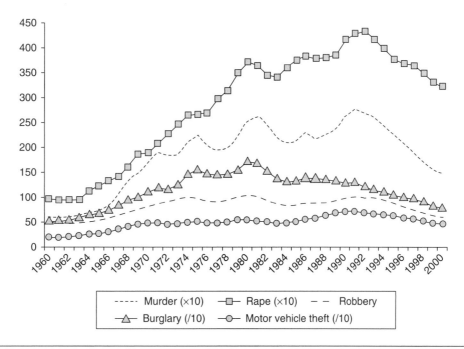

Figure 24.1 Reported Crime Rates, United States 1960–2000 (per 100,000 Population), Murder, Rape, Robbery, Burglary, and Motor Vehicle Theft

for new products, and since insurance premiums are actuarially calculated, the cost of the new television has been taken into account in setting the premium. Many victims, of course, lack insurance or have policies that make them pay part of the loss. There are also ancillary harms caused by thefts such as the inconvenience of being without something and having to take the time to replace it. Finally, thefts are unethical acts and undermine people's senses of confidence and security.

The harms caused by other crimes are even harder to characterize. For drug crimes, for example, it is hard to know whether drug use or drug law enforcement causes the greater harm. Many argue that the effects of use of drugs other than alcohol are relatively modest—some adverse health effects, some reduction in workforce participation, and some reductions in responsible parenting and citizenship—compared with the effects of drug law enforcement. Because drugs are illegal, they must be purchased from people willing to accept the risks of breaking the law, and prices are much higher as a result. Illegal drugs must be purchased under dangerous circumstances, and there are no assurances that they are what they are represented to be or that they are not contaminated. Many addicted users sell drugs, work as prostitutes, or commit burglaries or street crimes in order to buy drugs at artificially high prices. Police tactics in drug law enforcement raise difficult civil liberties questions. And the police, court,

and correctional costs of handling drug offenders in the United States total many billions of dollars. Many people, however, think of drug use primarily as a moral issue and that the kinds of costs and consequences described above are regrettable, but in the end necessary.

One last crime, DUI, illustrates why many crimes raise difficult policy dilemmas. No one questions that alcohol is much the most costly abused drug in the United States. Its abuse causes hundreds of thousands of deaths of users per year, leads to billions of dollars per year in lost economic productivity, and contributes annually to tens of thousands of motor vehicle accidents each year that lead to hundreds of thousands of injuries and 10,000 to 20,000 deaths. Yet alcohol use and sale remain legal, and the criminal justice system response is a combination of mass media consciousness-raising campaigns, small-scale mandatory jail term policies for DUI recidivists, and (usually, though not always, short) prison sentences for DUI-caused deaths. Americans clearly feel much more ambivalently toward alcohol than toward marijuana, heroin, or Ecstasy.

The differing kinds of harms that various crimes threaten illustrate why scholars study the social construction of crimes. For some kinds of property crimes, for example, plausible arguments exist that they cause relatively little economic harm, and yet they are everywhere made criminal. Conversely, plausible arguments exist that many violations of environmental laws cause very great social and economic harm, and yet they are seldom criminally prosecuted and less often result in prison sentences. The different ways the criminal law and the criminal justice system handle alcohol and marijuana provide even starker examples of how historical, economic and social class, and ideological influences shape how America addresses objectively parallel social problems.

Victimization

The data on American crime trends shown in Figure 24.1 are from the UCR that the FBI annually compiles. The FBI data have been available since the late 1920s. There are, however, a number of well-known problems with police data. They are underinclusive. Many crimes are never reported to the police, often because they are not serious or because victims believe the police can do nothing about them. Some crimes are reported to the police, but they do not enter the FBI data because the police do not record them; sometimes because they don't believe the crime occurred; sometimes because they don't think it was serious; and sometimes for reasons of inefficiency or official policy.

Victimization surveys were invented in the 1960s to serve as a second source of crime trends and to learn about crimes that are either not reported to the police or are not recorded by them. Since 1973, the U.S. Bureau of the Census, on behalf of the U.S. Bureau of Justice Statistics (BJS), has surveyed 40,000 to 60,000 households every six months to learn about crimes committed against household members. The sample of households is selected so that it is representative of the overall U.S. population. The survey is called the National Crime Victimization Survey (NCVS).

Police data on recorded crimes and victimization data are not exactly different measures of the same thing. Partly this is because many events that people consider crime victimizations are never reported to the police. More important, though, it is because many crimes do not have easily identifiable individual victims. This is true not only of white-collar and organized crime but also of drug crimes, many "morals" crimes (prostitution, illegal gambling, pornography), traffic crimes, and vandalism. Such actions are defined as crimes because legislators believe they cause damage to the community. In addition, businesses are the victims of many property crimes, including shoplifting, burglary, and embezzlement. Not having individual victims, none of these categories of crime are measured by victimization surveys.

Figure 24.2 shows NCVS victimization rates for six crimes for the period 1980 through 2000. As in Figure 24.1, some rates have been divided by 10 so they can all be shown in one figure. The patterns parallel those from UCR data shown in Figure 24.1. Reported victimization for all six offenses declined from around the early to mid-1990s, some from peaks (e.g., auto theft and assault), and others as extensions of long-term downward trends (e.g., rape, burglary, theft).

Victimization surveys can be done in many ways, including face-to-face interviews, telephone interviews, Internet questionnaires, and self-completed paper questionnaires. Each has advantages and disadvantages. In the NCVS, most interviews are face-to-face or by telephone. In the ICVS, most are by telephone.

Having one-on-one encounters, whether in person or over the phone, provides the opportunity to ask not only about crime but also about other subjects. The NCVS confines its questions to crime victimization and very closely related subjects, such as fear of crime and whether and why crimes are reported to the police. The ICVS and the British Crime Survey (BCS), the largest national victimization survey outside the United States, ask questions about a much wider range of subjects, including confidence in the police, courts, and other agencies; opinions about sentencing; and actions taken to prevent crime, such as installation of burglar alarms, staying in at night, and other self-protective measures. The next section discusses fear of crime. This one mentions a few other findings.

First, the BCS and the NCVS show that crime victimization is not equally spread. In English-speaking countries, men are more likely to be victimized by crime than are women, blacks than whites, Hispanics than non-Hispanics, and city dwellers than suburbanites and people living in small towns and rural areas. These patterns hold true overall and are even more pronounced for violent crimes.

Second, victimization is not randomly distributed by age. Both for violent crime and for theft, the most common property crime, in the United States, 16- to 19-year-olds have the highest victimization rates, followed by 12- to 15-year-olds and 20- to 24-year-olds.

The elderly, though the group most fearful about crime, have much the lowest likelihood of victimization.

Third, there are pronounced income patterns in crime victimization. Victimization risks are inversely correlated with income. The NCVS, for example, divides its respondents into seven household income bands from under $7,000 to over $75,000. The risk of violent crime

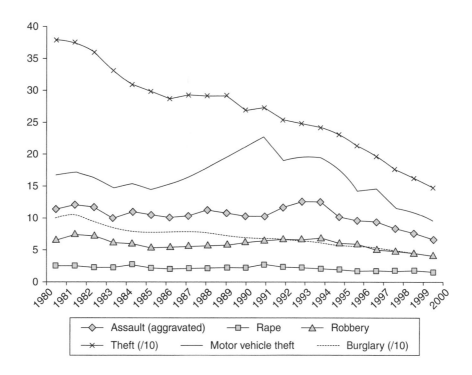

Figure 24.2   NCVS Crime Estimates, 1980–2000

victimization is highest for the lowest-income group and drops successively in each higher band. The violent risk for the lowest income group (7 percent are victimized) is 2.5 times that of the highest group (3 percent). For theft, victimization rates are highest for the lowest-income group and then decrease through the fifth group, after which they stabilize.

Fourth, approximately half of all crimes are reported to the police. Though the broad patterns of findings from all representative victimization surveys are similar, I use ICVS results for illustration. Results from a 1996 survey of 11 industrialized countries showed that, on average, 50 percent of victimizations were reported to the police. Swedish and Swiss respondents were at the high end, reporting 57 to 58 percent of victimizations to the police, and France and Northern Ireland were at the low end, reporting 47 to 48 percent. There were three principal reasons why crimes were not reported. Much the most common was that the crime wasn't serious enough or nothing was lost. The second most common was that people "solved it themselves" or it was otherwise just not appropriate to call the police. The third was that the "police could do nothing." The three most common reasons for not reporting in the United States in 2001 were similar: "reported to another [that is, not police] official," "private or personal matter," "object recovered; offender unsuccessful," and "not important enough."

American crime reporting rates are somewhat lower. In 2001, NCVS respondents indicated that they had reported 49 percent of violent crimes to the police and 37 percent of property crimes. Ordinary theft was the least likely crime to be reported (30 percent of the time), and auto theft the most likely (82 percent). Violent crimes, depending on what they were, were reported to the police 40 to 55 percent of the time.

Fear

Fear of crime in recent decades has worried policymakers almost as much as crime itself. There are several reasons for this. First, public opinion research in the 1990s showed that fear of crime remained high even though crime rates fell steadily. Ordinary citizens cannot be presumed to know much about crime statistics, but in the 1990s, the decline in crime rates was so great and received so much attention in both newspapers and television news shows that few people could not have heard. Why might fear of crime have remained persistently high? One reason might be that rates, though lower, remained above some absolute level that causes widespread fear. Another might be that politicians often in the 1980s and 1990s ran on "tough on crime" platforms, and the campaigning and related media attention created a false impression of a growing crime problem in people's minds. Whatever the reason, if citizens are fearful, policymakers are concerned that voters will hold them responsible.

A second reason why policymakers worry about high levels of fear of crime is that it weakens neighborhoods and communities. If people are fearful, they won't go out as often or at particular times, for example, at night. If they are fearful in the communities where they live, they are likely to go elsewhere for recreation and shopping, and their own neighborhoods will deteriorate.

Researchers evaluating police-patrolling experiments in the 1970s (police in cars versus on foot, one-versus two-officer police cars, high-visibility versus low-visibility patrolling) found that most of the experiments had no effects on crime rates but that more visible policing, especially foot patrol, reduced fear of crime. If fear of crime undermines communities and neighborhoods, the lesson was that more visible policing will reduce fear and some of the time, at least, strengthen neighborhoods.

The NCVS does not devote much attention to fear of crime. The closest proxy questions ask people whether they believe crime is increasing, decreasing, or staying about the same. People who think crime is getting worse will be more likely to be fearful, or to be more fearful, than people who think crime is decreasing. The Gallup Poll asked a representative sample of Americans this in 2001, when American crime rates had been falling for a decade. Overall, 41 percent thought crime rates higher, and 43 percent thought them lower. The breakdowns, however, are striking. Women (49 percent) were much more likely than men (33 percent) to think crime rates were higher, blacks (56 percent) than whites (40 percent), high school dropouts (54 percent) than people with graduate training (16 percent), and people who earned less than $20,000 (57 percent) than people who earned more than $75,000 (24 percent). The ICVS shows the same patterns in other countries.

Fear is based on information, whether true or false, and therefore often on stereotypes. People know about society in general from the mass media but know about their own communities and neighborhoods from personal experience. One consequence is that we tend to think things are worse elsewhere than where we live. In 2001, for example, a representative sample of Americans was asked whether crime nationally was better, worse, or about the same. Forty-one percent said there was more crime, 43 percent said there was less, and 10 percent said about the same. When the same question was asked about "your own area," 26 percent said there was more crime, 52 percent said there was less, and 18 percent said it was about the same.

The ICVS asks more questions about fear than does the NCVS. Its data offer a fuller picture. There are substantial national differences in the pervasiveness of fear of crime. In the most recent (2000) survey, 35 percent of respondents from Poland and Australia said they felt unsafe on streets in their neighborhoods at night, compared with around 15 percent in Canada, Sweden, and the United States. The average rate for 16 countries was 23 percent. The cross-national fear-of-crime findings on men versus women, majority versus minority residents, and rural versus urban respondents parallel those for the NCVS. Probably not surprisingly, people who have been victims of violence or of burglary are more fearful on the streets and at home than are people who have not been victims.

Victims' Burdens

Only in the past 30 years have collateral effects of crime and punishment received much attention from policymakers, researchers, and policy analysts. State systems of prosecution, trial, and punishment began to take shape hundreds of years ago, in part to bring crime within the province of the organized state and thereby to forestall vigilantism and private revenge. Crimes came to be seen as offenses against the state. The victim might have an important role to play as witness, but the legal action set the state against the defendant. A widespread conceptualization formed that the fundamental issue in a criminal case is whether the state can satisfactorily demonstrate, usually by proof beyond a reasonable doubt, that the defendant committed a crime and accordingly that the state has authority to deprive him of life, liberty, or property.

That image, though it is fundamentally important in a society that values individual liberty, does not allow much of a role for the victim. As a result, few governments had programs to help victims of crime deal with physical, emotional, and financial consequences of their victimization. Because the trial pitted the state against the defendant, pretrial procedures and trials were organized around the interests and convenience of the lawyers and the defendant. Thus, if the trial were continued many times, the victim might time after time take a day off work to testify at a trial only to find that it had been rescheduled. Similarly, because the victim was not a party to the prosecution, courts generally lacked authority to order offenders to pay restitution to victims.

To remedy these things, beginning in the 1970s, a number of initiatives occurred. Initially in a small number of American jurisdictions, but by the 1990s in most jurisdictions, courts and prosecutors established victim and witness offices. Their job was to help victims understand the court process, notify them when they had to appear in court and of changes in schedule, and sometimes to help arrange transportation to the courthouse.

By the early 1980s, the "victims rights" movement took shape and pressed a variety of claims: for victim restitution as part of the offender's sentence, for a right to testify in trials and sentencing and parole hearings, for the preparation of a "victim impact statement" in every case, for a right to be notified when "their" offender had a release hearing or was released, and eventually for enactment of a "Victim's Bill of Rights" as an amendment to the U.S. Constitution. The constitutional amendment never passed, but many states enacted victims' bills of rights and established many of the proposed victims' policies.

The federal Victims of Crime Act passed in 1984 and set up a Federal Crime Victims Fund that receives moneys paid by federal offenders as fines and as explicit victim compensation penalties. It also receives money forfeited by federal offenders, and, as many white-collar and drug defendants forfeit large amounts, the fund in the 1990s contained hundreds of millions of dollars. Much of this is paid out to states according to formulas and is supposed to be spent to fund state programs that address crime victims' needs. Otherwise, crime victims receive only whatever services and funds are available under general state and federal welfare programs. These are typically not generous in the United States, and crime victims are treated no better than anyone else who qualifies for help.

Victims of crime in other countries benefit both from state-funded services and support, such as that provided by England's Victim Support, and also from general state welfare and medical programs. As these are typically more generous and better funded than such programs in the United States, victims in other Western countries are better treated.

Crime causes emotional and physical suffering for victims. It also imposes financial costs, including lost earnings, out-of-pocket expenditures for medical and mental health care, the value of lost money or property, and costs of replacement and repair of lost or damaged property. Some efforts have been made to estimate these things, among other costs of crime and punishment. I discuss this in the next section.

Collateral Costs

A cost-benefit literature on the costs of crime emerged in the 1980s. Much imagination was invested in calculating the costs of crime and the criminal justice system, but no one thought to take the offender and his costs and suffering into account. The principal aim was to calculate whether "prison works" in the sense that the economic value of crimes prevented through locking people up outweighed the costs of operating the criminal justice system, including the prisons.

The earliest article, by Edwin Zedlewski of the U.S. National Institute of Justice, concluded that for one average prisoner, "A year in prison [at] total social costs of $25,000" would produce a saving of "$430,000 in [reduced] crime costs." Zedlewski assumed that each person locked up would commit 173 crimes per year if at liberty. His article provoked a fierce response. Should the costs of the police be included in the calculation, since every society has a police force? Should crime prevention costs, from burglar alarms to private security firms' fees, be included? Were the estimates of the numbers of crimes prevented per locked-up offender accurate or even remotely plausible? Should both incapacitative and deterrent effects be predicted, or only incapacitative effects?

Gradually, over time, the estimation techniques improved, and general agreements were reached about what should be taken into account. The most striking development, and the most influential, was a series of estimates of victims' direct out-of-pocket expenses, their pain and suffering, and their risk of death that were provided by economist Mark Cohen. For most crimes, the intangible costs of pain and suffering and risk of death far outweighed out-of-pocket costs. For rape, direct costs totaled $4,617, intangible costs $46,441. For personal robbery, direct costs totaled $1,114, intangible costs $11,480; for assault, it was $422 and $11,606. Cohen developed these estimates by adapting data from jury awards in tort (accident) cases and applying them to economic analyses of crime.

This was a cockamamie thing to do. Only very serious accidents result in jury awards (most are settled), and he was thus using data on the most serious accidents to estimate the costs of average crimes. Jury awards are inflated to include attorneys' fees (a third to a half of the total). Cohen's inflated estimates, however, soon became widely used. This is probably because they were the only ones around.

Whether Cohen's estimates are plausible, however, is not the point. What is important is what is missing. Nowhere in this literature, including even in vigorous critiques of its quality and value, did anyone take account of offenders. A prison sentence entails pain and suffering by the offender. During the period behind walls, he is denied liberty, deprived of the company of loved ones, and exposed to the dangers and degradations of prison life. When he is released, he will be stigmatized and face numerous obstacles to resuming a normal life. These range from ineligibility for many professions, inability to vote, and employer resistance to employing ex-cons. He will after prison have lower life chances, life expectancy, and lifetime earnings than if he'd not spent time in prison. His family also will have suffered, economically, socially, and psychologically, if it survived intact.

Social scientists did little better than economists in relation to the effects of punishment on offenders. My 1995 *Malign Neglect* was one of the first calls for attention to collateral effects of imprisonment for prisoners, their families, and their communities. When, in 1997, I commissioned an essay from John Hagan and Robin Dinovitzer on the collateral effects of punishment, they had to report that the literature was fragmentary and fugitive, though they did their best to pull it together. On many important subjects—for examples, the effects of a parent's imprisonment on children's development and well-being or the effects of imprisonment on offenders' later health and life expectancy—there was no respectable social science literature. The inattention is beginning to end, and work is beginning to appear on the effects of imprisonment on prisoners' communities and on collateral costs more generally.

Social workers and health care workers, of course, have long known about the collateral effects of imprisonment for prisoners and their families. When parents who formerly supported the family go to prison, families must often apply for food stamps and income support. When caregivers, usually mothers, go to prison, child care agencies must arrange foster care or placements with responsible relatives. When children raised in broken and impoverished homes fail in school, participate in gangs or drug abuse, and manifest mental health problems, state agencies must respond. Such consequences were known and, however inadequately, addressed by care providers, however little systematic attention they received from academics.

First, both quantitative and qualitative literatures show that imprisonment reduces offenders' job prospects and their average and lifetime earnings. Insofar as ex-prisoners support partners and children, they too experience reduced standards of living and often lesser life chances than they would otherwise have had. Reduced job prospects should be no surprise. Prisoners lose their jobs when they go to prison. When they come out, they bear the stigma of being ex-cons and find that many employers do not want to hire them at all, or only for low-pay dead-end jobs. Self-esteem and self-confidence plummet for many, and planning for the future becomes difficult. That family break-up, social failure, and mental health problems follow should be no surprise. These in their turn make prospects of good jobs and good earnings worse.

Second, as sociologist William Julius Wilson showed, though few researchers have followed this up, imprisonment impedes family formation and thereby undermines communities and increases the number of children raised in disadvantaged single-parent families. Wilson calculated, from census data, the number of "marriageable males" per 100 women of the same age and race in urban neighborhoods. By this, he meant employed men. He learned that the number of marriageable (employed) young black men for every 100 young black women had declined steadily throughout the 1970s and 1980s and was lowest for young blacks among all age-and-race combinations. A principal reason for this is that since the late 1980s, nearly a third of young black men are at any time in prison or jail or on probation or parole. In other words, because so many more black men were sent to prison in the 1970s and 1980s and suffered the stigma of being ex-convicts afterwards, there were simply fewer attractive potential marriage partners around for young urban black women than in earlier times. Chances of formation of two-parent families declined.

Third, sociologist Todd Clear and others have studied the effects on communities when large numbers of young men are removed and sent to prison. Clear found something surprising. That removal of young men reduces the number of potential partners for women and reduces the number of potential workers is not surprising. What Clear and his colleagues found, and more recently Jeffrey Fagan has confirmed, is that sending many young men to prison increases crime rates in the community. To laypeople, this should be counterintuitive. After all, people are sent to prison because they have committed crimes, so surely removal of criminals from a community should decrease crime rates. Instead, what Clear and colleagues and Fagan found, was that neighborhoods from which very large numbers of offenders were sent to prison experienced higher crime rates. The reasons were that removal of so many young men fundamentally undermined community cohesion—things fell apart—and that above some critical number, men who amass criminal records become positive role models for youth when there are so few or no conventional role models at all. Stating the last point differently, when many or most men in a community acquire prison records, going to prison stops being stigmatizing and prison stops serving even potentially as a deterrent to crime. Crime rates rise in a community as a result.

Fourth, in the United States, a country in which many millions of people have been convicted of felonies, disenfranchisement laws have greatly reduced voting and other participation in democratic and economic institutions. These laws vary from state to state. In some, people are barred from voting while in prison. In others, though, they are barred if they've ever had a felony conviction. Thus, in the 2000 presidential election in Florida, which George Bush won by a whisker, hundreds of thousands of state residents, mostly black men, were unable to vote because of their felony convictions. Demographic voting patterns (black people and poorer people tend to vote for Democrats) suggest that Bush would have lost the Florida election and therefore the presidency if Florida had not had a felon disenfranchisement law.

Felons, however, are in many states disqualified from other activities open to other citizens. These include occupational exclusion laws that forbid felons from becoming lawyers, barbers, or teachers. And they include laws that make felons ineligible for some educational and social service benefits. And federal law makes many felons who are immigrants vulnerable to deportation.

Conclusions

Crime thus is not one social problem, but many. In this chapter, I have identified and discussed some of the effects of crime that most people would consider social problems. These include the suffering, economic costs, and undesirable collateral effects of crime for victims, offenders, and communities. That is phrased in general terms. When we become more specific, hundreds of social problems appear that warrant analysis, understanding, and policy solutions. Most of them damage people's lives in ways that could be avoided or ameliorated. The life chances of children are diminished when they lose their parents or when their material conditions of life greatly worsen. The life expectancies of adults are lessened when, because they are ex-prisoners, they cannot get good jobs or earn adequate incomes, and because of that their self-esteem and hopes for the future plummet, and with that their mental and physical health.

There are many ways to address social problems associated with crime. One is to establish policies and programs aimed at remedying direct and collateral effects of crime.

Victims' programs, social work programs aimed at disadvantaged households and at-risk children, and parenting skills programs in prison exemplify the wide range of possible remedies. Or we can reduce the intrusiveness and severity of American crime and drug control policies and thereby make many of the collateral effects of crime less common and less likely.

Discussion Questions

1. What are the consequences of conceiving crime primarily as criminal harms perpetrated by immoral individuals?

   Policy responses focus on criminal behavior or motives, punishment, and base prevention on incapacitating and deterring offenders. The U.S. prison population has increased since 1972. There is little or no investment in treatment or rehabilitation programs, prevention efforts outside of the criminal justice system, or prisoner rights organizations.

2. Tonry argues for the importance of analyzing crime as a whole, examining fear, victims' burdens, and collateral costs in addition to criminal harms. Select and review two of these aspects and explain how it relates to crime as a social problem.

   Students should reflect on the fact that crime is not simply a single social problem and discuss the ways that fear, victims' burdens, and collateral costs are aspects of crime that affect victims, offenders, and communities.

Source: From Tonry, M. (2005). Crime. In G. Ritzer (Ed.), *Handbook of social problems: A comparative international perspective* (pp. 465–477). Thousand, Oaks, CA: Sage. Reprinted by permission of Sage Publications.

CHAPTER 25

Prison Health and the Health of the Public

Ties That Bind

Natasha H. Williams (2007)

Nearly 2.2 million men and women in the United States today are incarcerated. Natasha Williams takes a hard look at the U.S. prison system, focusing specifically on the health status of prisoners and the quality of health care provided by the U.S. criminal justice system. She contends that "the disparities experienced by individuals in U.S. jails and prison reflect the human and social consequences of political policies and cultural biases" and documents the disproportionate impact of these policies on racial-ethnic and minority communities.

Introduction: A Hard Look at the Health of Our Prisoners

The word "genocide" evokes images of horrors in other lands—of the Holocaust or deaths in Bosnia, Rwanda, and now, Darfur. All too often, in the aftermath of these atrocities, voices the world over will condemn the sluggish responses that allowed killing fields or gas chambers, the inattention or the apathy that ultimately permitted "deliberate and systematic destruction of a racial, political, or cultural group" (*Merriam-Webster Online Dictionary*, www.m-w.com).

In our nation, the sad saga of the Trail of Tears is an example of systematic destruction closer to home. The forced removal of Cherokee Indians from their North Carolina home-lands in 1838, and the attendant condemnation to illness and poverty and premature death, did not happen by chance. Laws were enacted, public policies enforced, and resources committed—even here, in the "land of the free." And however mindful we may be in the 21st century of the cruelty and injustice of the past, the people lost and families destroyed will never be recovered.

The best we can hope for is that understanding the consequences of past errors will prevent similar catastrophes—that the overwhelming shame and sadness engendered by genocidal policies will rouse us to demand respect for humanity from our leaders and governments.

Yet when we consider the plight of prisoners in the U.S. criminal justice system, the world could rightly question how well we have learned from the mistaken paths of our history. Nearly 2.2 million men and women are incarcerated in prisons and jails in the United States (Harrison & Beck, 2006). Many convicted of crimes in this country enter their cells infected with HIV/AIDS, hepatitis, or tuberculosis. Many more suffer from undiagnosed or untreated mental illness. Oftentimes, prisoners have poor oral health, dental cavities, and gum disease. And a great many live with chronic conditions, especially diabetes and hypertension. A growing body of evidence points to levels of ill health and inadequate treatment that suggest a willful disregard of prisoners' basic human rights. Whatever the length of individual sentences, taken as a group, prisoners are more likely to suffer serious illness and premature death. And those risks are compounded by the many systemic barriers to receiving needed health services once they are released.

At present, health care provided in the prisons across the United States varies greatly. Although standards of care for inmates are promulgated by the National Commission on Correctional Health Care (NCCHC) and other organizations, as well as various government agencies, compliance with these standards is voluntary and no one set of standards is universally accepted. Dr. Robert Greifinger, a health care policy and quality management consultant, notes a range of health programs that spans those "considered excellent to those that are shameful, not only in terms of what we do to the individuals but shameful in terms of the risks we expose our staff to and the risks to the public's health" (Commission on Safety and Abuse in America's Prisons, 2006, p. 38).

In general, overcrowded conditions and lack of resources to deliver adequate care aggravate prisoners' existing medical conditions. Chronic illnesses such as hypertension, diabetes, asthma, and heart disease require regular monitoring and consistent care to keep the diseases from escalating to crisis levels. Poor oral health can complicate and compound the ill effects of diabetes and cardiovascular disease (Treadwell & Formicola, 2005). With longer prison sentences, more men and women are growing old in prisons and developing the diseases of the elderly (respiratory illness, Alzheimer's disease, cardiovascular disease, arthritis, ulcer disease, mental health problems, and cancer). And as prevalent as these conditions are in the general inmate population, they appear to be more concentrated among older prisoners (Anno, Graham, Lawrence, & Shansky, 2004).

Once released, many former prisoners have no access to health insurance and thus no entrée to health services. Added to that, ex-offenders often return to the communities with the fewest resources—cities, towns, and neighborhoods that are already poor, overburdened, and with limited health resources. The effect is to exacerbate health disparities already present. And the implications for public health cannot be walled off or isolated to particular communities or neighborhoods. On the contrary, the unmet health needs of people in jails and prisons can threaten the well-being of their families, communities, and society as a whole. In a worst-case scenario, untreated or overlooked illness in a prison population can expose whole communities to the risk of epidemic. As an example, a multidrug resistant strain of tuberculosis that surfaced in New York City in 1989 was linked to inadequate treatment in prisons and jails (Commission on Safety and Abuse in America's Prisons, 2006; Mauer, 1999; NCCHC, 2002).

It also appears that the network of relationships interrupted by incarceration may be the conduit for ready transmission of diseases and conditions prevalent in prisons when prisoners are released. Many correlate the catastrophic rise in HIV cases among African American women with the return of HIV-positive men after release from prison (Adimora, Schoenbach, & Doherty, 2006; Clemetson, 2004). While incarcerated, inmates may engage in high-risk sexual behavior either consensually or by force. When they return to their communities, ex-offenders often resume relationships and unwittingly "bridge lower-risk community partners to higher-risk contacts developed in prison" (Adimora et al., 2006, p. S44).

Dire examples like these represent tangible health threats we can measure, track, and document. Less well understood are the intangible effects of inadequate health care on prisoners and their loved ones or on the way poor health translates into fewer options for employment and for productive contributions to family life and community. As we take an unflinching look at the current prison population, its health status, and the implications for public policies, let us keep in mind that men and women confined to prisons and jails are not held in a vacuum. Even under lock and key, they remain parents, husbands, wives, daughters, sons, and neighbors who will return to their homes once released. As such, their health is inextricably linked to the health of our society.

The People in Our Prisons and Jails

At the end of 2005, nearly 2.2 million men and women were incarcerated in jails and prisons in the United States—the rough equivalent of one out of every 136 U.S. residents. Of those inmates sentenced to at least 1 year in prison, 547,200 were African American males; this represents 40% of this population, compared with 35% for Whites and 20% for Hispanics. Moreover, African American males aged 25 to 29 years had the highest incarceration rate when compared with other racial and ethnic groups. In 2005, 8.1% of African American males in this age group were incarcerated compared with 2.6% Hispanic and 1.1% White (Harrison & Beck, 2006).

The same data show that women represented 7% of all prisoners, an increase from 6.1% in 1995. Even so, men were at least 14 times more likely than women to be incarcerated in state and federal prisons. And racial and ethnic disparities appear to be consistent among both women and men. Data indicate that African American women are more than twice as likely as Hispanic females to be imprisoned and three times as likely as White women (Harrison & Beck, 2006).

Rather than mirroring the general population, the proportion of people of color in U.S. prisons and jails mirrors economic and educational disparities in society as a whole. Many did not follow the path to prison of their own volition; they were pushed onto this pathway (Williams, 2006). But the ripple effect on communities economically and socially is significant, in particular because many of those in prisons are parents.

In 1999, more than 700,000 people incarcerated in state and federal prisons were parents. Data from 1997 indicate that before incarceration, more than 70% in both state (70.9%) and federal (73.5%) prisons were employed, taxpaying citizens. These wage-earning men and women were parents to at least 1.5 million minor children, most of them (58%) younger than the age of 10 with an average age of 8 (Mumola, 2000).

Looked at another way, these data indicate that only 2% of the 72 million children in the United States had an incarcerated parent. Yet according to analysis by the Bureau of Justice Statistics, "Black children were nearly nine times more likely to have a parent in prison than white children and Hispanic children were three times as likely as white children to have an inmate parent" (Mumola, 2000, p. 2). Unfortunately, that is where available data about incarceration and families end. At present there is limited research exploring how having a parent in prison might affect children—their mental health, their resilience, or their future well-being—and in particular their potential for incarceration themselves (Travis & Waul, 2003).

A trend toward more punitive practices in criminal justice—including mandatory sentencing, increased sentences for drug offenses, and the elimination of parole by many states—has resulted in inmates serving longer sentences and beginning to grow older in prison. Between 1992 and 2001, the number of inmates aged 50 years or older increased 172.6%, representing almost 8% of the prison population in 2001 (Anno et al., 2004). This graying of the prison population impacts both health care needs and possibilities for resocialization. As with the general population, the prevalence of chronic diseases associated with aging (such as diabetes, heart disease, and hypertension) increases among inmates, as well. In addition, extended separation from home makes it almost impossible for ex-offenders to reestablish meaningful relationships with family, children, and community.

Lack of health insurance after release compounds health consequences for the prison population. Because the United States does not guarantee coverage for the poor and unemployed or underemployed, many of these individuals face limited health care options. For example, a person working a low- or minimum-wage job with no insurance may not be able to sit in an emergency room for hours to wait to be seen by a physician. For the hourly worker, time is money and most cannot afford to sacrifice those precious hours of pay. Missed hours of work represent food, clothing, and housing—essentials for survival for the workers and their families. Moreover, some jobs may not allow employees to take time off for medical care, forcing the low-wage ex-offender to choose between health and a paycheck.

The inability to secure or maintain a job because of health issues may set in motion a sequence of events that leads back to prison. Unable to find employment, get housing, pay for medication, and reestablish family and community relationships, an individual may opt to return to the activities that led to confinement, thus perpetuating a vicious cycle of incarceration and release. The effect is to create a population of people condemned to either hardscrabble existence or repeated sentences. Resources must be provided to those reentering society through prerelease planning and once they return home to eradicate this destructive cycle.

More Prisoners, More Serious Health Care Needs

The U.S. domestic war on drugs had a staggering effect on the prison system from the 1980s onward. Between 1986 and 1991, the number of state prison inmates incarcerated for drug offenses rose from 9% to 21%. In the federal system, the drug offender population rose from 25% in 1980 to 61% in 1993. Overall, the state and federal prison population increased from 329,821 in 1980 to a stunning 1,053,738 in 1994 (Brown, 1997).

During this period, disparities in who went to prison and for how long became more pronounced. Whereas the number of White inmates increased 163% from 1980 to 1993, the roll of Black prisoners increased by 217% (Brown, 1997). Once arrested, African Americans served longer sentences than their White counterparts, with the average sentence for an African American drug offender in federal court at 89 months compared with that of a White offender at 70 months (Cole & Littman, 1997).

With increased incarceration of drug offenders came prison overcrowding and exposure to HIV and tuberculosis. The extensive health care needs of the swollen prison population dealt a heavy blow to prison health care systems across the nation. As the infection rates of HIV/AIDS, tuberculosis, and other diseases increased among the inmate population, the cost of intensive health care services also increased. The U.S. Department of Justice reported that state prisons spent $3.3 billion on inmate medical care in 2001, a 34% increase over 1996 (Stephan, 1999, 2004).

COMMUNICABLE AND CHRONIC DISEASES

The prevalence of communicable and chronic diseases among prisoners during incarceration and upon release is one way to gauge the extent of unmet health care needs. In 1997, approximately 107,000 to 137,000 incarcerated individuals had at least one sexually transmitted disease—syphilis, gonorrhea, or chlamydia—and among those released were an estimated 465,000 cases. Moreover, 36,000 inmates had hepatitis B, more than 300,000 had hepatitis C, and 130,000 had latent tuberculosis infection. Of prisoners released in 1996, 155,000 had hepatitis B infection, 1.4 million were infected with hepatitis C, and 566,000 had latent tuberculosis infection. In addition, 8.5% of inmates suffered from asthma, an estimated 4.8% from diabetes, and more than 18% from hypertension (NCCHC, 2002). Inmates with infectious diseases pose a risk not only to themselves but also to other inmates, correctional personnel, and their families when they return home (Commission on Safety and Abuse in America's Prisons, 2006).

Failure to provide prisoners with comprehensive medical care fuels public health crises both inside and outside of the correctional facility. Because inmates with chronic diseases are in poor health, lack health insurance, and generally do not have a continuum of care upon release, the correctional facility has the opportunity to provide health care that will stabilize and treat the inmate's condition before release. As researchers have concluded, "It is time for public health to go to jail" (Community Voices, 2005, p. 10).

ORAL HEALTH

The people incarcerated at disproportionately high levels are also those most often in need of oral health care. In the general population, African Americans, Hispanics, and Native Americans are less likely to have visited a dentist within the past year and more likely to have untreated dental caries than their White counterparts; African American males also have the highest incidence of oral and pharyngeal cancer (Satcher, 2003). In prison, the same

conditions prevail: Whites had fewer decayed teeth than Black inmates. The number of missing teeth increased with age (Mixon, Eplee, Feil, Jones, & Rico, 1990).

Unfortunately, having missing teeth is becoming a telltale sign of having been incarcerated. Poor oral health has serious health implications leading to nutritional problems and complicating chronic conditions such as diabetes, cardiovascular disease, and oral cancers. Equally important, poor oral health constrains social, professional, and personal relationships. A person with missing teeth or in poor oral health is less likely to be hired for a job. And for someone ill or in pain from a cavity, impacted tooth, or oral cancer, searching for a job is almost impossible. Though no direct correlative studies have been conducted, African American men have the highest death rate from oral cancer (Ahluwalia, Ro, Erwin, & Treadwell, 2005).

HIV/AIDS

In 2004, an estimated 23,046 people incarcerated in state and federal prisons were known to be infected with HIV. Of known cases, 21,366 state inmates and 1,680 federal inmates were HIV positive. In addition, there were 5,483 confirmed AIDS cases among inmates, with 4,842 in state prisons and 641 in federal prisons. The rate of confirmed AIDS among the prison population was 3 times higher than in the U.S. general population. In state prisons, 2.6% of all females were HIV positive compared with 1.8% of males (Maruschak, 2006).

Equally disconcerting is that people in prisons are more likely to die of AIDS than other Americans: Their rate is 1.5 times that of the general population between the ages of 15 and 54 in 2003. Maruschak (2006) estimates that among prisoners, 1 in 13 deaths could be traced to AIDS-related causes; in the general population, the figure would be closer to 1 in 23. At least two thirds of AIDS-related deaths were among Black inmates. In fact, Maruschak (2006) found that Black inmates in state prisons were about "2½ times more likely than Whites and 5 times more likely than Hispanics to die from AIDS-related causes" (p. 9).

These estimates may be low: In a 1996 report, only a handful of U.S. state and federal prison systems conducted mandatory screening of inmates (Braithwaite, Hammett, & Mayberry, 1996). But inmates clearly have higher rates of HIV/AIDS than the general population and a greater likelihood of dying from the disease—a stark reality seldom remarked on by public health officials, the public, or policymakers. Yet understanding what we now do about how to manage HIV/AIDS as a chronic illness, the death rate of prisoners is unnecessarily high and brings to light disparities between care inside of prison walls and in society as a whole.

To reverse this trend, prisoners need a continuum of care and counseling not only while they are incarcerated but also once they return home. Because many releasees do not have insurance or Medicaid coverage (reinstitution of their benefits can take weeks to months—if they are eligible at all), they do not have medical care or medication. Prerelease planning to manage HIV/AIDS could ensure that networks for payment and facilitated access to services be in place before an individual's return to the community. Outreach workers collaborating with parole and/or probation officers could mediate this process.

MENTAL HEALTH

Incarcerated people suffer from many mental health conditions. Data from 1997 indicate that inmates in state prisons had comparatively high rates of schizophrenia and another psychotic disorder (2% to 4%), anxiety disorder (22% to 30%), posttraumatic stress disorder (6% to 12%), major depression (13% to 19%), bipolar disorder (2% to 5%), and dysthymic disorder or chronic low-grade depression (8% to 14%). In federal facilities, the prevalence of these mental health conditions is lower, with approximately 2.5% suffering from schizophrenia or another psychotic disorder, 13% to 16% with major depression, 1% to 3% with bipolar disorder, 6% to 12% with dysthymia, 18% to 23% with an anxiety disorder, and 4% to 7% with posttraumatic stress disorder. Of inmates in jails, approximately 1% had schizophrenia or another psychotic disorder, 8% to 15% had major depression, 1% to 3% bipolar disorder, 2% to 4% dysthymia, 14% to 20% an anxiety disorder, and 4% to 9% posttraumatic stress disorder (NCCHC, 2002).

More recently, James and Glaze (2006) cite Bureau of Justice Statistics from 2005 indicating that more than 50% of all people in U.S. prisons and jails suffered from a mental health problem (psychotic disorders, major depression, and other conditions)—specifically, 705,600 inmates in state prisons (56%), 70,200 in federal prisons (45%), and 479,900 in local jails (64%). White inmates were more likely to have diagnosed mental health problems than Black or Hispanic inmates (among state prison inmates: 62% White, 55% Black, 46% Hispanic; among jail inmates: 71% White, 63% Black, 51% Hispanic).

Even though males have higher incarceration rates than females, incarcerated women have higher rates of mental illness than their male counterparts—in state prisons (73% of females compared to 55% of males), federal prisons (61% of females compared to 44% of males), and local jails (75% of females compared to 63% of males). Of women with mental health problems in state prisons, 68% reported past physical and sexual abuse (James & Glaze, 2006).

Many inmates with mental problems also have a co-occurring disorder of substance abuse. James and Glaze (2006) found that 63% of state prisoners with a mental health problem also used drugs in the month before their arrest. In general, rates of alcohol or drug abuse and dependence are high, with local jail inmates at 76%, state prisoners at 74%, and federal prisoners at 64%. Because many people self-medicate with marijuana, hashish, and alcohol, data also suggest that rates of substance use among inmates with mental health problems were high in the month before an offense; specifically, 46% among state prisoners, 41% among federal prisoners, and 43% among jail inmates. In addition, about 43% of state prisoners, 38% of federal prisoners, and 48% of jail inmates indicated they had participated in binge drinking in the past. Inmates with mental health problems also were twice as likely to be homeless in the year before their arrest (James & Glaze, 2006).

In a 2000 Bureau of Prisons (n.d.) analysis examining the co-occurrence of substance abuse disorders with depression and antisocial personality disorder (APD) among federal inmates, researchers noted that "38% of the male inmates dependent on one or more drugs had a diagnosis of APD as compared with 43% of the drug dependent women. In contrast, women were more likely to have a diagnosis of depression. Seventeen percent of the drug dependent males had a lifetime diagnosis of depression compared with one third of the drug dependent female inmates" (p. 1). These results indicate the need for greater monitoring and assessment for inmates who are dually diagnosed with substance abuse and mental health disorders.

Despite the prevalence of mental health conditions among inmates, many do not receive the treatment they need. In 2005, only one in three state prisoners and one in six jail inmates received treatment following admission (James & Glaze, 2006). Beck and Maruschak (2001) cite Bureau of Justice Statistics indicating that in 2000 only 1,394 of 1,558 state public and private adult correctional facilities provided mental health services. Of the facilities for state prisoners, Beck and Maruschak also noted, "70% of facilities housing state prison inmates screened inmates at intake; 65% conducted psychiatric assessments; 51% provided 24-hour mental health care; 71% provided therapy/counseling by trained mental health professionals; 73% distributed psychotropic medications to their inmates; and 66% helped released inmates obtain community mental health services" (p. 1). Furthermore, 10% of inmates were receiving psychotropic medications and fewer than 2% of state inmates were in a 24-hour mental health unit.

As stated earlier, inmates suffer from many mental conditions including depression, bipolar disorder, and schizophrenia. Some inmates also commit suicide. Mumola (2005), citing data from 2000 through 2002, notes that White jail inmates were six times more likely to commit suicide than Black inmates and more than three times more likely than Hispanic inmates. In the same analysis, males in local jails were 50% more likely than female inmates to commit suicide, and violent offenders had a suicide rate three times that of nonviolent offenders.

Screening techniques that are effective, culturally sensitive, and accurate must be developed to correctly detect and diagnose mental health problems, especially among African Americans and Hispanics (Baker & Bell, 1999; Borowsky et al., 2000). While incarcerated, those with mental health conditions need treatment regimes that provide for assessment to determine proper treatment modality, extensive case management, and discharge planning upon release. Once they reenter the community, they also need facilitated access to social services, medical services, housing, transportation, and employment and linkages to ongoing treatment programs (Welsh & Ogloff, 1998).

Substance Abuse

The extent of drug use and abuse among people in jails and prisons is well documented and provides another lens to consider the breadth of need for treatment. Mumola and Karberg (2006) note that in 2004, 56% of state inmates and 50% of federal inmates used drugs a month before committing the offense for which they were incarcerated. Writing about state inmates they note, "a third committed their current offense while under the influence of drugs, more than half used drugs within the month of their current offense, and two-thirds used drugs regularly" (p. 2). The most commonly used drugs by state inmates a month before their current offense were marijuana (40%), cocaine or crack (21%), stimulants (12%), heroin and other opiates (8%), and hallucinogens (6%). Of those inmates in federal prisons, 26% used drugs at the time of their current offense and 50% within a month of their current offense. Among federal prisoners, the most commonly used drugs a month before their current offense were marijuana (36%), cocaine or crack (18%), stimulants (11%), heroin and other opiates (6%), and hallucinogens (6%).

For state inmates, 53% to 58% of all racial/ethnic groups reported using drugs in the month before the offense. For federal inmates, 58% of Whites, 53% of Blacks, and 38% of Hispanics reported using drugs in the month before the offense. In federal prisons, Mumola and Karberg (2006) note, "men (50%) were slightly more likely than women (48%) to report drug use in the month before the offense in 2004" (p. 3). On the other hand, in state prisons, women (60%) were more likely to use drugs in the month before their current offense (56% for men). Of drug abusing inmates in state prisons, 14% were homeless the year before admission and 68% were employed in the month before incarceration. Of recent drug users in state prisons, 39% reported participation in a variety of drug abuse programs, including self-help groups, peer counseling, and drug abuse education programs. However, only 14% participated in drug treatment programs with a trained professional. Of federal inmates who were recently incarcerated drug abusers, 45% participated in drug abuse programs but only 15% received treatment provided by a trained professional (Mumola & Karberg, 2006).

Inmates with substance abuse problems before incarceration have a greater risk of contracting a variety of diseases, including HIV, multiresistant tuberculosis, hepatitis B and C, endocarditis, bloodstream bacterial infections, and sexually transmitted diseases (Cole & Littman, 1997). In 1999, the Bureau of Justice Statistics stated that there was a substantial link between drug use and HIV infection. Based on personal interviews with state prisoners, 2.3% of those who said they had ever used drugs were HIV positive, as were 2.7% of those who had used drugs in the month before their current arrest, 4.6% of those who had used a needle to inject drugs, and 7.7% of those who had shared a needle (Maruschak, 1999).

The possible health complications that put incarcerated drug abusers at risk include liver disease, renal failure, nasal perforation from snorting cocaine or smoking marijuana, and greater susceptibility to strokes and heart attacks from cocaine consumption (McCorkel, Butzin, Martin, & Inciardi, 1998).

Tearing Down Policy Barriers to Health Care for Inmates

According to the Commission on Safety and Abuse in America's Prisons (2006), there are several policy barriers that prevent inmates from receiving quality health care.

These impediments include inadequate funding of prison health care systems, lack of collaboration and partnerships of the correctional facilities with primary and public health care providers in the community, lack of consistent screening for infectious diseases, required co-payment by inmates for medical and oral health care, and the inability of inmates to receive Medicare and Medicaid while incarcerated. Specifically, the report states:

> No U.S. correctional institution receives federal Medicaid or Medicare reimbursement for health services provided to prisoners, even though most prisoners would qualify for these benefits and many were enrolled in these programs before incarceration. Medicaid is funded jointly by the federal and state governments, whereas Medicare is a federal program. Current law prevents the federal government from paying its share. (Commission on Safety and Abuse in America's Prisons, 2006, p. 50)

To overcome these barriers the Commission on Safety recommended the following:

- Forming partnerships between departments of corrections and community health providers to provide culturally competent health services to inmates
- Designing a health care delivery system where there is collaboration between medical, correctional, and security staff within the facility
- Identifying and providing comprehensive treatment for those inmates with mental illness
- Screening throughout all prisons and jails for infectious disease based on a national guideline to ensure a continuum of care once the inmate is released
- Repealing state laws that require inmates to pay a co-payment to receive medical treatment
- Changing Medicaid and Medicare rules that prohibit correctional facilities from receiving federal funds for the health care of inmates who may be eligible
- Making Medicare and Medicaid benefits available to eligible inmates immediately upon release

In addition to these recommendations, it is imperative to provide health care coverage, either through Medicaid or some other form of public coverage, as a part of a national access program.

Why We Must Act Now

Implementing the recommendations of the Commission on Safety would represent a bold step toward improving the treatment and care of men and women in prisons and jails and for those going home. But to truly improve the health of prison populations, we must address the stigma of incarceration as well because although it is seldom spoken aloud or acknowledged, the underlying belief that those convicted of crimes do not deserve comprehensive health care is the most solid barrier to improving health services to prisoners. Perhaps that is because although all Americans are laden by the social, economic, and health consequences of incarceration, some groups are more burdened than others. African American communities—and men in these communities, statistics show—bear the heaviest burden of all. This gives some in our society cover to ignore cruel inequities. "Why should we care?" these voices ask blandly. "Why should inmates have better health care than law-abiding Americans?"

The answer is twofold. First, the cost to incarcerate one individual for 1 year was almost $23,000 in 2001 compared to $5,700 for 1 year at community college (Stephan, 1999, 2004); U.S. Department of Education, 2006). Taxpayers want the greatest return on their valuable tax investments. Under the current criminal justice systems, the costs to taxpayers will only rise as the likely return diminishes. By contrast, paying attention to serious health issues during and after incarceration is an investment that can only benefit public health.

Second, even though the logistics may be complicated, the reason is simple: Because we must. Health care is a basic human right for those in prison, just as it is for those of us on the outside, whatever current payment systems may indicate to the contrary. As we formulate national health objectives for 2020, it is important ethically and morally to give priority to the most vulnerable—among them, people in prisons and jails. It is unthinkable that we in the richest nation in the world, the self-proclaimed "land of the free," would stand idly by watching people suffer and die from preventable diseases and conditions. So, although standards and practices to protect and treat prisoners are an important step, sufficient human caring must be part of policy as well. To do otherwise risks wanton indifference and neglect of a vulnerable population hidden behind bars in American jails and prisons.

Looked at from another angle, tackling prison health care is not only the right thing to do but also the smart thing to do, because to do otherwise puts our viability as a society at stake. If we do not act, the public health crisis and health care costs that will emerge—which we are beginning to witness with the skyrocketing HIV rates in African American women—will decimate our health care system and our communities and mortgage future generations.

Where to Improve the Health of Those Coming Home

Policymakers and practitioners must do the following to stop the unnecessary human suffering and death among the incarcerated for health and social justice reasons, and to end the alienation that is magnified by factors such as race, gender, and poverty:

Expand health care coverage. Provide coverage for comprehensive primary health care that includes mental health care, substance abuse treatment on demand, and oral health care for those returning to their communities from prison or jail. Coverage alone does not equate to accessible quality health care, so the discharge process should entail providing all releasees with health insurance cards, referring them to a specific community-based provider, and networking with a community outreach worker. This will remedy the coverage gaps experienced by many poor men, in particular those who are African American or Hispanic.

Eliminate co-payments. Co-payment for primary health care and oral health services received in prison must be discontinued because it is a disincentive for inmates to seek care when they cannot afford the co-payment.

Include oral health care. Oral health coverage must become an integral part of services required by the Centers for Medicare and Medicaid Services as a part of state benefits programs. Moreover, to ensure sufficient staffing in prison, jails, and underserved communities, as well as a culturally diverse workforce of dental professionals, recruitment efforts must be stepped up to meet the need for dentists and hygienists, and any restrictions that prevent hygienists from serving these populations should be removed.

Increase mental health training of health care providers. Primary care physicians and frontline workers (nurse practitioners and others in the nursing workforce) must

be trained through postsecondary and continuing education courses to screen for signs of mental distress using culturally sensitive screening regimens and to provide medications and referrals for community-based counseling.

Increase the number of providers. All graduate medical and nursing education institutions should be required to provide health services to correctional institutions and to the underserved communities where many inmates return until disparities are reduced in the areas of primary health care, mental health, and substance abuse treatment. Provision of such health services would act as a counterbalance to the support these institutions receive from local, state, and federal taxes.

Encourage collaboration. All federally funded and state-supported community-based clinics should develop plans to work collaboratively with jails and prisons, local district attorneys, and departments of corrections to address the needs of the incarcerated and especially those who are returning to their communities. Also, the U.S. Department of Justice should require that all criminal justice entities establish formal linkages with health, housing, social services, employment, and transportation agencies to facilitate the transition to community for former inmates.

Increase systematic and ongoing collection of data. A system of data collection must be initiated that integrates the health data of prisoners with the data of communities to provide an accurate assessment of the health disparities in the African American communities and, in particular, inmates and former inmates. Analysis of such data will foster systems changes that will lead to a more comprehensive system of health care for those communities and individuals in greatest need of care.

Promote the usage of national standards. An organization such as the Institute of Medicine should review and recommend standards for quality health care, promote their use, and enforce laws and regulations to ensure quality care. Another national entity should be charged with enforcing laws, regulations, and general standards related to access to comprehensive care, protection from rape, and other activities and services that will protect the health and human rights of those imprisoned, as guaranteed by the Constitution of the United States of America.

Address other barriers to reentry for releasees. Because inmate health does not exist in a vacuum, policymakers must address the other barriers and hidden sanctions that impact the health of inmates and of the communities to which they return. Recommendations include the following:

• To help incarcerated parents maintain family connections, free telephone calls should be permitted to enable them to foster social and parenting relationships with their children and their children's caregivers. In addition, for prisoners held more than 50 miles from home, their families must be given free transportation for periodic visits.

• Address barriers to housing by ensuring that verifiable housing is available to the individual leaving jail or prison and removing restrictions that prevent released inmates from returning to public housing.

• Federal and state governments must make more attractive their incentive programs to employers to hire releasees for positions that pay a living wage. They also should prohibit employers from barring individuals from employment based on their past felony conviction(s).

• Food security must be ensured by providing food stamps to individuals leaving prison and jail, and eligibility for continuing food stamps must be preauthorized as a part of the discharge process.

Prison health and the public's health are intertwined. We need immediate and determined action to address social institutions broken almost irretrievably. In making our laws and practices more humane and more just, we will demonstrate that the hard lessons of past and contemporary history have not been wasted.

References

Adimora, A. A., Schoenbach, V. J., & Doherty, I. A. (2006). HIV and African Americans in the southern United States: Sexual networks and social context. *Sexually Transmitted Diseases, 33*(Suppl.), S39–S45.

Ahluwalia, K., Ro, M., Erwin, K., & Treadwell, H. (2005). Racial disparities in oral cancer risks and outcomes. *Journal of Cancer Education, 20,* 70–71.

Anno, B. J., Graham, C., Lawrence, J. E., & Shansky, R. (2004). *Correctional health care: Addressing the needs of elderly, chronically ill, and terminally ill inmates.* Washington, DC: U.S. Department of Justice, National Institute of Corrections.

Retrieved November 2, 2006, from http://www.nicic.org/pubs/2004/018735.pdf

Baker, F. M., & Bell, C. C. (1999). Issues in the psychiatric treatment of African Americans. *Psychiatric Services, 50,* 362–368.

Beck, A. J., & Maruschak, L. M. (2001). *Mental health treatment in state prisons, 2000* (Bureau of Justice Statistics Special Report, NCJ 188215). Retrieved November 23, 2006, from http://www.ojp.usdoj.gov/bjs/pub/pdf/mhtsp00.pdf

Borowsky, S. J., Rubenstein, L. V., Meredith, L. S., Camp, P., Jackson-Triche, M., & Wells, K. B. (2000). Who is at risk of nondetection of mental health problems in primary care? *Journal of General Internal Medicine, 15,* 381.

Braithwaite, R., Hammett, T., & Mayberry, R. (1996). *Prisons and AIDS: A public health challenge.* New York: Jossey-Bass.

Brown, J. R. (1997). Drug diversion courts: Are they needed and will they succeed in breaking the cycle of drug-related crime? *New England Journal on Crime and Civil Confinement, 23,* 63–99.

Bureau of Prisons. (n.d.). *Antisocial personality and depression among incarcerated drug treatment participants executive summary—2000.* Retrieved September 1, 2006, from http://www.bop.gov/news/research–projects/current_projects/oretriadescomorbid.pdf

Clemetson, L. (2004, August 6). Links between prison and AIDS affecting blacks inside and out. New York Times. Retrieved November 21, 2006, from http://www.reentrymediaoutreach.org/pdfs/nytimes_august6.pdf

Cole, D., & Littman, B. (1997). Casualties of the drug war: An equality-based argument for drug treatment. In J. A. Egertson, D. M. Fox, & L. Luborsky (Eds.), *Treating drug abusers effectively* (pp. 281–309). Malden, MA: Blackwell.

Commission on Safety and Abuse in America's Prisons. (2006). Confronting confinement. Retrieved November 2, 2006, from http://www.prisoncommission.org/pdfs/Confronting_Confinement.pdf

Community Voices. (2005). *In need of correction: The prison cycle of health care.* Retrieved November 21, 2006, from http://www.communityvoices.org/Uploads/PrisonHealthForum_00108_00138.pdf

Harrison, P. M., & Beck, A. J. (2006). *Prisoners in 2005* (Bureau of Justice Statistics Bulletin, NCJ 215092). Retrieved November 30, 2006, from http://www.ojp.usdoj.gov/bjs/pub/pdf/p05.pdf

James, D., & Glaze, L. (2006). *Mental health problems of prison and jail inmates* (Bureau of Justice Statistics Bulletin, NCJ 213600). Retrieved November 2, 2006, from http://www.ojp.usdoj.gov/bjs/pub/pdf/mhppji.pdf

Maruschak, L. (1999). *HIV in prisons, 1997* (Bureau of Justice Statistics Bulletin, NCJ 178284). Retrieved November 23, 2006, from http://www.ojp.usdoj.gov/bjs/pub/ascii/hivp97.txt

Maruschak, L. (2006). *HIV in prisons, 2004* (Bureau of Justice Statistics Bulletin, NCJ 213897). Retrieved November 23, 2006, from http://www.ojp.usdoj.gov/bjs/pub/pdf/hivp04.pdf

Mauer, M. (1999). *Race to incarcerate.* New York: New York Press.

McCorkel, J. A., Butzin, C. A., Martin, S. S., & Inciardi, J. A. (1998). Use of health care services in a sample of drug-involved offenders: A comparison with national norms. *American Behavioral Scientist, 41,* 1079–1089.

Mixon, J. M., Eplee, H. C., Feil, P. H., Jones, J. J., & Rico, M. (1990). Oral health status of a federal prison population. *Public Health Dentistry, 50,* 257–261.

Mumola, C. (2000). *Incarcerated parents and their children* (Bureau of Justice Statistics Special Report, NCJ 182335). Retrieved November 2, 2006, from http://www.ojp.usdoj.gov/bjs/pub/pdf/iptc.pdf

Mumola, C. (2005). *Suicide and homicide in state prisons and local jails* (Bureau of Justice Statistics Special Report, NCJ 210036). Retrieved November 2, 2006, from http://www.ojp.usdoj.gov/bjs/pub/pdf/shsplj.pdf

Mumola, C., & Karberg, J. (2006). *Drug use and dependence, state and federal prisoners, 2004* (Bureau of Justice Statistics Special Report, NCJ 213530). Retrieved November 2, 2006, from http://www.ojp.usdoj.gov/bjs/pub/pdf/dudsfp04.pdf

National Commission on Correctional Health Care. (2002). *The health status of soon-to be-released inmates: A report to Congress.* Chicago: Author. Retrieved March 8, 2007, from http://www.ncchc.org/stbr/Volume1/Health%20Status%20(vol%201).pdf

Satcher, D. (2003). Overlooked and underserved: Improving the health of men of color. *American Journal of Public Health, 93,* 707–709.

Stephan, J. J. (1999). *State prison expenditures, 1996* (Bureau of Justice Statistics Special Report, NCJ 172211). Washington, DC: U.S. Department of Justice, Office of Justice Programs. Retrieved February 23, 2007, from http://www.ojp.usdoj.gov/bjs/pub/ascii/spe96.txt

Stephan, J. J. (2004). *State prison expenditures, 2001* (Bureau of Justice Statistics Report, NCJ 202949). Washington, DC: U.S. Department of Justice, Office of Justice Programs. Retrieved February 23, 2007, from http://www.ojp.usdoj.gov/bjs/pub/ascii/spe01.txt

Travis, J., & Waul, M. (2003). *Prisoners once removed: The impact of incarceration and reentry on children, families and communities.* Washington, DC: Urban Institute Press.

Treadwell, H. M., & Formicola, A. J. (2005). Improving the oral health of prisoners to improve overall health and well-being. *American Journal of Public Health, 95,* 1677–1678.

U.S. Department of Education, National Center for Education Statistics. (2006). *Digest of education statistics.* Retrieved November 21, 2006, from http://nces.ed.gov/fastfacts/display.asp?id=76

Welsh, A., & Ogloff, J. R. P. (1998). Mentally ill offenders in jails and prisons: Advances in service planning and delivery. *Current Opinion in Psychiatry, 11,* 683–687.

Williams, N. (2006). *Where are the men? The impact of incarceration and reentry on African-American men and their children and families* (Community Voices Policy Brief). Retrieved November 21, 2006, from http://www.communityvoices.org/Article.aspx?ID=396

Discussion Questions

1. Explain the relationship between rising incarceration rates (specifically for drug offenders) and the level of health needs among the prison population. How are minority and ethnic communities particularly impacted?

   The U.S. war on drug has increased the number of state and federal prisoners. The proportion of black prisoners increased and they serve longer sentences than their white counterparts. For example, an African American drug offender is federal court was sentenced an average of 89 months compared to 70 months for a white offender. With the increased incarceration of drug offenders, prison overcrowding and exposure to HIV and tuberculosis also increase.

2. How is the health of the prison population linked to public health?

   Williams explains how after they are released, many prisoners have no access to health insurance and thus, no access to health care. Ex-offenders return to communities with the fewest resources, to areas that are already poor, overburdened, and with limited health resources. Their unmet health needs can threaten the well-being of their families, communities, and society as a whole. The worst case scenario would be an untreated or overlooked illness in a prison population that could expose an entire community to an epidemic.

Source: From Williams, N. H. (2007). Prison health and the health of the public: Ties that bind. *Journal of Correctional Health Care, 13*(4), 80–92. Reprinted by permission of Sage Publications.

CHAPTER 26

The Global Impact of Gangs

John M. Hagedorn (2005)

John Hagedorn provides a unique perspective on American gangs by arguing that the study of gangs must be "rooted in a global context." He believes that gangs must be studied within a larger global context, examining the social, cultural, political, and economic factors that encourage their growth and maintenance.

Why study gangs? The short answer is that gangs are a significant worldwide phenomenon with millions of members and a voice of those marginalized by processes of globalization. Understanding these social actors is crucial to fashioning public policies and building social movements that can both reduce violence and erode the deep-seated inequalities that all too often are reinforced by present economic, social, and military policies.

The American study of gangs can no longer start and stop with local conditions but must also be rooted in a global context. How else do we come to grips with Jamaican posses in Kansas (Gunst, 1995), San Diego's Calle Trente and their past relationship to Mexico's Arellano brothers cartel (Rotella, 1998), the Russian "mafiya" in Chicago (Finckenauer & Waring, 1998), female Muslim gangs in Oslo (Lien, 2002), LA's MS-13 and 18th Street as the largest gangs in Honduras and El Salvador (Decesare, 2003), Nigerian drug smugglers coming through Ronald Reagan International Airport (Grennan, Britz, Rush, & Barker, 2000), Crips in the Netherlands (van Gemert, 2001), the ties of U.S. tongs to Chinese Triads (Booth, 1999), and other examples of a global web of gangs?

Gang research is important today for six related reasons:

1. Unprecedented worldwide urbanization has created fertile conditions for the growth of gangs, particularly in Latin America, Asia, and Africa.

2. Unlike the expansion of the state in the earlier industrial era, in the global era the state has retreated in the face of instantaneous financial flows and neoliberal monetary policy, while emphasizing punitive policies toward marginalized communities. Gangs and other groups of armed young men occupy the vacuum created by the retreat of the social welfare policies of the state.

3. The strengthening of cultural identities by men and women is a central method of resistance to marginalization. Whereas fundamentalist religion and nationalism have been adopted by many gang members, hip-hop culture and its "gangsta rap" variant also provide powerful resistance identities and influence millions.

4. Globalization's valorization of some areas and marginalization of others has meant the flourishing of an underground economy for survival and as profitable, internationally connected enterprises run by gangs, cartels, and similar groups.

5. The wealth of the global economy has led to the redivision of space in cities all across the globe. "Economic development," "making the city safe," and "ethnic cleansing" are among the reasons given for the clearing out of "the other" from urban spaces desired by dominant ethnic or religious majorities. These spatial changes have influenced the nature and activity of gangs.

6. Some gangs institutionalize and become permanent social actors in communities, cities, and nations rather than fading away after a generation. These gangs often replace or rival demoralized political groups and play important, albeit often destructive, social, economic, and political roles in cities around the world.

The Explosion of Urbanization

A UN-Habitat (2003) report finds that nearly one billion people live in slums in the world today. In developing nations, slum dwellers make up 43% of the total population compared with 6% in developed countries. Eighty percent of the population of Latin America is now urban. In sub-Saharan Africa, nearly three quarters of those who live in cities are slum dwellers. India has 25 cities of one million or more and China, as of this writing, has 166 (French, 2004).

The present urban population is greater than the entire population of the world in 1960 (Davis, 2004). Urbanization has accelerated worldwide in processes that were so well described by Robert Park, Frederic Thrasher, and the Chicago School as prime conditions for the growth of gangs. Malcolm Klein's (1995) argument that "the common varieties of street gang still are an essentially American product" (p. 3) leads in the wrong research direction. The vast majority of gangs and gang members are from Latin America, Africa, and Asia—recent products of urbanization.

Gangs did not originate in the United States. Dickens and others described London gangs long before their American cousins existed (Pearson, 1983). Even female gang members—scuttlers—may have roamed Manchester in the 19th century (Davies, 1998). Gangs have formed all over the world whenever and wherever industrialization and related processes drive people into cities.

For example, industrializing Third World countries like South Africa had gangs, or *skollies,* for most of the 20th century (Pinnock, 1984). "Number gangs" have been known in South African prisons for nearly a century (Shurink, 1986). In the wake of post-World War II urbanization, gangs like the rarry boys in Sierra Leone (Abdullah, 2002) were formed by the children of urban migrants. In New Zealand, Maori gangs have built a national network since the mid-20th century (Hazelhurst, in press). And one familiar figure, Yasser Arafat, learned guerrilla tactics as a street gang leader in Cairo in the 1940s (Aburish, 1998).

Other forms of the gang have been around even longer. In China, Triads began in the 18th century and morphed into gangster activity in Hong Kong, Shanghai, and other large Chinese cities (e.g., Booth, 1999). The mafia, originally a rural 19th-century Sicilian rebel force, took root in U.S. cities and transformed local gangs, like Chicago's Taylor Street crew, into powerful illicit organizations (Hobsbawm, 1969; Nelli, 1969).

Much of the current world literature on gangs, unlike the "at-risk youth" literature in the United States, does not use the label "gangs." The World Bank, for example, documents millions of "street children" around the world and that term includes various semiorganized forms (World Bank Institute, 2000). The "child soldiers" literature, newly supplemented by the category of "children in organized armed violence," is another source of reporting on gangs (Dowdney, 2003; Human Rights Watch, 2004). By perusing the global organized crime literature and the human rights studies (e.g., Amnesty International, 2004; UN Convention on Transnational Organized Crime, 2000), other snapshots of youth gangs can be garnered. The Social Science Research Council is currently organizing an international working group on "youth in organized armed violence."

But what is a gang? Group process definitions, from Thrasher (1927) to Short and Strodtbeck (1965) to Moore (1978), describe unsupervised youth developing organization through conflict with other groups and authorities. They pointedly exclude criminalization as a necessary characteristic of the definition of gangs as claimed by Klein (1971) and Miller (1982).

In today's cities, particularly in less developed countries, such unsupervised groups of youth are often "supervised" by a variety of criminal groups and recruited by nationalist and religious militias. Prisons both receive and create gangs that spread back to their communities, as in South Africa (Shurink, 1986), California (Moore, 1978), and Rio de Janiero (Dowdney, 2003). The present era has witnessed the proliferation of gangs and other groups who are outside the control of formal state authority. Thrasher's (1927) diagram of the various paths a "casual crowd" can take was prescient (p. 70).

The central issue is that gangs today are organizations of the socially excluded, most of whom come and go as their wild, teenage peer group ages. But a substantial number institutionalize on the streets, either through self-generated processes or with the assistance of already institutionalized armed groups.[1] The similarity of these institutionalized gangs to other groups of armed young men requires that the global study of gangs broaden its focus (see Hagedorn, in press-a). Although I am a theoretical soulmate of Short and Moore, it's clear that one central mechanism for the persistence of institutionalized gangs is participation in the underground economy.

There are no comprehensive, comparative studies of gangs across the world (but see Hagedorn, in press-b; Hazlehurst & Hazlehurst, 1998; Klein, Kerner, Maxsen, &Weitekamp, 2001; Kontos, Brotherton, &Barrios, 2003). However, it is possible to estimate that, depending on the definition, there are at least tens of millions of gang members in the world today.

Globalization and the Retreat of the State

The study of gangs began in an era of optimism about the role of the state in solving problems of poverty and diverting youth from delinquency (Thrasher, 1927; Wirth, 1928/1956). The social disorganization that accompanied immigration, the theory propounded, could be overcome by social programs, settlement houses, and the juvenile court "in loco parentis" (Addams, 1920/1960). The key to combating delinquency, Shaw and McKay (1942) argued, was the organization of communities to control delinquent behavior.

Gang studies in the 1960s argued for new social programs that stressed opportunity as part of a societal war on poverty (Cloward & Ohlin, 1960; Yablonsky, 1966). Much current gang literature continues to urge increased state intervention (e.g., Klein, 1995; Spergel, 1995), whereas others follow Shaw and McKay (1942) and stress community empowerment, in part through leveraging state resources (Bursik & Grasmick, 1993; Sampson & Groves, 1989).

Social disorganization theory is theoretically grounded in the Enlightenment notion of the progressive nature of history and belief that the secular state would continue to grow as religion and tradition were weakened by modern society (Elias, 1939/1994; Nisbet, 1980; see especially Touraine, 2000). The only way to overcome the loss of the bonds of old-world culture, Kornhauser (1978) argued, is to strengthen community institutions, an approach that continues to guide social theory today (Sampson, Raudenbush, & Earls, 1997; Wilson & Sampson, 1995). The role of the state has changed, however, and the gang literature has all but ignored the decline of the state and the rise of global cities that are at the cutting edge of urban political economy (see Castells, 1997; Sassen, 2002).

The vast transformation of the U.S. economy has resulted in economic restructuring that prioritizes information and services over heavy industry, contingent over unionized labor, and consumption over production (see, e.g., Bell, 1960; Castells, 1998). These developments have been accompanied by public policies that stress security and the needs of the new wealthy and fray the safety net for the poor and a weakened working class (Bourdieu, 1998; Touraine, 2001). In the wake of reduced opportunity for unskilled labor, many gang members have remained in their gangs as adults and gangs have become an important ghetto employer (Hagedorn, 2001).

These policies have been accelerated by the war on terror (Calhoun, Price, & Timmer, 2002). In Europe and other advanced countries, the Reagan-Thatcher agenda has been more controversial and contested (Hagedorn, 1999; Pitts, 2000; Wacquant, 1999). In the Third World, International Monetary Fund strictures to reduce social spending, pay on foreign debt, allow foreign capital penetration, and continue a strong military have resulted in the erosion of the social welfare policies of already weak states (Bauman, 1998; Castells, 1998) while increasing what Wacquant (2004) calls the "neoliberal penalty."

Latin American and African academics have long been skeptical about the progressive nature of development (e.g., de Soto, 1990; Frank, 1970). The retreat of the state in the Third World has created anew what might at first blush be considered conditions of "social disorganization," with weakened and delegitimized social institutions unable to contain a rapidly urbanizing population. As a result, various sorts of "armed young men" (Hagedorn, in press-a; Kaldor, 1999) including gangs, para-militaries, death squads, and drug cartels that parallel, replace, or complement public authority have proliferated.

The state in many countries can no longer be said to have a monopoly on violence, Weber's (1968) standard definition of the modern state. For example, in Rio de Janeiro, drug factions control and patrol the favelas and police enter only with massive armed force and then quickly withdraw (Dowdney, 2003). In Haiti, the state lost all capacity to control the populace and various types of groups of armed youth, leading to the deposing of Aristide and an uncertain status for the new state (Farmer, 1994; Kovats-Bernat, 2000). Recent press reports from Haiti tell of pro- and anti-Aristide youth gangs who now refuse to put down their arms and have turned full-time to crime (Children in Organised Armed Violence [COAV], 2004).

The proliferation of death squads in this sense is another indication that the state no longer can enforce its rule without resort to extra-legal violence. Like gated communities with their private security guards for the wealthy, armed groups or vigilantes, like the Bakassi Boys in Nigeria (Human Rights Watch, 2002), are filling a vacuum within poor communities, where the state is unable to maintain order. In many cases, the state, to preserve "plausible deniability," subcontracts tasks of violence to informal death squads (Campbell & Brenner, 2000). In Colombia, militias, cartels, revolutionaries, and the military all draw teenage warriors from the large pool of youth gangs in urban areas (COAV, 2003). Castells (2000) sums up this point:

> In a world of exclusion, and in the midst of a crisis of political legitimacy, the boundary between protest, patterns of immediate gratification, adventure, and crime becomes increasingly blurred. (p. 210)

This does not mean that gangs are the same thing as death squads or terrorists. It does mean, however, that social disorganization and juvenile delinquency are too narrow for the study of gangs. The structuralist emphasis of most U.S. gang studies is also undermined by the power of identity.

The Power of Identity

Globalization and the retreat of the state have meant more than a loss of social control. The failure of modern institutions and the lack of faith in the certainty of a better future have strengthened *resistance identities*—identities formed in opposition to the dominant culture and the uncertainties of an unstable modernity (Castells, 1997). Touraine (1995) argues that the modern era can be understood best as the clash between the unfettered power of the market and the resistance of national, ethnic, and religious identities.

Within poor communities, resistance identities are held by a wide assortment of people including gangs and other groups of armed youth. Nationalist, religious, and ethnic cultures have grown strong by resisting the homogenizing influences of westernization. Islamic fundamentalism today is but one example of the strength of cultural resistance identities.

Often overlooked is the resistance of women who share ethnic or religious identities but also challenge the male dominance of traditional culture. As Moore (in press) notes, there is scant literature on female gangs around the world, although such gangs may be increasing. Although most female gangs still appear to be adolescent groups, adult forms may differ markedly from adult male gangs, and both are woefully understudied (Chesney-Lind & Hagedorn, 1999). In the United States, the conflicted voices of women can be seen in gangsta rap music, where misogyny and violence reign, but female rappers strongly protest, while defending Black males against racist attacks on their music (hooks, 1994; Rose, 1994).

The power of rap music is not often discussed in gang studies, although its strong influence contradicts the premise that culture is everywhere in decline, and even more so in subcultures (Kornhauser, 1978; Park, 1940; but see Finestone, 1957, 1967). The present era is marked by the strength of culture, driven by the international dominance of the U.S. media, the resurgence and reinvention of traditional cultures, and the dominance of youth street cultures, even in Islamic countries. In Nigeria, gangs of Muslim youth enforce Sharia for the state, while wearing gold chains, using and selling drugs, and listening to rap music (Casey, 2002). Throughout Africa, Latin America, and Asia, homegrown styles of rap music have captured the imagination of youth.

Although media corporations promote gangsta rap to run up profits, and the lure of sex and violence celebrates values of the dog-eat-dog "cowboy capitalism" of globalization, the broader cultural power of hip-hop helps forge a more complex resistance identity for youth modeled after African American rebellion to White authority (see Short, 1996). Among the founders of hip-hop were former gang members, like Afrika Bambaata in the South Bronx, who consciously saw hip-hop as a way to pull youth away from gangs (Kitwana, 1994, 2002). The fact that rap now contains conflicting ideals of violence and anti-violence, consumerism and anti-consumerism, religion and antagonism to religion, and misogyny and feminism only attests to its overall power in identifying the locus of the struggle.

To say that gangs can be understood through the lens of hip-hop culture is different from saying that gangs are subcultures (Cloward & Ohlin, 1960; Cohen, 1955; Miller, 1958). Miller and Cohen (1955) both saw subculture as an ethnically neutral and temporary outlook of working or lower class youth and adults. Cloward and Ohlin (1960) saw the source of gang subculture in the particular characteristics of opportunity structures within kinds of neighborhoods and downplayed its ethnic dimensions.

Hip-hop culture, and its gangsta rap variant, is avowedly African American, with African and Jamaican roots. Originating in communal, life-affirming values (Rose, 1994), like all cultural goods today, it is also shamelessly exploited by media companies "merchandizing the rhymes of violence" (Ro, 1996). Gangsta rap is also nihilistic, worshiping destruction and violence in a way more extreme than Cohen's reaction formation, a paean to Black survival and a violent response to the no-way-out life of the ghetto.

However, the gangster identity exists within a broader, worldwide hip-hop culture and represents an outlook of millions of the socially excluded. This contested resistance identity is no longer a transient subculture of alienated youth but a permanent oppositional and racialized culture arising in the wake of the retreat of the state and the parallel strengthening of cultural identities. The power of gangsta rap within hip-hop culture attests to the importance of the global criminal economy to socially excluded youth.

The Underground Economy

The criminal economy has been estimated by the UN as grossing more than $400 billion annually, which would make it the largest market in the world, including oil. Peter Reuter's (1996) more conservative estimates (his low-ball figure of $150 billion in annual drug sales) are nevertheless breathtaking. The U.S. gang literature has often described drug dealing as unorganized, and low-paying, but the sale of drugs in the United States is tied to an international network of drug suppliers, cartels, and mafias that exercise enormous influence in communities and nations on a global scale (Castells, 1998).

The literature on gangs and the underground economy in the United States is extensive (Moore, 1991; Taylor, 1989; Venkatesh & Leavitt, 2000). But these are local studies and their emphasis, as in my own prior work, is on the insular world of drug dealing in a single city. These studies describe the importance of the drug market to both young gang members and to the community (see especially Pattillo, 1998; Venkatesh, 2000). They also describe drug-dealing gangs as the main street-level employer of youth in the poorest areas of cities, forsaken by industrial jobs (Hagedorn, 2001).

The underground economy, however, has changed over the decades. Portes, Castells, and Benton (1989) explain how globalization has transformed illegal markets into an integral part of the world system. The underground economy has survival functions in urban areas where the formal economy disappears, providing goods and services in unregulated ways that are in demand by more affluent customers. On the U.S. border, a crusading prosecutor who was later killed admitted, "It is sad to say, but while the drug lords are here the economy is strong. This money activates the economy, injects new money" (Rotella, 1998, p. 254). In many areas, profitable illegal markets in drugs are but one business among many that include arms sales and trafficking in women and children. When the formal economy falters, the informal steps in.

An important feature of the global era is the coexistence/convergence of different kinds of non-state actors, including groups of armed young men (see also Goldstone, 2002). Political movements often rely on the underground economy and many state security forces have been corrupted by massive profits derived from selling drugs and guns. As left-wing political movements wane, demoralization sets in and militants, many who have few skills outside of armed struggle, are faced with a dubious moral choice of unemployment or working for drug gangs. Thus, the inability of the new government in South Africa to assimilate all "Spear of the Nation" guerrillas into the police or military has led some former guerrillas into the world of crime. Protestant militias in Belfast, faced with the "greening" of Northern Ireland and what appears more and more certainly as a future reunification with the south, have turned their guns on one another in a war over drug turf. Mexico is the poster child for the integration of military and police forces with the local drug cartels. In Central America, journalist Silla Boccanero sadly reported, "Until recently, a rebellious youth from Central America would go into the mountains and join the guerrillas. Today, he leaves the countryside for the city and joins one of the street gangs engaged in common crime without political objectives" (COAV, 2002).

The informal underground economy is now a structural part of the world order, assured by the uneven development of globalization. Violence is not a necessary condition for illicit enterprises, but when regulation by peaceful means fails, gangs and other groups of armed youth rise in prominence.

Urban Redivision of Space

Peter Marcuse (1997) argues that the vast expansion of wealth in the world economy has produced global cities that are separated into the "citadel" and the "ghetto." Space in globalizing cities is redivided as the wealthy and well-paid "knowledge workers" hew out spaces for themselves near the banks and central business districts (see Sassen, 2002). This "yuppie" land grab is accompanied by renewed emphasis on safety, crime, and ethnic antagonisms. The spatial concentration of ethnic minorities—often people of African descent—in the poorest areas of old cities has meant that lands coveted by the wealthy must be "cleansed" of the criminal, the violent, and the "other." Thus, Chicago has displaced 100,000 African

Americans by demolishing the high-rise housing projects that were built to contain them less than half a century ago (Hagedorn & Rauch, 2004). São Paulo is compared to Los Angeles in Caldeira's (2000) brilliant study of the two cities erecting walls of segregation to keep the dark poor away from the White elite (see also Massey, 1996), the vast expansion of wealth in the global economy.

This worldwide trend has meant the politicization of policies on crime and violence, even though in most cities of the industrialized world, violence declined in the 1990s. In the United States, this law and order trend has targeted alienated and jobless African American youth, resulting in an unprecedented expansion of prison building. America's prisons, at least 50% Black in a country where African Americans make up about 12% of the population, can be seen as but another device for control of the "social dynamite" of the ghetto. Wacquant (2000) argues that the prison and the ghetto are but two nodes on a continuum of social control dating back to slavery. Although prisons are often built far from urban areas, they have become virtually contiguous to ghettoes and barrios, as gang leaders continue to run their organizations from their cells. Most gangs in both Rio de Janeiro and Chicago are run from the prison (Dowdney, 2003; Hagedorn, in press-a). Some gangs have their origins in prison, like La Eme, and later dominate the streets (Hayden, 2004).

The Institutionalization of Gangs

Violence in cities of the world varies widely, from very low rates of homicide in Europe, China, Japan, Oceania, and the Middle East to very high rates in cities of many countries in Africa, Latin America, and the Caribbean. Within the United States, as in South America, Asia, Eastern Europe, and Africa, some cities have very high rates, and some low.

Gangs are to be found in cities all over the world, in those with both low and high rates of violence. However, in some cities, gangs have institutionalized and have been present for decades. To say that a gang has institutionalized is to say that it persists despite changes in leadership (e.g., killed, incarcerated, or "matured out"), has organization complex enough to sustain multiple roles of its members (including roles for women and children), can adapt to changing environments without dissolving (e.g., as a result of police repression), fulfills some needs of its community (economic, security, services), and organizes a distinct outlook of its members (rituals, symbols, and rules).

That some cities are home to institutionalized gangs and others not reinforces the importance of local conditions. My research suggests that in every city in the world that has had persisting high rates of violence, there are institutionalized groups of armed youth—for example, Chicago, Los Angeles, Rio de Janeiro, Medillin, Caracas, Kingston, Cape Flats, Lagos, Mogadishu, and Belfast—although causality is likely to be recursive. The divided cities literature (Hagedorn & Perry, 2002; Marcuse, 1997) suggests that gangs or other groups of armed youth institutionalize in contested cities with high levels of racial, ethnic, or religious (rather than solely class) oppression, where demoralization and the defeat of political struggle have occurred, and in defensible spaces that provide natural protection opportunities for illegal economic activity.

Institutionalized gangs are more than a crime problem. Many are deeply involved with politics, real estate, religion, and community organizations and cannot be easily destroyed by suppression or repression of the drug economy. Drug sales also provide opportunities for large-scale corruption and the purchase of heavy weapons. Gangs thus are social actors, in Touraine's and Park's sense. As social actors within poor communities with weak mechanisms of formal social control, gangs, militias, factions, and cartels have the capacity not only to wage war but also to rein it in (see Brotherton & Barrios, 2003; Bursik & Grasmick, 1993; Hayden, 2004, for different elaborations of this thesis). Differences among cities (e.g., why Chicago and Los Angeles are home to institutionalized gangs and New York City is not) have not been satisfactorily explained. Understanding the factors underlying the institutionalization of gangs and the persistence of violence are among the most pressing reasons for studying gangs.

Conclusion: Gangs as Social Actors

The U.S. Justice Department war on terror has redirected funds for research (Savelsberg, Cleveland, & King, 2004), with the result that fewer social scientists will be doing gang research and perspectives are likely to be polarized. Federally funded studies are likely to stress gang links to terrorism, whereas non-federally funded studies may continue to "puncture stereotypes" and stress local conditions. A more realistic and productive future for gang research lies in neither of these directions. Instead, we should combine our sociological and anthropological orientations with urban political economy and the analysis of gangs and other organizations of the socially excluded in the globalizing city. Gangs cannot be understood outside of their global context, nor reduced to epiphenomena of globalization or cogs in an international terrorist conspiracy. To a far greater degree than in the past, we need to study the racialized identities of male and female gang members and the salience of culture.

Gangs are being reproduced throughout this largely urban world by a combination of economic and political marginalization and cultural resistance. We ignore organizations of the socially excluded at great risk. Although the collapse of socialism and demoralization of left-wing forces have been replaced by new social movements that show promise for social change (Castells, 1997; Touraine, 1995), in some places institutionalized gangs and other groups of armed youth have moved into the vacuum created by the demise of the left. These groups are cynical about politics and looking desperately for a better life today, not tomorrow. For them, the promises of modernity have proven to be illusory. Gangs are one price we pay for the failure of the modern project.

Institutionalized gangs are unlikely either to gradually die out or be eliminated by force. It might be profitable for social scientists to see them as partners at the table who need to be included in the polity, as Bursik and Grasmick (1993) controversially suggested a decade ago. In Touraine's sense, institutionalized gangs, too, are subjects. Dealing with gangs as social actors requires a policy of both intolerance of violence and tolerance of informal, nonviolent economic activity. It requires more negotiation and less suppression. How we deal with the reality of gangs and others among the socially excluded is one of those markers that will shape the nature, and the future, of civilization.

Note

1. Although women play roles in these gangs, overwhelmingly they are groups of armed young men, warriors fighting for masculinity, survival, and ethnic or religious identity.

References

Abdullah, I. (2002). Youth, culture, and rebellion: Understanding Sierra Leone's wasted decade. *Critical Arts: A Journal of South-North Cultural and Media Studies, 16*(2), 19–37.

Aburish, S. K. (1998). *Arafat: From defender to dictator* (1st U.S. ed.). New York: Bloomsbury.

Addams, J. (1960). *Twenty years at Hull-House.* New York: Signet. (Original work published 1920)

Amnesty International. (2004). *2004 report.* Retrieved November 14, 2004, from http://www.amnestyusa.org/annualreport/index .html

Bauman, Z. (1998). *Globalization: The human consequences.* New York: Columbia University Press.

Bell, D. (1960). *The end of ideology: On the exhaustion of political ideas in the fifties.* New York: Free Press.

Booth, M. (1999). *The Dragon Syndicates: The global phenomenon of the Triads.* New York: Carroll & Graf.

Bourdieu, P. (1998). *Acts of resistance: Against the tyranny of the market.* New York: New Press.

Brotherton, D., & Barrios, L. (2003). *Between black and gold: The street politics of the Almighty Latin King and Queen Nation.* New York: Columbia University Press.

Bursik, R. J., Jr., & Grasmick, H. G. (1993). *Neighborhoods and crime: The dimensions of effective community control.* New York: Lexington Books.

Caldeira, T. P. R. (2000). *City of walls: Crime, segregation, and citizenship in São Paulo.* Berkeley: University of California.

Calhoun, C., Price, P., & Timmer, A. (Eds.). (2002). *Understanding September 11.* New York: New Press.

Campbell, B., & Brenner, A. D. (2000). *Death squads in global perspective: Murder with deniability.* New York: St. Martin's.

Casey, C. (2002). *"States of emergency": Islam, youth gangs, and the politically unseeable.* Unpublished manuscript, University of California, Los Angeles.

Castells, M. (1997). *The information age: Economy, society and culture* (Volume 2: The Power of Identity). Malden, MA: Blackwell.

Castells, M. (2000). *The information age: Economy, society and culture* (Volume 3: End of Millennium). Malden, MA: Blackwell.

Children in Organised Armed Violence. (2002). *From guerrillas to gangs.* Retrieved November 18, 2004, from www.paranaonline .org.br

Children in Organised Armed Violence. (2003). *Country reports, Rio de Janeiro, Viva Rio.* Retrieved November 14, 2004, from http:// www.coav.org.br/

Children in Organised Armed Violence. (2004). *Youth gangs using arsenal inherited from Haitian government.* Retrieved November 14, 2004, from http://www.coav.org.br/frame.asp?url=/publique/ cgi/cgilua.exe/sys/start.htm?UserActiveTemplate= %5Fen&infoid=827&sid=38

Cloward, R., & Ohlin, L. (1960). *Delinquency and opportunity.* Glencoe, IL: Free Press.

Cohen, A. (1955). *Delinquent boys.* Glencoe, IL: Free Press.

Davies, A. (1998). Youth gangs, masculinity and violence in late Victorian Manchester and Salford. *Journal of Social History, 32,* 349–370.

Davis, M. (2004, March-April). Planet of slums. *New Left Review, 26.* Retrieved November 13, 2004, from http://www.newleftreview .net/NLR26001.shtml

Decesare, D. (2003). From Civil War to gang war: The tragedy of Edgar Bolanos. In L. Kontos, D. Brotherton, & L. Barrios (Eds.), *Gangs and society: Alternative perspectives* (pp. 283–313). New York: Columbia University Press.

de Soto, H. (1990). *The other path: The invisible revolution in the Third World.* New York: Harper & Row.

Dowdney, L. (2003). *Children of the drug trade: A case study of children in organized armed violence in Rio de Janeiro.* Rio de Janeiro: 7Letras.

Elias, N. (1994). *The civilizing process: The history of manners.* Oxford: Blackwell. (Original work published 1939)

Farmer, P. (1994). *The uses of Haiti.* Monroe, ME: Common Courage Press.

Finckenauer, J. O., & Waring, E. J. (1998). *Russian mafia in America: Immigration, culture, and crime.* Boston: Northeastern University Press.

Finestone, H. (1957). Cats, kicks, and color. *Social Problems, 5,* 3–13.

Finestone, H. (1967). Reformation and recidivism among Italian and Polish criminal offenders. *American Journal of Sociology, 72,* 575–588.

Frank, A. G. (1970). *Latin America: Underdevelopment or revolution.* New York: Monthly Review Press.

French, H. W. (2004, July 28). New boomtowns change path of China's growth. *New York Times,* p. 1.

Goldstone, J. A. (2002). States, terrorists, and the clash of civilizations. In C. Calhoun, P. Price, & A. Timmer (Eds.), *Understanding September 11* (pp. 139–158). New York: New Press.

Grennan, S., Britz, M. T., Rush, J., & Barker, T. (2000). *Gangs: An international approach.* Upper Saddle River, NJ: Prentice Hall.

Gunst, L. (1995). *Born fi' dead: A journey through the Jamaican Posse underworld.* New York: Henry Holt & Company.

Hagedorn, J. M. (1999). Gangs and globalization. In M. Klein, H-J. Kerner, C. L. Maxson, & E. G. Weitekamp (Eds.), *The Eurogang paradox: Street gangs and youth groups in the U.S. and Europe* (pp. 41–58). Dordrecht: Kluwer Academic.

Hagedorn, J. M. (2001). Gangs and the informal economy. In R. Huff (Ed.), *Gangs in America III* (pp. 101–120). Beverly Hills, CA: Sage.

Hagedorn, J. M. (in press-a). Gangs in late modernity. In J. M. Hagedorn (Ed.), *Gangs in the global city: Reconsidering criminology.* Champaign: University of Illinois Press.

Hagedorn, J. M. (Ed.). (in press-b). *Gangs in the global city: Reconsidering criminology.* Champaign: University of Illinois Press.

Hagedorn, J. M., & Perry, D. (2002). *Contested cities.* Paper presented at the annual meeting of the American Society of Criminology, Chicago.

Hagedorn, J. M., & Rauch, B. (2004). *Variations in urban homicide.* Paper presented at the City Futures Conference, Chicago.

Hayden, T. (2004). *Street wars: Gangs and the future of violence.* New York: New Press.

Hazlehurst, C. (in press). Observing New Zealand "gangs," 1950–2000: Learning from a small country. In J. M. Hagedorn (Ed.), *Gangs in the global city: Criminology reconsidered.* Champaign: University of Illinois Press.

Hazlehurst, K., & Hazlehurst, C. (Eds.). (1998). *Gangs and youth subcultures: International explorations.* New Brunswick, NJ: Transaction.

Hobsbawm, E. (1969). *Bandits.* New York: Pantheon.

hooks, b. (1994). *Misogyny, gangsta rap, and the piano.* Retrieved November 14, 2004, from http://eserver.org/race/misogyny.html

Human Rights Watch. (2002). *The Bakassi Boys: The legitimation of murder and torture.* Retrieved November 14, 2004, from http://www.hrw.org/reports/2002/nigeria2/index.htm#TopOfPage

Human Rights Watch. (2004). *Stop the use of child soldiers.* Retrieved November 14, 2004, from http://hrw.org/campaigns/crp/index.htm

Kaldor, M. (1999). *New and old wars: Organized violence in a global era.* Stanford, CA: Stanford University Press.

Kitwana, B. (1994). *Rap on Gangsta rap: Who run it?* Chicago: Third World Press.

Kitwana, B. (2002). *Hip hop generation: Young Blacks and the crisis of American culture.* New York: Basic Civitas.

Klein, M. W. (1971). *Street gangs and street workers.* Englewood Cliffs, NJ: Prentice Hall.

Klein, M. W. (1995). *The American street gang: Its nature, prevalence, and control.* New York: Oxford University Press.

Klein, M., Kerner, H.-J., Maxsen, C. L., & Weitekamp, E. G. (Eds.). (2001). *The Eurogang paradox: Street gangs and youth groups in the U.S. and Europe.* Dordrecht: Kluwer Academic.

Kontos, L., Brotherton, D., & Barrios, L. (Eds.). (2003). *Gangs and society: Alternative perspectives.* New York: Columbia University Press.

Kornhauser, R. R. (1978). *Social sources of delinquency: An appraisal of analytic models.* Chicago: University of Chicago.

Kovats-Bernat, J. C. (2000). Anti-gang, Arimaj, and the war on street children. *Peace Review, 12,* 415–421.

Lien, I. (2002). *The dynamics of honor in violence and cultural change.* Unpublished manuscript, Norwegian Institute for Urban and Regional Research, Oslo, Norway.

Marcuse, P. (1997). The enclave, the Citadel, and the ghetto: What has changed in the post-Fordist U.S. city. *Urban Affairs Review, 33,* 228–264.

Massey, D. S. (1996). The age of extremes: Concentrated affluence and poverty in the twenty-first century. *Demography, 33,* 395–412.

Miller, W. B. (1958). Lower class culture as a generating milieu of gang delinquency. *Journal of Social Issues, 14,* 5–19.

Miller, W. B. (1982). *Crime by youth gangs and groups in the United States.* Washington, DC: U.S. Department of Justice, Office of Justice Programs, Office of Juvenile Justice and Delinquency Prevention.

Moore, J. W. (1978). *Homeboys: Gangs, drugs, and prison in the barrios of Los Angeles.* Philadelphia: Temple University Press.

Moore, J. W. (1991). *Going down to the barrio: Homeboys and homegirls in change.* Philadelphia: Temple University Press.

Moore, J. W. (in press). Female gangs: Gender and globalization. In J. M. Hagedorn (Ed.), *Gangs in the global city: Criminology reconsidered.* Champaign: University of Illinois Press.

Nelli, H. S. (1969). Italians and crime in Chicago: The formative years, 1890–1920. *American Journal of Sociology, 74,* 373–391.

Nisbet, R. A. (1980). *History of the idea of progress.* New York: Basic Books.

Park, R. (1940). *Race and culture.* Chicago: University of Chicago.

Pattillo, M. E. (1998). Sweet mothers and gangbangers: Managing crime in a Black middle-class neighborhood. *Social Forces, 76,* 747–774.

Pearson, G. (1983). *Hooligan: A history of respectable fears.* New York: Shocken Books.

Pinnock, D. (1984). *The brotherhoods: Street gangs and state control in Cape Town.* Cape Town: David Philip.

Pitts, J. (2000). *The new politics of youth crime: Discipline or solidarity?* Basing-stoke: Palgrave.

Portes, A., Castells, M., & Benton, L. A. (Eds.). (1989). *The informal economy: Studies in advanced and less advanced countries.* Baltimore, MD: Johns Hopkins Press.

Reuter, P. (1996). The mismeasurement of illegal drug markets. In S. Pozo (Ed.), *Exploring the underground economy* (pp. 63–80). Kalamazoo, MI: Upjohn Institute.

Ro, R. (1996). *Gangsta: Merchandizing the rhymes of violence.* New York: St. Martin's.

Rose, T. (1994). *Black noise: Rap music and Black culture in contemporary America.* Hanover, NH: Wesleyan University Press.

Rotella, S. (1998). *Twilight on the line: Underworlds and politics at the U.S.-Mexico border* (1st ed.). New York: Norton.

Sampson, R. J., & Groves, W. B. (1989). Community structure and crime: Testing social-disorganization theory. *American Journal of Sociology, 94,* 774–802.

Sampson, R. J., Raudenbush, S. W., & Earls, F. (1997). Neighborhoods and violent crime: A multilevel study of collective efficacy. *Science, 277,* 918–924.

Sassen, S. (2002). Governance hotspots: Challenges we must confront in the post-September 11 world. In C. Calhoun, P. Price, & A. Timmer (Eds.), *Understanding September 11* (pp. 106–120). New York: New Press.

Savelsberg, J., Cleveland, L. L., & King, R. D. (2004). Institutional environments and scholarly work: American criminology, 1951–1993. *Social Forces, 82,* 1275–1302.

Shaw, C. R., & McKay, H. D. (1942). *Juvenile delinquency and urban areas* (1st ed.). Chicago: University of Chicago.

Short, J. F. (1996). Personal, gang, and community careers. In R. C. Huff (Ed.), *Gangs in America* (2nd ed., pp. 221–240). Thousand Oaks, CA: Sage.

Short, J. F., Jr., & Strodtbeck, F. L. (1965). *Group process and gang delinquency.* Chicago: University of Chicago Press.

Shurink, W. J. (1986). *Number gangs in South African prisons: An organizational perspective.* Paper presented at the Association for Sociology in Southern Africa, Durban, South Africa.

Spergel, I. A. (1995). *The youth gang problem: A community approach.* New York: Oxford University Press.

Taylor, C. (1989). *Dangerous society.* East Lansing: Michigan State University Press.

Thrasher, F. (1927). *The gang* (1st ed.). Chicago: University of Chicago.

Touraine, A. (1995). *Critique of modernity.* Oxford: Blackwell.

Touraine, A. (2000). *Can we live together? Equality and difference.* Stanford, CA: Stanford University Press.

Touraine, A. (2001). *Beyond neoliberalism.* Cambridge, UK: Polity Press.

UN Convention on Transnational Organized Crime. (2000). Retrieved November 14, 2004, from http://www.unodc.org/palermo.convmain.html

UN-Habitat. (2003). *Slums of the world: The face of urban poverty in the new millennium.* Nairobi, Kenya: United Nations Human Settlements Programme.

van Gemert, F. (2001). Crips in orange: Gangs and groups in the Netherlands. In M. Klein, H.-J. Kerner, C. L. Maxson, & E. G. Weitekamp (Eds.), *The Eurogang paradox: Street gangs and youth groups in the U.S. and Europe* (pp. 145–152). Dordrecht: Kluwer Academic.

Venkatesh, S. A. (2000). *American project: The rise and fall of a modern ghetto.* Cambridge, MA: Harvard University Press.

Venkatesh, S. A., & Leavitt, S. D. (2000). "Are we a family or a business?" History and disjuncture in the urban American street gang. *Theory and Society, 29,* 427–462.

Wacquant, L. (1999). Urban marginality in the coming millennium. *Urban Studies, 36,* 1639–1647.

Wacquant, L. (2000). The new "peculiar institution": On the prison as surrogate ghetto. *Theoretical Criminology, 4,* 377–389.

Wacquant, L. (2004). *Deadly symbiosis: Race and the rise of neoliberal penalty.* London: Polity Press.

Weber, M. (1968). *Economy and society* (Vol. 1). Berkeley: University of California Press.

Wilson, W. J., & Sampson, R. J. (1995). Toward a theory of race, crime, and urban inequality. In J. Hagan & R. D. Peterson (Eds.), *Crime and inequality* (pp. 37–54). Stanford, CA: Stanford University Press.

Wirth, L. (1956). *The ghetto.* Chicago: University of Chicago Press. (Original work published 1928)

World Bank Institute. (2000). *Street children: Latin America's wasted resource.* Retrieved November 14, 2004, from http://www1.worldbank.org/deboutreach/ summer00/article.asp?id=64

Yablonsky, L. (1966). *The violent gang.* New York: Macmillan.

Discussion Questions

1. In his article, Hagedorn argues that the creation and existence of youth gangs are determined by a set of universal global factors. Review and explain the importance of each factor.

   Students should consider the following factors in their discussion: urbanization, globalization, resistance identities, underground economy, the urban redivision of space, and institutionalization of gangs.

2. What does Hagedorn mean when he argues that in some cities gangs have "institutionalized"?

   According to Hagedorn, gangs have institutionalized when they persist over time despite changes in leadership so that they are able to adapt to changing environments and fulfill some community need. Institutionalization also refers to gangs' complex organizations that sustain multiple roles of their members and organizes the outlook of their members through rules, symbols, and rituals.

Source: From Hagedorn, J. M. (2005). The global impact of gangs. *Journal of Contemporary Criminal Justice, 21*(5), pp. 153–169. Reprinted by permission of Sage Publications.

PART X

ENVIRONMENT

CHAPTER 27

Nature's Trust

A Legal, Political and Moral Frame for Global Warming

Mary Christina Wood (2007)

> Mary Christina Wood argues that the subversion of environmental law by government and industry permitted environmental destruction and exacerbated the problem of global warming. Wood argues that to confront our current climate crisis, societies must begin to reframe environmental laws to include a commitment to "Nature's Trust."

Introduction

Melting icecaps. Raging wildfires. Widespread drought. 35,000 Europeans, dead from a heat wave. Jakarta, underwater. Drowning polar bears. West Nile virus. Species in mass exodus towards the poles. Hurricane Katrina.

Those are the headlines over the past few years. Yet many Americans are still asleep to climate crisis. They are in for quite a shock when they wake up to realize the consequences of ignoring this threat. Climate is the invisible currency of our lives. It supports our food supplies, water sources, private property, businesses, and recreation. Yet, for most of us, it has been an overlooked source of our security and comfort.

That is about to change.

In this decade, we will decide whether to hand over to future generations an imperiled world or a world on its way towards restored natural abundance.[1] At this pivotal moment in human history, our need to define government's obligations towards future generations has perhaps never been greater. Yet we lack a legal beacon to guide us through this time of decision. I hope to offer a way of thinking that draws on timeless principles of property law to characterize government's obligation to preserve the natural inheritance belonging to the future generations.

I

First, let me briefly explain the dynamics of global warming. Complex as it is, global warming can be presented in terms that the average American understands.[2] Through our emissions of greenhouse gases, we are literally creating a heat trap for ourselves and for all living things on Earth.[3] The sun sends a massive amount of energy that warms our planet. The energy then radiates back into space as heat, but some heat is held captive by heat-trapping gases in the atmosphere. These gases—including carbon dioxide and methane—regulate the temperature of Earth.[4] Before the Industrial Revolution, Nature had maintained a balance in the gases to keep the Earth's average surface temperature at fifty-nine degrees Fahrenheit.[5] It may be hard to appreciate the remarkability of a fifty-nine degree average until you consider that the ecosystems we know and depend on today evolved against this average temperature. Essentially, fifty-nine degrees is for Earth what 98.7 degrees is for our bodies.

Since the Industrial Revolution, Earth's populations have burned massive quantities of fossil fuels. In doing so, we literally have changed the composition of the atmosphere such that less heat can escape into space.[6] It is no great mystery why the great ice sheets of this planet are melting.

Just as an ice cube will melt in a warm room, so is the Polar Ice Cap, Greenland, and every major glacier of the world melting on our warming Earth.[7] Glacier National Park in Montana is losing its glaciers so fast that it may have none left by 2030—just twenty-three years from now.[8]

Carbon dioxide—the gas emitted from cars, coal fire plants, and gas heating[9]—has climbed to levels unknown in the past 650,000 years,[10] and we are still pumping it out at an annual increase of two percent per year.[11] According to the United Nations Intergovernmental Panel on Climate Change (IPCC), the average surface temperature on Earth will rise between 2.5 degrees and 10.4 degrees Fahrenheit within the next 100 years if our greenhouse gas emissions do not turn downward soon enough.[12]

Our prior carbon pollution has already locked us into an irrevocable temperature rise of up to two degrees Fahrenheit.[13] Two degrees does not sound like much at all until you realize that the Earth's average temperature has not varied by more than 1.8 degrees Fahrenheit in the last 10,000 years.[14] Just a few degrees of average temperature change makes the difference between an ice age and our current climate.[15] Temperatures only five to nine degrees Fahrenheit cooler than those today marked the end of the last Ice Age, when the northeast United States was under 3000 feet of ice.[16] In light of that fact, consider the effect of a ten degree difference on the hot side.[17] Once we understand the climate premium that every single degree Fahrenheit carries, we would no more dismiss a ten degree temperature rise for Earth than we would dismiss a 108 degree fever in our bodies.

So, what does all of this mean for us? In effect, you and I—along with all of the other people and species on this Earth—find ourselves in a greenhouse with climbing temperatures.[18] And this situation is bound to create hostility as Americans alone account for nearly thirty percent of the world's greenhouse gas emissions.[19] There is no magic Tylenol that will cure this temperature rise overnight, because carbon dioxide can persist in the atmosphere for up to a few centuries.[20]

Hurricane Katrina—which devastated the U.S. Gulf Coast in 2005—signaled what we can expect from the global warming already underway as a result of the carbon emissions that we cannot call back.[21] Scientists across multiple disciplines warn of crop losses,[22] food shortages,[23] flooding,[24] coastal loss,[25] wildfire,[26] drought,[27] pests,[28] hurricanes,[29] tornadoes,[30] heat waves,[31] landslides,[32] species extinctions,[33] vanishing snow pack,[34] increased disease vectors,[35] and other harms.[36]

An international climate research team recently warned of a need to prepare for as many as fifty million environmental refugees by 2010.[37]

If we do nothing to curb carbon emissions, we will commit ourselves to a future that most Americans cannot even imagine. Jim Hansen, the leading climate scientist for the National Aeronautics and Space Administration (NASA), presents the ten degree Fahrenheit scenario: it will send fifty percent or more species into extinction.[38] That is equivalent to the mass extinction that occurred fifty-five million years ago.[39] In his words, "Life will survive, but it will do so on a transformed planet."[40] A mere five-degree Fahrenheit temperature increase may cause an eighty foot rise in sea level.[41] Hansen points out: "In that case, the United States would lose most East Coast cities: Boston, New York, Philadelphia, Washington, and Miami; indeed, practically the entire state of Florida would be under water. Fifty million people in the U.S. live below that sea level."[42]

I could go on detailing how climate crisis will affect the lives of every human on Earth. What I have mentioned is just the tip of the iceberg—a phrase on its way out. British commentator Mark Lynas, author of *High Tide*, summarizes the Earth's situation this way: "Let me put it simply: if we go on emitting greenhouse gases at anything like the current rate, most of the surface of the globe will be rendered uninhabitable within the lifetimes of most readers of this article."[43]

II

As a group, Americans yearn to have peace of mind over the future for themselves and their children. Entire industries are premised on the inclination of Americans to sacrifice a little now in order to buy security in the future. We simply would not have insurance, estate planning, retirement accounts, or Social Security were it not for the strongly held preference on the part of Americans to pay for disaster avoidance.

As a society, we are now in the position of buying climate insurance. By most scientific accounts, we still have the ability to stabilize the Earth's temperature increase at two degrees Fahrenheit[44]—remember that two degrees, because it is the benchmark of your future. As Jim Hansen puts it, "further global warming exceeding two degrees Fahrenheit will be dangerous."[45] Here is the purchase price of that climate insurance: we have to curb drastically our greenhouse gas emissions, beginning immediately.[46]

As a planet, we have been at a similar danger point before. When it was discovered in the 1970s that chlorofluorocarbons (CFCs) were putting a hole in the atmosphere's ozone layer, we stopped using them, and the hole is now repairing itself.[47] While, at the time, the CFC industry tried to convince us that Western civilization would crumble without spray canisters,[48] that scenario proved not to be the case. The ozone layer is crucial, as it shields us from the harmful ultraviolet light coming from the Sun.[49] Looking back, are we not grateful that the decision-makers at the time decided not to trade out our Earth's ozone layer for CFCs?

Transitioning to a carbon-free society is more complicated than our previous experience with CFCs because it involves nearly every sector of society. This process is not going to be easy. Carbon is emitted all over the place. But the basic choice is still the same as that presented to humankind by the ozone hole discovery: do we take bold action now in order to buy climate security in the future? Or do we continue on our business-as-usual course with the knowledge that it will ultimately lead to catastrophe for ourselves and our children—that it will drain our descendants of the natural abundance and security that we all took for granted? This choice cannot be characterized as just another environmental issue. As author Ross Gelbspan puts it, "[T]he climate crisis is far more than just an environmental issue. It is a civilizational issue."[50]

Unfortunately, we have no latitude for indecision. Hansen states: "[W]e have at most ten years—not ten years to decide upon action, but ten years to alter fundamentally the trajectory of global greenhouse emissions."[51] You might wonder why the atmosphere is giving us so little time. It is because we have already pumped so much carbon into it that we are likely nearing a "tipping point" that will trigger irreversible dynamics.[52] After that tipping point, our subsequent carbon reductions, no matter how impressive, will not thwart long-term catastrophe.[53]

Let me be clear. I do not mean to imply that all climate catastrophes will visit us on January 1 of Year Eleven from now. The tipping point concept means this: if we continue business as usual, then at some point within this coming decade, and probably sooner rather than later, we will effectively place a lock on the door of our heating greenhouse and throw out the key. Our children and future generations are trapped in that greenhouse with rising temperatures, and they will have no way to get out. This ten-year action window we are now looking through means that, if we pour resources into the wrong strategy, we will not have time to go back and chart another course before this tipping point has come and gone.

State legislatures, federal agencies, and governors across the country should be burning the midnight oil (or, rather, fluorescent lights) figuring out solutions to get us to a carbon-free society in the short time we have left. But, with few exceptions,[54] our government is still sleeping

through climate crisis. So scientists are trying new ways—any ways they can think of—to wake people up to this urgency. In January 2007, the Harvard Medical School's Center for Health and Global Environment convened top climate scientists to hold a press conference in Washington, D.C., with national evangelical Christian leaders. They jointly delivered an "Urgent Call to Action" to the President of the United States to "protect Creation."[55] How many times have you seen scientists and Evangelicals holding a press conference together to protect Creation? They stated their "Shared Concern": "[T]he Earth . . . is seriously imperiled . . . .[W]e are gradually destroying the sustaining community of life on which all living things on Earth depend . . . .We declare that every sector of our nation's leadership . . . must act now . . . before it is too late . . . . Business as usual cannot continue yet one more day."[56]

The international community is sounding the same alarm. Three months ago British Prime Minister Tony Blair said to the world: 'This disaster is not set to happen in some science fiction future many years ahead, but in our lifetime. Unless we act now . . . these consequences, disastrous as they are, will be irreversible."[57] In February 2007, an international climate team released a report setting forth immediate policy initiatives to combat climate crisis, stating: "Humanity must act collectively and urgently to change course through leadership at all levels of society. There is no more time for delay."[58]

These are not the voices of Chicken Little and Henny Penny.[59] If someone dismisses climate warming to you as "sky is falling" kind of talk,[60] go back and read the book *Chicken Little* and see if you can find any intelligent comparison between mounting atmospheric heat-trapping gases and an acorn falling on a little chicken's head. The United Nations' Intergovernmental Panel on Climate Change (IPCC) issued a report in February 2007, stating that climate change is "unequivocal,"[61] A second report was issued in draft form in March 2007, discussing the catastrophic impacts of unchecked global warming.[62] These United Nations (U.N.) reports compile the conclusions of more than 1200 authors and 2500 expert reviewers, reflecting scientific expertise from more than 130 countries.[63] To be sure, there are those few global warming "contrarians" dismissing the threat, but before you place the future of your children in their hands, check out their affiliations with the fossil fuel industry.[64] When the U.N. report came out in February ending any debate on whether global warming existed,[65] the Exxon-funded American Enterprise Institute responded with an ad offering $10,000 to any scientist who could refute it.[66] Let us think about a logical way to process these contrarian views. If several doctors diagnosed your child with life-threatening bacterial meningitis, you would likely not waste time going back to debate the germ theory of medicine with them. You would start the antibiotics and hope or pray for the best.

The urgent warnings coming from all branches of science are intended to focus society on reaching a decision, now.

III

The global warming crisis, encompassing as it is, can be confronted by setting a firm national timeline for greenhouse gas reduction. You can think of this timeline as Nature's Carbon Mandate. Scientists have defined it very clearly. First, we must reverse the climbing trajectory of greenhouse gas emissions within the next decade.[67] Second, over the longer term, we must reduce emissions as much as eighty percent below 1990 levels by 2050.[68]

These goals are quantitative, not progressive. Making progress towards meeting Nature's Mandate is not enough. This is carbon math, and falling short means risking a temperature rise of up to ten degrees. If Americans are to secure the future for themselves and their children, they must understand this carbon math as readily as they understand that four quarters equal a dollar.

We simply cannot meet Nature's Mandate without governmental leadership. The carbon problem transcends all societal sectors—including transport, energy, housing, and industry. Government is the huge engine that propels our society. We have thousands of agencies—indeed more than any other nation in the world. They exist at the federal, state, and local levels. Collectively, these agencies hold immense expertise, authority, and staffing to solve environmental problems. If every one of these agencies made global warming a top priority, we might stand a chance of meeting Nature's Mandate head on. But to implement programs necessary to reverse our carbon emissions within ten years, government has to start now. With respect to this need to act, Prime Minister Blair stated, 'There is nothing more serious, more urgent, more demanding of leadership . . . in the global community.'[69]

European countries are well on the way to reducing carbon emissions.[70] But, what is the U.S. government doing? It is driving the United States towards *runaway* greenhouse gas emissions. County commissioners are approving trophy home subdivisions as if global warming does not exist.[71] State environmental agencies are approving air permits as if global warming does not exist.[72] The U.S. Forest Service is delivering timber sales, as if global warming does not exist.[73] Magnify this trend by the hundreds of government actions taken on a daily basis across the country. And consider this: The electric power industry is racing to build more than 150 new coal-fired power plants across the United States.[74] The industry investment in these plants reflects an assumption that our U.S. Environmental Protection Agency (EPA) will grant permits under environmental statutes allowing them to spew forth "hundreds of millions of tons of carbon dioxide into the atmosphere each year for decades to come" as if global warming does not exist.[75] You see, nearly every agency in the United States is acting as if global warming does not exist.

Political will grows overnight when citizens demand action. But those Americans who *are* awake to this crisis are focusing their energy on reducing their own carbon footprint rather than holding their leaders accountable. Our voluntary efforts are vitally important, but they also conceal a state of national chaos. We will not come into compliance with Nature's Mandate in the very short time we have left through voluntary efforts alone. The fact that Americans are trying to solve global warming on their own tells us that we have lost our sense of governmental accountability in environmental issues. In the next section, I will suggest why our system of law, as currently framed by government, will not respond to the climate crisis. Then I will propose how the American public can reframe our environmental law to demand the regulation necessary to meet Nature's Mandate.

IV

As we all know, to analyze a problem, we often need to go back to its roots. For the past three decades, we have looked to environmental law to address environmental problems. Environmental law consists of hundreds of statutes and regulations passed since the 1970s to protect our natural resources. Statutes give tremendous authority to officials at all levels of government to control just about any environmental harm.

But, before we turn to existing environmental laws to address global warming, we need to face one fact. Had environmental law worked, we would not have an ecological crisis on our hands. Environmental law delivered global warming and resource scarcity to our doorstep. Environmental law is crippled by enormous dysfunction, and if we fail to acknowledge this dysfunction, we will be looking for a solution in the same system that brought us this crisis.

The heart of the problem is this: While the purpose of every local, state, and federal environmental law is to protect natural resources, nearly every law also provides authority to the agencies to permit, in their *discretion*, the very pollution or land damage that the statutes were designed to prevent. Of course, the permit systems were never intended to subvert the goals of environmental statutes. But most agencies today spend nearly all of their resources to *permit*, rather than prohibit, environmental destruction. Essentially, our agencies have taken the discretion in the law and used it to destroy Nature, including its atmosphere.

Why would public servants who draw their salaries from the taxpayers do such a thing? It is because the call of private property rights is sounded in the halls of nearly every agency, nearly every day. Asphalt plant operators and chemical manufacturers, land developers and timber companies, automobile makers and coal-fired plant investors, and industrialists and individuals of all sorts call out to these agencies not to draw that regulatory line on their activity—because doing so would hurt their economic goals. This private property rights rhetoric has cowered officials at every level of government. Most officials are good, dedicated individuals, but as a group, they dread saying no to permits. So it is really no surprise that nearly every agency in America is still acting as if global warming did not exist.

Moreover, agencies have created so much complexity in their regulations, with meaningless acronyms and techno-jargon, that citizens are not speaking in the clear and forceful terms they need to in order to pose a counterweight to private property rights in this vast realm of agency discretion.

U.S. environmental law has created a thick veil of complexity behind which agencies serve private interests at the expense of the public. Our third branch of government—the judiciary—has been indifferent towards the politicization of agencies. Courts often defer to agency decisions on the false premise that agencies are neutral.[76] A compromised judicial check skews the Constitutional balance of power over the environment.

Without that third branch of government fulfilling its function, our democracy becomes an administrative tyranny over Nature, with dangerous results for our future.

V

You may be wondering how this subversion of environmental law could happen. The explanation lies in how government and industry have framed those laws. You can think of our environmental law, with all of its complicated statutes and regulations, as one big picture. The private property rights movement and agencies themselves have constructed a frame for that picture. The four sides of that frame are: discretion, discretion, discretion, and discretion—to allow damage to our natural resources. Though our statutes have aspirational goals of protecting our environment, when they are carried out through the discretion frame, these laws are used as tools to legalize damage to our resources. This usage is the source of species extinctions, air pollution, rivers running dry, dead zones in our oceans, toxic fish advisories, and global warming. Too much agency discretion can be a very dangerous thing.

Consider how our federal government is using this discretion frame to justify inaction in the face of climate crisis. EPA is the only federal agency charged by Congress to control air pollution.[77] Even though the Clean Air Act (CAA) provides EPA with the authority to regulate carbon dioxide,[78] EPA has steadfastly refused to do so.[79] Viewed through the frame that EPA has presented to the American public, the air is simply an object of regulation, a nebulous commons, and EPA can use its discretion to permit pollution by the oil, gas, coal, and automobile industries, despite the fact that this legalized pollution will degrade the atmosphere so much that it will no longer support human civilization as we know it.

Because the discretion frame never characterizes natural resources as quantified property assets, it allows government to damage the resources until they are all gone.

VI

How do we turn these agencies around and convince agency officials to use all of their authority to meet Nature's Mandate? Or, put another way, how do we convince officials to do what they currently consider to be political suicide? The public has to find a new frame for our existing statutes. Reframing environmental law does not mean throwing out existing environmental statutes. Again, those statutes give us a tremendous bureaucracy that we can steer back on course. Reframing means taking control of the language we use to hold government accountable under those statutes. As author George Lakoff says, "Reframing is changing the way the public sees the world. It is changing what counts as common sense."[80] Social frames can be destructive and oppressive, or they can embolden and inspire.

When Dr. Martin Luther King, Jr. urged Americans to take down another destructive frame in our history, he called out for all citizens to recognize the "fierce urgency of now."[81] Unbelievable as it may seem, the future of humanity rests on our generation being able to reframe government's obligation towards Nature.

VII

We can reframe environmental law by looking to timeless principles that reach far back on this and other continents. Indeed, such principles have grounded Supreme Court jurisprudence since the beginning of this country, but our agencies have lost sight of them in the last thirty years. In just that short period, these principles have been suppressed by thousands of pages of complex statutes and regulations that have proliferated across the legal landscape like an invasive species.

These foundational principles are as crucial today in the face of global warming as they were two hundred years ago, because they clearly define government's responsibility towards Nature and towards future generations. They do so by drawing upon ancient trust concepts originating in property law, not statutory law.

A trust is a fundamental type of ownership whereby one manages property for the benefit of another.[82] Long ago, the Supreme Court said that government, as the only enduring institution with control over human actions, is a trustee of Nature's resources.[83] What does this mean? You can imagine all of the resources essential to our human welfare and survival—including waters, wildlife, and air—as being packaged together in a legal endowment which I call Nature's Trust.[84] Our imperiled atmosphere is one of the assets in that trust. Government holds this great natural trust for all generations of citizens— past, present, and future.[85] We are all beneficiaries of this trust. Our great-grandparents were beneficiaries, and our great-grandchildren are beneficiaries, even though they are not yet born. We all hold a common property interest in Nature's Trust. You could think of this as Nature's treasure to be passed down through all generations of humankind.

With every trust there is a core duty of protection.[86] The trustee must defend the trust against injury.[87] Where it has been damaged, the trustee must restore the property in the trust.[88] Protecting our natural trust is more consequential than anything else government does. More consequential than jobs, health care, Social Security, education, or even defense, for this duty carries the weight not only of the present generation of citizens, but of all citizens to come.

It is not surprising that Nature's Trust principles were penned by judges long ago as the first environmental law

of this nation.[89] This fundamental doctrine of governance reaches back literally, to Justinian times and Roman law.[90] On this continent it reaches back even further, as much as 10,000 years. The native nations managed natural resources to ensure their availability in the same abundance for beneficiaries in distant generations.[91]

This ancient strand of law threads together all of our modern environmental statutes. In the National Environmental Policy Act (NEPA), Congress declared a national duty to "fulfill the responsibilities of each generation as trustee of the environment for succeeding generations."[92] When we invoke the trust to call upon government to protect our natural resources, we are not creating anything new.

Indeed, this sovereign trust over natural resources is so basic to governance that it is found in many other countries today. For example, in 1993, the Supreme Court of the Philippines invoked the trust to halt rainforest logging.[93] The Philippine government contended that it had complete discretion—remember discretion?— to allow private companies to cut the last 2.8% of remaining forest. Every government that is captured by special interests invokes the discretion frame because it conveniently and invisibly delivers the natural wealth of the nation to those interests. The Philippine Supreme Court enforced the peoples' trust and halted logging, stating:

> [E]very generation has a responsibility to the next to preserve that . . . harmony [of Nature] . . .
>
> . . .
>
> . . . [The] right [to a balanced ecology] concerns nothing less than self-preservation and self-perpetuation [,] . . . the advancement of which may even be said to predate all governments and constitutions.
>
> . . . [These principles] are assumed to exist from the inception of humankind.[94]

In other words, the trust frame forces government to hand down the endowment to future generations and not give it away to private interests that happen to be knocking loudly at government's door this generation.

These trust principles are engrained in government itself. Back in 1892, the U.S. Supreme Court said: 'The State can no more abdicate its trust over property in which the whole people are interested . . . than it can abdicate its police powers in the administration of government . . .'[95] The national chaos over global warming today is a direct result of our government abdicating its trust over our atmosphere.

VIII

Let us take a look at how the two frames I have described differ and their implications for humanity. In contrast to the discretion frame, the four sides of the trust frame are: obligation, obligation, obligation, obligation. We can take the very same set of environmental laws, and without changing a word of them, reframe our government's role with respect to Nature on a policy, legal, and moral level. By reframing, we can turn the government's *discretion* to destroy Nature into an *obligation* to protect Nature. But this principle works in reverse as well. We can pass any new law we want, and no matter what it says, if it is pressed through the discretion frame, the government will continue to impoverish natural resources until our society can no longer sustain itself.

So how do citizens reframe their government's role towards Nature at this pivotal time? They must expand their political imprint and use new words. They must speak in clear terms to their public officials at all levels of government.

An example of this type of discourse took place in McCall, Idaho, early 2007. Citizens there took down the discretion frame and put up the trust frame to protect their airshed. The Idaho Department of Environmental Quality (DEQ) proposed to issue an air permit for an asphalt plant that spews so much pollution into neighborhoods that mothers pull their kids inside day after day.[96] This permit, delivered by the hand of environmental law, would legalize the emission of fifty-four toxins right into the mountain air including lead, mercury, chromium six, dioxin, arsenic, and formaldehyde.[97] If you read the DEQ analysis of this proposed permit, you would be hard-pressed to find any sort of statement that this pollution would damage the airshed or the people living there, much less contribute greenhouse gas emissions. Instead, the analysis is filled with charts and incomprehensible technical statements. The reader is hit in the face with AACs, AACCs, TAP analysis, TRACT, HAPs, NESHAPs, SIP, MACT and more. Does the average citizen know what any of these terms mean? Amidst this gibberish, there is no core value driving governmental action.

There was a hearing in January 2007, to discuss this asphalt plant permit.[98] Normally, such hearings are filled with empty seats, and no wonder. But someone in McCall handed out flyers that said, quite simply, "Air for Sale," and the hearing room was packed with angry citizens. These were people drawn together by a common airshed—doctors, school kids, cancer victims, retirees, ski team coaches. Forest Service employees,

real estate brokers, teachers, mothers and fathers. When you translate the techno-jargon into "Air for Sale," you replace the discretion frame with the trust frame. Citizens suddenly feel that their property is being trampled by their own government. They start thinking, "Hey, that's my air, even if I share it with others." Pollution of that air becomes an infringement on American property. The frame makes a difference. It expresses our core expectations of government towards Nature.

IX

In this section, I would like to suggest how this trust frame helps in getting the American mind around the issue of global warming and, thus, how it becomes a coalescing force to confront climate crisis.

A

The first point has to do with Americans' feeling of entitlement towards Nature. The discretion frame, with all of its techno-jargon, gives no hint of environmental loss. The ARARs, TMDLs and TSDs, SIPs and HRSs, RPAs and PRPs, and the hundreds of other acronyms that our agencies use to hospice a dying planet really do not sound out any alarms to the public. These are neutral terms *because* they are incomprehensible. The public, then, is simply led to accept our degraded environment as a nebulous state of affairs. We never imagine that resources could be all spent down, all used up, or no longer there for us at some point in time. We seem unbothered even when our government leads us into global environmental catastrophe.

Yet, when we portray Nature as a trust rather than an ill-defined commons, we vest citizens with expectations of enduring property rights to a defined, bounded asset. Any loss of the trust becomes manifest. This frame resonates with and motivates the public because it taps into concepts that are familiar and important to Americans. Most people have heard of a trust. Kids know about college accounts. Adults know about retirement accounts. Americans are ferociously protective of their property rights. Once they understand they have a property right in something, they are inclined to protect it.

The trust frame has particular empowerment for youths, because it recognizes a property right of natural inheritance for the children of the world. It gives children an entitlement, as beneficiaries with no lesser standing than our own, to natural wealth, even though they are not yet old enough to exercise any voting power over their government. Children get angry when they think of our generation spending down a trust that they are entitled to take in the same abundance we have enjoyed.

B

Second, when we invoke the trust frame to explain global warming, we may be better able to overcome denial. The cruel irony is that the most disastrous manifestations of global warming may not occur until after our window of opportunity to avert the crisis has closed. A daunting obstacle we must confront is that most citizens do not perceive global warming as an immediate threat. For many Americans, the predictions are so extreme—like an ice age[99]—that they must seem like a science-fiction movie. Indeed, the more dire the environmental issue, the less likely it seems to be taken seriously in the United States. Many simply mock the messenger for spreading gloom. Global warming science is passed off as another doomsday scenario, and for some Americans that is all they need to hear in order not to take it seriously.

Without a sense of immediate loss, the public will not feel the urgency to demand government to take leadership in the short time frame we have left. Harvard professor Daniel Gilbert suggests that humans are hardwired by evolution to ignore threats like global warming.[100] Humans evolved to respond to immediate threats, like enemies coming over the hillside.[101]

The discretion frame put forth by our government capitalizes on this mental weakness and lures people into complacency. People operating within this frame think of air as "out there somewhere," way beyond that hillside. But people's perceptions change remarkably when they think of their trust being mismanaged. That is an immediate concern, even if the full effects will not be felt for years to come. Beneficiaries do not often sit idle when their trustee drains their trust. They hold their trustee accountable for the losses. And they worry about collapse scenarios. They understand stocks crashing. They understand a freewheeling grandfather spending down all of their rightful inheritance.

Recall the Philippines case mentioned earlier.[102] The Philippine Supreme Court brought forth the reality of a depleted natural trust by speaking in familiar terms of inheritance. It said simply, "[T]he day would not be too far when all else would be lost [for] generations which stand to inherit nothing but parched earth incapable of sustaining life."[103] There is no doomsday

language there. This is about intergenerational theft. We all know what theft is.

C

Third, by defining Nature in familiar property terms, the trust frame reconciles private property rights with environmental protection, which the discretion frame does not do. The discretion frame portrays environmental resources as nebulous features of the world in which we live. Private property rights carry the day in our agencies simply because they draw upon a language of property that is so deeply embedded in our national culture. To confront any environmental crisis today, including global warming, we have to be clear on how public resources and private property rights fit together in the scheme of things.

The trust frame is itself a property concept, so rather than pitting environment against property rights, you are fitting Nature into the system of property rights. The Nature's Trust frame is not anti-property rights. To the contrary, it affirms our collective property rights in assets that support humanity.

Every U.S. Supreme Court case invoking the trust makes clear that the government cannot allow private property rights to damage crucial public resources.[104] In 1907, the Supreme Court said, "[T]he state has an interest independent of and behind the titles of its citizens, in all the earth and air within its domain. It has the last word as to whether its mountains shall be stripped of their forests and its inhabitants shall breathe pure air."[105] And in 1892 when private enterprise threatened the shoreline of Lake Michigan, the Supreme Court said, "It would not be listened to that the control and management of [Lake Michigan]—a subject of concern to the whole people of the state—should . . . be placed elsewhere than in the state itself."[106] You can practically hear those same Justices saying today that "[i]t would not be listened to" that government would let our atmosphere be dangerously warmed in the name of individual, private property rights.[107]

Let us not for a moment think that just because private interests will have to be regulated and certain industries phased out entirely, the trust frame is anti-private property. In securing our public property, the trust also anchors our entire system of private property rights. All private property depends on Nature's infrastructure. When that infrastructure collapses, it causes natural disasters that make property boundaries irrelevant. Remember, private property deeds did not account for anything in the aftermath of Hurricane Katrina, and they will not account for anything along coastlines submerged by rising sea levels.

D

Finally, the trust frame has global reach. This is important because global warming is, after all, a global problem. When we portray it to the American public, we must be able to explain the role of foreign nations. Many people have heard about the Kyoto Protocol. They know that China is bringing massive numbers of coal-fired plants on line.[108] When Americans are asked to make changes in their own lives, they often reply that it will not make a difference because global warming is an international issue.

The trust framework positions all nations of the world in a logical relationship towards Nature. Transboundary assets like the atmosphere are shared as property among sovereign nations of the world. These nations are co-tenant trustees of the asset. In other words, they are all trustees, but they share the resource as co-tenants, bound by the same fundamental duties that organize, for example, the relationship of family members who share ownership of a mountain cabin as co-tenants.[109] Property law offers timeless principles to deal with common ownership. It has always imposed a responsibility on co-tenants not to degrade, or waste, the common asset.[110] This one concept lends definition to international responsibilities, whether we are talking about a shared fishery, an ocean, or the Earth's atmosphere.

Moreover, by embracing principles that are native to many other countries, the trust frame can be invoked by those citizens who are calling their own government to action. At a time when the world is so politically fractured, the trust frame offers hope that citizens across the entire planet can view Earth's resources in the same light and defend those resources in their many different languages, but with one voice.

Conclusion

If citizens seek a secure climate future for themselves and their children, they must call upon government to take immediate action. They must speak in clear terms through a powerful frame.

In *An Inconvenient Truth*, Al Gore presents climate crisis as a "moral and spiritual challenge" for our generation.[111] The trust frame is the obligation that springs from the heart of all humanity, pressed into the institution of government. The same trust principles that flow through a judge's pen can be preached from a pulpit or

spoken as the last words from a grandmother to her grandchildren anywhere in the world, because the trust encompasses a moral obligation that transcends all governments, cultures, and peoples on Earth. And that obligation is not just an attribute of this frame—it has been its enduring power through all of time, and it will be its enduring hope for all time to come.

Notes

1. *See* STERN REVIEW, THE ECONOMICS OF CLIMATE CHANGE, Summary of Conclusions, at vi (Cambridge University Press 2007), *available at* http://www.hm-treasury.gov.uk (follow "Independent Review" hyperlink; then follow "Stern Review on the Economics of Climate Change" hyperlink; then follow "Full Report" hyperlink) [hereinafter STERN REVIEW] (stating that if no action is taken to reduce emissions, the resulting temperature rise would cause "a radical change in the physical geography of the world . . . . "); *see also infra* notes 22–36.

2. For a full explanation of global warming dynamics, see Union of Concerned Scientists, Frequently Asked Questions About Global Warming, http://www.ucsusa.org/global_warming/science/global-warming-faq.html (last revised Mar. 8, 2007) [hereinafter Union of Concerned Scientists FAQ].

3. *Id.*

4. *Id.*

5. *See id.*

6. *Id.*

7. *See* UNITED NATIONS-SIGMA XI SCIENTIFIC EXPERT GROUP ON CLIMATE CHANGE, CONFRONTING CLIMATE CHANGE: AVOIDING THE UNMANAGEABLE AND MANAGING THE UNAVOIDABLE 1, 11 (2007), *available at* http://www.unfoundation.org/files/pdf/2007/SEG_Report.pdf [hereinafter U.N.-SIGMA XI REPORT]. For a comparison of historic and current photographs of glaciers, see AL GORE, AN INCONVENIENT TRUTH: THE PLANETARY EMERGENCY OF GLOBAL WARMING AND WHAT WE CAN DO ABOUT IT 42–59, 194–95 (2006). The mass of Greenland decreased by fifty cubic miles of ice in 2005. Jim Hansen, *The Threat to the Planet*, N.Y. REV. BOOKS, July 13, 2006, at 12, 13, *available at* http://www.nybooks.com/articles/19131. The Arctic sea ice is experiencing ice loss of about 38,000 square miles annually due to rising concentrations of greenhouse gases alongside natural variability. University of Colorado at Boulder, *Arctic Sea Ice Decline May Trigger Climate Change Cascade*, http://www.colorado.edu/news/releases/2007/109.html (Mar. 15, 2007) (summarizing research by National Center for Atmospheric Research and CU-Boulder's National Snow and Ice Data Center). Scientists have projected a seasonally ice-free Arctic Ocean between 2040 and 2050. *Id.* Recent research suggests that the Arctic ice may have already passed a "tipping point" whereby even "'natural climate fluctuations could send it into a tailspin.'" *Id.* (quoting Mark Serreze of CU-Boulder's Cooperative Institute for Research in Environmental Science). Scientists warn of a cascade of climate change reaching to other parts of the globe. *Id.*

8. U.S. Geological Survey, Melting Glaciers Signal Change in National Parks, http://www.nwrc.usgs.gov/world/content/land5.html (last modified Jan. 29, 2007); *see* GORE, *supra* note 7, at 48 ("Our own Glacier National Park will soon need to be renamed 'the park formerly known as Glacier.'"). In the last 150 years, the glaciated area of the Waterton-Glacier International Peace Park—a World Heritage

Site—has decreased by seventy-three percent. INT'L ENVTL. LAW PROJECT OF LEWIS & CLARK LAW SCH., PETITION TO THE WORLD HERITAGE COMMITTEE REQUESTING INCLUSION OF WATERTON-GLACIER INTERNATIONAL PEACE PARK ON THE LIST OF WORLD HERITAGE IN DANGER AS A RESULT OF CLIMATE CHANGE AND FOR PROTECTIVE MEASURES AND ACTIONS, at vii (2006), *available at* http://law.lclark.edu/org/ielp/objects/Waterton-Glacier Petition2.15.06.pdf. Of the 150 glaciers that were present in 1850, only twenty-seven remain today. *Id.* at 1.

9. *See* U.N.-SIGMA XI REPORT, *supra* note 7, at ix. Deforestation contributes substantially to carbon dioxide concentrations as well. *Id.*

10. GORE, *supra* note 7, at 66–67; Press Release, Union of Concerned Scientists, Authoritative Report Confirms Human Activity Driving Global Warming (Feb. 2, 2007), *available at* http://www.ucsusa.org/news/press_release/authoritative-report-confirms-0008.html (summarizing the findings of the United Nations).

11. Hansen, *supra* note 7, at 14 (noting increase of global carbon dioxide emissions of two percent each year during past ten years).

12. Union of Concerned Scientists FAQ, *supra* note 2 (summarizing the Intergovernmental Panel on Climate Change's (IPCC) Third Assessment Report); *see also* U.N.-SIGMA XI REPORT, *supra* note 7, at x–xi.

> If CO_2 emissions and concentrations grow according to mid-range projections . . . the global average surface temperature is expected to rise by 0.2°C to 0.4°C per decade [equivalent to 0.7° F. to 0.9° F.] throughout the 21st century and would continue to rise thereafter. The cumulative warming by 2100 would be approximately 3°C to 5°C [5.4° to 9° R] over preindustrial conditions.
>
> *Id.*

13. *See* U.N.-SIGMA XI REPORT, *supra note 7*, at x ("Even if human emissions could be instantaneously stopped, the world would not escape further climatic change. [A] further . . . rise in global-average surface temperature will take place as a result of the current atmospheric concentrations of greenhouse gases and particles."); Hansen, *supra* note 7, at 13.

14. Union of Concerned Scientists FAQ, *supra* note 2.

15. *See id.*

16. *Id.; see also* Hansen, *supra* note 7, at 13 (noting that the coldest ice ages had an average temperature of about ten degrees Fahrenheit less than today).

17. *See* U.N.-SIGMA XI REPORT, *supra* note 7, at x–xi. The report states:

> Accumulating scientific evidence suggests that changes in the average temperature of this magnitude are likely to be associated with large and perhaps abrupt changes in climatic patterns that, far more than average temperature alone, will adversely impact agriculture, forestry, fisheries, the availability of fresh water, the geography of disease, the livability of human settlements, and more.
> Id.

18. Global temperatures have already increased about 1.4 degrees Fahrenheit over pre-industrial levels. Robert Lee Hotz, A Call To Arms on Climate Shift, L.A. TIMES, Feb. 28, 2007, at 8 (summarizing the U.N.-Sigma XI Report).

19. GORE, supra note 7, at 250–51 (featuring a map depicting contributions across the globe); Hansen, supra note 7, at 16.

20. See Union of Concerned Scientists FAQ, supra note 2; see also James Hansen, foreword to AM. SOLAR ENERGY SOC'Y, TACKLING CLIMATE CHANGE IN THE U.S.: POTENTIAL CARBON EMISSIONS REDUCTIONS FROM ENERGY EFFICIENCY AND RENEWABLE ENERGY BY 2030 (Charles F. Kutscher ed., 2007), available at http://www.ases.org/climate

change/climate_change.pdf [hereinafter TACKLING CLIMATE CHANGE] (stating that a quarter of the carbon dioxide emissions from fossil fuel burning will persist in the atmosphere for more than 500 years).

21. Gore, supra note 7, at 92–93 (citing an MIT study and concluding that "[m]ajor storms spinning in both the Atlantic and Pacific since the 1970s have increased in duration and intensity by about 50 percent"); see U.N.-SIGMA XI REPORT, supra note 7, at x. The authors of the report pointed out:

> The seemingly modest changes in average temperature experienced over the 20th century have been accompanied by significant increases in the incidence of floods, droughts, heat waves, and wildfires, particularly since 1970. It now appears that the intensity of tropical storms has been increasing as well. There have also been large reductions in the extent of summer sea ice in the Arctic, large increases in summer melting on the Greenland Ice Sheet, signs of instability in the West Antarctic Ice Sheet, and movement in the geographic and altitudinal ranges of large numbers of plant and animal species.
>
> U.N.-SIGMA XI REPORT, *supra* note 7, at x.

22. NASA Goddard Space Flight Center, Computer Model Suggests Future Crop Loss Due to Potential Increase in Extreme Rain Events Over Next Century (Oct. 28, 2002), http://www.gsfc.nasa.gov/topstory/20021022cropdamage.html (projecting crop damage from water-logged soils leading to total losses of three billion dollars annually in the United States by 2030).

23. Associated Press, *Report Outlines Global Warming's Effects*, Mar. 12, 2007, *available at* http://www.christianpost.com/article/20070312/26266_Report_Oudines_Clobal_Warming's_Effects.htm [hereinafter A.P., *Report Outlines Global Warming's Effects*] (describing the U.N.'s IPCC Working Group II's conclusion that by 2080 between 200 and 600 million people could face starvation because of global warming); Philip Puella, *Global Warming Will Increase World Hunger*, REUTERS, May 27, 2005 (summarizing report by U.N. Food and Agricultural Organization); John Vidal & Tim Radford, *One in Six Countries Facing Food Shortage*, THE GUARDIAN, June 30, 2005, *available at* http://www.guardian.co.uk/climatechange/ story/0,12374,1517831,00.html (discussing U.N. report findings).

24. U.N.-SIGMA XI REPORT, *supra* note 7, at x, 1, 11; *see also id.* at v ("As the climate changes, . . . low-lying coastal communities worldwide will be flooded as sea level rises."); A.P., *Report Outlines Global Warming's Effects, supra* note 23 (stating that U.N. scientists conclude that by 2080, rising seas could flood about 100 million people worldwide each year).

25. U.N.-SIGMA XI REPORT, *supra* note 7, at 102. The U.N.-Sigma XI international team of climate scientists has called for a worldwide ban on coastal beachfront construction to minimize the hazards of climate-related disasters such as flooding and powerful storms. *Id.* at xvi; *see* Hotz, *supra* note 18 (summarizing the U.N.-Sigma XI Report)

26. Patrick O'Driscoll, *Study Says Global Warming Helps Extend Wildfire Season*, USA TODAY, July 7, 2006, at 3A (noting number of large wildfires in Idaho, Montana and Wyoming has increased sixty percent since 1987).

27. A.P., *Report Outlines Global Warming's Effects, supra* note 23 (stating U.N. scientists' conclusion that "within a couple of decades hundreds of millions of people won't have enough water" and that by 2050, more than one billion people in Asia could face water shortages). By 2080, water shortages could threaten 1.1 to 3.2 billion people if global warming continues. *Id.* The percentage of Earth's land area struck by serious drought more than doubled from the 1970s to the

early 2000s, according to the National Center for Atmospheric Research (NCAR). *See* Press Release, National Center for Atmospheric Research, *Drought's Crowing Reach: NCAR Study Points to Global Warming as Key Factor* (Jan. 10, 2005), *available at* http://www.ucar.edu/news/releases/2005/drought_research.shtml.

28. Blaine Harden & Juliet Eilperin, *On the Move to Outrun Climate Change*, Wash. Post, Nov. 26, 2006, at A10.

29. *See* U.N.-Sigma XI Report, *supra* note 7, at 28 (predicting "longer-lasting and more destructive hurricanes and typhoons"); Gore, *supra* note 7, at 92–107.

30. An increasing frequency of tornadoes seems to be occurring simultaneously with global warming, though scientists have not yet established a direct correlation. *See* National Oceanic and Atmospheric Association, *NOAA Reports Record Number of Tornadoes in 2004* (Dec. 30, 2004), http://www.noaanews.noaa.gov/stories2004/s2359.htm. *But see Reaping the Whirlwind: Extreme Weather Prompts Unprecedented Global Warming Alert*, Independent (UK), July 3, 2003, *available at* http://news.independent.co.uk/environment/article94497.ece (citing a report issued by the World Meteorological Organization linking extreme weather events, such as Switzerland's hottest June in 250 years and record number of tornadoes in United States, to climate change).

31. U.N.-Sigma XI Report, *supra* note 7, at 1 ("More frequent, longer-lasting, and more intense heat waves will cause many more deaths unless actions are taken to reduce vulnerability."). In 2003, a massive heat wave killed 35,000 people in Europe. *See* Shaoni Bhattacharya, *European Heatwave Caused 35,000 Deaths*, Newscientist.com, Oct. 10, 2003, http://www.newscientist.com/article.ns?id=dn4259. The U.S. Environmental Protection Agency (EPA) has issued a guide called the Excessive Heat Events Guidebook, which says, "Excessive heat events . . . are and will continue to be a *fact of life* in the United States." U.S. Envtl. Prot. Agency, Excessive Heat Events Guidebook, EPA # 430-B-06-005, 5 (2006), *available at* http://www.epa.gov/hiri/about/pdf/EHEguide_final.pdf (emphasis added).

32. *See* Alister Doyle, *Landslides Could Worsen with Global Warming*, Reuters, Jan. 18, 2006, *available at* http://www.enn.com/today.html?id=9688 (reporting conclusions of U.N. experts that if climate change predictions are correct, more intense and extreme rainfall will lead to increased landslides).

33. An international team of scientists has projected that between fifteen and thirty-seven percent of species on Earth will become extinct by 2050 because of global warming. *See* A.P., *Report Outlines Global Warming's Effects, supra* note 23 (quoting co-author of U.N. IPCC Working Group II Report, Dr. Terry Root of Stanford University, who stated that "[w]e truly are standing at the edge of mass extinction"); Carl Zimmer, *A Radical Step to Preserve a Species: Assisted Migration*, N.Y. Times, Jan. 23, 2007, at 4. Species are already migrating towards the poles in search of colder climates. *Id.; see also* Hansen, *supra* note 7, at 12. The Polar Bear has been proposed for listing under the Endangered Species Act. 12-Month Petition Finding and Proposed Rule to List the Polar Bear (Ursus Maritimus) as Threatened Throughout Its Range, 72 Fed. Reg. 1064, 1072 (proposed Jan. 9, 2007) (to be codified 50 C.F.R. pt. 17) (noting "[o]bserved and predicted changes in sea ice cover, characteristics, and time have profound effects on polar bears"); *see also* Juliet Eilperin, *U.S. Wants Polar Bears Listed as Threatened*, Wash. Post, Dec. 27, 2006, at A1 (stating summer sea ice on which polar bears depend for hunting could disappear by 2040). Coral reefs worldwide are bleaching and dying from pathogens that thrive in the warmer seas occurring as a result of climate heating. *See* Jonathan Amos, *Action Needed to Save Coral Reefs*, BBC News Online, Feb. 13, 2004, http://news.bbc.co.Uk/l/hi/sci/

tech/3487869.stm (summarizing report commissioned by Pew Center on Global Climate Change). Eighty percent of the coral reefs in the Caribbean Sea are already dead, an event "unprecedented on centennial and millennial scales." *Id.* (quoting coral expert Dr. Richard Aronso).

34. In 2003, the United Nations Environment Programme (UNEP) released a study predicting the ruin of many low-level ski resorts world-wide as a result of global warming. *See* United Nations Env't Programme, *Global Warming Threatens Many Low-Level Ski Resorts with Ruin—UN Study*, UN News Serv., Dec. 2, 2003, http://www.un.org/apps/news/printnewsAr.asp?nid=9035.

35. Climate warming is prompting disease vectors to move into new areas. Mosquitoes are invading higher elevation areas where they have never been, bringing with them diseases like malaria and yellow fever. *See* Associated Press, *Global Warming May Spread Diseases*, CBS News, June 20, 2002, *available at* http://www.cbsnews.com/stories/2002/06/20/tech/main512920.shtml.

36. For a broad discussion of global warming impacts, see Stern Review, *supra* note 1; U.N.-Sigma XI Report, *supra* note 7, at v. *See also* A.P., *Report Outlines Global Warming's Effects, supra* note 23 ("Changes in climate are now affecting physical and biological systems on every continent.") (quoting U.N. Draft report of IPCC Working Group II).

> Climate change is expected to have a widespread negative effect on water resources, natural ecosystems, coastal communities and infrastructure, air and water quality, biodiversity, coastal fisheries, parks and preserves, forestry, human health, agriculture and food production, and other factors that support economic performance and human well-being around the world.

U.N.-Sigma XI Report, *supra* note 7, at v.

37. U.N.-Sigma XI Report, *supra* note 7, at 99 (citing predictions by the U.N. University's Institute for Environment and Human Safety that fifty million people will be fleeing environmental degradation); *see* Hotz, *supra* note 18.

38. Hansen, *supra* note 7, at 12.

39. *Id.*

40. *Id.*

41. *Id.* At 13.

42. *Id.*

43. Mark Lynas, *Why We Must Ration the Future*, New Statesman, Oct. 23, 2006, at 12, *available at* http://www.newstatesman.com/200610230015. A leading team of economists has concluded: "Climate change threatens the basic elements of life for people around the world—access to water, food production, health, and use of land and the environment." Stern Review, *supra* note 1, Executive Summary, at vi.

44. Hansen, *supra* note 7, at 13. There appears to be substantial consensus among scientists worldwide that society can still thwart the most disastrous global warming by decreasing greenhouse gas emissions immediately. *See, e.g.*, U.N.-Sigma XI Report, *supra* note 7, at ix ("Significant harm from climate change is already occurring, and further damages are a certainty. The challenge now is to keep climate change from becoming a catastrophe. There is still a good chance of succeeding in this [effort] . . . . "); Stern Review, *supra* note 1, Summary of Conclusions, at vi ("There is still time to avoid the worst impacts of climate change, if we take strong action now.").

45. Hansen, *supra* note 7, at 14.

46. *See infra* notes 67–68 and accompanying text (explaining the reduction goals presented by the U.N. and scientists worldwide). *The Stern Review on the Economics of Climate Change*, a landmark economic report authored by Sir Nicholas Stern, former chief economist at the World Bank, concludes: The costs of stabili[z]ing the

climate are significant but manageable; delay would be dangerous and much more costly." STERN REVIEW, *supra* note 1, Summary of Conclusions, at vii.

47. *See* National Aeronautics and Space Administration, The Ozone Resource Page, http://www.nasa.gov/vision/earth/environment/ozone_resource_page.html (last visited Apr. 27, 2007) (citing a 2006 report by the World Meteorological Organization and the U.N. predicting the ozone would fully recover by approximately 2065); Brien Sparling, *Ozone Depletion, History, and Politics*, http://www.nas.nasa.gov/About/Education/Ozone/history.html (May 30, 2001).

48. Sparling, *supra* note 47.

49. NASA, The Ozone Resource Page, *supra* note 47.

50. Ross Gelbspan, Boiling Point: How Politicians, Big Oil and Coal, Journalists, and Activists are Fueling the Climate Crisis—and What We Can Do to Avert Disaster 1 (2004).

51. Hansen, *supra* note 7, at 16.

52. *See* STERN REVIEW, *supra* note 1, at 298 ("Recent scientific developments have placed more emphasis on the dangers of amplifying feedbacks of global temperature increases and the risks of crossing irreversible tipping points . . . ."); U.N.-SIGMA XI REPORT, *supra* note 7, at xi (stating that "increases beyond 2° C to 2.5° C above the 1750 level will entail sharply rising risks of crossing a climate 'tipping point' that could lead to intolerable impacts on human well-being . . . ."); Hansen, *supra* note 7, at 14 ("[B]ecause of the global warming already bound to take place as a result of the continuing long-term effects of greenhouse gases and the energy systems now in use, . . . it will soon be impossible to avoid climate change with far-ranging undesirable consequences. We have reached a critical tipping point.").

53. STERN REVIEW, *supra* note 1, at 298; U.N.-SIGMA XI REPORT, *supra* note 7, at xi; Hansen, *supra* note 7, at 14

54. California, for example, is a national leader in reducing greenhouse gas emissions. *See* Paul Krugman, *Global Warming Can Be Reduced Without Radical Change*, REGISTER GUARD (Eugene, Or.), Feb. 26, 2007, at A9.

55. *An Urgent Call To Action: Scientists and Evangelicals Unite to Protect Creation* (Jan. 17, 2007), *available at* http://www.conservation.org/ (follow "Conservation Programs" hyperlink; then follow "Conservation and Faith" hyperlink; then follow "Scientists and Evangelicals Unite to Protect Creation" hyperlink); Letter from Eric Chivian, M.D., Director, Ctr. for Health and the Global Env't, Harvard Med. Sch., and Rev. Richard Cizik, Vice President for Governmental Affairs, Nat'l Ass'n of Evangelicals, to President George W. Bush (Jan. 17, 2007) (on file with author) (enclosing *An Urgent Call to Action: Scientists and Evangelicals Unite to Protect Creation*); *see also* Rodrique Ngowi, *Evangelicals, Scientists Join Forces to Combat Global Warming*, BOSTON GLOBE, Jan. 14, 2007, *available at* http://www.boston.com (Search "Greater Boston" for "Evangelicals, Scientists Join Forces"; then follow "Evangelicals, Scientists Join Forces to Combat Global Warming" hyperlink).

56. *An Urgent Call to Action, supra* note 55.

57. Simon Hooper, *Report Sets Climate Change Challenge*, CNN.COM, Oct. 30, 2006, http://edition.cnn.com/2006/WORLD/europe/10/30/climate.costs/.

58. U.N.-SIGMA XI REPORT, *supra* note 7, at xviii.

59. *See generally* HELEN CRAIG, *Chicken Little, in* THE RANDOM HOUSE BOOK OF NURSERY STORIES 77 (1999) [hereinafter *Chicken Little*].

60. *See generally* Patrick J. Michaels, *Is the Sky* Really *Falling? A Review of Recent Global Warming Scare Stories, in* POL'Y ANALYSIS No. 576 (CATO Institute 2006), *available at* http://www.cato.org/pubs/pas/pa576.pdf. Patrick J. Michaels is an outspoken global warming

"contrarian" whose evaluation of climate science is informed by the following passage in the classic children's story *Chicken Little*. "One morning. Chicken Little was in the woods when an acorn fell on his head. 'Oh, my goodness! The sky is falling!' cried Chicken Little. 'I must go and tell the King.'" *Chicken Little, supra* note 59, at 77. The "contrarian" view has been marginalized by the worldwide scientific consensus on global warming. *See* Union of Concerned Scientists, Findings of the IPCC Fourth Assessment Report: Climate Change Science, http://www.ucsusa.org/global_warming/science/ipcc-highlightsl.html (last revised Feb. 23, 2007).

61. INTERGOVERNMENTAL PANEL ON CLIMATE CHANGE, CLIMATE CHANGE 2007: THE PHYSICAL BASIS, SUMMARY FOR POLICY MAKERS 5 (Feb. 5, 2007), *available at* http://www.ipcc.ch/SPM2feb07.pdf ("Warming of the climate system is unequivocal, as is now evident from observations of increases in global average air and ocean temperatures, widespread melting of snow and ice, and rising global average sea level."). This report, produced by IPCC Working Group I, is the first of three that comprise the full IPCC Fourth Assessment Report.

62. *See* A.P., *Report Outlines Global Warming's Effects, supra* note 23.

63. Union of Concerned Scientists, The IPCC: Who Are They and Why Do Their Climate Reports Matter?, http://www.ucsusa.org/global_warming/science/the-ipcc.html (last revised Mar. 8, 2007).

64. *See* Union of Concerned Scientists, *ExxonMobil's Tobacco-Like Disinformation Campaign on Global Warming Science*, http://www.ucsusa.org/global_warming/science/exxonmobilsmoke-mirrors-hot.html (last revised Feb. 12, 2007) (reporting that ExxonMobil has funneled nearly sixteen million dollars between 1998 and 2005 into a network of forty-five advocacy organizations seeking to confuse the public on global warming science).

65. *See* Hotz, *supra* note 18 (summarizing the U.N. IPCC report, and concluding that "[r]esearchers are no longer debating whether human-induced global warming is genuine").

66. Juliet Eilperin, *Climate Report Critics Offered Cash*, COLUMBIAN (Clark County, Wash.), Feb. 5, 2007, at A4; *see also* Kathleen Rest, *US Must Stop Ignoring Warming*, COLUMBIAN (Clark County, Wash.), Feb. 12, 2007 (discussing federal political interference with global warming science).

67. *See* Hansen, *supra* note 7, at 16; *see also supra* note 51 and accompanying text.

68. *See* TACKLING CLIMATE CHANGE, *supra* note 20, at 3; STERN REVIEW, *supra* note 1, Summary of Conclusions, at vii; Press Release, United Nations Framework Convention on Climate Change, UNFCCC Executive Secretary Calls for Speedy and Decisive International Action on Climate Change (Feb. 2, 2007) (summarizing the U.N. IPCC Report), *available at* http://unfccc.int (follow "Press" hyperlink; then follow "Press Releases" hyperlink; then follow hyperlink under 2 Feb 2007); *see also* Alan Zarembo, *Game Over on Global Warming?*, L.A. TIMES, Feb. 5, 2007.

Some individual states in the United States have set carbon reduction goals, but few outside of California have legislation to implement those goals. *See* 2006 Cal. Legis. Serv. 488 (codified at CAL. HEALTH & SAFETY CODE § 38,500, 38,550 (West 2006)) (mandating eighty percent reduction from 1990 level by 2050); Jon S. Corzine, Governor of N.J., Exec. Order No. 54 (Feb. 13, 2007) (mandating eighty percent greenhouse gas reduction below 2006 levels by 2050), *available at* http://www.state.nj.us/governor/news/news/approved/20070213a.html; GOVERNOR'S ADVISORY GROUP ON GLOBAL WARMING, OREGON STRATEGY FOR GREENHOUSE GAS REDUCTIONS, Executive Summary, at ii (2004), *available at* http://oregon.gov/ENERGY/GBLWRM/docs/GWReport-Final.pdf (detailing the goals of seventy-five percent reduction of greenhouse gas emissions below 1990 levels by 2050; arrest of growth of greenhouse *gas* emissions by 2010; ten percent reduction of emissions below 1990 levels by 2020). Some state goals, while seemingly ambitious, fall short. *See* Rachel La Corte, *Gregoire Signs Order on Climate-Change Goats for Washington*, Associated Press, Feb. 8, 2007 (outlining Washington Governor Chris Gregoire's Executive Order setting a goal of only fifty percent reduction below 1990 levels by 2050). For a complete list of carbon emissions targets set by states and foreign countries, see Pew Center on Global Climate Change, Emissions Targets: United States, http://www.pewclimate .org/what_s_being_done/targets/index.cfm (last visited Apr. 27, 2007).

69. Simon Hooper, *Report Sets Climate Change Challenge*, CNN.com, Oct. 30, 2006, http://www.cnn.com/2006/WORLD/europe/10/30/climate.costs/index.html.

70. *See* Euractiv.com, Parliament Wants 60–80% Less Greenhouse Gas Emissions by 2050, http://www.euractiv.com/en/sustainahility/parliament-wants-60–80-greenhouse-gasemissions-2050/article-148891 (Apr. 24, 2007) (describing the European Parliament's goal of a sixty to eighty percent reduction in greenhouse gas emissions by 2050); *see also* Stern Review, *supra* note 1, Summary of Conclusions, at viii; Richard Black, *New Law in the Climate Jungle*, BBC News, Mar. 13, 2007, http://news.bbc.co.uk/2/hi/science/nature/6445613.stm (describing Britain's proposed climate law).

71. Such decisions are made on a local basis. Information can generally be obtained by accessing minutes from proceedings of the county commissioners. Valley County, Idaho, provides an example of access to such information. Valley County Planning & Zoning, Meeting Minutes, http://www.co.valley.id.us/PZ_minutes.htm (last visited Apr. 27, 2007); *see also* Anne Wallace Allen, *EPA Comes to the Rescue of Town Overrun by Growth*, Oregonian, Dec. 25, 2005, at 1 (detailing EPA's involvement in local growth management issues in McCall, Idaho).

72. *See* Idaho Dep't of Envtl. Quality, Public Info and Input: Public Comment Opportunities, http://www.deq.idaho.gov/Applications/NewsApp/checkCommentCache.cfm (last visited Apr. 16, 2007) (providing a list of Idaho's pending air permits).

73. *See* Matthew Daly, *New Forest Service Chief Gets Rough Treatment in Congress*, Associated Press, Feb. 14, 2007 (detailing Forest Service plan to harvest up to 800 million board feet in Washington, Oregon, and Northern California in fiscal year 2008).

74. News Release, Nat'l Energy Tech. Lab., Department of Energy Tracks Resurgence of Coal-Fired Power Plants (Aug. 2, 2006), *available at* http://www.netl.doe.gov/publications/press/2006/06046-Coal-Fired_Power_Plants_Database.html ("Updated Database Shows 153 New Plants ... Proposed by 2025.").

75. *See* Jeff Goodell, *Big Coal's Dirty Move*, Rolling Stone, Jan. 25, 2007, *available at* http://www.rollingstone.com/ (Search "Big Coal's Dirty Move" in "All"; then follow "National Affairs: Big Coal's Dirty Move" hyperlink). Several scientists have called for a ban on new coal-fired plants that cannot capture and store the carbon dioxide they emit. *See* Hotz, *supra* note 18; Juliet Eilperin, *Governors Agree on Emissions Plan*, Register Guard (Eugene, Or.), Feb. 27, 2007, at E3.

76. Massachusetts v. U.S. Envtl. Prot. Agency, 415 F.3d 50, 58 (D. C. Cir. 2005) (holding that EPA has discretion not to regulate greenhouse gas emissions under the Clean Air Act (CAA)), *rev'd* Massachusetts v. U.S. Envtl. Prot. Agency No. 05-1120, 2007 U.S. Lexis 3785 (U.S. Apr. 2, 2007); *see infra* notes 77–79 and accompanying text.

77. *See infra* note 85; *see also* 42 U.S.C. § 7413 (2000) (describing federal enforcement powers).

78. For example, the CAA states the following in section 202(a)(1): "The [EPA] shall ... prescribe ... standards [for] any air pollutant from ... new motor vehicles ... which in [its] judgment cause, or contribute to, air pollution which may reasonably be anticipated to endanger public health or welfare." 42 U.S.C. § 7521(a)(1). In *Massachusetts v. EPA*, the Supreme Court found that this provision was "unambiguous" in giving EPA authority to regulate greenhouse gas emissions from new cars. No. 05-1120, 2007 U.S. LEXIS 2785, at *55.

79. *See generally Massachusetts v. EPA*, 415 F.3d at 50 (reviewing EPA's denial of petition to regulate greenhouse gases from new automobiles). The Supreme Court recently held, however, that EPA does not have "roving license to ignore the statutory text" of the CAA and must regulate greenhouse gas emissions if it finds that they endanger public health or welfare. *Massachusetts v. EPA*, No. 05-1120, 2007 U.S. LEXIS 3785, at *61 (citing 42 U.S.C. § 7521 (a) (1)). The Court, however, simply remanded the process back to EPA. *Id.* at *65.

80. George Lakoff, Don't Think of an Elephant! Know Your Values and Frame the Debate, at xv (2004).

81. Dr. Martin Luther King, Jr., "I Have a Dream" Address at the March on Washington for Jobs and Freedom (Aug. 28, 1963), *in* A Call to Conscience: The Landmark Speeches of Dr. Martin Luther King, Jr. 82 (Clayborne Carson & Kris Shephard eds., 2001) ("We have ... come to this hallowed spot to remind America of the fierce urgency of now. This is no time ... to engage in the luxury of cooling off or to take the tranquilizing drug of gradualism.").

82. 90 C.J.S. *Trusts* § 6, at 129 (2002).

83. Ill. Cent. R.R. Co. v. Illinois, 146 U.S. 387, 455 (1892) ("[T]he decisions are numerous which declare that such property is held by the State, by virtue of its sovereignty, in trust for the public."); Geer v. Connecticut, 161 U.S. 519, 525–29 (1896) (detailing ancient and English common law principles of sovereign trust ownership of air, water, sea, shores, and wildlife and stating that "the power or control lodged in the State, resulting from this common ownership, is to be exercised, like all other powers of government, as a trust for the benefit of the people"). For sources and materials on the public trust doctrine, see Jan G. Laitos, Sandra B. Zellmer, Mary C. Wood, & Daniel H. Cole, Natural Resources Law ch. 8.II, at 622–54 (2006).

84. *See* Mary Christina Wood, *Nature's Trust: Reclaiming an Environmental Discourse*, 25 Va. Envtl. L.J. (forthcoming spring 2007).

85. *See Geer*, 161 U.S. at 534 ("'[T]he ownership of the sovereign authority is in trust for all the people of the State, and hence by implication it is the duty of the legislature to enact such laws as will best preserve the subject of the trust and secure its beneficial use in the future to the people of the State.'") (quoting Magner v. Illinois, 1881 WL 10415 (Ill. Feb. 3, 1881)).

86. 76 Am. Jur. 2d *Trusts* § 404, at 455 (2005) ("One of the fundamental common-law duties of a trustee is to preserve and maintain trust assets. A trustee has the right and duty to safeguard, preserve, or protect the trust assets and the safety of the principal.").

87. States, for example, have protected their air trust by bringing nuisance lawsuits against polluters. *See, e.g.,* Georgia v. Tenn. Copper Co., 206 U.S. 230, 237-38(1907) ("This is a [nuisance] suit by a state for an injury to it in its capacity of quasi-sovereign .... It is a fair and reasonable demand on the part of a sovereign that the air over its territory should not be polluted on a great scale ... by the act of persons beyond its control ...."). California brought a nuisance suit against major automobile manufacturers for their contribution to global warming. *See generally* California v. Gen. Motors Corp., No. 3:06-CV-05755 (N.D. Cal. filed Sept. 20, 2006).

88. See Mary Christina Wood, Protecting the Wildlife Trust: A Reinterpretation of Section 7 of the Endangered Species Act, 34 Envtl. L. 605, 612–13 & n.27 (2004).

89. See Geer V. Connecticut, 161 U.S. 519, 529 (1896); Ill. Cent. R.R. Co. v. Illinois, 146 U.S. 387, 393 (1892).

90. Charles F. Wilkinson, The Headwaters of the Public Trust: Some of the Traditional Doctrine, 19 ENVTL. L. 425, 428–29 (1989).

91. See Mary Christina Wood, The Politics of Abundance: Towards a Future of Tribal-State Relations, 83 OR. L. REV. 1331, 1336 (2004).

92. 42 U.S.C. § 4331(b) (l) (2000). Federal pollution laws also designate sovereigns—federal, tribal and state governments—as trustees of natural resources for purposes of collecting natural resource damages. See generally Charles B. Anderson, Damage to Natural Resources and the Costs of Restoration, 72 TUL. L. REV. 417 (1997).

93. Oposa v. Factoran, G.R. No. 101083 (July 30, 1993) (Phil.). This opinion is excerpted in LAITOS, ZELLMER, WOOD & COLE, supra note 83, at 441–44.

94. Oposa, G.R. No. 101083, in LAITOS, ZELLMER, WOOD & COLE, supra note 83, at 443–44.

95. Ill. Cent. R.R. Co. v. Illinois, 146 U.S. 387, 453 (1892). The Court also held: "Every legislature must, at the time of its existence, exercise the power of the State in the execution of the trust devolved upon it." Id. at 460. In addition, the Court discussed public water assets:

> [T]he abdication of the general control of the State over [waterways] . . . is not consistent with the exercise of that trust which requires the government of the State to preserve such waters for the use of the public.
>
> . . . .
>
> . . . The ownership [of waterways] . . . is a subject of public concern to the whole people of the State. The trust with which they are held, therefore, is governmental and cannot be alienated . . . .
>
> Id. at 452–55.

96. See IDAHO DEP'T OF ENVTL. QUALITY, AIR QUALITY: PERMIT TO CONSTRUCT, No. P-060024 1, 4, available at http://www.deq.idaho .gov/air/permits_forms/pdfs/valley_paving_mccall_ptc_permit.pdf; IDAHO DEP'T OF ENVTL. QUALITY, PUBLIC HEARING RE: DOCKET No. AQ-0624– PERMIT NO. P-060024, 26, 29, 30, 64–65 (2007); Jennifer Church, Valley Paving Is a Nuisance, Should Not Receive Permit, Letter to the Editor, STAR-NEWS (McCall, Idaho), Jan. 18, 2007, at A-4.

97. See TRACY DROUIN, IDAHO DEP'T OF ENVTL. QUALITY, AIR QUALITY PERMITTING STATEMENT OF BASIS: PERMIT NO. P-060024, 19–21, 28–31 (2006), available at http://www.deq.idaho.gov/air/permits_forms/ pdfs/valley_paving_mccall_ptc_statement.pdf.

98. See News Release, Idaho Dep't of Envtl. Quality, DEQ Extends Comment Period on Proposed Air Permit to Construct for Valley Paving & Asphalt, McCall; Public Hearing Date Rescheduled (Dec. 14, 2006), available at http://vvww.deq.idaho/Applications/ NewsApp/check.NewsCache.cfm?news_id=1747.

99. See Peter N. Spotts, Ice Age to Warming—And Back?, CHRISTIAN SCIENCE MONITOR, Mar. 18, 2004, at 16.

100. See, e.g., Daniel Gilbert, Op-Ed., If Only Gay Sex Caused Global Warming: Why We're Mare Scared of Gay Marriage and Terrorism Than a Much Deadlier Threat, L.A. TIMES, July 2, 2006, at M1.

101 See id.

102. See supra Part VII.

103. Oposa V. Factoran, G.R. No. 101083 (July 30, 1993) (Phil), in LAITOS, ZELLMER, WOOD & COLE, supra note 83, at 444.

104. See, e.g., Ill. Cent. R.R. Co. v. Illinois, 146 U.S. 387 (1892).

105. Georgia V. Tenn. Copper Co., 206 U.S. 230, 237 (1907).

106. Ill. Cent. R.R. Co., 146 U.S. at 455.

107. The economic arguments militate against inaction. See STERN REVIEW, supra note 1, Summary of Conclusions, at vii-viii ("The costs of stabili[z]ing the climate are significant but manageable; delay would be dangerous and much more costly."); id. at viii ("Climate change is the greatest market failure the world has ever seen . . . .").

109. See Hotz, supra note 18.

109. For discussion of co-tenancy framework in natural resources such as a shared fishery, see Mary Christina Wood, The Tribal Property Right to Wildlife Capital (Part 1): Applying Principles of Sovereignty to Protect Imperiled Wildlife Populations, 37 IDAHO L. REV. 1, 86–101 (2000).

110. The term waste means "neglect or misconduct resulting in material damage to or loss of property." JOSEPH SINGER, PROPERTY LAW: RULES, POLICIES, AND PRACTICES 555 (4th ed. 2006). Waste is a spoil or destruction of "corporeal hereditaments." Lytle v. Payette-Or. Slope Irrigation Dist., 152 P.2d 934, 939 (Or. 1944). The court held, "Ill husbandry, carried to such extent as materially injures the rights of the . . . reversioner, constitutes waste." Id. (citation omitted).

111. See generally GORE, supra note 7, Introduction.

Discussion Questions

1. What contradictions exist between current environmental laws and environmental protection interests?

   Wood writes, "While the purpose of every local, state and federal environmental law is to protect natural resources, nearly every law also provides authority to the agencies to permit, in their discretion, the very pollution or land damage that the statues were designed to permit." Hiding behind the law, agencies and programs have the discretion to enforce environmental restrictions or prohibitions. Business interests and private property rights are often protected before the environment.

2. What is meant by the phrase "Nature's Trust"? Why, according to Wood, do we have an obligation to it?

   A trust is a type of ownership structure where one manages property for the benefit of another. All nature's resources (land, air, and water) could be considered as part of a legal trust for the benefit of all generations of citizens (past, present, and future). As a result, we must protect and restore the contents of the trust for our generation, as well as for future generations.

CHAPTER 28

Katrina and Power in America

Peter Dreier (2006)

Peter Dreier characterizes Hurricane Katrina as a human disaster. In this article, Dreier examines the conditions that led to this disaster and discusses the government's immediate response and plans for post-Katrina reconstruction. He concludes that the government response to this crisis represents a missed opportunity for significant and lasting regional renewal.

A few days after Katrina struck New Orleans, President George W. Bush told the press that the relationship between the federal, state, and local governments is "an important relationship, and I need to understand how it works better" (Bush 2005).

New Orleans Mayor Ray Nagin, desperate and frustrated, was a bit more straightforward in his assessment of how federalism works in practice: "I don't know whether it's the governor's problem," he said, "I don't know whether it's the president's problem. But somebody needs to get their ass on a plane and sit down, the two of them, and figure this out" ("Mayor to Feds" 2005).

But long before Katrina hit the city, New Orleans residents—and their counterparts in other cities around the country—already knew that the federal government had abandoned them. The president's response to the disaster simply put his indifference to the plight of cities in dramatic relief.

New Orleans's Race and Class Fault Lines

Katrina was *not* an equal opportunity disaster. In *Heat Wave: A Social Autopsy of Disaster in Chicago*, sociologist Eric Klinenberg (2002) reveals how that city's economic and social divisions were reflected in who died and who survived in a severe heat wave in July 1995. The poor, people of color, and the elderly—those most likely to be socially isolated and without resources—were the most likely to die.

Likewise, in New Orleans, the poorest neighborhoods were hit hardest by the hurricane. The Bush administration apparently assumed that people would evacuate New Orleans on their own, without giving much thought to who these people were, what resources they had, or where they would go. They acted as if everyone had an SUV full of gas and family or friends (or a second home) waiting to take them in somewhere safe.

In late August, the Census Bureau released two reports (Fronzcek 2005; DaNavas-Walt, Proctor, and Lee 2005) revealing that Mississippi (with a 21.6% poverty rate) and Louisiana (19.4%) are the nation's poorest states. New Orleans (with a 23.2% poverty rate) is the twelfth-poorest city in the nation. Its median household income in 2000 was only $27,133. Only 46.5% of its households own their own homes—one of the lowest big-city home-ownership rates in the South. Of the city's African-Americans, 35% do not own a car, compared with 15% of Whites.

While most Southern cities gained population since the 1960s, New Orleans declined like a rustbelt city. It reached its peak population, 627,525, in 1960. Between 1990, when it had 496,939 people, and 2000, with 484,674, it lost 2.5% of its population, while Louisiana grew by 5.9%. By 2004, it declined another 4.6%, to 462,269. Despite declining population, murders increased from 158 (32.6 per 100,000) in 1999 to 274 in 2003 (56.5 per 100,000). ("New Orleans," n.d.)

From 1980 through 2003, New Orleans lost more than 50,000 jobs (from 339,953 to 279,056). During that period, oil and gas prices dropped. The city's port lost business to Miami and Houston. Several major companies with headquarters in the city left town. By 2000, only one Fortune 500 firm—the city's power company—remained. Tourism, a low-wage industry whose major employers, such as hotel chains, are headquartered elsewhere, increased its importance as a source of jobs. The New Orleans area saw a faster exodus of jobs, as well as middle-class and wealthy families, to the suburbs than in other metropolitan areas, exacerbating the city's fiscal crisis. ("Katrina: Issues and the Aftermath" 2005)

New Orleans is not only one of the nation's poorest cities, but also among the most ghettoized. Among the nation's 100 largest metro areas, it ranks third in poverty concentration. In 2000, 23% of the poor in metro New Orleans lived in high-poverty neighborhoods (where at least 40% of the population live below the poverty line) (Pettit and Kingsley 2003).

Housing discrimination and the concentration of government-subsidized housing have contributed to the city's economic and racial segregation. Over two-thirds of New Orleans residents, but only one-fifth of suburban residents, are African-American. New Orleans ranked among the nation's most racially segregated urban areas. The metro area's dissimilarity index in 2000 was 69—meaning that 69% of Blacks would have to move to achieve an equal distribution of Blacks and Whites in every neighborhood ("Sortable List of Dissimilarity Scores" 2005).

Incompetence or Indifference?

Culturally, New Orleans is a unique city. But its economic and social conditions parallel those in most U.S. cities. Since World War II, federal housing and highway policies, the practices of private businesses (particularly developers, banks, and insurance companies), and local zoning and tax laws have combined to promote middle-class flight, racial and economic segregation, and chronic fiscal problems in America's cities. Federal assistance to improve urban conditions has fluctuated depending on who

controls the White House and Congress, but even with Democrats in charge urban aid has been dwarfed by policies that subsidize and encourage the flight of employers and middle-class residents from cities (Dreier, Mollenkopf, and Swanstrom 2005).

During the second half of the 1990s, economic and social conditions improved, due largely to an unprecedented national economic expansion, reinforced by federal policies that reduced unemployment, spurred productivity, lifted the working poor out of poverty (such as the Earned Income Tax Credit and a minimum wage increase), and targeted private investment (stimulated in part by stronger enforcement of the Community Reinvestment Act) to low-income urban areas. Since 2001, the indicators of urban revival—such as reductions in unemployment, poverty, crime, the number of families without health insurance, and the number of families paying more than they can afford for housing—reversed direction (Dreier, Mollenkopf, and Swanstrom 2005).

It is not difficult to understand why Bush has paid so little attention to New Orleans (before and after Katrina) and to urban America in general. In 2000 and 2004, Al Gore and John Kerry beat Bush among urban voters by wide margins. Bush's first Department of Housing and Urban Development (HUD) Secretary, Mel Martinez, told the *Washington Post* that "Housing issues are predominantly local issues. . . . The solution to meeting the nation's affordable housing needs will not come out of Washington" (Broder 2002, p. B7). Testifying before Congress in 2004 to justify proposed cuts for housing assistance, Bush's next HUD Secretary, Alphonso Jackson, claimed that, "being poor is a state of mind, not a condition" (Washington 2004, 5 A).[1] Both comments reveal the Bush administration's underlying view that urban problems are not really federal responsibilities and that poverty is due primarily to character flaws among the poor.

Conservative pundits and politicians have characterized Bush's mishandling of the disaster as the inherent inefficiency of "big government." But government—whether big or small—can be competent or incompetent. In fact, the federal government has a reasonably good track record of responding to so-called "natural" disasters like earthquakes, floods, and hurricanes. Remnick (2005) described how President Lyndon Johnson quickly and competently responded to Hurricane Betsy, a major hurricane that struck New Orleans in September 1965. More recently, the Clinton administration significantly professionalized and improved the Federal Emergency Management Agency (FEMA), appointed an experienced administrator (James Whitt), increased its budget, and developed close working relationships with governors, mayors, and their disaster management agencies. The Clinton administration's success in overseeing relief and reconstruction after the 1994 Los Angeles earthquake suggests that the federal government can act effectively and efficiently in times of crisis (Dreier and Rothstein 1994).

The Bush administration's actions might better be characterized as indifference rather than incompetence. It was a natural outgrowth of its fundamental hostility to government itself. A central tenet of conservative ideology is that government interferes with individual liberty, is less efficient than the private sector, and in many cases is simply unnecessary. Even so, many contemporary conservatives argue that (with the exception of military spending) we need to "starve the beast," mostly by reducing taxes (especially for the wealthy) so much that government in general, and the federal government in particular, will be virtually paralyzed (Krugman 2003).

As Americans saw on TV, Katrina revealed that when needed most, government was paralyzed.

We do not know the magnitude of the Bush administration's blunders and misjudgments, or their cost in human lives and property damage. What is clear is that its indifference toward New Orleans began long before Katrina struck. It cut the budget for FEMA and the Army Corps of Engineers. It folded FEMA into the Department of Homeland Security, diminishing its role as an emergency planning and relief agency while viewing it as simply another part of the administration's "war on terror." It failed to invest adequately in the infrastructure needed to prevent severe hurricane damage in New Orleans and Mississippi. The Bush administration was extremely slow in providing relief after the hurricane struck. In late October—two months after Katrina struck—at least 20,000 public school students from Louisiana (mostly from New Orleans) who were uprooted by the hurricane were still not attending any school. About 200,000 evacuees remained in hotels, while only 7,308 temporary trailers and 10,940 housing units had been occupied by victims in the three affected states. Many Medicaid recipients were unable to get benefits in their new locations (Lipton 2005).

Crony Capitalism and Disaster Profiteers

Bush has been justly faulted for his failure of leadership and his mishandling of the nuts and bolts of the Katrina relief effort. But on several matters involving posthurricane reconstruction, Bush was exceedingly decisive. The administration's failure to adequately prepare for Katrina, and then its botching of the evacuation and relief effort, was not simply a matter of hiring the wrong people for the job. Indeed, Bush used the Katrina disaster as a pretext for the administration's crony capitalism, corporate agenda, and disregard for the urban poor.

Post-Katrina, the Bush administration sought to enact conservative policies that it could not get through Congress under normal circumstances. Bush dusted off several free-market approaches—such as a "Gulf Opportunity Zone" (tax breaks for small businesses)—that have failed in the past (Vieth 2005). It lifted the requirement that contractors have affirmative-action plans. It proposed allowing the Environmental Protection Agency to waive environmental regulations, including provisions of the Clean Air Act, during the rebuilding. It promoted the use of school vouchers for children of Katrina evacuees. It rescinded rules governing the number of hours truckers can work.[2]

Many Republicans in Congress demanded that any supplemental funds to provide relief to Katrina's victims—now likely to cost more than $100 billion—be offset with budget cuts rather than tax increases. Only a few weeks after Katrina hit, Congressional Republicans called for over $50 billion in spending cuts, most from programs for the poor, such as Medicaid, food stamps, child care support, the earned-income tax credit, and Supplemental Security Income. Even so, Bush and the GOP leaders in Congress, including majority leader Senator Bill Frist, still want to adopt a $70 billion tax cut, mostly for the very rich (Sanger and Andrews 2005).

Bush decisively suspended federal rules to allow FEMA and the Army Corps of Engineers to extend no-bid contracts to corporations engaged in rebuilding. Companies with close political ties went to the front of the line. Bush then sweetened these contracts by suspending the federal Davis-Bacon Act, which requires federal contractors to pay local "prevailing wages" on construction projects. (In late October, after enormous public criticism of these actions, Bush reversed both decisions.)

Even Jack Kemp, the conservative HUD secretary under the first President Bush, criticized Bush's approach: "There has to be some federal leadership here," Kemp said. "Laissez-faire, Darwinian capitalism is not going to work. Markets do work, but they need the direction of government in situations like this" (Gosselin 2005).

Katrina is a disaster for the people of the gulf region and for the nation's economy. About 400,000 Americans will lose their jobs, according to the Congressional Budget Office (Gruber 2005). But for some companies, especially those with political connections, Katrina—like the war in Iraq—is a bonanza.

The reconstruction of New Orleans and the Gulf Coast unleashed a feeding frenzy of government contracts. FEMA and the Army Corps of Engineers (ACE) quickly suspended rules in order to allow no-bid contracts and speed up reconstruction.

Three companies—the Shaw Group, Kellogg Brown & Root (KBR, a subsidiary of Haliburton, whose former CEO is Vice President Dick Cheney), and Boh Brothers Construction of New Orleans—quickly scooped up no-bid ACE contracts to perform the restoration. Bechtel and Fluor (also with close GOP ties) also reaped huge contracts. The Department of Defense has been criticized for awarding Iraq reconstruction contracts to Haliburton and Bechtel without competition (Broder 2005).

As the *New York Times* reported, "From global engineering and construction firms like the Fluor Corporation and Haliburton, to local trash removal and road-building concerns, the private sector is poised to reap a windfall of business in the largest domestic rebuilding effort ever undertaken" (Broder 2005: A1).

According to the *Los Angeles Times* (Miller and Silverstein 2005), lobbyists representing energy, transportation, and other corporate sectors dominated the task forces created by Louisiana Senators David Vitter (a Republican) and Mary Landrieu (a Democrat) to advise them in drafting the Louisiana Katrina Reconstruction Act. The legislation included "billions of dollars' worth of business for clients of those lobbyists" (Miller and Silverstein 2005: A1).

Bush's first FEMA director, Joseph Allbaugh, resigned in 2003 to head New Bridge Strategies, a firm whose Web site boasts it is "a unique company that was created specifically with the aim of assisting clients to evaluate and take advantage of business opportunities in the Middle East following the conclusion of the U.S.-led war in Iraq." Allbaugh used his connections to help his clients, including KBR, win post-Katrina contracts, including a U.S. Navy contract to, according to the *Houston Chronicle,* "restore electric power, repair roofs and remove debris at three naval facilities in Mississippi damaged by Hurricane Katrina" and to "perform damage assessments at other naval installations in New Orleans as soon as it is safe to do so" ("Around the Region" 2005: 3).

Compounding this crony capitalism, Bush suspended the Davis-Bacon law for Katrina-damaged areas of Alabama, Florida, Louisiana, and Mississippi. Enacted in 1931, it sets a minimum pay scale for workers on federal contracts by requiring contractors to pay each region's

prevailing wages. The prevailing wage for a carpenter is about $12 an hour in New Orleans and $7 an hour in Gulfport, Mississippi, both far below the national average (Eisenbrey 2005).

The Bush administration, Congressional Republicans, and their corporate allies have long opposed the Davis-Bacon law. During the 2004 election cycle, the construction industry donated $71 million to candidates for the White House and Congress. According to the Center for Responsive Politics, a nonpartisan watchdog group, 72% of those contributions went to Republicans ("Your Guide to Money in U.S. Elections" 2005). They used Katrina to impose their agenda through the back door.

The suspension of Davis-Bacon was an open invitation to employers to pay low wages to people desperate for jobs. The Gulf Coast and New Orleans—which prior to Katrina had a tiny (3.1%) Latino population—saw an influx of Mexican and Central American immigrants, many of them undocumented, lured by the boom in construction work and service-sector jobs previously filled by residents who had evacuated the region. Most employers pay them far below prevailing wages; some failed to pay at all. Many of these immigrants had to live in overcrowded conditions.

Who Will Rule the New New Orleans?

To Americans watching events unfold on TV or reading newspapers and news magazines, the Katrina disaster revealed the meltdown of New Orleans's local government. Mayor Nagin appeared angry but helpless. Many of his police department's officers failed to report for duty, undermining the city's ability to protect lives and property. A handful of cops were even seen looting local retail stores. Patients at the private Tulane University hospital were quickly removed, while patients at the municipally run Charity Hospital were left for days to fend for themselves (Sternberg 2005). The city government had no evacuation plan in place before the disaster struck. While the White House and the federal EPA disagreed about whether the region's water was safe to drink, Nagin first urged people to return, then told them to stay away. To the casual observer, New Orleans's municipal government fit the worst stereotypes about urban politics.

In truth, no municipal government has the capacity to handle a disaster of Katrina's magnitude. Only the federal government has the resources to deal with the prevention, rescue, and rebuilding of areas faced with major disasters. For certain, the city government had a role to play. But New Orleans, even more than most cities, faced chronic fiscal problems, because so many of its residents are poor and so much of its economy is based on low-wage jobs. Because Louisiana is a right-to-work state, New Orleans lacks a strong local labor movement, which is often a key player in municipal politics elsewhere.

Occasionally, inchoate class conflicts surface in the political arena. For example, in 2002, New Orleans ACORN (a community organizing group) and the Service Employees International Union (SEIU) waged a grassroots campaign to get the city to adopt a municipal minimum wage that was $1 over the federal level, and would apply only to businesses with over $500,000 in revenues. The referendum passed with support from 63% of the voters. The law would have bene-fited about 70,000 low-income workers, mostly African-Americans, mostly employed in the tourism industry. After the vote, however, the region's business groups, which had led the opposition to the proposal, successfully filed suit in Louisiana Supreme Court to uphold a state law, passed a few years earlier, to pre-empt local minimum wage ordinances, overturning the people's will (Finch 2002; Pollin, Brenner, and Luce 2002; Yerton 2002).

In the wake of Katrina, class and race struggles will again rise to the surface. Which local stakeholders will play important roles in how federal funds are allocated for rebuilding the city, who will receive the funds, and how will those funds be used?

Although the Bush administration would prefer to circumvent state and local government (both run by Democrats) as well as local community and labor groups, and make most of these decisions without their input, Bush cannot simply ignore local players. National corpora-tions and local businesses with close ties to the Bush administration (and, in Mississippi, to Governor Haley Barbour, former Republican National Committee head)—as well as with the Congressional delegation, the governor, and the mayor—will have an advantage in shaping the agenda and getting federal reconstruction funds.

The *New York Times* (Rivlin 2005a and 2005b) profiled several such players. One is Joseph C. Canizaro, a major New Orleans developer who had been a big Bush fundraiser, is close to Mayor Nagin, and in 2000 created the Committee for a Better New Orleans (CBNO), which brought together more than 100 business and civic leaders to address the city's problems. Canizaro played a key role in helping Nagin pick the 17-member blue-ribbon task force to make recom-mendations on rebuilding the city. Another task force member, Donald Bollinger, is head of Bollinger Shipyards (based in nearby Lockport, Mississippi), is close to Bush and other Republicans, served as chair of the local United Way, and was president of CBNO.

Who speaks for New Orleans's poor, the people whose neighborhoods were hardest hit, who lost their jobs and their health insurance, and who are not represented on Mayor Nagin's commission?

One problem in answering this question is that more than one million New Orleans and Gulf Coast residents fled the region and now live in Baton Rouge, Houston, Jackson, and elsewhere. Many of their New Orleans houses and apartments may be uninhabitable. Their neighborhoods may be toxic health hazards for some time. Their old jobs may no longer exist, at least in the short-term.

How will the state and city deal with displaced voters? Will they retain their right to vote as Louisiana and New Orleans residents, even if they do not return for six months or a year? Or will state and local politicians try to remove them from the voting rolls? Even if they remain on the vot-ing lists, will the local politicians make a serious effort to find them and provide them with absentee ballots? Will there even be a public debate and struggle over these issues?

The Katrina exodus could dramatically shift the bal-ance of power in Louisiana and New Orleans. Governor Blanco's 2003 election victory and Senator Mary Landrieu's (D-Louisiana) 2002 reelection win had mar-gins of fewer than 60,000 votes. Overwhelming support from African-Americans constituted much of those margins (Fletcher and Hsu 2005).

Mayor Nagin and the entire City Council is up for re-election in February 2006. As the *Washington Post* noted: "The election will be one of the most important in the city's history, with the winners set to play a pivotal role in deciding how the city will be rebuilt. But with only a smattering of the city's 484,000 residents back home, it will also be an election in which voters will be difficult to find and residency hard to prove, leaving candidates unsure of how to campaign" (Fletcher and Hsu 2005: A7).

Public officials will focus primarily on the concerns of businesses and the affluent unless the poor and near-poor are mobilized to make demands and participate in elections. The major media have generally portrayed New Orleans-area residents as helpless victims, grateful for any handout from the Red Cross, FEMA, or other charities and government agencies.

The mainstream media virtually ignored the efforts of several community-organizing groups to mobilize resi-dents of New Orleans, as well as among the evacuees living in Houston, Baton Rouge, and elsewhere, to gain a voice in the post-Katrina deliberations. The three national orga-nizing networks—ACORN, IAF, and PICO—immediately began sending their local organizers to the Superdome in

New Orleans, the Astrodome in Houston, and other emergency shelters, talking with evacuees about their immediate and longer-term needs. They worked with churches, unions, community groups, and their own local members to find survivors and help them find emergency relief, housing, jobs, and other basic needs (Blumenthal 2005; Casey 2005; Hall 2005; Klein 2005; Riccardi and Zucchino 2005; Stiles 2005; Tisserand 2005).

ACORN, which has chapters in 75 cities around the country, organized the Katrina Survivors Association to give residents, including those who fled to other communities, a voice. Soon after Katrina hit, ACORN—whose national headquarters was located in New Orleans—began contacting members in over 35 cities who had escaped Katrina. It held meetings of survivors to distribute recovery information and began making demands on government officials, winning a number of important victories. In Dallas, for example, ACORN members marched on the mayor's office to protest the city's refusal to work with FEMA to provide housing for evacuees. After two weeks of public pressure, FEMA developed a plan to provide housing directly to survivors. On October 15, ACORN members staged a caravan into the Lower Ninth Ward to claim their right to return, posting "Do Not Bulldoze" signs on homes. In October, New Orleans ACORN, the Louisiana AFL-CIO, the Louisiana NAACP, and SEIU locals organized a march and rally in Baton Rouge to demand a resident voice in rebuilding. A delegation of ACORN's Katrina survivors traveled to Washington, D.C., where they met with Congressional leadership, held a rally at FEMA, and joined Senator Ted Kennedy in introducing the Rebuild and Respect Act, which embodies many of the rebuilding principles they have been fighting for. In November, ACORN organized a meeting at Louisiana State University that brought together its leaders, staff, and two dozen planners, housing developers, and economists to develop a comprehensive plan for post-Katrina reconstruction.

Soon after Katrina struck, Houston Mayor Bill White immediately invited The Metropolitan Organization (TMO), a well-regarded community-organizing group affiliated with the Industrial Areas Foundation, to participate in the city's efforts to deal with the tens of thousands of new residents in terms of health care, housing, education, and other needs. TMO's organizers and leaders organized meetings in local churches where survivors voiced their complaints and made demands in front of local officials, including the mayor, FEMA, and the Red Cross. TMO formed its own organization of residents and gathered thousands of signatures among evacuees to demand better treatment, especially for children, the elderly, and those in need of medical help.

The PICO organizing network sponsored a meeting of 1,000 refugees from New Orleans held in Baton Rouge in early October. Governor Blanco came and signed PICO's "reconstruction covenant."

What Kind of Reconstruction?

While the rescue and resettlement of Katrina's victims was just beginning, government officials and business leaders were already formulating reconstruction plans. The federal government approved more than $100 billion for hurricane relief and repair, the largest urban (and rural) renewal program in memory.

Will these funds be used primarily to provide a financial bonanza to politically connected corporations and developers? Or will they be used to help create strong and healthy communities that will do more than restore what was there before but will improve economic, social, and environmental conditions for the people who live and work there?

The answer to these questions depends in large measure on whether the residents of the region have a strong voice in shaping the rebuilding process. Through their community organizations, religious congregations, labor unions, and civic groups, residents should play a central role in determining how and where the money is spent. Many residents worry that the Bush administration, the governors, and the mayors will be influenced primarily by corporate powerbrokers, bankers, and builders.

The Gulf Coast has half of the nation's oil refineries. About 60% of oil imports come through Gulf ports. Within weeks of the disaster, repair of these facilities was underway. People also hope that much of the city's cultural life—its music venues, the French Quarter, its charming neighborhoods—can be restored. But what about the rest of the city and region? The people who return will need jobs, homes, and public services. The area will need to rebuild hospitals, health clinics, parks, playgrounds, and schools.

Should the federal government simply subsidize the reconstruction of the city's low-wage economy—its hotels, casinos, and other tourist and service industries? If a major hotel chain or casino is going to get millions in federal aid, should there be some quid pro quos—like requiring them to pay a living wage or provide other community benefits?

Should the federal government provide homebuilders and landlords with millions of dollars in federal funds to reconstruct apartment buildings without any guarantees that rents will be affordable to the families who need them?

In rebuilding New Orleans and its suburbs, should policy makers avoid isolating the poor in ghetto neighborhoods? In reconstructing the city's infrastructure, should they link where people live, work, and shop through improved public transit?

Political constituencies will have to be mobilized—nationally as well as in the Gulf Coast region—to ensure that New Orleans is eventually a more livable place than it was before, especially for its poor. If post-Katrina reconstruction is to proceed as a two-way street—bottom-up as well as top-down—government policy makers should take into account some guidelines and principles learned from previous successes and failures of urban and metropolitan policy.

Public health. Much of the region is now a huge toxic brownfield that could contaminate children, workers, and the elderly, producing permanent damage. Will the Bush administration resist pressures from big business, developers, and some residents to start putting shovels in the ground as soon as possible? Should construction of homes, schools, businesses, and other facilities occur before a comprehensive environmental and public health assessment has been done, to evaluate which areas are safe and which will require extensive environmental clean-up? Should toxic areas that endanger public health be declared Superfund sites and federal funds allocated to decontaminate them before people are permitted to live and work there?

Infrastructure. In New Orleans, much of the physical infrastructure—sewers, utilities, levees, and roads—was outdated and crumbling even before Katrina struck. In much of the rural parts of Louisiana, Mississippi, and Alabama, infrastructure was primitive. Before homes, businesses, and public facilities are constructed, should the federal government invest in infrastructure to ensure that the next hurricane does not destroy the region? Key to making conditions more livable is developing a *regional* plan for public transportation that includes bus, trolley, and automobile to limit congestion and to provide options for families without cars.

The federal government must rebuild the city's levee system to withstand Category 5 hurricanes. Insurance companies, lenders, and builders will be reluctant to invest in New Orleans—and especially its flood-prone low-income neighborhoods—if they think the levees are not strong enough. Or, if they do invest in New Orleans, they will charge outrageous premiums to consumers.

Any rebuilding effort in the region must take into account the erosion of the wetlands. Policies that allowed developers to build in the wetlands exacerbated flood conditions, harming the environment, making Louisiana's cities and towns more vulnerable to hurricane devastation.[3] The rebuilding of New Orleans needs to complement the rebuilding of the Louisiana coast, which used to act as a land buffer to slow down and weaken hurricanes as they came onshore. This is no longer the case, because much of Louisiana's coastline has sunk into the Gulf of Mexico.

Public facilities. The region's schools, nursing homes, hospitals, health clinics, and child care centers need to be rebuilt. These institutions are critical to a community's social fabric. Louisiana, Mississippi, and Alabama are among the nation's poorest states. Their schools were already among the most underfunded. Their populations ranked among the lowest in access to health insurance, a situation exacerbated by the disaster, because many people are now jobless, and the Bush administration proposed to deny Medicaid to many Katrina victims.

Housing. More than a million people were forced to flee New Orleans and the Gulf Coast. Many of their homes were destroyed or became uninhabitable and need to be razed. The *New York Times* reported that as many as 50,000 (out of 180,000) New Orleans homes may have to be demolished (Nossiter 2005b). Many New Orleans residents were evacuated to "temporary" trailer parks in Baton Rouge and elsewhere. Most want to return, but under what circumstances? Post-Katrina provides an opportunity to learn from past mistakes and create stronger communities and neighborhoods.

Among the poor, many homes were already physically substandard. It makes no sense to rebuild the region's residential areas just as they were before Katrina. In New Orleans, for example, federally subsidized housing for the poor was concentrated in a few areas, isolating the poor in economic and racial ghettoes. Instead, neighborhoods should include homeownership and rental housing, market-rate homes and homes affordable to low-income and middle-class families.

In September, Bush proposed giving away federally owned land to families by lottery if they were willing to build new homes on the sites, under an "urban homesteading" program (Chen and Curtius 2005). There is not enough federal land to make this plan practical. But even if there were, rebuilding the region one house at a time would be wasteful and inefficient. Entire neighborhoods need to be rebuilt. Experienced nonprofit and for-profit developers should be enlisted in this effort, guided by plans created by local residents.

Homeownership counseling by knowledgeable nonprofit community groups is critical. Otherwise, people could become unwitting victims of unscrupulous and predatory lenders and contractors, who prey on desperate people, do shoddy construction, and charge excessive fees. This would lead to large-scale foreclosures in a few years, as we have seen in other cities.

In areas of New Orleans, Baton Rouge, Houston, and elsewhere where there still may be housing vacancies, HUD can provide Section 8 rental vouchers to evacuees.

But something must be done to restrain the greed of speculators, who within days of Katrina were buying up properties throughout the region to take advantage of the housing shortage and of the federally subsidized bonanza. To limit price gouging during this emergency, we need temporary rent control or a freeze on real estate transactions until a rebuilding plan is in place. Soon after the hurricane hit, Governor Blanco announced an emergency ban on evictions for tenants who had fled their homes. But under pressure from the Greater New Orleans Apartment Association, Blanco lifted the ban less than a month later (Nossiter 2005a).

The state of Louisiana could create a nonprofit building supplies and materials cooperative to negotiate with suppliers and purchase building materials (lumber, tools, cement, bricks, even home appliances) at a discount. The cooperative would have enormous leverage over building suppliers, using the economies of scale of large-scale purchasing. It could make these discounted building supplies available to designated developers/contractors for reconstruction. Without such an entity, the competition for building materials will lead to enormous increases in costs, making residential reconstruction much more expensive. In this way, savings would focus on building supplies, not labor.

Jobs. The decade-long rebuilding of New Orleans and the Gulf Coast—plus the addition of new schools and other facilities in Houston, Baton Rouge, and elsewhere to accommodate their local population explosions—will generate tens of thousands of jobs, particularly in the construction of homes, roads, infrastructure, schools, hospitals, and businesses. Who will get those jobs and will they pay a living wage? Should local residents be given priority for jobs rebuilding their communities? Should federal funds be targeted to competent nonprofit organizations that have experience in job training so that people will have permanent skills?

Lessons for Urban Scholars and Practitioners

The Katrina disaster could have triggered a bold social experiment. In its wake, policy makers could have applied the lessons, learning from both successes and failures, of past urban policy to help rebuild New Orleans and the Gulf Coast region. More than $100 billion in federal funds alone will be targeted to the city and the region for housing, schools, infrastructure, parks, commercial districts, and transportation. Under different political circumstances, this could have been a remarkable moment for urban and regional planning and policy practitioners to work collaboratively with government officials, community groups, civic leaders, unions, and business to rebuild the New Orleans region as a more livable and sustainable area. The missing ingredient, however, was political will on the part of those with power—the Bush administration, the heads of Congressional committees, and key business leaders—to develop a common vision for the region's future that involved the residents and their organizations.

Some urban scholars, policy practitioners, and community activists hoped that the Katrina disaster would catalyze a renewed interest in urban policy, poverty, and racism. Indeed, for a few weeks after Katrina struck, these issues were back in the news. Newspaper and magazine articles highlighted the race and class fault lines exposed by the hurricane (Alter 2005; DeParle 2005: Connolly 2005; Brownstein 2005a; Brownstein 2005b; Maggs 2005; Henninger 2005; Keyssar 2005; Altman 2005; Kelman 2005).

But the public debate quickly faded as media stories began to focus on the finger-pointing between the federal, state, and local governments and the Bush administration's mishandling of evacuation and relief efforts. Exaggerated news reports of looting by New Orleans residents reinforced the conservative "blame the victim" stereotypes about urban problems.

It is instructive to compare the Katrina aftermath with the similar dynamic that occurred after the April 1992 Los Angeles riots. For years, urban scholars and activists had warned that our cities were ticking time bombs, waiting to explode. When the riots erupted—the worst civil disorder in American history—many hoped that it would catalyze a major national commitment to revitalize the cities—an urban Marshall Plan. The timing seemed perfect. The riots coincided with the end of the Cold War. When the Berlin Wall fell, and the Soviet Union collapsed, there was much public discussion about the prospects for a "peace dividend" to reorder national priorities and address long-unmet domestic needs. Moreover, the riots occurred in the midst of a national election for President and Congress. For a few weeks following the riots, America's urban crisis became a hot topic (Dreier 1992 and 2003). But soon the plight of America's cities returned to political obscurity. Pundits and politicians were divided between conservatives, who blamed the victims for their plight, and liberals, who called for modest increases in federal assistance to cities and the poor.

Many urbanists hoped that Bill Clinton's victory in November 1992 would usher in a new era of hope for the nation's cities. His victory was viewed as a mandate for a more activist government. But Clinton was elected without a majority mandate. He received only 43% of the overall vote. Equally important, his own Democratic Party, while capturing a majority of the seats in Congress, was deeply divided, with many members closely linked to big business interests who oppose progressive taxation, Keynesian pump-priming, and social spending. Early in the Clinton administration, Congress thwarted the president's efforts to enact a modest public investment plan, universal health insurance, and even a child immunization program. The Republican takeover of Congress in November 1994 exacerbated the political isolation of cities, symbolized by Clinton's proposal a month later to dramatically cut the HUD budget. Although urban conditions improved during the Clinton years, the plight of our cities has not been a prominent issue in presidential campaigns since then.

We cannot expect a major disaster—whether the Los Angeles riots or the Katrina disaster—to trigger a national debate over cities. Disasters, accidents, scandals, and other unexpected events such as Watergate, Enron, and the Santa Barbara oil spill often expose the things we take for granted (Molotch 1970). They force us to hold a mirror up to society and see it as it really is. The public is often shocked at the human consequences of such events. They tell pollsters that government officials need to "do something" to address the problem. They often lead to a shift in public opinion. But these events are rarely, on their own, catalysts for social change or major policy shifts. The immediacy of the tragedy soon recedes and people return to business as usual. The media soon loses interest when the political drama fades and the mundane tasks of recovery take over. The root causes and the chronic human suffering get pushed aside by stories about government turf battles and bureaucratic bungling, undermining public confidence in the capacity of government to solve problems (Dreier 2005).

What generally brings about positive change—especially for poor and working-class people—is the slow, gradual, difficult work of union organizing, community organizing, and participation in electoral politics. To the extent that Los Angeles is a better city today than it was ten years ago, it is due to the grassroots activists—and their allies among foundations, media, clergy, and public officials—who have worked in the trenches pushing for change against difficult obstacles (Gottlieb, Freer, Vallianatos, and Dreier 2004). Likewise, whatever positive things happen in the aftermath of Katrina will be due, in

large measure, to the long-term work of grassroots community and union-organizing groups who mobilized quickly after the disaster struck to provide a voice for the have-nots and who found allies among urban planning, engineering, and community-development experts to help formulate alternative plans to those developed by business and political elites.

The debate over post-Katrina reconstruction is not about "big government" versus "small government." It is about "big government" for whom? Will the main beneficiaries of federal funds be those with deep pockets and political connections? Or will federal funds focus on the needs of ordinary people and help them to rebuild their homes, neighborhoods, jobs, and lives? Unless those people have a voice in the decision making from the start, and unless the rebuilding follows the principles outlined above, the new New Orleans will look very similar (although perhaps smaller in population size, somewhat whiter, and more gentrified) to the old New Orleans. And public trust in government will sink even more than the levees.

In contrast to conservative ideology, the Katrina disaster reveals how much we need government to provide things that individuals and the private sector cannot. It is needed to build the public infrastructure necessary for a civilized society, protect people from health, environmental, and disaster risks, help relieve the immediate suffering, build dams, levees, bridges, roads, and public transit as well as schools, parks, and playgrounds, and help people and communities restore some level of normalcy and decency.

Katrina also highlights the importance of having *competent* government run by well-trained people. There were plenty of competent public servants who, given the opportunity and resources, could have prevented the disaster and/or dramatically limited its consequences. Katrina was a failure of will by high-ranking government leaders, not incompetence by middle-level managers and front-line staff in the military, FEMA, and other agencies.

The Katrina disaster has triggered the nation's largest population movement in memory. Some will return to their previous communities, but many will remain where they have relocated. These cities are now faced with enormous challenges. Where will these people live and work? Where will their children attend school? How will they get health care and nursing home care?

Should the burden for addressing these human needs and economic realities fall on the localities, or be left to the private market? Or should Washington play a significant role? Will the Bush administration and Congress view this resettlement the way it views immigration from abroad, forcing those cities and states with the vast majority of new immigrants (especially California, Texas, New Mexico, and Arizona) to provide for them?

Wherever they move, the evacuees from New Orleans and Mississippi are mostly poor. They will need jobs, housing, and health care, among other things. But so do millions of other Americans, including the 37 million who are poor, the 45.8 million without health insurance, the even larger number who pay more than they can afford to put a roof over their heads (DeNavas-Walt, Proctor, and Lee 2005). Why help the victims of Katrina but not the victims of government policies and business practices that have undermined the American Dream for so many people?

The Katrina disaster begs the larger question: What responsibility, if any, does the federal government have to provide Americans with decent housing, access to health care, and opportunities for work that pays a living wage? Should government help people cope with the vicissitudes of the business cycle, the inequities of the market economy, and just plain bad luck?

Building majoritarian support for a renewed federal effort to help cities is possible, but we cannot expect an event like Katrina to substitute for the hard political work that is necessary. The United States is now a suburban nation. More than half of all voters in presidential elections are suburbanites. We need to forge coalitions between urban voters and sectors of the suburban electorate that can win elections in a majority of Congressional districts. This requires reframing the way we think about cities as parts of metropolitan areas. It requires developing a national policy agenda that addresses issues such as public education, housing, transportation, the environment, health care, and others in ways that build common ground between cities and sectors of suburbia.

Both suburban sprawl and concentrated urban poverty are economically inefficient, socially unfair, and environmentally wasteful. Of course, we cannot turn back the clock. But just as we spent trillions of federal dollars to lure people and jobs to the suburbs, we must develop an equally ambitious plan to improve the fiscal condition of our cities and older suburbs, to limit the economic competition between municipalities (for the latest shopping mall or Wal-Marts, for example) that fuels further sprawl, to reduce widening economic disparities between the rich and poor, and to help lift the poor out of poverty with decent jobs, adequate health care, well-funded schools, and access to public transit and affordable housing outside ghettos and barrios (Dreier, Mollenkopf, and Swanstrom 2005; Rusk 1999).

Katrina unveiled the human disaster at hand as a result of several decades of the ascendancy of right-wing

ideas and corporate domination of the federal government, which extols market forces, individualism, and private charity over public responsibility and the common good. It underscores the need to reorder national priorities.

Notes

1. Jackson also triggered a controversy after Katrina struck when he said that parts of the low-lying Ninth Ward, a mostly African-American and low-income area, may never be rebuilt. "Whether we like it or not, New Orleans is not going to be 500,000 people for a long time," he said. "New Orleans is not going to be as Black as it was for a long time, if ever again" (Fletcher and Hsu 2005: A7; Havemann 2005: A14; Axtman 2005: 1).

2. President Bush's behavior is consistent. In the wake of the 9/11 tragedy, Bush used concerns over national security as a pretext for undermining workers' rights. His legislation sought to strip 170,000 federal employees being transferred to the new Department of Homeland Security of various workplace protections, including civil service regulations and collective bargaining rights. Similarly, the legislation federalizing about 56,000 airport screeners exempted them from union protections. Soon after 9/11, Bush also established a quota requiring government agencies to outsource at least 425,000 (later upped to 850,000) federal jobs to private contractors (many of which, it turns out, had contributed to his campaign). In December 2001, Bush also revoked rules prohibiting companies with a track record of violating federal labor laws—as well as environmental, consumer protection, civil rights and tax laws—from signing outsource employment contracts with federal agencies.

3. The *New Yorker* (Mayer 2005) reported that, according to Carol Browner, who ran the Environmental Protection Agency (EPA) during the Clinton administration, Senator Trent Lott of Mississippi fought EPA's efforts to limit construction of gambling casinos on Mississippi's environmentally sensitive wetlands. Will, in the wake of Katrina, the developers and their political allies heed those warnings?

References

Alter, J. (2005). "The other America; An enduring shame: Katrina reminded us, but the problem is not new. Why a rising tide of people live in poverty, who they are—and what we can do about it." *Newsweek,* September 19, p. 42.

Altman, D. (2005). "The disaster behind the disaster: Poverty." *New York Times* September 18, p. 3.

"Around the Region." (2005). *Houston Chronicle,* Business Section, September 2, p. 3.

Axtman, K. (2005). "In Ninth Ward, thoughts of leaving—for good: A permanent exodus from the district would alter the face of New Orleans." *Christian Science Monitor,* October 27, p. 1.

Blumenthal, R. (2005). "A grass-roots group Is helping hurricane survivors help themselves." *New York Times,* October 31, p. A12.

Broder, D. 2002. "Housing on the back burner." *Washington Post,* June 9.

Broder, J. 2005. "In storm's ruins, a rush to rebuild and reopen for business." *New York Times,* September 10, p. A1.

Brownstein, R. (2005a). "Katrina's aftermath; floodwaters lift poverty debate into political focus; Democrats call for renewed aid efforts, while Republicans fault traditional programs." *Los Angeles Times,* September 13, p. A1.

———. (2005b). "Liberals and conservatives hitch wagons to recovery." *Los Angeles Times,* September 25, p. A1.

Bush, G. W. (2005). President briefed on hurricane Rita preparations at FEMA. Washington, D.C., The White House, September 23.

Casey, R. (2005). "The Katrina coffee klatch." *Houston Chronicle,* September 6.

Chen, E., and M. Curtius. (2005). "Katrina's aftermath; Bush promises a massive rebuilding of Gulf Coast." *Los Angeles Times,* September 16, p. A1.

Connolly, C. (2005). "9th Ward: History, yes, but a future?; race and class frame debate on rebuilding New Orleans district." *Washington Post,* October 3, p. Al.

DeNavas-Walt, C., B. D. Proctor, and C. H. Lee. (2005). *Income, poverty and health insurance coverage in the United States: 2004.* Washington, D.C.: U.S. Census Bureau, August.

DeParle, J. (2005). "Liberal hopes ebb in post-storm poverty debate." *New York Times* October 11, p. A1.

Dreier, P. 1992. "Bush to cities: Drop dead." *Progressive* 56 (July): 20–23.

———. (2003). The urban crisis a decade since the LA riots. *National Civic Review* 92(1): 35–55.

———. (2005). How the Media Compound Urban Problems. *Journal of Urban Affairs* 27(2): 193–201.

Dreier, P., and R. Rothstein. (1994). "Seismic stimulus: The California quake's creative destruction." *American Prospect,* Summer.

Dreier, P., J. Mollenkopf, and T. Swanstrom. (2005). *Place matters: Metropolitics for the 21st century,* 2nd edition. Lawrence: University Press of Kansas.

Eisenbrey, R. (2005). "Gulf families' recovery at risk." Washington, D.C.: Economic Policy Institute, September 28, http://www.epi.org/content.cfm/webfeatures_snapshots_20050928 (accessed November 14).

Finch, S. (2002). "Minimum wage increase in N.O. upheld; Opponents to appeal to La. Supreme Court." *New Orleans Times-Picayune,* March 26: p. 1.

Fletcher, M. A., and S. S. Hsu. (2005). "Storms alter Louisiana politics; Population loss likely to reduce influence of black voters." *Washington Post,* October 14, p. A7.

Fronzcek, P., (2005). *Income, earnings and poverty from the 2004 American community survey.* Washington, D.C.: U.S. Census Bureau, August.

Gosselin, P. (2005). "Bush is in no hurry on Katrina recovery; The president's go-slow approach is called a recipe for chaos, even by fellow Republicans." *Los Angeles Times,* October 17, p. A1.

Gottlieb, R., R. Freer, M. Vallianatos, and P. Dreier. (2004). *The next Los Angeles: The struggle for a livable city.* Berkeley: Univ. of California Press.

Gruber, J. (2005). "Katrina will cost 400,000 Jobs." *USA Today,* September 7.

Hall, M. (2005). "Lack of FEMA data slows relief." *USA Today,* November 1.

Havemann, J. (2005). "A shattered Gulf Coast; New Orleans' racial future hotly argued; The U.S. housing chief expresses doubts about rebuilding, and draws anger and concern." *Los Angeles Times,* October 1, p. A14.

Henninger, D. (2005). "Wonder land: All the king's men cannot save New Orleans." *Wall Street Journal,* September 23, p. A16.

"Katrina: Issues and the aftermath." 2005. Washington, D.C.: Brookings Institution, Metropolitan Policy Program, http://www.brookings.edu/metro/katrina.htm (accessed November 13).

Kelman, A. (2005). "America's underclass exposed." *Christian Science Monitor,* September 12, p. 9.

Keyssar, A. (2005). "Reminders of poverty, soon forgotten." *Chronicle of Higher Education,* November 4, B6-B8.

Klein, N. (2005). "Let the people rebuild New Orleans." *The Nation,* September 26.

Klinenberg, E. (2002). *Heat wave: A social autopsy of disaster in Chicago.* Chicago: Univ. of Chicago Press.

Krugman, P. (2003). "Tax cut con." *New York Times Magazine,* September 14.

Lipton, E. (2005). "$11 Million a day spent on hotels for storm relief." *New York Times,* October 13, p. A1.

Maggs, J. (2005). "Creative destruction." *National Journal,* September 24, 2914–16.

Mayer, J. (2005). "High stakes." *The New Yorker,* September 19.

"Mayor to feds: 'Get off your asses.'" Transcript of radio interview with New Orleans' Nagin. (2005). CNN, September 2.

Miller, A. C., and K. Silverstein. (2005). "Long road to recovery; Lobbyists advise Katrina relief; A senate bill includes billions of dollars in projects for clients of 'experienced experts.'" *Los Angeles Times,* October 10, p. A1.

Molotch, H. (1970). "Oil in Santa Barbara and power in America." *Sociological Inquiry,* 40 (Winter): 131–144.

"New Orleans, Louisiana," http://www.city-data.com/city/New-Orleans-Louisiana.html (accessed November 14, 2005).

Nossiter, A. (2005a). "New Orleans landlords are pitted against tenants in court." *New York Times,* November 4, p. A20.

———. (2005b). "Thousands of demolitions near, New Orleans braces for new pain." *New York Times,* October 23, p. 1.

Pettit, K., and G. T. Kinglsey. (2003). *Concentrated poverty: A change in course.* Washington, D.C.: Urban Institute, May.

Pollin, R., M. Brenner, and S. Luce. (2002). "Intended versus unintended consequences: Evaluating the New Orleans living wage ordinance." *Journal of Economic Issues,* 36 (December)(4).

Remnick, D. (2005). "High water." *The New Yorker,* October 3, http://www.newyorker.com/fact/ content/articles/051003fa_fact (accessed November 13, 2005).

Riccardi, N., and D. Zucchino. (2005). "Long road to recovery; Now New Orleans is battered by layoffs." *Los Angeles Times,* October 5, p. A1.

Rivlin, G. (2005a). "A mogul who would rebuild New Orleans." *New York Times,* September 29, p. C1.

———. (2005b). "New Orleans Forms a Panel on Renewal." New York Times, October 1, p. A11.

Rusk, D. (1999). *Inside game/outside game.* Washington, DC: Brookings Institution Press.

Sanger, D. E., and E. L. Andrews. (2005). "Bush rules out a tax increase for gulf relief." *New York Times,* September 17, p. A1.

"Sortable List of Dissimilarity Scores." (2005). Albany, N.Y.: Lewis Mumford Center, SUNY-Albany, http://mumford.albany.edu/census/WholePop/WPsort/sort_d1.html (accessed November 13).

Sternberg, S. (2005). "For city's historic hospital, help is needed in a hurry." *USA Today,* September 1.

Stiles, M. (2005). "Groups want all to get equal chance at available services." *Houston Chronicle,* September 8.

Tisserand, M. (2005). "Beyond shelters." *The Nation,* November 7.

Vieth, W. (2005). "Little data to support Gulf Enterprise Zone's promise; The Bush proposal may need a leap of faith, given that no one is sure that such business tax breaks actually work." *Los Angeles Times,* October 25, p. A8.

Washington, L. (2004). "Ducking all responsibility ruled in 2004." *Philadelphia Tribune,* December 28, p. 5A.

Yerton, S. (2002). "N.O. voters approve minimum wage increase." *New Orleans Times-Picayune,* February 3, p. 1.

"Your guide to money in U.S. elections." (2005). Washington, DC: Center for Responsive Politics, http://www.opensecrets.org (accessed November 14).

Discussion Questions

1. Dreier writes, "Katrina was not an equal opportunity disaster." What evidence does he provide to support this statement?

   For example, Mississippi and Louisiana are the nation's poorest states. New Orleans is the 12th poorest city; median household income in 2000 was $27,133. Less than half of the households (46.5%) own their own homes. Among the city's African Americans, 35% do not own a car, compared with 15% of whites.

2. How were class and power conflicts evident in rebuilding efforts?

   Dreier identifies how national corporations and local businesses with close ties to the Bush administration have an advantage in shaping the agenda and getting federal reconstruction funds. With more than one million displaced residents, the rebuilding efforts are likely to remain focused on businesses and the affluent, unless the poor and near-poor are able to mobilize, make demands, and participate in city and state elections. The mobilization efforts on behalf of the displaced and poor have also received less media attention.

Source: From Dreier, P. (2006). Katrina and power in America. *Urban Affairs Review, 41*(3), 528–549. Reprinted by permission of Sage Publications.

CHAPTER 29

Integrating Environmental Justice and the Precautionary Principle in Research and Policy Making

The Case of Ambient Air Toxics Exposures and Health Risks Among Schoolchildren in Los Angeles

Rachel Morello-Frosch, Manuel Pastor Jr., and James Sadd (2002)

Morello-Frosch and her colleagues integrate two environmental policy frameworks— environmental justice and the precautionary principle—in their examination of toxic air exposures and health risks among schoolchildren in the Los Angeles Unified School District. Their data reveal that racial-ethnic minority children bear the highest burden of estimated cancer and noncancer health risks associated with ambient air toxic exposures.

Environmental justice embraces the principle that all people and communities are entitled to equal protection of environmental and public health laws and regulations.

—Bullard (1996)

When an activity raises threats of harm to human health or the environment, precautionary measures should be taken even if some cause and effect relationships are not fully established scientifically.

—Raffensperger and Tickner (1999)

Hazards are produced by business operations, to be sure, but they are defined and evaluated socially— in the mass media, in the experts' debate, in the jungle of interpretations and jurisdictions, in courts or with strategic-intellectual dodges, in a milieu of contexts.

—Beck (1992)

The emergence of two policy frameworks during the past two decades—environmental justice and the precautionary principle—has begun to transform traditional approaches to environmental policy making, research, and community organizing related to public health. Yet despite the burgeoning literature on both of these frameworks, and the fact that they share some important tenets, environmental justice and the precautionary principle have not always been well integrated at either the theoretical or the policy levels. In this article, we examine the foundations of environmental justice and the precautionary principle and propose ways in which these concepts could be better integrated to reshape environmental health policy making to protect public health, particularly for vulnerable populations, such as poor communities of color. We attempt to elucidate the implications of environmental justice and the precautionary principle for policy making by discussing some results from our research on environmental inequality in ambient air toxics exposures and associated health risks among schoolchildren in Southern California. We conclude by suggesting possible future paths of inquiry for research and policy making.

Environmental Justice and the Framework for Precaution

The principle of environmental justice emerged out of a vibrant social movement that has challenged biases within environmental policy making and regulation along with exclusionary land use and economic development decision making that create disparities in the prevalence of hazardous pollution among the poor and communities of color (Morello-Frosch 2002). Environmental justice advocates contend that despite seemingly neutral and uniform regulations, legislation, and performance standards, formal and informal dynamics may affect the daily operations of regulatory activities in unexpected ways that produce and perpetuate discriminatory outcomes. Indeed, situations where there is leeway for bureaucratic discretion in the implementation of environmental policies can lead to regional and community differences in the extent of regulatory enforcement efforts. The fact that working-class and minority interests are poorly represented within regulatory circles can perpetuate these discriminatory outcomes (Gelobter 1992; Lavelle and Coyle 1992).

With its emphasis on public health, social inequality, and environmental degradation, environmental justice provides a framework for public policy debates about the impact of discrimination on the environmental health of diverse communities in the United States. The issue of environmental justice also raises the challenging question of whether disparities in exposures to environmental hazards may play an important, yet poorly understood, role in the complex and persistent patterns of disparate health status among the poor and people of color in the United States (Ecob and Smith 1999; Haan, Kaplan, and Camacho 1987; Haan 1985; Hahn et al. 1996; Kawachi and Marmot 1998; Krieger et al. 1993; Kubzansky et al. 1998; Lazarus 1993; Navarro 1990; Robinson 1984, 1987; Syme and Berkman 1976; U.S. Department of Health and Human Services 1990).

The movement has also catalyzed a surge of academic inquiry into whether and how discrimination creates disparities in the distributions of environmental hazards among diverse communities. Research on environmental inequality varies widely, ranging from anecdotal and descriptive studies to rigorous statistical modeling that quantifies the extent to which race and/or

class explain disparities in environmental hazards among diverse communities (Boer et al. 1997; Bowen et al. 1995; Bullard 1983; Burke 1993; Commission for Racial Justice 1987; Hersh 1995; Kraft and Scheberle 1995; Lavelle and Coyle 1992; Mohai and Bryant 1992; Pastor, Sadd, and Hipp 2001; Pollock and Vittas 1995; Pulido, Sidawi, and Vos 1996; Sadd et al. 1999; Wernette and Nieves 1991; Zimmerman 1993). Much, although not all, of the evidence points to a pattern of disproportionate exposures to toxics and associated health risks among communities of color and the poor, with racial disparities often persisting across economic strata.

Social science researchers examining environmental inequalities have generally limited their inquiries to evaluating differences in the location of pollution sources between population groups, while placing less emphasis on evaluating the distribution of exposures or, more important, potential health risks. Activists have pushed environmental health researchers and regulatory authorities in particular to move beyond chemical-by-chemical or facility-by-facility analysis toward a cumulative exposure approach that accounts for the exposure realities of diverse populations and that better elucidates how race and class discrimination can increase community susceptibility to environmental pollutants (Morello-Frosch, Pastor, and Sadd 2001).

Nevertheless, causally linking the presence of environmental pollution with potentially adverse health effects is an ongoing challenge in the environmental health field, particularly in situations where populations are chronically exposed to complex chemical mixtures (Institute of Medicine 1999). Environmental organizations, including environmental justice activists, have powerfully argued that in the never-ending quest for better data and unequivocal proof of cause and effect, some researchers and regulators have lost sight of a basic public health principle—namely, the importance of disease prevention (Bullard 1994; Lee 2002). As a result, activist organizing and models of community-based participatory research have encouraged some academics and regulators to integrate and operationalize the precautionary principle into their work (Brown and Mikkelsen 1997, 134–38). Practically, this means that in the face of uncertain but suggestive evidence of adverse environmental or human health effects, regulatory action is needed to prevent future harm. Known as the precautionary principle, this perspective seeks to mobilize environmental and public health policy making that otherwise can be paralyzed when implementation is too dependent on scientific certainty.

The essence of the precautionary principle promotes planning, alternatives assessment, and anticipatory action with the aim of promoting disease prevention and avoiding environmental health and ecological calamities due to industrial production and other potentially harmful activities. Instead of presuming that specific chemicals or production processes are safe until data and research prove they are hazardous, the precautionary principle favors a more cautious regulatory and policy approach that prioritizes the protection of human and environmental health. In short, "the absence of evidence of harm is not the same thing as evidence of the absence of harm" (Kriebel et al. 2001, 873). Equally important, the precautionary principle also seeks to shift the burden of hazard assessment, monitoring, and data generation activities onto those who propose to undertake potentially harmful activities or chemical production (Kriebel and Tickner 2001; Steingraber 2000). The notion of precaution has been used to justify the development and implementation of innovative policies at the international, national, and local levels to address a range of environmental problems, including acid rain, water pollution, global warming, exposure to electromagnetic fields, and children's exposure to pesticides (Foster, Vecchia, and Repacholi 2000; Raffensperger and Tickner 1999, 3; World Health Organization 2002; Calver 2000).

Recently, children's health advocates have put forth recommendations for implementing the precautionary principle to protect children from the adverse effects of environmental hazard exposures (Tickner and Hoppin 2000; Schettler et al. 1999). Indeed, scientific evidence indicates that children are more susceptible to the effects of environmental pollution than adults because of fundamental differences in their physiology, metabolism, and absorption and exposure patterns (Crom 1994; Guzelian, Henry, and Olin 1992; Kaplan and Morris 2000; National Research Council 1993; Parkinson 1996; Schettler et al. 1999). Certain childhood diseases (e.g., respiratory illnesses such as asthma) are significant health issues (Leikauf et al. 1995; Mannino, Homa, and Pertowski 1998), and air pollution could be aggravating these problems (Burg and Gist 1998; Leikauf et al. 1995; Ware et al. 1993). Anecdotal, epidemiologic, and exposure studies suggest potential short-and long-term health effects among children from outdoor and indoor air pollutants (Gilliland et al. 1999; Guo et al. 1999; Jedrychowski and Flak 1998; Ritz et al. 2002; Schettler et al. 2001; Van Vliet et al. 1997), potentially hazardous facilities (Ginns and Gatrell 1996; Gomzi and Saric 1997), and pesticides (Landrigan et al. 1999; Northwest Coalition for Alternatives to Pesticides 2000; U.S. General Accounting Office 1999). Partly because of this research, Executive Order 13045, issued in 1997,

directs federal agencies to consider the particular vulnerability of children to environmental health risks (White House 1997). Consistent with the concerns of environmental justice, there is increasing evidence that children of color bear the burden of exposures to environmental hazards and their potentially adverse health effects (Clark et al. 1999; Gold et al. 1993; Schwartz et al. 1990; Sexton and Adgate 1999).

Environmental Justice and Children's Exposure to Ambient Air Toxics in Los Angeles

While children's health may certainly be affected by environmental hazards in their homes and neighborhoods, they spend much of their day in schools—and these schools may or may not be located in the communities where they live, particularly given magnet programs and cross-town busing in major urban areas. We sought to examine the issue of children's environmental health through the lens of environmental justice with a preliminary analysis of estimated outdoor air toxics exposures and associated health risks among schoolchildren in the Los Angeles Unified School District (M. Pastor, J. L. Sadd, and R. Morello-Frosch 2002). The Los Angeles Unified School District is the second largest school district in the country, spanning 704 square miles and enrolling more than 700,000 students. Given suggestive evidence of a link between childhood respiratory problems associated with air pollution and diminished academic performance (Bener et al. 1994; Diette et al. 2000; Fowler, Davenport, and Garg 1992; Perera et al. 1999), we have also conducted a preliminary assessment of the potential relationship between estimated respiratory risks associated with air toxics and overall school academic performance (M. Pastor, J. Sadd, and R. A. Morello-Frosch 2002).

METHOD AND DATA SOURCES

All school locations were geocoded to host census tracts and linked to a set of environmental hazard indicators, including tract-level estimates of lifetime individual cancer risk and a respiratory hazard index, both associated with ambient exposures to air toxics from mobile and stationary emission sources. Estimated cancer risk and respiratory hazard indices were derived by combining modeled estimates of ambient air toxics concentrations with corresponding toxicity data information from the U.S. Environmental Protection Agency and the California Environmental Protection Agency. The methodology for calculating these cancer and noncancer risk estimates is discussed extensively elsewhere (Caldwell et al. 1998; Morello-Frosch, Pastor, and Sadd 2001; Morello-Frosch et al. 2000). Exposure data were derived from a modeling analysis undertaken by the U.S. Environmental Protection Agency's Cumulative Exposure Project, which estimated long-term average concentrations for 1990 of 148 air toxics for every census tract in the contiguous United States (U.S. Environmental Protection Agency 1998). Emissions data used in the model take into account large stationary sources (such as Toxic Release Inventory facilities), small area service industries and fabricators (such as dry cleaners, auto body paint shops, and furniture manufacturers), and mobile sources (such as cars, trucks, and air craft). The modeling algorithm takes into account meteorological data and simulation of atmospheric processes (Rosenbaum et al. 1999; Rosenbaum, Ligocki, and Wei 1999).

Cancer risk estimates were derived using inhalation unit risk estimates, which are a measure of carcinogenic potency for each pollutant (U.S. Environmental Protection Agency 1986). Cancer risks for each pollutant in each census tract were derived with the following formula:

$$R_{ij} = C_{ij} \times IUR_j,$$

where R_{ij} is the estimate of individual lifetime cancer risk from pollutant j in census tract i, C_{ij} is the concentration of hazardous air pollutant j in micrograms per cubic meter ($\mu g/m^3$) in census tract i, and IUR is the inhalation unit risk estimate, or cancer potency, for pollutant j in $(\mu g/m^3)^{-1}$. The cancer risks of different air toxics were assumed to be additive and were summed together in each census tract to estimate a total individual lifetime cancer risk in each tract.

For respiratory health risks, pollutant concentration estimates were divided by their corresponding reference concentration for chronic respiratory effects to derive a hazard ratio (Dourson and Stara 1983). Respiratory hazard ratios for each pollutant in each census tract were calculated using the following formula:

$$HR_{ij} = C_{ij}/RfC_j,$$

where HR_{ij} is the hazard ratio for pollutant j in tract i, C_{ij} is the concentration in $\mu g/m^3$ of pollutant j in census tract i, and RfC_j is the reference concentration for pollutant j in $\mu g/m^3$. An indicator of total respiratory hazard

was calculated by summing the hazard ratios for each pollutant to derive a total chronic respiratory hazard index:

$$HI_i = \sum_j HR_{ij},$$

where HI_i is the sum of the hazard ratios for all pollutants (j) in census tract i. This measure assumes that multiple subthreshold exposures may result in an adverse health effect.

School-level information came from the October 1999 California Basic Educational Data System, an annual data collection program administered by the California Department of Education Demographic Research Unit that includes basic school information as well as data on 1997–1998 enrollment and ethnic makeup of the student population by school (M. Pastor, J. L. Sadd, and R. Morello-Frosch 2002).

RESULTS

Estimated lifetime cancer risks associated with outdoor air toxics exposures in Los Angeles were found to be ubiquitously high, often exceeding the Clean Air Act goal of one in 1 million by between one and three orders of magnitude (Morello-Frosch, Pastor, and Sadd 2001).[1] Respiratory hazards, although not as high, exceeded health benchmarks in many locations (Morello-Frosch et al. 2000). Moreover, on average, a major portion of the estimated health risks are coming from pollutants generated from mobile and small area source emissions as compared to large point sources (Morello-Frosch, Pastor, and Sadd 2001).

Figure 29.1 shows the average lifetime cancer risk and the average chronic respiratory hazard index by schoolchildren of different racial and ethnic groups. The graph indicates that Latino and African American students bear the greatest burden of lifetime cancer risks associated with ambient air toxics, but Asian schoolchildren also face higher risks than Anglos. A similar pattern emerges for estimates of respiratory hazard (M. Pastor, J. L. Sadd, and R. Morello-Frosch 2002).

We then examined the relationship between school demographics and cancer and noncancer health risks associated with air toxics using multivariate regression (see Table 29.1). Estimated respiratory and cancer risks were modeled as a function of the proportion of students of color within each school as well as location-specific (or tract-level) characteristics, including percentage of land devoted to industrial use, population density, median household income, and the proportion of home

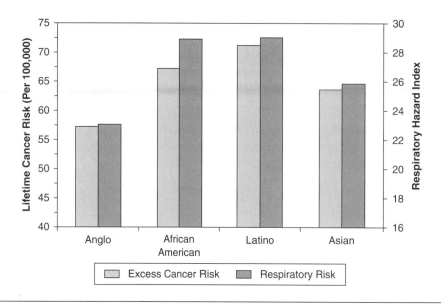

Figure 29.1 Cancer and Respiratory Risks for Schoolchildren, by Race—Los Angeles Unified School District

Table 29.1 Relationships of School Demographics to Estimated Health Risks Associated with Ambient Air Toxics—Los Angeles Unified School District

| | *Ordinary Least Squares Regression* | | | |
| | *Cancer Risk* | | *Respiratory Risk* | |
Demographic	*Coefficient*	*T-Score*	*Coefficient*	*T-Score*
Percentage of land devoted to industrial land use	0.121	2.701***	0.039	1.402*
Population density per square mile	0.086	8.169***	0.033	5.005***
Median household income	−0.033	−1.080	−0.011	−0.565
Rate of home ownership	−0.168	−3.407***	−0.067	−2.173**
Minority students as percentage of school site	0.117	2.111**	0.078	2.274**
F value/log likelihood	96.8***		41.2***	
Adjusted or Nagelkerke R^2	.456		.260	
n	572		572	

*Significant at the .20 level. **Significant at the .05 level. ***Significant at the .01 level.

ownership. Although this is not an explicitly causal model, these regressions provide an assessment of the relationship between school demographics and estimated health risks after controlling for other key factors, which may indicate whether there are issues of environmental inequality among Los Angeles schoolchildren. Regression results show that after controlling for key covariates, the proportion of students of color at a school site continues to be a statistically significant factor for increased estimated cancer and respiratory risks associated with ambient air toxics exposures (M. Pastor, J. L. Sadd, and R. Morello-Frosch 2002).

To assess whether environmental hazards and estimated respiratory risks may affect student school performance, we assessed the relationship between school educational outcomes and estimated respiratory risk. To do this, we utilized California's Academic Performance Index, a summary score of school performance based on the Stanford 9 achievement test given as part of the state's mandated testing program (M. Pastor, J. Sadd, and R. A. Morello-Frosch 2002). It is important to note that we do not have measures of individual student performance but rather a score for the entire school that helps in ranking a particular school in question against other schools.[2] Such school-level studies are increasingly common because of the way in which states and school districts have focused on schools as the unit of accountability, which requires an emphasis on aggregate performance (Bickel and Howley 2000; Fowler and Herbert 1991).

The map in Figure 29.2 shows the geographic pattern when we compare the estimated cumulative respiratory hazard ratio, split into thirds, to quartiles of school performance; the visual correlation between higher

risk estimates and lower scores is striking. Figure 29.3 helps to contextualize this map by showing the average school Academic Performance Index score for schools, ranked by lowest respiratory hazard to highest respiratory hazard associated with ambient air toxics, with the risk groups each reflecting one-third of all schools. As can be seen, the differences are substantial as schools located in tracts with the highest estimated respiratory hazard have a performance differential of about 20 percent compared

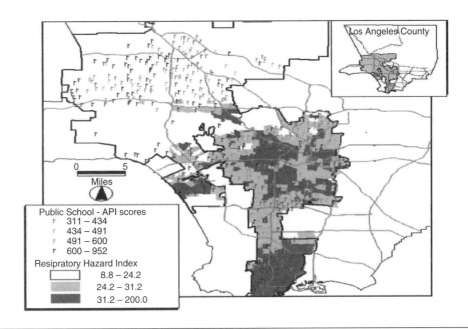

Figure 29.2 Public School Academic Performance Index (API) and Estimated Cumulative Respiratory Risk From Ambient Air Toxics Exposure—Los Angeles Unified School District

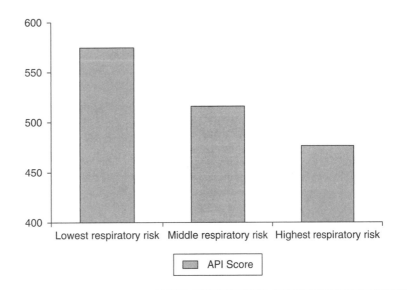

Figure 29.3 Academic Performance Index (API) Score, by Respiratory Hazard Ranking

to schools located in tracts with the lowest risk level. This 20 percent differential is sizable, roughly matching the average difference between the bottom third and middle third of schools in terms of academic performance.

These preliminary results, showing a correlation between estimated respiratory risks and Academic Performance Index scores, are likely to be influenced by other demographic characteristics that affect student academic performance. A stepwise regression approach found that increasing estimated respiratory risks has a negative and statistically significant impact on overall school performance on the Academic Performance Index, even when controlling for the other factors that should explain such indicators of academic achievement. Key factors that were entered into the model included the percentage of children receiving free school lunches (see Krueger 1999; Orfield 1997), the percentage of teachers with emergency credentials (an indicator of teaching quality), average class size and school size, whether schools were on year-round schedules, the percentage of students who are just learning English,[3] a measure of student mobility (the number of students who are new to a school that year), and parents' educational attainment level with all variables also coming from the state's Academic Performance Index database (M. Pastor, J. Sadd, and R. A. Morello-Frosch 2002).

Thus, this cross-sectional study indicates that minority students, particularly African Americans and Latinos, are more likely to bear the burden of attending school in locations where estimated cancer and respiratory risks from air toxics tend to be highest. Moreover, after controlling for demographic covariates, it appears as if indicators of respiratory risk associated with air toxics are associated with diminished school performance.

Implications of Results for Policy Making

Preliminary results from our analysis indicate that there may be serious environmental justice concerns for minority students attending public schools in Los Angeles. While all Los Angeles schoolchildren face problematic outdoor air toxics exposures and associated health risks, minority (especially African American and Latino) youth seem to bear the largest share of the burden. Moreover, these estimated respiratory hazards associated with air toxics appear to negatively affect indices of school performance. While the causal chain and biological mechanisms are not clearly specified, the association, even after controlling for other important

covariates, is problematic given the existing tendency of predominantly minority and poor schools to underperform academically.

While our results cannot be meaningfully generalized beyond Los Angeles, our study offers some useful policy lessons and has implications for future research on the intersection of environmental justice and children's health. First, our study results reinforce the need to take a more holistic approach to environmental health and justice research. As more comprehensive data become available, future studies need to move away from locational and pollutant-by-pollutant analysis and toward a cumulative exposure approach that gets at the ultimate question of what disparities in exposures mean for potential inequities in health risks. Due to a paucity of comprehensive epidemiological data to answer this question, we are often left with the tools of risk assessment, which even within an equity analysis framework remains controversial among the public and policy makers alike (Kuehn 1996; Latin 1988). However, we sought to use risk assessment comparatively to assess the distribution of health risks associated with ambient air toxics exposures among schoolchildren in Los Angeles. Although the analysis focused on one exposure media, air pollution, it characterized potential health risks from cumulative exposures to multiple chemicals from multiple sources (e.g., mobile and stationary sources). Results here show that with a paucity of good epidemiological data, risk assessment can provide crucial information for communities and policy makers who are grappling with potentially high-stakes environmental equity issues related to school siting decisions.

Moreover, with student enrollments spiraling and mounting pressure to ease severe overcrowding in Los Angeles schools, the district is faced with the Herculean task of building more than eighty new schools during the next five years (Trotter 2002). This scenario, which is occurring in urban districts across the country, raises challenges for balancing the need to enhance educational opportunities for students in the district, most of whom are students of color, with the need to address legitimate environmental health concerns about siting new facilities. The difficulties of resolving this conflict came to light during a recent controversy in 1999 over construction of the Belmont Learning Complex, a state-of-the-art school designed to relieve overcrowding in a largely Latino immigrant section of the city. Unfortunately, the school was sited in a former oil field with active methane gas leaks and soil contaminated with carcinogenic compounds (Anderson 2000).

In the wake of the Belmont controversy, some have forcefully argued that building schools in densely populated urban areas may require the use of brownfield land and that slowing down construction or failing to quickly identify sites will have a negative impact on the educational opportunities and futures of minority school-children (Blume 2000; Hernandez 1999; Metropolitan Forum Project 1999). Yet preliminary data from our study showing demographic disparities in health risks associated with air toxics exposures among schoolchildren should encourage precaution on the part of critics who argue against strict and potentially costly environmental standards for siting new schools. Indeed, both environmental justice concerns and the precautionary principle would promote the notion that any future construction plans should take into account the disparities in environmental hazard distributions among minority schoolchildren in the district, particularly given the overall poorer health status of these populations (U.S. Environmental Protection Agency 1992). These environmental inequalities have implications for public policy in terms of future zoning, siting decisions, and general school-based intervention strategies aimed at improving the health status and educational opportunities of minority students. At a minimum, this situation of environmental inequity should not be further aggravated by future expansion plans.

One lesson learned from the Belmont controversy and our preliminary study results is that environmental health concerns must always be part of the equation when deciding how to site new school facilities. Standards for acquiring and cleaning up brownfields for school construction should be clarified and take into account the particular vulnerability of children to environmental hazards. A positive outgrowth of the Belmont controversy is a new requirement that potential sites for school construction must pass an environmental review by California's Department of Toxic Substances Control. This development is a key step in the right direction in terms of proceeding with caution to ensure that children's environmental health concerns are adequately addressed. However, it also raises a polemical social justice issue for urban districts that face unique challenges in finding suitable sites for school construction but are also pressured to expedite the siting and construction process to ensure that they receive adequate and timely state funding to support new projects. Until recently, California's system for allocating state funds to support massive school construction initiatives such as those desperately needed in Los Angeles functioned on a first-come, first-served basis. This seemingly neutral and fair policy had the unintended effect of placing urban school districts at a severe financial disadvantage and created a

strong disincentive to integrate the precautionary principle and environmental justice concerns when weighing the merits and pitfalls of potentially new sites for future schools. Currently, the funding allocation system is being overhauled to accommodate urban districts facing unique and difficult challenges, both in acquiring suitable property and redeveloping industrial land to build new schools. Further efforts to address the overwhelming challenges faced by the Los Angeles Unified School District in accommodating the space needs of its rapidly expanding student body will require leadership and collaboration between impacted communities, the school district, city and state officials, and even the private sector to ensure that the environmental health and educational needs of children of color are effectively addressed.

Conclusion: The Promise of Precaution and Environmental Justice for Policy Making

The issue of children's environmental health has been used as the quintessential example for making the case to support environmental justice and the precautionary principle in environmental regulation and policy making (Bullard 1994; Tickner and Hoppin 2000). The persistent and tragic problem of childhood lead poisoning highlights the need to better integrate both of these frameworks to better protect children's environmental health. Indeed, historical failures in policy making to exercise precautions and to decisively act to eliminate lead from paint and gasoline has created a situation in which currently 1 million U.S. children continue to exceed the benchmark for blood lead level exposure that affects development (Schettler et al. 2001). This failure to enact precaution has had a disparate impact on urban children of color, who tend to have the highest average blood lead levels, and their attendant neurological and developmental effects.

Our study results on the environmental justice implications of air toxics exposure among Los Angeles schoolchildren provide some preliminary and suggestive data to justify the development of policy strategies in the district that uphold both environmental justice and the precautionary principle. Creating a process to assess the environmental hazards of new construction sites, coupled with changing the statewide school bond funding allocation system to address the needs of urban districts serving predominantly minority students, demonstrates how these two principles can be effectively integrated in the policy-making arena. In addition, the Los Angeles Unified School District's recent integrated pest management policy to decrease pesticide use in the schools further demonstrates how community organizing can effectively create significant local policy shifts that protect children, particularly children of color (Prussel and Tepperman 2001).

Purposeful strategies for integrating environmental justice and the precautionary principle are key if we are to effectively protect vulnerable populations and eliminate persistent race- and class-based disparities in environmental hazard exposures and health outcomes. Although it is important to acknowledge the unique histories of community organizing and policy advocacy that underlie these two distinct policy principles, environmental justice and the precautionary principle have some important overlapping goals, which are delineated in Table 29.2. These include (1) *Public health and disease prevention for environmental justice*, i.e., protecting communities of color from the environmental health effects of institutional and social discrimination. For the

precautionary principle, this goal implies a commitment to preventing harm to human health or ecosystems in the face of inadequate scientific tools and incomplete, but suggestive, data. *(2) Shifting the burden of proof*: environmental justice advocates reject the notion that claims of environmental inequality must demonstrate a pattern of discriminatory intent and disparate impact, a requirement that creates formidable barriers to communities seeking remedies or policy action to address disparities in environmental hazard exposures. Similarly, the precautionary principle proposes that chemicals should not be considered innocent until proven guilty but rather that proponents of a proposed new activity rather than the public must bear responsibility for demonstrating that a new product or chemical is safe. *(3) Procedural justice and democratic decision making*: here environmental justice and the precautionary principle offer divergent yet complementary objectives for ensuring public participation in decisions that affect community environmental health. Environmental justice proposes a political

Table 29.2   A Framework for Integrating the Precautionary Principle and Environmental Justice

Environmental Justice Principle	*Principle of Integration*	*Precautionary Principle*
Protect communities of color and the poor against environmental inequality and the disparate impact of toxics	Public health and disease prevention	Prioritize prevention of harm and public health in the face of uncertain science and incomplete data
Eliminate the discriminatory intent standard in favor of a disparate impact standard to trigger regulatory action or remediation for environmental harm against communities of color	Shifting the burden of proof	Uphold the principle of reverse onus, which requires that proponents of a potentially harmful activity, rather than the public, bear responsibility for showing that a new product or chemical is safe
Democratize environmental, regulatory, social, and economic policy making, which requires community decision-making power in a. Environmental regulation activities, e.g., facility siting, sanctioning activities, and pollution monitoring strategies; b. Regional and economic development policy, e.g., industrial and housing development, zoning and land use, transportation planning, job creation and labor markets, and community revitalization	Procedural justice and democratic decision making on issues affecting community environmental health	Democratize environmental regulation and industrial production decisions **Employ principle of least harmful alternative:** Require implementing an open, democratic, and informed process of evaluating viable alternatives to a potentially hazardous activity Assess must examine adverse as well as beneficial effects of proposed activity Fully disclose who is affected by proposed activity All of which can be a requirement for government agencies (e.g., National Environmental Policy Act) or industry (e.g., Massachusetts Toxic Use Reduction Act)

economy perspective that asserts the need to enhance community capacity to shape environmental policy making and regulatory enforcement and to influence regional and economic development activities in systematic ways that benefit (or at least do not harm) its residents. The precautionary principle emphasizes procedural justice by promoting the concept of alternatives assessment, which entails a democratic, open, and transparent process to examine viable alternatives to potentially harmful activities. This process can be applied to government, through requirements of the National Environmental Protection Act, for example, which requires an environmental impact statement that describes the adverse and beneficial consequences of federally funded projects and their alternatives. Alternatives assessment is also the key element of the Massachusetts Toxic Use Reduction Act, which requires industries using a threshold quantity of certain chemicals to periodically undergo a process to identify alternatives to reduce chemical use. Both of these approaches to alternatives assessment allow for a certain level of public disclosure, comment, and input.

The integration of environmental justice and the precautionary principle offers possibilities for new and innovative approaches to addressing issues of children's environmental health. Community participation is key for developing long-term regulatory, enforcement, and economic development initiatives that are sustainable and that protect the health of diverse and vulnerable communities. Moreover, decision making about regulatory action in the face of inadequate scientific tools and uncertain data must be transparent and democratic, particularly given that polemical questions of whether and how to regulate hazards often transcend the realm of science, data, and risk assessment and become political, socioeconomic, and moral judgment calls. The challenge for advocates, scientists, and policy makers alike is to keep in mind that environmental policy making is generally carried out in a milieu where the distinction between the scientific and sociopolitical realms is often unclear. Integrating some of the overarching goals of environmental justice and the precautionary principle offers a new path and framework to create concrete policy tools that promote public health, disease prevention, and a safer future for everyone.

Notes

1. In 1990, Congress established a health-based goal for the Clean Air Act: to reduce lifetime cancer risks from major sources of hazardous air pollutants to one in 1 million. The act required that over time, U.S. Environmental Protection Agency regulations for major sources should "provide an ample margin of safety to protect public health" (Clean Air Act Amendments 1990).

2. For a general review of the quality of such educational indicators, see Koretz (1997).

3. English proficiency affects the overall Academic Performance Index scores, which are not adjusted for this variable. The underlying exams used to calculate the Academic Performance Index are administered in English due to the passage in California of a 1998 statewide initiative that limits bilingual instruction and testing.

References

Anderson, S. (2000). The school that wasn't: Politics and pollution in LA. *Nation*, p. 32.

Beck, Ulrich. (1992). From industrial society to the risk society: Questions of survival, social structure and ecological enlightment. *Theory, Culture and Society* 9 (1): 97–123.

Bener, A., Y. M. Abdulrazzaq, P. Debuse, and A. H. Abdin. 1994. Asthma and wheezing as the cause of school absence. *Journal of Asthma* 31 (2): 93–98.

Bickel, R., and C. Howley. (2000). The influence of scale on school performance: A multi-level extension of the Matthew principle. *Education Policy Analysis Archives* 8 (22). Retrieved from http://epaa.asu.edu/epaa/v8n22/.

Blume, H. (2000). No vacancy: The school district's space crunch is much worse than you know. And no one has a plan that will fix it. *LA Weekly*, 9–15 June. Retrieved from http://www.laweekly.com/ink/00/29/features-blume.php.

Boer, T. J., M. Pastor, J. L. Sadd, and L. D. Snyder. (1997). Is there environmental racism? The demographics of hazardous waste in Los Angeles County. *Social Science Quarterly* 78 (4): 793–810.

Bowen, W. M., M. J. Salling, K. E. Haynes, and E. J. Cyran. (1995). Toward environmental justice: Spatial equity in Ohio and Cleveland. *Annals of the Association of American Geographers* 85 (4): 641–63.

Brown, P., and E. J. Mikkelsen. (1997). *No safe place: Toxic waste, leukemia, and community action.* Berkeley: University of California Press.

Bullard, Robert. (1983). Solid waste sites and the black community. *Sociological Inquiry* 53:273–88.

Bullard, R. D. (1994). Overcoming racism in environmental decision-making. *Environment* 36 (4): 10–44.

———. 1996. Environmental justice: It's more than waste facility siting. *Social Science Quarterly* 77 (3): 493–99.

Burg, J., and G. Gist. (1998). The National Exposure Registry: Analysis of health outcomes from the Benzene subregistry. *Toxicology and Industrial Health* 14 (3): 367–87.

Burke, L. M. (1993). Race and environmental equity: A geographic analysis in Los Angeles. *Geo-Info Systems* October: 44–50.

Caldwell, J. C., T. J. Woodruff, R. Morello-Frosch, and D. A. Axelrad. (1998). Application of health information to hazardous air pollutants modeled in EPA's Cumulative Exposure Project. *Toxicology and Industrial Health* 14 (3): 429–54.

Calver, M. C. (2000). Lessons from preventive medicine for the precautionary principle and ecosystem health. *Ecosystem Health* 6 (2): 339–47.

Clark, N. M., R. W. Brown, E. Parker, T. G. Robins, D. G. Remick, M. A. Philbert, G. Keeler, and B. Israel. 1999. Childhood asthma. *Environmental Health Perspectives* 107 (Suppl. 3): 421–29.

Clean Air Act Amendments. § 112(f), Standard to Protect Health and the Environment (1990).

Commission for Racial Justice, United Church of Christ. 1987. *Toxic wastes and race in the U.S.: A national report on the racial and socio-economic characteristics of communities with hazardous waste sites.* New York: United Church of Christ.

Crom, W. R. (1994). Pharmacokinetics in the child. *Environmental Health Perspectives* 102 (Suppl. 11): 111–17.

Diette, G. B., L. Markson, E. A. Skinner, T. T. Nguyen, P. Algatt-Bergstrom, and A. W. Wu. (2000). Nocturnal asthma in children affects school attendance, school performance, and parents' work attendance. *Archives of Pediatrics and Adolescent Medicine* 154 (9): 923–29.

Dourson, M. L., and J. F. Stara. (1983). Regulatory history and experimental support of uncertainty (safety) factors. *Regulatory Toxicology and Pharmacology* 3 (3): 224–38.

Ecob, R., and G. Davey Smith. (1999). Income and health: What is the nature of the relationship? *Social Science & Medicine* 48:693–705.

Foster, K. R., P. Vecchia, and M. H. Repacholi. (2000). Science and the precautionary principle. *Science* 288 (5468): 979–81.

Fowler, M. G., M. G. Davenport, and R. Garg. (1992). School functioning of US children with asthma. *Pediatrics* 90 (6): 939–44.

Fowler, W. J., Jr., and J. W. Herbert. (1991). School size, characteristics, and outcomes. *Educational Evaluation and Policy Analysis* 13 (2): 189–202.

Gelobter, M. (1992). Toward a model of environmental discrimination. In *Race and the incidence of environmental hazards: A time for discourse,* edited by B. Bryant and P. Mohai. Boulder, CO: Westview.

Gilliland, F. D., R. McConnell, J. Peters, and H. Gong. (1999). A theoretical basis for investigating ambient air pollution and children's respiratory health. *Environmental Health Perspectives* 107 (Suppl. 3): 403–7.

Ginns, S. E., and A. C. Gatrell. (1996). Respiratory health effects of industrial air pollution: A study in east Lancashire, UK. *Journal of Epidemiology and Community Health* 50 (6): 631–35.

Gold, D. R., A. Rotnitzky, A. I. Damokosh, J. H. Ware, F. E. Speizer, B. G. Ferris, and D. W Dockery. 1993. Race and gender differences in respiratory illness prevalence and their relationship to environmental exposures in children 7 to 14 years of age. *American Review of Respiratory Disease* 148:10–18.

Gomzi, M., and M. Saric. (1997). Respiratory impairment among children living in the vicinity of a fertilizer plant. *International Archives of Occupational and Environmental Health* 70 (5): 314–20.

Guo, Y. L., Y. C. Lin, F. C. Sung, S. L. Huang, Y. C. Ko, J. S. Lai, H. J. Su, C. K. Shaw, R. S. Lin, and D. W Dockery. 1999. Climate, traffic-related air pollutants, and asthma prevalence in middle-school children in Taiwan. *Environmental Health Perspectives* 107 (12): 1001–6.

Guzelian, P., C. Henry, and S. Olin. (1992). *Similarities and differences between children and adults: Implications for risk assessment.* Washington, DC: ILSI Press.

Haan, M., G. Kaplan, and T. Camacho. (1987). Poverty and health: Prospective evidence from the Alameda County study. *American Journal of Epidemiology* 125:989–98.

Haan, M. N. (1985). *Socio-economic position and health: A review.* Berkeley: California State Department of Public Health.

Hahn, R., E. Eaker, N. Barker, S. Teutsch, W Sosniak, and N. Krieger. (1996). Poverty and death in the United States. *International Journal of Health Services* 26 (4): 673–90.

Hernandez, J. (1999). Is Belmont High School's legacy racist environmental standards? *Planning Report* 13(3). Available from www.ablinc.net/trp.

Hersh, R. (1995). *Race and industrial hazards: An historical geography of the Pittsburgh region, 1900–1990.* Washington, DC: Resources for the Future.

Institute of Medicine. (1999). *Toward environmental justice: Research, education, and health policy needs.* Washington, DC: Committee on Environmental Justice, Health Sciences Policy Program, Health Sciences Section, Institute of Medicine.

Jedrychowski, W., and E. Flak. (1998). Separate and combined effects of the outdoor and indoor air quality on chronic respiratory symptoms adjusted for allergy among preadolescent children. *International Journal of Occupational Medicine and Environmental Health* 11 (1): 19–35.

Kaplan, S., and J. Morris. (2000). Kids at risk: Chemicals in the environment come under scrutiny as the number of childhood learning problems soars. *U.S. News & World Report,* p. 1.

Kawachi, I., and M. G. Marmot. (1998). Commentary: What can we learn from studies of occupational class and cardiovascular disease? *American Journal of Epidemiology* 148 (2): 160–63.

Koretz, Daniel. (1998). Indicators of educational achievement. In *Indicators of children's well-being,* edited by R. M. Hauser, B. V. Brown, and W. R. Prosser, 208–34. New York: Russell Sage.

Kraft, M. E., and D. Scheberle. (1995). Environmental justice and the allocation of risk—The case of lead and public health. *Policy Studies Journal* 23 (1): 113–22.

Kreibel, D., and J. Tickner. (2001). Reenergizing public health through precaution. *American Journal of Public Health* 91 (9): 1351–54.

Kriebel, D., J. Tickner, P. Epstein, J. Lemons, R. Levins, E. L. Loechler, M. Quinn, R. Rudel, T. Schettler, and M. Stoto. 2001. The precautionary principle in environmental health science. *Environmental Health Perspectives* 109 (9): 871–76.

Krieger, N., D. L. Rowley, A. A. Herman, B. Avery, and M. T. Phillips. 1993. Racism, sexism, and social class: Implications for studies of health, disease, and well-being. *American Journal of Preventive Medicine* 9 (6): 82–122.

Krueger, A. B. (1999). Experimental estimates of educational production functions. *Quarterly Journal of Economics* 114 (2): 497–532.

Kubzansky, L. D., L. F. Berkman, T. A. Glass, and T. E. Seeman. (1998). Is educational attainment associated with shared determinants of health in the elderly? Findings from the MacArthur Studies of Successful Aging. *Psychosomatic Medicine* 60 (5): 578–85.

Kuehn, R. R. (1996). The environmental justice implications of quantitative risk assessment. *University of Illinois Law Review* 13 (1): 103–72.

Landrigan, P. J., L. Claudio, S. B. Markowitz, G. S. Berkowitz, B. L. Brenner, H. Romero, J. G. Wetmur, T. D. Matte, A. C. Gore, J. H. Godbold, and M. S. Wolff. (1999). Pesticides and inner-city children: Exposures, risks and prevention. *Environmental Health Perspectives* 107 (Suppl. 3): 431–37.

Latin, H. (1988). Good science, bad regulation, and toxic risk assessment. *Yale Journal of Regulation* 5 (1): 89–148.

Lavelle, M., and M. Coyle. (1992). Unequal protection. *National Law Journal* 21: S2.

Lazarus, R. J. (1993). Pursuing "environmental justice": The distributional effects of environmental protection. *Northwest University Law Review* 87 (3): 787–845.

Lee, C. (2002). Environmental justice: Building a unified vision of health and environment. *Environmental Health Perspectives* 110 (Suppl. 2): 141–44.

Leikauf, G. D., S. Line, R. E. Albert, C. S. Baxter, D. I. Bernstein, and C. R. Buncher. (1995). Evaluation of a possible association of urban air toxics and asthma. *Environmental Health Perspectives* 103 (Suppl. 6): 253–71.

Mannino, D., D. Homa, and C. Pertowski. 1998. Surveillance for asthma—United States, 1960–1995. *Morbidity and Mortality Weekly Report* 47 (SS-1): 1–28.

Metropolitan Forum Project. (1999). *What if? New schools, better neighborhoods, more livable communities.* Los Angeles: Metropolitan Forum Project.

Mohai, P., and B. Bryant. (1992). Environmental racism: Reviewing the evidence. In *Race and the incidence of environmental hazards: A time for discourse*, edited by B. Bryant and P. Mohai. Boulder, CO: Westview.

Morello-Frosch, R. (2002). The political economy of environmental discrimination. *Environment and Planning C: Government and Policy* 20 (4): 477–96.

Morello-Frosch, R. A., M. Pastor, and J. L. Sadd. (2001). Environmental justice and Southern California's "riskscape": The distribution of air toxics exposures and health risks among diverse communities. *Urban Affairs Review* 36 (4): 551–78.

Morello-Frosch, R. A., T. J. Woodruff, D. A. Axelrad, and J. C. Caldwell. (2000). Air toxics and health risks in California: The public health implications of outdoor concentrations. *Risk Analysis* 20 (2): 273–91.

National Research Council. (1993). *Pesticides in the diets of infants and children.* Washington, DC: National Research Council.

Navarro, V. (1990). Race or class versus race and class: Mortality differentials in the United States. *Lancet* 226:1238–40.

Northwest Coalition for Alternatives to Pesticides. 2000. *Unthinkable risk: How children are exposed and harmed when pesticides are used at school.* Eugene, OR: Northwest Coalition for Alternatives to Pesticides.

Orfield, M. (1997). *Metropolitics: A regional agenda for community and stability.* Washington, DC: Brookings Institution.

Parkinson, A. (1996). *Casarett and Doull's toxicology, the basic science of poisons*, edited by C. Klaassen. New York: McGraw-Hill.

Pastor, M., J. Sadd, and J. Hipp. 2001. Which came first? Toxic facilities, minority move-in, and environmental justice. *Journal of Urban Affairs* 23 (1): 1–21.

Pastor, M., J. Sadd, and R. A. Morello-Frosch. (2002). Reading, writing and toxics: Children's health, academic performance and environmental justice in Los Angeles. Working Paper, Center for Justice, Tolerance, and Community, University of California, Santa Cruz.

Pastor, M., J. L. Sadd, and R. Morello-Frosch. (2002). Who's minding the kids? Pollution, public schools, and environmental justice in Los Angeles. *Social Science Quarterly* 83 (1): 263–80.

Perera, F. P., W. Jedrychowski, V. Rauh, and R. M. Whyatt. (1999). Molecular epidemiological research on the effects of environmental pollutants on the fetus. *Environmental Health Perspectives* 107 (Suppl. 3): 451–60.

Pollock, P. H., and M. E. Vittas. (1995). Who bears the burden of environmental pollution? Race, ethnicity, and environmental equity in Florida. *Social Science Quarterly* 76 (2): 294–310.

Prussel, D., and J. Tepperman. 2001. Tackling health hazards at school action alliance for children, 2001. Retrieved 26 May 2002 from http://www.4children.org/news/901toxic.htm.

Pulido, L., S. Sidawi, and R. O. Vos. (1996). An archeology of environmental racism in Los Angeles. *Urban Geography* 17 (5): 419–39.

Raffensperger, C., and J. Tickner, eds. 1999. *Protecting public health and the environment: Implementing the precautionary principle.* Washington, DC: Island Press.

Ritz, B., F. Yu, S. Fruin, G. Chapa, G. M. Shaw, and J. A. Harris. (2002). Ambient air pollution and risk of birth defects in Southern California. *American Journal of Epidemiology* 155 (1): 17–25.

Robinson, J. C. 1984. Racial inequality and the probability of occupational-related injury or illness. *Milbank Quarterly* 62 (4): 567–90.

———. 1987. Trends in racial inequality and exposure to work-related hazards. *Milbank Quarterly* 65 (2): 404–19.

Rosenbaum, A., D. A. Axelrad, T. J. Woodruff, Y. Wei, M. P. Ligocki, and J. P. Cohen. (1999). National estimates of outdoor air toxics concentrations. *Journal of the Air & Waste Management Association* 49:1138–52.

Rosenbaum, A., M. Ligocki, and Y. Wei. (1999). Modeling cumulative outdoor concentrations of hazardous air pollutants: Revised final report Systems Applications International, Inc. Retrieved May 2000 from http://www.epa.gov/CumulativeExposure/resource/resource.htm.

Sadd, J. L., M. Pastor, T. Boer, and L. D. Snyder. (1999). "Every breath you take . . .": The demographics of toxic air releases in Southern California. *Economic Development Quarterly* 13 (2): 107–23.

Schettler, T., G. Solomon, M. Valenit, and A. Huddle. (1999). *Generations at risk: Reproductive health and the environment.* Cambridge, MA: MIT Press.

Schettler, T., J. Stein, F. Reich, and M. Valenti. (2001). *In harm's way: Toxic threats to child development.* Boston: Greater Boston Physicians for Social Responsibility. Available from http://www.igc.org/psr.

Schwartz, J., D. Gold, D. W Dockery, S. T. Weiss, and F. E. Speizer. (1990). Predictors of asthma and persistent wheeze in a national sample of children in the United States: Association with social class, perinatal events and race. *American Review of Repiratory Disease* 142:555–62.

Sexton, K., and J. L. Adgate. (1999). Looking at environmental justice from an environmental health perspective. *Journal of Exposure Analysis and Environmental Epidemiology* 9 (1): 3–8.

Steingraber, S. (2000). The social production of cancer: A walk upstream. In *Rethinking the environmental debate: The politics of health in a toxic culture*, edited by R. Hofrichter. Cambridge, MA: MIT Press.

Syme, S., and L. Berkman. (1976). Social class, susceptibility and sickness. *American Journal of Epidemiology* 104 (1): 1–8.

Tickner, J. A., and P. Hoppin. (2000). Children's environmental health: A case study in implementing the precautionary principle. *International Journal of Environmental Health* 6 (4): 281–88.

Trotter, A. (2002). Los Angeles revives beleaguered Belmont project. *Education Week on the Web* 21 (27): 5. Retrieved 21 May from http://www.edweek.org/ew/newstory.cfm?slug=27belmont.h21.

U.S. Department of Health and Human Services. (1990). *Age-adjusted death rates for selected causes of death, according to sex and race: United States, selected years, 1950–87.* Washington, DC: U.S. Department of Health and Human Services.

U.S. Environmental Protection Agency. (1986). *Guidelines for carcinogenic risk assessment.* Washington, DC: U.S. Environmental Protection Agency, Federal Register.

———. 1992. *Environmental equity: Reducing risk for all communities.* Washington, DC: U.S. Environmental Protection Agency.

———. 1998. *Cumulative Exposure Project.* Retrieved from www.epa.gov/CumulativeExposure.

U.S. General Accounting Office. (1999). *Pesticides: Uses effects and alternatives to pesticides in schools.* Washington, DC: U.S. General Accounting Office.

Van Vliet, P., M. Knape, J. de Hartog, N. Janseen, H. Harssema, and B. Brunekreef. (1997). Motor vehicle exhaust and chronic respiratory symptoms in children living near freeways. *Environmental Research* 74 (2): 122–32.

Ware, J. H., J. D. Spengler, L. M. Neas, J. M. Samet, G. R. Wagner, D. Coultas, H. Ozkaynak, and M. Schwab. 1993. Respiratory and irritant health effects of ambient volatile organic compounds: The Kanawha County Health Study. *American Journal of Epidemiology* 137 (12): 1287–1301.

Wernette, D. R., and L. A. Nieves. (1991). Minorities and air quality non-attainment areas: A preliminary geo-demographic analysis. Paper presented at the Socioeconomic Energy and Research Conference, Baltimore.

White House. 1997. *Protection of children from environmental health risks and safety risks.* Executive order 13045. Washington, DC: White House.

World Health Organization. (2002). *Precautionary policies and health protection: Principles and applications: Report on a WHO workshop.* Rome: World Health Organization.

Zimmerman, Rae. 1993. Social equity and environmental risk. *Risk Analysis* 13 (6): 649–66.

Discussion Questions

1. Define environmental justice and the precautionary principle.

   Environmental justice emphasizes public health, social inequality, and environmental degradation and provides a framework for public policy debates about the impact of discrimination on the environmental health of diverse communities.

   Precautionary principle promotes planning, alternatives assessment, and anticipatory action with the aim of promoting disease prevention and avoiding environmental health and ecological calamities due to industrial production and other potentially harmful activities.

2. Based on Morello-Frosch and her colleagues' research, who is at higher risk to environmental exposure and hazards?

   According to researchers, minority students, particularly African American and Latinos, are more likely to bear the burden of attending schools in locations with higher cancer and respiratory risks.

3. What policy implications are identified in the article? In your opinion, are any viable? Why or why not?

   Study results emphasize the need to take a holistic approach to environmental health and justice research. Environmental health concerns must always be considered when deciding where and how to build new school facilities. Standards for acquiring and cleaning brownfields for school construction should be clarified and should consider the vulnerability of children to environmental hazards.

Source: Morello-Frosch, R., Pastor, M., Jr., & Sadd, J. (2002). Integrating environmental justice and the precautionary principle in research and policy making: The case of ambient air toxics exposures and health risks among schoolchildren in Los Angeles. *The Annals of the American Academy of Political and Social Science, 584*(1), 47–68. Reprinted by permission of Sage Publications.

PART XI

WAR AND VIOLENCE

CHAPTER 30

Poverty, Inequality, and Youth Violence

Ronald C. Kramer (2000)

Ronald Kramer explores the role poverty, economic inequality, and social exclusion play in shaping the problem of youth violence in the United States. A summary of sociological theory and research is presented.

The problem of school violence exploded into public consciousness in the United States in the late 1990s with a rash of highly publicized school shootings like the one at Columbine High School in Littleton, Colorado. Because these shooting incidents took place in suburban or semirural settings, they touched off "a national mood of self-searching about the roots of youth violence that a decade of inner-city carnage had not" (Currie 1999, 234).

Despite the horrific nature of these specific acts, there is no evidence to suggest that the overall level of school violence in America has increased dramatically in recent years (Chandler et al. 1998). In fact, serious youth violence, particularly homicide, has actually declined in the United States during the past few years (Blumstein and Rosenfeld 1998). Lethal violence in America, however, is still exceedingly common and one of our most serious social problems. As Zimring and Hawkins (1997) demonstrate, "Lethal violence rather than high rates of crime is the disabling problem that sets the United States apart from other developed countries in the 1990s" (1).

Given this "American exceptionalism" concerning violence (Messner and Rosenfeld 1997) and the fact that violent acts disproportionately involve young people aged 15 to 24, we should indeed engage in some self-searching about the roots of youth violence. This article will examine some of the more general social, economic, and cultural conditions that give rise to serious crime

and violence in the United States. Specifically, the article will explore the role of poverty, economic inequality, and social exclusion in shaping the problem of youth violence by summarizing and integrating the recent theory and research of a number of sociological criminologists, such as Elliott Currie, John Hagan, and Francis Cullen.

Poverty, Inequality, and Social Exclusion

Why does the United States have exceptionally high rates of violent crime, particularly youth homicide, compared to other industrial nations? Conservative commentators frequently assert that it is a lenient criminal justice and juvenile justice system that causes high crime rates or that crime and violence are the result of cultural decline and something called moral poverty. But the American justice system is one of the harshest in the world, and, although the cultural and moral condition of American families and communities is important to take into account in understanding crime, these conditions are strongly affected by larger social and economic forces. These larger social structural conditions are the factors that sociological criminologists point to as the roots of violence. As Currie (1998) observes, "For there is now overwhelming evidence that inequality, extreme poverty, and social exclusion matter profoundly in shaping a society's experience of violent crime. And they matter, in good part, precisely because of their impact on the close-in institutions of family and community" (114).

When we look at the research on poverty and economic inequality, we find that the United States has by far the highest poverty rate and the biggest gap between the rich and the poor of any of the developed nations (Kerbo 1996). Currie (1998) notes the findings of the Luxembourg Income Study (LIS), an international survey of poverty, inequality, and government spending in industrial countries (Rainwater and Smeeding 1995). The LIS shows that the United States, while a very wealthy society, has far more inequality and is far less committed to providing a decent life for the poor than are other developed nations. The LIS also demonstrates that, in particular, children and families in the United States are far more likely to be poor than those in other industrial democracies. Furthermore, poor American children are more likely to be extremely poor compared to children in other advanced countries.

According to the LIS and other studies, there are several reasons why poor children and families in the United States find themselves in such a plight. First, many Americans in the so-called urban underclass are trapped in a system of concentrated unemployment that results in an increasingly isolated poverty (Wilson 1996). Second, those who do work, primarily in the secondary labor market, earn very low wages compared to their counterparts in other countries. This creates the problem of the working poor. Finally, the United States provides fewer government benefits to either the underclass or the working poor to offset the problems of concentrated unemployment and poor wages. Recent changes in the welfare system are likely to aggravate the situation.

This deprivation and social exclusion are related to the high rates of violence found in the United States. Currie reviews both studies of international differences in violent crime and studies of violence within the United States and other countries to demonstrate the connection. Cross-national studies show that countries with a high degree of economic inequality have higher levels of violence (Gartner 1990). Other studies show that, even within a generally deprived population, it is the most deprived children who face the greatest risks of engaging in crime and violence (Werner and Smith 1992). Finally, Currie notes the research of Krivo and Peterson (1996), who suggest that it is the link between extreme disadvantage and violence that underlies much of the association between race and violent crime in the

United States. After reviewing these and other studies, Currie (1998) concludes,

> The links between extreme deprivation, delinquency, and violence, then, are strong, consistent, and compelling. There is little question that growing up in extreme poverty exerts powerful pressures toward crime. The fact that those pressures are overcome by some individuals is testimony to human strength and resiliency, but does not diminish the importance of the link between social exclusion and violence. The effects are compounded by the absence of public supports to buffer economic insecurity and deprivation, and they are even more potent when racial subordination is added to the mix. And this . . . helps us begin to understand why the United States suffers more serious violent crime than other industrial democracies, and why violence has remained stubbornly high in the face of our unprecedented efforts at repressive control. (131)

But how do these social and economic forces cause violence? In what specific ways do poverty, inequality, and social exclusion act to produce violent crime by young people? To help answer these questions, I suggest that we utilize the general organizing concepts of social support and informal social control. It is the absence of these two important social processes, in urban, suburban, or rural settings, that allows for the infliction of social and psychic pain on young people and the development of negative attitudes and emotions that can easily lead to violence.

The Absence of Social Support and Informal Social Control

In his presidential address to the Academy of Criminal Justice Sciences in 1994, Francis T. Cullen suggested that a lack of social support is implicated in crime. Cullen argued that social support, if approached systematically, can be an important organizing concept for criminology. He defined social support as "the perceived or actual instrumental and/or expressive provisions supplied by the community, social networks, and confiding partners" (Cullen 1994, 530). Cullen went on to develop a series of propositions, supported by criminological research, about the relationship between the lack of social support and the presence of crime at societal, community, family, and relational levels of analysis.

According to Cullen, a distinction should be made between the concepts of social support and informal social control. Informal social control involves all the sanctions and constraints used in an effort to control another individual's behavior (to make him or her conform to social norms) that fall outside of formal, legal, and bureaucratic systems. Informal social control is generally exercised by significant others, families, friends, neighbors, and community networks. The breakdown or absence of informal social control has also long been cited by criminologists as a factor in the involvement of persons in criminal behavior.

In the following sections, I will review theory and research that examine the relationship between broad structural conditions like poverty, inequality, and social exclusion; institutional-level social support and informal social control; and the problem of youth violence. First I will consider social support as an organizing concept and then informal social control.

SOCIAL SUPPORT

One of the most significant ways in which economic deprivation and social exclusion can lead to youth violence is by inhibiting or breaking down the social supports that affect young people. Cullen (1994) reviews research that supports his proposition that "America has higher rates of serious crime than other industrial nations because it is a less supportive society (531). He notes studies that have demonstrated the corrosive effect of America's culture of excessive individualism and pursuit of material gain without regard to means (Messner and Rosenfeld 1997). This competitive pursuit of the American Dream not only encourages individuals to obtain material goods "by any means necessary"; it also inhibits the development of a "good society" in which concern for community and mutuality of support dominate. Cullen (1994) also points out that "economic inequality can generate crime not only by exposing people to relative deprivation but also by eviscerating and inhibiting the development of social support networks" (534).

Moving down from the national level, Cullen (1994) argues that "the less social support there is in a community, the higher the crime rate will be" (534). He reviews evidence that "governmental assistance to the poor tends to lessen violent crime across ecological units," and research that reveals "that crime rates are higher in communities characterized by family disruption, weak friendship networks, and low participation in local voluntary organizations" (534–35). Finally, Cullen notes

quantitative and ethnographic research on the "underclass" that documents that powerful social and economic forces have created isolated innercity enclaves. These enclaves fray the supportive relations that once existed between adults and youths, supportive relations that previously offered protection to those youths from involvement in crime. We will return to this body of research later in a review of the work of John Hagan (1994).

Next, Cullen (1994) addresses the issue of the role of the family in offering social support. He asserts that "the more support a family provides, the less likely it is that a person will engage in crime" (538). This is the critical link between poverty, inequality, exclusion, and violence. Recall Currie's argument that these social forces matter precisely because of their impact on the close-in institutions like the family. As Cullen (1994, 538) notes, there is a considerable amount of evidence that parental expressive support diminishes children's risk of criminal involvement. He cites Loeber and Stouthamer-Loeber's (1986) comprehensive meta-analysis of family correlates of delinquency that clearly shows that indicators of a lack of parental support increase delinquent behavior. This study concludes that youth crime is related inversely to "child-parent involvement, such as the amount of intimate communication, confiding, sharing of activities, and seeking help" (Loeber and Stouthamer-Loeber 1986, 42).

Both Cullen and Currie warn that any discussion of families and crime must avoid the "fallacy of autonomy—the belief that what goes on inside the family can usefully be separated from the forces that affect it from the outside: the larger social context in which families are embedded for better or for worse" (Currie 1985, 185). While any family, regardless of its socioeconomic status, can be affected, both Cullen and Currie stress the social and economic forces like poverty and inequality that have transformed and, in many cases, ripped apart families, particularly families of the underclass, in ways that have reduced their capacity to support children. The Panel on High-Risk Youth (cited in Cullen 1994, 539) states:

Perhaps the most serious risk facing adolescents in high-risk settings is isolation from the nurturance, safety, and guidance that comes from sustained relationships with adults. Parents are the best source of support, but for many adolescents, parents are not positively involved in their lives. In some cases, parents are absent or abusive. In many more cases, parents strive to be good parents, but lack the capacity or opportunity to be so.

In his review of the research on the connections between family deprivation and violent crime, Currie (1998, 135–39) highlights four key findings: "1) extreme deprivation inhibits children's intellectual development; 2) extreme deprivation breeds violence by encouraging child abuse and neglect; 3) extreme poverty creates multiple stresses that undermine parents' ability to raise children caringly and effectively; and 4) poverty breeds crime by undermining parents' ability to monitor and supervise their children." Findings 1 through 3 provide more specific articulation about the ways in which poverty and inequality shape youth violence through the lack of social support. Stunted intellectual development that cripples children's ability to be successful in school or at work, violence and abuse that create angry and fearful children, and the lack of parental care and nurturance all contribute to the production of young people who are prone to strike out at the world through violent acts.

Social and Cultural Capital

Another important perspective on the relationship between social and economic conditions, the lack of social support, and youth crime is contained in the work of John Hagan. In presenting a "new sociology of crime and disrepute," Hagan (1994) develops the concepts of human, social, and cultural capital and capital disinvestment processes to help us understand the connections between inequality, social institutions, and violent crime. According to Hagan, the general concept of human capital refers to the skills, capabilities, and knowledge acquired by individuals through education and training that allow them to act in new ways. To this he adds the concept of social capital, which "involves the creation of capabilities through socially structured relationships between individuals in groups" (67). Social groups such as intact nuclear and extended families, well-integrated neighborhoods, stable communities, and even nation-states are the sites for the development of social capital in individuals that provides them with the resources and capacities to achieve group and individual goals. These supportive social networks can lead to the formation of cultural capital such as the credentials of higher education and involvement in high culture like the arts and their supporting institutions. As Hagan points out, "In these community and family settings, social capital is used to successfully endow children with forms of cultural capital that significantly enhance their later life changes" (69).

The ability to endow children with social and cultural capital, however, is linked to economic position. As Hagan (1994) notes, in less advantaged community and social settings, which lack abundant forms of social and cultural capital, parents are far less able to provide resources, opportunities, and supports to their children. Thus, "the children of less advantageously positioned and less-driven and controlling parents may more often drift or be driven into and along less-promising paths of social and cultural adaptation and capital formation" (70). These "less-promising paths of social and cultural adaptation," of course, include embeddedness in the criminal economy of drugs and other forms of gang activity and delinquent behavior.

Hagan (1994) emphasizes that "disadvantaging social and economic processes" in the community and broader society, what he calls "capital disinvestment processes," are destructive of social and cultural capital and often produce deviant subcultural adaptations (70). The three capital disinvestment processes that "discourage societal and community level formations of conventional social capital" are residential segregation, race-linked inequality, and concentrations of poverty (70–71). Hagan describes these destructive structural conditions and the dislocations that they produce in community settings. He then reviews a considerable body of new ethnographic and quantitative research that documents and articulates the ways in which these community-level processes of capital disinvestment disrupt and destroy the social capital of families, diminishing their capacity to provide the human and cultural capital their children need to improve their life chances and become stable and productive members of the community. Thus these children are at a much greater risk of becoming embedded in the criminal economy of drugs and the violence that it often entails, as well as becoming involved in other forms of conventional criminality. As Hagan observes, "In communities that suffer from capital disinvestment and in families that have little closure of social networks and social capital to facilitate investment in their children, youths are more likely to drift into cultural adaptations that bring short-term status and material benefits, but whose longer-term consequences include diminished life-chances" (93).

Informal Social Control

As noted previously, Currie found that the lack of effective parental supervision has a strong relationship to delinquency. This raises the important issue of informal social control. The ability of adults to monitor and supervise, impose sanctions, shame, and otherwise keep young people in line through face-to-face interaction within important social institutions is an important variable in delinquency prevention. There is a considerable amount of criminological evidence that suggests that these informal mechanisms of social control, operating within families, schools, neighborhoods, workplaces, and social networks, play an important role in preventing youth crime and violence. As Minor (1993) points out, "Research has demonstrated that, during the course of childhood and adolescent socialization, the more meaningfully integrated persons become [into] those social institutions which promote informal social control, such as the family, school, and work, the lower the likelihood of delinquency" (59).

As with the lack of social support, social structural forces such as poverty and social exclusion can inhibit or erode the exercise of informal social controls within these intermediate institutions. With the erosion of these controls, the chances for young people to become involved in violent crime increases. As Minor (1993) observes,

Through their impact on social institutions, the macro forces emanating from a society's political economic organization shape the quantity and quality of behavioral choices available to individuals. By diminishing the capacity of institutions, especially the family, to positively influence the choices made by youths and by rendering youths vulnerable to delinquent socialization in peer groups, macro forces can weaken informal mechanisms of social control. (59)

In his excellent review of the theory and research on the political and economic context of delinquency in the United States, Minor (1993) identifies three macro forces that have had important consequences for the problem of youth violence. These forces are the socially defined position of youth, the impact of market relations, and poverty and inequality. First, compulsory education, child labor laws, and the emergence of the juvenile justice system combined to promote youth segregation, impose labor market restrictions on young people, and increase the importance of peer group socialization. Market relations led to the penetration of economic norms into all spheres of life and the fostering of a competitive individualism that undermined interpersonal cooperation and collective social welfare. Poverty and inequality had a disintegrative effect on social institutions through the lack of resources and emotional stress. According to Minor, these three forces evolved together as part of the transformation of the American economy to monopoly capitalism, and they have acted collectively to weaken informal mechanisms of social control and therefore increase youth violence.

Another perspective on the impact of cultural and structural forces on the ability of social institutions such as the family to control youth crime comes from Messner and Rosenfeld (1997). Building on Robert Merton's concept of anomie, Messner and Rosenfeld assert that the core features of the social organization of the United States—culture and institutional structure—shape the high levels of American crime. At the cultural level, they argue that the core values of the American Dream (achievement, individualism, universalism, monetary success) stimulate criminal motivations while promoting weak norms to guide the choices of means to achieve cultural goals (anomie). As Messner and Rosenfeld point out, "The American Dream does not contain within it strong injunctions against substituting more effective, illegitimate means for less effective, legitimate means in the pursuit of monetary success" (76).

At the institutional level, Messner and Rosenfeld (1997) observe that the economy tends to dominate all other social institutions and that this imbalance of institutional power fosters weak social control. There are two ways that this imbalance of power weakens social control. First, social institutions such as the family and the schools are supposed to socialize children into values, beliefs, and commitments other than those of the economic system. However, as Messner and Rosenfeld note, "as these noneconomic institutions are relatively devalued and forced to accommodate to economic considerations, as they are penetrated by economic standards, they are less able to fulfill their distinctive socialization functions successfully" (77). Thus, economic domination weakens the normative control associated with culture.

The imbalance of power also weakens the external type of social control associated with social structure. As Messner and Rosenfeld (1997, 78) point out, "External control is achieved through the active involvement of individuals in institutional roles and through the dispensation of rewards and punishments by institutions." When these noneconomic institutions are devalued and rendered impotent, then the attractiveness of the roles they offer to young people is diminished, and the incentives and penalties they can offer for prosocial behavior are limited.

Messner and Rosenfeld conclude by noting that the problem of external control by major social institutions is inseparable from the problem of the internal regulation of social norms (anomie):

Anomic societies will inevitably find it difficult and costly to exert social control over the behavior of people who feel free to use whatever means prove most effective in reaching personal goals. Hence, the very sociocultural dynamics that make American institutions weak also enable and entitle Americans to defy institutional controls. If Americans are exceptionally resistant to social control—and therefore exceptionally vulnerable to criminal temptations—it is because they live in a society that enshrines the unfettered pursuit of individual material success above all other values. In the United States, anomie is considered a virtue. (79)

Sampson and Laub's innovative reassessment (1993) of the longitudinal data gathered by Sheldon and Eleanor Glueck in the 1940s also supports the proposition that poverty and inequality undermine the ability of informal social controls within the family and school to contain delinquent behavior. Sampson and Laub develop an age-graded theory of informal social control. Their basic thesis is that "structural context mediated by informal family and school controls explains delinquency in childhood and adolescence" (7). Their unified model of informal family social control focuses on three dimensions: discipline, supervision, and attachment. They observe that "the key to all three components of informal family social control lies in the extent to which they facilitate linking the child to family and ultimately society through emotional bonds of attachment and direct yet socially integrative forms of control, monitoring, and punishment" (68).

The second part of Sampson and Laub's theory suggests that structural background factors, such as poverty, influence youth crime largely through their effects on family process. The empirical findings support their theory. They find that negative structural forces have little direct effect on delinquency but instead are mediated by intervening sources of informal social controls in the family and the school. They offer the following summary:

> We found that the strongest and most consistent effects on both official and unofficial delinquency flow from the social processes of family, school, and peers. Low levels of parental supervision, erratic, threatening, and harsh discipline, and weak parental attachment were strongly and directly related to delinquency. . . . Negative structural conditions (such as poverty or family disruption) also affect delinquency, but largely through family and school process variables. (Sampson and Laub 1993, 247)

What Sampson and Laub find in their reassessment of the Gluecks' data on white children born in the 1920s and 1930s is supported by a more recent study of urban black children conducted by Shihadeh and Steffensmier

(1994). They studied the links between economic inequality, family disruption, and urban black violence in more than 150 cities across the country. They found that as economic inequality increases, so do arrests of black youths for violent crimes. Shihadeh and Steffensmier suggest that the link between inequality and violence, however, is indirect. Greater income inequality increases the number of black single-parent households, and the increase in single-parent households is related to the level of youth violence. Single parents, with more stress and fewer resources, have a more difficult time monitoring and supervising their children and, in general, exercising effective social control. Rutter and Giller (1983) and Larzelere and Patterson (1990) provide additional evidence on the connection between poverty and poor parenting skills.

A final perspective on the relationship between economic conditions, informal social control, and violent delinquent behavior that should be mentioned is the work of Colvin and Pauly (1983). They develop an integrated structural-Marxist theory of delinquency production that focuses on the structures of control in several locations in the economic production and social reproduction processes: workplaces, families, schools, and peer groups. They argue that "the more coercive the control relations encountered in these various socialization contexts tend to be, the more negative or alienated will be the individual's ideological bond and the more likely is the individual to engage in serious, patterned delinquency" (515). Working-class parents who experience coerciveness in workplace control structures develop alienated bonds, which in turn contribute to the development of more coercive family control structures. Children who experience coercive family control structures develop alienated initial bonds that lead them to be placed in more coercive school control structures, which reinforce the juveniles' alienated bonds. This, in turn, leads to greater association with alienated peers, who form peer group control structures that interact with various community opportunity structures to produce delinquency.

Prom Inequalities to Youth Violence

Even though the rates of violent crime committed by young people have declined in recent years, youth violence remains a serious social problem in the United States. While many factors must be taken into account as we search for ways to deal with youth violence in general, and school violence in particular, it is imperative to understand the broader social and economic forces that play a critical role in shaping America's experience with this problem. The theory and research that have been reviewed in this article make a compelling case for the thesis that poverty, economic inequality, and social exclusion are causal agents in the production of crime and violence by young people in the United States. Although these structural conditions do not often have a direct effect in producing violent crime, they are important because of the impact they have on social institutions like the family, the school, and the community. While families, schools, and neighborhoods in middle-class, suburban areas can also become disrupted, the evidence shows that poverty, inequality, and exclusion decisively undermine the ability of those close-in institutions to provide the social support and informal social control that produce healthy, well-functioning children and prevent serious violent crime. When these institutions, in whatever socioeconomic setting, are unable to socialize children properly, care for them appropriately, and provide them with human and social capital, violence is a possible result. When these institutions, in whatever socioeconomic setting, are unable to effectively monitor, supervise, and sanction juveniles, violent crimes can take place.

This violence by young people seems to generally take one of three forms: predatory economic crimes, drug industry crimes, or social relationship violence. The first of these forms of violence occurs in the pursuit of monetary or materialistic goals by any means necessary. Given the intense cultural pressures for monetary success in America, economically disadvantaged youths who are blocked from less effective, legitimate means are often inclined to select more effective, illegitimate means to pursue the American Dream. As Messner and Rosenfeld (1997) point out, "This anomic orientation leads not simply to high levels of crime in general but to especially violent forms of economic crime, for which the United States is known throughout the industrial world, such as mugging, car-jacking, and home invasion" (76).

The second form of youth violence, involvement in the illegal drug industry, also stems from the pursuit of monetary success through effective, illegitimate means. Hagan (1994) points out that participation in the illegal drug industry is a sub-cultural adaptation to processes of capital disinvestment, in effect, a form of recapitalization, an effort to use available (albeit illegal) resources to achieve economic goals. As he notes, "During the period of capital disinvestment when access to legitimate job networks linked to core sector jobs declined in many distressed minority communities, networks of contacts into the world of drugs and drug-related crime proliferated, paving the way for

many youths to become embedded in the criminal economy" (96). Hagan also points out that today's illegal drug industry is much more violent and unstable than those of the past. As more young people became embedded in the criminal economy of drugs, the more violent they became as gangs battled for drug markets. Rates of serious violence, including homicide, skyrocketed in the late 1980s and early 1990s, in particular with the rise of the crack cocaine epidemic. In fact, the recent reductions in violent crime rates are often attributed to the stabilization of the crack markets in the mid-1990s (Blumstein and Rosenfeld 1998).

The final form of youth violence is the violence that often flares within the context of frayed and volatile social relationships. Youths who are powerless, angry, frustrated, and alienated often act out in violent ways. For those who are rendered powerless by the social and economic structure, violence within social relationships is one way to reassert power and control in their lives (Pfohl 1994, 407). Youths who experience the structural humiliation of poverty and inequality and lack the support and controls of a protective family or community often attempt to transcend their humiliation and shame through violence (Braithwaite 1992; Gilligan 1996). As John Braithwaite (1992) asserts, "When inequality of wealth and power is structurally humiliating, this undermines respect for the dominion of others. And a society where the respect for dominion is lost will be a society riddled with crime" (80). Additionally, Katz (1988) has observed that humiliation can lead to the embrace of righteous violence, which resolves the humiliation "through the overwhelming sensuality of rage" (24). Inequality and social exclusion, among other social and cultural forces, can shred the bonds of community that tie young people to others and can foster the use of violence within their close-in social relationships in the family, at school, or on the street corner.

One final note about these forms of violence. All of them are more likely to become lethal due to the overwhelming presence of guns in American society. The mugging, the bad drug deal, the schoolyard fight—all are more likely to turn deadly due to the easy availability of firearms in the United States. The recent school shooting deaths in Colorado and elsewhere were all made possible by the easy access of these youths to guns. As Zimring and Hawkins (1997) point out, firearms are a contributing cause of violent death and injury from intentional attacks. They note that "current evidence suggests that a combination of the ready availability of guns and the willingness to use maximum force in interpersonal conflict is the most important single contribution to the high U.S. death rate from violence" (122–23).

Policy Implications

In her influential book, *Deadly Consequences,* Deborah Prothrow-Stith (1991) urges that we take a public health approach to the problem of youth violence. A public health approach emphasizes the need for prevention. Rather than waiting for the violence to occur and then intervene, as we often do in the formal criminal justice approach, the public health approach argues that we need to intervene as early in the process as possible, in a variety of ways, to keep the harm from happening in the first place. A prevention strategy toward violence not only saves victims from being victimized; it also saves offenders from the consequences of their involvement in violent crime. It invests money at the front end of the problem in order to keep from paying a lot more at the back end in victimization and criminal justice process costs. In the long run, prevention saves both money and lives.

The problem is that we often do not think about prevention strategies or any type of long-term solutions. We are so caught up in reacting to the high levels of violence occurring all around us that we grab whatever short-term solutions appear to be available at the time. As Currie (1985) notes, we frequently find ourselves in the position of trying to mop up the flood on the bathroom floor while the tub is overflowing and the faucet is still running. We mop as hard as we can, and we buy increasingly expensive mops to help battle the flood, but until we learn how to turn off the faucet and stop the tub from overflowing we had better be prepared to do an awful lot of mopping.

Given what we know about the connections between poverty, inequality, and social exclusion and the social problem of youth violence, what can we do to begin to turn off the faucet of this violence? What are the policy implications of the theory and research that have been reviewed in this article for the prevention of violence by our nation's youths? Public health professionals like Prothrow-Stith (1991, 140) stress three levels of intervention: primary, secondary, and tertiary. Primary prevention focuses on the larger social or physical environment that contributes to the problem. Secondary prevention involves interventions with people who are at high risk, identifying practices and situations that put them at risk. Tertiary prevention focuses on those who are already afflicted and seeks to minimize the consequences of the problems they are experiencing. The work reviewed in this article has important implications for strategies of primary and secondary prevention of youth violence.

A primary prevention approach to youth violence would focus on the larger structural conditions that shape the problem. It would target what Hagan (1994) referred to as "disinvestment processes," social and economic forces that often lead to violent crime. Specifically, a primary prevention approach would concentrate on the need to reduce poverty and inequality and develop more inclusionary public policies. Space limitations prevent any extended discussion of how to achieve these ambitious goals, but the most important point is that we need to make a commitment to long-run, permanent intervention in the labor market itself. Currie (1985) has argued that "a commitment to full and decent employment remains the keystone of any successful anticrime policy" (263). He points out that we need direct public job creation, policies to upgrade wages and narrow existing disparities in earnings, an improved national system of job training, greater support for workplace organization through the labor movement, policies to spread the social costs of the transfer of jobs abroad, and legislation to shorten work hours and spread available work time (Currie 1996, 1998).

In addition to these labor market interventions to reduce poverty and inequality, we need to attack the social exclusion that breeds violent crime. Barkan (1997) argues that we need to "provide government economic aid for people who cannot find work or who find work but still cannot lift themselves out of poverty" (538). Currie (1998) suggests "providing more generous, universal social services, particularly in the two areas that most distinguish us from less volatile industrial societies—child care and health care" (157). We need only look to these other industrial democracies to see that more inclusionary government welfare programs can have a major impact on families and communities and prevent serious youth violence (Eitzen and Leedham 1998). Measures to end racial segregation in housing and restore the social integration of urban neighborhoods would also constitute primary prevention strategies (Hagan 1994; Barkan 1997).

While primary prevention focuses on structural conditions like poverty and economic inequality, secondary prevention strategies involve the close-in institutions of the family, school, and community and the developmental processes that occur within them. A secondary prevention approach to youth violence would point to the need to establish early-childhood intervention programs for high-risk children and their families (Barkan 1997), invest serious resources in the prevention of child abuse and neglect (Currie 1998), improve urban schools beset by "savage inequalities" (Kozol 1991), and invest in skill-building programs for vulnerable adolescents (Currie 1998).

Three recent federal reports review a wide array of secondary prevention programs that have been attempted, and they note numerous programs that seem to work and many others that show some promise (Howell and Bilchik 1995; Muller and Mihalic 1999; Sherman et al. 1997). However, the Maryland Report (Sherman et al. 1997) points out that many crime prevention programs are most likely to work in communities that need them the least. Secondary prevention programs are much less likely to work in urban centers with a high concentration of poverty that are already swamped by much violent crime. According to Walker (1998), this proves that "the heart of the crime problem lies in the underlying structural conditions in high-crime areas" (277). Thus, primary prevention programs that attack these underlying structural conditions should have the highest priority if we are interested in reducing the amount of youth violence in our society.

But we all know that programs designed to reduce poverty and economic inequality in the United States do not have a high priority these days. As Wilson (1996) observes, there has been a "dramatic retreat from using public policy as a means to fight social inequality" (208). Most legislative proposals to provide greater social inclusion through public programs are met with scorn and are doomed to failure. A conservative moral and political philosophy holds sway, arguing that social inequality is necessary to encourage individual initiative and economic efficiency. This leads to a noninterventionist laissez-faire approach to government that relies heavily on the discipline of largely unregulated market forces backed up by a reliance on severe criminal sanctions (Hagan 1994). As long as this ideology dominates political discourse in the United States, the retreat from public policy as a way to alleviate problems of poverty and inequality will continue, with "profound negative consequences for the future of disadvantaged groups such as the ghetto poor" (Wilson 1996, 209). The violence will continue, and more children will die. The tub is still overflowing, and none of our political leaders appears to have the courage to reach in and turn off the faucet.

References

Barkan, Steven E. (1997). *Criminology: A Sociological Understanding.* Upper Saddle River, NJ: Prentice Hall.

Blumstein, Alfred and Richard Rosenfeld. (1998). Assessing the Recent Ups and Downs in U.S. Homicide Rates. *National Institute of Justice Journal* Oct.:9-11.

Braithwaite, John. (1992). Poverty, Power, and White-Collar Crime: Sutherland and the Paradoxes of Criminological Theory. In *White-Collar Crime Reconsidered,* ed. Kip Schlegel and David Weisburd. Boston: Northeastern University Press.

Chandler, Kathryn A., Christopher D. Chapman, Michael R. Rand, and Bruce M. Taylor. (1998). *Students' Reports of School Crime: 1989 and 1995.* Washington, DC: Department of Education, Department of Justice.

Colvin, Mark and John Pauly. (1983). A Critique of Criminology: Toward an Integrated Structural-Marxist Theory of Delinquency Production. *American Journal of Sociology* 89:513–51.

Cullen, Francis T. (1994). Social Support as an Organizing Concept for Criminology: Presidential Address to the Academy of Criminal Justice Sciences. *Justice Quarterly* 11:527–59.

Currie, Elliott. (1985). *Confronting Crime: An American Challenge.* New York: Pantheon.

———. (1996). Missing Pieces: Notes on Crime, Poverty, and Social Policy. *Critical Criminology* 7:37–52.

———. (1998). *Crime and Punishment in America.* New York: Metropolitan Books.

——— (1999). Children Killing Children. In *Britannica Book of the Year* Chicago: Encyclopedia Britannica.

Eitzen, D. Stanley and Craig S. Leedham. 1998. *Solutions to Social Problems: Lessons from Other Societies.* Boston: Allyn & Bacon.

Gartner, Rosemary. (1990). The Victims of Homicide: A Temporal and Cross-National Comparison. *American Sociological Review* 55:92–106.

Gilligan, James. (1996). *Violence: Reflections on a National Epidemic.* New York: Vintage Books.

Hagan, John. (1994). *Crime and Disrepute.* Thousand Oaks, CA: Pine Forge Press.

Howell, James C. and Shay Bilchik. (1995). *Guide for Implementing the Comprehensive Strategy for Serious, Violent, and Chronic Juvenile Offenders.* Washington, DC: Department of Justice, Office of Justice Programs, Office of Juvenile Justice and Delinquency Prevention.

Katz, Jack. 1988. *Seductions of Crime: Moral and Sensual Attractions of Doing Evil.* New York: Basic Books.

Kerbo, Harold R. (1996). *Social Stratification and Inequality: Class Conflict in Historical and Comparative Perspective.* 3d ed. New York: McGraw-Hill.

Kozol, Jonathan. (1991). *Savage Inequalities: Children in America's Schools.* New York: HarperPerennial.

Krivo, Lauren J. and Ruth D. Peterson. (1996.) Extremely Disadvantaged Neighborhoods and Urban Crime. *Social Forces* 75:619–50.

Larzelere, Robert E. and Gerald R. Patterson. 1990). Parental Management: Mediator of the Effect of Socioeconomic Status on Early Delinquency. *Criminology* 28:301–23.

Loeber, Rolf and Magda Stouthamer-Loeber. (1986). Family Factors as Correlates and Predictors of Juvenile Conduct Problems and Delinquency. In *Crime and Justice: An Annual Review of Research,* ed. M. Tonry and N. Morris. Vol. 7. Chicago: University of Chicago Press.

Messner, Steven F. and Richard Rosenfeld. (1997). *Crime and the American Dream.* 2d ed. Belmont, CA: Wadsworth.

Minor, Kevin I. (1993). Juvenile Delinquency and the Transition to Monopoly Capitalism. *Journal of Sociology and Social Welfare* 20:59–80.

Muller, Janine and Sharon Mihalic. (1999). *Blueprints: A Violence Prevention Initiative.* Washington, DC: Department of Justice, Office of Justice Programs, Office of Juvenile Justice and Delinquency Prevention.

Pfohl, Stephen. (1994). *Images of Deviance and Social Control: A Sociological History*. 2d ed. New York: McGraw-Hill.

Prothrow-Stith, Deborah. (1991). *Deadly Consequences: How Violence Is Destroying Our Teenage Population and a Plan to Begin Solving the Problem*. New York: HarperPerennial.

Rainwater, Lee and Timothy M. Smeeding. 1995. *Doing Poorly: The Real Income of American Children in a Comparative Perspective*. Syracuse, NY: Syracuse University, Maxwell School of Citizenship and Public Affairs.

Rutter, Michael and Henri Giller. (1983). *Juvenile Delinquency: Trends and Perspectives*. New York: Guilford Press.

Sampson, Robert J. and John H. Laub. (1993). *Crime in the Making: Pathways and Turning Points Through Life*. Cambridge, MA: Harvard University Press.

Sherman, Lawrence W., Denise Gottfredson, Doris MacKenzie, John Eck, Peter Reuter, and Shawn Bushway. (1997). *Preventing Crime: What Works, What Doesn't, What's Promising*. Washington, DC: Department of Justice, Office of Justice Programs.

Shihadeh, Edward S. and Darrell J. Steffensmier. (1994). Economic Inequality, Family Disruption, and Urban Black Violence: Cities as Units of Stratification and Social Control. *Social Forces* 73:729–51.

Walker, Samuel. (1998). *Sense and Nonsense About Crime and Drugs: A Policy Guide*. 4th ed. Belmont, CA: West/ Wadsworth.

Werner, Emily E. and Ruth S. Smith. (1992). *Overcoming the Odds: High Risk Children from Birth to Adulthood*. Ithaca, NY: Cornell University Press.

Wilson, William Julius. (1996). *When Work Disappears: The World of the New Urban Poor*. New York: Knopf.

Zimring, Franklin E. and Gordon Hawkins. (1997). *Crime Is Not the Problem: Lethal Violence in America*. New York: Oxford University Press.

Discussion Questions

1. How are economic inequality and social exclusion related to youth violence? How are they related to social support and social control?

Kramer describes economic inequality and social exclusion as "the roots of violence," attributing their influence on violence via their impact on the family, education, and community. He argues that social and economic forces cause violence through the absence of social support and social control. Students should review the literature cited by Kramer supporting the relationship between economic inequality and social exclusion with violence.

Economic deprivation inhibits or destroys the social supports that affect youth. The competitive pursuit of the American dream encourages individualism (i.e., the pursuit of material goods by any means), but also inhibits the development of society where community and mutual support are valued. Extreme poverty undermines parents' ability to raise, support, and monitor their children.

The same social forces that limit support structures affect informal social controls (family, peers, community). (Note: More formal social controls would include police.) Informal social controls effectively monitor, supervise, and sanction inappropriate behavior. The chances for youth to become involved in violent crime increase as informal social controls decrease.

2. What policy recommendations would you recommend?

Kramer proposes three prevention levels. Primary prevention would focus on the larger social or physical environment. Secondary prevention considers interventions with high risk youth. Finally, tertiary prevention focuses on those who are already afflicted and attempts to minimize the consequences of the problems they are experiencing. Students should identify policies for all three levels and discuss which level would be most effective (considering long term vs. short term impact).

Source: From Kramer, R. (2000). Poverty, inequality, and youth violence. *The Annals of the American Academy of Political and Social Science*, *567*(1), 123–139. Reprinted by permission of Sage Publications.

CHAPTER 31

Learning War/Learning Race

Fourth-Grade Students in the Aftermath of September 11th in New York City

Maria Kromidas (2004)

Based on ethnographic research with fourth-grade students from a Brooklyn, New York, public school, Maria Kromidas studies how these children constructed and negotiated meaning after September 11, 2001. Children revealed a racialization of a far-away and ill-defined enemy that was also evident in their own interactions and friendships. Kromidas cautions that the events of September 11 have produced a culture of fear with lasting and as yet unintelligible effects on racial dynamics in the United States.

Immediately after September 11th there was a veritable outpouring in the media from adults who deal with children—child psychologists, religious leaders, politicians, pediatricians, educators, school counselors and parents. In one way or another, they all asked: how are "we," "as a society," going to address these issues with children and what *should* children know? Polite suggestions quickly become political and controversial when it comes to curricular directives for public schools. There is one issue that has taken center-stage in this respect, making simmering culture wars in schools erupt into a boiling national debate. This has been the debate that has been framed as that between the values of teaching "multiculturalism" or teaching "patriotism."[1] The debate is re-ignited in the media periodically, and it is doubtful that it will be buried any time soon. What should teachers teach and students learn at the two-year anniversary of the attack? At the ten-year anniversary? Stepping back from the heat of the controversy, however, reveals how much those on either side of the debate share in the form of their most basic assumption—that students are somehow empty receptacles waiting to be filled by the

educators. What children do actually know has rarely been considered in these conversations.

Rather than seeing children as blank slates, the goal of this research with a class of fourth-grade students (nine-year-olds) in East New York, Brooklyn departs from critiques of dominant socialization models and instead seeks to view children as *bricoleurs* in their own right, actively constructing and negotiating meaning from the resources available to them, "multicultural" or "patriotic" discourses being among those resources. Simply stated, my purpose was to figure out what children actually *do* know and what lasting impact, if any, there was on their daily lives almost six months after September 11th. For this purpose, I investigated students' modes of speaking and writing about these events. Although my work with the students spanned various topics that are all interesting in their own right, what emerged again and again in discussions with students was their racialization of a far-away and ill-defined enemy. My observations of the children's social interactions reveal how this racialization was also evident in their interactional patterns and friendship networks. The point of this article is thus to consider the shifting terrain of race in the children's daily lives after September 11th in terms of the local dynamics and the wider social and historical context that in many respects frames it.

While I argue that matters of race are always rooted in the local historical patterns of interaction, I also suggest that the issues of race, racialization, racial discrimination and xenophobia that were evident in this fourth-grade classroom of 23 students are related to wider, nation-wide patterns of discrimination. By looking at nation-wide reports of personal, institutional and state violence directly related to September 11th and its aftermath, as well as political mobilization of targeted groups, I suggest that one of the many effects of this rupturing event is a shift in the racial dynamics in the United States. The most obvious shift is in the increased visibility of Arabs, Muslims, and those attributes that are in the popular understanding related to them by virtue of skin color and vague notions of "foreignness," including religion. While the increased visibility and lumping together of these "brown" people may be considered in some respects "new," it is most productive to view these reverberations in the racial dynamics in terms of processes that have long been entrenched in the history of race relations in the United States. And while the long-term effects on the racial (dis)order are not completely intelligible, this analysis suggests that the soil is well tilled for the exacerbation of racial tensions by fear, real and/or imaginary, in the continuing crisis and internal war on terrorism as well as the [then] impending war with Iraq.

The School and the Surrounding Neighborhood

First it is necessary to very briefly sketch out the school and its surrounding neighborhood. Public School 999[2] in East New York, Brooklyn (Community School District 19, Community District 8) is located in a multi-floored building straddling relatively quiet residential streets on three of its sides, and a busy and speeding expressway on the other, back side of the building. The zoned neighborhood serving the school includes the three-to four-family homes surrounding the school as well as the imposing five building projects across the expressway. The children who live in the projects are mostly African-American and second- and third-generation Latino, while most of the children who live in the unattached homes are recent and first-generation immigrants who mirror the changing immigration base of New York. Three of the top five sending countries to NYC in

the 1990s (Dominican Republic, Jamaica, and Guyana), as well as new groups whose increasing immigration is due to the new "diversity" provisions in immigration law—Nigeria and Bangladesh (Bangladeshis are now the sixth largest group entering New York under the diversity visa program)—are well represented in the school and surrounding neighborhood (NYC Dept of City Planning, 1999). Twelve percent of the students have come to the United States within the last three years (NY State Education Dept, 2001). A traditional breakdown of the school population into the major racial/ethnic categories (28 percent black, 1 percent white, 46 percent Hispanic and 25 percent Asian [NY State Education Dept, 2001]) does not capture the spatial organization of these categories, nor does it appreciate the diversity within them. Approximately 85 percent of the students in the school are eligible for free lunch (NY State Education Dept, 2001), which is commonly interpreted by state and federal agencies as the poverty level index of the students' families. Most of the students' parents or guardians work in the lowest rungs of the service sector ladder—as dishwashers in fancy hotels, security guards for financial companies, janitors in airports, maids for wealthier households. By contrast, the Bengali immigrants have a slightly different pattern—most of the women do not work and a larger percentage of the men are self-employed or employed in "semi-skilled" labor. Like schools with similar demographics throughout the city, the school is identified as a "high-need" school, with most students scoring far below the achievement goals set by the city and state on standardized exams.[3] The classroom in which I conducted fieldwork was considered the lowest-performing of the seven fourth-grade classrooms and was set up as a "reading intervention" class, and thus had a larger percentage of recent immigrants. My choice of this site was at the same time practical (I had previously taught in the school for three years and thus had familiarity with the neighborhood and relative ease of gaining permission from the administration), methodological (a culturally diverse site) and moral/ethical (these students are rarely given the opportunity for open and critical discussions).

While the dominant media and Bush administration's portrayals of "evil" terrorists, the evil governments that support them, and the general rhetoric of "evildoers" that we must "rid the world of" had somewhat prepared me to excavate issues of cultural (mis)essentialism and the like, it was evident from my first day with the children that I need not bring my pick and axe; these matters were not only plainly visible on the surface, but deeply consequential in the students' daily lives. These were the reasons that I altered the focus of my investigation as well as my teaching.

In the Classroom

Within the first three minutes in the classroom, responding to my question of "What's going on in the world right now?" one student stood up to declare "We fighting those ugly people," to the laughter and amusement of most of the class. Later that afternoon, it was the students' continuous shorthand use of the word "they" in the ensuing discussion of war and September 11th that needed clarification. One example, arising after the class was brought together from small discussion groups, follows:

Example 1

Sheri: We were talking about who started it first, and if they kill a lot of white people. . . . I mean a lot of people, we got to go to war right then.

MK: Who are they?

Sheri: The Indians.

MK: The Indians?

Sheri: I don't know—that's what I call them.

Jonathan: The Pakistans!

MK: The Pakistans?

Sodiq: The Afghanistans!

MK: The Afghanistans?

Joseph: The terrorists.

Later that afternoon:

Example 2

Sheri: I feel sorry for the Afghanistan people.

Susanna: Why do you feel sorry after what they did?

Sheri: Because they gonna die! (Most of the class breaks up with laughter)

Latisha: (standing up) I feel happy! (laughter)

Latisha: No, no, no . . . because they want to kill our people, they're going to die too. They want to have a party when we die, so we should celebrate!

Anupa: If they die, it will be better for us.

MK: Who are they?

Anupa: The Araback people.

Marisela: The Afghanistans have always hated the Americans. I know because I always watch the news.

In Example 1, the enemy or "they" referred to Indians, Pakistanis or Afghanistanis; while in Example 2, "they" became again the Afghanistanis, then the Palestinians (I hold strongly that the people that were having a "party" refers to the film recording of Palestinians repeatedly aired in the media), and eventually all Arabic (Araback) people. The students' labeling of the enemy as "Araback" or "Indian" can be considered a racialization—a lumping together of unrelated peoples by virtue of their skin color, and a racialization that was woven with—not surprisingly—xenophobia. It is quite easy to dismiss this racial lumping together as a result of the students' immaturity or ignorance of these matters; it is just children's babble. Two points make this dismissal unacceptable. First, that it is not unlike the sort of racial and xenophobic lumping and labeling that is going on in the wider culture and, second, that this kind of talk made sense in the classroom. Indeed, it made so much sense that it elicited laughter (some uproarious, some mischievous, some nervous) from many classmates, as in the first question I posed, and as in Example 2. So much sense that the students were exasperated with me when I kept asking them to clarify who "they" referred to (Example 1). The students knew what Sheri was talking about, they knew that I knew what Sheri was talking about; the adult was just playing with technicalities. In a sense, the students were just "playing" themselves. For even after I had clarified that the only acceptable reference to "they" was "terrorist," Latisha continued to use the "wrong" signifier.

Example 3

Latisha: The Indians, *I* call them Indians . . .

MK: Who?

Latisha: The people that was in the airplane. They said that God told them to do this. (throwing up her hands and moving her head in mock frustration) Why would he tell them . . .?

Teacher: (Interrupting) You see, they had certain beliefs, but . . .

Latisha quite adeptly used the "wrong" signifier as an additional way to belittle the terrorists as part of her theatrical display to make her classmates laugh. And they did. What is interesting is not what Sheri or Latisha knew or believed in their heads to be the proper identification of "terrorists" (the case could in fact be made that Latisha certainly "knew" the terrorists were not Indians), but rather that they effectively made use of an emerging and available racial construct – successfully in that it made so much sense that it elicited laughter for the audience of students. The activities of fun, "making fun," playing and laughing are clearly an important context where learning occurs, especially learning race, as will be discussed below, but it is important to point out that that not all are playing, not all are having fun, and not all are laughing.

"Difference Multiculturalism"

My initial response to the students' discriminatory remarks was to put forth a few clarifications in the form of a "lesson" about the diversity of peoples who profess Islam; using maps, pictures, literature, etc. I then asked the students to write what they know and might want to know about Muslim people, in order to gauge where and how far I should take this inquiry. The Muslim students in the class wrote about Islamic beliefs, practices, holidays, cultural practices and traditions. A few students earnestly tried to write all of the little they did know, and asked questions about what the religion is like and about the languages Muslims speak. However, the bulk of the responses from the non-Muslim students were frightening to me, to say the least. Here are a few of these written responses.

> They don't talk English. They like money. They like to kill people. They own different kind of stores. (Susanna)

> I don't know any thing about the Muslim people. The only thing that I know is that they are poor and they eat out of dirty pot and the Muslim people stink and they got rotting teeth and they take a bath once a year and the ugly people try to bomb the U.S.A. (Anthony)

> They like to fight other people. They fight the people in their own country. They drink dirty water. They poor. They don't get along. They sleep in bushes. If they are mean they go to hell. (Sheri)

> Muslims kill people. They are terrorist. (Anupa)

> The Muslim like money. They like to kill people. The Muslims is bad. The Muslims like to [go to] war. Muslim people is like bin Ladin. Why do Muslim people stink? Muslim people has long hair. (Chaitram)

What is initially striking about the students' written responses is how perceptions that were obviously new for the students and directly arising from the events and aftermath of September 11th are grafted on to previously existing prejudices, to be discussed in the next section. But also important to note here is the context in which these remarks made sense. I was employing and making available to the students the discourse of "difference multiculturalism." While this is the most popular form of multicultural discourse employed by schools, it has been shown that the espousal of this discourse actually has a divisive effect on students' friendship groups (Fine et al., 1997; Goode, 2001; Goode et al., 1992). This effect was evident from just one multicultural lesson, and the students' "play" with it clearly shows the danger involved in the use of such discourse. Through my talk about Muslims, I was inadvertently singling out this group, reifying their "difference" and justifying talk about "them." But "they" were not just out there, "they" were also in the classroom.

The Students' Social Interactions

It was during this class period that two Bengali girls approached to tell me that some students were "making fun of my country." Although I found out later that this had been an issue with these girls (and others) for some time, the classroom teacher was completely unaware of it. The teacher should not in any case be blamed for this, for these are the informal processes that often go unnoticed within the increasingly formalized world of public education.[4] The following should illustrate to ethnographers of education that children's informal learning may be just as important, or in some cases more important, to consider than the official classroom lessons. Because I was not under the ordinary formal constraints of a teacher—the students were not going to be tested on the material I was teaching, and neither my skills nor my job were at stake[5]—I had the luxury of stepping back, observing and responding to the informal processes taking place.

"Making fun of my country" actually referred to the statement "you sleep in bushes" or "your family sleeps in bushes," as recorded in Sheri's responses to the exercise above. The girls perceived that this was a remark directed not at their individual families, but to their families' background, or rather some imagined aspect of it. I would agree with the girls' perception of this remark for two reasons: the context in which these remarks were made (during a formal lesson about Muslim people) and the students to whom these remarks were directed. This derogatory remark was picked up by many students in the class (it is not known whether Sheri had started this or not) and aimed at students that were from Bangladesh or Guyana, regardless of whether they were Muslim or not. The non-Muslim Guyanese were loudly proclaiming that they were not Muslim, nor were they from Bangladesh—and to make their case they began using the remark in reference to others to whom they felt it applied more appropriately (the Bengali Muslims). Other students continued to make fun of these non-Muslim students as if they did indeed "sleep in the bushes." Anupa (non-Muslim Guyanese) later complained to me: "They always think I'm from their country and I always tell them that I'm not." The questions that arise, then, are—what is the import of the country Anupa is from? What is the function of a statement such as "You sleep in the bushes"?

Quite simply, statements such as these function as forms of exclusion—they indicate to the recipient that she or he is somehow unlike the rest of the group. "You sleep in the bushes" or "you are from Bangladesh" take on a level of significance that the statement "you are from Ecuador" does not, regardless of where the individual is from. It is an accusation of not only being somehow unlike the group, but not worthy of participation in the group's activities. For instance, during a group science project that I was observing, the students in Chaitram's group complained that they did not want to work with him because "he doesn't speak English," "he speaks Bengali." This would not be such an interesting point if it were not that English was Sayab's native and only language! Indeed he did have a Guyanese accent, but the Jamaican accent of another classmate did not arouse any such exclusionary tactics. Thus being from Bangladesh, speaking Bengali or looking as if you do is the new marker for not belonging in this classroom. As folklorist Winslow noted:

> Uncomplimentary and hateful names have always served as a protest against social change and thus as a means of social control. A new name, derogatory or otherwise, is always an indication of flux. Old names are sufficient until a nameless variation emerges, then new identifications are made. After the new thing is located, it is pigeonholed to enable the rest of the group to handle it. (1969: 261)

While the children have not made up a "new name," they are clearly at work constructing and labeling a group with racist and xenophobic tools. This is a space that clearly shows the children as *bricoleurs*—adopting constructs from the media, their families, the neighborhood and the school, grafting new perceptions on to

previously existing ones, reconciling these often contradictory discourses from the private and public realms, and applying them to their classmates. What must be emphasized is that the singling out of South Asian and Muslim students is in many ways new, and that the indicative "flux" must be accounted for in terms of both ongoing processes as well as the rupture point of September 11th. Before September 11th, the Bengali and South Asian diasporic students' presence can be characterized as almost invisible for the other students. Guyanese and Trinidadian students of South Asian descent formed friendship networks with Bengali students and these networks rarely overlapped with those of other students. It cannot be assumed that this pattern of clustering was due to any similarity in immigration status, country of origin, culture or religion of the students, for these networks were composed of a diversity of these characteristics. It may then be presumed that these students were racialized as belonging together and not quite belonging with the black and Latino majority. To illustrate, in the midst of the 1999–2000 school year, I received a new student from Trinidad. She immediately became included and included herself as a part of one group of black and Latino girls rather than the group of South Asian diasporic girls that included another Trinidadian immigrant. Thus, racialization was a relevant process at work in the students' friendships, but this process can be better characterized as *non-inclusionary* rather than *exclusionary*. The key difference is the discriminatory and derogatory elements that are missing from the first as opposed to the second. The first seemed to proceed "naturally" while the second proceeds with force. What follows is another instructive example concerning the marked difference in the significance of a headscarf in the two time periods.

In the midst of the 1999–2000 school year, Shelley, a normally exuberant fourth grader (she wanted to be a singer), approached me tearfully in the morning about how upset she was that she had to start wearing a headscarf. She was nervous that everyone was going to make fun of her and that she looked "ugly." She came back to my classroom after school, her normally chipper self, reporting that everything was fine, except that she felt a bit hot during gym class. Shelley's experience contrasts sharply with Sonia's, who arrived at PS 999 already wearing a headscarf. Nevertheless, she reported to me that this was an issue that she was continually bothered with—"Every day they always ask me why I wear my scarf and every day I tell them that it's my religion." However "invisible" this group may have been for the students before September 11th, points of tension did exist for the adults around them.

For the parents, the Bengalis became visible only at moments of tension, as during a proposed re-zoning of students due to overcrowding or during a meeting concerning the collapsing of one kindergarten class in order to construct another bilingual Bengali class. To many of the parents, it was inevitably the immigrant families from Bangladesh that were to blame for these inconveniences. One parent had even proposed during a meeting that only they should be re-zoned. This pattern of intolerance and blaming the newcomer for structural problems is a phenomenon documented for other neighborhoods in New York (Kim, 2000; Sanjek, 1998; Susser, 1982). Other points of tension and intolerance were evident, for example, parents groaning when meetings were translated into Bengali, or when some parents walked out of a graduation ceremony when it was translated into Bengali (there were no such moans during the Spanish portion). Another point of stress is the fact that many of the small businesses in the neighborhood are owned by Bengalis in a neighborhood with very few black-owned businesses. Evidently the students picked up on this fact from their written responses above such as "they like money" and "they own different kinds of stores." The point I wish to make is that these previously existing tensions moved from the private sphere and became exacerbated in the very public domain of harassment and discrimination.

"Radical Multiculturalism"

I decided it would be more fruitful to direct our attention less towards issues concerning 9/11 and the war, and to focus instead on discrimination—not only as it applied to Muslim-Americans, but as it might be an issue in all their lives. I began by presenting to the students their own uncritical talk about freedom, with the goal of linking it to their discriminatory views. As might be expected, the children had picked up on the current rhetoric about freedom to justify both the war and the events of September 11th. Across the board, the students believed that the World Trade Center was attacked because "we have freedom," that we were at war "to get freedom."[6] Jumping off from their own universalistic definitions of freedom, I led into a historical inquiry as to the exclusionary nature of freedom in the history of the United States (see Foner, 1998). I addressed the struggles of Native Americans, African-Americans, women, immigrants and labor leaders to challenge the boundaries of

freedom, as well as the definition of freedom itself. I also tried to make clear Foner's (1998, 2001) timely insights of how the racial dimensions of freedom and nationalism are exacerbated during periods of crisis through a discussion of Second World War internment of Japanese-Americans. Whereas one of my immediate goals in all of this was to connect our historical inquiry with the present discrimination faced by Muslim-Americans and those that "look like them" as well as the students' own discriminatory attitudes, I chose not to limit our conversations to this group so as not to reinforce some students' "Otherizing" practices, as shown above.[7] My attempt to make things concrete was to have students craft their own stories about a discriminatory event. This process took several days of brainstorming, revising, and editing during which I would continually give feedback to individual students and the entire class.[8] This project was hopefully an exercise in learning for the students, but, for the purpose of this investigation, it also reveals how the students understand the issues of our entire inquiry. I see these stories as indexing how students experience the issue of discrimination, either as victims, witnesses or perpetrators.

The Students' Stories

Although I led a short group discussion on the differences between the institutional and individual forms of discrimination that we had been studying, all but two chose to write stories about individual forms of discrimination, as children of this age tend to write about things that are more concrete in their daily lives. Thus these coded stories reveal how students see and experience the issue of discrimination personally. Indeed, half of all the created characters that were victimized were of the same race or ethnicity as the author, and half of the students that did not infuse their characters with some aspect of their subjectivities created characters that were Muslim or were from Bangladesh. Table 31.1 summarizes each of the students' stories in terms of the main character/victim of discrimination and the perpetrator of the discriminatory act.[9]

Two of the African-American girls in the class wrote stories about white-on-black violence. For instance, Latisha's story is about a character named Joe who got beat up "by a lot of white kids." In the end, "all the black people had a meeting. They were fighting back. And they won." Notably, this is the only story that has grassroots political resistance in response to victimization. Sheri's story about a black woman and her daughter getting shot by a white man ends on a less positive note—"the police came but

Table 31.1 Students' Stories

Student	Race/Ethnicity/Country of origin	Discriminated characteristic of main character	Relevant characteristic of perpetrator
Sherezad	Bangladesh; first generation	Unmarked girl	Unmarked girls
Farana	Bangladesh; immigrated within past three years	Bengali girl wearing head-covering	Unmarked other girls
Amena	Bangladesh; immigrated within past three years	Bengali girl	"Black man"
Sabrina	Haitian; immigrated before school age	N/A	N/A
Sheri	African-American	"Black" kid	"White kids"
Jorge	Latino, second/third generation	"Gang member"	Police
Marisela	Latino; first generation Dominican	"White" girl	"Black people"
Sodiq	Nigeria; immigrated before school age	N/A	N/A
Auriana	Ecuador; immigrated within past three years	Dominican girl	Unmarked "pilot" of an airplane
Chaya	Guyana; immigrated within past three years	N/A	N/A
Susanna	Latino; Puerto Rican	Bengali girl	Unmarked man
Danny	Latino; Puerto Rican	"Fat" boy	Big-eared boy
Marisela	Latino; Puerto Rican	Bengali girl, "black" and "ugly"	Unmarked boy
Anupa	Guyana; immigrated before school age	Girl "from Africa"	Unmarked "kids"
Anthony	Jamaica; immigrated over three years ago	Bengali woman, language status	Unmarked man
Latisha	African-American	"Black" woman and her daughter	Unmarked man
Joseph	Latino; first-generation Dominican	Young Dominican man	"American" men
Jonathan	Latino; Puerto Rican	Muslim woman and her daughter	Unmarked "guy"
Jesmin	Bangladesh; immigrated via the United Arab Emirates within past three years	Bengali girl	"Black boy," her fellow classmate Anthony
Chaitram	Guyana; immigrated within past three years	Immigrant boy told to "go back to your country"	Unmarked boys
Daniel	Guyana; first generation	N/A	N/A
Sonia	Guyana; immigrated within past three years	"Japanese-American" boy	Unmarked boys
Matthew	Latino; first-generation Ecuadorian	"José who came from Peru"	Unmarked boys

they didn't know [what] happened." Sheri's story took place on "March 3, 1776," and conforms to the pattern of some students supposing racial violence is a thing of the past.

The Latino students who used their own ethnicity had perpetrators who were either unmarked or simply "American," as in Joseph's story about a 20-year-old named Tommy "that goes to his job everyday." The men who "were saying the F word to him" and eventually shot him "were Americans." What is interesting to note is that the three Latino students who created main characters conforming to their own ethnicity were all either first generation or immigrants themselves. Of the seven students who are Puerto Rican or second or third generation, none created characters that were Latino. Marisela, after many drafts of stories about friends fighting with each other, finally crafted a story where a girl was not allowed to see her mother in the hospital—"The man said you can not come in the room because you are white and there are only black people." There were other instances where Latino students referred to themselves or other Latino students as "white" or as having "white-skin." While they often remarked on their national origin, there was also evidence that they had some sort of pan-ethnic identity, which they referred to as "Spanish."[10]

Chaitram was the only Guyanese student whose character was possibly related to himself. His story is about a boy told to "go back to your country." Chaitram was one of the students who was having difficulty crafting a story; throughout the week he said he "didn't know what to write." His story was written during a class session when I was discussing coded racist speech and acts such as anti-immigrant and English-only initiatives. This conversation was effective in that many of the students have heard this kind of racist speech, but had not connected it to the issues we were writing and talking about. Six other students incorporated such coded speech into their writings, a few of whom were also having difficulties writing a story.

It is interesting that none of the five Guyanese students chose to write about Muslim discrimination, as in our conversations and in their written responses they were (with the exception of the two Muslim girls) the most vociferously racist against Muslims in general and the Bengalis specifically.

Perhaps they were trying to distance themselves from the Bengali students because they were being identified with them, as discussed above.

Half of the students who did not infuse their main character with their own subjectivities instead created a Muslim or Bengali character. This is significant if we hold to the assumption that the children tend to write about the concrete rather than the abstract, or what they may have experienced in their daily lives. It should not be surprising then that three of the four Bengali girls used Bengali characters in their stories, two of which are woven with true events. Farana's is one such story, although she added her own little twist at the end.

One day my cousin went to her class. 4 girls came and tell her "why [do] you wear this scarf?" She tell them this is our religion. They told her "You look ugly with your scarf." And they told her to take it off. They were teasing her. . . . Then the next day the girl forgot to wear her pants and everybody was laughing at her and she was crying. Then my cousin tell her "when somebody teasing you, you cry but do you know how people feel when you teasing them?"

Jesmin is also from Bangladesh, but came to the USA via the United Arab Emirates where she lived for two years. She is also Farana's cousin. While Jesmin tried to craft a fictional story, she shifted into the first person. You will be hearing more about her fellow classmate Anthony.

One day Yeasmin was at the lunchroom. A boy named [Anthony] [said] that in Bangladesh people don't live in houses they live in the woods on the floor. They're nasty. They're ugly. They're stupid and they don't know anything. They're poor. They speak a stupid language. And that boy is a black boy. . . . And this is the person who teased me . . .

Anthony indeed caused quite a few problems in the class, but unlike some of the other students who were using racist and xenophobic speech, he went about it in a covert manner. I only found out from students complaining directly to me. My one-on-one talks with him did not seem to matter either—it was only when his friend Matthew (a very "cool" kid) humiliated another student for using racist speech that Anthony's harassment seemed to decrease, according to the reports of his victims. Anthony was born in Jamaica and came to the USA about four years ago. However his immigrant experience has obviously not made him any more sensitive. Although black Caribbean-Americans' resistance to being identified as black Americans has been documented as one of the relevant identity paths for black immigrants (Kasinitz, 1992; Waters, 1999; Zéphir, 2001), it is clear that blackness gives Anthony a way to be "American." Anthony never talked about his early childhood in Jamaica, nor did he ever contribute anything in our class discussions of our or our family's experience with immigration or migration. It is interesting that his story picked up on the language difference of the Bengali victim—as that is an issue not applicable to him. His story is about a girl who gets cut by a man while walking down the street.

She said why did you cut me and the man said because you are from Bangladesh and you speak a different language and you are in America and you should speak English.

The last two stories that I will include here are especially interesting because of the racialization of the victim, more so when they are juxtaposed. Marisela, Puerto Rican and proudly so, wrote a story about a 14-year-old girl from Bangladesh. On her way to school a boy said to her: "You are very ugly and very black. . . . You are the ugly girl. You are an ugly Bangladesh. You got that dress because my sister put it in the trash . . ." Ameena, who is from Bangladesh, also wrote a story about a girl from Bangladesh.

My friend was going to the store to buy some clothes. Her name is Sume. She is smart. She has black hair and brown eyes. . . . When she walk[ed] to the store she was looking at the clothes. Suddenly she saw a black man. He told her that he will kill her. She was white and he was black. She yell[ed] for help and the manager came. . . . The police came to arrest the black man. She was so happy.

That Marisela's Bengali character is "black" and Ameena's is "white" is another instance of the (dis)order of the children's understanding of the racial structure. Indeed, this is the point that I want to emphasize—that however the children may racialize themselves, their peers, and others in their world, there is nothing coherent or definite about the children's view of the racial order. Race is a somewhat messy principle, but still a principle that they are constructing and resisting out of the raw materials of their lives—and the larger racial polarity/hierarchy of white/black, while not quite clear, is still one such material.

Conclusion

In this article I have tried to show the connection between the students' hazy understanding of a far-away enemy and their categorization of their South Asian diasporic classmates, in the context of their overall racial understandings. Briefly I have outlined how, in this neighborhood that is almost 100 percent minority, the South Asians (including Guyanese) are constructed by blacks and Latinos as a brown foreign Other, while some Latinos refer to them as black. The Bengalis in turn distance themselves from black people, while the Guyanese resist being categorized with the Bengalis, vociferously putting forward their own racist views. I have called

attention to the impact that learning about war, and a brown and foreign enemy, has had in this neighborhood where some children are made to feel they belong by excluding others, and other children are pushed beyond the margins of belonging. The events of September 11th brought home war in a very specific way to these children—learning about war is always learning about an enemy, and this "enemy" is very much a racial one: brown, foreign, strange and Muslim. And while the children do not consider their Muslim classmates as "evil" or as "terrorists," their identities are taken note of as never before. Students who are themselves immigrants or bilingual perpetrate hateful acts towards their classmates, even the children that are lumped together with these students. But I want to make clear that the specific dynamics that I have described is a description of the local level in East New York, a neighborhood with few whites and a neighborhood where a large portion of the newest immigrants are from Bangladesh.

Thus far, I have primarily discussed only one relatively small realm of the local level of experience—the racializations of a group of children's discourse and friendship networks within the institution of the school. Based on this research, I have staked a rather large claim—that the lumping of Arabs, South Asians and Muslims is a "new" racial formation in the "post September 11th" world. How can this claim be substantiated?

It is quite easy to dismiss these dynamics, putting them down to the students' immaturity or ignorance of these matters—that is, until one confronts both the acts of violence daily being perpetrated against "browns" or "nonwhites/nonblacks" since September 11th and the racist practices of the state and other major institutions. As pertains to interpersonal violence, a report compiled in the immediate aftermath of September 11th (SAALT, 2001) shows that, rather than being a scattered and random phenomenon, the violence inflicted upon Muslims, South Asians and other "brown" peoples was much more widespread than it was presented to be by the mainstream media. By looking instead to local press, SAALT uncovered 645 incidents of backlash in the week following September 11th alone, which does not include police reports not covered by the media and the many other incidents that presumably went unreported. While it is obvious, as the SAALT report points out, that "perception played a major role in determining backlash victims," in support of which they cite incidents where the victims were not Muslims or Arab-Americans, the issue is obviously not who has been "correctly identified" or not. Rather there are larger issues, exacerbated and uniquely intertwined in the aftermath of September 11th: the racial structure of the United States and the precarious and at times paradoxical position of South Asian-Americans and Arab-Americans within it (Kibria, 1999; Koshy, 1998, 2001; Naber, 2000; Prashad, 2000; Shilpa et al., 1999), coupled with the profound historical misunderstanding and vilification of Muslims and the Arab world in the American popular understanding (Shaheen, 2001). In this respect, the state could be considered the most powerful actor in the racial drama.

The persecution and degradation of civil liberties faced by members of this group at the hands of police, airport security, the Justice Department, Congressional legislation and the Immigration and Naturalization Service (INS) further substantiate that the events of September 11th have facilitated the consolidation of a new racialized category of those who "look" like the enemy (Ahmad, 2002; Volpp, 2002). In reaction to the practices of racial profiling of public institutions and private citizens, some members of this group have stood up to declare themselves mistakenly identified (e.g. Sikhs who protest: "We are not Muslim!"), while others have participated in multi-racial, multi-ethnic activities of grassroots organizations to protest the domestic atrocities of the aftermath of September 11th.[11]

By now it is quite banal to point out the diversity between those lumped together—the crosscutting lines of class, gender, nationality, religion and language among them. It is not essence but political relations and processes, conflict and struggle, that constitute race. While shared experiences of oppression do not *necessarily* build unity, that is one trajectory amongst others. Whatever long-term effects this new racism of a not-white, not-black but brown and foreign Other will have on future coalitions and race relations in America remains to be seen. What is clear, however, is that this cultural and political economy of fear shows no trace of subsiding—duct tape, orange alerts and evacuation drills are daily reminders that somewhere among us an enemy lurks.[12] Glued to the news of our own disaster on CNN, we are comforted by an advertisement for a home radiation detector—one that can detect traces of radiation long before we would even hear of the attack on CNN! As the alarm beeps, the white couple jumps into their SUV, whizzing off to the mountains, leaving the city and its Others far behind.

Notes

1. The broad range of advice and directives for educators can be categorized in three ideal-types: radical, neo-liberal and neo-conservative. Three publications can serve as paradigmatic cases of each of these categories. They are, respectively, *Rethinking Schools*, the *New York Times* and *Scholastic Magazine*. All have dedicated sections of their website to September 11th and the ensuing "war on terrorism." Available online: *Rethinking Schools* [http://www.rethinkingschools. org/special_reports/sept11/index.shtml]; *New York Times* [http://www.nytimes.com/learning/teachers/lessons/ archive.html (search terrorism or September 11th)]; *Scholastic Magazine* [http://teacher.scholastic.com/professional/breaking_news/leading .htm.].

2. This is a pseudonym. All names have been changed to protect the anonymity of the school, teacher and students.

3. Compare District 19's achievement to other schools in the New York City Board of Education [http://www.nycenet.edu].

4. Especially in this and other "failing" or "high-need" schools, much attention is devoted to the raising of test scores. Students and teachers are inundated with school and district-wide pre-tests, post-tests, testing of individual skills ("main idea," "drawing conclusions," etc.) as well as increasingly scripted teaching methods. So intense is this pressure on the participants of the school that, for example, in the school year of 1997–8 the new superintendent prohibited all class trips so that everyone could concentrate on testing.

5. Results of testing are aggregated by class and often presented next to the individual teacher's name, often bringing into question the teacher's ability if the class did not score as well as other classes. In pre- and post-test situations, which represent how much the students improved on a particular skill, this phenomenon of "accountability" or blaming the teacher is further exaggerated.

6. The students' families also used this discourse of freedom. In the first two weeks of my research, the students, with my guidance, made up questions to interview their family and friends about the war. While we came up with 20 or so "good" questions, most of the students asked their interviewee about six questions. Many students did more than one interview; their subjects were mothers, older siblings, aunts, grandmothers, family friends and their own friends. The one question that most students asked in their interviews was: "Why do some people hate the US?" The responses were, across the board with only one exception (from a student's tutor who answered: "They maybe hate the US because they think the US has helped their enemies and has put them into poverty"), that people were jealous of the US because of our wealth, our technology, our equality and our freedom.

7. Countering the sense that groups fought and "now we have freedom," and talking about current forms of racism, proved to be the most difficult and sensitive aspect of my teaching/fieldwork.

8. For instance, I noticed at the beginning of our project that three or four students were confusing forms of discrimination with other forms of teasing and fighting amongst friends. Another point that I had to address with the whole class was the endings of their stories. All of the students' stories ended on a terribly negative note – their main character dead, beaten up, or running home and crying. I reminded them of the resistance to discrimination that we had discussed, and although this was not quite applicable to their personal stories, the endings changed to characters fighting back, telling authorities, confronting the perpetrators, etc.

9. Of the 23 students, four students did not do the work involved, no matter what tactics I resorted to. Of the 19 stories that students wrote, nine used their own race or ethnicity, six did not, three were about non-racial discriminatory forms of teasing or did not make sense (friends fighting, a boy getting teased because of his

weight, a girl not allowed in a hospital because "she is white"), one was about a gang member getting ignored by the police when he was shot (which was apparently a true story), and one was ambiguous about the racial or ethnic identity of the victim.

10. See Oboler's "Hispanics and the Dynamics of Race and Class" (1995: Ch. 5), which deals with her research on how first-generation immigrants from Latin American used, negotiated and resisted the pan-ethnic label of Hispanic.

11. For instance, the organization DRUM (Dezis Rizing Up and Moving) attempts to build coalitions of South Asian, Arab, Muslim, black and Latino organizations. See the DRUM website [http://www.drumnation.org]. For information on their community projects directly related to the aftermath of September 11th, see: [http://www.drumnation.org/911selfdefense.html]. These projects include the "Racial Violence and INS Disappearance Hotline," "YouthPower! Self Defense & Know Your Rights" and "Multi-Racial Anti-War Organizing." Also see Varghese (2002).

12. Davis (2001) contextualizes the current "globalization of fear" in his historical parody/critique of the apocalyptic currents within cities. His point is to link this fear with the unprecedented surveillance that urban dwellers are currently experiencing.

References

Ahmad, Muner (2002). "Homeland Insecurities: Racial Violence the Day after September 11," *Social Text* 20(3): 101–15.

Davis, Mike (2001). "The Flames of New York," *New Left Review* 12: 34–50.

Fine, Michelle, Louise Weis and Linda C. Powell (1997). "Communities of Difference: A Critical Look at Desegregated Spaces Created for and by Youth," *Harvard Educational Review* 67(2): 247–84.

Foner, Eric (1998). *The Story of American Freedom.* New York: W.W. Norton.

Foner, Eric (2001). "The Most Patriotic Act," *The Nation* 8 October.

Goode, J. (2001). "Teaching Against Cultural Essentialism," pp. 434–56 in I. Susser and T.C. Patterson (eds) *Cultural Diversity in the United States.* Malden, MA: Blackwell.

Goode, Judith, Jo Anne Schneider and Suzanne Blanc (1992). "Transcending Boundaries and Closing Ranks: How Schools Shape Interrelations," pp. 173–214 in L. Lamphere (ed.) *Structuring Diversity: Ethnographic Perspectives on the New Immigration.* Chicago, University of Chicago Press.

Kasinitz, P. (1992). *Caribbean New York: Black Immigrants and the Politics of Race.* Ithaca, NY: Cornell University Press.

Kibria, Nazil (1999). "The Racial Gap: South Asian American Racial Identity and the Asian American Movement," in Lavina D. Shankar and Rajini Srikanth (eds) *A Part Yet Apart: South Asians in Asian America.* Philadelphia, PA: Temple University Press.

Kim, C. (2000). *Bitter Fruit: The Politics of Black-Korean Conflict in New York City.* New Haven, CT: Yale University Press.

Koshy, Susan (1998). "Category Crisis: South Asian Americans and Questions of Race and Ethnicity," *Diaspora* 7(3): 285–320.

Koshy, Susan (2001). "Morphing Race into Ethnicity: Asian Americans and Critical Transformations of Whiteness," *Boundary 2* 28(1): 153–94.

Naber, Nadine (2000). "Ambiguous Insiders: An Investigation of Arab American Invisibility," *Ethnic and Racial Studies* 23(1): 37–61.

NY State Education Department (2001). *2000–2001 Annual School Report.* New York: New York State Education Department, Division of Assessment and Accountability.

NYC Dept of City Planning (1999). *Newest New Yorkers 1995–1996: An Update of Immigration to the City in the Mid-90s.* New York: NYC Dept of City Planning.

Oboler, Suzanne (1995). *Ethnic Labels, Latino Lives: Identity and the Politics of (Re)Presentation in the United States.* Minneapolis: University of Minnesota Press.

Prashad, Vijay (2000). *The Karma of Brown Folk.* Minneapolis: University of Minnesota Press.

SAALT (South Asian American Leaders of Tomorrow) (2001). American Backlash: Terrorists Bring Home War in More Ways Than One. Available: [www.saalt.org/biasreport.pdf].

Sanjek, Roger (1998). *The Future of Us All: Race and Neighborhood Politics in New York City.* Ithaca, NY: Cornell University Press.

Shankar, Lavina D. and Rajini Srikanth, eds (1999). *A Part Yet Apart: South Asians in Asian America.* Philadelphia, PA: Temple University Press.

Shaheen, Jack (2001). *Reel Bad Arabs: How Hollywood Vilifies a People.* New York: Olive Branch Press.

Shilpa, Dave, Pawan Dhingra, Sunaina Maira, Partha Mazumdar, Lavina D. Shankar, Jaideep Singh and Rajini Srikanth (2000). "De-privileging Positions: Indian Americans, South Asian Americans, and the Politics of Asian American Studies," *Journal of Asian American Studies* 3(1): 67–100.

Susser, I. (1982). *Norman Street: Poverty and Politics in an Urban Neighborhood.* New York: Oxford University Press.

Varghese, Romy (2002). "The New New Yorkers: DRUMing up Support," *New York Newsday, Queens Edition* 2 January.

Volpp, Leti (2002). "The Citizen and the Terrorist," *UCLA Law Review* 49(June).

Waters, M.C. (1999). *Black Identities: West Indian Immigrant Dreams and American Realities.* Cambridge, MA: Harvard University Press.

Winslow, D.J. (1969). "Children's Derogatory Epithets," *The Journal of American Folklore* 82(325): 255–63.

Zéphir, F. (2001). *Trends in Ethnic Identification Among Second-generation Haitian Immigrants in New York City.* Westport, CT: Bergin and Garvey.

Discussion Questions

1. Review Kromidas' methodology. Identify her study setting and subjects.

   Kromidas utilized qualitative research methodology—interviews, discussion, and story analysis. Her subjects are students in a fourth-grade class at Public School 999 in East New York, Brooklyn. The school is located between a residential area and a busy expressway. Her subjects are mostly African American and second and third generation Latino. Other students are either immigrants or the children of immigrants from the Dominican Republic, Jamaica, Guyana, Nigeria, and Bangladesh.

2. How did students' racialized conceptualization of the enemy affect their interaction with others?

   Kromidas documents how students categorized, discriminated, and excluded others based on racist constructs and perceptions they learned from the media, their families and community. They singled out South Asian and Muslim students, separating them from African American and Latino friendship groups. There was evidence of increasing intolerance toward Bengali immigrants and their children from students (picking on a student wearing a headband, not wanting to work with a student since he didn't speak English) and among community members (expressing displeasure when materials or events included Bengali translation).

Source: From Kromidas, M. (2004). Learning war/learning race: Fourth-grade students in the aftermath of September 11th in New York City. *Critique of Anthropology, 24*(1), 15–33 (2004). Reprinted by permission of Sage Publications and the author.

CHAPTER 32

Combat Casualties and Race

What Can We Learn From the 2003–2004 Iraq Conflict?

Brian Gifford (2005)

Though African Americans are overrepresented among volunteers for the U.S. Armed Forces, they are less likely to die in combat when compared with white military personnel. Brian Gifford argues that the racial composition of combat casualties reflects three factors: the social processes that sort volunteers into various units and occupational specialties, the mix of units and specialties that participate in military operations, and the battlefield conditions they encounter. His analysis is based on data from the 2003–2004 Iraq conflict.

Since the end of the draft in 1973, African Americans have been overrepresented among volunteers for the U.S. Armed Forces.[1] While many commentators have hailed the military as a uniquely egalitarian avenue for social and economic advancement in a society beset with racial inequities, the high participation rate among blacks has periodically led to concerns that they (and more recently, other ethnic minorities such as Hispanics) would disproportionately suffer from casualties in the event of military hostilities.[2] However, after numerous U.S. military engagements since the 1970s, these fears have not been borne out. In fact, African Americans seem less likely to die in combat than their overall representation in uniform would suggest. Taken at face value, the racial composition of U.S. combat casualties stands in stark contrast to the racial pattern of morbidity and mortality in the larger society, where African Americans as a group fare worse than whites on measures such as death rates, infant mortality, and life expectancy.[3]

It would seem that, as a comparatively disadvantaged group, African Americans in the all-volunteer era have reaped the benefits of military service without unduly bearing its ultimate burdens. However, explanations for the unexpectedly low African American casualty rate have not been rigorously examined. Furthermore, assessing the racial equity of military service based on historical casualty patterns assumes that future combat operations will closely resemble those that have occurred since Vietnam—an assumption that in this new century looks increasingly untenable.

Extending the work of Martin Binkin and his collaborators,[4] this study argues that the racial composition of combat casualties reflects three factors: the social processes that sort volunteers into various military units and occupational specialties; the mix of units and specialties that participate in military operations; and the battlefield conditions they encounter. Or put another way, given a particular environment within which armed conflict occurs, the probability of any person becoming a casualty is a function of their representation in those units most likely to make hostile contact with enemy forces. Following this, the underrepresentation of African Americans in the units most involved in combat operations since Vietnam may partly explain the disjuncture between their military participation and casualty rates. By extension, the higher propensity of whites to serve in combat capacities could explain their higher-than-expected, post-Vietnam casualty rate. The same may be true of ethnic Hispanics, who are also overrepresented in the combat arms, though their reasons for volunteering for such assignments may differ from those of their non-Hispanic white counterparts.

The short duration of post-Vietnam U.S. ground combat engagements such as Panama and Somalia—as well as the prominent roles played by special operations and light-infantry units for which blacks are less likely to volunteer[5]—has thus far prevented a rigorous evaluation of such propositions. However, the 2003-2004 conflict in Iraq presents one opportunity to assess the race distribution of U.S. casualties under varying combat conditions. First, compared to other combat engagements since Vietnam, many diverse military units have been operating in Iraq for a relatively long time. Second, the U.S. military experience in Iraq has been, broadly speaking, marked by differing conflict environments. In the relatively brief opening period, coalition ground combat forces (mainly U.S. and British infantry and armor) rapidly penetrated deep into enemy territory and carried out offensive actions primarily against Iraqi military forces. The subsequent—and ongoing—mission involves efforts by combat and noncombat personnel (e.g., intelligence, police, logistical, and civil affairs) to consolidate U.S. control, restore civil order, pacify hostile forces, and administer occupied areas.

This study assesses the racial equity of military service by examining the racial distribution of U.S. casualties in Iraq for the first twelve months since the invasion by U.S. and coalition forces. To better understand how different conflict environments impact racial and ethnic groups with different occupational patterns, the Iraq conflict is divided into two periods, delineated by President George W. Bush's declaration on May 1, 2003, of an end to "major" combat operations. This distinction is important because it signaled a shift in tactics by both coalition and hostile Iraqi forces, and thus altered the risk exposure of U.S. troops with different operational missions. Moreover, in the latter period, the distinction between front lines and rear areas has been blurred, if not eradicated. The conflict environment, operationalized by the different phases of the U.S. mission and by measures of combat intensity, is thus the major statistical control.

Data from the Iraq conflict also permit an analysis of casualties among Hispanics, a diverse group with growing significance within both U.S. society and the

military, but whose enlistment patterns and combat experiences have been underexamined and undertheorized, and for whom little prior casualty data exist. The analysis of Hispanic casualties may thus be considered largely exploratory, although some attempt is made to link the findings back to the theoretical discussion of the relative burdens faced by white and African American military personnel.

It bears repeating that casualties of the Iraq conflict do not collectively comprise a randomly drawn sample. Notwithstanding measurement error, the racial distribution of the individuals killed in Iraq has its own specific reality; enumerating their deaths directly reveals the comparative burdens of those in uniform. Nonetheless, a fundamental assumption of this study holds that casualties on any particular battlefield reflect the social representation of the troops who find themselves there. Observed casualties are therefore treated as a sample from which we may speculate about future U.S. military engagements and about the final casualty distribution of the Iraq conflict.

The organization of the article is as follows: following a brief review of the literature on African-American military casualties, the intersection of enlistment patterns and battlefield conditions is discussed. A third section further extends the argument to Hispanics. These conceptual sections are followed by formal hypotheses, a description of the data and analytical results, and concluding remarks.

African Americans in Uniform: Benefits and Burdens

African Americans have served in the U.S. Armed Forces since the Revolutionary War. Prior to the Korean War, blacks' military participation was intermittent; they were drafted or recruited into uniform only when available white manpower dwindled, and were typically assigned to noncombat support duties. African American combat casualties have thus historically been much lower than their representation in either U.S. society or its armed forces. This pattern changed dramatically during the Vietnam War. African Americans accounted for almost 21 percent of the combat casualties in 1965–1966, but only about 12 percent of the U.S. Army and Marine Corps. In response to public criticisms over these high casualty rates, the Pentagon redistributed some African American troops away from front line units.[6] By the war's end, black casualties were

Table 32.1 Blacks Killed in Action Since Vietnam

Military operation	Total killed	Blacks killed	Blacks as percentage of total killed
Mayaguez (1975)	14	1	7.1
Lebanon (1983)	254	46	18.1
Grenada (1983)	18	0	0
Panama (1989)	26	1	4.3
Gulf War (1991)	182	28	15.4
Somalia (1992–93)	29	2	6.9
Total	520	78	15.0

Source: Moskos and Butler (1996), table 1.2, p. 8.

proportional to their representation in those units that saw most of the fighting on the ground.

With the end of conscription in 1973, commentators both within and outside of the armed forces expressed concerns about the potential overreliance on African American labor. On one hand, commanders and military planners worried about the effects of racial discord within the ranks and an influx of substandard recruits on the readiness of military units.[7] On the other hand, some leaders of the black community expressed concerns that African Americans pursuing military careers in the absence of better civilian alternatives would bear a disproportionate burden of any U.S. combat engagements. While African Americans did volunteer in relatively large numbers, the institution of policies designed to promote racial harmony within the ranks, and the overall performance of African American, largely mitigated concerns about the erosion of military readiness.

However, this did not assuage underlying concerns about African American "cannon fodder" that publicly resurfaced with the massive buildup of force in preparation for the 1991 Persian Gulf War.[8] Yet by and large, fears of excessive black casualties were not borne out; nor were they for other post-Vietnam military operations. Charles C. Moskos and John Sibley Butler[9] analyzed U.S. combat casualties between 1975 and 1993 and report that of five hundred twenty deaths in six hostile situations, only 15 percent were black—a figure slightly higher than their representation in the age-appropriate population, but lower than their percentage in the active-duty military (Table 32.1 reproduces their findings). Moskos and Butler conclude that "no serious case can be made that Blacks suffer undue casualties in America's wars and military interventions."[10]

Environments of Conflict, Race, Military Specialty, and Combat Intensity

In effectively refuting the cannon-fodder argument, Moskos and Butler provide no explanation for the low rate of African American casualties relative to their overall participation in uniform. Unlike during the Vietnam War, there has been no explicit policy of equilibrating the risks among service members of various races and ethnicities.[11] What seems to matter is the composition of the forces used in the fight, and the battlefield conditions they encounter. Martin Binkin argues that the low African American casualty rate in the Persian Gulf War reflects its short duration and the limited exposure of U.S. ground forces to intense combat conditions. He further proposes that, had Iraqi forces posed stiffer resistance, conventional ground units would have suffered higher casualties, which would have in turn driven up the proportion of black casualties.[12]

Binkin's basic insight points to the importance of conflict environments—the political goals, battlefield missions and tactics, and degrees and types of enemy resistance—that expose military units to varying levels of combat risk. For general theorizing, one useful conceptual distinction is between *high-intensity* and *low-intensity* conflict environments.[13] High-intensity conflict environments bring to mind what most people think of as "war." The immediate goal of cobelligerent armed forces is first and foremost the reduction of the other's will and capacity to fight, usually through application of massed military firepower against enemy formations, fortifications, and materièl. Thus units and personnel primarily organized, equipped, and trained for lethal combat are most likely to make contact with enemy forces, particularly when executing offensive tactics.

By contrast, in low-intensity environments—referred to in the past as *limited war*, and which today often goes by the term *operations other than war*—both immediate goals and the means of achieving them are more ambiguous than what is observed in conventional war scenarios. While precise definitions of low-intensity conflict are highly contested, the term has come to denote a range of activities including peacekeeping and peacemaking interventions, occupation duties, internal security operations and counterinsurgency, counter- and antiterror efforts, and civil affairs operations designed to "win the hearts and minds" of indigenous populations. Military forces remain policy instruments, but military tactics frequently take a backseat to political considerations, and there are few clear distinctions between front line and rear areas. Intuitively, the expanded participation of noncombat forces in support and civil affairs activities increases their likelihood of making hostile contact with enemy forces.[14]

Explaining the low rate of post-Vietnam African American casualties thus entails understanding the units most involved in hostilities, the battlefield conditions they encountered, and the representation of African Americans within them. The engagements analyzed by Moskos and Butler (see Table 32.1) were mostly short, intense operations conducted primarily by elite, lightly equipped, rapidly deployable light infantry and commando units (such as Army Rangers, special operations forces, paratroopers, and Marine expeditionary units). Moreover, the tactics employed by such units dictate that they operate with little direct support (at least in the short run) from noncombat units.

African Americans are typically underrepresented in these types of units and specialties, and have instead been more concentrated in noncombat support positions.[15] For example, in 2001, only one in eight African Americans was in a combat specialty, compared to just under one in five whites. This pattern is not atypical of the all-volunteer era, and could explain African Americans' low post-Vietnam casualty rates.

The possible exceptions to the near-exclusive risk exposure of elite combat personnel are Lebanon and the Persian Gulf War. In Lebanon, most of the U.S. casualties occurred in one unprecedented terror attack against a Marine Corps barracks;[16] in the Persian Gulf, heavy armored forces required extensive logistical support, and Iraqi missile attacks into coalition rear areas caused many casualties among support personnel. It is telling that these two engagements claimed both the majority of post-Vietnam casualties (until 2003) and saw the highest percentages of African American casualties.[17]

The low participation rate of African Americans in the most likely combatant units partly reflects the reasons for which they enter the military. The propensity to volunteer for the armed forces has been linked to individual socioeconomic circumstances and macroeconomic conditions.[18] On the whole, military volunteers tend to have fewer educational and human capital advantages than their age-appropriate peers who do not join. Yet more so than their white counterparts, African Americans enlist in the armed forces for economic and social advancement[19]. For example, black youths are more likely to cite pay as a reason for considering military employment, and less likely to cite "other career interests" as a reason not to join.[20] Whites also cite "money for education" and "job training" as reasons to join more often than do blacks, perhaps signifying a preference for shorter enlistment commitments. This is further borne out by higher reenlistment rates among African Americans.[21] Blacks are also almost twice as likely as whites to cite "threat to life" as a reason not to join. In short, combat specialties and rapidly deployable units—with their frequent deployments, high-stress environments, and occupational hazards such as training and combat injuries—may be less attractive to blacks pursuing a stable military career in the absence of more promising civilian alternatives. Ultimately, the social process that sorts military volunteers into various military units and occupational specialties plays a key role in the race distribution of casualties.

Hispanics in Uniform

In contrast to the well-researched military experiences of African Americans, we have much less systematic information on post-Vietnam era Hispanic American service members.[22] Nor do reliable data on Hispanic casualties exist for past combat engagements. Although they represent a diversity of ethnic backgrounds, persons of Hispanic and Latino heritage now collectively comprise the largest and fastest-growing minority group in the United States. They are therefore a potentially important source of military labor.

Like African Americans, Hispanics tend to earn less and have less wealth and education than whites.[23] However, the economic similarities between African Americans and Hispanics have not translated into similar military participation rates or occupational patterns. Among U.S. sixteen- to twenty-four-year-olds with no prior military service, Hispanics show the highest propensity to enlist in the armed forces, even when controlling for educational attainment. Like blacks, Hispanics were less likely than whites to cite "other career interests" as a reason for avoiding the military.[24] Yet Hispanics are more similar to whites in their attitudes towards pay, job training, educational benefits, and the life-threatening nature of military service. Of all three groups, Hispanics seem the least dissuaded by the military lifestyle. Important for this study, Hispanics volunteer for combat units and specialties—particularly those of the Marine Corps—at about the same rate as whites. For example, in 2001, 18 percent of all Hispanic military applicants attempted to enlist in the Marine Corps, a figure statistically higher than the proportions of any other racial group.[25]

However, compared to the military-age population, Hispanics are underrepresented in the U.S. Armed Forces as a whole. This partly reflects educational and language requirements that render many young Hispanics effectively ineligible for service. About one-half of enlistment-age Hispanics are immigrants, and they tend to attain less education than their native-born counterparts.[26] Such recruits would be in a disadvantaged position when taking the Armed Forces Qualification Test.[27] This makes it difficult to confidently assert that the structure of employment opportunities influences casualties among Hispanics in the same manner as African Americans; explaining their propensity toward combat specialties is also beyond the scope of this study. At best, we can postulate that the social processes that influence Hispanic enlistment patterns are different than those for either whites or blacks. Describing observed casualty rates is thus the first step in developing new theoretical insights about the Hispanic military experience in the all-volunteer era.

Hypotheses

To summarize, persons of different races and ethnicities exhibit different propensities to volunteer for the armed forces and to select combat specialties and units. In turn, in any given conflict environment, military personnel serving in different units and trained in different skills will likely face varying levels of combat hazards. These propositions suggest specific testable hypotheses about the racial distribution of casualties under different conditions.

Hypothesis 1: The racial distribution of casualties will differ between the early phase of the Iraq conflict—when U.S. personnel encountered high-intensity conditions resembling war—and the later phase, which is characterized primarily by low-intensity operations other than war.

Hypothesis 2: During the early phase of the conflict, the racial distribution of casualties will reflect the racial composition of ground combat forces.

Hypothesis 3: During the later phase of the conflict, the racial distribution of casualties will resemble the racial composition of the military as a whole.

Hypotheses 2 and 3 imply that blacks and whites will be overrepresented compared to the U.S. population, while Hispanics will be underrepresented. However, hypothesis 2 implies that compared to the military overall, whites and Hispanics will be overrepresented, and blacks underrepresented. The relationships are reversed in hypothesis 3. Given that the majority of the casualties have occurred in this latter period, the total casualties for the Iraq conflict should follow the pattern described in hypothesis 3.

These hypotheses are offered with some important caveats. The latter portion of the Iraq engagement has been beset by continued casualties, caused mainly by insurgents' ambushes, bombings, and suicide attacks against coalition military forces and civilian targets. Coalition forces have periodically responded with aggressive air-supported ground assaults. The danger to combat troops thus remains high. On the other hand, unlike shorter, small-scale interventions such as Panama and Grenada, heavy armor and mechanized infantry units carried out the bulk of the initial ground assaults in Iraq. Providing these forces with fuel, rations, ammunition, and other materièl brought noncombat support troops into close proximity of battle areas, and required them to travel along extensive, vulnerable supply lines. Both of these situations could mediate differences in the casualty distribution between the two phases. I therefore use quantitative measures of combat intensity across the phases of the conflict, and within the latter period to test the following hypothesis:

Hypothesis 4: As the intensity of conditions on the ground increase, casualties will resemble the racial composition of ground combat forces. This implies the racial casualty patterns described for hypothesis 2.

Data

The data come from the U.S. Department of Defense's (DoD) Directorate for Information Operations and Reports, Statistical Information Analysis Division (DIOR/SIAD). They cover all casualties incurred in Operation Iraqi Freedom since the opening of the conflict on March

19, 2003, through April 8, 2004. Data were collected from the DIOR/SIAD Web site[28] on April 12, 2004. A list of all casualties provides basic information for each individual (such as name, age, branch, component, hometown), but no information on race. However, aggregated data are crosstabulated by race and branch, and by race and the date range in which the casualty occurred.

Casualty data include information on 3,276 wounded U.S. personnel, as well as on 643 deaths. However, as is generally recognized in medical care and public health studies, deaths are a more reliable and easily interpretable measure of outcomes than most other health indicators. DoD reporting on the racial composition of deaths also appears somewhat more rigorous than for wounded. About 8.8 percent of wounded cases were listed as "multiple races, pending, or unknown," compared to only eight cases (1.2 percent) among deaths. The proportions in this category account for much of the variation between the two groups. When the "unknown" group is excluded, differences in the racial distributions among wounded and dead are reduced (the χ^2 shrank from 72.1 to 17). Therefore, only deaths among U.S. personnel are analyzed. Deaths include those resulting from hostile enemy action (four hundred fifty) and from nonhostile causes (one hundred ninety-three, including accidents, illnesses, three homicides, and twenty-three confirmed suicides). Including both categories is necessary because the data do not crosstabulate race by casualty type.

DoD categorizes casualties by race/ethnicity. Values include "white," "black or African-American," "Hispanic or Latino," "Asian," "American Indian or Alaska Native," "Native Hawaiian or Pacific Islander," and "Multiple races, pending, or unknown." Because they are relatively small in number, and to better compare with existing data on military populations, the latter four categories are aggregated into a single category, "other race."[29] The data are crosstabulated by the four major branches of the military: Army, Navy, Air Force, and Marine Corps. Large numbers of reserve and National Guard personnel have played a role in the Iraq theater (comprising perhaps as many as one-quarter of personnel in the later period),[30] but casualties among these troops are aggregated to their parent branches.

I compare the racial distribution of combat casualties to three populations: all U.S. active-duty military forces, all personnel in U.S. Army and Marine Corps occupational specialties listed as "infantry, gun crews and seamanship" (alternately referred to as "ground combat troops" or "Army/Marine Corps combat personnel"),[31] and the U.S. population between the ages of eighteen and thirty-four. It is important to compare to more than one relevant population because any given distribution of

casualties has multiple implications for assessing the equity of military service. A casualty distribution that differs from the general U.S. population may reflect both inequitable processes that sort people into the armed forces (such as economic and labor market inequities) and differences in preferences and eligibility for military service. Likewise, casualties may differ from the military as a whole to the degree that vocational preferences and aptitudes for differentially risky occupations and specialties are stratified by race. Finally, within particular occupational categories, casualties may reflect relative risks inherent to the military rank structure, between branches of service, and in the assignment of duties.

Data on military populations come from DoD's *Population Representation in the Military Services, Fiscal Year 2001*. Casualties are compared to the entire active-duty armed forces for consistency with other studies focusing on race in the military, even though the Navy and Air Force committed comparatively few troops on the ground.[32] Data on the U.S. population come from the U.S. Census Bureau's 2000 decennial census. Racial categories represent the proportions identifying themselves by one race. Census definitions allow Hispanics or Latinos to define themselves as any race. This confounds comparisons with casualties, who are categorized by one race only, or by an unspecified combination of racial or ethnic categories. Estimates of the U.S. Hispanic population are derived by subtracting the proportional number of Hispanics from each racial category, and aggregating them into a distinct Hispanic category. I use the age group eighteen to thirty-four for comparability with the estimates provided by Moskos and Butler.

For analytical purposes only, I label the period through President George W. Bush's declaration of an end to "major" combat operations on May 1, 2003, as the "war phase," and from May 2 onward the "occupation phase." These labels characterize the overall mission of U.S. military forces in each period. In the war phase, U.S. forces worked primarily toward the elimination of the existing Iraqi authority structure. In the occupation phase, the military supports a more diffuse project of administering Iraqi territory and promoting the conditions conducive to the reestablishment of Iraqi civil and political society.

The occupation phase has been marked by periodic, often large-scale clashes between coalition and insurgent guerrilla forces. I therefore examine the average daily casualty rate as an additional measure of combat intensity.[33] There was an average of 3.1 casualties per day in the war phase, compared to 1.5 per day between May 2, 2003, and April 8, 2004. Within the occupation period, the daily casualty rate climbed to 2.8 in October-November 2003—coinciding with the downing of three

Table 32.2   Casualties by Phases of the Iraq Conflict and Race, March 19, 2003–April 8, 2004

Race	March 9, 2003 May 1, 2003 War Phase	May 2, 2003 April 8, 2004 Occupation Phase	March 19, 2003 April 8, 2004 Total Iraq Conflict
White	84	361	445
	60.9%	71.5%	69.2%
Black	26	67	90
	16.7%	13.3%	14.0%
Hispanic	22	50	72
	15.9%	9.9%	11.2%
Other	9	27	36
	6.5%	5.3%	5.6%
N	138	505	643
Average casualties per day	3.1	1.6	1.8

Source: U.S. Department of Defense

U.S. helicopters and the commencement of an aggressive U.S. counteroffensive dubbed Operation Iron Hammer— and climbed again to 3.5 in April 2004 as U.S. forces confronted large-scale Shiite uprisings in several cities.

Table 32.2 summarizes the racial distribution of casualties for the distinct phases analyzed, and for the conflict as a whole.

Analysis

TOTAL CASUALTIES

We begin with an overview of casualties in the Iraq conflict. Table 32.3 presents the racial distribution of total U.S. casualties incurred over the entire period from March 19, 2003, to April 8, 2004. These are compared to the racial composition of the age-appropriate U.S. population and selected military populations. I first calculate chi squared (χ^2) values to assess whether the observed casualty distribution differs significantly from the comparison population. I then conduct standard-error-of-proportions tests to determine whether the observed proportion in each racial category differed significantly from the proportion in the comparison population.

Table 32.3 indicates that the percentage of total black casualties (14.0) exceeds the percentage of blacks in the eighteen- to thirty-four-year-old U.S. population (13.4). The same is true of whites (69.2, compared to

63.9). Hispanics are comparatively underrepresented at 11.1 percent. If the Iraq conflict had ended on April 8, 2004, one could accurately state that whites and blacks disproportionately bore the burden of the fighting (assuming no measurement error of race).

However, the observed proportion of black deaths is not significantly different from the expected number of casualties based on the percentage of blacks in the U.S. population, and falls significantly below their share of the overall military. The data do not suggest disproportionately high black casualties, either going forward in the Iraq conflict or in unspecified future military engagements. The values of χ^2 thus far do not support hypothesis 3; the racial distribution of total casualties does not resemble the active-duty military, but instead looks like the racial makeup of ground combat troops. Compared to the active-duty military, whites and Hispanics are overrepresented, while blacks are underrepresented.

CASUALTIES BY PHASES OF THE CONFLICT

Table 32.4 shows the racial distribution of casualties by the two phases of the conflict, compared to the age-appropriate U.S. population and selected military populations. As predicted by hypothesis 1, the data suggest that the tactical conditions faced by U.S. military personnel influence the racial composition of casualties. The distributions

Table 32.3 Percentage of Total Iraq Conflict Casualties by Race, Compared to Military and U.S. Populations, March 19, 2003–April 8, 2004 (N = 643)

| | % of total deaths | Comparison population | | |
		U.S. population, ages 18–34	All active-duty military	Army/Marine Corps combat personnel
White	69.2	63.9**	65.2*	68.4
Black	14.0	13.4	20.3**	15.2
Hispanic	11.1	16.2**	8.6*	10.7
Other	5.6	6.5	5.9	5.7
χ2 (df = 3)		13.6**	19.2**	0.84

Two-tailed *p* values: * < .05, ** < .01

Note: For U.S. totals, Hispanics may be of any race

differ between the war and occupation phases but the relationship is weak ($\chi^2 = 6.5$; $df = 3$; $p = .09$). This unanticipated similarity stems from the fluctuations in combat intensity during the latter phase (discussed below).

Looking at casualties in the war phase (panel A), hypothesis 2 receives mixed support. Comparing χ^2 values, casualties resemble ground combat troops more than the military as a whole. However, the racial distribution of deaths differs dramatically from the expected outcome. Compared to their representation among Army and Marine combat troops, whites are underrepresented by about 11 percent of the expected value ($p = .056$). Black

casualty figures exceed their percentage of ground combat troops by about 10 percent, but not significantly so.

By far, the most striking support for hypothesis 2 is the finding that the casualty rate among Hispanics during the war is 49 percent higher than their representation in the ground combat forces would suggest ($p = .002$), and 85 percent higher than Hispanics on active duty ($p = .044$). As expected, Hispanic war casualties fall below their portion of the U.S. population (though this may reflect circumstances that effectively render many young, non-English-speaking Hispanics ineligible for military service).

Table 32.4 Percentage of Iraq Conflict Casualties by Race and Phase of Conflict, Compared to Military and U.S. Populations

| | | % of deaths | Comparison population | | |
			U.S. population, ages 18–34	All active-duty military	Army/Marine Corps combat personnel
Panel A:	White	60.9	63.9	65.2	68.4 †
March 19–May 1,	Black	16.7	13.4	20.3	15.2
2003 war deaths	Hispanic	15.9	16.2	8.6**	10.7*
(N = 138)	Other	6.5	6.5	5.9	5.7
	χ^2 (df = 3)		1.30	9.98*	5.13
Panel B:	White	71.4	63.9**	65.2**	68.4
May 2, 2003–	Black	13.3	13.4	20.3**	15.2
April 8, 2004					
occupation deaths	Hispanic	9.9	16.2**	8.6	10.7
(N = 505)	Other	5.3	6.5	5.9	5.7
	χ^2 (df = 3)		17.8**	16.5**	2.3

Two-tailed *p* values: † < .10, * < .05, ** < .01

For U.S. totals, Hispanics may be of any race

As was observed in Table 32.3, panel B of Table 32.4 provides little solid support for hypothesis 3. Again, casualties more closely resemble ground combat forces than they do the active-duty military as a whole. Compared to active-duty forces, whites are overrepresented by 10 percent ($p = .003$), but blacks are unexpectedly underrepresented by about 34 percent ($p < .001$). Nor are black casualties disproportionately high compared to the black U.S. population. However, the observed pattern for Hispanics again conforms with hypothesized outcomes; the percentage of Hispanic casualties drops dramatically after May 1, 2003, and is consistent with their presence in both military populations.

We may largely exclude the rank distribution of casualties as an explanation for the observed racial patterns. As Table 32.5 shows, Hispanics are overrepresented in the enlisted ranks of the Army and Marine Corps, blacks are overrepresented among noncommissioned officers (NCOs), and whites are overrepresented among officers. Table 32.6 further reveals that enlisted personnel made up the majority of casualties in the war and occupation phases, but their proportions did not appreciably vary, nor did they differ significantly from the Army and Marines as a whole. NCOs saw significantly lower-than-expected casualties during the war phase, while officer deaths were higher. Neither of these patterns supports the contention that the unexpectedly high rate of Hispanic war casualties reflects an inordinately high number of

junior or senior enlisted casualties, nor did the high casualty rate among officers in the war phase translate into appreciably higher white casualties.

CASUALTIES IN HIGH-INTENSITY AND LOW-INTENSITY ENVIRONMENTS

Since the data are not crosstabulated by military specialties, it is not clear that combat troops suffer disproportionately high casualties in both periods. Furthermore, given their high propensity for combat specialties, the low rate of white deaths prior to May 1, 2003, contradicts this explanation, as does the low rate of Hispanic casualties after May 2. The proportional increase in white casualties during the occupation may reflect an increased involvement of reserve and National Guard Units drawn from regions with relatively small minority populations; the drop in Hispanic casualties coincides with the virtual withdrawal of Marine Corps units from the combat theater until late March 2004. More than half of all Marine casualties occurred prior to May 2, compared to less than one-eighth of Army casualties ($\chi^2 = 107.3$). About 29 percent of all Hispanic casualties were Marines, and about 62 percent of Hispanic Marine fatalities occurred prior to May 2. There may also be race-specific differences in the nonhostile death rate within similar types of units and occupational specialties, although it is difficult to speculate why this would be the case.

Table 32.5 Race Distribution of Ranks (Percentages), Compared to Total Army and Marine Corps Personnel

	Enlisted	NCO	Officer	Total Army and Marines
White	61.1	53.3	79.4	61.0
Black	21.1	31.3	10.8	23.3
Hispanic	12.3	8.8	4.5	10.0
Other	5.4	6.5	5.3	5.8

Source: U.S. Department of Defense

Table 32.6 Percentage of Iraq Conflict Casualties by Rank, Compared to Total Army and Marine Corps Personnel

	Total deaths	Pre May 1 war deaths	Post May 1 occupation deaths	Total Army and Marines
Enlisted	54.1	55.1	53.9	52.1
NCO	31.7	25.4*	33.5	35.2
Officer	14.2	19.6*	12.7	12.7
χ^2 ($df = 2$)	1.40	9.10*	0.50	
n	643	138	505	

Two-tailed p values: † $< .10$, * $< .05$, ** $< .01$

More likely, using May 1 as the cutoff point between the war and occupation is a somewhat arbitrary delineation, even if the overall U.S. mission effectively changed thereafter. As noted above, U.S. troops faced guerrilla tactics such as suicide bombs during the invasion, and continued to pursue enemy formations after the declared end of major combat operations. The point is underscored by comparing the racial distribution of casualties to the intensity of contact with enemy forces. Figure 32.1 shows the racial distribution of casualties incurred during each period for which DIOR/SIAD provided cumulative totals and the average daily casualties.[34] Hypothesis 4 receives mixed support. While there is evidence of temporal variation, in general, the proportion of white casualties tends to fall as the average daily casualty rate rises. Again, the patterns observed for the Hispanic group conform most closely to expected outcomes. Hispanic deaths tend to increase with average daily casualties; the same is apparent for blacks, though in a seemingly less linear fashion.

The racial distributions of the war phase and the periods in which U.S. forces mounted major counterinsurgency efforts (Oct. 23–Nov. 20, 2003, and March 19–April 8, 2004) are essentially the same ($\chi^2 = 4.2$, $df = 6$). Taken together, these high-intensity periods differ significantly from the other periods as a whole ($\chi^2 = 13.9$, $df = 3$, $p = .003$). These results can not be easily dismissed with reference to the small sample sizes in the periods after August 2003 (which could result in fewer observed minority cases). Whites are overrepresented in the fourth bar of the chart, which has the most cases of all the periods.

In short, the racial similarities between casualties and the military overall can be expected to ebb and flow with the intensity of the conditions on the ground, if not necessarily in ways predicted by existing theory.

Discussion: Toward a New Discussion of Race and National Sacrifice

Concerns over the racial composition of the U.S. armed forces reflect that society's ambivalence about the voluntary basis of military service itself. On one hand, deep and widespread antipathy towards compulsory military service has lingered since the Vietnam War. On the other hand, national security is a collective good. In a nation with tremendous income and wealth inequalities, many are uncomfortable with the idea that individuals who voluntarily provide this good do so in large part because they face comparatively few vocational and economic options. The recognition that many volunteers also come from historically disadvantaged racial and ethnic groups compounds this discomfort.

It is recognized here that death and physical injury represent merely the worst among a range of hardships faced by individuals at war. Separation from loved ones, loss of income (for many reservists and National Guard members), strained personal relations, and long-term psychological or emotional problems are all inequitably experienced when the military does not resemble society as a whole. Yet the results of this analysis conditionally support Moskos and Butler's (1996) position that African

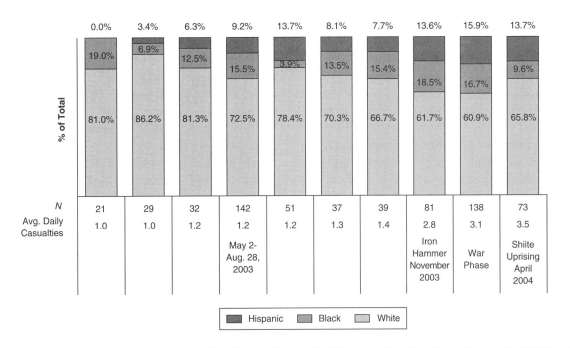

Figure 32.1 Percentage of Iraq Conflict Casualties by Race and Average Daily Casualties

Americans do not disproportionately bear the *ultimate* burden of U.S. military operations, nor do other racial or ethnic minorities. Whites comprise the majority of combat casualties, in keeping with their majority status on active duty and their high representation in U.S. Army and Marine Corps combat specialties.

Binkin's proposition that combat casualties ultimately reflect the conditions faced by the units in the fight also receives some support from the temporal variation in casualty patterns, and remains a useful theoretical starting point. However, conceptualizing and measuring these conditions require further analytical effort and richer data than were employed in this study. Additionally, while the data indicate that tactical conditions within different conflict environments produce different patterns of casualties, a too-narrow focus on white-black racial dichotomies contributed to erroneous predictions about relative military burdens. Blacks make up a larger percentage of the war deaths than they do the U.S. population between the ages eighteen to thirty-four, but nonetheless fall within an expected range. In the occupation phase, they are underrepresented compared to the active-duty military.

If any group of minority service members faces an elevated risk of casualties, it is Hispanics under high-intensity combat conditions. Observed patterns of Hispanic casualties conform well to hypothesized outcomes, and generally follow what has been traditionally expected for whites: when U.S. tactics dictate a more active, aggressive role in finding and attacking enemy targets, Hispanics incur casualties in excess of their participation in ground combat units. In less intense environments, the Hispanic casualty rate more closely resembles their presence in the military as a whole. Explaining these stark patterns will require studies that explicitly theorize the Hispanic military experience, rather than rely on insights from the white and African American experiences. If such research properly incorporates themes such as culture, geography, citizenship, and socioeconomics, bringing Hispanics into the debates about military benefits and burdens may shed some unique light on who chooses to serve, in what capacity, and why. Given that Hispanics now collectively comprise the largest minority group in the United States, such a research agenda is long overdue.

Notwithstanding the evidence that whites have borne excessive casualties in U.S. post-Vietnam military operations, it is difficult to ignore the high percentage of deaths incurred by minorities during the heaviest fighting in Iraq. Until the urban battles that characterized the Shiite uprisings of April 2004, few would have denied that the over-throw of the Hussein regime involved far greater risks for U.S. troops than the subsequent occupation. The

higher-than-expected minority death rate under conditions where U.S. ground forces saw the most intense and prolonged large-scale fighting in over a decade poses a troubling puzzle that will only be solved when more information on individual casualties becomes available to researchers.

The racial breakdown of casualties may in fact measure the offensive capability of U.S. forces relative to Iraqi defenders. Deaths among (disproportionately white) combat troops may have been minimal in the war phase, coupled with an unexpectedly high number of (disproportionately black) noncombat support casualties. Assaulting predetermined targets in force and being supported by considerable suppressive firepower (aircraft, artillery, mortars, cruise missiles, etc.) may enhance the survivability of combat-trained and equipped troops, while simultaneously contributing to conditions that endanger less-well-trained and less-well-armed noncombat personnel who support them. When contact with enemy forces becomes incidental and unexpected—as occurs frequently in the occupation phase—the advantage afforded to trained combat troops may diminish. Yet this explanation runs counter to an official army review of its conduct in the war phase, which documented shortages of both support troops and materièl through the opening offensives.[35] It also fails to explain the high Hispanic death rate during the war phase. For now, it is premature to conclude that minority combat troops were placed in inordinately risky situations—by mistakes of omission or commission—or that noncombat troops providing logistical support were inadequately prepared for the fluid violence that characterized the invasion phase of the Iraq conflict.

It is impossible to speculate confidently about the character of the U.S. military's future combat engagements. Yet as ongoing conflicts ebb and flow and other potentially hostile situations develop, understanding which segments of society will pay the ultimate price of U.S. foreign policy decisions can facilitate honest debates about the equity of our system of military service. The current Iraq conflict provides a case in point. Now that Iraq's sovereignty has formally passed back to Iraqi officials, the support mission of the U.S. military may involve intermittent combat engagements that claim the lives of personnel on a steady, if somewhat small-scale, basis. Under such circumstances, expectations of disproportionate minority casualties would be unwarranted. The national dialogue on the equity of military service may shift back to the social process that impels whites—particularly those from the lower socioeconomic strata—into the ranks. However, should U.S. troops resume large-scale offensive campaigns against a number of seemingly growing and increasingly well-organized insurgent threats, casualties among blacks and Hispanics may creep up to a point where the fairness of military sacrifice again becomes an uncomfortable racial issue.

On a final note, the findings of this study are not germane only to the military experiences of the United States. As of 2000, several advanced industrial democracies with long histories of conscription had abandoned the practice in favor of voluntary service, or had plans to phase it out by 2004.[36] Some nations with rising immigration rates have experienced increased racial and ethnic diversity in their volunteer militaries,[37] while others (such as Spain and France) actively recruit foreign volunteers. At the same time, conflicts such as Kosovo in 1999 and contemporary operations in Afghanistan and Iraq have subjected the militaries of many nations to their first hostile fire in decades (for example, coalition casualties in Iraq include personnel from Italy, Spain, Poland, Denmark, and Bulgaria). To the degree that ethnic enlistment patterns are similarly structured by socioeconomic factors, debates about military equity and recruitment policies in the U.S. case may presage similar dialogues elsewhere.

Notes

1. See, for example, table D-17, U.S. Department of Defense, *Population Representation in the Military Services, Fiscal Year 2001* (Washington, DC: Office of the Under Secretary of Defense, Personnel and Readiness, 2003).

2. See Martin Binkin, *Who Will Fight the Next War?* (Washington, DC: The Brookings Institution, 1993); Morris Janowitz, "The Social Demography of the All Volunteer Armed Force," *Annals of the American Academy of Political and Social Science* 406 (March 1973): 86-93; Charles C. Moskos, John Sibley Butler, Alan Ned Sabrosky, and Alvin J. Schexnider, "Symposium: Race and the United States Military," *Armed Forces & Society* 6, 4 (Summer 1980): 586-613; Martin Binkin, Mark J. Eitelberg, Alvin J. Schexnider, and Marvin M. Smith, *Blacks and the Military* (Washington, DC: The Brookings Institution, 1982); Robert K. Fullinwider, "Choice, Justice, and Representation," in *Who Defends America? Race, Sex, and Class in the Armed Forces*, ed. Edwin Dorn (Washington, DC: Joint Center for Political Studies Press, 1989); Ruben Castaneda, "War Would Hurt Minorities, Activists Charge," *Washington Post*, November 9, 1990; Juan Williams, "Race and the War in the Persian Gulf," *Washington Post*, January 20, 1991; David J. Armor, "Race and Gender in the U.S. Military," *Armed Forces & Society* 23, 1 (Fall 1996): 7-27; Andrew Gumbel, "Pentagon Targets Latinos and Mexicans to Man the Front Lines in War on Terror," *The Independent*, September 10, 2003, 11.

3. See, for example, Institute of Medicine, *Unequal Treatment: Confronting Racial and Ethnic Disparities in Health Care*, ed. Brian D. Smedley, Adrienne Y. Stith, and Alan R. Nelson (Washington, DC: National Academies Press, 2002).

4. Binkin, *Who Will Fight the Next War?*; Binkin et al., Blacks and the Military.

5. See Margaret C. Harrell, Sheila Nataraj Kirby, Jennifer Sloan, Clifford M. Graf, Christopher J. McKelvey, and Jerry M. Sollinger, *Barriers to Minority Participation in Special Operations*

Forces (Santa Monica, CA: Rand, 1999); Department of Defense, *Population Representation*, table B-30.

6. Binkin, *Who Will Fight the Next War?*

7. Charles C. Moskos, "The American Dilemma in Uniform: Race in the Armed Forces," *Annals of the American Academy of Political and Social Science* 406 (March 1973): 94-106.

8. Castaneda, "War Would Hurt Minorities"; Williams, "Race and the War in the Persian Gulf."

9. Charles C. Moskos and John Sibley Butler, *All That We Can Be: Black Leadership and Racial Integration the Army Way* (New York: Twentieth Century Fund, 1996).

10. Ibid., 9.

11. In fact, during the Persian Gulf War, Gen Colin L. Powell, then Chairman of the Joint Chiefs of Staff, publicly expressed disdain for such policies, asking rhetorically, "if the whole force accepts casualties, what would you wish me to do? Move the blacks from the positions they're in so that they will have a lower percentage of casualties?" Cited in Arch Puddington, "Black Leaders vs. Desert Storm," *Commentary* 91, 5 (1991):28–34.

12. Binkin, *Who Will Fight the Next War?*, p. 86. See also Binkin et al., *Blacks and the Military*.

13. For general discussions of these categories, see M.L.R. Smith, "Guerrillas in the Mist: Reassessing Strategy and Low Intensity Warfare," *Review of International Studies* 29 (2003):19-37; J.J.A. Wallace, "Manoeuvre Theory in Operations Other Than War," *Journal of Strategic Studies* 19, 4 (1996): 207-226; Loren B. Thompson, "Low Intensity Conflict: An Overview," *Low-Intensity Conflict: The Pattern of Warfare in the Modern World*, ed. Loren B. Thompson (Lexington, MA: Lexington Books, 1989); Harry G. Summers, "A War is a War is War is a War," ibid. These categories are not exhaustive of all types of organized armed conflict, nor are they representative of all combatants' perspectives. They are theoretically rooted in the study of foreign policy options within a larger geopolitical context, and presuppose states' autonomous capacity for military action. In the contemporary context, the distinction is therefore most appropriate to interstate wars and the expeditionary activities of military and industrial powers.

14. The distinction between high- and low-intensity environments is seldom neat, and any particular conflict may contain elements of both types. For example, few hostile engagements have exhibited the clear distinction between war and operations other than war observed in the Second World War and the subsequent occupations of Japan and Germany. In Algeria during the 1950s and '60s, French military forces performed gendarmerie, occupation, and counterinsurgency duties in urban areas such as Algiers, while mounting conventional mountain and desert offensives against insurgents in the countryside. Thus the character of conflict may vary across both time and space.

15. See Harrell et al., *Barriers to Minority Participation*.

16. In 1983, blacks made up 18.9 percent of the U.S. Marine Corps, compared to 28.7 percent of the Army. The corresponding percentages in 2001 were 14.9 and 26.2, respectively.

17. In fact, looking at these two engagements alone, African American casualties comprise about 17 percent of the total, a figure that is significantly larger than the 13.1 percent of the 1990 population of eighteen- to thirty-four-year-olds cited by Moskos and Butler for comparison ($z = 2.39, p = .017$), but still smaller than their presence in the ranks.

18. See Jerald G. Bachman, David R. Segal, Peter Freedman-Doan, and Patrick M. O'Malley, "Who Chooses Military Service? Correlates of Propensity and Enlistment in the U.S. Armed Forces," *Military Psychology* 12, 1 (2000): 1–30; David R. Segal, Thomas

J. Burns, William W. Falk, Michael P. Silver, and Bam Dev Sharda, "The All-Volunteer Force in the 1970s," *Social Science Quarterly* 79, 2 (1998):390–411; Jay D. Teachman, Vaughn R.A. Call, and Mady W. Segal, "The Selectivity of Military Enlistment," *Journal of Political and Military Sociology* 21 (1993):287–309; Charles Dale and Curtis Gilroy, "Determinants of Enlistments: A Macroeconomic Time-Series View," *Armed Forces & Society* 10, 2 (1984): 192–210; Charles Brown, "Military Enlistments: What Can We Learn From Geographic Variation?" *The American Economic Review* 75, 1 (1985): 228–234.

19. Moskos and Butler, *All That We Can Be*; Moskos, "The American Dilemma."

20. Michael J. Wilson, James B. Greenlees, Tracey Hagerty, D. Wayne Hintze, and Lerome D. Lehnus, *Youth Attitude Tracking Study: 1998 Propensity and Advertising Report* (Arlington, VA: Defense Manpower Data Center, 2000).

21. Binkin, *Who Will Fight the Next War?*; Moskos and Butler, *All That We Can Be*; Brenda L. Moore, "African-American Women in the U.S. Military," *Armed Forces & Society* 17, 3 (1991): 363–384.

22. However, see Javier Hernandez, "An Exploratory Study of Hispanic Officer Recruiting in the Mexican-American Community of South Central Los Angeles: Implications for the Officer Corps of the Future" (master's thesis, Naval Postgraduate School, 2003).

23. U.S. Bureau of the Census, *Statistical Abstract of the United States 2002*. CD-ROM.

24. Wilson et al., *Youth Attitude Tracking Study*.

25. DoD, *Population Representation in the Military Services*.

26. Wilson et al., *Youth Attitude Tracking Study*; see also Pew Hispanic Center, "Fact Sheet: Hispanics in the Military," March 27, 2003.

27. Hispanics with low test-taking acumen may also be less likely to apply for enlistment. Hispanic applicants for enlistment in 2001 were 2.6 times more likely than whites to score in the two lowest AFQT categories. Black applicants were 3.1 times more likely than whites to score in these categories. See *Population Representation in the Military Services*.

28. U.S. Department of Defense (DIOR/SIAD), "U.S. Military Casualties—Operation Iraqi Freedom," http://web1.whs.osd.mil/mmid/mmidhome.htm, accessed April 12, 2004.

29. The category is retained for completeness. Nonetheless, the lack of theoretically developed propositions prevents any in-depth analysis of "other races" throughout this study.

30. See Global Security.org, "U.S. Forces Order of Battle, http://www.globalsecurity.org/ military/ops/iraq_orbat.htm, accessed December 2, 2003. See also Eric Schmitt and Thom Shanker, "Reserve and Guard Ordered to Alert More Troops for Iraq," *New York Times*, November 20, 2003.

31. Combat personnel comprise less than 17 percent of the active-duty enlisted members and noncommissioned officers. The category applies only to these ranks, which make up about 84 percent of the active-duty forces.

32. Given the breadth and scale of the mission in Iraq, and the diversity of military units participating, there is little reason to expect that the racial composition of U.S. forces there differs from the active-duty forces as a whole. One mediating factor might be the regional character of reservists and National Guard units in the Iraq theater.

33. A second measure of combat intensity, the ratio of hostile to nonhostile casualties, was also tested. Results were similar. The analysis below is therefore limited to average daily casualties, which are subject to less measurement ambiguity and probably more reliable.

34. These data are not available on the DIOR/SIAD website, but were provided to the author by Roger V. Jorstad, Director of the Statistical Information Analysis Division. The pattern is similar when the number of average daily casualties is substituted with the alternate measure of conflict intensity, the ratio of hostile to nonhostile casualties.

35. Eric Schmitt, "Army Study of Iraq War Details a 'Morass' of Supply Shortages," *New York Times*, February 3, 2004, A1.

36. Christopher Jehn and Zachary Selden, "The End of Conscription in Europe?" *Contemporary Economic Policy* 20, 2 (2002): 93–100.

37. See, for example, Christopher Dandeker and David Mason, "The British Armed Services and the Participation of Minority Ethnic Communities: From Equal Opportunities to Diversity?" *Sociological Review* 49, 2 (2001): 219–235; and Christopher Dandeker and David Mason, "Diversifying the Uniform? The Participation of Minority Ethnic Personnel in the British Armed Services," *Armed Forces & Society* 29, 4 (2003): 481-507; Catherine Miller, "The Death of Conscription," *BBC News Online*, June 29, 2001, http://news.bbc.co.uk

Discussion Questions

1. Though African Americans are overrepresented in the U.S. Armed Forces, their casualty rates are not as high as white soldiers. Discuss why, according to Gifford, this disparity exists.

   Gifford's analysis reveals how whites comprise the majority of combat casualties, consistent with their majority status on active duty and U.S. Army and Marine Corps combat specialties. In contrast, African Americans and other racial or ethnic minorities are assigned to non-combat support units, at lower risk to combat injuries.

2. Examine the enlistment and combat experiences of Hispanics compared to other racial groups. What differences or similarities can you identify?

   Gifford explains how among U.S. 16- to 24-year-olds with no prior military service, Hispanics show the highest propensity to enlist in the armed forces, even when controlling for educational attainment. Hispanics are more similar to whites in their attitudes towards pay, job training, educational benefits, and the life-threatening nature of military service. Hispanics under high-intensity combat situations face an elevated risk of causalities when compared to other minority service members.

INTERNET RESOURCES

Part I . The Sociology of Social Problems

The Martin Luther King Research and Education Institute

http://www.stanford.edu/group/King/index.htm

The institute sponsors the MLK Papers Project, a collection of all his speeches, sermons, and articles. The institute's Web site also features materials from the Liberation Curriculum and information on teacher development workshops that utilize online documentary materials concerning nonviolent movements to achieve social justice, transformation, and reconciliation.

American Sociological Association

http://www.asanet.org

A nonprofit national association, the American Sociological Association is dedicated to advancing sociology as a discipline and as a profession serving the public good. From the main page, select "Students" for undergraduate and graduate student materials and links.

Society for the Study of Social Problems

http://www.sssp1.org

The Society for the Study of Social Problems is a nonprofit national association dedicated to promoting and protecting sociological research and teaching on significant problems of social life, to stimulating the application of the scientific method and theory to the study of vital social problems, and to the application of scientific sociological findings to the formulation of social policies.

Part II. The Fragmentation of Social Life

Civic Engagement in America

http://www.bowlingalone.com

This Web site features ongoing research and discussion on social capital in the United States and globally. Several organization and programs are linked, including information from the Saguaro Seminar: Civic Engagement in America, based at the JFK School of Government at Harvard University.

The Story of Stuff

http://www.storyofstuff.com/?gclid=COer1-6Bo5ACFRscawod4TEL7A

Annie Leonard's 20-minute film on the "materials economy" is available from this Web site. In this educational and entertaining piece, Leonard examines the economic, environmental, and personal consequences of all the "stuff" we consume in society.

Part III. The Global Fragmentation of Social Life

Global Policy Forum

http://www.globalpolicy.org

Global Forum is a nonprofit organization, with consultative status at the United Nations. Its goal is to "promote accountability of global decisions. Educate and mobilize for global citizen participation, and advocate on vital issues of international peace and justice." The site contains a number of articles and resources about current global events, economic and social policies, and data on varied aspects of globalization such as demographic change, economic integration and technology, and cultural change. The Web site also includes links to other important sites and resources including the International Forum on Globalization and the World Watch Institute.

International Organization for Migration

http://www.iom.int/jahia/jsp/index.jsp

Since its establishment in 1951, International Organization for Migration (IOM) has been the leading intergovernmental organization in the field of migration. Working with more than 100 member states and countries, IOM is dedicated to promoting human and orderly migration. The organization posts migration news, information, and research on its Web site.

Migration Policy Institute

http://www.migrationpolicy.org

Migration Policy Institute is a nonpartisan, nonprofit organization dedicated to the study of the movement of people across the globe. This Web site offers research and reports on issues and policies related to immigration and immigrants. In addition, the Migration Policy Institute "data hub" provides data about historical and contemporary migration flows and trends.

Part IV. Media

Adbusters

http://www.adbusters.org/home

Based in Vancouver, British Columbia, Canada, Adbusters represents "a global network of artists, activists, writers, pranksters, students, educators and entrepreneurs who want to advance the new social activist movement of the information age." The aim of the organization is to "topple existing power structures and forge a major shift in the way we will live in the 21st century." The site includes information on the organization's magazine, as well as on its advocacy programs.

Project Censored

http://www.projectcensored.org

Project Censored is a media research group based at Sonoma State University. The group of faculty, students, and community members publishes an annual list of 25 news stories of social significance that have been overlooked, underreported or self-censored by the major national news media.

Part V. Work

U.S. Department of Labor Bureau Statistics

http://www.bls.gov

This Web site provides information about such labor and economic topics as wages, benefits, and unemployment rates. It is an excellent source of information for those interested in finding out about the state of the U.S. labor force.

Human Trafficking.org

http://www.humantrafficking.org

The Web site brings governments and NGOs (nongovernment organizations) in East Asia and Pacific together to "cooperate and learn from each other's experiences in their efforts to combat human trafficking." The site provides country-specific information, such as national laws and action plans on human trafficking and contact information for governmental agencies. Information from the United States is also available from the site.

Economic Policy Institute

http://www.epi.org

The Economic Policy Institute is a "nonprofit, nonpartisan think tank that seeks to broaden the public debate about strategies to achieve a prosperous and fair economy." Included on this Web site are data and reports about some of the most pressing economic issues facing individuals and families today, including "issue guidelines" on topics such as the living wage, offshore production, unemployment, social security, and welfare.

Part VI. Education

Department of Education – No Child Left Behind

http://www.ed.gov/nclb/landing.jhtml

Legislation, regulations, and research related to No Child Left Behind (NCLB) are available on this Department of Education Web site. Reading and math proficiency test results are reported for all states, including current NCLB programming and budgeting information.

Global Education Database

http://qesdb.cdie.org/ged/index.html

This site is sponsored by the Office of Education of the U.S. Agency for International Development (USAID). The site contains a wealth of information about education across the globe and international education statistics compiled by the UNESCO Institute for Statistics and the Demographic and Health Surveys (DHS).

Part VII. Health Care

National Center for Health Statistics Fast Stats from A to Z

http://www.cdc.gov/nchs/fastats/Default.htm

This Web site provides statistical data about the health status of people living in the U.S. Topics are organized alphabetically and include links to state information.

World Health Organization (WHO)

http://www.who.int/topics/en

Serving as the public health arm of the United Nations, the World Health Organization directs health programs and policies globally. The organization collects statistical data about global health, all of which is available at this site.

Part VIII. Poverty and Social Welfare Policy

World Bank Poverty Net

http://web.worldbank.org/WBSITE/EXTERNAL/TOPICS/EXTPOVERTY/0,,menuPK:336998~pagePK:149018~piPK:149093~theSitePK:336992,00.html

The World Bank is an international organization providing financial and technical assistance to developing countries throughout the world. Through Poverty Net, the organization "provides an introduction to key issues as well as in-depth information on poverty measurement, monitoring, analysis, and on poverty reduction strategies for researchers and practitioners."

U.S. Census Bureau Poverty Statistics

http://www.census.gov/hhes/www/poverty/poverty.html

This Web site provides historical and current data about poverty in the United States. The Bureau's most recent poverty document is available at this site (*Income, Poverty, and Health Insurance in the United States 2006*).

Area Poverty Research Centers

http://wcpc.washington.edu - University of Washington (West)

http://www.ukcpr.org - University of Kentucky (South)

http://www.irp.wisc.edu/home.htm - University of Wisconsin (Midwest)

These three poverty centers are sponsored by the Office of the Assistant Secretary for Planning and Evaluation (ASPE) in the U.S. Department of Health and Human Services. Each center supports research on the causes and consequences of poverty and inequality. Regional data and publications are available from each Web site. Each also posts information on current events, workshops, and seminars.

Part IX. Criminal Justice

Bureau of Justice Statistics (BJS)

http://www.ojp.usdoj.gov/bjs/welcome.html

The primary source for U.S. criminal justice statistics, the Bureau of Justice Statistics provides current and historical data on crime, criminal offenders, victims of crimes, and the operation of the U.S. justice system. Statistical information can be accessed by selecting topics from the BJS home page.

Youth Gang Prevention Initiative

http://ojjdp.ncjrs.gov/programs/antigang

This is the main Web site for the Department of Justice's Youth Gang Prevention Initiative. The site includes information on current Department of Justice research, program initiatives, and anti-gang strategies.

Part X. Environment

Environmental Protection Agency Global Warming Site

http://yosemite.epa.gov/oar/glob alwarming.nsf/content/index.html

The EPA Web site provides background on global climate change. It also includes suggestions on what you can do to help curb it.

The Simple Living Network

http://www.simpleliving.net/main

The Simple Living Network provides "resources, tools, examples and contacts for conscious, simple, healthy and restorative living." This for-profit organization posts information on how to access a number of (free or paid) resources to help you explore ways and thoughts about simple living (also known as voluntary simplicity).

Friends of the Earth

http://www.foe.org/index.html

Friends of the Earth is an "international network of grassroots groups in 70 countries" dedicated to efforts to create a "more healthy, just world." The Web site provides information and updates on environmental issues, as well as environmental campaigns.

Part XI. War and Violence

Amnesty International

http://www.amnesty.org

Amnesty International is a "worldwide movement of people who campaign for internationally recognized human rights for all." The organization works to improve human rights through campaigning and international solidarity. Their Web site offers in-depth reports on a wide range of issues and countries, appeals for action, and international campaigns.

Iraq Body Count

http://www.iraqbodycount.org

Motivated by the belief that "war is an abomination whose defining characteristic is the organised killing of humans" and that the "human costs of war must be recorded," this site documents the number of violent civilian deaths since the 2003 military intervention in Iraq. Its public database includes "deaths caused by US-led coalition forces and paramilitary or criminal attacks by others."

Women Watch

http://www.un.org/womenwatch

WomenWatch provides information and resources on the promotion of gender equality and the empowerment of women "throughout the United Nations system, including the United Nations Secretariat, regional commissions, funds, programmes, specialized agencies and academic and research institutions." Informational topics include women and violence, women and poverty, women and armed conflict, the human rights of women, trafficking, and women and peace and security.

INDEX

A&P, 18
ABC, 83–84
Abernathy, Ralph, 16
Abramovitz, Mimi, 198
Absolute poverty, 119
Academic Performance Index, 304–306
Accumulation by dispossession, 55–56, 59
Adoption and Safe Families
        Act (ASFA), 203
Advertising
    brand symbolism, 45–46
    pharmaceuticals, 179–180
    sex in, 97
    social dynamics force, 43
    underage girls in, 100–101
Affirmative action, 29–30
Africa
    debt-to-GNP, 73
    migrant workers from, 72
    See also specific countries
African Americans
    air pollution risks, 306–307
    barrier-beliefs study, 142–148
    challenges (1960s), 19–21
    combat causalities, 337–339
    families, 7, 14
    hip-hop culture, 267–268
    HIV/AIDS, 255
    immigrant labor and, 137
    imprisonment of, 252
    income inequality, 120–121
    inferiority, 14
    military, 336–339
    poverty, 62
    in prison, 256, 260
    protests, 21–22
    southern society architecture, 16–17
    urban displacement of, 268–269
    welfare reform and, 207
    working poor, 122
Age
    child labor by, 227 *table*, 228–229
    crime victims, 248–249
Agriculture, 69–70, 129–130
Aguilera, Christina, 99
Aid to Dependent Children (ADC), 199
Aid to Families with Dependent Children
        (AFDC), 11, 199

Air pollution study
    data sources, 302–303
    methods, 302–303
    overview, 302
    policy implications, 306–307
    results, 303–306
Air traffic controllers, 54
Allbaugh, Joseph, 291
Allen, Paul, 28
Allende, Salvador, 50
Amazon.com, 94
American Federation of Television and Radio
        Artists (AFTRA), 107
America Online (AOL), 94
American Chamber of Commerce, 52
American Dream, 34, 318
American exceptionalism, 314
Anomic societies, 318–319
Anti-Slavery International, 127
Apple, Michael, 162
Aquino, Corazon, 75
Arafat, Yasser, 265
Argentina
    artists from, 187–188
    military takeover, 51
    neoliberal policies in, 55
Aristide, Jean-Bertrand, 266
Armed forces
    African Americans in,
        336–339
    Latinos in, 339–340
    racial composition, 336
    volunteers, 338–339
Army Corps of Engineers, 290
Arnold, Matthew, 50
Asia
    Americas from, 37
    labor-exporting programs,
        74–75
    neoliberalism in, 55
    See also specific countries
Asian economic crisis, 57
Association of Community Organizations for Reform
        Now (ACORN), 292
AstraZeneca, 173
AT&T, 79, 89
Audit culture, 165–166
Aufderheide, Patricia, 84

Baby Phat, 100
Bagdikian, Ben, 92–93
Baker, Carroll, 98
Ballmer, Steve, 28
Bambaata, Afrika, 267
Bangladesh
    child labor in, 229–235
    foreign exchange in, 73
    immigrants from, 325, 328–332
    labor-exporting program, 75
Barbour, Haley, 292
Barilli, Ademar, 128–129
Barrymore, Drew, 98
Baycol, 178
Beckerman, Gal, 104
Behavior
    class-based, 45
    classroom, 155
    criminal, 245–246
    delinquent, 316–317
    gay, 30
    individualistic, 27
    sexual, 14, 99–101, 255
    young girls, 100–101
Belmont Learning Complex, 306–307
Bilanovic, Branco, 65
Binkin, Martin, 338
Blackness, idea of, 20
Blair, Tony, 276
Blaming the Victim (Ryan), 6–15
Blanco, Kathleen, 292, 295
Boccanero, Silla, 268
Boh Brothers Construction, 291
Bollinger, Donald, 292
Book stores, 94
Bosnia, 126–127
Bourdieu, Pierre, 44
Bozell, L. Brent, 107
Bracero program, 136
Brand symbolism, 45–46
Bremer, Paul, 50
Bretton Woods, 51
Bricoleurs, 324, 328
British Crime Survey (BCS), 248
Brown, Bob, 18
Bryant, William Cullen, 24
Busfield, Joan, 172
Bush, George W.
    defense strategy, 49
    economic inequity views, 153–154
    election of, 253
    Hurricane Katrina, 288, 290
    Iraq War declaration, 341
    poverty views, 151
    terrorist's portrayals by, 325–326
Business processing outsourcing (BPO), 116
Business Round Table, 52–53
Butler, John Sibley, 338

Cable television, 93, 95
Caldwell, Melissa, 107
Calle Trente gang, 264
Cancer risk, 303–306
Canizaro, Joseph C., 292
Cannibalization, 39–40
Capital. See Social capital
Capitalism
    basic goal, 32–33
    class nature of, 66
    classes and, 33–34
    contradictions, 66–67
    corporate, 33
    crony, 290–291
    domination of, 62
    gender inequality and, 35
    golden age, 51
    inequality and, 33
    means of production, 66
    output bias, 38
    racism and, 34–35
    social context, 36
    workers and, 33
    See also Global capitalism
Carbon dioxide, 275
Career-barriers research
    discussion, 147–148
    future research, 148
    hypotheses, 143
    limitations, 148
    measures, 144–145
    methods, 143–144
    overview, 142–143
    procedure, 144
    purpose, 143
    results, 145–147
Castro, Fidel, 22
CBS. See Viacom/CBS merger
Center for Digital Democracy, 107
Center for Responsive Politics, 291
Channel One, 167
Charity Hospital, 291
Cheney, Dick, 291
Chester, Jeffrey, 107
Chief Executive Officers (CEOs), 28
Child abuse
    impact, 159
    incidents, 245
    poverty and, 159
    prevention, 321
Child exclusion, 200–203
Child labor
    by age and gender, 227 table
    defined, 227
    determinants, 232–233
    household means comparisons, 232 table
    literature, 226–227, 232–233
    scale of, 227–228

Child labor (Bangladesh)
   adult work potential, 232–234, 234
   determinants, 233–235
   household contributions, 230
   poverty impact, 234
   preliminary analysis, 229–232
   school attendance and, 229–230
   sectorial distribution, 228–229
   study results, 233–235
Children
   as bricoleurs, 324, 328
   debt slavery and, 127
   delinquent behavior, 316–317
   deprived, 6–7
   drug trials on, 176
   environmental health risks,
      302, 306–307
   environmental trust of, 280–281
   informal learning, 327–328
   news impact on, 324
   pare with parents in prison, 256
   poor, 28, 62–63
   population, 206
   racial discrimination by, 327–328
   September 11 reactions, 324–334
   sexualization of. *See* Sexualized children
   trafficking of, 75–76
   violent. *See* Youth violence
   welfare policy and, 199–203
Children's Defense Fund, 124
Chile
   coup d'état, 51
   neoliberal economics in, 50, 56
China
   gangs in, 265
   GDP, 66
   immigrants from, 34
   population, 65
Chinese triads, 128, 265
Chlorofluorocarbons (CFC), 275–276
Christopher, Warren, 27
Cities
   Black displacement in, 268–269
   as cultural construct, 154
   revitalization efforts, 295–296
   See also Communities
Citizen schools, 168
Citizenship Education Program, 17
Civil rights, 29–30
Clark, Septima, 17
Class inequality
   in education, 152
   by ethnicity, 119–121
   income, 116–118
   poverty, 118–124
   by race, 119–121
   wealth, 118
   working hours, 121–122

Class system. *See* Social classes
Clear, Todd, 252
Clinton, Bill
   disaster management under, 289–290
   telecommunications law, 106
   urban renewal mandate, 296
   volunteerism initiative, 26
   welfare reform by, 205
Clinton, Hillary, 105
Coalition of Immokalee Workers (CIW), 129–130
Cockburn, Andrew, 126
Code Pink, 105
Cohen, Mark, 251–252
Collins, Patricia Hill, 37
Collins, Stephanie Baker, 212
Columbine High School, 314
Comcast, 78
Commission of Safety and Abuse in America's Prison, 260
Committee for a Better New Orleans, 292
Commodities, 44
Common Cause, 106
Common property rights, 56
Communities
   caring, creating, 155–156
   consumerism and, 39–40
   divisions in, 29
   public health, 301
   suburban, 27
   See also Cities
Computer aided design (CAD) systems, 113
Conservative modernization, politics of, 165–168
Consumer debt, 124
Consumer products
   demand for, 113
   health care, 205
   pharmaceuticals, 173, 179
   sexuality and, 95, 97
Consumer society, 38
Consumerism
   community and, 39–40
   defined, 38
   environmental impact, 39
   individualistic model, 43
   norms escalation, 39
   rap music and, 267
   work and spend cycle, 40–41
Consumers
   advertising to, 95, 97, 179–1'60
   debt, 124
   labor of, 166–167
Consumers Union, 107, 108
Consumption
   escalation of, 39
   media influence, 42
   private, 39
   status competition, 41
Cooper, Mark, 107

Copps, Michael J., 108
Core status commodities, 44
Corporate capitalism, 33, 138
Corporations
    agricultural, 129–130
    crimes, 57, 320
    cronyism, 290–292
    downsizing, 34
    employment policies, 114
    fragmentation, 60
    media, 78–80, 84–86, 90–96
    neoliberal ideology, 53–57
    political action committees, 52–53
    taxes, 57
    technology, 70
Cotton, Dorothy, 17
Coyotes. *See* Trafficking mafias
Crime Victims Survey (ICVS), 246
Crimes
    behavior, 245–246
    collateral costs, 251–253
    collateral effects, 250
    drug, 246–247
    fear of, 249–250
    gang-related, 265–270
    harms caused by, 246–248
    insurance against, 246–247
    literature, 251
    patterns, 248–249
    politics of, 253
    predatory economic, 320
    prevention, 245
    punishment effect, 244
    rates, 247 *figure*
    reporting of, 249
    as social problems, 244–246
    victims of, 245–246
Crisis management, 57
Cross-border migrations
    economic links, 69–72
    ethnic networks, 70–72
    governments role, 74–75
    history, 69
    organized efforts, 72–76
    recruitment, 70–72
    rise in, 134
    See also Immigrants
Croteau, David, 78
Cullen, Francis T., 315
Cultural capital, 317
Cultural homicide, 20
Culture
    distribution mechanism, 167
    globalization and, 115–116
    hip-hop, 267
    selection mechanism, 167
Cunningham, Victoria, 105

Dark, Gregory, 98
Darwin, Charles, 12

Dassault, 113
Davis-Bacon Act, 290–291
Deadly Consequences (Prothrow-Stith), 321
Death squads, 266–267
Debt
    credit card, 34, 45
    crisis, 39, 57
    municipal, 53–54
    remittances and, 136
    service, 73
    slavery, 126–128
Deregulation
    goal of, 204
    impact of, 56–57
    media, 83–85
Developing countries
    gangs in, 265
    HIPCs, 73
    migrant labor from, 72–76
    pharmaceutical industry in, 172–173
    social disorganization in, 266
De-Voicing of Society, The (Locke), 27
Devolution, 204
Dialectical materialism, 23
Digital data, 86, 89
Dinovitzer, Robin, 252
Discretion frame, 281
Discrimination, 29, 329–330
Disinvestment process, 321
Diversity, 29–30
Domestic violence, 245
Domination matrix, 37
Dottridge, Mike, 127
Dreier, Peter, 288
Driving under the influence (DUI), 247
Drug crimes
    corporate, 320
    harms caused by, 247
    social view of, 246
Drugs. *See* Pharmaceuticals
Duesenberry, Jim, 41
Dunst, Kirsten, 98
Durbin, Deanna, 98
Durkheim, Emile, 3

Early childhood intervention, 321
Eckbo, Garrett, 5
Economic inequality
    capitalism and, 33, 62–67
    globalization and, 62–67
    insecurity and, 123–124
    military volunteers, 339
    poverty and, 118–124
    violence link, 314–315
    vulnerability, 123–124
    wealth and, 118
Economic threats, 51
Economic Value of Education Questionnaire, 144
Economics
    Chicago school, 50

cross-border migrations, 69–72
fiscal discipline, 53–54
importance, 32
neoliberal policies, 48–60
power, 20
predatory crimes, 320
redistribution, 58
resource alternatives, 39
security, 21
social movements, 57, 59, 67
trickle down, 43–44, 204
Economy
    capitalistic, 23
    deregulation policies, 56–57
    inequality and, 29
    nation-state role, 48
    post–World War II, 112–113
    unemployment and, 5
Edison Schools, 167
Educating the Right Way: Markets, Standards, God, and Inequality (Apple), 162, 164
Education
    academic performance index, 304–306
    achievement gaps, 151–152
    adequate yearly progress, 164
    audit culture, 165–166
    child labor and, 229–230
    class inequality in, 152
    compensatory, 8
    failure, poverty role, 154
    informal, 327–328
    military volunteers, 340
    neoliberal assault on, 53
    policy analysis, 151–159
    privatization, 56
    research universities, 54
    segregation, 20
    sex, 201
    Westernized, 70
    workload intensification, 166
    See also No Child Left Behind Act (NCLB); Schools
Eitzen, D. Stanley, 26
Elderly, 176
Elementary and Secondary Act. *See* No Child Left Behind Act
Energy, 39
England's Victim Support, 251
Environment
    conflict, 338–339
    consumerism's impact, 39
    global warming and, 274–282
Environmental justice
    air pollution and, 302–307
    foundations of, 300–301
    impact of, 300
    laws, 277–280
    precautionary principle integration, 308–309
    principle of, 301
    public policy and, 306–309
Ethnicity. *See* Race/ethnicity

Exceptionalism
    American, 314
    defined, 11
    universalistic application of, 13
Exchange rates, floating, 51

Fagan, Jeffrey, 252
Fairness Doctrine, 106
Families
    African Americans, 7, 14
    economic survival, 124
    fragmentation, 28
    income, 121 *table*
    migration links, 71
    post–World War II image, 113
    social support from, 316
    supervisory role, 317
    welfare, 7
    See also Children; Single mothers
Family cap, 200
Family Support Act, 199
Family values, 207
Federal Communication Commission (FCC)
    deregulation and, 83
    media mergers, 84
    ownership rules, 104–109
    regulation role, 94
Federal Crime Victims Fund, 251
Federal Emergency Management Agency (FEMA), 289–291
Ferree, Kenneth, 108
Feuerbach, Ludwig Andreas, 23
Financialization, 56–57
Fluor Corporation, 291
Food and Drug Administration (FDA), 175–176
Food co-operatives, 214, 222
For-profit schools, 167
Foster, Jody, 98
Foucault, Michael, 101
Fowler, Mark, 106, 167
Framework for Understanding Poverty, A (Payne), 155
Fraser, Nancy, 163
Free Press, 108
Freedom, 49, 221
Frey, William, 29
Friedman, Milton, 50
Frist, Bill, 290
Functional participation, 215

Gaining Early Awareness and Readiness for Undergraduate Programs (GEAR UP), 143
Galbraith, James K., 29, 65
Galbraith, John Kenneth, 21
Gangs
    defined, 265
    identity and, 267–268
    institutionalization, 269
    literature on, 265–266
    organization, 265–266
    origins, 265

research on, importance, 264–265
social context, 269–270
social disorganization theory, 266–267
space redivision and, 268–269
underground economy, 268
urbanization and, 265–266
Gangsta rap, 267
Gates, Bill, 28
GDP. *See* Gross domestic product (GDP)
Gelbspan, Ross, 276
Gender
child labor by, 227 *table,* 228–229
inequality, 35
social jeopardy of, 36–37
stereotypes, 198, 200
See also Women
General Electric, 78
Generic pharmaceutical companies, 173
Genocide, 254
George, Henry, 21
Germany. *See* West Germany
Germino, Laura, 130
Gersl-Pepin, Cynthia I., 151
Gifford, Brian, 336
GlaxoSmithKline, 173
Global capitalism
class power in, 52
class relationships in, 138
hegemonic system, 51
labor pool serving, 134–135
political economy and, 137
specter of, 132
volatility of, 52
Global warming
denial and, 281
discretion frame, 281
dynamics of, 274–275
environmental laws and, 279–280
insurance against, 275–276
politics of, 278–279
response to, 276–278
trust frame, 280–282
UN reports, 276–277
Globalization
class inequality, 116–118
cultural changes, 115–116
evaluation, 49
gang activity and, 264–270
identity and, 267–268
immigrant labor and, 134–136
in disarray, 51–52
income gaps and, 65–66
inequality in, 62–67
manufacturing and, 114–115
media integration and, 79, 90–91
migrant labor and, 72–76
neoliberal strategies, 54
pharmaceuticals impact, 173
poverty and, 64–65, 122–124
service industry and, 115–118

space redivision and, 268–269
technology and, 113–114
U.S. workers and, 113–114
underground economy and, 268
Gore, Al, 282, 289
Governments
big vs. small, 296
competency, 289
global warming response, 277
marriage promotion by, 200–203
nature trustee role, 279
recruitment of labor by, 70–71
resources, 73
responsibility of, 297
worker exportation by, 74–75
See also Nation states
"Great American Boycott 2006/A Day Without an
      Immigrant, The," 132
Great Britain
neoliberal policies, 54–55
welfare state in, 52
White racism in, 34
See also Thatcherism
Great Society, 204
Greenhouse gases, 274–275, 277
Greifiner, Robert, 255
Gross domestic product (GDP), 66
Gross national products (GNP), 73
Group of Seven (G7), 54
Gucci, 100–101
Guest worker programs, 136
Gulf Opportunity Zone, 290

Hagan, John, 252
Hagedorn, John, 264
Haiti, 266
Halcion, 176, 178
Haliburton, 291
Hall, John A., 30
Hansen, Jim, 275
Harrington, Michael, 30
Harvard's Center for Health and Global
      Environment, 276
Harvey, David, 48
Hate crimes, 133
Health care
access to, 184, 186
affordable, 189–190
barriers to, 193
costs, 124, 177, 179, 205
improving coverage, 261–262
insurance, 188, 192
poverty, 7–8, 63
remedial aspects, 63
social problems, 10
universal, 26, 56, 168
See also Inmate health care
Healthy Marriage Initiative (HMI), 202
Hearst corporation, 85–86
Hearst, William Randolph, 85

Heat Wage: A Social Autopsy of Disaster in Chicago
    (Klinenberg), 288
Heavily indebted poor countries (HIPCs), 73
Hegel, Georg Wihelm, 23
Heritage Foundation, 53
High Tide (Lynas), 275
Hill, Henry, 5
Hip-hop culture, 267–268
HIPCs. *See* Heavily indebted poor countries (HIPCs)
HIV/AIDS, 254–255, 257–258
Hofstadter, Richard, 12
Homeland Security, 290
Homelessness, 28–29
Homosexuals, 30, 36
Horizontal integration
    characterization, 86
    digital data and, 86, 89
    vertical integration and, 90
Household Expenditure Survey (HES), 226, 228
Households
    competitive consumption, 42
    income, child labor and, 230
    savings rate, 39
    wealth, 34
Housing
    costs of, 29
    low-income, 19
    post-Katrina, 294–295
    slum, 7
Housing Development Corporation, 19
Hoynes, William, 78
Humanitarianism, 13–14
Hurricane Betsy, 289
Hurricane Katrina
    disaster profiteers and, 290–291
    evacuation fault lines, 288–290
    global warming and, 275
    lessons from, 295–297
    local government's role, 291–293
    reconstruction following, 293–297
    welfare reform and, 203
Hustler magazine, 98
Hytrek, Gary, 112

Idaho Department of Environmental Quality, 280
Identity
    ethnic/racial, 35, 331, 334
    power of, 267–268
    victim-blaming and, 8–9
    wealth, 218–219
Ideology
    social problems and, 9–11
    victim blaming, 9–13
    victim-blaming, 7
Illegitimacy bonus, 200
Immigrant policy reform, 136
Immigrants
    Bangladeshis, 325, 328–332
    barrier-beliefs study, 142–148
    deportability, 135–136

hate crimes against, 133
labor, 134–136
mobilizations, 132–134
remittances sent by, 73
rights movement, 138
struggles of, 137–138
tango, 184–193
trafficking mafias and, 127–128
See also Cross-border migrations
Imperialism, 54
Imprisonment, 252
Inconvenient Truth, An (Gore), 282
Income
    class inequality, 116–118
    distribution, 44
    groups, descriptions, 218–219
    growth, 63
    household, 230–232
    inequality gap, 28–29, 62–64
    leisure time and, 41
    low, 154
    top one percent, 51–52
    trends, 117–118
    See also Wages
Income poverty measures, 212
India
    GDP, 66
    income estimates, 64
    population, 65
Individualism
    excessive, 26–27
    neoliberal support of, 54
    neoliberal theory, 49
Individualistic model, 43
Industrial Areas Foundation, 293
Inequality
    data on, 29
    gender, 35
    increases, 28–29
    prom, 319–320
    See also Class inequality;
            Economic inequality
Information technology
    competition and, 113
    jobs and, 114–115
    service sector and, 116
Inmate health care
    communicable/chronic diseases, 257
    HIV/AIDS, 257–258
    mental health, 258–259
    needs, 256–257
    oral health, 257
    policy change recommendations, 260–261
    post-release, 261–262
    substance abuse treatment, 259
Inner city, 154
Integration
    horizontal, 86–89
    media, 85–86
    vertical, 89–94

Interfaith Social Assistance Reform
        Coalition (ISARC), 220
Intergovernmental Panel on Climate Change (IPCC),
        275–276
International Monetary Fund (IMR)
        function of, 48–49
        neoliberal influence, 53
        opposition to, 57
        sex tourism view, 75
International Police Task Force (IPTF), 127
Internet
        growth, 95
        media impact, 80, 83
        media sites, 86
        mergers, 81–82 *table*
Interview with the Vampire, 98
Intolerance
        racial, 29–30
        religious, 30
        sexual, 30
Iraq War casualty study
        analysis, 342–344
        background, 337–340
        data, 340–345
        discussion, 345–347
        hypotheses, 340
Iraq War, neoliberal agenda and, 50
Ireland, migrant labor from, 71–72
Is America Breaking Apart? (Hall, Lindholm), 30
Isolation, 27–28
Italy, 71–72

Jackson, Alphonso, 289
Japan
        migrant workers in, 70
        neoliberal policies, 54–55
Japanese Americans, internment of, 329
Jim Crow, 29
Johnson, Allan G., 32
Johnson, Lyndon, 289
Just-in-time labor force, 114
Just-in-time production, 113–114

Katrina. *See* Hurricane Katrina
Kellogg Brown & Root, 291
Kemp, Jack, 290
Kennedy, John F., 29
Kennedy, Ted, 133, 293
Kerry, John, 289
Keynes, J. M., 116
Keynes, John Maynard, 199
Keys, Alicia, 100
Kimmelman, Gene, 107
King, Martin Luther, Jr., 16, 278–279
Kissinger, Henry, 50
Klinenberg, Eric, 288
Koogle, Timothy, 28
Korean War, 337
Kramer, Ronald, 314
Kromidas, Maria, 324

Krugman, Paul, 63
Ku Klux Klan, 133

Labor
        capitalism and, 33
        extended definition, 227
        global, politics, 137–138
        globalization and, 114
        immigrants, 134–136
        income inequality, 116–117
        manufacturing sector changes, 114–115
        mass layoffs, 114
        migrant (*See* Cross-border migrations)
        neoliberal policies and, 58–59
        occupational mobility, 34
        social pact, 67
        unionized, 20, 123
        work and spend cycle, 40
        working poor, 122–123
        See also Child labor
Labor-force participation, 122
Lakoff, George, 278
Landrieu, Mary, 291, 292
Latin America
        debt-to-GNP, 73
        migrant workers from, 69
        neoliberalism in, 136–137
        See also specific countries
Latinos
        air pollution risks, 306–307
        barrier-beliefs study, 142–148
        educational attitudes, 340
        immigration issues activism, 132–134
        income inequality, 120–121
        Iraq war casualties, 344–345
        in military, 339–340
        population increase, 339
        poverty, 62
        transitional migration, 136–137
        victimization of, 248
        welfare reform and, 207
        working poor, 122
Latour, B., 174–176
Lauren, Ralph, 46
Lazos, Grigoris, 127–128
Lead poisoning issue, 13
Leather, 39
Leaving Child Left Behind? (Hess, Finn), 162–163
Lecky, W. E. H., 3
Leisure time, 38, 41
Lethal violence, 314, 320
Limbaugh, Rush, 26–27
Lindholm, Charles, 30
Literacy
        empowerment, 156–158
        redefinition of, 164
Locke, John L., 27
Lolita (Nabokov), 97
Loncaric, Josip, 128
Los Angeles riots, 295–296

Los Angeles Unified School District
    air pollution study, 303–306
    characterization, 302
Lott, Trent, 106
Luxembourg Income Study (LIS), 315
Luxury markets, 44–45
Lynas, Mark, 275
Lyon, Sue, 98

Madonna, 100
Mail-order bride agencies, 74–75
Malign Neglect (Leon-Guerrero), 252
Mangan, Mona, 108
Manifest Destiny, 29
Maniscalco, Francis J., 105, 109
Mannheim, 9
Mannheim, Karl, 3
Manufacturing
    internationalization, 69–70
    sector changes, 114–115
    technological changes, 113–114
Many Children Left Behind (Meier, Wood), 162, 164, 168
Maori gangs, 265
Maquiladoras, 135, 137
Marc Jacobs, 100–101
Mark, Karl, 23
Marriages
    government promotion of, 200–203
    healthy, 201
    social imagination view, 5
Martinez, Mel, 289
Marx, Karl, 3
Mass layoffs, 114
Massachusetts Toxic Use Reduction Act, 309
Matrix of domination, 37
Matrix of privilege, 37
McCain, John, 133
McChesney, Robert, 107
Means-testing, 205
Meat consumption, 39
Media
    class interests and, 55
    consumption and, 42
    digital data, 86, 89
    disaster coverage, 295
    life world balance and, 43
    literacy framework, 97–102
    neoliberal assault on, 53
    options, 94
    sexualized children in, 98–102
    terrorist's portrayals, 325–326
    See also specific outlets
Media Access Project, 107
Media industry
    changes in, 78–79
    deregulation, 83–85
    growth, 79–80
    horizontal integration, 86–89
    integration, 85–86
    market perspective, 94–95

    mergers, 77–79
    new technology, 80, 83
    ownership, 91–94, 104
    public sphere perspective, 79, 95–96
    sector domination, 93
    structural trends, 79–86
    vertical integration, 89–94
    See also Viacom/CBS merger
Media Monopoly, The (Bagdikian), 92–93
MediaOne, 79
Medicine. *See* Pharmaceuticals
Mellon, Andrew, 57
Mental health
    prison cases, 258–259
    social problems, 10
Merskin, Debra, 97
Metanarratives, 152, 158–159
Metropolis, 5
Mexico
    immigrants from, 133–134
    migrant workers from, 69
    neoliberal policies in, 55
    trafficking mafias in, 128–129
    Zapatista uprising, 57, 59
Microsoft, 78
Middle class
    income distribution, 44–45
    norms, 155
    U. S domination by, 62
    upper, 45
Migrations. *See* Cross-border migrations
Milakovic, Milorad, 126–127
Military. *See* Armed Forces
Mills, C. Wright, 2, 9–10
Mills, Hayley, 98
Minuteman, 133
Monbiot, George, 64
Moral Majority, 53
Morello-Frosch, Rachel, 300
Moskos, Charles C., 338
Mostel, Zero, 6
MoveOn, 108
Movies, 98
MTV, 91, 92 table
Multiculturalism, 327
Multiplexiality
    defined, 185
    social networks, 188, 193
Munoz, Juan, 129–130
Muslims, 327–329

Nabokov, Vladimir, 97
Nagin, Ray, 288, 292
Narrative policy analysis
    advantages, 153
    characterization, 152
    key components, 152–153
    metanarrative, 158–159
    methods, 153
    NCLB, 152–158

Nation at Risk, A, 151
Nation states
    economic role, 48
    power of, 56
    recruitment of labor by, 70–71
    redistribution policies, 58
    retreat of, 266–267
    See also Governments
National Aeronautics and Space Administration
    (NASA), 275
National Crime Victimization Survey (NCVS), 248–249
National Environmental Policy Act (NEPA), 279
National Environmental Protection Act, 309
National Health Service (British), 52
National Institute for Clinical Excellence (NICE), 179
National Institute for Occupational Safety
    and Health, 124
National Organization for Women (NOW), 108–109
National Rifle Association, 108
National Welfare Rights Organization, 198
Native Americans, 34
Nature's Mandate, 277
NCLB. *See* No Child Left Behind Act (NCLB)
Neoliberalism
    accumulation by dispossession, 55–56, 59
    alternatives, 58–60
    ascendency, 48–49
    class power and, 52–54
    contradictions in, 60
    creative destruction, 54–58
    crisis management/manipulation, 57
    defined, 48
    economic system, 48–49
    financialization, 56–57
    in Latin America, 136–137
    naturalization of, 49–51
    privatization, 56
    rise of, 51–52
    state redistribution, 58
    welfare reform and, 203–208
Net worth, 118, 119 *table*
New Bridge Strategies, 291
New Deal programs, 204
New Orleans
    community actors, 292–294
    cultural uniqueness of, 289–290
    fiscal problems, 292
    housing, 294–295
    housing discrimination in, 289
    infrastructure, 294
    jobs, 295
    population decline, 288–289
    poverty rate, 288
    public facilities, 294
    public health, 294
    reconstruction of, 291, 293–295
    unemployment in, 289
    See also Hurricane Katrina
New poor, 122
New York City debt crisis, 53

New York Times, 99
New Zealand, 48
Newspapers, 89, 93
Niagara Falls women, 214–224
Niagara Social Assistance Reform Committee, 222
Nichols, John, 107
Nietzche, Friedrich, 20
Nigeria, 64, 266–267
Nixon, Richard, 52
No Child Left Behind Act (NCLB), 151–152
    complexity, 163–165
    conservative modernization politics of, 165–168
    knowledge, 153
    literacy empowerment, 156
    literature review, 162–163
    policy narrative shaping, 153–154
    social justice narrative, 151–152
No Child Left Behind? (Peterson, West), 162
Nonstandard work arrangements, 114
Nonstories, 152, 154–158
Nonviolence, 21–22
North American Free Trade Agreement
    (NAFTA), 128
Number gangs, 265
Nursing Relief Act, 74

Occupational mobility, 34
Offshore labor, 70, 116
Operation Breadbasket, 17–19
Opren, 178
Oral health care, 257, 261
Organization of Petroleum Exporting
    Countries (OPEC), 74
Otherizing practice, 329
Output bias, 38
Outsourcing. *See* Offshore labor
Overspent American, The (Schor), 41
Overworked American, The (Schor), 40

Panel on High-Risk Youth, 316–317
Parents Television, 109
Parents Television Council, 107
Pariser, Eli, 108
Participatory Poverty Assessment (PPA)
    change catalyst in, 222
    functional to interactive transition, 215–216
    income group descriptions, 218–219
    methodology, 213–214
    Niagara Falls lessons, 216–223
    overview, 212–213
    power and participation in, 222–223
    procedures, 213–214
    quality of life dimension, 216–217
    recruitment, 214–215
    seasonally dimension, 217–218
    social assistance dimension, 219–222
Paxon, Lowell "Bud," 84
PAX-TV, 84
Penthouse magazine, 98
Persian Gulf War, 338

Personal isolation, 27–28
Personal savings, 123
Pharmaceutical industry
    corporate headquarters, 172
    dev in developing countries, 172–173
    globalization, 172–173
    ideological advantage, 179
    power of, 172, 174
    pre-approval drug development, 175–178
    regulatory capture, 177
    revenues, 172–173
Pharmaceuticals
    effectiveness testing, 176–177
    generics, 173
    inconspicuous consumption, 173
    marketing, 179
    patients, 172, 175
    post-approval evaluation, 178–180
    pre-approval process, 175–178
    production, 173–174
Philippines, 74–75, 279
Philippines Overseas Employment
        Administration (POEA), 74
Pickford, Mary, 98
PICO National Network, 293
Pinochet, Augusto, 50
Playboy magazine, 98
Policy. *See* Public policy; Social policy
Policy analysis. *See* Narrative policy analysis
Political action committees, 52–53
Politics
    conservative modernization, 165–168
    deregulation, 83–85
    global labor, 137–138
    media ownership, 104–105
    power, 20
    religious right, 53
    voting patterns, 253
Pollution, 302–306
Poverty
    absolute, 119
    child labor and, 226, 234
    children in, 28
    class inequality and, 118–124
    complexity, 154
    cycle of, 7
    defined, 62–63
    education role, 154
    global economy and, 62–67
    incidence of, 62–63
    income measures, 212
    metanarrative of, 158–159
    narrative policy analysis, 152–159
    PPA study, 212–223
    rate, 119
    relative, 119
    U.S. rate, 315
    understanding, 155–156
    violence link, 314–315
    women in, 202

    World Bank assessment, 220
    See also Inequality; Wealth
Powell, Lewis, 52
Powell, Michael, 104, 106–108
Power
    absence of, 21
    class, 52–54
    defined, 20
    identity, 267–268
    nation states,' 56
    participation and, 222–223
    pharmaceutical industry, 172, 174
PPA. *See* Participatory Poverty
        Assessment (PPA)
Precautionary principle
    environmental justice integration,
        308–309
    essence of, 301–302
    impact of, 300
Pretty Baby, 98
Prisons
    gender and, 255–256
    health care in, 254–262
    racial disparities, 256
Pritchett, Lance, 66
Private consumption, 39
Private property rights, 281
Privatization, 56, 204
Privilege, systems of, 36–37
Producer capture, 163
Productivity, 33
Project SHARE
    growth of, 222
    participants, 214–215
    protests against, 220
Prom inequalities, 319–320
Property crimes
    harm from, 246
    rates, 249
    reporting of, 249–250
Property rights, 56
Prostitution
    criminal harm, 246
    debt slavery, 126–128
    See also Sex industry
Prothrow-Stith, Deborah, 321
Psychotropics, 173
Public health, 301
Public policy
    debate framework, 301
    environmental inequalities, 307
    family values in, 204
    retreat from, 322
    See also Social policy
Public school 999 study
    classroom interviews, 326–327
    conclusions, 332–333
    multiculturalism in, 327
    neighborhood surrounding,
        325–326

social interactions, 327–329
    student stories, 329–332
Public sphere perspective, 79, 95–96
Punishment, effect of, 244

Quality of life
    assessment, 216–217
    poor, 217
    relationships and, 218–219
    social assistance and, 219–222

Race/ethnicity
    class inequality and, 119–121
    DoD categorization, 341
    drug use and, 259
    incarceration rates and, 256
    interaction, historical patterns, 325
    Katrina response and, 288–289
    neutral social policy, 207
    segregation, 16
    semantics and, 20
    social fragmentation and, 29–31
    social jeopardy of, 36
    war causalities and, 327, 340–347
    war on terror and, 325–327, 329, 332
    See also specific groups
Racialization, 328, 332
Racism. *See* White racism
Radio stations, 93, 106
Ramos, José Luis, 130
Ramsey, Jon Benet, 102
Rap music, 267
Rawls, John, 30
RCA, 78
Reading instruction, 164
Reagan, Ronald, 53–54, 167, 203
Reaganism
    media deregulation, 83–84
    neoliberal theory, 48, 50
    trickle down theory, 43–44, 204
Rebuild and Respect Act, 293
Redistribution, economic, 58
Reframing, 279–282
Regulatory capture, 177
Reich, Robert, 29
Relative poverty, 119
Religious intolerance, 30
Remittances, 136
Replacement cost coverage, 246
Republican Party, 52–54
Research
    career-barriers, 142–148
    and development, 175
    gang, 264–265
    universities, 54
    See also specific studies
Resources, 184–185
Rethinking Schools, 168
Reuther, Walter, 20
Reverse depreciation, 188

Revolutions, internal, 22
Robinson, James, 19
Robinson, William, 132
Rockerfeller, John D., 12
Rohatyn, Felix, 53
Rolling Stone magazine, 99
Ross, E. A., 3
Ruling classes, 51
Rumsfeld, Donald, 105
Ryan, William, 6

Salaries. *See* Wages
Salinas de Gortari, Carlos, 55
SARC. *See* Interfaith Social Assistance Reform Coalition
        (ISARC)
Satellite television, 95
Savings rate, 39
Schools
    behavior in, 155
    change process, 158–159
    citizen, 168
    curricular directives, 324
    for-profit, 167
    producer capture, 163
    violence in, 314–315
    See also Education; Public school 999 study
Schor, Juliet, 38
Schumpeter, Joseph, 3
Schwartzman, Andrew, 106, 107
Science in Action (Latour), 174
Scientific facts, 174
Seagram's, 78
Seasonally, 217–218
Seeley, John, 9
Semantics, racial, 20
Sensenbrenner, James, 133
Service Employees International Union (SEIU), 292
Service sector, 115–118, 122
Sex education, 201
Sex industry
    economic importance of, 72
    growth in, 75
    organized crime in, 76
Sexual orientation, 30, 36
Sexuality
    adolescent, 100
    in advertising, 97
    cultural divisions, 29–31
    innocence and, 102
    social construction of, 99
Sexualized children
    in advertising, 100–101
    criminal aspects, 102
    ideology, 98–99
    in literature, 99
    phenomenon of, 97
Shaw Group, 291
Shields, Brooke, 98
Shrimp consumption, 39
Shulman, Beth, 123

Simmel, Georg, 43–44
Simmons, Russell, 100
Simon, William, 53
Single mothers
 demonizing, 201
 family values, 207
 historical overview, 199 *table*
 programs for, 205
 stigmatizing, 198
Skollies, 265
Slater, Philip, 27
Slavery
 justification, 12
 racism and, 34
 twenty-first century, 126–131
Slum housing, 7
Smith, Adam, 26
Social Assistance Advisory Committee, 222
Social assistance system. *See* Welfare
Social capital
 absence of, youth crime link, 317
 benefits of, 193–194
 defined, 184, 185
 literature on, 184
 reverse depreciation, 188
 social networks and, 190
 source, 184–185
 unmet expectations and, 192–193
Social classes
 capitalism and, 33–34
 global economy and, 138
 income, 44–45, 65
 interest, 14
 Katrina response and, 288–289
 media and, 55
 power of, restoration, 52–54
 ruling, 51
 social jeopardy of, 36
 struggles, 59–60
 See also specific groups
Social control, 317–319
Social Darwinism, 12
Social democratic compromise, 59
Social disorganization theory, 266–267
Social exchange, 189
Social exclusion, 314–315
Social expenditures, 54
Social imagination, 3–5
Social life
 basis, 32
 consumption competition and, 42
 fragmentation, 26–31
Social movements
 class-based, 60
 economic-based, 57, 59, 67
 grassroots activists, 292–293, 296
 immigrant rights, 138
 student, 49
 victims' rights, 251
 welfare state and, 207–208

Social networks
 characterization, 184–185
 diversity, 193–194
 multiplexial, 188
 social capital and, 184, 190
 tango immigrants, 188–189
Social policy
 crime and, 250
 crisis management, 57
 exceptionalist view, 11
 immigration, 136
 inmate health care, 259–260
 race neutral, 207
 welfare, 202
 youth violence and, 321–322
 See also Narrative policy analysis; Public policy
Social problems
 crimes as, 244–246
 defining, 9
 ideology and, 9–11
Social relationships
 quality of life and, 218–219
 reciprocity, 189–191
 resource access via, 184–185
 youth violence and, 320
Social Security Act, 199
Social structures
 global, 138
 public issues, 4
 support, 315–319
 term use, 5
Social webs, 185
Society
 inequality's effect, 29
 study of, 3–4
 zero-sum, 34
South Africa, 48, 58
South Korea, 58, 74–75
South Park, 95
Southern Christian Leadership Council (SCLC), 17, 19
Spears, Britney, 98, 101
Spencer, Herbert, 3, 12
Spy magazine, 99
Star Trek, 86
Status competition, 41
Status quo, 9, 12
Stereotypes
 gender, 198, 200
 origins of, 250
 racial, 7, 17, 198, 200, 203
 terrorists, 327
 welfare reform and, 203, 207
 youth gangs, 269
Stewart, Martha, 46
Stigma, 7–8
Stress, 217
Structural Adjustment Programs (SAPs), 72
Student movement, 49
Substance abuse, 259
Suburban communities, 27

Sumner, William Graham, 12
Suplee, Curt, 27
Supreme Court, 281
Sweden, 48

Tango immigrants
    field study, 185–187
    health care, 188, 192
    social networks, 188–189
    social reciprocity and, 189–191
    venues for, 187–188
Taxes, 57, 204
Taxi Driver, 98
Technology
    globalization and, 113–114
    information, 113
    isolation and, 27
    media mergers and, 80, 83
Telecommunications Act
    antiregulatory sentiment and, 84
    impact of, 95–96
    media concentrations and, 93
    ownership rule changes, 85 *table*
Television
    cable, 93, 95
    com as commodity, 167
    ownership concentration, 93
    programs, 83–84
    satellite, 95
    sexual advertising in, 97
    social influence of, 43
Temporary Aid to Needy Families (TANF),
        199, 203, 205
Terrorists
    identification of, 327
    portrayal of, 325–326
    stereotypes, 327
Thatcher, Margaret, 50, 52
Thatcherism
    neoliberal theory, 48, 50, 52
    trickle down theory, 43–44
Metropolitan Organization, The (TMO), 293
Think tanks, 53
Thurow, Lester, 29, 34
Tillmon, Johnnie, 198
Time Inc., 83
Tonry, Michael, 244
Tourism, sex, 75
Trade unions, 123, 206
Trade-related Aspects of Intellectual Property Rights
        (TRIPS), 56
Trafficking mafias, 127–128
Trail of Tears, 254
Triads, 265
Trickle down economics, 43–44
Trickle down economics, 204
Tristani, Gloria, 107
Trust frame, 280–282
Trust, loss of, 192–193

Underclasses, 316
Underground economy, 268
Unemployment, 4–5, 269
UN-Habit report, 265
U.N. Human Development Report, 65
Uniform Crime Reports (UCR), 246, 248
United States
    antiregulatory sentiment, 84
    consumer debt, 124
    diversity, 29–31
    ethnic immigration, 71–72
    federal revenues, 204
    federal spending, 204–205
    globalization and, 113–114, 123–124
    imperial tradition, 54
    income inequality, 63
    middle class domination in, 62
    migrant workers in, 69
    neoliberalism in, 52–55
    personal savings in, 123
    poverty rate, 315
    prison population, 245, 252–253
    slavery in, 34
    status competition in, 41
    welfare reform, 198–208
Universalism, 11, 13
University of Texas Project, 65
Urbanization
    in China, 58
    defined, 9
    gang activity and, 264–265
    See also Cities
Urban Marshall Plan, 295
U.S. Bureau of Justice, 248
U.S. National Defense Strategy, 49–49
Utopia, 9

Veblen, Thorstein, 3, 43–44
Vertical integration
    characterization, 89–90
    globalization and, 90–91
    Viacom/CBS merger, 90
Viacom/CBS merger
    deregulation and, 84
    globalization aspects, 91
    holdings after, 87–89 *table*
    impact, 78–79
    media integration and, 86
    perspectives of, 79
    size of, 78
    vertical integration, 90
Victim blaming
    class interest, 14
    generic process, 7–9
    humanitarian concerns and, 13–14
    identification process, 8–9
    ideological process, 9–15
    logic of, 6–7
    psychological aspects, 14

Victims
burdens, 250–251
deprived children, 6–7
support for, 245–246
surveys on, 248–249
"Victim's Bill of Rights," 251
Victims of Crime Act, 251
Victims of Trafficking and Violence
Protection Act, 130
Vietnam War, 337–338
Viladrich, Anahi, 183
Violence
American exceptionalism, 314
crimes associated with, 246, 248–249
gang, 269
lethal, 314, 320
reporting of, 249–250
against women, 245
See also Youth violence
Vioxx, 177–178
Vitter, David, 291
Voting patterns, 253

Wages
CEOs,' 28
class inequality and, 116–117
falling, 206
immigrant labor, 71
workers, 33
Walt Disney Company, 83–84
Wars
causality data, 337–347
cultural, 324
environments, 338–339, 344–345
privatization, 56
racism and, 325–327, 329, 332
social imagination view, 5
See also Armed forces; specific conflicts
Washington Consensus, 51
Watts Riot 1965, 21–22
Wealth
capitalism and, 32–35
concentration of, 52, 55, 57
educational achievement, 57
global expansion of, 264, 266, 268–269
household, 34
image of, 218–219
natural, 279, 281
tax rate and, 204
See also Inequality; Poverty
Weber, Max, 3
Weld, Tuesday, 98
Welfare
decline of, 205–206
discretionary spending on, 205–206
families on, 7
means-testing, 205
name change, 199
neoliberal assault on, 52, 54

privatization, 56
social movements and, 207–208
surveillance issues, 219–222
Welfare reform
child exclusion, 200–203
family values and, 207
goals, 198
illegitimacy bonus, 200
key provisions, 199–203
lower labor costs and, 206
marriage promotion, 200–203
neoliberalism and, 203–208
overview, 199
race and, 207
Reaganomics and, 204
support for, 205–206
work enforcement, 199–200
West Germany, 54–55
Westinghouse, 78
Wexler, Celia, 106–107
White racism
capitalism and, 34–36
children views, 326–327
origins, 32
use of, 35
Whiteness, idea of, 34–35
Whitt, James, 289
Wideman, John Edgar, 63
Widow's Pension, 199
Will, George, 30
Williams, Hosea, 17
Williams, Natasha, 254
Wilson, William Julius, 252
Women
child-like media image, 97–98
consumption by, 40
debt slavery and, 127
domestic, 245
drug trials on, 176
drug use by, 259
in gangs, 267
government programs for, 205
illegal trafficking of, 72, 75–76
low-wage jobs, 206
mental illness among, 258
Niagara Falls, 214–224
population, 206
in poverty, 202
in prison, 255–256
role of, 35
sex trade and, 74
underage girls, 100–101
wealthy, 202
welfare reform and, 199
working, 124
See also Single mothers
Wood, Mary Christina, 274
Work and spend cycle, 40–41
Workers. See Labor

Workfare, 199–200
Working classes
    immigrant/nonimmigrant divisions, 135
    labor movements, 53
    material interests of, 53
Working poor, 122–123
World Bank
    antipoverty efforts, 64–65
    gang label, 265
    global income estimates, 64
    income inequality estimates, 65–66
    sex tourism view, 75
World Bank Participatory Poverty Assessment, 220
World Social Forum, 59
World Trade Organization (WTO), 49, 54
Writers Guild, 107, 109

Yates, Michael, 62
Youth violence
    fire arm access and, 320
    inequality link, 314–315
    policy implications, 321–322
    poverty link, 314–315
    prevention, 321–322
    prom inequalities and, 319–320
    societal links, 314–320
Youth, low-income, 142–143

Zadora, Pia, 98
Zapatista uprising, 57, 59
Zedlewski, Edwin, 251
Zentegraf, Kristine, 112
Zero-sum society, 34